Modeling Evolution

Modeling Evolution

an introduction to numerical methods

Derek A. Roff

OXFORD

UNIVERSITY PRESS

OXFORD
UNIVERSITY PRESS

Great Clarendon Street, Oxford OX2 6DP

Oxford University Press is a department of the University of Oxford.
It furthers the University's objective of excellence in research, scholarship,
and education by publishing worldwide in

Oxford New York

Auckland Cape Town Dar es Salaam Hong Kong Karachi
Kuala Lumpur Madrid Melbourne Mexico City Nairobi
New Delhi Shanghai Taipei Toronto

With offices in

Argentina Austria Brazil Chile Czech Republic France Greece
Guatemala Hungary Italy Japan Poland Portugal Singapore
South Korea Switzerland Thailand Turkey Ukraine Vietnam

Oxford is a registered trade mark of Oxford University Press
in the UK and in certain other countries

Published in the United States
by Oxford University Press Inc., New York

British Library Cataloguing in Publication Data
Data available

Library of Congress Cataloging in Publication Data
Data available

Typeset by SPI Publisher Services, Pondicherry, India
Printed in Great Britain
on acid-free paper by
CPI Antony Rowe Chippenham, Wiltshire

ISBN 978-0-19-957114-7

3 5 7 9 10 8 6 4 2

Contents

3 Invasibility analysis   *165*

CHAPTER 1

Overview

1.1 Introduction

1.1.1 The aim of this book

Computer modeling is now an integral part of research into evolutionary biology. The advent of increased processing power in the personal computer, coupled with the availability of languages such as R, S-PLUS, Mathematica, Maple, Mathcad, and MATLAB, has ensured that the development and analysis of computer models of evolution is now within the capabilities of most graduate students. However, there are two hurdles that, in my experience, discourage students from making full use of the power of computer modeling. The first is the general problem of formulating the question in a manner that is amenable to programming and the second is its implementation using one of the aforementioned computer languages. This is because the learning curve of each of these languages is quite steep, unless one already has prior computing experience as an undergraduate.

Presently available texts on modeling evolutionary problems typically do not focus on the issue of implementation. The same problem formally confronted students learning statistical analysis. However, in contrast to books on modeling in evolution, many statistical texts now give numerous examples and demonstrate the statistical analyses using available programs. This is particularly true for statistical texts based on S-PLUS or R (e.g., Crawley [2002, 2007]; Krause and Olson [2002]; Venables and Ripley [2002]; Roff [2006]). The philosophy, of providing coding as an integral part of the explanation, has guided the writing of this book. The present book is designed to outline how evolutionary questions are formulated and how, in practice, they can be resolved by analytical and numerical methods (the emphasis being on the latter). The general structure of each chapter consists of an introduction, in which the general approach and methods are described, followed by a series of scenarios demonstrating the different techniques and providing coding in R and, in two chapters (2 and 6), MATLAB. This coding is available on my Web site (http://www.biology.ucr.edu/people/faculty/Roff.html). Each scenario commences with a list of general assumptions of the model. These assumptions are then given precise mathematical meaning, followed by the available methods of analysis. I have chosen scenarios that highlight particular aspects of evolutionary modeling, the aim being to allow these models to be used as templates for other models. At the end of the chapter a list of exemplary papers is given: These papers have been selected on the basis of how well they explain and illustrate the techniques discussed in the chapter.

1.1.2   Why R and MATLAB?

Both R and MATLAB are readily available and extensively used. The program R has two major advantages over MATLAB: first it is free, and second it is a highly sophisticated statistical package. Thus a student who learns R can use it to do modeling and to address the statistical questions that will arise following experiments to test such models. MATLAB appears to be generally faster than R, except perhaps in the complex statistical analyses. On the other hand, MATLAB is not cheap and although it has statistical routines, these are not its forte and I would not recommend it as a general means of statistical analysis. Although the symbols of the two languages are different (e.g., "<-" in R vs. "=" in MATLAB), in most cases the basic structures are very similar and it is not difficult to navigate between the two, once the general concepts are understood. While I personally prefer R, MATLAB does have some significance: Therefore, in Chapters 2 and 6 I provide coding in both R and MATLAB and in the other chapters I give the coding only in R. The problems addressed in Chapter 2 typically involve the calculus for which MATLAB is particularly useful and may involve somewhat different coding to that of R. In contrast, the problems addressed in Chapter 6 use coding that is essentially the same, and the MATLAB code can be obtained from the R code in large measure by relatively little editing (see later). This is the case for the other chapters, which, in the interests of clarity, is why I have omitted the MATLAB code (the primary coding changes generally involve graphical output). Throughout the book computer code is given in courier font to distinguish it from the rest of the text. Appendix 1 lists all the R functions used in this book and, where available, the MATLAB equivalents. In general, R code can be largely converted to MATLAB code by global editing in a text-editor such as Word. The general changes that will have to be made are as follows:

1. Replace the assignment symbol "<-" with "=".
2. Replace the comment symbol "#" with "%".
3. For ease of reading I frequently use a "." in my variable names, as for example, X.Matrix. This is not permitted in MATLAB and so I replace "." with the underscore character "_".
4. Matrices in R use square brackets, for example, X[1,1]; replace these with parentheses, that is, X(1,1).
5. Concatenation uses the symbol c(variables); in MATLAB use square brackets [variables].
6. Loops in R use the brackets "{' and '}". MATLAB does not use these, so delete them and replace "}" with "end".
7. In MATLAB, functions go in separate files. See Appendix 1 and Section 3 (Step 10) for differences in construction of functions.

8. For MATLAB code place ";" at the end of each line that you do not want to be echoed back.

9. Supplied functions may differ in name: check Appendix 1 for such changes. The codes in Chapter 2 are most dissimilar and require care, whereas those in Chapter 6 are very readily changed.

1.2   Operational definitions of fitness

In modeling evolution we must clearly define the term "fitness," not only in an abstract sense but, more importantly, in an operational sense. In this section I present an overview of such definitions, which are expanded upon in the relevant chapters.

A central idea of Darwin's theory is that organisms vary in their ability to leave descendants, a phenomenon that is now generally called "Darwinian fitness" or simply "fitness." In the simplest case the term "descendants" might refer to immediate offspring but more generally the time horizon is longer than a single generation and takes into account the differential rate of increase of genotypes in a population. This concept is pivotal to our understanding of evolution and in the design and analysis of evolutionary models. There is certainly no real issue with the basic concept of fitness, but it has proven a rich source of discussion when implementing operational definitions of fitness in evolutionary models (Brommer 2000; Brommer et al. 2002). Such models attempt to determine the equilibrium trait values and, in some cases, their evolutionary trajectory, under the influence of natural selection. Evolutionary models may be classified along five broad dimensions: (*a*) finite versus infinite (or very large) population size, (*b*) type of environment (constant, fixed length, temporally stochastic, temporally predictable, spatially stochastic, and spatially predictable), (*c*) Density-dependent or density-independent, (*d*) inherent population dynamics (equilibrium, cyclical, and chaotic), and (*e*) frequency-dependent or frequency-independent. Considerable theoretical attention has been given to a subset of these combinations but it is probably possible to find models that include all combinations, at least for particular models. Here I shall focus upon those combinations of dimensions for which there is a relatively strong theoretical justification for the fitness criterion and where possible suggest the fitness criterion for other combinations.

Operational measures of fitness have developed largely from the fundamental equation of fitness from the demographic model of Fisher (1930). Fisher took an actuarial approach, assuming a population at a stable-age distribution in which case the rate of growth of the population, r, can be described by the age-specific schedules of reproduction and survival as brought together in the characteristic (or Euler) equation

$$\int_0^\infty e^{-rx}l(x)m(x)dx = \int_0^\infty e^{-rx}V(x)dx = 1 \qquad (1.1)$$

where $l(x)$ is the survival to age x and $m(x)$ is the number of female births at age x. The above equation can also be written in discrete form (see Chapter 2): which model is to be preferred will depend upon the details of the underlying biological model. Qualitative results are not affected by this type of variation and I shall not explicitly distinguish between the two cases in this overview, but examples of both are discussed in this book. For a homogeneous population at stable equilibrium r equals zero and the characteristic equation reduces to

$$\int_0^\infty l(x)m(x)dx = \int_0^\infty V(x)dx = 1 \qquad (1.2)$$

In the absence of density-dependence, we have the net reproduction rate R_0:

$$R_0 = \int_0^\infty l(x)m(x)dx = \int_0^\infty V(x)dx \qquad (1.3)$$

This parameter is one of the most widely used operational metrics of fitness (e.g., Clutton-Brock [1988]; Roff [1992]; Stearns [1992]; Charnov [1993]) but, as discussed in Section 1.2.4, its use implies a particular definition of the biological scenario, which is often not overtly acknowledged.

Fisher argued that selection will favor the particular life history that maximizes r, which he termed the **Malthusian parameter** in honor of Thomas Malthus, who in his "Essay on the Principle of Population" (Malthus 1798) pointed out that populations increase geometrically. This parameter is also referred to as the **intrinsic rate of increase** or simply the **rate of increase** (hence the present use of the symbol r or sometimes specifically r_0 to distinguish it from rates of increase calculated with other factors is included). The characteristic equation was derived earlier (see Lotka [1907]; Sharpe and Lotka [1911]) but Fisher was the first to see its importance as a measure of fitness: "The Malthusian parameter will in general be different for each different genotype, and will measure the fitness to survive of each" (Fisher 1930, p. 46). As pointed out by Charlesworth (1970), it is not really desirable to equate r with a genotype as segregation and recombination will be changing the frequency of genotypes in the population. However, it is true, as discussed later, that under the circumstances considered by Fisher the parameter r will increase until an equilibrium is reached. While the operational definitions of fitness may vary under different scenarios, they all have equation (1.3) as their basic root, that is, fitness is a function of the long-term growth rate of genotypes in a population. Invasion by a mutant form is contingent on its long-term growth rate relative to the resident population.

Fisher, who was clearly concerned about the genetical basis of evolution, never provided a rigorous mathematical argument for r as the appropriate measure of fitness in genetical models. This lacuna was filled only relatively recently by the work of Charlesworth (1994, for the collected analyses) and Lande (1982). In many cases it is not necessary to include the genetical basis of the traits under investigation, because, in general, sufficient genetic variation is available to permit evolution to proceed. In all models a central assumption is that there is a set of phenotypic trade-offs that limit the scope of trait combinations. Incorporation of genetic models may be important in determining the evolutionary trajectory or as a numerical means of locating the optimal combination (see Chapters 4 and 6). For convenience, I shall divide the following sections according to the primary focus of the analyses described therein.

1.2.1   Constant environment, density-independent, and stable-age distribution

This is the situation modeled by Fisher (1930), for which the characteristic equation provides the appropriate fitness criterion, although, as noted earlier, he did not provide a formal mathematical proof of this. Charlesworth (1994) showed that in a population genetical framework, a mutant allele will spread in a resident population if the mutation increases the intrinsic rate of increase of a genotype possessing the mutation. Lande (1982) showed that for a quantitative genetic model with weak selection and a nearly stable-age distribution "life history evolution continually increases the intrinsic rate of increase of the population, until an equilibrium is reached" (Lande 1982, p. 611; see also Charlesworth [1993]).

The general discrete mathematical model for this scenario is the **Leslie matrix**, which comprises the age-specific fecundities and survival probabilities. The finite rate of increase, λ $(=e^r)$ is given by the **dominant eigenvalue** of the Leslie matrix (see Chapter 3). For the continuous case, as given in equation (1.1) either an analytical solution can be found from the functional form of $V(x)$ or numerical methods are employed (see Chapter 2).

1.2.2   Demographic stochasticity

As noted earlier, implicit in the characteristic equation is the assumption of a constant environment, a stable-age distribution, and an infinite (or very large) population so that variation due to demographic stochasticity can be ignored. The question of a spread of a mutant allele in a finite population has been considered in great detail in the population genetics literature (Wright 1931, 1969; Crow and Kimura 1970; Hedrick 2000; Gillespie 2006). In such models fitness is mathematically defined with respect to a genotype: thus for the single locus, two-allele case we have w_{AA}, w_{Aa}, and w_{aa}, where the subscripts refer to the genotypes. Relative fitness is then obtained by setting the largest w to 1 and the others as proportions of the largest value. This characterization of fitness is typical of population genetic models. The most important implicit assumption of most of these models is that generation length is fixed, which greatly simplifies analytical approaches.

Demetrius and Ziehe (2007) tackled the problem by dividing r into two components:

$$r = H + \Phi \tag{1.4}$$

where

$$H = -\frac{\displaystyle\int_0^\infty e^{-rx}V(x)\ln[e^{-rx}V(x)]dx}{\displaystyle\int_0^\infty xe^{-rx}V(x)dx} \equiv \frac{S}{T}$$

$$\Phi = \frac{\displaystyle\int_0^\infty e^{-rx}V(x)\ln[V(x)]dx}{\displaystyle\int_0^\infty xe^{-rx}V(x)dx} \equiv \frac{E}{T}$$

(1.5)

The parameter T is the mean generation time. S is called the **demographic entropy**: It is a measure of the uncertainty of the age of a newborn's mother. It measures the degree of iteroparity: small values of S specify late age at maturity, small progeny sets, and extended reproductive spans and large values the opposite. H is called the **evolutionary entropy**: It characterizes the **robustness** of the population, that is, the ability of the population to retain its phenotypic characteristics in the face of random perturbations in its phenotypic state. H is negatively correlated with the coefficient of variation in population size. E is called the **net reproductive index**: It describes the net-offspring production $\ln[V(x)]$, averaged over all age classes. Φ is called the **reproductive potential**.

To relate the Malthusian parameter with demographic stochasticity, Demetrius and Ziehe (2007) introduce a demographic parameter called the **demographic variance**, defined as

$$\sigma^2 = \frac{\displaystyle\int_0^\infty e^{-rx}V(x)\{-x\Phi + \ln[V(x)]\}dx}{\displaystyle\int_0^\infty xe^{-rx}V(x)dx}$$

(1.6)

A mutant can be characterized by its effect on r and σ^2:

$$\Delta r = r^* - r$$
$$\Delta\sigma^2 = \sigma^{*2} - \sigma^2$$

(1.7)

where * denotes the mutant, and the selective advantage of the mutant, s, is given by

$$s = \Delta r - \frac{1}{N}\Delta\sigma^2$$

(1.8)

where N is the population size. Note that as population size approaches infinity, the selective advantage converges to the Fisherian model. The present analysis takes into account that populations are of finite size, whereas the usual, unstated, assumption is that the population is very large. Predicted outcomes can be determined given the signs of Δr and $\Delta\sigma^2$ (Table 1.1).

Table 1.1 Predicted outcome of a mutant with specified effects on r and demographic variance σ^2

Δr	$\Delta \sigma^2$	N	Invasion	Extinction
Positive	Negative	Does not matter	Highly likely	
Negative	Positive	Does not matter		Highly likely
Positive	Positive	$>\Delta\sigma^2/\Delta r$	Highly likely	
Positive	Positive	$<\Delta\sigma^2/\Delta r$		Decreasing with N
Negative	Negative	$>\Delta\sigma^2/\Delta r$		Highly likely
Negative	Negative	$<\Delta\sigma^2/\Delta r$	Decreasing with N	

1.2.3 Environments of fixed length (e.g., deterministic seasonal environments)

An example in this case is a univoltine life cycle in a seasonal environment that shows no interannual variation. One fitness metric in this instance is the number of offspring that a female produces at the end of the season (Roff 1980). This measure may have to be modified to take into account the quality of the offspring in which case the measure may be redefined as the reproductive success of the offspring of a female. If multiple generations are possible the fitness criterion becomes the reproductive success of the descendants passing into the next season of offspring of a female that originated at the start of the season. By adding the mathematical constraints of a cutoff, these definitions can be subsumed under the more general fitness criterion of invasibility, which will be discussed shortly.

1.2.4 Constant environment, density-dependence with a stable equilibrium

This case was studied extensively by Charlesworth (1972), who showed that the focus of selection is the age group or groups in which the density-dependence occurs, called the **critical age group**: Selection will favor the strategy that maximizes the number of individuals in the critical age group. If the population model is written as a projection matrix the maximum fitness is given by the **dominant Lyapunov exponent** (van Dooren and Metz 1998; also see Chapter 3). Metz et al. (1992), and later Ferriere and Gatto (1995), asserted that the dominant (also called the leading) Lyapunov exponent is an appropriate general criterion of invasibility. Rand et al. (1994) called this parameter the **invasion exponent**. As this criterion measures the long-term growth rate of a population (Ferriere and Gordon 1995) it relates directly to the Malthusian parameter. In some cases, an easier and equivalent fitness measure is the **net reproduction rate**, which is the expected offspring production by a female (see equation (1.3); also see van Dooren and Metz [1998]).

The question of the relationship between equilibrium population size and relative fitness has risen repeatedly, commencing with the concept of r and K selection (see review in Roff [1992]). It is clear from the critical age group that fitness cannot be evaluated to population size nor would we expect that relative selection pressures could be evaluated from total population size. Caswell et al. (2004) explored this problem and produced a general theorem on density-dependent sensitivity in matrix population models. The **effective equilibrium density**, $\tilde{N}$, is not the census number but rather a weighted value of each stage, the weights being a function of the contribution to density-dependence and the effect of the stage on λ (= the dominant eigenvalue of the density-dependence matrix). At equilibrium $\lambda = 1$. The effect of variation in some parameter θ on λ is measured by its **elasticity**, which is defined as the proportional change in λ resulting from an infinitesimal proportional change in θ. For detailed discussion of elasticity, see Grant (1997), Grant and Benton (2000, 2003), Caswell (2002), and Van Tienderen (2000). The elasticity of λ to θ is proportional to the elasticity of $\tilde{N}$ to θ

$$\frac{\theta}{\lambda}\frac{\partial \lambda}{\partial \theta}\bigg|_{\theta_0,\tilde{n}} = \frac{\theta}{\lambda}\frac{\partial \tilde{N}}{\partial \theta} = \tilde{N}\frac{\theta}{\tilde{N}}\frac{\partial \tilde{N}}{\partial \theta} \tag{1.9}$$

Any change that increases λ will increase $\tilde{N}$ but not necessarily the total census population. The sensitivity of the invasion exponent to a change in the parameter θ, is given by the elasticity of λ to θ

$$\frac{1}{\lambda}\frac{\partial \lambda}{\partial \theta}\bigg|_{\theta_0,\tilde{n}} \tag{1.10}$$

from which it is evident that the invasion of a mutant will increase the effective equilibrium density and the **ESS** (**Evolutionarily Stable Strategy**, a strategy that cannot be invaded by another mutant) will maximize the effective equilibrium density.

As noted earlier, for a homogeneous population at stable equilibrium r equals zero and the characteristic equation reduces to equation (1.2) and ignoring the density-dependent effect we have the net reproduction rate, R_0 (see equation [1.3]). This parameter is one of the most widely used operational metrics of fitness (e.g., Roff [1992]; Stearns [1992]; Charnov [1993]; see Chapter 2) but its use implies a particular definition of the biological scenario, which is often not overtly acknowledged. In order for R_0 to be an appropriate definition of fitness *either the density-dependence is selectively neutral* or *the density-dependence is neutral with respect to the trait under study* (Roff 1992, p. 39). Determination of the optimal life history using r may give a different answer to that obtained using R_0 (Roff 1992, pp. 183–184; Stearns 1992, pp. 31–33): Both answers cannot be right and the correct one (if either is correct) depends upon the population dynamical assumptions. If the population is assumed to be at equilibrium and the above assumption(s) of density-dependence hold, then R_0 is appropriate. On the other hand, if the population is in a growing phase and again the above assumption(s) of density-dependence hold, then r is appropriate. If density-dependence is not selectively neutral, then neither metric is appropriate and the analysis must take the selective effects of the density-dependence into account (Mylius and Diekmann 1995; Benton and Grant 2000; Brommer 2000).

1.2.5 Constant environment, variable population dynamics

Even in a constant environment a population may still show fluctuations as a result of the deterministic properties of the population model. A general and much used example of this is the Ricker function (see Chapter 3):

$$N_{t+1} = \lambda N_t e^{-MN_t} \tag{1.11}$$

where N_t is the population size at time t, λ is the finite rate of increase at low population numbers, and M is a parameter that could be the mortality of juveniles resulting from competition or cannibalism by the parents. Depending on the value of λ, the population is either stable ($1 \le \lambda \ge 2$), oscillates with a period of 2^n (where n is a positive integer, the value of n depending on the value of λ, with $e^2 < \lambda < e^{2.6924}$) or displays chaotic fluctuations ($\lambda > e^{2.6924}$).

What we would like to know is whether a mutant can invade such a population, which is generally termed the resident population. To find this out we consider the situation at the beginning of the process when the mutant is so rare that it cannot have a significant effect on the dynamics of the system. If under these circumstances the mutant can increase in frequency, then we presume that it will increase to fixation in the population. Note that this assumption presupposes no frequency-dependence. Nor does it suppose that there is necessarily a unique parameter set that is resistant to invasion by all other mutants (see below and Chapter 3 for further discussions). We can write the trace for the resident population as

$$\begin{aligned} N_{R,t} &= \lambda_R e^{-M_R N_{R,t}} N_{R,t-1} \\ N_{R,t-1} &= \lambda_R e^{-M_R N_{R,t-2}} N_{R,t-2} \\ N_{R,t} &= N_{R,0} \lambda_R^t \prod_{i=0}^{t} e^{-M_R N_{R,i}} \end{aligned} \tag{1.12}$$

where the subscript R designates the parameters of the resident population. Taking logs gives

$$\ln N_{R,t} - \ln N_{R,0} = t \ln \lambda_R - M_R \sum_{i=0}^{t} N_{R,i} \tag{1.13}$$

Taking limits gives

$$\ln \lambda_R - M_R \frac{\sum_{i=0}^{t} N_{R,i}}{t} = \lim_{t\to\infty} \frac{1}{t} E(\ln N_{R,t} - \ln N_{R,0}) \tag{1.14}$$

which is the dominant Lyapunov exponent, given the symbol s by Ferriere and Gatto (1995). Because a mutant will be in insignificant numbers in the initial invasion, the trace of population numbers is given by the trace of population numbers of the resident population, that is, $\sum_{i=0}^{t} N_{R,i}$. Thus, the invasion (Lyapunov) exponent of a mutant, s_m, is given by

$$s_m = \ln \lambda_m - M_m \frac{\sum_{i=0}^{t} N_{R,i}}{t} \tag{1.15}$$

and the condition for the mutant to invade is

$$\frac{\ln\lambda_m}{M_m} > \frac{\ln\lambda_R}{M_R} \qquad (1.16)$$

In the above example, it is possible to derive an exact expression for the invasion (Lyapunov) exponent: This will frequently not be the case and numerical methods will have to be employed (see Chapter 3). Nothing in the above theory precludes the existence of a polymorphism, and indeed the origin of the theory for temporal variation, discussed later, was initiated by the presence of dimorphism for dormancy in plants (Cohen 1966).

1.2.6 Temporally stochastic environments

Environments are rarely if ever temporally stable and such variation is likely to be reflected in variation in vital rates. In general, a population growth rate converges to a fixed quantity, which Tuljapurka (1982) labeled a to distinguish it from the Malthusian parameter. In a constant environment a is equivalent to the Malthusian parameter. Population size at some time t can be represented by

$$\begin{aligned}
N_t &= \lambda_{t-1}N_{t-1} \\
N_{t-1} &= \lambda_{t-2}N_{t-2} \\
N_t &= N_0 \prod_{i=0}^{t} \lambda_i
\end{aligned} \qquad (1.17)$$

Taking logs gives

$$\ln N_t = \ln N_0 + \sum_{i=0}^{t} \ln[\lambda_i] \qquad (1.18)$$

As noted earlier, under relatively unrestricted conditions – namely, (a) demographic weak ergodicity, (b) the random process generating vital rates is stationary and ergodic, and (c) the logarithmic moment of vital rates is bounded (Tuljapurkar 1989; see Tuljapurkar [1990] for a definition of demographic weak ergodicity) – the value of $N(t)$ becomes independent of the initial condition, N_0, and the long-run growth rate and hence the fitness of a particular life history is given by Cohen (1966), Tuljapurkar and Orzack (1980), and Caswell (2001):

$$\ln\lambda = \lim_{t\to\infty} \frac{1}{t} E(\ln N_t - \ln N_0) \qquad (1.19)$$

Fitness is measured by the **geometric mean** of the finite rate of increase. The geometric mean rate of increase, $\bar{r}_G$, is a function of the arithmetic mean finite rate of increase, $\bar{\lambda}$, and its variance, σ_λ^2. Using a Taylor series expansion an approximate formula is (Lewontin and Cohen 1969)

$$\bar{r}_G = E(\ln\lambda) \approx \ln\bar{\lambda} - \frac{\sigma_\lambda^2}{2\bar{\lambda}^2} \qquad (1.20)$$

The important point is that increases in the variance in the rate of increase decrease fitness and thus selection will favor strategies that both increase the arithmetic rate of increase and decrease it variance. One such manner in which the latter can be achieved is by producing variation in offspring phenotypes. This concept appears to have been put forward at least three times since 1966. It is implicit in Cohen's analysis (1966) of the optimal germination rate in a randomly varying environment, was explicitly advanced verbally by den Boer (1968), who referred to it by the term "**spreading the risk,**" and finally discussed by Gillespie (1974, 1977) in the context of variation in offspring number. Slatkin (1974), in reviewing Gillespie's work, labeled the phenomenon as "**bet-hedging,**" a term that has stuck. The forgoing arguments apply to populations of infinite size, but we might expect from the analysis of Demetrius and Ziehe (2007) that this fitness measure may break down at low population sizes. Indeed, for a particular scenario in which there is a common and a rare environment (King and Masel 2007) showed that bet-hedging would not be favored when

$$N < \sqrt{2(s+1)/(s\theta)} \tag{1.21}$$

where N is the population size, s is the selective advantage associated with switching in the rare environment, and θ is the rate of encountering the rare environment.

With age structure, the equivalent measure of the long-term population growth rate in relation to the arithmetic average is (Orzack and Tuljapurkar 1989)

$$a \approx \ln\lambda - \frac{\mathbf{S}^{\mathrm{T}}\mathbf{V}\mathbf{S}}{2} \tag{1.22}$$

where $\ln\lambda$ is the dominant eigenvalue of the average Leslie matrix, $\mathbf{S}$ is a column vector of the sensitivities of λ to a fluctuation in the matrix elements (i.e., $S_{ij} = \partial\ln\lambda/\partial x_{ij}$, where x_{ij} is the ij element), $\mathbf{S}^{\mathrm{T}}$ is its transpose, and $\mathbf{V}$ is a variance–covariance matrix of the elements (x_{ij}).

Equation (1.22) can be illustrated with a simple two-age class model described by Tuljapurkar (1989). Population change is described by the equation

$$\mathbf{N}_{t+1} = \mathbf{A}_t\mathbf{N}_t \tag{1.23}$$

where

$$\mathbf{N}_t = \begin{pmatrix} N_{1,t} \\ N_{2,t} \end{pmatrix} \text{ and } \mathbf{A}_t = \begin{pmatrix} \dfrac{m_1}{x} & \dfrac{m_2}{x} \\ S & 0 \end{pmatrix} \tag{1.24}$$

Fecundity at age i equals m_i and survival from age class 1 to age class 2 equals S. Uncorrelated temporal variability is described by the parameter x which follows a gamma distribution with probability density function:

$$P(x) = \frac{v^v}{(v-1)!}x^{v-1}e^{-vx} \tag{1.25}$$

The parameter x measures the variance, with the variance increasing as v approaches zero and x approaching 1 as v approaches infinity. If the parameters are fixed at their average values the ratio m_2N_t/m_1N_t converges to a stable value, say R^*. The growth rate of the population is then given by

$$r = \ln \bar{\lambda} = \ln\left[\left(\frac{m_2S}{m_1}\right)R^*\right] \tag{1.26}$$

The long-run average growth rate of the population with temporal variability, a, is approximately

$$a \approx r - \left(\frac{1}{2x\lambda^2C^2}\right)\left(m_1 + \frac{m_2}{\lambda}\right)^2 \tag{1.27}$$

where $C = 2 - \{m_1x/[(x-1)\lambda]\}$. As in the case of equation (1.20) the average growth rate is diminished by variability in the vital rates. Thus it is insufficient to determine the most fit life history using the growth rate from the averaged values of the life history.

While the fate of a gene or mutant can be determined by the geometric mean or long-run growth rate, and thus fitness can be so defined for the sake of modeling, Lande (2007, p. 183) has shown that "these measures fail to describe the expected short-term dynamics of gene frequencies or mean phenotypes, by which expected selection coefficients and expected relative fitnesses should be defined." The expected relative fitness of an individual is the Malthusian fitness of the genotype or phenotype in the average environment minus the covariance of its growth rate with that of the population. A consequence of this is that the expected relative fitness is frequency-dependent (Land 2007). This result is important in correctly defining fitness but, as noted earlier, this does not change the utility of the geometric mean or long-run growth rate as a metric by which to calculate the optimal combination of trait values.

1.2.7 Temporally variable, density-dependent environments

From the following discussions the most appropriate measure of fitness is the invasion exponent. Given the complexity of the interactions it is likely that analytical solutions will not be typically available and one will have to resort to simulation analysis. Benton and Grant (2000) investigated the reliability of alternate measures of fitness for models in which there was both density-dependence and temporally uncorrelated variation. Four models of density-dependence were investigated: Beverton and Holt-type, Ricker-type, Usher-type with gradual onset of density-dependence, and Usher-type with sudden onset of density-dependence. Beverton and Holt-type models produce a stable equilibrium, whereas the Usher-type with sudden onset of density-dependence generally produces chaotic behavior. The dynamical behavior of the other two depends on parameter values, though Benton and Grant (2000, p. 773) state that "the vast majority of other combinations of density-dependence … resulted in equilibrium dynamics." Given the predicted differences between models with equilibrium versus nonequilibrium dynamics it is unfortunate that the analysis did not divide the results both according to the four-model types and the two-dynamical behaviors. Benton and Grant (2000) considered the following "surrogate" measure of fitness: r, R_0, and a estimated both with and without density-dependence effects and the average (both arithmetic and geometric) population size, K.

First, Benton and Grant simulated constant environments and found, as expected, that for the chaotic models none of the fitness criteria performed well. On the other hand, the $DI - R_0$ and K performed well for the Beverton–Holt model, which does not exhibit chaotic behavior. In a stochastic environment the best predictor of the invasion exponent was K, although it has to be remembered that the density-dependence in the models was a direct function of total population size. The general message from the analyses is that if the population is expected to show variable dynamics, either due to environmental fluctuation or intrinsic population dynamical properties, and density-dependence is not a consequence of a response to total population number. the only viable measure of fitness is the invasion exponent. However, the result in a model with chaotic population dynamics may also depend upon the mode of inheritance (compare Scenario 3 of Chapter 3 with Scenario 5 in Chapter 4). In populations showing more or less stable equilibria the density-independent R_0 appeared to be a reasonable measure, which is reassuring, given the considerable number of analyses based on this fitness measure.

1.2.8   Spatially variable environments

Starting with Levene (1953) there has been a considerable number of population and quantitative genetic analyses of the conditions required for the maintenance of genetic variation (reviewed in Roff [1997]). So far as I am aware, these analyses have assumed nonoverlapping generations (i.e., no age structure). The solution to defining fitness when the environment is spatially variable and there is a stable-age distribution was enunciated independently by Houston and McNamara (1992) and Kawecki and Stearns (1993). The critical realization in deriving the solution was that fitness must be measured over the entire environment simultaneously and not patch by patch. Thus, if we take r as the appropriate fitness measure (meaning that we assume an equilibrium population) the measure that selection will maximize is the rate of growth of the population as a whole

$$\int P(h) \int V(x,h)e^{-r_{\text{Pop}}x}dx = 1 \qquad (1.28)$$

where r_{Pop} is the rate of growth of the entire population (as opposed to the rates of growth within each patch), $P(h)$ is the probability of patch of type h occurring, and $V(x, h)$ is the value of $l(x)m(x)$ for patch of type h. One would expect that in a spatially variable world a reaction norm would evolve to modify the life history patterns in response to the habitat parameters, the evolutionary change obviously being dependent on the presence and predictability of cues that indicate habitat type. Nevertheless, the maximization of fitness within each patch is subject to the constraint imposed by equation (1.28).

For density-dependent populations in which equilibrium is attained and for which density-dependence is assumed to be selectively neutral the appropriate criterion is the **net reproduction rate**, R, and the fitness criterion becomes

$$R_{\text{Pop}} = \int P(h) \int V(x, h)dx \qquad (1.29)$$

meaning that selection will favor the life history that maximizes R for the population s as a whole (Charlesworth 1994). If density-dependence is not selectively neutral, then equation (1.29) must include those effects.

1.2.9 Social environment

In the environments so far discussed, the relationship between individuals is of no consequence because social interactions are absent. In this book I shall not explicitly consider the social environment, although it can be accommodated within the various analytical frameworks. When survival or reproduction depends upon interactions between individuals that might be related it is necessary to take into account the increment of fitness accruing to the individual by virtue of such interactions. Two relatively well-studied social phenomena are altruism (Koenig 1988; Dugatkin and Reeve 1994, 1998; Thorne 1997; Ratnieks and Wenseleers 2008) and "helpers-at-the-nest" behavior (Koenig et al. 1991; Bshary and Bergmueller 2008; Carranza et al. 2008).

The overall fitness, inclusive of interactions among relatives, was termed **inclusive fitness** by Hamilton (1964), though, because of the obscurity of Hamilton's definition, it was, at least initially, frequently interpreted incorrectly (Grafen 1982). Operationally, inclusive fitness can be defined, or replaced by, Hamilton's rule, which states that organisms are selected to perform actions for which

$$r^*b - c > 0 \qquad (1.30)$$

where r^* is relatedness, and b, c refer to the effects of an allele on offspring production: bearers of this allele behave in such a manner that each has c fewer offspring, and the bearer's sib has b more offspring (Grafen 1984). Queller (1996) noted that it is phenotypes that interact not genotypes and suggested replacing r^* with $\text{Cov}(G_A, P_O)/\text{Cov}(G_A, P_A)$, where G_A is the genetic value of the "actor" or focal individual, P_A is its phenotypic value, and P_O is the phenotypic value of the average phenotype. For other formulations of the relatedness coefficient see Pepper (2000). Taylor et al. (2006) expanded Hamilton's rule to a class-structured model, while Gardner et al. (2007) provide a multilocus version of the rule. Oli (2002) provides a method of estimating inclusive fitness in an age-structured population using a Leslie matrix formulation. For other modifications of Hamilton's rule that have been advanced to account for such things as nonadditivity of fitnesses see Fletcher and Zwick (2006).

More generally, b and c in equation (1.30) are referred to as the benefits and costs, respectively. A potential problem with using Hamilton's rule is in operationally defining these costs and benefits, leading some to attempt to use a more direct definition of inclusive fitness, which in turn has led to discussion over how to correctly calculate this quantity. The issue lies in the verbal description given by Hamilton (1964) that inclusive fitness is the sum of the fitness that would be obtained in the absence of the social environment (e.g., helpers at the nest) and the added increment due to the presence of the social environment. The problem is in calculating the former quantity. Creel (1990) pointed out that a potential paradox can arise if the social environment is essential for successful reproduction, as is almost the case for the dwarf mongoose, *Helogale parvula*. Stripping away the social environment leaves the reproductive individual with zero fitness, all the fitness being attributed to the helpers. Thus there should be contest to be helpers and not reproductives, which is clearly not the case and makes no sense genetically. Creel's solution to this paradox was shown by Queller (1996) to be inappropriate and that the solution resides in recognizing that Hamilton's rule applies strictly only when fitnesses are additive, which in the mongoose case they are not. The paradox is removed when nonadditive versions of Hamilton's rule are used (Queller 1996; Pepper 2000; West et al. 2002).

1.2.10 Frequency-dependence

A reasonably general definition of frequency-dependent selection is that given by Ayala and Campbell (1974, p. 116): "The selective value of a genotype is frequency dependent when its contribution to the following generation relative to alternative genotypes varies with the frequency of the genotype in the population." There are, however, other definitions, which though similar, can be subtlety different, or more restrictive in the sense that stable coexistence is required (Heino et al. 1998). There is no reason why a stable equilibrium frequency of genotypes should be a requirement of frequency-dependent selection and some very simple games such as "Rock-Paper-Scissors" which are clearly frequency-dependent do not have a stable equilibrium (Maynard Smith 1998; see Chapter 6). Most models of frequency-dependent selection assume either competition between clones or Mendelian inheritance with a fixed generation time. In either case fitness is defined in terms of the contribution of types (genotype or phenotype) to the subsequent generation.

An example of frequency-dependence is the occurrence of two types of males in several fish species, particularly salmon: One type of male is territorial whereas the other is typically smaller, matures earlier, cannot maintain a territory, and attempts to sneak fertilizations (Gross 1982, 1985; Hutchings and Myers 1988). The analysis of the equilibrium combination of the two types in the population has either used R_0 as the fitness measure (Gross and Charnov 1980) or r (Hutchings and Myers 1994). A more frequently used approach is that of Game theory, in which the relative fitness of each type when interacting either with another of its type or another type is represented by a payoff matrix. The classic example of this approach is the Hawk-Dove game (Maynard Smith 1982): In this scenario there is a 2×2 payoff matrix indicating the payoff to a hawk when it interacts with either another hawk or a dove and the payoff to a dove when it interacts with either a hawk or a dove. The game is frequency-dependent because although a hawk interacting with a dove has a higher fitness than the dove, a hawk interacting with another hawk suffers a decrement in fitness. The equilibrium frequency of hawks and doves in the population depends upon the relative values in the payoff matrix and is called an ESS. It is obtained simply by equating the payoff to hawks with the payoff to doves: at equilibrium the two must be equal. In simple terms an ESS is one that cannot be invaded by a mutant playing an alternate strategy (see Hammerstein [1998] for a more formal definition). Game theoretic models are discussed in detail in Chapter 6.

1.3   Some general principles of model building

Models are not replicas of nature: If they were they would be just as complicated and equally hard to understand. The purpose of a model is to extract the essential elements that define the problem under study. Having done this we investigate the impact of the model components and compare the predictions of the model with nature. Should there be an obvious discrepancy we return to the model and examine the underlying assumptions: A model is simply the logical outcome of the assumptions and thus any failure to fit reality is a failure of the assumptions. Having modified the model we again compare predictions and observations, repeating the process until a satisfactory fit is obtained.

In constructing a model the following should be kept very much to the fore:

1. Keep the model as simple as possible and focus upon the problem. Modeling the mechanism for telling time provides an instructive example of this process. The modern digital watch is a highly complex affair and seemingly vastly different from the earliest mechanical clocks. Further, when one looks at the history of clocks and watches one sees an enormous variety of mechanisms. Yet under all this complexity and variety, all mechanical or electrical clocks have five elements in common that determine how time is monitored: "(1) a source of energy (spring or battery); (2) an oscillating controller (balance or quartz crystal); (3) a counting device (escapement or solid state circuit); (4) transmission (wheelwork or electric current); (5) display (hands or liquid crystal segments)" (Landes 1983, p. 377). All mechanical or electrical clocks must satisfy these requirements. Thus to find out how a clock works one must strip away the extraneous details such as the size of the clock, whether it gives the date or altitude or compass direction and look for these five preceding elements.

2. Make assumptions explicit. Verbal models are frequently "preferred" because they seem less confined than a mathematical model but in reality verbal models are generally full of "hidden" assumptions that may well result in any conclusions to come crashing down once these assumptions are noted. In this book I adopt the policy of beginning with a general conceptual model and then move to a mathematical construct based on the general assumptions. For example, we might assume that there is a negative relationship between the size and number of offspring that a female produces. This statement is very

general and might be sufficient in some analyses but most cases an analysis will require a more detailed specification such as that the number of offspring is proportional to the reproductive biomass divided by offspring size.

3. This book is primarily concerned with numerical analysis of models: If an analytical solution is possible, then it is to be preferred. Such solutions may be possible only on very simplified versions of the model and numerical analysis of more complex scenarios may reveal inadequacies in the simple analytical solution.

4. While simplicity is desirable it is important to maintain a reasonable level of realism. In this regard it is important to provide operational definitions of all parameters and variables in the model. If a variable cannot be measured, then it is not useful and an alternate approach should be sought.

5. As much as possible, write the model incrementally and as a series of modules that can be examined and debugged separately.

To illustrate these points the next section constructs a model of the evolution of migration in a spatially and temporally heterogeneous environment.

1.4   An introduction to modeling in R and MATLAB

The purpose of this section is twofold: First, it is to outline, by using a simple example, the process of creating a model to address an evolutionary question, and second to illustrate the most important R and MATLAB codes used in the remainder of the book.

The problem we shall consider is that of the evolution of migration in a heterogeneous environment. As used in all the scenarios throughout this book we begin first by outlining a conceptual model and then convert this model into one that can be programmed.

1.4.1   General assumptions

1. The environment is heterogeneous in time and space.

2. This heterogeneity affects population dynamics by causing variation in the vital statistics of the population (e.g., fecundity and survival) and the carrying capacity of the environment.

These two assumptions are too general to be programmed as such and must be converted into a suitable form by addressing the underlying mathematical assumptions, which will necessarily restrict the model to some extent. While we could pose a mathematical model that included the processes outlined above it would include factors, such as age structure, that may not be important to the central issue but could complicate the analysis. Thus to start we begin with a very simple model and ask if in this case spatial and temporal heterogeneity could be an important selective agent. This does not prove that such variation is an important selective agent but does demonstrate that an empirical investigation is warranted.

Our first objective is to examine the hypothesis that environmental variation is plausibly a significant factor in population persistence: If we find this to be the case then it would seem reasonable to suppose that such variation will favor particular life histories, the next step being then to examine what trait might be favored. As noted earlier, we build the computer program incrementally, ensuring that at each step the model is performing as specified by the mathematical assumptions. We begin with the simplest possible model, assuming no environmental variation and then add temporal variation. Our initial model assumes the following.

1.4.2   Mathematical assumptions of model 1

1. There is no age structure.

2. Generations do not overlap.

3. The environment is constant in space and time.

4. Growth per generation is a constant.

An appropriate mathematical model given the above is

$$N_{t+1} = \lambda N_t \tag{1.31}$$

where N_t is the population size at time t and λ is the per generation rate of increase. The above equation is called a **recursive equation**. To program this in R or MATLAB we proceed as follows.

Step 1: Clearing memory

One of the advantages of R and MATLAB is that values are retained in memory even after the program has finished. This can be very useful in that it allows programs to be run sequentially, where one program utilizes the output of the preceding program (e.g., one program might generate values and the second program display them graphically). On the other hand, it can cause problems if one runs another unrelated program that contains parameters with the same name but which have not, due to error, been assigned values (e.g., suppose one ran a program that contained the parameter `Afit` and then a second program that also contained `Afit` but this parameter was inadvertently not assigned a value). In this case the program will pick up the wrong parameter values, most probably leading to incorrect solutions. Unless one wishes to retain values in memory, the best practice is to wipe the memory at the start of each program by having the first line of coding read:

R CODE: `rm(list=ls())`

MATLAB CODE: `clear all`

Step 2: Annotating programs

At the time of writing a computer program the structure and logic might (should) appear clear. However, upon returning to the code after a week or so it is a common experience that the lines of coding have reached a level of obscurity that may necessitate considerable time and effort in clarifying. It is thus very important to annotate the program to a degree that may well seem absurd while constructing the original code. In general, every line of code should have an annotation. Blocks of code that carry out a particular operation should also be annotated at the beginning with a description of the process. In both R and MATLAB remarks can either be on their own line or on the same line as but following a coding instruction. Remarks in R are designated by # and in MATLAB by %. I also like to try to align the text in the coding for ease of reading. Thus for the above two codes clearing memory one should type

```
R CODE:          rm(list=ls())     #  Clear memory

MATLAB CODE:        clear all         %  Clear memory
```

Step 3: Assigning values to parameters and variables

A parameter is defined by the Oxford dictionary as a "quantity constant in case considered, but varying in different cases" whereas a variable is "able to assume different values." Thus in equation (1.31), λ is a parameter but N is a variable. However, variables are considered as parameters when passed to a function (discussed in Step 8), which makes the definitions somewhat murky. The assignment of values to parameters and variables is the basic operation in any program. Consider the task of assigning the value 3 to a variable X. In the usual mathematical notation we write $X = 3$. This is the method used in MATLAB but in R and S-PLUS the "=" sign is replaced by an arrow "<−". (The "=" sign can be used in R but it has a more restricted definition than "<−", as described in the R help dialogue: "The operators <− and = assign into the environment in which they are evaluated. The operator <− can be used anywhere, whereas the operator = is only allowed at the top level [e.g., in the complete expression typed at the Code prompt] or as one of the subexpressions in a braced list of expressions.")

Thus in R we write X <- 3. In like manner any operation on the right is assigned to the variable on the left: for example, $X = a + b$, where a and b are previously assigned parameter values of, say, 1 and 4, respectively, is written as follows:

R CODE:

```
a    <- 1           # Assign the value of 1 to a
b    <- 4           # Assign the value of 4 to b
X    <- a + b       # Assign the sum of a and b to X
```

MATLAB CODE:

```
a = 1;       % Assign the value of 1 to a
b = 4;       % Assign the value of 4 to b
X = a + b;   % Assign the sum of a and b to X
```

Notice that in the MATLAB statements each line before the comment statement is ended with the symbol ";". If this symbol is not appended to the line MATLAB echoes the result of the assignment statement. While this can be a simple and convenient method to print results, it can give very messy output when there are a lot of lines of coding and iterations.

It is good practice to make the names of parameters and variables meaningful so that the code is not too obscure. In the present case we need to assign the number of generations the model will run, the rate of increase, and the initial population size. Now it is possible to insert the first two values in all the relevant locations in the program, but a better approach is to assign the values to parameters, which means that we need only change a single line when changing either value. This is not only easier than altering all lines but eliminates the problem of missing a line and having different values in different parts of the program.

R CODE:

```
MAXGEN  <-  100     # Set maximum number of generations
N.init  <-  20      # Initial population size
LAMBDA  <- 1.1      # Rate of increase
```

MATLAB CODE:

```
MAXGEN  = 100;      % Set maximum number of generations
N.init  = 20;       % Initial population size
LAMBDA  = 1.1;      % Rate of increase
```

Step 4: Creating space to store the output: c(...), vectors, matrices, etc.

For any model there will be information that is generated by the program that we will want to analyze at the end of the simulation. While it is possible to dynamically allocate space, a better method is to preassign the space at the start of the simulation. Information can be stored in a matrix, a vector, an array, a data frame, or a list.

A **matrix** is a two-dimensional (2-D) structure that contains only information of the same type (e.g., only numerical information). A **vector** is simply a matrix with a single column or row. Examples of a vector and a matrix are as follows:

$$A.vector = \begin{bmatrix} 1 \\ 3 \\ 5 \end{bmatrix} \quad A.matrix = \begin{bmatrix} 1 & 6 & 0 \\ 2 & 4 & 2 \\ 4 & 8 & 1 \end{bmatrix}$$

To assign 1, 3, 5 to the vector A.vector we can use the concatenate code c(...) in R and square brackets in MATLAB

R CODE:

```
A.vector  <- c(1, 3, 5)    # Assign values
A.vector                   # print result
```

MATLAB CODE:

```
A.vector = c[1, 3, 5]   % Assign values and print result
```

which will produce the row vector 1 3 5, or we can use the R matrix code

```
A.vector  <- matrix(c(1,3,5), nrow=1, ncol=3)
```

which will produce the same output. The designators `nrow=` and `ncol=` can be omitted as R uses the position to determine which are the row and column counts (putting `nrow=` and `ncol=` in the code does make reading easier). To produce a column vector we can simply switch row and column counts

```
A.vector  <- matrix(c(1,3,5), nrow=3, ncol=1); A.vector
```

Note that in the above construct the two commands are entered not on separate lines but separated by a ";": this can be convenient in compressing code. To create the matrix `A.matrix` we first note that in R the default for filling in a matrix is to fill by columns and hence the sequence of entries is given column-wise

```
A.matrix  <- matrix( c(1,2,4,6,4,8,0,2,1),3,3); A.matrix
```

which produces the output

```
     [,1] [,2] [,3]
[1,]   1    6    0
[2,]   2    4    2
[3,]   4    8    1
```

An **array** is an extension of the matrix in that there can be more than two dimensions. A **data frame** is like a matrix except that it can contain data of different modes: For example, one column might contain character data such as population names and another column could contain numeric data. Data frames are used extensively in statistical analysis but most of the programs in this book use matrices, because the output is typically numeric only. Finally, a **list** is a construction that concatenates a variety of information. Most statistical output in R comes as a list which can be deconstructed to obtain the relevant pieces of information: for more on lists, see Steps 11 and 12.

In the present case we want to store the population size at each generation. There are several possible ways to do this: we shall consider two.

Approach 1: Two vectors
We create two vectors, one that holds the generation number and the second that holds the population size. We know that the generations will run from 1 to MAXGEN and hence we can use the following codes:

R CODE:

```
Generation   <- seq(from=1, to=MAXGEN) # Generation vector
```

MATLAB CODE:

```
Generation = 1:MAXGEN;              % Generation vector
```

To create the vector for population size we first create a matrix with 1 column filled with zeros and then insert our initial population size in the first space.

R CODE:

```
Npop     <- matrix(0,MAXGEN,1) # Generation vector
Npop[1] <- N.init               # Store initial population size
```

MATLAB CODE:

```
Npop     = zeros(MAXGEN);  % Generation vector
Npop(1) = N_init;          % Store initial population size
```

Approach 2: One matrix

An alternate approach is to create a matrix, which I shall call OUTPUT, that has MAXGEN rows and two columns, the first holding the generation number and the second the population size. This can be done in a single call but for clarity I prefer splitting the process

R CODE:

```
OUTPUT     <- matrix(0,MAXGEN,2)    # Pre-assign output space
OUTPUT[,1] <- seq(from=1, to=MAXGEN)# Assign gen nos to col 1
OUTPUT[1,2]<- N.INIT                 # Assign initial popn size
```

MATLAB CODE:

```
OUTPUT       = zeros(MAXGEN,2);  % Pre-assign output space
OUTPUT(:,1) = 1: MAXGEN);         % Assign gen nos to col 1
OUTPUT(1,2) = N_INIT;             % Assign initial popn size
```

Step 5: Iterating over generations: loops

The use of loops is discouraged in any programming language: This is not because loops are intrinsically bad (in fact, they are frequently the most obvious way of writing code) but because no one has come up with a method of making them efficient in terms of speed. R and MATLAB are object-oriented languages and hence in many cases loops can be replaced with an object-oriented approach: For example, suppose we have a vector, X, of N values to which we wish to add the value 3. Using a loop we can write

R CODE:

```
for  (i in 1: N) {X[i]  <- X[i]+3}        # Add 3 to X
```

MATLAB CODE:

```
for i   = 1:N              % ; not required here
X(i)    = X(i) + 3;        % Add 3 to X
end                        % end loop
```

In both R and MATLAB the above construct can be replaced by

R CODE:

```
X <- X + 3
```

MATLAB CODE:

```
X = X + 3;
```

However, recursive equations are best dealt with using a loop structure. In the present case, we wish to iterate from 1 to MAXGEN applying the recursive formula of equation (1.31). I have omitted the remark statement.

R CODE:

```
      for (i in 2:MAXGEN){Npop[i]       <- LAMBDA*Npop[i-1]}
OR    for (i in 2:MAXGEN){OUTPUT[i,2]  <- LAMBDA*OUTPUT[i-1,2]}
```

MATLAB CODE:

```
   for i    = 2:MAXGEN
   Npop(i) = LAMBDA*Npop(i-1);
   end
OR   for i = 2:MAXGEN
     OUTPUT(i,2) = LAMBDA*OUTPUT(i-1,2);
     end
```

Step 6: Plotting the results: 2-D graphs

In general, a graphical output is desirable to see if there is anything obviously wrong with the program. There are many "bells and whistles" that can be added to the graph. The default is a graph that plots the x, y data as points. Neither R nor MATLAB is as convenient as a dedicated graphical package such as SigmaPlot and my own preference is to plot "working graphs" in R and then dump the data into a text file to create better quality plots using SigmaPlot. The graphs given in this book are such "working graphs" and while perfectly satisfactory for visual analysis are not of publishable quality: these are used here to keep the coding simple and to show the reader what the actual output will look like. In the present program, we want (a) a line plot and (b) specified labels on the axes. The appropriate coding is

R CODE:

```
plot(Generation, Npop, xlab='Generation', ylab='Population
size', type='l')
```

OR

```
plot(OUTPUT[,1],OUTPUT[,2], xlab='Generation', ylab='Popula-
tion size', type='l')
```

MATLAB CODE:

```
    plot(Generation, Npop);
    xlabel('Generation');
    ylabel('Population size');
```

OR

```
    plot(OUTPUT(:,1),OUTPUT(:,2));
    xlabel('Generation');
    ylabel('Population size');
```

Putting all of this together gives the R code

```
    rm(list=ls())                           # Clear memory
    MAXGEN      <- 100                       # Set maximum number of
                                               generations
    N.init      <- 20                        # Initial population
                                               size
    LAMBDA      <- 1.1                       # Rate of increase
    Generation <- seq(from=1, to=MAXGEN)    # Generation vector
    Npop        <- matrix(0,MAXGEN,1)        # Generation vector
    Npop[1]     <- N.init                    # Store initial
                                               population size
# Iterate over generations
    for (i in 2: MAXGEN){ Npop[i]   <- LAMBDA*Npop[i-1]}
plot(Generation, Npop, xlab='Generation', ylab='Population
size', type='l')
    print(Npop[MAXGEN])                      # Print last population size
```

Note that I have added a print statement to print out the last population size. In this instance the word print is not required and the same result would be obtained if I had written Npop[MAXGEN]. However, the print function is required in some instances, such as within a loop, and so, as a general rule, I prefer to use it. The graphical output is shown in Figure 1.1. As expected, population growth is exponential with the printout showing that the population has expanded to 250,556.6 individuals. We now move on to the next step and add temporal heterogeneity in model 2.

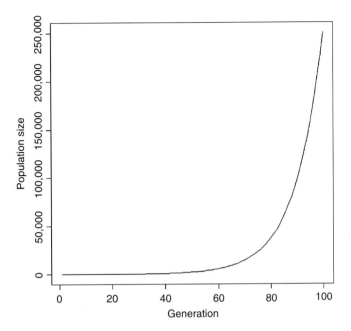

Figure 1.1 Output from model 1 showing exponential increase in population size.

1.4.3   Mathematical assumptions of model 2

1. Assumptions 1 and 2 of model 1 remain the same.

2. There is temporal heterogeneity in the rate of increase λ. For the present pedagogical purpose, I shall assume that λ is a random uniform variate from 0 to MAX.LAMBDA. The mean value of λ, $\bar{\lambda}$, under this scenario is LAMBDA/2.

If MAX.LAMBDA=2.2, then $\bar{\lambda} = 1.1$, the same value as in the constant environment. As the mean growth rate exceeds unity we might, naively, expect that the population would still grow without bound. The expected population size after MAXGEN generations is N.init*LAMBDA^(MAXGEN−1), which in the present case would be the same as in model 1, namely 250,556.6. However, as the numerical analysis will show this is not a correct assessment.

Step 7: Seeding a random number generator

To add temporal variation to the rate increase we use a uniform random number generator (functions `runif` in R and `rand` in MATLAB). All random number generators are pseudorandom numbers in that they are based on a formula that generates numbers that are random for at least a subset of numbers (typically, the generators cycle such that the same sequence is generated after a large number [e. g., 63,000] of generations). Unless and otherwise specified, the generator takes its initial value from some varying component such as the computer clock. For the purposes of debugging a program, it is useful to be able to recreate the same

sequence of random numbers: To do this we "seed" the random number generator, which means that it always starts at the same point and generates the same
sequence.

R CODE:

```
set.seed(100)  # set seed
```

MATLAB CODE:

```
rand('twister', 100);  % set seed
```

In the above code, the integer 100 is arbitrary and set by the user (see the "help"
menus in each language for further details): the important point is that changing
the integer will change the random number sequence generated.

Step 8: Adding a random element: functions `runif` and `rand`
According to the earlier assumptions λ varies between 0 and MAX.LAMBDA. This
means that we must change the variable LAMBDA from a constant to a vector of
random uniform elements. To do this in R we replace

```
LAMBDA        <- 1.1   # Rate of increase
```

with

```
MAX.LAMBDA <- 2.2                   # Maximum rate of increase
LAMBDA       <- runif(MAXGEN, min=0, max=MAX.LAMBDA) # Random
                                                        lambdas
```

In MATLAB we use

```
MAX_LAMBDA = 2.2;                   % Maximum rate of increase
LAMBDA       = Max_LAMBDA*rand(MAXGEN, 1); % Random lambdas
```

The new R coding is

```
rm(list=ls())                    # Clear memory
set.seed(100)                    # set seed
MAXGEN        <- 100             # Set maximum number of generations
N.init        <- 20             # Initial population size
MAX.LAMBDA <- 2.2               # Maximum rate of increase
LAMBDA        <- runif(MAXGEN, min=0, max= MAX.LAMBDA) # Random
                                                          lambdas
Generation <- seq(from=1, to=MAXGEN) # Generation vector
Npop    <- matrix(0,MAXGEN,1)    # Generation vector
Npop[1] <- N.init                # Store initial population size
for (i in 2: MAXGEN) { Npop[i] <- LAMBDA[i-1]*Npop[i-1] }
plot(Generation,  Npop,  xlab='Generation',  ylab='Population
size', type='l')
print(Npop[MAXGEN])              # Print last population size
```

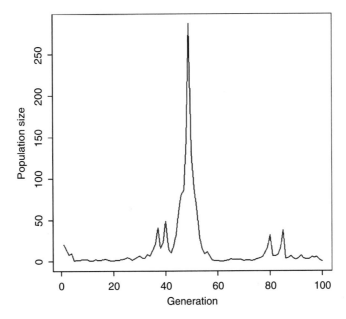

Figure 1.2 Output from a single run of model 2.

Contrary to our naive expectation, the population has a peak at less than 300 and finishes the simulation at only a population size of 0.09446408, much less than the expected value of 250,556.6 (Figure 1.2). The question that immediately arises is whether this is just a fluke of the random number seed we chose: by varying this seed it is easy to see that this is not the case. It is perhaps unreasonable to allow the population size to drop below a single individual and we should assume that the population is extinct at this point.

Step 9: Adding a conditional statement: the `while` loop

One approach to stop the simulation if the population falls below 1 individual is to change the loop to a `while` loop (an alternative possibility is the use of an "if" statement. In the present case this is slower). The `while` construct cycles through the instructions enclosed by {...} until a specified condition is met. We could replace the `for` loop in the model by a `while` loop (ignoring for the present the issue of population sizes less than 1):

R CODE:

```
Gen         <- 1         # Set the generation counter to 1
while (Gen<MAXGEN)
{
Gen         <- Gen+1     # Increment the generation counter
Npop[Gen] <- LAMBDA[Gen-1]*Npop[Gen-1] # new population size
}                        # End of while loop
```

MATLAB CODE:

```
Gen      = 1;              % Set the generation counter to 1
while (Gen<MAXGEN);
Gen        = Gen+1;        % Increment the generation counter
Npop(Gen) = LAMBDA(Gen-1)*Npop(Gen-1); % new population size
end;                       % End of while loop
```

This gives exactly the same output as previously (i.e., Figure 1.3). To add the population size condition we change the `while` statement to

```
while  (Gen<MAXGEN && Npop[Gen]>1)      # R code
while  (Gen<MAXGEN && Npop(Gen)>1);     % MATLAB R code
```

The cycle continues so long as `Gen` is less than `MAXGEN` and `Npop` of the previous cycle is greater than 1. Because we have preassigned zeros to the population numbers, if the simulation stops before the maximum number of generations is reached the plot still shows the population at zero for the remaining generations. An alternative method would be to plot only the data from 1 to `Gen`, which is the last generation of the simulation:

```
plot(Generation[1:Gen],  Npop[1:Gen],   xlab='Generation',
ylab='Population size', type='l')
```

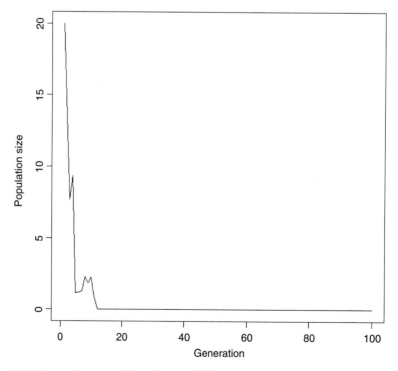

Figure 1.3 Output from model 2 using a while loop to stop the simulation if the number of individuals falls below 1.

We now have two types of output from the model, the final population size and the persistence time (Gen or MAXGEN) for a given run. What we want to do now is to determine the frequency distribution of population sizes and minimum persistence times. Thus, we need to run many replicates.

Step 10: Running multiple simulations: functions

While we could enclose the above coding in an outside loop that ran through the iterations we need, a faster method is to write the model as a function and then use a function such as apply in R (for simplicity I use a loop for MATLAB code). Functions have already been introduced in terms of those supplied by the program (e.g., in R we have used seq, runif, print, set.seed). Here we create our own function. As in Los Vegas, what happens in a function stays in the function, unless passed back to the main program. A function has a name and a set of variables that can be passed to it. If a variable occurs in the function but is not passed to the function the R program uses the value set elsewhere. For example, consider a function called TEST that adds numbers a and b

```
rm(list=ls())
TEST   <- function(x,y) {x+y}    # Function to add two numbers
# Main program
a   <- 5; b   <- 3               # Define numbers
TEST(a,b)                        # Call function
print(c(a, b, a+b))              # Print a, b and their sum
```

Running this program gives the output
```
>  TEST(b)
[1] 8
> print(c(a,b,  a+b))
[1] 5 3 8
```

Now suppose we change the function so that only b is passed and a is incremented within the function
```
rm(list=ls())
TEST <- function(y) {a <- a+1; a+y}  # Function to add two numbers
# Main program
a <- 5; b <- 3                       # Define numbers
TEST(b)                              # Call function
print(c(a, b, a+b))                  # Print a, b and their sum
```

This program gives
```
> TEST(b)  # Call function
[1] 9
> print(c(a, b, a+b))# Print a, b and their sum
[1] 5 3 8
```

The function correctly sets the initial value of a to 5 and increments it to give the summed value of 9 but the value of a is not changed in the main program. This property means that it is not actually necessary to name all variables that are used in the function: However, it is a good practice and avoids possible errors to pass all variables in the function call.

In the present model we want the final population size. Thus we do not need to store the intermediate values. I shall call the function POP (in this book I use all capitals for "user-supplied" functions to distinguish them from the R-supplied functions, which are generally in lower case) and pass to it all the initial parameters (MAXGEN, Npop, MAX.LAMBDA), and receive back the final population size and minimum persistence time. Note that the names in the function call are arbitrary, but it is useful to at least have them similar for readability: thus I have used (Maxgen, Npop, MAX.Lambda). I could equally have used (MAXGEN, Npop, MAX.LAMBDA). The important point is that parameter names in the function match by order the parameter names in the function declaration. The population size and generation are concatenated into a vector for return to the main program. The function should be placed above the main program otherwise R will not find it. However, the clear code (rm(list=ls())) needs to be the first line or it will delete the function from the workspace. In MATLAB, the function is placed in a separate file and has a different opening structure.

R CODE:

```
  POP <- function(Maxgen, Npop, MAX.Lambda) # Population function
{
   Gen <- 1                # Set the generation counter to 1
# Generate Maxgen random lambdas
   LAMBDA <- runif(Maxgen, min=0, max= MAX.Lambda)
# Cycle through until MAXGEN or extinction
   while (Gen<Maxgen && Npop > 1)
  {
   Gen <- Gen+1                # Increment the generation counter
   Npop <- LAMBDA[Gen-1]*Npop # New population size
  }                          # End of while loop
# Concatenate and return the final population size and persistence
   time
   return (c(Npop, Gen))
} # End of function
```

MATLAB CODE:

```
function [Npop, Gen] = POP(Maxgen, Npop, MAX_Lambda) % Population
                                                            function
   Gen  = 1                      % Set the generation counter to 1
% Generate Maxgen random lambdas
   LAMBDA = rand(Maxgen, 1)*MAX.Lambda;
```

```
# Cycle through until MAXGEN or extinction
    while (Gen<Maxgen && Npop > 1)
    Gen = Gen+1;                   % Increment the generation counter
    Npop = LAMBDA (Gen-1) *Npop; % New population size
    end                            % End of while loop
% End of function
```

To access this function we simply call it with the appropriate parameters.

R CODE:

```
set.seed(100)             # set seed
MAXGEN      <- 100        # Set maximum number of generations
N.init      <- 20         # Initial population size
MAX.LAMBDA  <- 2.2        # Maximum rate of increase
POP(MAXGEN, N.init, MAX.LAMBDA )     # Call function POP
```

MATLAB CODE:

```
rand('twister',100)    % set seed
MAXGEN      = 100;     % Set maximum number of generations
N_init      = 20;      % Initial population size
MAX_LAMBDA  = 2.2;     % Maximum rate of increase
[Npop, Gen]   = POP(MAXGEN, N_init, MAX_LAMBDA ) % Call function POP
```

which gives the output $0.8325039\ 11.0000000$. In this case the population size should actually be set to zero (and one could argue that the persistence time is 10 not 11): we shall deal with these issues below.

Step 11: Running multiple simulations: the `apply` function

Suppose we wish to run NREP replicate runs: one way would be to use a loop.

R CODE:

```
    Nrep  <- 10 # Set the number of replicates
# Pre-assign space for the final popn values and generation values
# Column 1 will hold the population and column 2 the generation
    Output  <- matrix(0,Nrep,2)
    for (Irep in 1: Nrep)          # Iterate over replicates
{
    Output[Irep,]  <- POP(MAXGEN, N.init, MAX.LAMBDA)  # Call POP
}                                  # End of replicate loop
```

MATLAB CODE:

```
    Nrep - 10 % Set the number of replicates
% Pre-assign space for the final popn values and generation values
% Column 1 will hold the population and column 2 the generation
    Output = zeros (Nrep,2);
```

```
for (Irep = 1: Nrep)                % Iterate over replicates
[Npop, Gen] = POP(MAXGEN, N_init, MAX_LAMBDA); % Call POP
Output[Irep,1:2] = [Npop, Gen]; % Store output
end                                 % End of replicate loop
```

The full coding in R (lines omitted from POP) is

```
rm(list=ls())                       # Clear memory
POP <- function(Maxgen, Npop, MAX.Lambda) {enter lines as above}
################### MAIN PROGRAM ###################
set.seed(100)            # set seed
MAXGEN           <- 100  # Set maximum number of generations
N.init           <- 20   # Initial population size
MAX.LAMBDA       <- 2.2  # Maximum rate of increase
Nreps            <- 10   # Set the number of replicates
# Pre-assign space for the final popn values and generation values
# Column 1 will hold the population and column 2 the generation
Output <- matrix(0,Nreps,2)
for (Irep in 1: Nreps)   # Iterate over replicates
{
Output[Irep,] <- POP(MAXGEN, N.init, MAX.LAMBDA)  # Call POP
} # End of replicate loop
Output                   # print out matrix called Output
```

The data are stored in the matrix called Output, the first column holding the population sizes and the second column the generation times. The last line prints out the matrix Output:

```
> Output
              [,1]    [,2]
 [1,]   0.8325039    11
 [2,]   0.8863995     5
 [3,]   0.4853632    29
 [4,]   0.5199308    65
 [5,]   0.1201204    18
 [6,]   0.4594043    14
 [7,]   0.6047426     4
 [8,]   0.1101742    17
 [9,]   0.4876619     7
[10,]   0.7386976     3
```

An alternate approach in R that is quicker is the use of the R function apply. Its use in this instance is somewhat unusual in that it is used simply to generate replication whereas it is more typically used to apply a function to the rows or columns of a matrix. The general structure of the function apply is apply(X, MARGIN, FUN, ...), where X is the array to be used, MARGIN is a vector giving the subscripts which the function will be applied over (1 indicates rows, 2 indicates columns, and `c(1,2)` indicates rows and columns), `FUN` is the function to be applied, and ... denotes optional arguments to `FUN`.

Before showing how the apply function can be used to run multiple replicates I shall give an example of its more typical use: suppose we wished to examine the effect of different maximum rates of increase, specifically, `MAX.LAMBDA = 2.1`, 2.2, 2.3, and 2.4. First, we create a matrix holding these values:

```
Maximum.Lambdas  <-  matrix(c(2.1,2.2,2.3,2.4))
```

This matrix is the matrix X to be supplied to the `apply` function. The matrix is a 4 × 1 matrix and hence `MARGIN=1` (i.e., use rows). The function to be supplied is `POP` but we have to make a change to the function declaration sequence because `apply` expects the first component of the sequence to be the value supplied by X: thus we rewrite `POP` as

```
POP  <-  function(MAX.Lambda, Maxgen, Npop)
```

and supply `Maxgen` and `Npop` as optional arguments in `apply`

```
Output  <-  apply(Maximum.Lambdas, 1, POP, MAXGEN, N.init)
```

The function cycles through the matrix `Maximum.Lambdas` and applies the function `POP`, storing the results in `Output`. Printing `Output` gives

```
> Output
        [,1]        [,2]        [,3]        [,4]
[1,]  0.96059   0.8863995   0.9807614   732.6482
[2,]  5.00000   5.0000000  31.0000000   100.0000
```

R is "intelligent" enough to place the two values returned on each cycle in separate rows, meaning that population size occupies the first row and generation number the second row. We can extract these separately by

```
Npops <- Output[1,1:4]; Gens <- Output[2,1:4] # Separate output
```

Returning now to the issue of using `apply` to run multiple replicates: We do not actually wish to supply different values of the three variables in the declaration sequence but simply to call the function multiple times. Therefore, to do `Nreps` replications we create an `Nreps` × 1 (called, say, `MaxL`) matrix with the same value of the first parameter in the function declaration in each cell: so assuming that, as above, `MAX.Lambda` is the first parameter we create `MaxL` using the replicate function `rep`

```
Nreps  <-  10          # Set the number of replications
MaxL   <-  matrix(rep(MAX.LAMBDA, times = Nreps)) # Create
                                                    matrix
                                                    for
                                                    apply
```

We can now call `apply` using `MaxL` as the X array

```
Output <- apply(MaxL, 1, POP, MAXGEN, N.init)   # Call apply
Npops  <- Output[1,1:Nreps]; Npops    # Extract populations
Gens   <- Output[2,1:Nreps]; Gens     # Extract generations
```

The full coding reads

```
    rm(list=ls())   # Clear memory
    POP  <-  function(MAX.Lambda, Maxgen, Npop, ) {enter lines as
above}
################### MAIN PROGRAM ###################
  set.seed(100)        # set seed
  MAXGEN        <- 100    # Set maximum number of generations
  N.init        <-  20    # Initial population size
  MAX.LAMBDA  <- 2.2    # Maximum rate of increase
  Nreps         <- 10    # Set the number of replicates
  MaxL  <- matrix(rep(MAX.LAMBDA, times = Nreps)) # Create matrix
                                               for apply
# We can now call apply using MaxL as the X array
  Output      <- apply(MaxL, 1, POP, MAXGEN, N.init) # Call apply
  Npops  <- Output[1,1:Nreps]; Npops       # Extract populations
  Gens        <- Output[2,1:Nreps]; Gens   # Extract generations
which generates the output
>  Npops      <- Output[1,1:Nreps]; Npops
   [1] 0.8325039 0.8863995 0.4853632 0.5199308 0.1201204 0.4594043
   [7] 0.6047426 0.1101742 0.4876619 0.7386976
>  Gens        <- Output[2,1:Nreps]; Gens
[1] 11 5 29 65 18 14 4 17 7 3
```

Despite the large expected value, the ten replicates become extinct within less than 100 generations. To better examine the statistical distribution of these two types of output we must run many more simulations, 1,000 being a reasonable number for a first analysis. Before doing this we shall return to the issue of setting population sizes of those populations that go extinct to zero and decreasing the displayed generation by 1 to reflect the actual generation at which extinction occurred.

Step 12: Matrix-wide comparisons

Our object is to change all population values less than 1 to zero and subtract 1 from the generations if the population goes extinct before the end of the simulation. While the former could be done using a loop and an "if" statement, a much better approach is to use the following object-oriented construction:

```
Npops[Npops<1] <- 0 # R Set all pop sizes < 1 to 0
Npops(Npops<1) = 0; % MATLAB Set all pop sizes < 1 to 0
```

This statement can be read as "set all values of Npops less than 1 in the matrix Npops to zero." We could do the same for the 2-D matrix Output. In this case we want to examine only the entries in the first column as it is this column that contains the population sizes. The appropriate coding is

```
Output[Output[,1]<1,]   <- 0  # Examine all entries in the
                                 first column
Output(Output[:,1]<1,:] = 0;  % Examine all entries in the
                                 first column
```

which would give the output

```
> Output
     [,1] [,2] [,3] [,4] [,5] [,6] [,7] [,8] [,9] [,10]
[1,]    0    0    0    0    0    0    0    0    0     0
[2,]   11    5   29   65   18   14    4   17    7     3
```

A value of 1 can be subtracted from each element by the matrix-wide operation:

```
Gens <- Gens-1 # R Subtract 1 from each element of Gens
Gens  = Gens-1; % MATLAB Subtract 1 from each element of Gens
```

OR

```
Output[2,] <- Output[2,] −1  # R Subtract 1 from each element of
                               row 2
Output(2,:) = Output[2,:] −1 % MATLAB Subtract 1 from each ele-
                               ment of row 2
```

However, this operation would also subtract 1 from those runs in which the population persisted. To exclude these cases we can write a two-step operation:

R CODE:

```
Gens <- Gens-1           # Subtract 1 from all generations
Gens[Gens==MAXGEN-1] <- MAXGEN # If generation = MAXGEN-1
                               set to MAXgEN
```

MATLAB CODE:

```
Gens = Gens-1;           % Subtract 1 from all genera-
                           tions
Gens(Gens=MAXGEN-1) = MAXGEN; % If generation = MAXGEN-1
                               set to MAXGEN
```

The first line subtracts 1 from all generations, while the second line restores this value if the subtraction gives MAXGEN−1, meaning that the simulation had run its full course in this replicate.

Step 13: Summarizing and plotting the results: functions `hist`, `summary`, `length`

To obtain sufficient replicates to accurately depict the distributions requires at least 1,000 replicates: here I use 10,000 (i.e., `Nreps <- 10000`). A simple graphical display is produced by the histogram function `hist` in both R and MATLAB. There are three graphs that are worth producing: (*a*) the distribution of population sizes for the entire data set, (*b*) the distribution of persistence times, and (*c*) the distribution of population sizes for those populations that persisted the full length of the simulation. To obtain the third group we extract the data from the full set of population sizes:

```
Pops.not.extinct <- Npops[Npops>0] # Extract all populations that
                                             persisted
```

For reasons that will become clear I also plot the log of population size of those populations that persisted. To display all four graphs on the same page we split the graphics page into four sections using

```
par(mcol=c(2,2))          # Split the graphics page into quadrats
```

which tells R to plot the graphs by columns (thus the sequence of plotting will be top left, bottom left, top right, and bottom right. To plot across rows use `par (mfrow=c(2,2))`. The four histograms are plotted with

```
hist(Npops)                 # Histogram of population sizes
hist(Gens)                  # Histogram of persistence times
hist(Pops.not.extinct)      # Histogram of surviving pop sizes
hist(log10(Pops.not.extinct))# Histogram of log surviving pops
```

It is clear from visual inspection of the histograms (Figure 1.4) that the vast majority of populations become extinct before the end of the simulation and that persistence times are generally less than 20 generations. To get a better idea of the numerical results we use the R function `summary` (a similar function is available in the statistics toolbox of MATLAB). This function is a generic function in that it supplies information depending on the R object supplied to it: Thus supplying it with a set of numbers, as in this case, causes it to send back a set of standard summary statistics, whereas supplying it with the object obtained from an analysis of variance causes it to send back an analysis of variance table and associated information. In most cases the information is stored as a list but in this particular case the mode is numeric (to determine the mode of an object use the code `mode(Object name)`). The result of being a numeric rather than a list mode is that the way one extracts information is different. To illustrate the method in the present case we call `summary` and store it as an object:

```
# Get summary data
  Data.Npops            <- summary(Npops)
  Data.Pops.not.extinct <- summary(Pops.not.extinct)
  Data.Gens             <- summary(Gens)
```

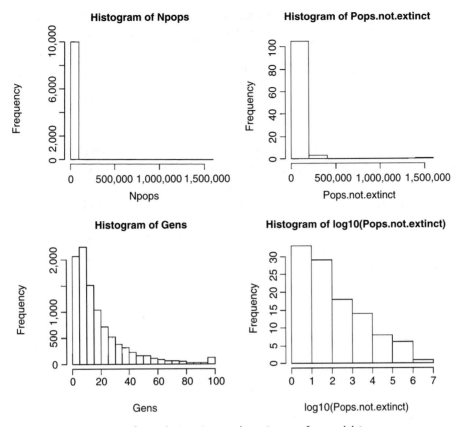

Figure 1.4 Histograms of population sizes and persistence for model 2.

To print out the entire summary information we simply type the object name (I have inserted print statements to make the output more readable):

```
print ( "Summary data for population sizes" ) ;  Data.Npops
print ( "Summary data for Pops.not.extinct"); Data.Pops.not.extinct
print ( "Summary data for persistence times") ;  Data.Gens
```

which generates

```
> print ( "Summary data for population sizes" ) ; Data.Npops
[1] "Summary data for population sizes"
     Min.   1st Qu.   Median      Mean   3rd Qu.        Max.
      0.0       0.0      0.0     315.7       0.0  1574000.0
> print ( "Summary data for Pops.not.extinct"); Data.Pops.not.ex-
tinct
[1] "Summary data for Pops.not.extinct"
     Min.   1st Qu.  Median      Mean   3rd Qu.        Max.
1.498e+00 5.556e+00 5.884e+01 2.896e+04 1.072e+03 1.574e+06
```

```
> print ("Summary data for persistence times");Data.Gens
[1] "Summary data for persistence times"
     Min.    1st Qu.    Median     Mean    3rd Qu.     Max.
     1.00      6.00     13.00    19.09     25.00    100.00
```

Before discussing this output let us return to the summary objects. The summary object in the present case contains six pieces of information: the minimum value, the first quantile, the median, the mean, the third quantile, and the maximum. These components can be accessed separately: suppose, for example, we only wanted the mean value of Npops, which is the fourth entry in Data.Npops: to get this we simply use Data.Npops[4].

Returning to the above output: the mean population size is only 315.7, which is far below the expected value of 250,556.6, though the maximum population size is 1,570,0000, which is far above the expected population size. Unfortunately, the summary function does not give the sample sizes and so it is not possible from this information to assess how many populations persisted through the entire simulation. To extract this information we can use the R function length, which gives the number of elements in an object:

```
length(Pops.not.extinct) # number of populations that persisted
```

which gives 109: so out of 10,000 replications only 1.09% persisted for 100 generations.

Step 14: Further model analysis: more on lists

It is clear that the predicted population size from the deterministic model (model 1) does not match the result from the stochastic model with the same mean rate of increase (model 2). To further illustrate the list construct let us statistically compare the population sizes from model 2 with the size predicted by model 1. For simplicity I shall use a single sample t-test, recognizing that the extreme skew in the distribution makes such a test suspect (but this is for illustration of lists not statistical rigor). This test is available in the statistics toolbox of MATLAB. The R code, saving the output as an object called T.results, is

```
Data         <- Npops-250556.6   # Subtract predicted value
T.results    <- t.test(Data)      # T test with null of zero
T.results                         # Print out results of t test
```

The result is

```
      One Sample t-test
data: Data
t = -1501.757, df = 9999, p-value < 2.2e-16
alternative hypothesis: true mean is not equal to 0
95 percent confidence interval:
-250567.6 -249914.3
sample estimates:
mean of x
-250240.9
```

Obviously the difference is highly significant, even given the skew in the data. The object `T.results` consists of a list of items that can be accessed individually in a number of ways. First, to determine what items are in the list we issue the code

```
names(T.results) # Names of the items in the object T.results
```

with the result

```
[1] "statistic"  "parameter"  "p.value"  "conf.int"  "estimate"
[6] "null.value"  "alternative"  "method"  "data.name"
```

The estimate is located in position 5 and can be accessed in the following ways:

```
T.results[5]
T.results[[5]]
T.results$"estimate"
```

which give three slightly different outputs (but not different values):

```
> T.results[5]
$estimate
mean of x
−250240.9
- - - - - - - - - - -
> T.results[[5]]
mean of x
−250240.9
- - - - - - - - - - -
> T.results$estimate
mean of x
−250240.9
- - - - - - - - - - -
```

If one wishes to use the resulting variable the second two methods are preferred since, for example, `T.results[5]^2` results in the error message "`Error in T.results[5]^2 : non-numeric argument to binary operator`". If one wished to convert the value to a simple numerical value and eliminate the accompanying label "mean of x" use the function `as.numeric`, as in, for example,

```
a <- as.numeric(T.results$estimate) # Convert value to numeric
```

Step 15: An analytical aside: what is going on?

The present model results indicate that the arithmetic mean growth rate does not appear to be a good index of population persistence in a temporally stochastic environment. If this is the case then perhaps the arithmetic mean growth rate is also not an appropriate measure of fitness in a stochastic environment. Haldane and Jayakar (1963) and Cohen (1966) showed that the appropriate measure is the geometric rate of increase. The reason for this resides in the difference between the geometric and arithmetic means (Lewontin and Cohen 1969). In our model population size at time t is given by

$$N_{t+1} = N_0 \lambda_1 \lambda_2 \lambda_3 \ldots \lambda_t = N_0 \prod_{i=1}^{t} \lambda_i \tag{1.32}$$

We assumed that λ_i is a random, uncorrelated variable with mean $\bar{\lambda}$. The expected population size at time t is then given by the product of the initial population size, N_0, times the expectation of the product $\lambda_1 \lambda_2 \lambda_3 \ldots \lambda_t$. Because the λ's are uncorrelated, the expected value of the product is equal to the product of the expected values, giving

$$E\{N_t\} = N_0 E\{\prod_{i=1}^{t} \lambda_i\} = N_0 \prod_{i=1}^{t} E\{\lambda_i\} = N_0 \bar{\lambda}\, t \tag{1.33}$$

At first glance the above result suggests that an appropriate measure of fitness is $\bar{\lambda}$, which is the arithmetic mean of the finite rates of increase (i.e., $\bar{\lambda} = \sum_{i=1}^{t} \lambda_i$) not the geometric, which is given as $\bar{\lambda}_g = (\prod_{i=1}^{t} \lambda_i)^{\frac{1}{t}}$. However, the behavior of populations in a temporally randomly varying environment has the curious property that the expectation of population size will grow without bound whenever $\bar{\lambda} > 0$ but the probability of extinction within a few generations can be virtually certain (Lewontin and Cohen 1969; Levins 1969; May 1971, 1973; Turelli 1977). This paradoxical behavior can be illustrated with a simple example: suppose that λ can take two values, 0 or 3, with equal frequency. The expected value of λ is $(0 + 3)/2 = 1.5$, and hence the expected population size increases without bound as t increases. For example, starting from a single female, after 10 generations $E\{N_{10}\} = 1.50^{10} = 57.7$ but either $N_{10} = 59,049$ or $N_{10} = 0$ and the probability that the population persists for the 10 generations is $(0.5)^{10} = 0.00098$, a very small probability indeed! The geometric mean is always smaller than the arithmetic and the two are related by the approximation $E(\ln \lambda) \approx \ln \bar{\lambda} - \frac{\sigma_\lambda^2}{2\bar{\lambda}^2}$ (Lewontin and Cohen 1969), where $E(\ln\lambda)$ is the geometric mean, $\bar{\lambda}$ is the arithmetic mean, and σ_λ^2 is the variance. Selection should operate to increase the arithmetic mean and decrease its variance, which will increase the geometric mean.

Step 16: Adding spatial heterogeneity

The important conclusion from the model so far is that temporal heterogeneity could be an important selective agent favoring particular types of life history. Our impetus for this analysis was the hypothesis that migration is an important evolutionary response to environmental heterogeneity. Thus the next step of the analysis is to introduce spatial variation, initially keeping all subpopulations isolated.

1.4.4   Mathematical assumptions of model 3

1. The habitat is divided into a number of discrete patches.
2. Rates of increase are stochastically variable and uncorrelated among patches.
3. There is no migration of animals among patches.

There is no conceptual difference between this model and the previous model but there are two avenues by which it could be programmed:

1. Each population is run over its entire simulation within the function as previously done, with the main program iterating over patches.

2. The function could compute the single generation change for all populations and the function called iteratively for each generation of the simulation.

In the subsequent model we wish to introduce migration between habitats at each generation which could not be done under the first approach. Thus the second approach is appropriate in this instance. The coding is a straightforward extension of the previous approach with the following changes:

1. Within the POP function the number of random LAMBDA values generated is equal to the number of patches, not the number of generations.

2. The mean population size (called Npop.Sizes) is followed, which is obtained using the R and MATLAB function mean:

```
Npop.Sizes[Igen] <- mean(Npop)    # R code
Npop_Sizes(Igen) = mean(Npop);    % MATLAB code
```

where Npop is the vector of population sizes at generation Igen.

3. The simulation is stopped when either the maximum number of generations is reached or the mean population size is zero (i.e., all populations are extinct).

4. In addition to mean population size the program also keeps track of the number of extinct populations over time, N.extinct[Igen] (another example of matrix-wide comparison). The R and MATLAB codes are, respectively,

```
N.extinct[Igen] <- length(Npop[Npop==0]) # Store number of
                                              extinct popns
N.extinct(Igen) = length(Npop(Npop=0));  % Store number of
                                              extinct popns
```

The full coding in R is
```
rm(list=ls())     # Clear memory
POP <- function( MAX.Lambda, Npop, N.patches )  # Population
                                                   function
{
LAMBDA <- runif(N.patches, min=0, max=MAX.Lambda) # Generate
                                                     lambdas
Npop <- Npop*LAMBDA # Generate new population size for all patches
Npop[Npop<1] <- 0  # Check for extinction
return (Npop)         # Return the vector of new population sizes
} # End of function
################### MAIN PROGRAM ###################
set.seed(100)         # set seed
MAXGEN      <- 100    # Set maximum number of generations
N.init      <- 20     # Initial population size
MAX.LAMBDA  <- 2.2    # Maximum value of lambda
N.patches   <- 10     # Number of patches
Npop   <- matrix(N.init, N.patches, 1) # Initialise populations
Npop.Sizes <- matrix(0,MAXGEN)     # Pre-assign storage for
                                      mean popn size
```

```
    Npop.Sizes[1] <-  mean(Npop) # Store first generation mean
                            popn size
    N.extinct      <- matrix(0,N.patches,1)   # Storage for nos of
                                     extinct popns
    Igen           <- 1          # Initialize generation counter
    while ( Igen<MAXGEN && Npop.Sizes[Igen]>0) # Start while loop
{
    Igen           <- Igen+1            # Increment generation
    Npop <- POP(MAX.LAMBDA, Npop, N.patches) # New population sizes
    Npop.Sizes[Igen] <- mean(Npop)  # Store mean population size
    N.extinct[Igen]  <- length(Npop[Npop==0]) # Store number of
                                     extinct popns
    }                              # End of while loop
    par(mfcol=c(1,2))          # Divide graphics page into two
# Plot Mean population size over generations and nos extinct per
generation
    plot(seq(1, Igen), Npop.Sizes[1:Igen], xlab="Generation",
ylab="Mean population size", type="l")
    plot(seq(1, Igen), N.extinct[1:Igen], xlab="Generation",
ylab="Mean population size", type="l", ylim=c(0,N.patches))
```

OUTPUT: (Figure 1.5)

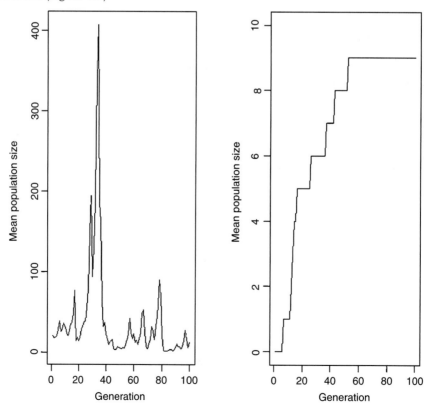

Figure 1.5 Population size and number of extinct populations for model 3.

The output from this model is the same as simply running 10 replicates of model 2 and thus although persistence time is increased the increase is of little evolutionary consequence, most populations becoming extinct within 50 generations. The importance of this model is as a stepping stone to the next model in which we introduce migration among patches.

Step 17: Adding migration

We shall make the simplest possible assumption concerning migration, namely that migrants are distributed among the patches in equal numbers. More complex models are possible (e.g., random assignment, distance-related, etc.) but one should always begin with the simplest model that is biologically not unreasonable.

1.4.5 Mathematical assumptions of model 4

1. All the assumptions of model 3 remain the same in model 4 except that there is now migration among patches.

2. Migrants enter a "common" pool and are then distributed in equal number among the patches.

3. A fixed proportion, P_{mig} (= 0.8 in the present simulation) of the population migrates.

4. Migrants survive migration at the fixed rate of P_{surv} (= 0.95 in the present simulation).

5. Reproduction occurs after migration.

From the above assumptions we get the following recursive equation for the population size in the ith patch at generation $t+1$:

$$N_{t+1,i} = \lambda_{t,i} \left[N_{t,i}(1 - P_{mig}) + \frac{P_{surv}P_{mig}\sum_{j=1}^{n} N_{t,i}}{n} \right] \tag{1.34}$$

where n is the number of patches (N.patches in the coding). The R code for this is

```
Emigrants   <- Npop*P.mig                          # Nos leaving
Immigrants <- sum(Emigrants)*P.surv/N.patches # Immigrants
per patch
Npop <- Npop - Emigrants + Immigrants # Distribute migrants
Npop <- Npop*LAMBDA                    # new population sizes
```

The full coding in R is

```
rm(list=ls())                         # Clear memory
POP   <- function(MAX.Lambda, Npop, N.patches,P.mig,P.surv)
                                      # Pop func
{
LAMBDA   <- runif(N.patches, min=0, max= MAX.Lambda)   # n random
                                                        lambdas
```

```
    Emigrants   <-  Npop*P.mig                      # Nos leaving
    Immigrants <-  sum(Emigrants)*P.surv/N.patches # Immigrants
per patch
    Npop  <- Npop - Emigrants + Immigrants  # Distribute migrants
    Npop  <- Npop*LAMBDA                      # new population sizes
    Npop[Npop<1] <-  0                  # Check for extinction
    return (Npop)                      #  Return the vector of new
population sizes
} # End of function
################### MAIN PROGRAM ###################
    set.seed(100)                         #  set seed
    MAXGEN            <-  1000           # Set maximum number of
                                             generations
    N.init           <- 20              #  Initial population size
    MAX.LAMBDA       <- 2.2            #  Maximum value of lambda
    N.patches        <- 10             #  Number of patches
    P.mig            <- 0.5            #  Proportion migrating
    P.surv           <- 0.95          # Survival rate of migrants
    Npop  <- matrix(N.init,N.patches,1)# Initialise populations
    Npop.Sizes       <- matrix(0,MAXGEN)  # Pre-assign storage
    Npop.Sizes[1]    <- mean(Npop)     # Store first generation
                                         mean population size
    N.extinct <- matrix(0,N.patches,1)  # Storage for nos extinct
                                          popns
    Igen             <- 1              #  Initial generation
  while ( Igen<MAXGEN && Npop.Sizes[Igen]>0)  # Start while loop
{
    Igen             <- Igen+1          # Increment generation
    Npop        <- POP(MAX.LAMBDA, Npop, N.patches, P.mig, P.surv)
                                        # New popn sizes
    Npop.Sizes[Igen] <-  mean(Npop)    # Store mean population
                                         size
    N.extinct[Igen]  <- length(Npop[Npop==0]) # Number of extinct
                                              populations
}                                            # End of while loop
  par(mfcol=c(1,2))                   # Split page into two
  plot(seq(1, Igen), log10(Npop.Sizes[1:Igen]), xlab="Genera-
tion", ylab="Mean population size", type="l")
  plot(seq(1, Igen), N.extinct[1:Igen], xlab="Generation",
ylab="Number of pops extinct", type="l", ylim=c(0,N.patches))
```

OUTPUT: (Figure (1.6)

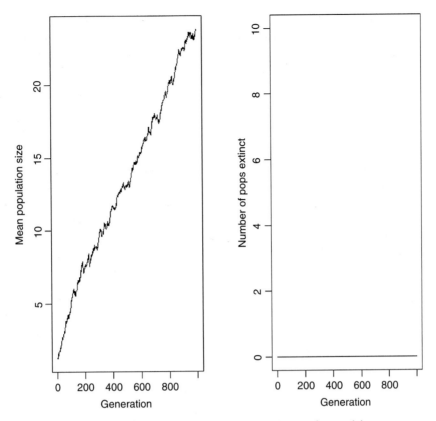

Figure 1.6 Population size and number of extinct populations for model 4.

The output is shown in Figure 1.6. The effect of migration is so great that the plot of population size is best shown on a log scale. Whereas the population crashed quickly in the absence of migration, the presence of migration prevents extinction and the population size increases to the unreasonably large value of 10^{15}.

Step 18: Controlling population growth: model 5

The mean population size reached after the addition of migration is unrealistic but demonstrates the potential evolutionary importance of migration. Before considering a model that allows migration rate to evolve we first add a carrying capacity to constrain population size.

1.4.6 Mathematical assumptions of model 5

1. All assumptions of model 4 apply to model 5 except that there is now a limitation to population size.

2. Population size is limited to a maximum of 1,000 individuals.

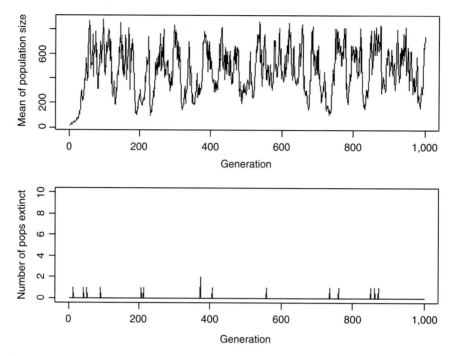

Figure 1.7 Population size and number of extinct populations for model 5 (model 4 plus a carrying capacity). For display purposes the graph page has been split horizontally using `par(mfcol=c(2,1))`. Note that population size is not log transformed.

Assumption 2 is coded as

```
Npop[Npop>1000]   <- 1000  # R code setting limit at 1000
Npop(Npop>1000)   = 1000;  % MATLAB code setting limit at 1000
```

Incorporation of this restriction produces a dramatic drop in population size, an increase in the number of temporally extinct populations, but no indication of a significant decline in population persistence (Figure 1.7). The mean population size over the last 100 generations, obtained from the code `mean(Npop.Sizes [900:1000])` is only 473.2975, which is less than one half of the carrying capacity. Thus, the imposition of a carrying capacity in a heterogeneous environment can have profound effects on population size even though a naive census would suggest that the carrying capacity was not being exceeded (see Roff [1974a, 1974b]).

Step 19: More on graphics: functions `expand.grid, outer, contour, persp`

Many analyses will require investigation of effects due to variation in multiple parameters: one method of graphically viewing such variation is to use a contour plot and a 3-D perspective plot. There are several ways to generate such plot: here I shall present two approaches. Before applying either method to the present model I shall consider a much simpler model to better illustrate the procedures. The object is to plot the equation of a circle:

$$z = \sqrt{x^2 + y^2}, \, -10 < x < 10, 0 < y < 10 \qquad (1.35)$$

First we define the function for z.

R CODE:

```
FUNC.Z  <- function(x,y) {sqrt(x^2+y^2)}
```

MATLAB CODE:

```
function z = FUNC_Z(x,y)
z = sqrt(x^2+y^2)
```

The ranges of x and y are divided into 10 parts (this will generate a matrix of 100 values):

R CODE:

```
n1 <-  4; n2 <-  3
x   <- seq(from=-10, to= 10,  length=n1)
y   <- seq(from=0, to = 10,   length=n2)
```

MATLAB CODE:

```
n1 = 4;
n2 = 3;
x  = linspace(-10, 10, n1);
y  = linspace(0, 10, n2);
```

Now we generate the matrix of z values for all combinations of x and y. In R this can be done by either of the following:

1. Using the R function `expand.grid` which takes the two vectors and generates a two-column matrix of all combinations, with the x variable changing most rapidly:

```
d  <- expand.grid(x,y)      # x values vary first
z  <- FUNC.Z(d[,1], d[,2])  # Create z
```

The two-column matrix is now converted into the appropriate matrix:

```
z.matrix  <- matrix(z,n1,n2)
```

2. An alternate method is to use the function `outer`

```
z.matrix  <- outer(x, y, func.z)
```

The equivalent in MATLAB is `meshgrid` and rather than the function `FUNC_Z` described above, I use here vectorization to give

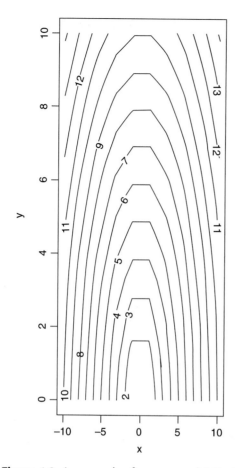
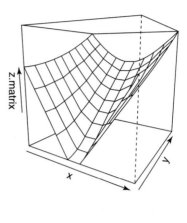

Figure 1.8 An example of contour and 3-D plots.

$$[\text{xx}, \text{yy}] \quad = \quad \text{meshgrid}(\text{x}, \text{y})$$
$$\text{zz} \qquad = \quad \text{x.}^2 + \text{y.}^2$$

The data are now in a format suitable for plotting the contours using `contour` or a 3-D plot using the R function `persp` (Figure 1.8) or `surfc` in MATLAB.

R CODE:

```
par(mfrow=c(1,2))                    # Divide graphics page into two
contour(x,y, z.matrix, xlab="x", ylab="y")   # Contour plot
persp(x, y, z.matrix, theta=30, phi=10)      # 3-D plot
```

The parameters `theta` and `phi` are angles defining the viewing direction: `theta` gives the azimuthal direction and `phi` the colatitude.

MATLAB CODE:

```
subplot(1,2,1); % Divide graphics page in two and plot contour in left
[C,h] = contour(x, y, zz)  % Create contour plot
```

```
% clabel(C,h) rotates the labels and inserts them in the contour
lines
clabel(C,h);
xlabel('x'); ylabel('y'); % Add text
subplot(1,2,2); % Divide graphics page in two and plot contour on
                right
surfc(xx,yy,zz); % Plot a 3-D surface
xlabel('Foraging'); ylabel('Vigilance'); zlabel('Fitness') % Add text
```

Now consider the analysis of variation in P.mig and P.surv in model 5. In this case I want to plot variation in mean population size for the ranges

```
P.mig  <- seq(from=0.1,to=0.9,length=10) # Proportion migrating
P.surv <- seq(from=0.8,to=0.9,length=10) # Survival rate of mi-
                                           grants
```

To do this I make the previous main program into a function

```
MAIN.PROG  <-  function(D)
{
P.mig     <-  D[1]
P.surv    <-  D[2]
```

Same lines as previously except for deletion of plotting codes

```
} # End of function MAIN.PROG
```

I have left the set.seed code in MAIN.PROG which means that the same sequence of random numbers is used for each combination: thus I replicate exactly the same environmental variation for each simulation. Now I can use expand.grid to generate the necessary variation and pass this to MAIN. PROG. However, if I do this exactly as before I will get an error message, because I need to pass only one combination at a time. To pass only one combination per run use the R function apply telling the function to use rows:

```
d           <- expand.grid(P.mig,P.surv)
z           <- apply(d, 1, MAIN.PROG)
z.matrix    <- matrix(z, length(P.mig), length(P.surv))
par(mfrow=c(1,2))
contour(P.mig, P.surv,z.matrix, xlab ="P.mig", ylab="P.surv")
persp(P.mig, P.surv, z.matrix, theta=20, phi=20)
```

OUTPUT: (Figure 1.9)

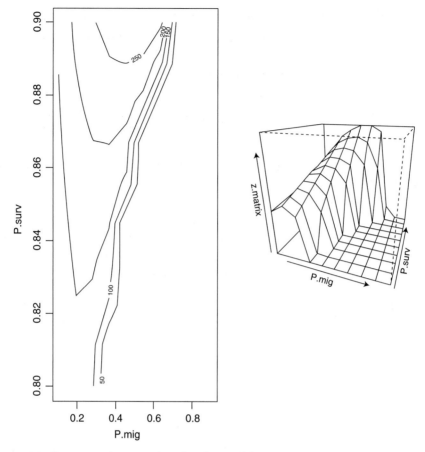

Figure 1.9 Contour and perspective plots for model 5.

The results plotted in Figure 1.9 show that population size increases with P.surv (not surprisingly) and that it is largest at an intermediate value of P.mig.

Step 20: Adding inheritance: functions `pnorm`, `dnorm` and numerical integration

The observation from the above analysis of the potential importance of migration in a heterogeneous environment raises the question of what is the optimal migration rate. This question is made difficult to answer analytically because at the metapopulation level fitness is frequency-dependent (Roff 1994a). Migrants can be reasonably assumed to suffer an increased mortality rate (in models 4 and 5) and a decrease in reproductive opportunities by a lack of time and by the allocation of energy to migration, both in terms of the energy used in migration and the energy sequested for the capability of migration, as found in wing-dimorphic insects (Roff 1996; Roff and Fairbairn 2007). For the present analysis I shall use a threshold model for the genetic basis of migrant and nonmigrant phenotypes.

1.4.7 Mathematical assumptions of model 6

1. Assumptions of model 5 hold for model 6 except that migration propensity is inherited.

2. Mating is at random and occurs prior to migration.

3. Individuals can be divided into two classes, nonmigrants and potential migrants. Individuals in the latter class migrate with a probability P_{mig} and survive the migratory episode with probability P_{surv}. Additionally, potential migrants suffer a reduction in reproductive fitness because of their allocation of resources to the capability of migration (e.g., presence or absence of a functional flight apparatus in wing-dimorphic insects).

4. Migratory propensity is inherited as a quantitative trait as specified by the threshold model. According to this model there is a continuously normally distributed underlying trait called the liability: individuals above a threshold develop into one type of morph, while individuals below the threshold develop into the alternate (Figure 1.10). Without loss of generality, we can set the threshold at zero and the variance of the distribution at 1. Assuming, again without loss of generality, that nonmigrants are those individuals lying above the threshold the proportion of nonmigrants in the population is given by the normal distribution function

$$P = \int_{0}^{\infty} \phi\left(x - \mu\right)dx, \text{where } \phi(x) = \frac{1}{\sqrt{2\pi}}e^{-\frac{1}{2}x^2} \tag{1.36}$$

where μ is the mean value of the liability. This function cannot be integrated symbolically but there is an R function `pnorm` and a MATLAB function `normcdf` that provide a solution. The integral from zero to infinity, given a mean of `Mu` (which can also be vector of values) is obtained as

```
P  <- pnorm( 0, mean= -Mu, sd=1) # R code
P  = normcdf(0, -Mu, 1);% MATLAB code
```

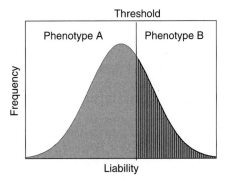

Figure 1.10 Graphical illustration of the threshold model. Individuals with liabilities below the threshold develop into phenotype A, whereas individuals with liabilities above the threshold develop into phenotype B.

The function $\phi(x)$ can be calculated using the R function `dnorm` or the MATLAB function `normcdf`. Numerical integration can be done in R using the function `integrate` and in MATLAB the functions `int` or `quad` (see, e.g., Scenario 4 of chapter 2). The mean values of nonmigrants, X_{NM}, and potential migrants, X_{PM}, can be calculated from the respective truncated normal distributions, giving

$$X_{NM} = \mu + \frac{\phi(\mu)}{P}, \quad X_{PM} = \mu - \frac{\phi(\mu)}{1-P} \tag{1.37}$$

Given random mating prior to migration, the phenotypic value of the liability of nonmigrants, Y_{NM}, and potential migrants, Y_{PM}, is (Roff 1994)

$$Y_{NM} = \mu + \frac{\phi(\mu)h^2}{2P}, \quad Y_{PM} = \mu - \frac{\phi(\mu)h^2}{2(1-P)} \tag{1.38}$$

which can be coded in R as (respectively)

```
Y.nonmigrants  <- Mu + dnorm(0, mean=Mu, sd=1)*h2/(2*P)
Y.migrants     <- Mu - dnorm(0, mean=Mu, sd=1)*h2/(2*(1-P))
```

where h^2 is the heritability of liability (set at 0.5 in the present model). The mean phenotypic value of offspring in the ith patch at generation $t+1$, $\mu_{t+1,i}$ is given by (Roff 1994)

$$\mu_{t+1,i} = \frac{N_{t,i}[Y_{NM,t,i}P_{t,i} + Y_{PM,t,i}(1-P_{t,i})(1-P_{mig})C] + \frac{Y_t^*}{n}}{N_{t,i}[(1-P_{t,i}) + (1-P_{mig})C] + \frac{N_{t,T}}{n}} \tag{1.39}$$

where n is the number of patches, C is the "cost" incurred by potential migrants for the ability to migrate (whether done so or not) and set to 0.6 in the present simulation (this cost is consistent with the loss in fecundity of the winged morph of the sand cricket [Roff 1984a]), $N_{t,i}$ is the number in the ith patch before migration, $N_{i,T}$ is the total number of migrants, and Y_t^* is the weighted phenotypic value of the offspring from migrants. The latter two variables are defined as

$$N_{t,T} = CP_{surv}P_{mig}\sum_{i=1}^{n}N_{t,i}(1-P_{t,i})$$
$$Y_t^* = CP_{surv}P_{mig}\sum_{i=1}^{n}N_{t,i}Y_{PM,t,i}(1-P_{t,i}) \tag{1.40}$$

Equations (1.39) and (1.40) can be coded in R as

```
Emigrants     <- P.mig*Npop*(1-P)          # Nos of emigrants
Nos.migrants  <- P.surv*sum(Emigrants)     # Nt,T
Y.star        <- P.mig*sum(Npop*P.surv*Y.migrants*(1-P))
Mu            <- (Npop*(Y.nonmigrants*P+Y.migrants*(1-P)*(1-P.
                 mig)*Cost) + (Y.star/N.patches))/(Npop*(P+(1-
                 P)*(1-P.mig)*Cost) + Nos.migrants/N.patches)
```

Finally, we compute the change in population size within each patch and return the new population size and new mean liability for each population:

```
#  New population size before reproduction
  Npop              <- Npop - Emigrants + Nos.migrants/N.patches
  Npop              <- Npop*LAMBDA         # Population size before
                                              constraints
  Npop[Npop<1]    <-  0               # Check for extinction
  Npop[Npop>1000] <-  1000            # Carrying capacity
# Return the vector of new population sizes and means
  return (c(Npop,Mu))
```

The full coding is

R CODE:

```
  rm(list=ls())                                    #Clearmemory
# Population and inheritance function
  POP   <-function(MAX.Lambda, Npop, N.patches, Mu, P.surv, P.mig)
{
  h2   <-  0.5; Cost <- 0.6                      # parameters
  LAMBDA <-runif(N.patches,min=0,max=MAX.Lambda) #randomlamb-
                                                     das
  P   <-  pnorm( 0, mean= -Mu, sd=1) # Proportion of nonmigrants
  Y.nonmigrants    <- Mu + dnorm(0,mean=Mu, sd=1)*h2/(2*P)
  Y.migrants       <- Mu - dnorm(0, mean=Mu, sd=1)*h2/(2*(1-P))
  Emigrants        <- P.mig*Npop*(1-P)      # vector of surviving
                                               emigrants
  Nos.migrants   <- P.surv*sum(Emigrants)# =N(t,T)
  Y.star          <- P.mig*sum(Npop*P.surv*Y.migrants*(1-P))
  Mu     <-  (Npop*(Y.nonmigrants*P+Y.migrants*(1-P)*(1-P.mig)
      *Cost)  +  (Y.star/N.patches))/(Npop*(P+  (1-P)*(1-P.
      mig)*Cost) + Nos.migrants/N.patches)# Calculate Nos in
      new populations
  Npop              <- Npop - Emigrants + Nos.migrants/N.patches
  Npop <- Npop*LAMBDA        # Population size before constraints
  Npop[Npop<1] 0             # Check for extinction
  Npop[Npop>1000] <- 1000    # Carrying capacity
  return (c(Npop,Mu)) #Return the vector of new popn sizes and means
} # End of function

################## MAIN PROGRAM ##################
  set.seed(100)         # set seed
  MAXGEN        <- 2000    # Set maximum number of generations
  N.init        <- 20     # Initial population size
  MAX.LAMBDA    <- 2.2    # Maximum value of lambda
  N.patches     <- 10     # Number of patches
  P.surv        <- 0.95   # Survival rate of migrants
  P.mig   <-.8   # Proportion of potential migrants migrating
  Mu <- matrix(0,N.patches,1)  # Initial mean liability values
  Npop <- matrix(N.init, N.patches,1) # Initialise populations
```

```
    Npop.Sizes<- matrix(0,MAXGEN)  # Pre-assign storage for means
    Npop.Sizes[1] <- mean(Npop)              #  Store 1st generation
                                                mean population size
    N.extinct     <- matrix(0,N.patches,1)# Assign storage for nos
                                                extinct
# Pre-assign space for mean propn non-migrants
    Mean.nonmig <- matrix(0,MAXGEN) # Storage for propn nonmigrants
# Mean propn nonmigrants
    Mean.nonmig[1] <- mean(pnorm( 0, mean= -Mu, sd=1))
    Mean.mig      <- matrix(0, MAXGEN) # Storage for propn migrants
    Mean.mig[1]     <- 1-Mean.nonmig[1]   # Proportion migrants
    Igen            <- 1             # Initial generation number
    while ( Igen<MAXGEN && Npop.Sizes[Igen]>0)  # Enter while loop
{
    Igen            <- Igen+1      # Increment generation counter
# Get new population sizes and mean liabilities
    OUT     <- POP(MAX.LAMBDA, Npop, N.patches, Mu, P.surv, P.mig)
    Npop     <- OUT[1:N.patches]  # Vector of Population sizes
    n1 <- N.patches+1; n2 <-2*N.patches  # Range for mean liabilities
    Mu            <- OUT[n1:n2]      # Mean liabilities
    P.nonmigrants  <- pnorm( 0, mean=-Mu, sd=1)  # Vector of prop
                                                nonmigrants
# Mean proportion of nonmigrants in metapopulation
    Mean.nonmig[Igen] <- sum(Npop*P.nonmigrants)/sum(Npop)
                    # mean proportion of population migrating
    Mean.mig[Igen] <- sum(Npop*(1-P.nonmigrants)*P.mig)/sum(Npop)
    Npop.Sizes[Igen]  <- mean(Npop) # Store mean population size
    N.extinct[Igen]     <- length(Npop[Npop==0])  # Store nos of ex-
                                                tinct popns
}
    par(mfcol=c(2,2))  # Divide graphics page into four quadrants
    Gen <- seq(1,Igen)  # vector of generation numbers
    plot(Gen, Npop.Sizes[1:Igen], xlab="Generation", ylab="Mean
population size", type="l") # Mean population size over generations
plot(Gen, N.extinct[1:Igen], xlab="Generation", ylab="Number of
pops extinct", type="l", ylim=c(0,N.patches))  # Nos extinct
over generations
    plot(Gen, Mean.nonmig[1:Igen], xlab="Generation", ylab="Mean
Proportion of nonmigrants", type='l') # Mean proportion of nonnon-
                                    migrants over generations
    plot(Gen, Mean.mig[1:Igen], xlab="Generation", ylab="Mean
Proportion of migrants", type-'l')  # Mean proportion of migrants
over generations
```

OUTPUT: (Figure 1.11)

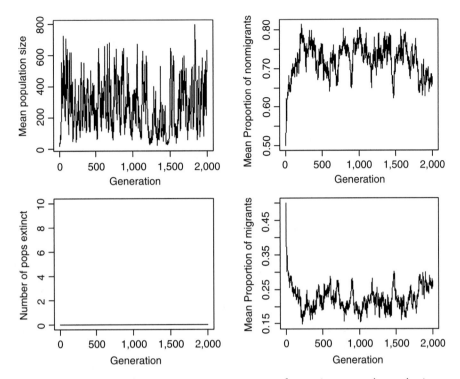

Figure 1.11 Mean population size, mean proportion of nonmigrants and actual migrants, and number of extinct populations for model 6. For display purposes the graph page has been split into four quadrats using `par(mfcol=c(2,2))`.

In addition to the population size data the program also plots the mean proportion of nonmigrants and the mean proportion of the population that actually migrate. As expected from the contour analysis, the system evolves to an intermediate level of migration. An interesting question, which I leave the reader to address is whether or not the evolutionarily stable proportion maximizes population size.

1.5   Summary of modeling approaches described in this book

1.5.1   Fisherian optimality analysis (Chapter 2)

Fisher's general analysis of evolution was based on the characteristic equation and the maximization of the Malthusian parameter, r (see Section 2.2). This approach has formed the backbone of much of the study of the evolution of trait variation. While I do not wish to imply that Fisher used only this approach, I think that he can be acknowledged as its originator. To distinguish this type of analysis from others in the book, which are also optimality models in one sense or another, I shall refer to it as "Fisherian" optimality analysis. The general assumptions of these models are

1. Stable-age distribution.

2. If density-dependence occurs it does not affect the trait under study.

3. Selection is frequency-independent.

4. In a stable environment fitness is maximized by r, R_0, or a fitness component whose maximization also maximizes one of the aforementioned fitness measures. The way these fitness measures are calculated depends upon the type of environment.

5. In a temporally variable environment the appropriate operational measure of fitness is the geometric mean of r. With age structure the appropriate fitness measure is the dominant Lyapunov exponent and is most readily analyzed using invasibility analysis (see Chapter 3).

6. Spatial variation can be handled by this approach using the framework developed simultaneously by Houston and McNamara (1992) and Kawecki and Stearns (1993), as described by equations (1.28) and (1.29). This assumes an equilibrium population.

Examples: Age at first reproduction and allocation to reproduction.

1.5.2   Invasibility analysis (Chapter 3)

Invasibility analysis is a technique that determines if a clone showing an alternate suite of characteristics (generally differences in parameter values) can invade a population. While it can be used for unstructured populations its strength lies primarily in addressing the evolution of traits in structured populations in which density-dependence occurs. The general properties are

1. The population is age-structured or stage-structured. Typically, the model is written in matrix form (e.g., a Leslie matrix).

2. The population may be at equilibrium or show variable behavior (e.g., cyclic or chaotic). If equilibrium can be assumed, then the model may be better analyzed using the methods for "Fisherian" optimality models.

3. Density-dependence may occur and may be an important selective factor.

Examples: Evolution of parameters in density-dependent functions (e.g., the Ricker function) and delayed maturity in a stage-structured model.

1.5.3   Genetic models (Chapter 4)

The preceding methods of analysis presume that the genetic mode of inheritance is not an impediment to the population evolving to the optimal combination of trait values. "Fisherian" optimality analysis focuses upon the optimal combination and has little to say about the trajectory or time course from one combination to another. Invasibility analysis can follow the change in frequency of mutant clones but whether this is relevant to other modes of inheritance is not addressed (in fact, as shown in Chapter 3, the genetic mode of inheritance can profoundly influence the outcome of evolution). In Chapter 3 I consider three types of genetic models, one focused at the population level and the other two focused on individual-based models. Potential advantages of genetic models are

1. The evolutionary trajectory can be followed.

2. Variation about the equilibrium combination can be assessed.

3. Density-dependence and frequency-dependence are easily incorporated into the individual-based approaches (examples of the latter are given in Chapter 6).

4. Age structure is readily accommodated (though bookkeeping can be tedious).

5. The model is itself a simple numerical method of locating the optimal combination. Used in this sense the actual genetic parameters may be irrelevant and can be selected to minimize the "search" time (e.g., set genetic correlations to zero). In rare cases parameter values may alter the equilibrium combination, but this can be easily investigated by varying parameter values.

Examples: Evolution of multiple traits in density-dependent populations and trait variation under the impact of stabilizing or directional selection.

1.5.4 Game theoretic models (Chapter 5)

Game theoretic models deal with interactions among individuals, typically between pairs of individuals. Such interactions, or "games," may be frequency-independent or frequency-dependent. In both cases fitness is defined by a payoff matrix that gives the increment (or decrement) in fitness associated with all possible pairs of interactions. The frequency-independent case is really a subset of "Fisherian" optimality analysis and most game theoretic models involve frequency-dependent games. General characteristics of game theoretic models are

1. Typically, population dynamics is not an important factor, a stable population being a frequent, but unspecified, assumption.

2. In simple models analytical solutions are possible but in more complex cases an individual-based models are used.

3. Clonal or explicit genetic models can be used.

Examples: Hawk-Dove game and territorial–satellite behavior.

1.5.5 Dynamic programming (Chapter 6)

Individuals are continually faced with decisions that affect their fitness. For example, a parasitic wasp must make a decision (I do not imply that this is a conscious act) on how many eggs to lay in a host: Too many larvae could compete with each other and hence have a reduction in fitness, but the female might not find another host and so laying too few larvae in the present host could result in a reduced fitness. In some cases the optimal decision set can be estimated using one of the previous approaches but in many cases the sequence of decisions to be made during the life of an organism is so complex that these approaches are inefficient methods of analysis. For such cases the method of dynamic programming is most appropriate. Such models generally include the following elements:

1. Fitness is a consequence of a series of "decisions" through the life (or specified period) of the organism. In the case in which only a single "decision" is made, such as when to leave a nest, "Fisherian" optimality modeling is generally an easier approach. Dynamic programming is the most appropriate approach when there are a series of decisions, such as how to distribute eggs in relation to the age of the female, the quality of patches in which the offspring will grow, and the time taken to locate suitable patches.

2. Fitness is measured by the maximization or minimization of some terminal variable, most typically survival or offspring production.

3. Selection is frequency-independent.

4. Population dynamics is assumed not to influence the decisions.

Examples: Optimal foraging and stopovers on a migration route.

CHAPTER 2

Fisherian Optimality Models

2.1 Introduction

This type of model is a development of Fisher's original approach to the study of evolutionary questions in which he took the Malthusian parameter, r, as the measure of fitness. As noted in Chapter 1, this measure is inappropriate under conditions in which a stable age distribution cannot be assumed, density-dependence or frequency-dependence is an important factor in the evolution of the traits under study, population dynamics is chaotic or fitness depends on the social setting. Even given these restrictions this type of model has proven to be a highly productive approach to the analysis of evolutionary questions and the generation of testable predictions. We first consider, in a little more detail than in Chapter 1, the fitness metrics assumed by models dealt with in this chapter. Next, I present a general scenario for analyses followed by illustrative scenarios (summarized in Table 1), and finally exemplary papers. MATLAB code for the scenarios is given in Section 2.18.

2.1.1 Fitness measures

The three most commonly used metrics for the type of model examined in this chapter are the Malthusian parameter, r, net (or lifetime) reproductive success, R_0, and a fitness component whose maximization also maximizes fitness. Of the three, the first has received the most theoretical study and can be considered to be the most general (Lande 1982; Charlesworth 1993, 1994). The Malthusian parameter is the rate of population increase achieved by a population that is in a stable age distribution and is given by the characteristic, (also called the Euler) equation

$$\int_0^\infty e^{-rt}l(x)m(x)dx = 1 \tag{2.1}$$

where t is age, $l(x)$ is survival to age x, and $m(x)$ is the number of female births at age x (typically equal sex ratios are assumed but this is not required). In the absence of density-dependence it is intuitively obvious that a mutation that increased r would increase in frequency, though proving this mathematically was no mean feat (for the mathematical justification see Charlesworth [1994]). If there is density-dependence then the appropriate measure of fitness is the relative number of individuals that pass out of the period in which the density-dependence acts. For example, suppose density-dependence occurred in the immature stage and that we wish to compute the fitnesses of two types of individuals, A and B. If the number of adult A exceeds the number of adult B then the former is necessarily the most fit. The analysis of such a situation can be made more complicated if the success through this period depends not simply on density but also on frequency of types in the population. The models examined in this chapter assume that density-dependence can be ignored in that it does not influence the traits under study. This is a reasonable assumption if the density-dependence is uncorrelated with the traits of interest. For example, suppose types A and B increased at rates r_A and r_B but after a specified time increment the sum of the two groups were reduced to a size N, with mortality being independent of type. In this case the most fit type would be that type with the highest r.

If the population is not increasing in size then a plausible measure of fitness is the net reproductive rate

$$R_0 = \int_0^\infty l(x)m(x)dx \tag{2.2}$$

which is sometimes called **expected lifetime reproductive success**. The assumption here is that if A has a higher R_0 than B then A will have the higher fitness. Density-dependence is implicitly assumed not to affect the traits of interest. When there are stochastic fluctuations that move the population out of a stable age structure neither r nor R_0 can be assumed to be an appropriate measure of fitness (Benton and Grant 2000). This situation is considered in Chapter 3.

In some cases, particularly behavioral studies, our interest is in a particular trait and to simplify analysis it is assumed that maximization of some component of the life history is equivalent to maximization of fitness. For example, we might wish to determine the optimal allocation of foraging time among patches that vary in resource quality. A common assumption is that the maximization of resources gathered per unit time is equivalent to maximizing fitness (Roff 1992). Care needs to be taken, because ignoring other components of the life history may produce erroneous conclusions. Two famous examples of this error are Cole's paradox and the Lack hypothesis.

In his landmark 1954 paper Cole suggested that there was an apparent paradox because "*For an annual species, the absolute gain in intrinsic population growth which could be achieved by changing to the perennial reproductive habit would be exactly equivalent to adding one individual to the average litter size*" (p. 118, Cole's italics). If Cole's assertion were true we would expect that perennials would be rare, which they certainly are not. The problem was that Cole failed to include differences in adult and juvenile survival, his analysis implicitly assuming survival rates of 1 for both stages (Roff 2002, pp. 190–192).

Lack (1947) hypothesized that in birds "*the average clutch-size is ultimately deter-mined by the average maximum number of young which the parents can successfully raise in the region and season in question*" (p. 319). Lack's hypothesis assumes that the only important interactions are negative density-dependent interactions between sib-lings within a clutch and predicts that the most productive clutch should also be the most frequent clutch observed, which is not the case. Lacking in Lack's hypothesis is the possibility that later survival of the offspring and adult survival will be affected by the number of offspring raised. Experimental manipulation of brood sizes in birds, mammals, reptiles, fishes, and plants has demonstrated negative effects of increased brood size on future survival of adults and/or off-spring (Roff 2002, pp 132–144). Incorporation of such effects predicts that the optimal brood size will be less than the Lack value (Roff 2002, pp. 243–248).

2.1.2 Methods of analysis: introduction

The focus of analyses is on equilibrium conditions and not the evolutionary trajectory taken to this (see Chapters 4 and 5 for examples of analyses involving evolutionary trajectories). As described above, density-dependence is not explicit-ly considered. Frequency-dependence is also assumed to be absent. The model formulation we would like to arrive at is

$$W = f(\theta_1, \theta_2, \ldots, \theta_k, x_1, x_2, \ldots, x_n) \tag{2.3}$$

where W is fitness $\theta_1, \theta_2, \ldots, \theta_k$ are parameters and $x_1, x_2, \ldots, x_n$ are traits. The above is to be read as "Fitness is a function of k parameters and n traits." A guiding rule is "Keep the number of parameters and traits to a minimum." Suppose we have five parameters and we decide to examine model performance over all combinations. Dividing each parameter into 10 parts, which is not an unreason-able division, will give use $10^5 = 100,000$ combinations to examine! While this is possible and may be necessary it is certainly not a preferable route, if it can be avoided.

The fitness function will invariably be made up of a number of component functions, such as described in Scenario 1, in which fitness is the product of fecundity and survival and these are functions of body size. These functions may produce a nice smooth fitness function which can be subject to analysis using the calculus or the fitness function may have discontinuities or be in some other way difficult to analyze (i.e., a "rugged" surface) using the calculus. Care needs to be taken in examining the model for discontinuities and places in which model components can take physically impossible values. In the first scenario survival is given as a negative linear function of body size, which means that above a particular body size survival will become negative, which is not possible. In the scenario given, this does not become a problem because fitness will be negative in this case. However, suppose the model contained the product of two survival functions that could mathematically be less than zero. Now it is possible that the two negative values will produce a positive and a fitness value that might not be seen to be wrong.

There are three general classes of models: First, fitness can be written as a function of the traits of interest and differentiation is not a problem; second, fitness can be written as a function of the traits of interest but differentiation is problematic; and third, the fitness function cannot be written such that fitness is isolated.

2.1.3   Methods of analysis: $W = f(\theta_1, \theta_2, \ldots, \theta_k, x_1, x_2, \ldots, x_n)$ and well-behaved

Assuming the fitness function to be well behaved and differentiable (a "smooth" fitness surface), we find the optimal trait value by differentiating with respect to the trait and setting the resultant to zero. For example, suppose, as in Scenario 1, the fitness function is a quadratic function:

$$W = f(\theta_1, \theta_2, \theta_3, x) = \theta_1 + \theta_2 x + \theta_3 x^2$$
$$\frac{dW}{dx} = \theta_2 + 2\theta_3 x$$
$$\frac{dW}{dx} = 0 \text{ when } x = \frac{-\theta_2}{2\theta_3}$$

(2.4)

Note that an intermediate fitness maximum requires that $\theta_3 < 0$ and $\theta_2 > 0$. Naively one might be tempted to require simply that $\frac{\theta_2}{\theta_3} < 0$: however, the condition $\theta_3 > 0$ and $\theta_2 < 0$ defines a function that in convex and hence the turning point is a minimum not a maximum. **Wherever possible, the function should be plotted to ensure that an appropriate turning point exists** (see Scenario 12 for a case in which prior plotting is essential). If the function is complex and/or contains many terms (e.g., Scenario 3) differentiation can become very tedious and care must be exercised that terms are not accidentally omitted or signs changed. Both R and MATLAB have routines for differentiation and it is wise to check one's results using one of these.

2.1.3.1   R code for differentiation

The code for R is simple but the output may appear somewhat obscure. As an example, suppose we wish to differentiate the quadratic $a + bx + cx^2$, which has the derivative of $b + 2cx$. The R code, saving the output in a variable y, is

```
y <- deriv(~ a+b*x+c*x^2,"x" ) # Compute differential and save in y
y                              # Print y
```

The output is

```
> y <- deriv(~ a+b*x+c*x^2,"x")
> y
expression({
    .value <- a + b * x + c * x^2
    .grad <- array(0, c(length(.value), 1L), list(NULL, c("x")))
    .grad[, "x"] <- b + c * (2 * x)
```

```
    attr(.value, "gradient") <- .grad
    .value
})
```

The derivative is given in the line `.grad[, "x"] <- b + c * (2 * x)`. To actually calculate the gradient at some value requires a few extra lines of code, as illustrated in Scenario 1. In some cases the output is split into separate expressions. For example, for the derivative of the equation $e_{ax}+bx+cx^2$, which has the derivative $ae^{ax}+b+2cx$, we get

```
> y <- deriv(~ exp(a*x)+b*x+c*x^2,"x")
> y
expression({
    .expr2 <- exp(a * x)
    .value <- .expr2 + b * x + c * x^2
    .grad <- array(0, c(length(.value), 1L), list(NULL, c("x")))
    .grad[, "x"] <- .expr2 * a + b + c * (2 * x)
    attr(.value, "gradient") <- .grad
    .value
})
```

The derivative is now found from lines 2 and 5 of `expression`, namely (`.expr2 <- exp(a * x)`) and (`.grad[, "x"] <- .expr2 * a + b + c * (2 * x)`)

2.1.3.2 MATLAB code for differentiation

The output in MATLAB is simpler than that given by R but all symbolic variables must be declared as such. Unless told otherwise, MATLAB uses a built-in hierarchy to decide which is the relevant variable. In the present example the variable that MATLAB assumes is the one to be used is x. The code for the first example is

```
syms x a b c;            % Define symbols
y=diff(a+b*x+c*x^2)      % Differentiate, save in y and echo result
```

and the output is

```
y =
b+2*c*x
```

The code for the second example is

```
syms x a b c;                    % Define symbols
y=diff (exp(a*x)+b*+c*x^2)  % Differentiate, save in y and echo
result
```

and the output is

```
y =
a*exp(a*x)+b+2*c*x
```

2.1.3.3 General approach

Regardless of the language used, the general pattern of code to solve models of this type is to

1. Define the fitness function.

2. Iterate over values of x to plot W versus x (e.g., Scenarios 1–5). Plotting is an important first step in the analysis to ensure that a maximum actually does occur and that there are no discontinuities or odd behaviors that could lead to erroneous results (see Scenario 9 for such a case). For two traits a contour plot is produced (W plotted on x_1, x_2; e.g., Scenarios 9, 12, and 13). Three traits cannot be readily visualized (e.g., Scenario 14), though pair-wise plots may be useful.

3. If the function has already been differentiated define a function for the differential.

4. Find the optimum by calling a library routine (e.g., in R `uniroot` if the differential is supplied, `optimize` or `nlm`, if the turning point is to be found numerically as shown in Step 6). As an example, suppose the fitness function is the quadratic $4x-2x^2$, which has a maximum at $x = 1$. The differential is $4-4x$. To use `uniroot` we first define a function for the differential and then call `uniroot`.

```
DIFF <-function(x){x-4*x}        # Function defining differential
# Call uniroot requesting the value of the root as designated by $root
  uniroot(f=DIFF, interval=c(-10,10))$root
```

OUTPUT:
```
[1] 1
```

In MATLAB the appropriate function is called solve:

```
solve(4-4*x)
```

OUTPUT:
```
  ans = 1
```

5. If the function has not been differentiated call a library routine, as described above, to do the differentiation, and then do Step 4.

6. To find the turning point without resorting to differentiation we can use `nlm` or `optimize`. The R function `nlm` computes the minimum of a function and hence we take the negative of fitness. The R function `optimize` can find a minimum or maximum, the former being the default. Both functions generate an output set from which we need to extract the relevant data. The `$estimate` and `$minimum` attached to the call does this. We first define a function `MINUS`. `W` that calculates the negative of fitness and then passes this function to `nlm` or `optimize`:

```
MINUS.W <-function(x){2*x^2-4*x}    # Function to calculate -W
                                       for a given x
# Call nlm function passing function and initial estimate called p
  nlm(f=MINUS.W, p=0)$estimate
# Call optimize function, passing function and interval for parameter
  optimize(f=MINUS.W,interval=c(-10,10))$minimum
```

OUTPUT:
```
> nlm(f=MINUS.W, p=0)$estimate
[1] 0.9999998
> optimize(f=MINUS.W,interval=c(-10,10))$minimum
[1] 1
```

In MATLAB the routine fminbnd acts like optimize but only finds a minimum. To call fminbnd we can either define an anonymous function or an inline function:

```
FITNESS =@(x)(-(2*x^2+4*x));           % anonymous function
FITNESS = inline('-(-2*x^2+4*x)','x'); % inline function
fminbnd(FITNESS,-10,10)                % search limits at -10,10
```

OUTPUT:
```
ans = 1.0000
```

Scenario 1 provides a simple example of the above process.

2.1.4 Methods of analysis: $W = f(\theta_1, \theta_2, \ldots, \theta_k, x_1, x_2, \ldots, x_n)$ and not well-behaved

If the function contains discontinuities (e.g., Scenario 12 and Figure 2.12), or is a set of instructions that define a model but not an explicit function, or is a recursive equation (e.g., Scenario 13), differentiation may not be possible or at least not give reliable answers. For such cases a numerical approach, which I shall refer to as the "Brute force approach," can be employed:

1. Follow Steps 1 and 2 as before.

2. Use a library routine that searches for the minimum or maximum of a function (e.g., in R optimize or nlm and fminbnd in MATLAB) and pass the fitness function to this routine.

3. If Step 2 fails (e.g., Scenario 12 in which there are abrupt changes) or is not feasible a brute force approach can be employed (e.g., Scenarios 6, 12, 13, and 14). In the simplest brute force approach we generate a set of estimates separated by the smallest difference that we require and pick that combination that has the largest fitness. For a single trait the process can be made more efficient by commencing at a value that is known to be to the left of the fitness peak and iterating until fitness declines. For example, suppose we have a single variable

x and we wish to locate the optimum x such that it is within $\pm\varepsilon$ of the true value. From the previous plots we know that the optimum is greater than x_{min}. We now iterate from x_{min} in steps of ε until fitness declines. The optimum value of x is then either this value or the previous value of x, the choice being that value which gives the highest fitness. In general, the value of ε can be selected such that there is no practical difference in the choice and in the scenarios presented the code selects the previous value of x. When there are several variables it may be computationally easier to simply generate all combinations located within the region of the optimum combination. In this case the step used must equal the increment that matches the desired accuracy (see Scenario 12 for an example).

To illustrate this process we shall consider the simple quadratic fitness function $4x-2x^2$ (a brute force method is obviously not required in this case but it serves to illustrate the method. For a more complex example see Scenarios 12). The code is divided into three parts: a function called FITNESS that calculate fitness, a function called Wdiff that calls the fitness function for x and $x + Step$, where *Step* is the increment length, and the main program that calls function Wdiff. The final answer and difference in fitness values between the last two selected values of x are printed out.

R CODE:

```
rm(list=ls()) # Remove all objects from memory
FITNESS <- function(x) { W= 4*x-2*x^2} # Fitness given x
WDIFF   <- function (x, Step)           # W for x and x+Step
{
 W1        <- FITNESS(x)        # Fitness given x
 W2        <- FITNESS(x+Step)   # Fitness given x+Step
 Wdiff2 <- W2-W1               # Diff between fitnesses
 return (Wdiff2)               # x will eventually be the best x
}
# MAIN PROGRAM
 x     <- 0                 # Set initial x
 Step <- 0.001             # Set Step length
 DIFF <- WDIFF(x, Step)    # Calculate difference between W at two x
 while (DIFF>0)            # If DIFF > 0 then W still increasing
{
 x       <- x + Step        # Increment x
 DIFF    <- WDIFF(x, Step)  # Calculate difference in fitness
}
# Out of loop and thus x is taken to be optimal
 print(c(x,DIFF)) # Print out x and Difference in fitnesses at end
```

OUTPUT:

```
[1] 1e+00 -2e-06
```

MATLAB CODE:

```
function w=FITNESS(x) % Fitness at x
  w   =4*x-2*x^
function Wdiff2 = WDIFF(x, Step)      % W for x and x+Step
  W1 = FITNESS(x);                    % Fitness given x
  W2 = FITNESS(x+Step);               % Fitness given x+Step
  Wdiff2 = W2-W1;                     % Diff between fitnesses
% MAIN PROGRAM
clear all;
  x = 0;                         % Set initial x
  Step = 0.001;                  % Set Step length
  DIFF = WDIFF(x, Step);         % Calculate difference between W at two x
while (DIFF>0)                    % If DIFF > 0 then W still increasing
  x = x + Step;                  % Increment x
  DIFF = WDIFF(x, Step); % Caluclate difference in fitness
end
% Out of loop and thus x is taken to be optimal
  [x,DIFF] % Print out x and Difference in fitnesses at end
```

OUTPUT:

```
ans =
     1.0000 -0.0000
```

Note that the difference is shown as zero because the default number of digits is too few.

2.1.5 Methods of analysis: $g(W) = f(\theta_1, \theta_2, \ldots, \theta_k, x_1, x_2, \ldots, x_n, W)$

In some cases it may not be possible to write the fitness function with fitness on one side and all other variables and parameters on the other. This is very likely to be the case when using an age-structured model with r as the measure of fitness (e.g., Scenario 5). Differentiation may still be possible using implicit differentiation leading to $W = f(\theta_1, \theta_2, \ldots, \theta_k, x_1, x_2, \ldots, x_n)$ or a function $h(\theta_1, \theta_2, \ldots, \theta_k, x_1, x_2, \ldots, x_n, W)$ that can be set to zero (since it is the differential and the maximum occurs when $dW/dx=0$) and hence solved numerically. A further complication may be that the fitness function must be integrated, which will usually be the case when using r. Integration is frequently much more difficult than differentiation and may not even be possible. For such cases we resort either to symbolic integration, which can be done in MATLAB but not R, or numerical integration, which can be done in either program. The general model is likely to be of the form

$$\int_0^\infty e^{-rt}\,(\theta_1, \theta_2, \ldots, \theta_k, x_1, x_2, \ldots, x_n)dt = 1 \tag{2.5}$$

Thus the steps to follow are

1. Define the fitness function. If the function can be integrated we will arrive at a function in which fitness, r, is on the left, for example, $r = f(\theta_1, \theta_2, \ldots, \theta_k, x_1, x_2, \ldots, x_n)$ or a function in which fitness cannot be separated, for example, $f(\theta_1, \theta_2, \ldots, \theta_k, x_1, x_2, \ldots, x_n, r) = 1..$ In the former case the model can be solved as discussed earlier. For the purposes of generality I shall assume that r cannot be separated out and that integration of equation (2.5) is to be done within the program. For clarity I shall consider the particular model considered in detail in Scenario 5:

$$\int_1^\infty e^{-rt}16xe^{-(1-0.5x)t}dt = 1 \tag{2.6}$$

2. The first computer function we define is one which I shall call INTEGRAND that gives the value of the function to be integrated, for example, in the above equation the function would give the value of $e^{-rt}16xe^{-(1-0.5x)t}$, which requires that we pass to it r, t, and x. In R t is a reserved word and so we rename it as age:

```
INTEGRAND <- function(age,x,r) { exp(-r*age)*16*x/exp((1-0.5*x)
*age)}
```

3. The second function, INTEGRAL, is one that calls the R function integrate to integrate the above with respect to age (the first variable passed) and subtract 1 so that we can use a root-finding function to solve for r:

```
INTEGRAL <- function(r,x) {1-integrate(INTEGRAND(1,Inf,x,r)$value}
```

4. The third function, RCALC, calls the R function uniroot to find the value of r that satisfies equation (2.6) for a given value of x:

```
RCALC <- function(x){uniroot(INTEGRAL, interval=c(1e-7,10),x)$root)}
```

5. All that now remains is to find the value of x that maximizes r. Good practice dictates that we first iterate over values of x to ensure that r is a concave function of x. Having satisfied ourselves that this is the case (see Scenario 5) we use the R function optimize, which can locate either a minimum (the default) or a maximum:

```
optimize(f=RCALC, interval=c(1.3,1.8), maximum=TRUE)$maximum
```

2.2   Summary of scenarios (Table 2.1)

1. Scenario 1 illustrates the analysis of the simplest type of optimality model, namely one in which the interaction of traits produce a concave function of fitness with the trait of interest. The example used is that in which body size, the trait of interest, is a positive function of fecundity and a negative function of survival. A semelparous life history is assumed, making analysis very simple. Scenarios 2–8 consider variants of Scenario 1.

2. In Scenario 2 age structure is added in such a manner that the analysis is unaffected, illustrating the principle that additional complications to a model may be mathematically neutral.

3. Scenario 3 also includes only the addition of age structure but in such a manner that the optimum trait value is affected.

4. Scenario 4 is the same as Scenario 3 except that the fitness function is a continuous rather than a discrete function of the trait of interest.

5. In Scenarios 1–4 fitness is measured by R_0 which makes analysis relatively simple. Scenario 5 considers the analysis of the model with r as the fitness function.

6. Scenarios 1–5 assume that parameter values are constant. Scenarios 6–8 consider models in which one or more of the parameters are variable. Scenario 6 assumes stochasticity in one or more parameters within but not among generations. In this case fitness is the arithmetic mean fitness. An important point made by this example is that mean fitness is not calculated simply using the means of the parameters.

7. Scenarios 7–8 assume that parameter values are temporally variable, in which case the fitness measure is the geometric mean rather than the arithmetic. Scenario 7 considers discrete temporal variation parameter values.

8. Scenario 8 examines the consequences of continuous temporal variation in parameter values.

9. Scenarios 9–14 illustrate the analysis of models in which two traits are of interest. In Scenario 9 the two traits are vigilance and foraging rate.

10. Scenario 10 illustrates that the two traits of interest may be independent even though fitness is a function of both.

11. Scenarios 11 and 12 examine a prominent problem in life history theory, namely the coevolution of propagule and clutch size. Scenario 11 illustrates a circumstance in which one trait is determined by the value of the second and hence the problem is reduced to the analysis of a single trait.

12. Scenario 12 expands Scenario 11 such that the two traits (propagule size in clutches 1 and 2 of a three-clutch life history) covary and cannot be reduced to a single trait. An important feature of this analysis is the illustration of the brute force method. It also illustrates the importance of plotting the fitness surface to determine if it is "smooth" or "rugged".

Table 2.1 Summary of principle model assumptions in the scenarios (S) described in the text

S	Focal trait(s)	Constraining traits	W	Scenario feature
1	Body size	Fecundity and survival	R_0	Simplest model
2	Body size	Fecundity and survival	R_0	No effect of age structure
3	Body size	Fecundity and age-specific survival	R_0	Discrete age structure and optimum changed
4	Body size	Fecundity and age-specific survival	R_0	Continuous age function and optimum changed
5	Body size	Fecundity and age-specific survival	r	Fitness cannot be isolated on one side of fitness function
6	Body size	Fecundity and age-specific survival	Arithmetic mean R_0	Stochastic variation in parameters
7	Body size	Fecundity and age-specific survival	Geometric mean R_0	Discrete temporal variation in a parameter
8	Body size	Fecundity and age-specific survival	Geometric mean R_0	Continuous temporal variation in a parameter
9	Vigilance and foraging rate	Survival	Survival	Simple two-trait model
10	Body size and fecundity	Propagule size and survival	R_0	Optima independent and hence each trait analyzed separately
11	Clutch sizes 1 and 2	Reserves, fecundity, and propagule size	R_0	Two traits but analysis reduces to that of a single trait
12	Age-specific clutch sizes	Reserves, fecundity, and propagule size	R_0	Importance of plotting to examine fitness surface and illustration of a brute force method
13	Age at first reproduction and single reproductive allocation	Continuous growth, weight-specific fecundity, and adult mortality	R_0	Recursion dictates use of brute force approach
14	Age at first reproduction, age-specific reproductive allocation	Continuous growth, weight-specific fecundity, and adult mortality	R_0	Expansion of analysis to more than two traits

13. Scenario 13 illustrates the analysis of models that involve recursion and which may require a brute force approach. The specific problem considered is that of finding the optimal age at maturity and allocation to reproduction in an iteroparous organism.

14. Scenario 14 expands the problem considered in the forgoing scenario by allowing the allocation to reproduction to change with age, thereby increasing the number of traits to the number of mature age classes plus one (age at maturity).

2.3   Scenario 1: A simple trade-off model

This scenario illustrates the analysis of the case in which there is no age structure and fitness is a simple quadratic function of the trait under study. Because of its simplicity, its visualization and analysis is readily accomplished. Given the ease with which this type of model can be analyzed it is worthwhile, if possible, to commence with such a model. Following the analysis of this model further biological assumptions, such as age structure as in Scenarios 2 and 3, can be added. This approach allows one to assess the importance of particular assumptions.

The present model considers the case of a semelparous organism in which the trait under investigation varies positively with one fitness component and negatively with another. A priori, one might be tempted to assume that this will necessarily result in a function that has a maximum at some intermediate trait value. This is not necessarily the case, suppose, for example the two fitness functions are

$$
\begin{aligned}
y_1 &= e^{ax} \\
y_2 &= e^{-bx}
\end{aligned}
\tag{2.7}
$$

where y_1 and y_2 are two traits such as fecundity and survival, a and b are constants, and x is the trait under study (e.g., body size). Let us suppose that fitness is the product of y_1 and y_2 (which is quite reasonable): fitness, W, is then given by

$$
W = y_1 y_2 = e^{(a-b)x}
\tag{2.8}
$$

which has no intermediate optimum. In the scenario discussed below an intermediate optimum is not assured but does occur for particular parameter values.

2.3.1   General assumptions

1. The organism is semelparous.
2. Fecundity, F, increases with body size, x.
3. Survival, S, decreases with body size, x.
4. Fitness, W, is a function of fecundity and survival.

The above assumptions describe a very general situation. To make a prediction we must convert these assumptions into mathematical expressions. But even before doing this we can make a general statement. Because one fitness component, fecundity, increases with body size, whereas the second component, survival, decreases with body size then in many (but not all) circumstances we can expect that there will be an optimum body size that maximizes fitness. To investigate this we shall give explicit mathematical expressions to the three assumptions.

2.3.2 Mathematical assumptions

1. Fecundity increases linearly with body size:

$$F = a_F + b_F x \tag{2.9}$$

where a_F and b_F are constants.

2. Survival decreases linearly with body size:

$$S = a_S - b_S x \tag{2.10}$$

3. Fitness, W, is the expected lifetime reproductive success, R_0, given as the product of fecundity and survival:

$$
\begin{aligned}
W &= R_0 = FS \\
&= (a_F + b_F x)(a_S - b_S x) \\
&= a_F a_S - b_F b_S x^2 + (a_S b_F - a_F b_S)x
\end{aligned}
\tag{2.11}
$$

The above equation describes a parabola that is concave down, that is, has a maximum value at some body size, say x^*. Thus for this model we already know that there is an optimal body size, though we do not know if this occurs at a plausible body size. The first step in the analysis is to plot W versus x to visually confirm that a maximum exists and show that it occurs at a value to be expected for the species or taxa under study.

2.3.3 Plotting the fitness function

It is usually a good idea to plot the function to visually examine its behavior. While we know that in the present case the function is a quadratic that is concave down we do not know if the optimum trait value is plausible given biologically plausible parameter values. Thus we must assign parameter values. For the purposes of illustration, let us suppose that reasonable values are $a_F = 0$, $b_F = 4$, $a_S = 1$, $b_S = 0.5$. The fitness equation can now be written as

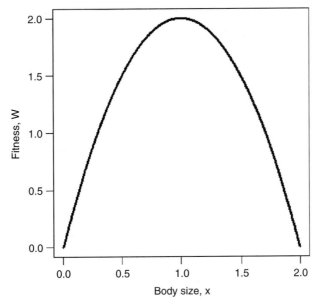

Figure 2.1 Scenario 1: Fitness versus body size.

$$W = 0 \times 1 - 4 \times 0.5x^2 + (1 \times 4 - 0 \times 0.5)x$$
$$= -2x^2 + 4x$$

(2.12)

R CODE:

```
rm(list=ls())              # remove all objects from memory
x <- seq(0,2,length= 1000) # Create a vector of length 1000 be-
                             tween 0, 2
W <- (-2*x^2 + 4*x) # Create a vector W using the fitness function
# Plot the data using 'l' to designate a line
# las=number orientation on axes, lwd = line width
plot(x,W,type='l',xlab='Body size, x', ylab='Fitness, W',
las=1,lwd=3)
```

From the plot of the fitness function (Figure 2.1) it can be seen that there is a maximum at or around 1.

MATLAB CODE: See Section 2.18.1.

2.3.4 Finding the maximum using the calculus

We can now proceed in one of two ways:

1. Find the optimal body size by the calculus.
2. Use a numerical method without resorting to the calculus (Section 2.3.5).

To obtain x^* using the calculus we differentiate the equation, set the result to zero and find the value of x that satisfies this condition. In the present case the differentiation can be easily accomplished using the rules given in Appendix 2:

$$\frac{dW}{dx} = -4x + 4$$

$$\frac{dW}{dx} = 0 \text{ when } -4x + 4 = 0, \text{i.e., } x = 1 \tag{2.13}$$

R CODE:

Symbolic differentiation in R can be done using deriv:

```
y <- deriv(~-2*x^2+4*x,"x") # Take the derivative and store in y
```

As discussed in the Introduction, the output is not particularly clear as it returns the expression for the evaluation of the derivative:

```
y # Print y
```

OUTPUT:

```
expression({
    .value <- -2 * x^2 + 4 * x
    .grad <- array(0, c(length(.value), 1L), list(NULL, c("x")))
    .grad[, "x"] <- 4 - 2 * (2 * x)
    attr(.value, "gradient") <- .grad
    .value
})
```

The value at which the derivative is zero can now be determined using the function uniroot. We set the derivative as a separate function to be called by uniroot:

```
rm(list=ls())                  # remove all objects from memory
# Function to obtain the gradient at a value w
FUNC <- function(w)
{
y <- deriv(~-2*x^2+4*x,"x")    # Get the derivative
x <- w                         # Set x equal to w
z <- eval(y)                   # Evaluate the derivative at w
d <- attr(z,"gradient")        # Assign the gradient value to d
return(d)                      # Return d to the main program
}
# MAIN PROGRAM
# Root must be enclosed by the limits set by the user, here set at
-2 to 4
B <- uniroot(FUNC, interval= c(-2,4))
B$root # Print out the value found
```

MATLAB CODE: See Section 2.18.2.

2.3.5 Finding the maximum using a numerical approach

In many cases the function may not be easily differentiable: for example, the function might consist of a simulation model or it may have discontinuities. We shall encounter such cases shortly. The present model can be used to illustrate the general approach.

The available routines typically locate the minimum value of a function. In our case we wish to find the maximum. To use the minimization routines we simply take the negative value of our function. Thus, instead of seeking the maximum of $4x-2x^2$ we seek the minimum of $2x^2-4x$. There are generally several routines that find minima. We shall, in this case, use `nlm` in R (an alternate is `optimize`) and `fminbnd` in MATLAB.

R CODE:

```
# Create function to evaluate fitness function
  FITNESS <- function(x) (2*x^2-4*x)
  nlm(FITNESS, p=-2)   # Call nlm with initial guess for x of -2
```

MATLAB CODE: See Section 2.18.3.

2.4 Scenario 2: Adding age structure may not affect the optimum

We increase the complexity of the problem by introducing age-structure, which we might expect to change the solution. In fact, they do not: **Increasing complexity need not change either the qualitative or quantitative conclusions**.

2.4.1 General assumptions

1. The organism is iteroparous.
2. The following assumptions are the same as in Scenario 1.
3. Fecundity, F, increases with body size, x, which does not change after maturity (e.g., as in insects).
4. Survival, S, decreases with body size, x.
5. Fitness, W, is a function of fecundity and survival.

2.4.2 Mathematical assumptions

1. Maturity occurs at age 1 after which no further growth occurs.
2. Fecundity increases linearly with size at maturity, resulting in fecundity being a uniform function of age, t:

$$F_t = a_F + b_F x \tag{2.14}$$

3. Survival to the age at first reproduction, here 1, decreases linearly with body size and is thereafter constant per time unit and independent of body size. Survival to age t is then given by

$$S_t = (a_S - b_S x)e^{-M(t-1)} \qquad (2.15)$$

where M is the instantaneous mortality rate that is independent of age.

4. Fitness, W, is the expected lifetime reproductive success, R_0, given as the cumulative product of survival and fecundity:

$$W = R_0 = \sum_{t=1}^{\infty} F_t S_t = \sum_{t=1}^{\infty} (a_F + b_F x)(a_S - b_S x)e^{-M(t-1)} \qquad (2.16)$$

Although the above equation looks a lot more complicated than equation (2.11) it actually contributes no new information that changes the optimal size, **because those components that depend on size do not depend on age and hence can be moved out of the summation sign.** Consequently, we have that the fitness equation specified above is simply equation (2.11) multiplied by a constant. Thus the optimal size remains unchanged.

2.5   Scenario 3: Adding age-specific mortality that affects the optimum

We retain the same general assumptions as before but introduce a mathematical change to the survival function that will alter the optimal size.

2.5.1   General assumptions

1. The organism is iteroparous.
2. Fecundity, F, increases with body size, x, which does not change after maturity (e.g., as in insects).
3. Survival, S, decreases with body size, x.
4. Fitness, W, is a function of fecundity and survival.

2.5.2   Mathematical assumptions

1. Maturity occurs at age 1 after which no further growth occurs.
2. Fecundity increases linearly with size at maturity, resulting in fecundity being a uniform function of age:

$$F_t = a_F + b_F x \qquad (2.17)$$

3. The instantaneous rate of mortality increases linearly with the body size attained at age 1 and is constant per time unit. Under this assumption, survival to age t is given by

$$S_t = e^{-(a_S + b_S x)t} \tag{2.18}$$

Note that to make survival a declining function of body size, given the exponential function, we replace the previous $a_S - b_S x$ with $a_S + b_S x$.

4. Fitness, W, is the expected lifetime reproductive success, R_0, given as the cumulative product of survival and fecundity:

$$W = R_0 = \sum_{t=1}^{\infty} F_t S_t = \sum_{t=1}^{\infty} (a_F + b_F x) e^{-(a_S + b_S x)t} \tag{2.19}$$

We cannot now factor out the age-dependent effects from body size and hence the optimal body size will not be the same as found previously.

2.5.3 Plotting the fitness function

Before seeking the turning point we first plot the fitness function to verify that it has a turning point and the function is not oddly shaped such that the routines locating the maximum will not home in on a single value, regardless of the starting points. We shall assume the same parameter values as before ($a_F = 0$, $b_F = 4$, $a_S = 1$, $b_S = 0.5$), and thus $W = \sum^{\infty} 4xe^{-(1+0.5x)t=1}$.

R CODE (Figures 2.2 and 2.3):

The above summation is taken to infinity, which is generally not an option with a numerical analysis. Thus first, we have to decide on how many ages, n, we need to consider in the summation. To do this we set body size, x, at some arbitrary but reasonable value, say $x = 1$. The following commands do the summation and plot the results as a function of the number of ages. The program consists of a separate function called SUMMATION that calculates the value of equation (2.19) from 1 to n. It does this by

1. Generating an integer sequence from 1 to n and assigning this to a vector called Age.
2. It then creates another vector called Wt, which is the age-specific component of equation (2.19), namely $4xe^{-(1+0.5x)t}$
3. Finally it computes the sum of the vector Wt using the R function sum.

The main program is as follows:

1. First sets the maximum number of ages, nmax, to use at 20.
2. Creates a single column matrix called n with the integer sequence 1 to nmax.

3. While we could use a loop to calculate the summed value for each value of n, a faster method is the use of the R function `apply` (whenever possible object-oriented programming should be used).

4. Finally the results are plotted using the R function plot.

```
  rm(list=ls()) # remove all objects from memory
# Function to calculate the summation of equation (2.19)
  SUMMATION <- function(n)
{
  x    <- 1                      # As before we set x = 1
  Age <- seq(from=1, to=n)       # Sequence from 1 to n
  Wt <- 4*x*exp(-(1+0.5*x)*Age)  # Vector of fitness at age t
  return(sum(Wt))                # Return the summed value
}
# MAIN PROGRAM
  nmax <- 20                              # Set maximum value for n
  n    <- matrix(seq(from=1, to=nmax)) # Vector of n values
  W    <- apply(n,1,SUMMATION) # Apply function SUMMATION to each row
# Plot W vs n using 'l' to designate a line
# las=number orientation on axes, lwd = line width
  plot(n,W,type='l', xlab='Age, n', ylab='Weight, Wt', las=1,
  lwd=3)
```

The summation quickly approaches its asymptotic value (Figure 2.2) and setting the maximum age at 20 should be adequate for all reasonable values of x. Now we change the summation function to sum for different values of x and plot the result (Figure 2.3):

```
  rm(list=ls()) # Remove all objects from memory
# Function to calculate the summation as a function of x
SUMMATION <- function(x)
{
  Age <- seq(from=1, to=20)       # Sequence from 1 to 20
  Wt  <- 4*x*exp(-(1+0.5*x)*Age)  # Vector of fitness at age t
  return(sum(Wt))                 # Return the summed value
}
# MAIN PROGRAM
  x<-matrix(seq(from=0, to=5, length=100)) # Vector from 0-5 of length 100
  W <- apply(x,1,SUMMATION)   # Apply function SUMMATION to each row
                              # Plot W vs x using 'l' to designate a
                              #   line
                              # las=number orientation on axes, lwd
                              #   = line width
  plot(x,W,type='l', xlab='Body size, x', ylab='Fitness, W',
las=1,lwd=4)
```

MATLAB CODE: See Section 2.18.4.

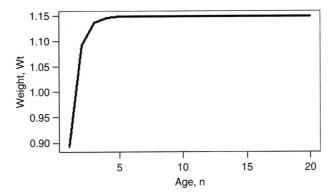

Figure 2.2 Scenario 3: Effect of varying length of summation on weight.

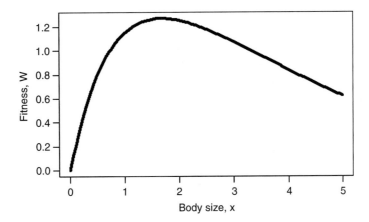

Figure 2.3 Scenario 3: Fitness versus body size.

2.5.4   Finding the maximum using the calculus

We are now assured that there is a maximal fitness, we know its approximate value and can thus set the limits of the search. The summation is, in this case, solvable and so we shall start by examining the exact solution.

A series that frequently occurs in life history models is the geometric series:

$$\sum_{i=1}^{\infty} a^{i-1} = 1 + a + a^2 + a^3 + \ldots = \frac{1}{1-a} \tag{2.20}$$

where $|a|<1$ (i.e., absolute value of a is less than one). In the present case the mortality function is a geometric series. For notational simplicity, let $a_F + b_F x = A$ and $a_s + b_s x = B$, which then gives

$$W = \sum_{t=1}^{\infty} F_t S_t = \sum_{t=1}^{\infty} (a_F + b_F x) e^{-(a_s + b_s x)t} = A \sum_{t=1}^{\infty} e^{-Bt} \qquad (2.21)$$

To convert this into the form of equation (2.20) we note that e^{-Bt} can be written as $e^{-B} e^{-B(t-1)}$ and thus $a = e^{-B}$ then equation (2.21) becomes

$$W = A \sum_{t=1}^{\infty} e^{-Bt} = A e^{-B} \sum_{t=1}^{\infty} e^{-B(t-1)} = \frac{A e^{-B}}{1 - e^{-B}} \qquad (2.22)$$

We now have a simple function that can be differentiated, although it is a tedious process and care has to be taken. The derivative using the chain rule (see Appendix 2) is the rather nasty looking equation:

$$\frac{dW}{dx} = \frac{(b_F) e^{-(a_s + b_s x)}}{1 - e^{-(a_s + b_s x)}}$$
$$+ \frac{(a_F + b_F x)[-b_s e^{-(a_s + b_s x)}]}{1 - e^{-(a_s + b_s x)}} \qquad (2.23)$$
$$+ \frac{(a_F + b_F x) e^{-(a_s + b_s x)}(-1)[b_s e^{-(a_s + b_s x)}]}{[1 - e^{-(a_s + b_s x)}]^2}$$

We need to find the value of x at which $\frac{dW}{dx} = 0$,, which allows us to simplify the equation a little since $\frac{e^{-(a_s + b_s x)}}{1 - e^{-(a_s + b_s x)}}$ is common to all three terms. So the equation we have to solve is

$$(b_F) + (a_F + b_F x)(-b_s) + \frac{(a_F + b_F x)(-1)[b_s e^{(a_s + b_s x)}]}{[1 - e^{-(a_s + b_s x)}]} = 0 \qquad (2.24)$$

To solve the above we use uniroot in R and solve in MATLAB.

R CODE:

Define a function FUNC that gives the value of equation (2.24) for a given value of x. In the main program call uniroot to find the value of x at which FUNC(x) is zero:

```
# Set up function to be evaluated
FUNC <- function(x) { (4)+(0+4*x)*(-0.5)+(0+4*x)*(-1)*(0.5*exp
(-(1+0.5*x)))/(1-exp(-(1+0.5*x)))}
# MAIN PROGRAM
  B <- uniroot(FUNC, interval= c(0,4))# Find root
  B$root                              # Print out the value found
```

OUTPUT:

```
[1] 1.682812
```

Because we are only interested in positive values the lower limit is set at 0, excluding the possible negative root. If there were two positive roots the one closest to the lower limit would be given. We know in the present case, from the plot (Figure 2.3) that there is only a single positive root and hence we do not need to investigate further.

MATLAB CODE: See Section 2.18.5.

2.5.5   Finding the maximum using a numerical approach

For generality, we shall consider only the summation model.

R CODE:
We use the same summation function as before except that we take the negative value, because the R function nlm finds the minimum of a function. The function, nlm requires an initial estimate, p, which here we set at 1:

```
 rm(list=ls()) # Remove all objects from memory
# Function to calculate the summation as a function of x
SUMMATION <- function(x)
{
  Age <- seq(from=1, to=20)      # Sequence from 1 to n
  Wt <- 4*x*exp(-(1+0.5*x)*Age)  # Vector of fitness at age t
  return(-sum(Wt))               # Return the negative summed value
}
# Main program
  nlm(SUMMATION, p=1)$estimate  # Call nonlinear routine nlm
```

OUTPUT:
```
[1] 1.682810
```

MATLAB CODE: See Section 2.18.6.

2.6   Scenario 4: Adding age-specific mortality that affects the optimum and using integration rather than summation

In using a summation we are making a statement about when the census is taken, namely at time steps 1, 2, 3, etc. An alternate assumption is that the process is more continuous and an integral is appropriate. Reiterating the assumptions:

2.6.1   General assumptions

1. The organism is iteroparous.
2. Fecundity, F, increases with body size, x, which does not change after maturity (e.g., as in insects).

3. Survival, S, decreases with body size, x.

4. Fitness, W, is a function of fecundity and survival.

2.6.2 Mathematical assumptions

1. Maturity occurs at age 1 after which no further growth occurs.

2. Fecundity increases linearly with size at maturity, resulting in fecundity being a uniform function of age:

$$F_t = a_F + b_F x \qquad (2.25)$$

3. The instantaneous rate of mortality increases linearly with the body size attained at age 1 and is constant per time unit. Under this assumption, survival to age t is given by

$$S_t = e^{-(a_S + b_S x)t} \qquad (2.26)$$

Note that to make survival a declining function of body size, given the exponential function, we replace the previous $a_s - b_s x$ with $a_s + b_s x$.

4. Fitness, W, is the expected lifetime reproductive success, R_0, given as the cumulative product of survival and fecundity:

$$W = \int_1^\infty F_t S_t dt = \int_1^\infty (a_F + b_F x) e^{-(a_S + b_S x)t} dt \qquad (2.27)$$

As noted above, we cannot now factor out the age dependent effects from body size.

2.6.3 Plotting the fitness function

There are two approaches to plotting W versus x: first, we could integrate equation (2.27) exactly to give W as a function of x, and second, we could use a numerical integration routine. The former is generally to be preferred but integration is frequently either not possible or extremely difficult. MATLAB has a symbolic integration routine but R does not.

Noting that $\int e^{-Bt} dt = \frac{-e^{-Bt}}{B}$ equation (2.27) can be integrated to give

$$W = (a_F + b_F x) \left[\frac{-e^{-(a_S + b_S x)t}}{a_S + b_S x} \right]_1^\infty = 0 + \frac{a_F + b_F x}{a_S + b_S x} e^{-(a_S + b_S x)} \qquad (2.28)$$

R CODE (Figure 2.4):

We shall use the numerical integration function `integrate`, passing to it the function to be integrated in a function which we shall call `INTEGRAND`, which contains the expression to be integrated (i.e., $(a_F + b_F x)e^{-(a_s+b_s x)t}$). Note that the integration is over `Age` but that `x` is also needed. Further, note that because we have to pass a single value of x we use a loop rather than `apply`. Parameter values are `Af = 0`, `Bf = 8`, `As = 1`, and `Bf = 0.5`.

```
  rm(list=ls())                       # Remove all objects from memory
# Function to do numerical integration
  INTEGRAND <- function(age,x)
{
  Af <- 0; Bf <- 8 ; As <- 1 ;Bs <- 0.5            # parameter values
  return ((Af-Bf*x)*exp(-(As+Bs*x)*age))       # return function
}
# MAIN PROGRAM
  n       <- 100                      # Number of points
  z       <- seq(0,3,length=n)        # Create a vector for z 0 to 3
  W       <- matrix(0,n,1)            # Create a vector W to hold results
for (i in 1:n)                        # Iterate over n "body sizes"
{
  x       <- z[i]                     # Set value of x
# Integrate from 1 to infinity and add to W
  W[i]  <- integrate(INTEGRAND,1,Inf,x)$value
}
  plot(z,-W,type='l', xlab='Body size, x', ylab='Fitness, W',
las=1,lwd=4)
```

MATLAB CODE: See Section 2.18.7.

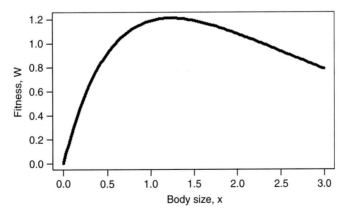

Figure 2.4 Scenario 4: Fitness versus body size.

2.6.4   Finding the maximum using the calculus

Taking the derivative of W with respect to x gives

$$\frac{dW}{dx} = \frac{b_F}{a_S + b_S x} e^{-(a_S + b_S x)} - \frac{(a_F + b_F x)b_S}{a_S + b_S x} e^{-(a_S + b_S x)} - \frac{(a_F + b_F x)b_S}{(a_S + b_S x)^2} e^{-(a_S + b_S x)}$$

$$= \frac{e^{-(a_S + b_S x)}}{a_S + b_S x} \left\{ b_F - (a_F + b_F x)b_s - \frac{(a_F + b_F x)b_s}{a_S + b_S x} \right\}$$

(2.29)

This can also be obtained using `deriv` in R or `diff` in MATLAB.

R CODE:

```
y <- deriv(~(0+4*x)*exp(-(1+0.5*x))/(1+0.5*x),"x")
y # OUTPUT y
```

OUTPUT:

```
expression({
.expr3 <- -0 + 4 * x
.expr5 <- 1 + 0.5 * x
.expr7 <- exp(-.expr5)
.expr8 <- .expr3 * .expr7
.value <- .expr8/.expr5
.grad <- array(0, c(length(.value), 1L), list(NULL, c("x")))
.grad[, "x"] <- (4 * .expr7 - .expr3 * (.expr7 * 0.5))/.expr5 -
    .expr8 * 0.5/.expr5^2
attr(.value, "gradient") <- .grad
.value
})
```

We do not need to interpret the output, merely store it as a variable, say `y`. To find the value of x at which $\frac{dW}{dx} = 0$, we find the value of x that makes the components within {} of equation (2.29) equal to zero.

R CODE:
Two possible routes are shown. In the first the derivative is supplied directly in the function FUNC, whereas in the second the derivative is obtained in FUNC using the R function deriv. In either case the main program calls `uniroot` to find the root:

```
rm(list=ls())                       # Remove all objects from memory
# Function to evaluate {} in eqn (2.29)
FUNC <- function(x){4+0.5*(0-4*x)-(0+4*x)*0.5/(1+0.5*x)}
B <- uniroot(FUNC, interval=c(0,4))# Set lower interval = 0
B$root                              # Print out the value found
```

OR using R to obtain the derivative:

```
# Using R to obtain the derivative
rm(list=ls()) # Remove all objects from memory
```

```
# Function to obtain the gradient at a value w
  FUNC <- function(w)
{
y <- deriv(~ (0+4*x)*exp(-(1+0.5*x))/(1+0.5*x),"x") # Get the derivative
x <- w                        # Set x equal to w
z <- eval(y)                  # Evaluate the derivative at w
d <- attr(z,"gradient")       # Assign the gradient value to d
return(d)                     # Return d to the main program
}
# MAIN PROGRAM
# Root must be enclosed by the limits set by the user, here set at 0 to 4
B <- uniroot(FUNC, interval= c(0,4))
B$root                 # Print out the value found
```

OUTPUT:

`[1] 1.236068`

In the present scenario we can actually go a step further and find an exact solution. First we place all terms enclosed by {} in equation (2.29) over $a_s+b_s x$ to give

$$b_F - (a_F + b_F x)b_S - \frac{(a_F + b_F x)b_S}{a_S + b_S x} = \frac{-a_F b_S a_S - x(b_F b_S a_S + a_F b_S^2) - x^2 b_F b_S^2}{a_S + b_S x} \qquad (2.30)$$

The numerator is a quadratic equation $(ax^2+bx+c+=0)$ for which the roots can be obtained exactly from the standard formula, $x = \frac{-b \pm \sqrt{b^2-4ac}}{2a}$, which gives 1.236068, the same as found previously. Notice that the optimum body size, x, is not the same as found using the summation formula. Whether one uses an integral or a sum will depend on the biological assumptions. In the present case the integral model can be more readily solved and thus if there are no strong reasons to prefer one model over the other then the integral model is clearly the better choice. Think carefully about the biological assumptions in relation to the ease with which the model can be solved, but never sacrifice necessary biological realism for mathematical convenience.

MATLAB CODE: See Section 2.18.8.

2.6.5 Finding the maximum using a numerical approach

R CODE:

We use the two R functions `integrate` and `nlm`. The function value for a given age and x, $(a_F + b_F x)e^{-(a_S+b_S x)age}$, is determined from the user-supplied function `INTEGRAND`. Remember that we have to return the negative of fitness, because we are finding the minimum! To obtain the integral the user-supplied function `FUNC`, calls the R function `integrate`, passing to it `INTEGRAND`. The optimum x is found by passing `FUNC` to `nlm`:

```
rm(list=ls())               # Remove all objects from memory
# Function to supply components for numerical integration
   INTEGRAND <- function(age,x) # Calculate function value
{
   Af <- 0; Bf <- 4 ; As <- 1 ;Bs <- 0.5 # parameter values
   return (-(Af+Bf*x)*exp(-(As+Bs*x)*age)) # return function value
}
# Function to call integration routine
   FUNC <- function(x){integrate(INTEGRAND,1,Inf,x)$value}
# Minimization routine
   nlm(FUNC,p=1)$estimate
```

OUTPUT:

[1] 1.236067

MATLAB CODE: See Section 2.18.9.

2.7   Scenario 5: Maximizing the Malthusian parameter, *r*, rather than expected lifetime reproductive success, *R*₀

Thus far we have assumed that the appropriate measure of fitness is the expected lifetime reproductive success, R_0. Whereas this measure of fitness may be appropriate for a stable population a more general fitness measure is the Malthusian parameter, r, which is equal to the population rate of increase at a stable age distribution:

$$\int_0^\infty e^{-rt}l(t)m(t)dt = 1$$

$$\sum_{t=1}^\infty e^{-rt}l_t m_t = 1$$

(2.31)

where $l(t)$, l_t are the probabilities of survival to age t and $m(t)$,m_1 are the age specific female births (= fecundities/2, assuming an equal sex-ratio). The different notations used in the two equations are generally of little or no consequence (the difference equation could equally well have been written in the same manner as the integral equation) and used here simply to illustrate that differences in notation should not be taken to imply differences in interpretation. Note that the difference equation is commenced at the end of the first time period, since we necessarily assume that fecundity is zero at birth (of course we could start from zero if we simply set m_0=0). Although these equations do not directly encompass the male contribution we could write a similar equation for males by relating his mating success to the population growth rate. The assumption underlying the use of r is that any mutation that increased r would increase in frequency in the population. This assumption is intuitively reasonable and has been verified (Lande 1982; Charlesworth 1994).

We shall make the same assumptions as in the previous scenario, except that the fitness measure will be taken to be r.

2.7.1 General assumptions

1. The organism is iteroparous.
2. Fecundity, F, increases with body size, x, which does not change after maturity (e.g., as in insect).
3. Survival, S, decreases with body size, x.
4. Fitness, W, is a function of fecundity and survival.

2.7.2 Mathematical assumptions

1. Maturity occurs at age 1 after which no further growth occurs.
2. Fecundity increases linearly with size at maturity, resulting in fecundity being a uniform function of age:

$$F_t = a_F + b_F x \tag{2.32}$$

3. The instantaneous rate of mortality increases linearly with the body size attained at age 1 and is constant per time unit. Under this assumption, survival to age t is given by

$$S_t = e^{-(a_S + b_S x)t} \tag{2.33}$$

Note that to make survival a declining function of body size, given the exponential function, we replace the previous $a_s - b_s x$ with $a_s + b_s x$.

4. Fitness, W, is the Malthusian parameter r. Taking r to be the measure of fitness, the fitness function is given by the solution of the characteristic equation:

$$\int_1^\infty e^{-rt}(a_F + b_F x)e^{-(a_S + b_S x)t}dt = 1 \tag{2.34}$$

where the initial value of the integral is set at 1, as this is the age of first reproduction.

The two exponents can be absorbed into a single term, giving

$$\int_1^\infty (a_F + b_F x)e^{-(a_S + b_S x + r)t}dt = 1 \tag{2.35}$$

Now the above equation has the same general form as equation (2.28) and so can be integrated to give

$$1 = (a_F + b_F x)\left[\frac{-e^{-(a_S + b_S x + r)t}}{a_S + b_S x + r}\right]_1^\infty = 0 + \frac{a_F + b_F x}{a_S + b_S x + r}e^{-(a_S + b_S x + r)} \tag{2.36}$$

2.7.3   Plotting the fitness function

To plot r, our fitness measure, as a function of x we must solve equation (2.35) or (2.36) for each value of x. We shall first examine methods to estimate r without ourselves doing the integration (i.e., using equation (2.35)) and then methods using equation (2.36).

2.7.3.1   Using the program to do the integration

R CODE (Figure 2.5):
We first consider numerical integration to estimate r. The strategy is to iterate over a range of x and for each value calculate r.

1. INTEGRAND calculates $(a_F + b_F x)e^{-(a_s+b_s x+r)\text{age}}$.

2. INTEGRAL calls the R function integrate to obtain the integral, passing to it INTEGRAND.

3. The function RCALC uses the R function uniroot to find the value of r which satisfies the characteristic equation (2.35) for a given x.

4. The main program creates a single column matrix of x values and uses the R function apply to use RCALC on each x value (row of matrix x) to get the requisite value of r, stored in the vector r.

5. The vectors x and r are then used in plot to display the relationship between r (fitness) and x (body size). In sequence, for a given x, RCALC calls uniroot which calls INTEGRAL which in turn calls INTEGRAND.

```
rm(list=ls())                      # Remove all objects from memory
# Function to output function to be integrated
INTEGRAND <- function(age,x,r)
{
Af <- 0; Bf <- 4*4 ; As <- 1 ;Bs <- 0.5   # parameter values
return ((Af+Bf*x)*exp(-(As+Bs*x+r)*age)) # return function
}
# Function to integrate characteristic equation and return 1-its
  value
  INTEGRAL <- function(r,x)
{ 1-integrate(INTEGRAND,1,Inf,x,r)$value}  # 1-Characteristic
                                                      equation
# Function to find r given x
  RCALC   <- function(x){uniroot(INTEGRAL, interval=c(1e-7,10),
x)$root}
# MAIN PROGRAM
  x <- matrix(seq(0.5,3, length=100))   # x ranging from 0.5 to 3
                                              length=100
  r <- apply(x,1,RCALC)                     # Calculate r for given x
plot(x,r,type='l',   xlab='Body   size,   x',   ylab='Fitness,
r',las=1,lwd=4)
```

OUTPUT: Plot shown in Figure 2.5.

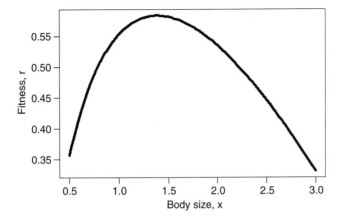

Figure 2.5 Scenario 5: Fitness versus body size.

MATLAB CODE: See Section 2.18.10.

2.7.3.2 User supplied solution to the integral

Using the integrated function shown in equation (2.36) is simpler. However, because many functions cannot be integrated analytically, it is less general.

R CODE (Figure 2.5):

```
  rm(list=ls())                        # Remove all objects from memory
# Function to evaluate equation (2.36)
  FUNC <- function(r,x)
{
  Af <- 0; Bf <- 4*4 ; As <- 1 ;Bs <- 0.5 # Parameter values
  S  <- exp(-(r+As+Bs*x))*(Af+Bf*x)/(As+Bs*x+r) # RHS of equation
  return(1-S)                            # Subtract 1
}
# Function to find r given x using uniroot
  RCALC <- function(x){uniroot( FUNC, interval=c(1e-07,10),x)$root}
# MAIN PROGRAM - same as previous
  x <- matrix(seq(0.5,3, length=100)) # X ranging from 0.5 to 3
  r <- apply(x,1,RCALC)               # Calculate r for given x and store
  plot(x, r, type='l', xlab="Size,x", ylab="Fitness, r",las=1,lwd=4)
```

MATLAB CODE: See Section 2.18.10.

2.7.4 Finding the maximum using the calculus

Our fitness measure is no longer on one side of the equation, and the equation cannot be simplified to make this so. The equation can be differentiated using implicit differentiation (see Appendix 2). For convenience we first take logs to convert the function into one that is additive:

$$0 = \ln\left(a_F + b_F x\right) - (a_S + b_S x + r) - \ln(a_S + b_S x + r)$$
$$= T1 - T2 - T3 \qquad (2.37)$$

Now taking each term separately we have

$$T1: \quad \frac{dr}{dx} = \frac{b_F}{a_F + b_F x}$$

$$T2: \quad \frac{dr}{dx} = b_S + \frac{dr}{dx} \qquad\qquad (2.38)$$

$$T3: \quad \frac{dr}{dx} = \left(\frac{1}{a_S + b_S x + r}\right)\left(\frac{dr}{dx}\right) + \frac{b_S}{a_S + b_S + r}$$

Gathering the terms together and rearranging we arrive at

$$\frac{dr}{dx}\left(1 + \frac{1}{a_S + b_S x + r}\right) = \frac{b_F}{a_F + b_F x} - b_S - \frac{b_S}{a_S + b_S x + r} \qquad (2.39)$$

Now $\frac{dr}{dx} = 0$ when the right-hand side equals zero, provided the term in parentheses on the left-hand side does not also equal zero, which will not generally be the case. Thus we can rearrange the right-hand side to make r a function of the parameters and x:

$$r^* = \frac{b_S(a_F + b_F x^*)}{b_F - b_S a_F - b_S b_F x^*} - b_S x^* - a_S \qquad (2.40)$$

where r^* is the maximum value of r, obtained at x^*. To find x^* we substitute equation (2.40) into equation (2.37) to obtain:

$$0 = \ln\left(a_F + b_F x^*\right) - (a_S + b_S x^* + r^*) - \ln\left(a_S + b_S x^* + r^*\right)$$

$$0 = \ln\ \left(a_F + b_F x^*\right) - \left[a_S + b_S x^* + \frac{b_S(a_F + b_F x^*)}{b_F - b_S a_F - b_S b_F x^*} - b_S x^* - a_S\right]$$

$$-\ln\left[a_S + b_S x^* + \frac{b_S(a_F + b_F x^*)}{b_F - b_S a_F - b_S b_F x^*} - b_S x^* - a_S\right] \qquad (2.41)$$

which can be solved numerically.

R CODE:
I here illustrate three functions that can be used to locate the required value of x.

2.7.4.1   Use of uniroot

The first is `uniroot`. Note that the limits are set fairly close to the required value. If the limits are set too far apart (e.g., `uniroot(f=RFUNC,interval=c (1.2,3))$root`) the function may fail, R returning the error message:

```
Error in uniroot(f = RFUNC, interval = c(1.2, 3)) :
  f.upper = f(upper) is NA
In addition: Warning message:
In log(As + Bs * x + r) : NaNs produced
```

The above failure emphasizes the importance of making a preliminary plot to determine the approximate value of x at which r is a maximum:

```
rm(list=ls())                    # Remove all objects from memory
# Function to calculate value of equation (2.41) for a given value of x
RFUNC <- function(x)
{
  Af <- 0;Bf<-4*4;As<-1;Bs<-0.5              # Set parameter va-
lues
  r  <- Bs*(Af+Bf*x)/(Bf-Bs*Af-Bs*Bf*x)-Bs*x-As # r from eqn (2.40)
  return(log(Af+Bf*x)-(As+Bs*x+r)-log(As+Bs*x+r))
}
# MAIN PROGRAM
  uniroot(f=RFUNC,interval=c(1.2,1.8))$root
```

OUTPUT:

```
[1] 1.389974
```

2.7.4.2 Use of nlm

An alternate approach is to use nlm by taking the absolute value in FUNC, in which case the minimum must be zero.

```
rm(list=ls())                    # Remove all objects from memory
# Function to calculate value of equation (2.41) for a given value of x
RFUNC <- function(x)
{
  Af<-0;Bf<-4*4;As<-1;Bs<-0.5               # Set parameter values
  r  <- Bs*(Af+Bf*x)/(Bf-Bs*Af-Bs*Bf*x)-Bs*x-As # r from eqn (2.40)
  return(abs(log(Af+Bf*x)-(As+Bs*x+r)-log(As+Bs*x+r)))
}
# MAIN PROGRAM
  nlm(RFUNC, p=1.2)$estimate
```

Because x is not constrained, this method is not very satisfactory and although the correct answer is found warning messages are generated.

OUTPUT:

```
[1] 1.389943
```

```
Warning messages:

1: In log(As + Bs * x + r) : NaNs produced
2: In nlm(RFUNC, p=1.2) : NA/Inf replaced by maximum positive value
```

2.7.4.3 Use of optimize

The third method is to use the routine optimize, which can find either a minimum or maximum and allows one to enter upper and lower limits for the search. As in the case of nlm we use the absolute value of the function.

```
   rm(list=ls())                # Remove all objects from memory
# Function to calculate value of equation (2.41) for a given value of x
   RFUNC <- function(x)
{
   Af<-0;Bf<-4*4;As<-1;Bs<-0.5          # Set parameter values
   r<-Bs*(Af+Bf*x)/(Bf-Bs*Af-Bs*Bf*x)-Bs*x-As   # r from eqn (2.40)
   return(abs(log(Af+Bf*x)-(As+Bs*x+r)-log(As+Bs*x+r)))
}
   optimize(f=RFUNC, interval=c(1.2,1.8),maximum=FALSE)$minimum
```

OUTPUT:

`[1] 1.389956`

As with `nlm`, if the limits are too broad a warning message may be generated:

`optimize(f = RFUNC, interval = c(1.2,3),maximum = FALSE)$minimum`

OUTPUT:

```
[1] 1.389951
Warning messages:
1: In log(As + Bs * x + r) : NaNs produced
2: In optimize(f = RFUNC, interval = c(1.3, 3), maximum = FALSE) :
NA/Inf replaced by maximum positive value
```

Note that the four outputs are close but not exactly the same.

MATLAB Code: See Section 2.18.11.

2.7.5   Finding the maximum using a numerical approach

We shall consider two approaches: first, using the solved integral equation (2.36) and second, using numerical integration to solve the original model (equation [2.35]). The latter method is the most general but will also be the most time consuming. Even if the integral can be solved, it is good practice to use the latter method as a check on the correctness of the integration.

2.7.5.1   Using the integrated function (equation [2.36])

The main program uses the R function `optimize`, giving it RCALC which uses `uniroot` to find the root of the function specified in FUNC.

```
   rm(list=ls())                # Remove all objects from memory
# Function to get integral value
   FUNC <- function(r,x)
{
   Af <- 0; Bf <- 4*4 ; As <- 1 ;Bs <- 0.5 # parameter values
   S <- exp(-(r+As+Bs*x))*(Af+Bf*x)/(As+Bs*x+r) # Function value
   return(1-S)
}
```

```
# Function to find r given x
  RCALC <- function(x){uniroot( FUNC, interval=c(1e-07,10),x)
$root}
# MAIN PROGRAM
# Use optimize which allows us to constrain the search
# Tell optimize that we want the maximum
optimize(f = RCALC, interval = c(.5,3),maximum = TRUE)$maximum
```

OUTPUT:

[1] 1.389946

2.7.5.2 Using numerical integration of the function.

The main program uses `optimize`, giving it `RCALC` which uses `uniroot` to find the root of the function specified in `FUNC`, which itself calls `INTEGRAND` to obtain the integral.

```
  rm(list=ls())           # Remove all objects from memory
# Function to do numerical integration of eqn (2.34)
  INTEGRAND <- function(age,x,r)
{
  Af <- 0; Bf <- 4*4 ; As <- 1 ;Bs <- 0.5          # parameter values
  return ((Af+Bf*x)*exp(-(As+Bs*x+r)*age))   # return function
}
# Function to integrate characteristic equation
  FUNC <- function(r,x){1-integrate(INTEGRAND,1,Inf,x,r)$value}
# Function to find r given x
  RCALC <- function(x){uniroot(FUNC, interval=c(1e-07,10),x)$root}
# MAIN PROGRAM
  optimize(f=RCALC, interval=c(1.2,1.8),maximum=TRUE)$maximum
```

OUTPUT:

[1] 1.389934

MATLAB CODE: See Section 2.18.12.

2.8 Scenario 6: Stochastic variation in parameters

Within any generation there is likely to be stochastic variation in parameter values. The scenario considered here is that in which one or more parameters vary within generations according to some probability distribution with the same distribution among generations. For variation in a single parameter, θ, fitness for a given value of x is given by $\int P(\theta) f(\theta, x) d\theta$, where $P(\theta)$ is the probability density function and $f(\theta, x)$ is the fitness function for a given θ and x. A possible model would be a normal density function, so that the probability of a value of θ is given by $P(\theta) = \frac{1}{\sigma_\theta \sqrt{2\pi}} e^{-\frac{1}{2}\left(\frac{\theta - \mu_\theta}{\sigma_\theta}\right)^2}$, where $\mu(\theta)$ is the mean parameter value and σ_θ^2 is its variance. Such a function could be problematic for traits such as survival that can only vary between zero and one, because the probability function must either be truncated or values less than zero set to zero and values greater than one set to one. The problem with adopting such a model is that the probability distribution could show unlikely rises at zero and one. Considerable care should be taken in the selection of a probability function and in general it is advisable to use several functions or one that can take a wide variety of shapes to ensure that the results are not uniquely dependent on the function chosen. The analysis of temporal variation in a single parameter is dealt with in the following two scenarios, the methods discussed in these scenarios are readily adapted to the present. Here I shall consider the somewhat more complex case, but that which is most likely to be appropriate for stochastic variation, in which several parameters vary. If there is variation in several parameters we need to take into account possible correlations between parameter values. This becomes a particular concern when the parameters are themselves traits, where genetic and phenotypic correlations may be highly likely. For two parameters the general form is a simple extension of the one trait case, namely $\int \int P(\theta_1, \theta_2) f(\theta_1, \theta_2, x) d\theta_1 d\theta_2$. Extension to more parameters is obvious but solving such equations can prove difficult. A brute force approach will always work but could be time consuming if the model is very detailed. To illustrate the general approach using brute force I shall consider the case of variation in two uncorrelated parameters. The case considered here is conceptually the same as in Scenario 1, except that variation is assumed for the parameters of the survival function.

2.8.1 General assumptions

1. The organism is semelparous.
2. Fecundity, F, increases with body size, x.
3. Survival, S, decreases with body size, x.
4. Two of the parameters in the functions describing the above two traits are variable within generations but the same distribution occurs among generations.
5. Fitness, W, is a function of fecundity and survival.

2.8.2 Mathematical Assumptions

1. As before, fecundity increases linearly with body size:

$$F = a_F + b_F x \tag{2.42}$$

where a_F and b_F are constants.

2. Survival decreases linearly with body size:

$$S = a_S - b_S x \qquad (2.43)$$

where both a_S and b_S, vary within generations and are specified by independent probability density functions. We shall assume the simplest probability function, namely a uniform function, which is defined as $P(\theta) = c$, where c is a constant determined from the minimum, θ_{min}, and maximum, θ_{max}, values of the parameter θ by the cumulative probability function:

$$\int_{\theta_{min}}^{\theta_{max}} c\theta = 1$$
$$[\theta]_{\theta_{min}}^{\theta_{max}} = 1 \qquad (2.44)$$
$$c(\theta_{max} - \theta_{min}) = 1$$
$$c = 1/(\theta_{max} - \theta_{min})$$

In the present case the two functions are defined as $P(a_s) = c_{as}$ and $P(b_s) = c_{bs}$.

3. As noted above, the appropriate measure of fitness is the average of the fitness values:

$$W = \int_{a_{min}}^{a_{max}} \int_{b_{min}}^{b_{max}} P(a_S)P(b_S)(a_F + b_F x)(a_S - b_S x)\, da_S db_S \qquad (2.45)$$

Because a_S and b_S are independent one might be led to think that the mean fitness will indeed be equal to the fitness using the mean values. This would indeed be true if the variable parameters were a_F and b_F (i.e., the mean of $a_F + b_F x$ is simply equal to $\mu_{af} + \mu_{bf} x$, where μ stands for the mean). However, survival must vary within the range 0–1 and hence there are combinations in equation (2.45) that are not permissible (and hence this equation as written is not strictly correct). For any given x value the set of pairs of a_S and b_S must be restricted to those that ensure that survival does not fall outside 0–1. For combinations in which survival is less than zero, survival is set to zero and for combinations in which survival is greater than 1, survival is set to 1.

2.8.3   Plotting the fitness function

The basic approach is to generate two vectors containing values of a_S and b_S generated from the appropriate probability distributions (or multivariate distribution if the parameters are correlated). The uniform distribution is generated in R by `runif` and in MATLAB by `rand`. It is generally useful to set the seed prior (`set.seed(n)` in R and `rand('twister', n)` in MATLAB, where n is set by the user) to the use of any random number generator as this allows the replication of runs, which can be very useful in debugging. After generation of the two values the vector of survival probabilities is calculated and values checked that they fall within the acceptable range (0–1). In addition to calculating mean fitness as a function of x (body size), the following code also calculate fitness using the mean parameter values. For each parameter vectors of 1,000 random values are generated. These vectors are then used in calculating the fitness for a given body size x. The survival vector `Surv` is 1,000 units long. For simplicity and without loss of significant run time a loop is used to iterate over values of body size.

R CODE (Figure 2.6):

```
rm(list=ls())            # Remove all objects from memory
Af   <- 2; Bf <- 2       # Invariant parameter values
Amin <- 0.3; Amax <- 1   # Min and max values of as
Bmin <- 0; Bmax <- 0.2   # Min and max values of bs
Amean <- (Amax+Amin)/2 # Mean value of as
Bmean <- (Bmax+Bmin)/2 # Mean value of bs
# Calculate n parameter combinations
n      <- 1000           # Number of values of as and bs to generate
# We are assuming a uniform distribution of values
set.seed(10)             # Set the random number seed
# Generate n random numbers from Bmin to Bmax
Bs <- runif(n, min=Bmin, max=Bmax)
# Generate n random numbers from Amin to Amax
As <- runif(n, min=Amin, max=Amax)
x <- seq(from=0, to=6, length=100)  # Body sizes from 0 to 6
W <- matrix(0,100,2)              # Matrix to take fitness values
for ( i in 1: 100)               # Iterate over x values
{
Surv <- As-Bs*x[i]               # Vector of survivals
# Check that no survival < 0. If so then set to zero
Surv[Surv<0]   <- 0
# Check that no survival > 1. If so then set to 1
Surv[Surv>1] <- 1
# Column 1 contains fitness for variable parameters
W[i,1] <- mean((Af+Bf*x[i])*Surv)
# Col 2 contains fitness using mean parameter values
W[i,2] <- (Af+Bf*x[i])*(Amean-Bmean*x[i])
}
# Plot fitness=W vs x for both columns on same graph
plot(x,W[,1], xlab='Body size, x', ylab='Fitness, W',las=1,
lwd=4)                   # Dots
lines(x,W[,2], lwd=4) # Line
```

MATLAB CODE: See Section 2.18.13.

Notice that the two parameter vectors are outside of the loop over x. This is important for two reasons: first, because only one pair of vectors is calculated, it speeds up

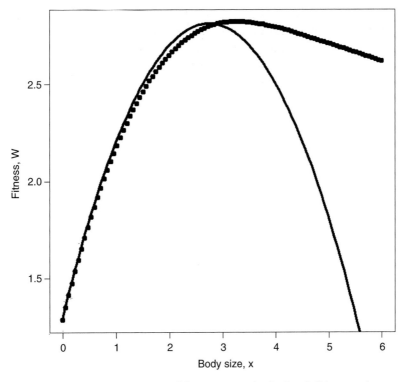

Figure 2.6 Scenario 6: Two measures of fitness versus body size. Solid curve shows results of using mean values (incorrect) and beaded lines shows correct curve.

the program and second, the fitnesses for the different values of x are compared against the same set of parameters. It is quite evident from the two plots in Figure 2.6 that the optimum body size cannot be calculated using the parameter means.

2.8.4 Finding the maximum using the calculus

In some cases it may be possible to integrate the fitness function and then solve the resultant function either analytically or numerically. In this particular case this is actually rather difficult because the integration limits are actually functions of x and there may be discontinuities because of setting survival equal to 1 if the survival function exceeds 1. Integration of equation (2.45) as written actually leads to the prediction that the optimal value of x is the same as that using the mean parameter values, which is clearly incorrect (Figure 2.6). Here I shall use the numerical integration routines in R and MATLAB. The multidimensional integration routine in R is called `adapt` and must be loaded as a separate package (since the first printing of this book this package has been moved to the R archive. Either retrieve it from there and load it into the library folder of R, or use the source code that is now on my website). It was necessary to adjust some of the default values in the routines `adapt` and `nlm` to get something approaching convergence to a consistent value. The integration routine `adapt` works by generating a grid of As and Bs values set by `Amin`, `Amax`, `Bmin`, and `Bmax` and using these to numerically evaluate the integral, where the function is defined in the function INTEGRAND.

Note that this function does not consist of a single equation but a series of steps that evaluate whether survival after being calculated according to As – Bs*x should be reset to 0 or 1. The function adapt calls INTEGRAND and adapt is called by the function FITNESS, which is itself called by nlm or optimize in the main program.

R CODE:

```
rm(list=ls())                  # Remove all objects from memory
library(adapt)                 # Make sure that adapt is loaded
INTEGRAND <- function(Y,x)     # Define function to be integrated
{
 Af <- 2; Bf <- 2              # Invariant parameter values
 Ca <- 1/0.7; Cb <- 5
# Y[1] = As and Y[2] = Bs
 Surv <- Y[1]-Y[2]*x           # Vector of survivals
# Check that no survival < 0. If so then set to zero
 Surv[Surv<0] <- 0
# Check that no survival > 1. If so then set to 1
 Surv[Surv>1] <- 1
 return((Af+Bf*x)*Surv*Cb*Ca)
}
 FITNESS<- function(x)    # Function that calls adapt for a given x
{
 Amin <- 0.3; Amax <- 1        # Min and max values of $a_S$
 Bmin <- 0; Bmax <- 0.2        # Min and max values of $b_S$
 W <- adapt(2, lo=c(Amin,Bmin), up=c(Amax,Bmax), minpts = 1000,
functn=INTEGRAND, x=x)
 return(-W$value)              # Return negative of fitness
}
# MAIN PROGRAM
 nlm(FITNESS,p=1,steptol = 1e-5)   # Note change in steptol
 optimize(f=FITNESS,interval=c(1,4), maximum=FALSE) #Alternate
                                                     method
```

OUTPUT: (modified slightly)

```
> nlm(FITNESS,p=1,steptol = 1e-5)
$minimum              [1] -2.897318
$estimate             [1] 3.324141
$gradient             [1] -0.01254321
$code                 [1] 2
$iterations           [1] 13
> optimize(f=FITNESS,interval=c(1,4), maximum=FALSE)
$minimum              [1] 3.368978
$objective            [1] -2.897131
```

The two routines nlm and optimize give slightly different answers. The termination code for nlm indicates that it is not clear that a minimum has been attained.

In fact it was necessary to change the default step tolerance steptol from 1e-6 to 1e-5 to achieve this (further changes did not change the result). Notice also that minpts in adapt has been changed from its default of 100 to 1,000. These changes were made to try and make the two optimization routines agree as much as possible. It is very important to carefully check the results of numerical methods by several pathways, if at all possible.

MATLAB CODE: See Section 2.18.14.

2.8.5 Finding the maximum using a numerical approach

The approach used here is a mixture of a brute force approach and non-linear optimization. For each value of x 10,000 values are calculated and nlm then used to locate the value of x at which fitness is maximized (i.e., $-W$ is minimized). To check on consistency the process is replicated 10 times and the mean and standard deviation calculated. Note that the random number seed is given outside the replication loop (or we would just be generating the same sequence each time) and that the same set of random parameter values are used within a replicate run.

R CODE:
```
  rm(list=ls())                    # Remove all objects from memory
FITNESS <- function(x,As,Bs)
{
  Af   <- 2; Bf <- 2               # Invariant parameter values
  Surv <- As-Bs*x                  # Vector of survivals
# Check that no survival < 0. If so then set to zero
  Surv[Surv<0] <- 0
# Check that no survival > 1. If so then set to 1
  Surv[Surv>1] <- 1
  W <- mean((Af+Bf*x)*Surv)
return(-W)
}
# MAIN PROGRAM
Amin <- 0.3; Amax <- 1      # Min and max values of aS
Bmin <- 0; Bmax <- 0.2      # Min and max values of bS
# Calculate n parameter combinations
n <- 10000                  # Number of values of a_S and b_S to generate
# We are assuming a uniform distribution of values
# Make several runs. Here we use 10
REP <- matrix(0,10)         # Create matrix to hold replicate
set.seed(10)                # Set seed for random number generator
for(i in 1:10)              # Iterate over replicates
{
  Bs     <- runif(n, min=Bmin, max=Bmax) # Vector of values of Bf
  As     <- runif(n, min=Amin, max=Amax) # Vector of values of As
  REP[i]<- nlm(FITNESS,p=REP[i],As,Bs)$estimate # Optimum for
                                               this run
```

```
}
  print(c(mean(REP), sd(REP))) # Print mean and standard deviation
```

OUTPUT:

```
[1] 3.36934528 0.03739426
```

The mean of the 10 replicate runs closely matches that obtained using `optimize` (3.368978). Because of the time required to do the numerical integration, there was little difference in run time between the two approaches.

MATLAB CODE:See Section 2.18.15.

2.9   Scenario 7: Discrete temporal variation in parameters

In the real world values will vary among generations either because of genetic or environmental variation. In this scenario we shall consider the consequences of discrete temporal stochastic variation in a single parameter. Within each generation the parameter takes a particular value for all individuals. As in Scenario 6, the particular case is conceptually the same as in Scenario 1, except that a parameter of the survival function varies temporally.

2.9.1   General assumptions

1. The organism is semelparous.
2. Fecundity, F, increases with body size, x.
3. Survival, S, decreases with body size, x.
4. At least one of the parameters in the functions describing the above two traits is temporally variable.
5. Fitness, W, is a function of fecundity and survival.

2.9.2   Mathematical assumptions

1. Fecundity increases linearly with body size:

$$F = a_F + b_F x \tag{2.46}$$

where a_F and b_F are constants.

2. Survival decreases linearly with body size:

$$S = a_S - b_{S,i} x \tag{2.47}$$

where $b_{S,i}$ varies from generation to generation, as indexed by i. In this particular case b_S takes one of the following values with the probability, P_i, shown in parentheses: 0.10 (0.1), 0.12 (0.3), 0.14 (0.4), or 0.2 (0.2). Note that the sum of the probabilities must be 1.

3. In a deterministic world fitness, W, is the expected lifetime reproductive success, R_0, given as the product of Fecundity and Survival. However, in a

temporally variable environment the appropriate measure of fitness is the geometric average (Roff, 2002, chapter 1):

$$W = \prod_{i=1}^{i=4} [(a_F + b_F x)(a_S - b_{S,i} x)]^{P_i} \tag{2.48}$$

Working with products is generally not a good policy as the numbers can quickly become very small or large. It is more convenient to take logs, thus converting the product into a summation:

$$\log W = \log \left\{ \prod_{i=1}^{i=4} [(a_F + b_F x)(a_S - b_{S,i} x)]^{P_1} \right\}$$
$$= \sum_{i=1}^{i=4} P_i \log[(a_F + b_F x)(a_S - b_{S,i} x)] \tag{2.49}$$

As always, we first ask if fitness has a maximum value at an intermediate value of x.

2.9.3 Plotting the fitness function

Because we have converted the fitness function to a summation there is nothing new introduced here. Parameter values are given in the function. An important aspect is that W approaches minus infinity as x approaches 3 and so the range in x is kept below 3.

R CODE:

```
rm(list=ls())               # Remove all objects from memory
FITNESS <- function(x)      # Function to calculate log of fitness
{
  Af  <- 2; Bf <- 2 ; As <- 0.6      # Parameter values
  pBs <- c(0.1,0.3,0.4,0.2)          # Vector of probabilities for Bs
  Bs  <- c(0.1,0.12,0.14,0.2)        # Vector of Bs values
  W.ind <- (Af+Bf*x)*(As-Bs*x)  # Fitness values for each Bs value
  log.W <- -sum(pBs*log(W.ind)) # log Fitness
  return(log.W)
}
# MAIN PROGRAM
  x <- matrix(seq(0,2.99,length=100))# Values. Note W =INF at x=3
  LOG.W <- apply(x,1,FITNESS)         # Calc log(fitness) values
# Plot fitness=exp(-W) vs x
  plot(x,exp(-LOG.W),xlab="Body  size,  x",ylab="Fitness,  W",
type='l',las=1, lwd=3)
```

Fitness is maximized in the vicinity of 1.5 (Figure 2.7) and body size can never equal or exceed 3.0, as fitness becomes negative.

MATLAB CODE: See Section 2.18.16.

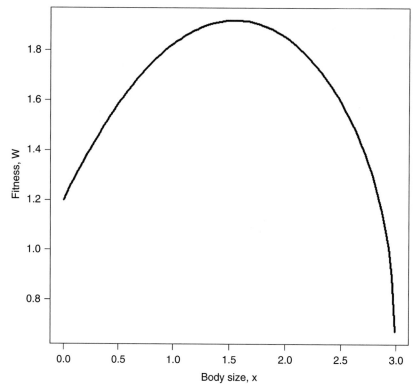

Figure 2.7 Scenario 7: Fitness versus body size.

2.9.4 Finding the maximum using the calculus

To discuss the general approach to the analysis of the type of equation shown in (2.49) we shall write it in a more general form as

$$\log W = \sum P_i \log[f(\theta_i, x)] \qquad (2.50)$$

where $f(\theta_i, x)$ means "a function of x (the trait of interest) and θ_i the variable parameter (in the present case $= b_{S,i}$)." In this form the equation presents no difficulty as it can readily be differentiated with respect to x for all individual values of θ_i:

$$\frac{d\log W}{dx} = \sum P_i \frac{d\log[f(\theta_i, x)]}{dx} \qquad (2.51)$$

which in the present scenario gives

$$logW = \sum_{i=1}^{i=4} P_i \log[(a_F + b_F x)(a_S - b_{S,i} x)]$$

$$= \sum_{i=1}^{i=4} P_i \log[a_F a_S + (a_S b_F - a_F b_{S,i})x - b_F b_{S,i} x^2] \qquad (2.52)$$

$$\frac{dlogW}{dx} = \sum_{i=1}^{i=4} P_i \frac{(a_S b_F - a_F b_{S,i}) - b_F b_{S,i} 2x}{a_F a_S + (a_S b_F - a_F b_{S,i})x - b_F b_{S,i} x^2}$$

Below I first present a code to calculate the optimum using equation (2.52) and secondly, a code which also computes the derivative using the fitness function directly.

2.9.4.1   Calculating the optimum using equation (2.52)

R CODE (using equation [2.52]):

```
rm(list=ls())          # Remove all objects from memory
DERIV <- function(x)  # Function to calculate value of derivative
{
  Af <- 2; Bf <- 2 ; As <- 0.6  # Parameter values
  pBs <- c(0.1,0.3,0.4,0.2) # Vector of probabilities for Bs
  Bs <- c(0.1,0.12,0.14,0.2) # Vector of Bs values
# Derivative
  D <- sum(pBs*(As*Bf-Af*Bs-Bf*Bs*2*x)/((Af+Bf*x)*(As-Bs*x)))
  return(D)
}
# MAIN PROGRAM
uniroot(DERIV,interval=c(1,2)) # Call uniroot function
```

OUTPUT: (slightly modified)

```
$root        [1]  1.545735
$f.root      [1]  1.355284e-06
$iter        [1]  4
$estim.prec  [1]  6.103516e-05
```

The optimal body size is at 1.545735

MATLAB CODE: See Section 2.18.17.

2.9.4.2   Computing the derivative using the fitness function directly

An alternative is to use R or MATLAB to calculate the derivative for us and then use uniroot in R and fzero in MATLAB.

R CODE:

Note that in FUNC the gradient is the sum of the derivatives over all
four values of Bs.

```
  rm(list=ls()) # Remove all objects from memory
FUNC <- function(w) # Function to obtain the gradient at a value w
{
  Af   <- 2; Bf <- 2 ; As <- 0.6   # Parameter values
  pBs  <- c(0.1,0.3,0.4,0.2)    # Vector of probabilities for Bs
  Bs   <- c(0.1,0.12,0.14,0.2) # Vector of Bs values
# Iterate over values of Bs and sum values of derivatives
  d    <- 0                # Derivative value
  for( i in 1:4)
{
  Bsi  <- Bs[i]   # Value of Bs
  pBsi <- pBs[i]  # Probability of this Bs
  y    <- deriv(~pBsi*log((Af+Bf*x)*(As-Bsi*x)),"x")  # Get the
                                                        deriva-
                                                        tive
  x    <- w                   # Set x equal to w
  z    <- eval(y)             # Evaluate the derivative at w
  d    <- d+attr(z,"gradient") # Assign the gradient value to summed d
}
  return(d) # Return d to the main program
}
# MAIN PROGRAM
# Root must be enclosed by the limits set by the user, here set at 1 to 2
  uniroot(FUNC, interval= c(1,2))$root
```

OUTPUT:

`[1] 1.545735`

MATLAB CODE: See Section 2.18.17.

2.9.5   Finding the maximum using numerical methods

This is readily done using the function previously used for plotting. For R we can
use either `nlm` or `optimize`.

R CODE:

```
  rm(list=ls()) # Remove all objects from memory
  FITNESS <- function(x) {Same code as in plotting function}
# MAIN PROGRAM
  nlm(FITNESS, p=1)
  optimize(f=FITNESS,interval=c(1,2), maximum=FALSE)
```

```
> nlm(FITNESS, p=1)
$minimum              [1] -0.6522457
$estimate             [1]  1.545738
$gradient             [1] -5.264757e-08
$code                 [1]  1
$iterations           [1]  4
w> optimize(f=FITNESS, interval=c(1,2), maximum=FALSE)
$minimum              [1]  1.545735
$objective            [1] -0.6522457
```

OUTPUT: (slightly modified)

MATLAB CODE: See Section 2.18.18.

2.10   Scenario 8: Continuous temporal variation in parameters

In the previous scenario the parameter varied in discrete states (four). A more likely condition is for the parameter to follow a continuous probability distribution. Applying this to the former scenario we have the following assumptions.

2.10.1   General assumptions

These remain the same as in Scenario 7.

2.10.2   Mathematical assumptions

1. As before, fecundity increases linearly with body size:

$$F = a_F + b_F x \tag{2.53}$$

where a_F and b_F are constants.

2. Survival decreases linearly with body size:

$$S = a_S - b_S x \tag{2.54}$$

where b_S varies from generation to generation and is specified by a probability density function. To avoid undue complexity confusing the approach illustrated I shall assume the simplest probability function, namely a uniform function, which is defined as $P(b_s)=c$, where c is determined as explained in Scenario 6. Parameters values are set at $b_{max}= 0.2$ and $b_{min}= 0$, giving $c = 1/0.2 = 5$.

3. As before, the appropriate measure of fitness is the geometric average. For computational convenience we work with $logW$:

$$\begin{aligned}
\log W &= \int_{b_{\min}}^{b_{\max}} P(b_S)\log[(a_F + b_F x)(a_S - b_S x)]db_S \\
&= \int_{b_{\min}}^{b_{\max}} c\log[(a_F + b_F x)(a_S - b_S x)]db_S
\end{aligned}$$

$$(2.55)$$

2.10.3 Plotting the fitness function

Integration is generally more "tricky" than differentiation and not all functions can be integrated. One also has to be careful that the function exists across the range of integration. This is potentially problematic in the present model, because the log of a negative number does not exist and thus we must ensure that this does not occur. Thus we require the inequality $a_S - b_S x > 0$, leading to $x < \frac{a_S}{b_S}$. Using the limits of b_S gives $x < 0.6/0 = \infty$ and $x < 0.6/0.2 = 3$. There is a symbolic integration routine in MATLAB, called int but not one in R. Therefore, we shall plot the function using the numerical integration routine integrate in R, passing to it the fitness function defined in the function INTEGRAND. A loop is used rather than apply, because a single value of x has to be passed to INTEGRAND.

R CODE (Figure 2.8):

```
rm(list=ls())                    # Remove all objects from memory
 INTEGRAND <- function(Bs,x)  # Function to do numerical integration
{
Af <- 2; Bf <- 2 ; As <- 0.6; c<- 5        # Parameter values
return (c*log((Af+Bf*x)*(As-Bs*x)))  # return function
}
# MAIN PROGRAM
 n <- 100                         # Number of points
 z <- seq(1.0,3,length=n)  # Create a vector for from 1 to 3
 log.W <- matrix(0,n,1)     # Create a vector log.W to hold results
 Bmin  <- 0; Bmax <- 0.2    # Limits of integration
 for (i in 1:n)                   # Iterate over n "body sizes"
{
   x           <- z[i] # Set value of x (body size)
# Integrate from Bmin to Bmax and add to W
  log.W[i] <- integrate(INTEGRAND,Bmin,Bmax,x)$value
}
# Plot fitness=exp(log.W) vs x
plot(z,exp(log.W),type='l', xlab='Body size, x', ylab='Fitness,
W',las=1,lwd=4)
```

MATLAB CODE: See Section 2.18.19.

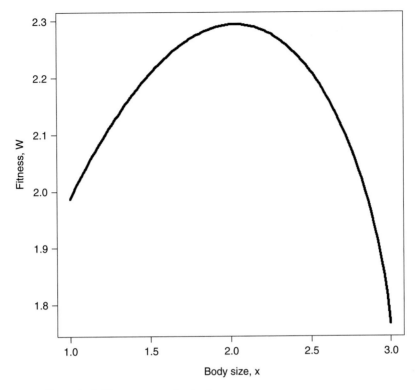

Figure 2.8 Scenario 8: Fitness versus body size.

2.10.4 Finding the maximum using a numerical approach

The main program calls both R functions `nlm` and `optimize` (to illustrate that either can be used) passing to the function the user-supplied function `FITNESS` which calls the R function `integrate` (which does the numerical integration from b_{min} to b_{max}), which calls the user-supplied function `integrand` which calculates the value of `c*log((Af+Bf*x)*(As−Bs*x))`: `nlm` (and `optimize`) calls `FITNESS` calls `integrate` calls `INTEGRAND`

R CODE:

```
rm(list=ls())                # Remove all objects from memory
INTEGRAND <- function(Bs,x)  # Function for numerical integration
{
  Af <- 2; Bf <- 2 ; As <- 0.6; c<- 5       # Parameter values
  return (c*log((Af+Bf*x)*(As−Bs*x))) # return function
}
# Fitness function integrates over limits
  FITNESS <- function(x) # Calculate −log fitness
  {
```

```
    Bmin <- 0; Bmax <- 0.2                    # Limits of integration
    W <- integrate(INTEGRAND,Bmin,Bmax,x)$value # Value of integral
    return(-W)
}
# MAIN PROGRAM Using two routines
    nlm(FITNESS, p=1)
    optimize(f=FITNESS,interval=c(1,3), maximum=FALSE)
```

OUTPUT: (slightly modified)

```
> nlm(FITNESS, p=1)
$minimum              [1]  -0.830392
$estimate             [1]   2.032337
$gradient             [1]  -5.402699e-08
$code                 [1]   1
$iterations           [1]   5
> optimize(f=FITNESS, interval=c(1, 3), maximum=FALSE)
$minimum              [1]   2.032344
$objective            [1]  -0.830392
```

MATLAB CODE: See Section 2.18.20.

2.11   Scenario 9: Maximizing two traits simultaneously

Thus far we have considered models in which there is only a single variable to be optimized. We now examine a case in which there are two variables, vigilance and foraging rate. Suppose that the probability of surviving through some period, such as a winter, depends on the amount of resources gathered prior to this period. At the same time the organism must keep watch for predators. Doing one activity necessarily detracts from the other. The problem is to find the combination of vigilance and foraging rate that maximizes survival.

2.11.1   General assumptions

1. Survival through some period depends upon the amount of resources gathered. Holding all other things constant, survival increases with foraging rate.

2. Survival through some period also depends upon the amount of vigilance. Holding all other things constant, survival increases with vigilance.

3. There is a trade-off between vigilance and foraging rate.

4. Fitness is measured by the survival through the given period.

2.11.2 Mathematical assumptions

1. Ignoring the trade-off between vigilance and foraging rate, survival, S_0, is proportional to the product of vigilance, x, and foraging rate, y:

$$S_0 = a_{xy}xy - a_0 \tag{2.56}$$

The above equation assumes that there is a required minimum amount of vigilance and foraging rate to survive. In the present model $a_{xy} = 0.4$ and $a_0 = 0.8$.

2. Overall survival, which is here also fitness, W, is equal to S_0 minus effects due to the interaction between foraging rate, S_{xy}, and vigilance S_{yx}:

$$W = S_0 - S_{xy} - S_{yx} \tag{2.57}$$

3. The term S_{xy} is the reduction in survival attributable to forage rate (Figure 2.9):

$$S_{xy} = -b_{xy}x + c_{xy}x^2 \tag{2.58}$$

where $b_{xy} = 0.8$ and $c_{xy} = 0.4$. From $x = 0$ to $x = 1$ the effect is increasingly negative. Thus an increase in foraging rate increases survival. However, above $x = 1$ the effect reverses because increased foraging causes a decrease in vigilance which decreases survival with increased foraging.

4. For simplicity I shall assume the same effect of increasing vigilance on survival (Figure 2.9):

$$S_{yx} = -b_{yx}y + c_{yx}y^2 \tag{2.59}$$

where $b_{yx} = 0.8$ and $c_{yx} = 0.4$.

5. Thus fitness, W (= survival) is equal to

$$
\begin{aligned}
W &= S_0 - S_{xy} - S_{yx} \\
&= a_{xy}xy - a_0 - (-b_{xy}x + c_{xy}x^2) - (-b_{yx}y + c_{yx}y^2) \\
&= a_{xy}xy - a_0 + b_{xy}x - c_{xy}x^2 + b_{yx}y - c_{yx}y^2
\end{aligned}
\tag{2.60}
$$

The above equation describes an ellipsoid. As noted above, for simplicity we shall assign the following values to the coefficients: $a_0 = b_{xy} = b_{yx} = 0.8$ and $a_{xy} = c_{xy} = c_{yx} = 0.4$.

Before proceeding with attempts to plot the function or look for optima given specific parameter values, we should investigate, if possible, the dependency of the optimum of one variable on the other. To do this we take the two partial derivatives (so called because we take the derivative of one variable while keeping the other one constant). To find the two separate optima we find those combinations at which both partial derivatives are equal to zero (i.e., $\frac{\partial W}{\partial x} = 0$ and $\frac{\partial W}{\partial y} = 0$):

$$\frac{\partial W}{\partial x} = a_{xy}y + b_{xy} - 2c_{xy}x \quad \text{and} \quad \frac{\partial W}{\partial y} = a_{xy}x + b_{yx} - 2c_{yx}y \tag{2.61}$$

The derivative can also be determined using MATLAB (see Section 2.18.21). It is clear from the above that the joint optima depend on both x and y.

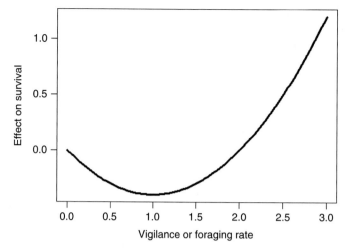

Figure 2.9 Plot of reduction in survival as a consequence of the interaction between vigilance or foraging rate. Because the effects are assumed to be the same the independent variable is either foraging rate or vigilance.

R CODE:

```
rm(list=ls())  #  remove all objects from memory
#  Set parameter values
  A0   <-Bxy   <-Byx    <- 0.8
  Axy <-Cxy   <-Cyx    <- 0.4
  x    <- seq(from=0, to=3,length=100)             #  vector of x
  Sxy  < - -Bxy*x+Cxy*x^2        # Vector of reduction in survival
  plot (x, Sxy, xlab='Vigilance of Foraging rate',ylab='Effect on
survival', type='1', las=1, lwd=3)
```

2.11.3 Plotting the fitness function

The most useful plot is the contour plot, which shows quite clearly the position of the optimum combination (Figure 2.10). Two alternative plots are first, a plot of W versus x for several values of y, and second a three-dimensional (3-D) plot (in R use `persp(x,y,w)` and in MATLAB use `surfc`).

R CODE:

To avoid looping we make use of the routine `expand.grid` which takes the x and y vectors and creates a 2 column matrix of all combinations. Following the calculation of fitnesses for these combinations the vector of fitnesses (`Wtemp`) is converted into an $n \times n$ matrix for plotting.

```
# CONTOUR PLOT
  rm(list=ls()) # Remove all objects from memory
# Function to calculate fitness, passing parameters to it
  FITNESS <- function(X,Axy,A0,Bxy,Cxy,Byx,Cyx)
```

```
{
  x    <- X[1]                # x = Vigilance
  y    <- X[2]                # y = Foraging
  S0   <- Axy*x*y-A0          # Eqn (2.56)
  Sxy <- -Bxy*x+Cxy*x^2       # Eqn (2.58)
  Syx <- -Byx*y+Cyx*y^2       # Eqn (2.59)
  W    <- S0-Sxy-Syx          # Fitness function (2.60)
  return(W)
}
# MAIN PROGRAM
# Parameter values
  A0 <- Bxy<-Byx<-0.8            # Assign parameter values
  Axy <- Cxy<-Cyx<-0.4           # Assign parameter values
  n <- 20                        # Matrix for contour plot=nxn
  x <- seq(from=1, to=3, length=n) # Generate Vigilance values
  y <- seq(from=1, to=3, length=n) # Generate foraging values
  d <- expand.grid(x,y)          # Expand to all combinations
# Create a vector of fitness values for all combinations
  Wtemp <- apply(d,1, FITNESS, 0.4,0.8,0.8,0.4,0.8,0.4)
# Convert into matrix
  W <- matrix(Wtemp,n,n,byrow=T)
# Set plotting page to put graphs side by side and not distorted
# Make plotting surface consist of four panels
  par(mfrow=c(2,2))
# Plot contour. las=orientation of axis labels
# lwd= line width, labcex=size of contour labels
contour(x,y,W, xlab='Foraging, x', ylab='Vigilance, y',las=1,
lwd=3,labcex=1)
# Plot perspective plot
persp(x,y,W,xlab='Foraging, x', ylab='Vigilance, y', zlab='Fit-
ness, W',theta = 50, phi = 25,lwd=2)
```

OUTPUT: (Figure 2.10)

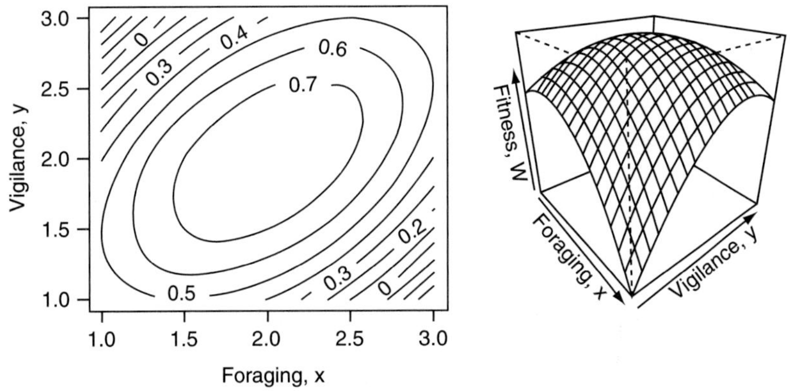

Figure 2.10 Scenario 9: Contour and perspective plots.

MATLAB CODE: See Section 2.18.22.

2.11.4   Finding the maximum using the calculus

We have already done the differentiation, which gives us two equations in x and y to solve, say $f_{xy}(x, y)$ and $f_{yx}(y, x)$. In the present case this can be readily done by hand. First, we rearrange one of the equations to a form in which one variable is a function of the other, such as $y=f(x)$, and then we substitute this into the other equation to arrive at a single equation in a single unknown. In the present scenario we can rearrange the first equation to give $x = \dfrac{a_{xy} + b_{xy}}{2c_{xy}}$, which after substitution in the second equation and rearranging gives

$$y = \frac{-2c_{xy}b_{yx} - a_{xy}b_{xy}}{a_{xy}^2 - 4c_{yx}^2} \tag{2.62}$$

R CODE:

Obviously if one can solve the above equation there is no need to resort to any computer methods other than simple calculation. However, it may be that the pair of equations cannot be so easily resolved. The following is a simple way to find the solution to any pair of equations, assuming that a solution exists, which one should already know, because of the prior plotting exercise. To find x and y take the absolute value, $|f_{xy}(x,y)| + |f_{yx}(y,x)|$, and use `nlm`:

```
# Solving the equation using the calculus
   FUNC <- function(x) {abs( 0.4*x[2]+0.8-2*0.4*x[1])+abs(0.4*x
[1]+0.8-2*0.4*x[2])}
   nlm(FUNC,p=c(1,1))$estimate # Call nlm to find minimum
```

OUTPUT:
```
[1] 1.999986 1.999972
```

MATLAB CODE: See Section 2.18.23.

2.11.5   Finding the maximum using a numerical approach

The approach here is the same as for the case of a single variable but we pass two variables rather than one.

R CODE:

```
   rm(list=ls()) # Remove all objects from memory
# Fitness function
   FITNESS <- function(x,Axy,A0,Bxy,Cxy,Byx,Cyx)
{
   W <- Axy*x[1]*x[2]-A0+Bxy*x[1]-Cxy*x[1]^2+Byx*x[2]-Cyx*x[2]^
2
   return(-W) # Return -W so nlm can find minimum
}
# MAIN PROGRAM
# Find estimates and store in vector called Traits
# Note that the coefficient values are passed as extra parameters
```

```
  Traits <- nlm(FITNESS,p=c(.5,.5),0.4,0.8,0.8,0.4,0.8,0.4)$estimate
# Calculate fitness at the optimum combination
  Wmax   <- -FITNESS(Traits,0.4,0.8,0.8,0.4,0.8,0.4)
  print(c(Traits, Wmax)) # Print out estimates and fitness value
```

OUTPUT:

[1] 1.999999 1.999999 0.800000

MATLAB CODE: See Section 2.18.24.

2.12   Scenario 10: Two traits may covary but optima are independent

It can easily happen that fitness depends on the combined effect of two traits but the optimum for each trait is independent of the other, in which case the separate optima can be found using the methods described above for single traits. The general strategy to test for this is to take the partial derivatives and see if each is independent.

2.12.1   General assumptions

1. The organism is semelparous.

2. Fecundity increases with final body size.

3. Fecundity is a decreasing function of propagule size (i.e., large propagules reduce fecundity).

4. Survival to the adult stage decreases with final body size.

5. Small and large propagules have a decreased survival (e.g., small propagules have few reserves while large propagules attract more predators).

6. Fitness, W, is a function of fecundity and survival from propagule to adult.

2.12.2   Mathematical assumptions

1. Fecundity increases linearly with body size, x:

$$F = a_F + b_F x \tag{2.63}$$

2. Fecundity is inversely proportional to propagule size, y:

$$F = \frac{a_F + b_F x}{y} \tag{2.64}$$

3. Survival decreases linearly with body size:

$$S = a_S - b_S x \tag{2.65}$$

4. Propagule survival, S_P, is a quadratic function of propagule size:

$$S_P = a_P + b_P y + c_P y^2 \qquad (2.66)$$

Propagule survival is zero at the two roots of the above equation:

$$S_{P,MIN} = \frac{-c_P + \sqrt{b_P^2 - 4a_P c_P}}{2c_P}, \quad S_{P,MAX} = \frac{-c_P - \sqrt{b_P^2 - 4a_P c_P}}{2c_P} \qquad (2.67)$$

5. There is a minimum positive propagule size below which survival is zero, i.e., $S_{P,MIN} > 0$

6. Fitness, W, is the expected lifetime reproductive success, R_0, given as the product of fecundity and survival:

$$
\begin{aligned}
W = R_0 &= FSS_P \\
&= (a_F + b_F x)(a_S - b_S x)(a_P + b_P y + c_P y^2)/y \qquad (2.68)\\
&= [a_F a_S - b_F b_S x^2 + (a_S b_F - a_F b_S)x](a_P + b_P y + c_P y^2)/y
\end{aligned}
$$

As before, the first task is to determine if the two optima are dependent on an interaction between the two traits. This is readily observable from the above equation and can be made obvious if we take logs:

$$\ln W = \ln[a_F a_S - b_F b_S x^2 + (a_S b_F - a_F b_S)x] + \ln(a_P + b_P y + c_P y^2) - \ln y \qquad (2.69)$$

It can now be seen that $\ln(W)$ is made up of a linear combination of terms and that each term involves only one of either variable. To make it clearer still we can write

$$\ln(W) = f(x) + g(y) \qquad (2.70)$$

where $f(x)$ stands for the first term and $g(y)$ stands for the second two terms. Taking the two partial derivatives gives

$$\frac{\partial W}{\partial x} = \frac{\partial f(x)}{\partial x}, \frac{\partial W}{\partial y} = \frac{\partial g(y)}{\partial y} \qquad (2.71)$$

Thus we need to proceed no further with respect to the question of covariation, though the question of individual optima can still be addressed. This latter question can be answered using the techniques described in Scenario 1.

2.13   Scenario 11: Two traits may be resolved into a single trait

In some cases it is possible to resolve a fitness function of two variables into a single variable. Should this be possible the problem is reduced to the analysis of a single trait. To illustrate this, I shall consider a model by Begon and Parker (1986) that demonstrates one circumstance in which propagule size decreases with each clutch produced. For this particular scenario I shall consider an organism that produces two clutches. The problem is to find the optimum propagule size for each clutch. Thus the two variables are propagule size in clutch 1 and propagule size in clutch 2.

2.13.1 General assumptions

1. An adult female accumulates a total reserve prior to reproduction, to be distributed among the subsequent clutches.
2. The survival rate is less than one, meaning that the probability of surviving to produce the second clutch is less than survival to the first.
3. Egg size is invariant within clutches but can vary between clutches.
4. Clutch size is invariant.
5. Each female produces two clutches.
6. The expected fecundity of offspring is an asymptotic function of propagule size.
7. Generations are nonoverlapping and hence fitness is equivalent to the per generation expected rate of increase.

2.13.2 Mathematical assumptions

1. Given a fixed reserve, R, and an invariant clutch size of N, propagule size is given by

$$Nx_1 + Nx_2 = R \tag{2.72}$$

where x_1 is the size of propagules in the first clutch and x_2 is the size of propagules in the second clutch.

2. Survival probabilities to the first and second clutches are S_1 and S_2, respectively, and $S_1 > S_2$.

3. The expected fecundity of offspring from propagules of size x_i, F, is the asymptotic function:

$$F_{\max}(1 - e^{-ax_i}) \tag{2.73}$$

where $F_{\max}$ and a are constants.

4. Fitness, W, is equal to the per generation rate of increase:

$$W = NS_1(1 - e^{-ax_1}) + NS_2(1 - e^{-ax_2}) \tag{2.74}$$

The object is to determine the optimal propagule sizes in the first and second clutches. We first note from equation (2.72) that, because of the constraint of a fixed resource pool

$$x_2 = \frac{R - Nx_1}{N} = \frac{R}{N} - x_1 \tag{2.75}$$

and hence the problem resolves itself to finding only the optimal value of x_1 using

$$W = NS_1F_{\max}(1 - e^{-ax_1}) + NS_2F_{\max}\left[1 - e^{-a\left(\frac{R}{N}-x_1\right)}\right] \qquad (2.76)$$

Begon and Parker (1986) predicted that under this model the propagule size in the second clutch will be less than in the first. It is instructive to continue the analysis of this scenario to illustrate the computational approach (for a theoretical justification of the model see Box 4.10 in Roff [2002]). Parameter values are set at $S_1 = 0.005$, $S_2 = 0.002$, $F_{\max} = 2$, $a = 1$, $R = 400$, and $N = 100$.

2.13.3   Plotting the fitness function

Because the total reserve is fixed, the size of the propagules in the first clutch cannot exceed $R/N = 400/100 = 4$, and the size of the propagules in the second clutch cannot exceed $(R/N) - x_1$. If $x_1 > 4$ then fitness is set to zero (this state can be avoided by not exceeding 4 in the program) and if $x_2 > (R/N) - x_1$ the expected fecundity of offspring from the second clutch is set to zero simply by setting egg size to zero (Figure 2.11).

R CODE (Figure 2.11):

Note the use of `max` to ensure that egg size is not smaller than 0.

```
rm(list=ls())            # Remove all objects from memory
FITNESS <- function(x1) # Fitness function
{
# Parameter values
S1       <- 0.005; S2 <- 0.002; Fmax <- 2; a <- 1; N <- 100; R <- 400
ExpFec1 <- Fmax*(1-exp(-a*x1))  # Expected fecundity from 1st
                                  clutch
x2 <- (R/N)-x1                  # Propagule size in 2nd clutch
x2 <- max(x2,0)                 # If x2 <0 set x2=0
ExpFec2 <- Fmax*(1-exp(-a*x2))  # Expected fecundity from 2nd
                                  clutch
W <- N*(S1*ExpFec1+S2*ExpFec2)  # Fitness
# Check to see if x1 is acceptable size
Xmax <- N*x1
if(Xmax>R) {W<-0 }              # if x1 too big set fitness to zero
return(W)                       # Return fitness
}
# MAIN PROGRAM
x <- matrix(seq(from=0, to=4, length=100)) # Vary x1 from 0 to 4
W <- apply(x,1,FITNESS)             # Calculate and store W
# Plot results
plot(x,W, type='l', xlab='Propagule size, x1', ylab='Fitness,
R0',las=1,lwd=3)
```

MATLAB CODE: See Section 2.18.25.

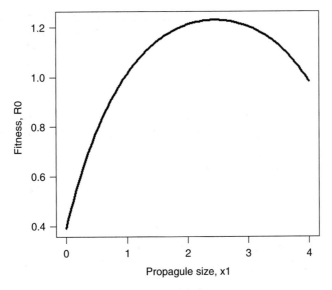

Figure 2.11 Scenario 11: Fitness versus propagule size.

2.13.4   Finding the optimum using the calculus

Equation (2.76) can be differentiated with respect to x_1 and the optimum value of x_1 found by setting the derivative equal to zero:

$$\frac{dW}{dx_1} = aNF_{max}\left[S_1 e^{-ax} + S_2 e^{-a\left(R/_N - x_1 \right)} \right]$$

$$\frac{dW}{dx_1} = 0 \text{ when } S_1 e^{-ax} + S_2 e^{-a\left(R/_N - x_1 \right)} = 0$$

(2.77)

The resultant answer must be checked to ensure that it is within the constraints. First, we make use of the above derivative directly and second, use R or MATLAB (see Section 2.18.26) to obtain it.

2.13.4.1   Using the derivative directly

R CODE:

```
rm(list=ls())        # Remove all objects from memory
DFUNC <- function(x) # Derivative function
{
# Parameter values
  S1 <- 0.005; S2 <- 0.002; a <- 1; N <- 100; R <- 400
  return(S1*exp(-a*x)-S2*exp(-a*(R/N-x))) # Return deriv value
}
```

```
    X1 <- uniroot(DFUNC,interval=(c(0,3)))$root # Call uniroot to
                                                        find root
# Calculate x2 for optimum x1
  N   <- 100; R<- 400 # Parameter values
  X2  <- (R/N)-X1     # Size of 2nd propagule
  print(c(X1,X2))
```

OUTPUT:

[1] 2.458153 1.541847

MATLAB CODE:

```
  function y=DFUNC(x)                      % Derivative function
% Parameter values
  S1 = 0.005; S2 = 0.002; a = 1; N = 100; R = 400;
  y=(S1*exp(-a*x)-S2*exp(-a*(R/N-x)));  % Return deriv value
```

Call function *DFUNC* with `fzero` to locate optimum *x*:

```
clear all;                               % Clear the workspace
fzero(@DFUNC,1) % Call root-finding function with initial value at 1
```

OUTPUT:

ans = 2.4581

2.13.4.2   Getting the derivative using R or MATLAB

R CODE:

```
rm(list=ls()) # Remove all objects from memory
# Function to obtain the gradient at a value w
FUNC <- function(w)
{
# Set parameter values
  S1 <- 0.005; S2 <- 0.002;a <- 1; N <- 100; R <- 400; Fmax<- 2
# Get the derivative of equation (2.76)
  y <- deriv(~ N*(S1*Fmax*(1-exp(-a*x))+S2*Fmax*(1-exp(-a*(R/
N-x)))),"x")
  x <- w                   # Set x equal to w
  z <- eval(y)             # Evaluate the derivative at w
  d <- attr(z,"gradient")  # Assign the gradient value to d
  return(d)                # Return d to the main program
}
# MAIN PROGRAM
# Root must be enclosed by the limits set by the user, here set at 0 to 3
X1 <- uniroot(FUNC, interval= c(0,3))$root
                        # Calculate x2 for optimum x1
N  <- 100; R<- 400      # Parameter values
X2 <- (R/N)-X1          # Size of 2nd propagule
print(c(X1,X2))
```

```
[1] 2.458153 1.541847
```

As predicted, the optimal size of a propagule in the second clutch is less than that in the first clutch.

2.13.5   Finding the optimum using a numerical approach

Here we use the routine `optimize`, setting it to find the maximum. The fitness function routine is the same as that used for plotting.

R CODE:
```
rm(list=ls()) # Remove all objects from memory
FITNESS <- function(x1) {This is the same as given in the plotting section}
# MAIN PROGRAM
# Calculate the optimum x1 using optimize
X1 <- optimize(f=FITNESS, interval=c(1,8),maximum=TRUE)$maximum
# Calculate x2 for optimum x1
  N  <- 100; R<- 400 # Parameter values
  X2 <- (R/N)-X1     # Size of 2nd propagule
  print(c(X1,X2))
```

OUTPUT:
```
[1] 2.458146 1.541854
```

The results are not exactly equal to the values obtained using the calculus but certainly close enough.

MATLAB CODE: see Section 2.18.27.

2.14   Scenario 12: The importance of plotting and the utility of brute force

In the previous scenario we were able to reduce the model to a single trait. We now examine the same model with the addition of a third clutch. This addition to the model means that there are two, relatively independent, traits ("relatively," because they are free to vary only within specified limits). In all previous plots there has been a single, well-defined peak on the fitness surface. In this scenario the surface turns out to be rugged, such that the optimization routines can get "stuck" at a point that is not the maximum.

2.14.1   General assumptions

The general assumptions remain as in the previous scenario and so will be omitted here.

2.14.2 Mathematical assumptions

1. Given a fixed reserve, R, and an invariant clutch size of N, propagule size is given by

$$Nx_1 + Nx_2 + Nx_3 = R \tag{2.78}$$

where x_i is the size of a propagule in the ith clutch ($i = 1$, 2, and 3).

2. Survival probabilities to the first, second, and third clutches are S1, S2, and S3, respectively, and S1 > S2 > S3.

3. The expected fecundity of offspring from propagules of size x_i, F, is given by the asymptotic function:

$$F_{max}(1 - e^{-ax_i}) \tag{2.79}$$

where F_{max} and a are constants.

4. Fitness, W, is equal to the per generation rate of increase:

$$\begin{aligned} W &= NS_1(1 - e^{-ax_1}) + NS_2(1 - e^{-ax_2}) + NS_3(1 - e^{-ax_3}) \\ &= \quad\quad W_1 \quad\quad + \quad\quad W_2 \quad\quad + \quad W_3 \end{aligned} \tag{2.80}$$

The object is to determine the optimal propagule sizes in the first and second clutches. The size of the third clutch is determined by the allocations to the first two clutches:

$$x_3 = \frac{R}{N} - (x_1 + x_2) \tag{2.81}$$

As noted previously, Parker and Begon (1986) predicted that under this model the propagule size in each clutch will be less than in the preceding clutch. For the present analysis parameter values are set at $S_1 = 0.035$, $S_2 = 0.030$, $S_3 = 0.025$, $F_{max} = 2$, $a = 1$, $R = 400$, and $N = 100$.

2.14.3 Plotting the fitness function

Because the total reserve is fixed, the size of the propagules in the first clutch is limited by the inequality $x_1 \leq R/N$ or, equivalently, $x_1 N \leq R$: therefore, when this inequality occurs fitness is set to zero. For the second clutch the propagule size is limited by the amount remaining after the expenditure on the first clutch: $(x_1 + x_2)N \leq R$. If this inequality is not satisfied fitness is equal to the fitness only from the first clutch (assuming that this is greater than zero). A similar constraint can be applied to the third clutch.

The fitness surface, as shown by the contour plot is rugged and the R commands do not easily portray it in three dimensions: therefore, for this purpose, I dumped the data as x,y,W triplets into a text file and plotted the 3D surface using Sigma-Plot. Note the use of the R routine `expand.grid(x, x)`, which creates a $2 \times n^2$

matrix of all x by x values, with the first column changing most rapidly. Fitness is then calculated for each row using the R function `apply`.

R CODE:

```
  rm(list=ls())            # Remove all objects from memory
  FITNESS <- function(x) # Function to calculate fitness
{
# x[1] = Propagule size in 1st clutch
# x[2] = Propagule size in 2nd clutch
# Set parameter values
  N <- 100; R <- 400
  S1 <- 0.035; S2 <- 0.030; S3 <- 0.025
  Fmax <- 2; a <- 0.1
  W1<-W2<-W3<-0 # Set fitnesses to zero. This is not necessary.
# Check if first clutch mass exceeds reserves
  if(N*x[1]>R) W <- 0 # Propagule too large
else{
# Calculate first fecundity
  W1 <- N*S1*Fmax*(1-exp(-a*x[1]))
# Calculate size of propagules in 2nd clutch and see if reserves exceeded
if(N*(x[1]+x[2])>R) W <- W1 # Propagules in 2nd clutch too large
else{
  W2 <- N*S2*Fmax*(1-exp(-a*x[2])) # Calculate 2nd fecundity
# Calculate the size of Propagules in 3rd clutch
# Note that there must be reserves remaining at this stage
  x3 <- (R-N*(x[1]+x[2]))/N
  W3 <- N*S3*Fmax*(1-exp(-a*x3)) # Calculate 3rd fecundity
  W   <- W1+W2+W3
} # End 2nd else
} # End 1st else
  return(-W) # Return negative of fitness
}
# MAIN PROGRAM
  n <- 20                          # Number of rows and columns
  x <- seq(from=1, to=5, length=n) # Range for propagule sizes
  d <- expand.grid(x,x)       # Create a matrix of all combinations
  W <- apply(d,1,FITNESS)     # Apply FITNESS to each combination
  W <- matrix(W,n,n)          # Convert W from a vector into a matrix
  contour(x,x,-W,xlab='Propagule size in 1st clutch',ylab='-
Propagule size in 2nd clutch') # Plot contour making W positive
```

OUTPUT: (Figure 2.12)

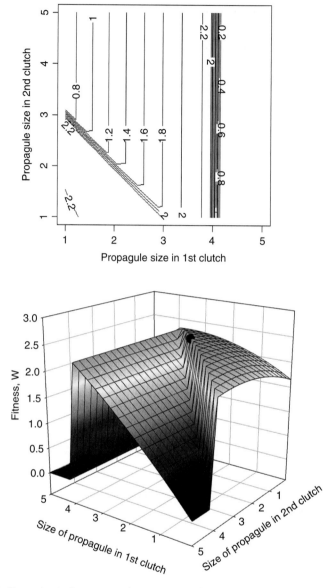

Figure 2.12 Scenario12: Contour and perspective plots. The dot in the 3D plot shows the approximate position of maximum fitness. The 3-D was made using SigmaPlot.

It is evident from the contour and 3D plots (Figure 2.12) that there exists an optimum value, but it is perched precariously close to, or on the edge of, a dramatic fitness decline, and there is a large parameter space over which there is little variation in fitness.

MATLAB CODE: see Section 2.18.28.

2.14.4 Finding the maximum using the calculus

The first task is to write the fitness function in a form suitable for partial differentiation with respect to x_1 and x_2. We can do this by substituting equation (2.81) into equation (2.80):

$$W = NS_1(1 - e^{-ax_1}) + NS_2(1 - e^{-ax_2}) + NS_3\left\{1 - e^{-a\left[\frac{R}{N} - (x_1 + x_2)\right]}\right\} \tag{2.82}$$

At this point we ignore the restriction that $Nx_1 + Nx_2 + Nx_3 = R$ and proceed with differentiation

$$\frac{\partial W}{\partial x_1} = NS_1 a e^{-ax_1} - NS_3 a e^{-a\left(\frac{R}{N} - (x_1 + x_2)\right)}$$

$$\frac{\partial W}{\partial x_2} = NS_2 a e^{-ax_2} - NS_3 a e^{-a\left(\frac{R}{N} - (x_1 + x_2)\right)} \tag{2.83}$$

Setting $\dfrac{\partial W}{\partial x_1} = 0, \dfrac{\partial W}{\partial x_2} = 0$ and equating the two equations leads to

$$x_1 = \frac{1}{a}\ln\left(\frac{S_1}{S_2}\right) + x_2 \tag{2.84}$$

We can substitute the above equation into equation (2.82) to obtain an equation in x_2, say $f(x_2)$ (there is no need here to write out the full equation because it does not simplify to anything that can be analytically resolved). Now x_3 is still defined by equation (2.81) and must exceed zero: thus only combinations of x_1 and x_2 that satisfy this requirement are permitted (i.e., set $W = 0$ in these cases). Plotting W versus x_2 shows that fitness (W) increases with x_2 until a critical value at which point W drops to zero due to the allocation exceeding the reserves available. The optimal propagules sizes can be found numerically using the following code, in which the code for the fitness function differs somewhat from that used in the plotting routine instructions. The program seeks the optimal propagule size in the second clutch using the R function $\mathtt{nlm}$ subject to the constraints enumerated above.

2.14.4.1 Using R or MATLAB to find the optima given the differential

This function differs from that used for plotting in that only a single variable, x_2, is passed. The function FITNESS takes x_2 as its input, calculates x_1 using equation (2.84) and then x_3 subject to the constraint that x_3 is positive. Fitness, W, is calculated according to the rules previously given and -W returned. The main program uses $\mathtt{nlm}$ to locate the optima, using x_2 as the input variable. All three trait values are calculated within FITNESS: these values can be obtained by simply printing them out within FITNESS or by writing the results to a file, which is read back after the optimization is finished. To write the data to a file we must specify the path at the start of the program: in the present case this is

```
setwd("C:/Documents and Settings/Administrator/My Documents/
Computer modelling/Chapter 2")
```

but the exact path will be user-specific. To write the data to a text file called
PROPAGULE.txt we use

```
write(c(x1,x2,x3), file="PROPAGULE.txt")
```

and to retrieve the data to a file called Propagules we use

```
Propagules <- read.table(file="PROPAGULE.txt")
```

Note that lines are overwritten and so the data file consists of a single line. To add
lines after the previous lines we need to specify that append is true.

R CODE:

```
rm(list=ls()) # Remove all objects from memory
setwd("C:/Documents and Settings/Administrator/My Documents/
Computer modelling/Chapter 2") # Set the folder into which to put
the data
   FITNESS <- function(x2)        # Function to calculate fitness.
# Differs from that used in plotting in only a single variable being
input
{
# Set parameter values
   N       <- 100;     R <- 400
   S1      <- 0.035; S2 <- 0.030; S3 <- 0.025
   Fmax   <- 2;      a    <- 0.1
   x1      <- 10*log(S1/S2)+x2    # x1 given the value of x2
   x3      <- (R-N*(x1+x2))/N     # Value of x3
   if (x3<0) W<-0                 # Check that x3 exists
else{
# Check if first clutch mass exceeds reserves
   if(N*x1 > R) W <- 0            # Propagule too large
else{
   W1 <- N*S1*Fmax*(1-exp(-a*x1)) # Calculate first fecundity
# Calculate size of propagules in 2nd clutch and see if reserves
exceeded
   if(N*x2 > R) W <- W1           # Propagules in 2nd clutch too large
else{
   W2 <- N*S2*Fmax*(1-exp(-a*x2)) # Calculate 2nd fecundity
# Calculate the size of Propagules in 3rd clutch
# Note that there must be reserves remaining at this stage
   W3      <- N*S3*Fmax*(1-exp(-a*x3)) # Calculate 3rd fecundity
   W       <- W1+W2+W3
} # End 3rd else
} # End 2nd else
} # End 1st else
```

```
# print (c (x1,x2,x3))
  write (c (x1,x2,x3) , file=" PROPAGULE.txt") # Print results into file
  return (-W)          # Return negative of fitness
}
# MAIN PROGRAM
# Locate optimum x2 and calculate x1 and x3
# Note that parameter values are given within function FITNESS
# Find optimum values of propagules
  nlm (FITNESS, p=1) # Use nlm to find optimum x2
  Propagules  <-  read.table (file=" PROPAGULE.txt")   #  Read  in
                                                             results

  print (Propagules)
```

OUTPUT: (format modified slightly)

```
$minimum                   [1] −2.388036
$estimate                  [1] 1.229245
$gradient                  [1] −0.06119668
$code                      [1] 2
$iterations                [1] 24
> Propagules <- read.table (®le=" PROPAGULE.txt") # Read in results
> print (Propagules)
V1          V2          V3
1 2.770753 1.229246 9.797043e−07
```

Here, code = 2, given at the end of the search, means "successive iterates within tolerance, current iterate is probably solution." Inspection of the gradient suggests that it is close to but not exactly at the proper solution. However, given the "cliff edge" form of the function this is not surprising. As predicted from theory, propagule size declines across the clutches.

MATLAB CODE: See Section 2.18.29.

2.14.4.2   Using R or MATLAB to do the calculus

The above code assumed that the derivative could be explicitly found. Using the R function $deriv$ we can get R to evaluate the derivative for us and use this to locate the optima. Because MATLAB has a symbolic differentiation routine, $diff$, the code is somewhat simpler but the conceptual approach remains the same. There are two user-defined functions.

1. GRADIENT: Finds the absolute difference in the gradient at values w and y, which in this case are x_1 and x_2. Thus GRADIENT gets the value
$$AbsDiff = |\frac{\partial W}{\partial x_1} - \frac{\partial W}{\partial x_2}|.$$

2. FITNESS: This is the same function as used above except that x_1 is now estimated by taking the value of x_2 and using nlm to find the optimum value of x_1 by passing to it GRADIENT: the optimum is to be found where $AbsDiff = 0$.

After getting the optimum x_1 the function calculates the value of x_3. It then checks that the values of x_1, x_2, and x_3 are permissible values. Finally, fitness, W, is calculated and its negative value returned.

The main program estimates the propagule size of the second clutch by calling nlm with FITNESS as the function to be minimized using x_2 as the variable. Recall that FITNESS finds the optimum value of x_1 given x_2: thus nlm within the main program locates the set of optimum values of x_2. As before, the values of x_1, x_2, and x_3 can be obtained by simply printing them out within FITNESS or by writing the results to a file, which is read back after the optimization is finished.

R CODE:

```
rm(list=ls()) # Remove all objects from memory
setwd("C:/Documents and Settings/Administrator/My Documents/
Computer modelling/Chapter 2") # Set the folder into which to put
                            the data
# Function to obtain the gradient at a value w for a given value of y
GRADIENT <- function(w,y)
{
# Set parameter values
  N     <- 100; R    <- 400
  S1    <- 0.035; S2 <- 0.030; S3 <- 0.025
  Fmax  <- 2;     a <- 0.1
# Calculate derivative, called Dx1x2, with respect to both x1 and x2
# x1 is 1st propagule x2 is 2nd propagule
   Dx1x2 <- deriv(~(N*S1*Fmax*(1-exp(-a*x1))+N*S2*Fmax*(1-exp
(-a*x2))+N*S3*Fmax*(1-exp(-a*(R/N-(x1+x2))))),c("x1","x2"))
   x1 <- w                  # Set x1 equal to w
   x2 <- y                  # Set x2 equal to y
   z  <- eval(Dx1x2)        # Evaluate the derivative at w
   G  <- attr(z,"gradient") # Assign the gradient values to AbsDiff
AbsDiff <- abs(G[1]-G[2])   # Calculate the absolute difference
  return(AbsDiff)           # Return AbsDiff to the main program
}
# Fitness function given x2, and calling nlm to find x1
  FITNESS <- function(x2)
{
# Set parameter values
N  <- 100; R <- 400
S1 <- 0.035; S2 <- 0.030; S3 <- 0.025
  Fmax <- 2;    a <- 0.1
# Find value of x1 given x2 using nlm to set derivatives to zero
# This line is the only difference from the previous FITNESS
function
```

```
x1          <- nlm(GRADIENT,p=1,x2)$estimate
# Now calculate x3 and fitness
    x3    <- (R-N*(x1+x2))/N          # Determine x2
    if (x3<0) W<-0                    # Check if x3 exists (>0)
else{
# Check if first clutch mass exceeds reserves
  if(N*x1 > R) W <- 0 # Propagule too large
else{
  W1   <- N*S1*Fmax*(1-exp(-a*x1))  # Calculate first fecundity
                                    # Calculate size of propagules
                                        in 2nd clutch and see if re-
                                        serves exceeded
  if(N*x2 > R) W <- W1              # Propagules in 2nd clutch too large
else{
  W2   <- N*S2*Fmax*(1-exp(-a*x2))   # Calculate 2nd fecundity
# Calculate the size of Propagules in 3rd clutch
# Note that there must be reserves remaining at this stage
  W3   <- N*S3*Fmax*(1-exp(-a*x3))   # Calculate 3rd fecundity
  W    <- W1+W2+W3                   # Sum fitness components
}   # End 3rd else
}   # End 2nd else
}   # End 1st else
# print(c(x1,x2,x3))
  write(c(x1,x2,x3), file="PROPAGULE.txt") # Print results into file
  return (-W)
}
# MAIN PROGRAM
# Find optimum values of propagules
  nlm(FITNESS, p=1) # Use nlm to find optimum x2
  Propagules <- read.table(file="PROPAGULE.txt") # Read in results
  print(Propagules)
```

OUTPUT: (format modified slightly)

```
$minimum          [1] -2.388037
$estimate         [1]  1.229246
$gradient         [1]  9713.389
$code             [1]  3
$iterations       [1]  37
> Propagules <- read.table(file="PROPAGULE.txt")
> print(Propagules)
V1        V2        V3
1 2.77063 1.229123 0.0002468677
```

Previous estimate:

```
1 2.770753 1.229246 9.797043e-07
```

In this case, code = 3, meaning that " last global step failed to locate a point lower than estimate. Either estimate is an approximate local minimum of the function or `steptol` is too small." The two sets of estimates are very close, the propagule size in clutch 3 differing somewhat, but either value is so small as to be effectively zero.

MATLAB CODE: See Section 2.18.29.

2.14.5 Finding the maximum using a numerical approach

Because of the rugged nature of the fitness surface it is possible that `nlm` (or `fminsearch`) will not home in on the appropriate combination. Therefore, in addition to the use of this function I shall also present an alternative approach, the "Brute force" method. First, what results do we get using nlm or fminsearch?

2.14.5.1 Using nlm (R) or fminsearch (MATLAB)

R CODE:
```
  rm(list=ls())          # Remove all objects from memory
  FITNESS <- function(x) # Function to calculate fitness
{This function is the same as that used for plotting}
# MAIN PROGRAM
# Call nlm passing fitness function with initial estimates
  ANS  <- nlm(FITNESS, p=c(0.1,0.1))
  X    <- ANS$estimate              # Store estimates in X
# Calculate x3
  R    <- 400; N <- 100             # Parameter values
  x3   <- (R-N*(X[1]+X[2]))/N       # x3
  ANS                               # Print out Stats for nlm
  print(c(X[1],X[2], x3))           # Propagule sizes
```

OUTPUT: (modified slightly)
```
$minimum      [1] -2.386848
$estimate     [1]  2.621084 1.378914
$gradient     [1]  2.948550e+05 -2.271604e-02
$code         [1]  2
$iterations   [1]  32
> print(c(X[1],X[2], x3)) # Propagule sizes
[1] 2.621084e+00 1.378914e+00 2.299669e-06
```

Previous results:

```
1 2.770753 1.229246 9.797043e-07 (using derivatives)
1 2.77063 1.229123 0.0002468677 (using R to get derivatives)
```

The present results differ from the previous results in giving a smaller x_1 and larger x_2. Fitnesses calculated at the three estimates, given in the above order, are 2.388, 2.388, and 2.387. Based on the evaluated fitnesses, the first two approaches are equivalent and the best, followed closely by the numerical approach.

MATLAB CODE: See Section 2.18.30.

2.14.5.2   The Brute force approach

We now consider the "Brute force" approach. From the initial plotting we know that the optimum occurs within limits of, say, $x_{1,min}$ to $x_{1,max}$ and $x_{2,min}$ to $x_{2,max}$. Suppose we wish to obtain an estimate that is ± 0.005: we can try all values within the foregoing ranges that differ by ± 0.005. The number of combinations we will need to try is roughly $\left(\dfrac{x_{1,max} - x_{1,min}}{0.005}\right)\left(\dfrac{x_{2,max} - x_{2,min}}{0.005}\right)$. Alternatively, we could simply try a large number of values within the specified range and then, if necessary, use the resulting output to refine our range. This is illustrated in the code below where I generate 10,000 combinations. Rather than generate a matrix to hold W the code below uses the R function expand.grid to generate a two column matrix called d with the appropriate combinations. In R the routine order is then used to find the row with the highest fitness.

R CODE:

```
rm(list=ls())             # remove all objects from memory
 FITNESS <- function(x)   # Function to calculate fitness
{This function is the same as that used for plotting, except that W
not -W is returned
  return(W) }
# MAIN PROGRAM
# Create vectors to produce an n by n matrix of combinations
 n <- 100                    # Number of rows and columns
 x <- seq(from=0, to=5, length=n)
 y <- x
 d <- expand.grid(x,y)    # Create 2xn² matrix of all combinations
 W <- apply(d,1,FITNESS) # Use apply to calculate fitnesses
# Now find position of row that has the highest fitness
# Row is stored in first row of Best, Best[1]
 Best <- order(W, na.last=TRUE, decreasing=TRUE)
 x1    <- d[Best[1],1]     # Best x1
 x2    <- d[Best[1],2]     # Best x2
# Calculate x3
 R   <- 400; N <- 100             # Parameter values
 x3  <- (R-N*(x1+x2))/N # x3
 print(c(x1,x2,x3,W[Best[1]])) # Propagule sizes and W
```

OUTPUT:

```
[1]    2.77777778    1.21212121    0.01010101    2.38771586
```

Previous results:

```
1 2.770753  1.229246  9.797043e-07  (using derivatives)
1 2.77063   1.229123  0.0002468677  (using R to get derivatives)
1 2.621084  1.378914  2.299669e-06  (nlm on fitness function)
```

Using the brute force results to refine the search (replace with the following lines)

```
y <- seq(from=1.0, to=1.3, length=n)
x <- seq(from=2.7, to=2.8, length=n)
```

gives
```
[1]    2.769697    1.230303    0.000000    2.388037
```

Fitness at optimum combination:
2.388   (using derivatives)
2.388   (using R to get derivatives)
2.387   (nlm on fitness function)
2.388   (brute force)
2.388   (brute force using first results to shrink ranges)

All methods give essentially the same answer. The one chosen will depend upon the ease with which the model can be differentiated either symbolically or numerically. The brute force method is the simplest and guaranteed to work, even if relatively slow. For this particular model it took only a couple of seconds to run through the 10,000 combinations. Obviously, as a model gets more complex the run time will increase and brute force may prove impractical. Nevertheless, it is certainly worthwhile to keep this approach in mind: it may be crude but it is very simple and, as shown in the above scenario, it can be very effective.

MATLAB CODE: See Section 2.18.30.

2.15   Scenario 13: Dealing with recursion by brute force

A recursive function is one that calls itself: for example, growth in one year is typically a function of previous growth, i.e., $W_{t+1} = f(W_t)$. Recursive functions can be particularly difficult to deal with except by the brute force method. To illustrate a possible approach I shall use a simplified model of the optimal age at first reproduction and reproductive allocation discussed in Roff et al. (2006).

2.15.1   General assumptions

1. The organism is iteroparous.

2. Reproduction occurs annually.

3. Size in year $t+1$ is a function of size in year t.

4. The increment in growth is a function of the allocation to reproduction.

5. Annual mortality is a function of the allocation to reproduction.

6. Fecundity increases with the allocation to reproduction.

7. Fitness is a function of reproduction and survival.

2.15.2 Mathematical assumptions

1. In the absence of reproduction the organism increases in weight by a fixed amount:

$$\begin{aligned}
W_0 &= 0 \\
W_1 &= W_0 + A \\
W_2 &= W_1 + A = 2A \\
&\vdots \\
W_{\alpha-1} &= W_{\alpha-2} + A = (\alpha - 1)A
\end{aligned} \tag{2.85}$$

where α is the age of first reproduction. Note that this growth function ceases at $\alpha-1$, because the allocation to reproduction, described below, occurs during the year preceding maturation.

2. At maturity a female allocates a constant fraction, G, of its biomass to reproduction:

$$W_{t+1} = W_t + A - GW_t, \quad t \geq \alpha - 1 \tag{2.86}$$

As noted above, the allocation is made in the year prior to reproduction.

3. Fecundity is proportional to weight and the allocation to reproduction:

$$F_t = aGW_t \tag{2.87}$$

where a is a constant.

4. In the absence of reproduction, the instantaneous (juvenile) mortality rate is M_J and hence the annual juvenile survival is e^{-M_J}.

5. The adult mortality rate, M_A, is a linear function of the allocation to reproduction:

$$M_A = M_J + M_a G \tag{2.88}$$

Where M_a is a constant. Thus annual survival, commencing in the year immediately prior to reproduction, is given by $e^{-M_A} = e^{-(M_J + M_a G)}$.

6. Fitness, W, is the expected lifetime fecundity:

$$W = \sum_{t=\alpha}^{\infty} aGW_t e^{-M_J(\alpha-1)} e^{-M_A(t-\alpha+1)} \tag{2.89}$$

The problem we wish to address is that of finding the values of α and G that maximize fitness. If the recursive equation can be converted into a simple function the above equation presents no problem, for example, suppose the weight-at-age function is $W_{t+1} = A + BW_t$, then we could write

$$W_{t+1} = W_\infty(1 - e^{-k}) + W_t e^{-k} \tag{2.90}$$

where $A = W_\infty(1-e^{-k})$ and $B = e^{-k}$. The above equation is a version of the von Bertalanffy growth function and it is equivalent to the non-recursive function:

$$W_t = W_\infty(1-e^{-kt}) \tag{2.91}$$

The present growth model cannot be reduced to such an equation and hence our analysis must deal with the recursive form. Given only a few terms it is feasible to apply the methods of calculus, but if, as in the present case, there are many terms, such an approach would at best be very tedious. A further problem with a recursive equation is that the function changes by unit steps, which generally precludes the use of a search routine such as nlm.

2.15.3   Plotting the fitness function

Even though α changes by unit steps we can still use contour (R or MATLAB) to plot the computed results: it must, however, be remembered that only integer values are possible and hence that the correct optimum combination is shifted relative to the peak portrayed in the contour plot. The summation limit is set to an age of 30, which calculates fitness to within fractions of a percentage point of its asymptotic value. Parameter values used are given in the function FITNESS.

R CODE:

```
  rm(list=ls())          # Remove all objects from memory
# Function to calculate fitness given Alpha
  FITNESS <- function(x)
{
  G         <- x[1]       # G values
  Alpha     <- x[2]       # Alpha value
# Set parameter values
  Mj        <- 0.05       # Background mortality rate
  Ma        <- 0.4        # Constant of mortality function
  Age.max <- 30           # Maximum age (arbitrary)
  a         <- 0.05       # Fecundity constant
  A         <- 10         # Wt increase/annum without reproduction
  A.minus.1 <- Alpha-1             # Year before first reproduction
  S           <- matrix(0,Age.max) # Annual survival
# Growth prior to reproduction is linear
# To include cases in which growth is more complex I here use a for
loop
  Wt        <- matrix(0,Age.max,1) # Initialize Wt vector
  S[1]      <- exp(-Mj)            # Survival to age 1
# Calculate Wt and Survival from age 2 to alpha-1
  for(i in 2:A.minus.1)
{
  Wt[i]     <- Wt[i-1]+A           # Weight
  S[i]      <- S[i-1]*exp(-Mj)     # Annual survival
```

```
}
# Now calculate change in wt and survival for age alpha to max age
  for(i in Alpha:Age.max)
{
  Wt[i]    <- Wt[i-1]+A-G*Wt[i-1]    # Weight
  S[i]     <- S[i-1]*exp(-(Mj+Ma*G)) # Annual survival
}
  W <- a*sum(S[Alpha:Age.max]*Wt[Alpha:Age.max]*G) # Fitness
  return(-W) # Return negative of fitness
}
# MAIN PROGRAM
  n.G <- 11                                 # Number of G values
  G    <- seq(from=0.01, to=0.5, length=n.G) # G vector, 0.01 to 0.5
  alpha    <- seq(from=3, to=20) # Alpha vector from 3 to 20
  n.alpha <- length(alpha)        # Get length of alpha vector
  d    <- expand.grid(G,alpha)  # Expand to a 2xn.g*n.alpha matrix
  W    <- apply(d,1,FITNESS)    # Calc fitness for each combination
  W    <- matrix(W,n.G,n.alpha) # Convert to a n.g x n.alpha matrix
# Contour plot
  contour(G,alpha,-W,    xlab="G",    ylab="ALPHA",las=1,lwd=3,
labcex=1)
```

OUTPUT: (Figure 2.13)

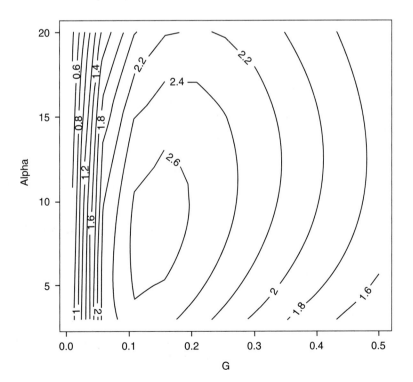

Figure 2.13 Scenario 13: Contour plot showing fitness as a function of G and α.

Fitness is maximized by combinations at approximately $G = 0.12$ and $\alpha = 10$ (Figure 2.13).

MATLAB CODE: See Section 2.18.31.

2.15.4   Finding the maximum using the calculus

This is not a practical method in this case and we move directly to numerical methods.

2.15.5   Finding the maximum using a numerical approach

The age of first reproduction is an integer and thus it is not possible to use `nlm` to find the value of α that maximizes W, but it can be used to find the optimal allocation for a given α. From the contour plot it is evident that there is a single peak and hence a simple approach is to begin with a low value of α and increase it until W decreases below its previous value (code presented at end of section). In fact, the present model runs so quickly that a simpler approach is to vary α from 3 to 20 and then use the function `order` to find the best combination.

2.15.5.1   Brute force using many values

R CODE:

```
rm(list=ls()) # Remove all objects from memory
# Function to calculate fitness given Alpha
  FITNESS <- function(G,Alpha){This function is the same as in the
plotting code, except that G and Alpha are passed rather than x }
# MAIN PROGRAM
# Create vector for alpha values
  alpha      <- seq(from=3, to=20) # alpha vector
  n.alpha    <- length(alpha)       # Length of vector
  G     <- matrix(0,n.alpha) # Create vector to store best G values
  W     <- matrix(0,n.alpha)  # Create vector to store W values
  for ( i in 1:n.alpha)        # Iterate over alpha vector values
{
# Find best G for this alpha by calling nlm
  G[i]   <- nlm(FITNESS,p=.2,alpha[i])$estimate # Store best G
  W[i]   <- -FITNESS(G[i],alpha[i])# Get W at best G for given alpha
}
# Now locate best combination and write out values
  Best            <- order(W, na.last = TRUE, decreasing = TRUE)
  Alpha.best   <- alpha[Best[1]]    # Best alpha
  G.best   <- G[Best[1]]            # Best G
  W.best   <- W[Best[1]]            # W at best alpha, best G
  print(c(Alpha.best,G.best,W.best))
```

OUTPUT:
```
[1] 8.0000000  0.1345672  2.6848553
```

MATLAB CODE: See Section 2.18.32.

2.15.5.2 Brute force using iteration

This presumes a single maximum. The strategy here is to compare W at $\alpha = t$ with W at $\alpha = t + 1$ (function = BESTG): if the difference is negative then the maximum must be at $\alpha = t$.

R CODE:

```
  rm(list=ls()) # Remove all objects from memory
# Function to calculate fitness given Alpha
  FITNESS <- function(G,Alpha) {This function is the same as in the
plotting code, except that G and Alpha are passed rather than x }
# Function to get best G for consecutive pairs of alpha
  BESTG <- function (alpha)
{
# Results for alpha
  G1    <- nlm(FITNESS,p=.1,alpha)$estimate  # Best G given alpha
  W1    <- -FITNESS(G1,alpha)                    # Fitness
# Results for alpha+1
  G2    <- nlm(FITNESS,p=.1,alpha+1)$estimate # Best G given
                                                      alpha+1
  W2    <- -FITNESS(G2,alpha+1)               # Fitness
  Wdiff <- W2-W1                              # Diff between fitnesses
  return (c(Wdiff,W1,G1))        # G1 will eventually be the best G
}
# MAIN PROGRAM
  ALPHA <- 5                # Set initial alpha
  DIFF  <- BESTG(ALPHA) # Calculate difference between W at two alphas
  while (DIFF[1]>0)     # If DIFF[1] > 0 then W still increasing
{
  ALPHA <- ALPHA+1
  DIFF <- BESTG(ALPHA)
}
# Out of loop and thus ALPHA is the best
  print(c(ALPHA,DIFF[3],DIFF[2])) #Print out alpha, G, W
```

OUTPUT: (same as before)
[1] 8.0000000 0.1345672 2.6848553

MATLAB CODE: See Section 2.18.32.

2.16 Scenario 14: Adding a third variable and more

With two variables it is possible to graphically display fitness as a function of both variables simultaneously. When the model includes three variables this is no longer possible. A reasonable approach is to plot two variables, keeping the third constant. The general method of analysis is the same as with two variables. To illustrate this I shall extend the foregoing model to include possible variation in age-specific allocation to reproduction. I shall assume that the organism lives N years after maturity. Life history theory predicts that, in general, allocation to reproduction will increase with age (Roff 2002). We commence by considering the case of $N = 2$ and thence more than 2.

2.16.1 General assumptions

1. The organism is iteroparous but survives only 2 years following maturity ($N = 2$).
2. Reproduction occurs annually.
3. Size in year $t + 1$ is a function of size in year t.
4. The increment in growth is a function of the allocation to reproduction.
5. Annual mortality is a function of the allocation to reproduction.
6. The allocation to reproduction is not constrained to be a constant.
7. Fecundity increases with the allocation to reproduction.
8. Fitness is a function of reproduction and survival.

2.16.2 Mathematical assumptions

1. In the absence of reproduction the organism increases in weight by a fixed amount:

$$W_{t+1} = W_t + A, \quad t < \alpha - 2 \tag{2.92}$$

where $W_0 = 0$ and α is the age of first reproduction. This growth function is the same as previous.

2. After maturity a female allocates an age-specific fraction, G_t, of its biomass to reproduction:

$$W_{t+1} = W_t + A - G_t W_t \quad t \geq \alpha - 1 \tag{2.93}$$

Note that, as before, the allocation is made in the year prior to reproduction.

3. Fecundity is proportional to weight and the allocation to reproduction:

$$F_t = a G_t W_t \tag{2.94}$$

where a is a constant.

4. In the absence of reproduction, the instantaneous (juvenile) mortality rate is M_J and hence the annual juvenile survival is. e^{-M_J}

5. The adult mortality rate, M_A, is a linear function of the age-specific allocation to reproduction.

$$M_{A,t} = M_J + M_a G_t \tag{2.95}$$

where M_a is a constant. Thus annual survival, commencing in the year immediately prior to reproduction, is given by $e^{-M_A} = e^{-(M_J + M_a G_1)}$.

6. Fitness, W, is the expected lifetime fecundity:

$$W = \sum_{t=\alpha}^{\alpha+1} a G_t W_t e^{-M_J(\alpha-1)} e^{-M_{A,t}(t-\alpha+1)} \tag{2.96}$$

2.16.3 Plotting the fitness function

As we have already seen that an optimal combination exists for a G that is not age-specific and α, it is not necessary here to plot the data.

2.16.4 Finding the maximum using the calculus

This is not practical in this case and we move directly to numerical methods.

2.16.5 Finding the maximum using a numerical approach

As noted previously, the age of first reproduction is an integer and thus it is not possible to use `nlm` to find the value of α that maximizes W. From the previous contour plot it is evident that there is a single peak and this is likely to hold for variable G, which can be verified by plotting it for several combinations of G_1, G_2. The following code follows the same strategy as previously in beginning with a low value of α and increasing until W decreases below its previous value. The fitness function is modified from that given previously as indicated by bold font, although with slight modification the present code will also work for the previous case (an illustration that there are generally several ways of coding a program. This is a good reason to abundantly annotate the code so that one can follow it when returning after several days, weeks, or months). An important change in the fitness function is that it now accepts a vector of G values.

R CODE:

```
rm(list=ls())                # Remove all objects from memory
# Function to calculate fitness given Alpha
FITNESS <- function(G,Alpha,N) # G IS NOW A VECTOR WITH N ENTRIES
{
# Set parameter values
Mj       <- 0.05        # Background mortality rate
Ma       <- 0.4         # Constant of mortality function
Age.max <- Alpha+1     # Maximum age
```

```
   a             <- 0.05        # Fecundity constant
   A             <- 10          # Wt increase/annum without reproduction
   A.minus.1 <- Alpha-1    # Year before first reproduction
   S             <- matrix(0,Age.max)     # Annual survival
# Growth prior to reproduction is linear
# To include cases in which growth is more complex I here use a for
loop
Wt            <- matrix(0,Age.max,1)     # Initialize Wt vector
S[1]          <- exp(-Mj)                # Survival to age 1
# Calculate Wt and Survival from age 2 to alpha-1
   for(i in 2:A.minus.1)
{
   Wt[i]          <- Wt[i-1]+A            # Weight
   S[i]           <- S[i-1]*exp(-Mj)      # Annual survival
}
# Now calculate change in wt and survival for age alpha to max age
# Accumulate W. W is now accumulated in the loop rather than after
   W <- 0
   for ( J in 1:N) # Iterate over the adult ages
{
   i       <- Alpha + J - 1              # Get age i = Alpha, Alpha+1
   Wt[i]   <- Wt[i-1]+ A- G[J]*Wt[i-1]   # Wt
   S[i]    <- S[i-1]*exp(-(Mj+Ma*G[J]))  # Annual survival
   W       <- W + a*S[i]*Wt[i]*G[J]      # Cumulative fitness
}
     return(-W)     # Return negative of fitness
}
# Now function BESTG
# Function to get best G for consecutive pairs of alpha
     BESTG <- function (alpha)
{
# Results for alpha
   N  <- 2                               # Number of mature ages
   G1 <- nlm(FITNESS,p=rep(.1,times=N),alpha,N)$estimate #N values
                                                          of G
   W1    <- -FITNESS(G1,alpha,N)
# Results for alpha+1
   G2    <- nlm(FITNESS,p=rep(.1,times=N),alpha+1,N)$estimate
   W2    <- -FITNESS(G2,alpha+1,N)
   Wdiff <- W2-W1
   return (c(Wdiff,W1,G1)) # G1 will eventually be the best G
}
# MAIN PROGRAM
   ALPHA <- 5 # Set initial alpha
   DIFF  <- BESTG(ALPHA) #Calculate difference between W at two alphas
   while  (DIFF[1]>0)    # If DIFF[1] > 0 then W still increasing
```

```
{
  ALPHA <- ALPHA+1
  DIFF <- BESTG(ALPHA)
}
# Out of loop and thus ALPHA is the best
  print(c(ALPHA,DIFF)) #Print out alpha, Wdiff, G1, G2..GN
```

OUTPUT:

[1]19.0000000000−0.00029716701.16930152210.34970195350.4835085056

As predicted, the allocation to reproduction increases with age (i.e., 0.35 versus 0.48). To increase the number of ages and hence the number of variables we simply alter N in the above code. Suppose we set N<−5, giving 6 variables to be estimated. The result is

OUTPUT:

[1] 18.000000000 −0.004169547 1.805390129 0.216575802 0.246302065
[6] 0.291752438 0.366635909 0.509802881

Again, as predicted, the allocation to reproduction increases with age (i.e., 0.22, 0.25, 0.29, 0.37, and 0.51). Using the "while" approach as shown in the above code is much faster than the brute force approach.

MATLAB CODE: See Section 2.18.33.

2.17 Some exemplary papers

Roff, D. A. 1981. On being the right size. *American Naturalist* 118:405–422.

Problem: Optimal adult size in *Drosophila melanogaster*

Fitness measure: r

Gilchrist, G. W.1995. Specialists and generalists in changing environments. I. Fitness landscapes of thermal sensitivity. *American Naturalist* 146:252–270.

Problem: Evolution of two components of thermal adaptation

Fitness measure: Geometric mean of r

Orzack, S. H. and S. Tuljapurkar. 2001. Reproductive effort in variable environments, or environmental variation is for the birds. *Ecology* 82:2659–2665.

Problem: Optimal clutch size in a temporally variable environment

Fitness measure: Long-term growth rate of population

Simons, A. M. and M. O. Johnston. 2003. Suboptimal timing of reproduction in *Lobelia inflata* may be a conservative bet-hedging strategy. *Journal of Evolutionary Biology* 16:233–243.

Problem: Evolution of timing of reproduction in the plant *Lobelia inflate*

Fitness measure: Fecundity

Roff, D. A., E. Heibo, and L. A. Vollestad. 2006. The importance of growth and mortality costs in the evolution of the optimal life history. *Journal of Evolutionary Biology* 19:1920–1930.

Problem: Evolution of the age at maturity and reproductive effort in fish

Fitness measure: R_0

Rudolf, V. H. W. and M. O. Rodel. 2007. Phenotypic plasticity and optimal timing of metamorphosis under uncertain time constraints. *Evolutionary Ecology* 21:121–142.

Problem: Optimal timing and size at metamorphosis in amphibians

Fitness measure: r

2.18   MATLAB code

2.18.1   Scenario 1: Plotting the fitness function

```
clear all
ezplot('-2*x^2+4*x',[0,2]) % the [0,2] defines the min and max
values of x
xlabel('Body size'); ylabel('Fitness')
```

OR

```
clear all
x = 0:0.01:2;              % Create vector from 0 to .2 in steps of 0.01
plot(x,-2*x.^2+4*x)   % Plot function using vector notation
xlabel('Body size');  % Label x axis
ylabel('Fitness');    % Label y axis
```

2.18.2   Scenario 1: Finding the maximum using the calculus

Symbolic differentiation can be done in MATLAB with the command diff:

```
% To differentiate the function and store the result in y
    syms x; y=diff(-2*x^2+4*x);
% Print solution
    y
```

OUTPUT:

```
y = -4*x+4
```

The value at which the derivative is zero (i.e., y = 0) can now be found using the command

```
solve
```

```
% Find value at which y = 0
  solve(y)
```

OUTPUT:

```
ans = 1
```

2.18.3   Scenario 1: Finding the maximum using a numerical approach

```
% Find minimum using the routine fminbnd setting the search limits
  at -2, 4
% Define function such that minimum is turning point
% and pass function directly to fminbnd
  fminbnd('-(-2*x^2+4*x)',-2,4) % search limits at -2, 4
```

OR

```
% Define the anonymous function such that minimum is turning point
  FITNESS =@(x)(-(-2*x^2+4*x));
  fminbnd(FITNESS,-2,4) % search limits at -2, 4
```

OR

```
% Define the inline function such that minimum is turning point
    FITNESS = inline('-(-2*x^2+4*x)','x');
    fminbnd(FITNESS, -2,4) % search limits at -2, 4
```

2.18.4   Scenario 3: Plotting the fitness function

All commands are placed into the main program and summation is done using the symbolic summation routine symsum. In this case a loop is used to calculate the summed value for each value of n.

```
clear all        % Clear workspace
syms t;          % Define t as a symbol for the summation routine
nmax=20;         % Set the maximum number of ages
n = 1:nmax;      % Create a vector of n from 1 to nmax
% Create an equal length vector to store the sums.
% Present values will be replaced
s = 1: nmax;     % Vector called s
x = 1;           % Set value of x to 1
for n1 = 1:nmax;   %Iterate from n=1 to n=nmax
% Call symsum for summation 1,n1
  s(n1) = symsum(4*x*exp(-(1+0.5*x)*t),1,n1);
end
plot(n,s)        % Plot results
xlabel('MAXIMUM AGE'); ylabel('SUM') % Label axes
```

The plot is, of course, identical to the previous, from which we concluded that $n = 20$ would be a sufficient interval of summation. To plot fitness, W, as a function of size, x, we proceed as follows:

1. Create a function that makes use of the symbolic summation routine symsum and store this in an M file called FITNESS.m:

```
function w=FITNESS(x)         % Function to do symbolic summation
   syms t;                    % Define t as a symbol
   w=symsum(4*x*exp(-(1+0.5*x)*t),1,20); % Sum over ages 1 to 20
```

OR

Create a function that makes use of `sum` to do the summation explicitly and store this in an M file called `FITNESS.m.`:

```
function w=FITNESS(x)                % Function to do summation
  Age = 1:20;                        % Create a vector of ages 1 to 20
  w = sum(4*x*exp(-(1+0.5*x)*Age));  % Create vector of fitness
and sum it
```

2. Use fplot to increment over values of *x* and plot the result:

```
clear all                         % Clear the workspace
fplot(@FITNESS,[0,5])% call FITNESS function lower and upper lim-
its=0,5
xlabel('SIZE'); ylabel('FITNESS'); % Label axes
```

2.18.5   Scenario 3: Finding the maximum by the calculus

Because the right hand side of the equation is zero it can be omitted in solve:

```
solve('(4)+(0+4*x)*(-0.5)+(0+4*x)*(-1)*(0.5*exp
(-(1+0.5*x)))/(1-exp(-(1+0.5*x))))')
```

OUTPUT:
```
ans =   1.6828113208739212756932093160250
        -4.29238644124116517047741220570427
```

2.18.6   Scenario 3: Finding the maximum using a numerical approach

We shall use the explicit summation function. Note that, as above, because we will be using a minimization routine, we take the negative value of the sum:

```
function w=FITNESS(x)            % Function to do summation
Age = 1:20;                      % Create a vector of ages 1 to 20
w = -sum(4*x*exp(-(1+0.5*x)*Age));   % Create vector of fitness
                                      and sum it
```

We now use the previously used minimization routine `fminbnd`, setting the limits at 0.5 and 2, as found from the graph (Figure 2.3):

```
fminbnd(@FITNESS,0.5,2) % Note the @ placed before the function
name
```

OUTPUT:
```
ans = 1.6828
```

2.18.7   Scenario 4: Plotting the fitness function

MATLAB has a symbolic integration routine `int`:

```
int('(Af+Bf*x)*exp(-(As+Bs*x)*t)','t')
```

OUTPUT:
```
ans =-1/(As+Bs*x)*(Af+Bf*x)*exp(-(As+Bs*x)*t)
```

To obtain a somewhat nicer looking output we can use the command `pretty`:

```
pretty(int('(Af+Bf*x)*exp(-(As+Bs*x)*t)','t'))
```

OUTPUT:

```
ans =              (Af + Bf x) exp(-(As + Bs x) t)
            -    -------------------------------
                           As + Bs x
```

To use `int` to plot *W* versus *x* we first make a function stored in `FITNESS.m`:

```
function w=FITNESS(x) % Function to evaluate fitness
  syms t                              % Make t a symbol
  f = (0+4*x)*exp(-(1+0.5*x)*t);      % Create function
  w=int(f,1,100);  % Call function that calculates integral 1 to 100
```

We then call this function in the following program:

```
clear all                % Clear the workspace
 x = linspace(0,5,100);   % 100 equal spaced values from 0 to 5
% Create a vector of fitnesses the same length as x
% Note that these initial entries are replaced
   W = x;                 % Preallocate space to W
for i =1:100              % iterate over all values of x
   W(i)=FITNESS(x(i));
end;                      % End of loop
plot(x, W)                % Plot W as a function of size
xlabel('SIZE'); ylabel('FITNESS');  % Label axes
```

If the integral is one that cannot be integrated symbolically then one can use one of the numerical integration functions, such as `quad`. First create the fitness function `FITNESS` stored in an M file:

```
   function w=FITNESS(x) % Function to evaluate fitness numerically
% Call function that calculates integral 1 to 100
   w=quad(@(t)(0+4*x)*exp(-(1+0.5*x)*t),1,100);
```

Then to plot we use

```
clear all                % Clear the workspace
fplot(@FITNESS,[0,5])% Call fplot to plot FITNESS function
xlabel('SIZE'); ylabel('FITNESS');   % Label axes
```

2.18.8 Scenario 4: Finding the maximum using the calculus

```
syms x;
y = diff((0+4*x)*exp(-(1+0.5*x))/(1+0.5*x))
```

OUTPUT:

```
y = 4*exp(-1-1/2*x)/(1+1/2*x)-2*x*exp(-1-1/2*x)/(1+1/2*x)
-2*x*exp(-1-1/2*x)/(1+1/2*x)^2
```

The above expression is formidable looking but, as with the R code, it can be stored in y and need not be shown.

As with the R code two routes are possible, supplying the derivative directly and letting MATLAB calculate it. The roots are then found using solve:

```
solve('4-0.5*(0+4*x)-(0+4*x)*0.5/(1+0.5*x)')   % Finding the
                                                       roots
```

OR

```
syms x;
y = diff((0+4*x)*exp(-(1+0.5*x))/(1+0.5*x))
vpa(solve(y),5) % Find the roots, outputting value to 5 decimal
places
```

OUTPUT: (from first code, second code giving only 5 decimal places)

```
ans =    -3.2360679774997896964091736687313
          1.2360679774997896964091736687313
```

As before, only the second answer is physically possible.

2.18.9   Scenario 4: Finding the maximum using a numerical approach

First create the function FITNESS:

```
function w=FITNESS(x)
w=-quad(@(t)(0+4*x)*exp(-(1+0.5*x)*t),1,100);   %  Numerical
                                                    integra-
                                                    tion
```

We now use the previously used minimization routine fminbnd setting the limits at 0.5 and 2, as found from the graph (Figure 2.4):

```
fminbnd(@FITNESS, 0.5, 2)
```

OUTPUT:
```
ans =  1.2361
```

2.18.10   Scenario 5: Plotting the fitness function

Using the program to do the integration

We use the function quad to do the numerical integration of the characteristic (also called the Euler) function and pass 1 minus its value back. This function does not accept infinity and so we set the upper integration limit at a large value, here 100. Note that we pass x and r:

```
function y=EULER(r,x)    % Function to evaluate 1-Euler equation
Af=0;Bf=16;As=1;Bs=0.5;  % Set parameter values
y=1-quad(@(t)(Af+Bf*x)*exp(-(As+Bs*x+r)*t),1,100);%1-integral
```

Now we iterate over values of *x* using `fzero` to find value of *r* (= fitness = *W*) for each value of *x*:

```
clear all                    % Clear the workspace
x=linspace(0.5,3,100);       % Generate 100 values between 0 and 3
W=x;                         % Preallocate values to w. Will be changed
for i = 1:100;               % Iterate over values of x
  % 1-Euler value is in function Euler
  W(i)=fzero(@(r) EULER(r,x(i)),0.5); % Use fzero to calculate r
end;
plot(x,W);                            % Plot fitness=r on x
xlabel('SIZE'); ylabel('FITNESS');    % Label axes
```

User supplied solution to the integral

```
function y=EULER(r,x)        % Function to evaluate fitness
Af=0;Bf=16;As=1;Bs=0.5;      % Set parameter values
y =1-exp(-(r+As+Bs*x))*(Af+Bf*x)/(As+Bs*x+r);  % 1-RHS of
                                                      equation
```

As with the R commands, the MATLAB main program is not changed.

2.18.11   Scenario 5: Finding the maximum using the calculus

First define a function called FITNESS to calculate equation (2.41):

```
function w=FITNESS(x);       % Function to evaluate fitness
Af=0;Bf=16;As=1;Bs=0.5;      % Set parameter values
r = Bs*(Af+Bf*x)/(Bf-Bs*Af-Bs*Bf*x)-Bs*x-As;  % r from eqn (2.40)
w = (log(Af+Bf*x)-(As+Bs*x+r)-log(As+Bs*x+r)); % equation (2.41)
```

Call function with

```
clear all                    % Clear the workspace
x=fzero(@FITNESS,[1.2,1.8])  % Use fzero to calculate r
```

OUTPUT:

x = 1.3899

2.18.12   Scenario 5: Finding the maximum using a numerical approach

We define two functions, `EULER`, which calculates 1-characteristic equation given *r* and *x* (two versions given below) and `RFUNC` which calculate the value of *r* using `fzero` calling `EULER`. The optimal value of *x* is found by calling `fminbind`:

```
function y=EULER(r,x)        % Function to evaluate 1-Euler equation
Af=0;Bf=16;As=1;Bs=0.5;      % Set parameter values
y=1-quad(@(t)(Af+Bf*x)*exp(-(As+Bs*x+r)*t),1,100);  % 1-inte-
                                                         gral
```

OR using the integrated function
```
function y=EULER(r,x)                    % Function to evaluate fitness
```

```
Af=0;Bf=16;As=1;Bs=0.5;          % Set parameter values
y =1-exp(-(r+As+Bs*x))*(Af+Bf*x)/(As+Bs*x+r);%1-RHS of equation
```

Above called by

```
function Rvalue=RFUNC(x)
Rvalue = fzero(@(r) EULER(r,x),0.5); % Use fzero to calculate r
Rvalue = =Rvalue;                    % Pass -r back
```

Main Program:

```
clear all;                    % Clear the workspace
fminbnd(@RFUNC,1.2,1.8);    % Use fminbnd to find minimum of -fitness
```

OUTPUT:

```
ans = 1.3899
```

2.18.13   Scenario 6: Plotting the fitness function

This is essentially the same as the R code.

```
clear all;                  % Clear the workspace
Af    = 2;      Bf = 2;     % Invariant parameter values
Amin  = 0.3;    Amax = 1;   % Min and max values of aS
Bmin = 0;       Bmax = 0.2; % Min and max values of bS
Amean = (Amax+Amin)/2;      % Mean value of aS
Bmean = (Bmax+Bmin)/2;      % Mean value of bS
% Calculate n parameter combinations
n     = 1000;               % Number of values of aS and bS to generate
% We are assuming a uniform distribution of values
rand('twister', 10);      % Set the random number seed
% Generate n random numbers from Bmin to Bmax
Bs  =   Bmin+(Bmax-Bmin)*rand(n,1);
% Generate n random numbers from Amin to Amax
As  = Amin+(Amax-Amin)*rand(n,1);
x   = linspace(0,6,100); % Body sizes from 0 to 6
W   =  zeros(100,2);     % Matrix to take fitness values
for i  =  1: 100         % Iterate over x values
    Surv  =  As-Bs*x(i); % Vector of survivals
% Check that no survival < 0. If so then set to zero
  Surv(Surv<0)    = 0;
% Check that no survival > 1. If so then set to 1
  Surv(Surv>1)    = 1;
% Column 1 contains fitness for variable parameters
  W(i,1)    = mean((Af+Bf*x(i))*Surv);
% Col 2 contains fitness using mean parameter values
  W(i,2)    = (Af+Bf*x(i))*(Amean-Bmean*x(i));
end
```

```
% Plot fitness=W vs x for both columns on same graph
  plot(x,W(:,1))           % Plot first line
  xlabel('Body size, x');ylabel('Fitness, W');
  hold on                  % Keep plot for next line
  plot(x,W(:,2),':')       % Plot second line with dashes
```

2.18.14   Scenario 6: Finding the maximum using the calculus

As with the R code there is a function, INTEGRAND, to generate the fitness value
for a given x and a function, FITNESS, that calls the numerical integration routine
dblquad which takes INTEGRAND as its input. Two points are worth noting. First,
we have to pass an extra parameter, x to the integration routine and second we
have to compress the fitness equation given in INTEGRAND into a single line. This
is done by making use of the routines min and max. The survival equation is
As−Bs*x, except that it is bounded at 0 and 1. This is specified by nesting the
min and max routines: min (max ((As−Bs*x), 0), 1). The inner routine
ensures that survival does not go below 0 and the outer routine ensures that it
does not exceed 1 (we could have used the same code in R but it is not as clear and
makes little difference to the speed of execution).

```
function f=INTEGRAND(As,Bs,x)   % Function to integrate function
Af  =2; Bf  =2; Ca  =1/0.7; Cb  =5;  % Invariant parameter values
f=(Af+Bf*x)*min(max((As−Bs*x),0),1)*Cb*Ca;% Fitness vector
```

Function to calculate fitness:

```
function W=FITNESS(x)     % Function to evaluate fitness
Amin  = 0.3; Amax  = 1;   % Min and max values of As
Bmin  = 0; Bmax  = 0.2;   % Min and max values of Bs
% Double integral. Note that x is passed also
W =dblquad(@ (As,Bs) INTEGRAND(As,Bs,x),Amin,Amax,Bmin,Bmax);
W=-W;                      % Negative of fitnessc
```

Main Program:

```
clear all;                % Clear the workspace
fminsearch(@FITNESS,2)    % Find minimum, starting with 2
```

OUTPUT:
ans =   3.3703

The answer given by MATLAB agrees with that obtained using optimize in R.

2.18.15   Scenario 6: Finding the maximum using a numerical approach

The fitness function uses the same general structure as previously used in INTE-
GRAND:

```
function W=FITNESS(x,As,Bs)   %  Function to evaluate fitness given
                                         Alpha
Af=2;  Bf=2;  Ca=1/0.7;  Cb=5; % Invariant parameter values
W = mean((Af+Bf*x)*min(max((As-Bs*x),0),1)*Cb*Ca);  % Fitness
                                                          vector
W = -W;                              % Return negative of fitness
```

Main Program:

```
  clear all;                 % Clear the workspace
  Amin = 0.3; Amax = 1;      % Min and max values of As
  Bmin = 0; Bmax = 0.2;      % Min and max values of Bs
% Calculate n parameter combinations
  n = 10000;                 % Number of values of As and Bs to generate
%   We are assuming a uniform distribution of values
%   Make several runs. Here we use 10
   REP = zeros(10,1);        % Create matrix to hold replicate
% We are assuming a uniform distribution of values
  rand('twister', 100);              % Set the random number seed
for i = 1:10                         % Iterate over replicates
  Bs = Bmin+(Bmax-Bmin)*rand(n,1);  % Vector of values of Bf
  As = Amin+(Amax-Amin)*rand(n,1);  % Vector of values of As
  REP(i)= fminsearch(@(x) FITNESS(x,As,Bs), 2); % Pass As,Bs as
                                                    well as x
end
  [mean(REP) std(REP)]       % Print mean and standard deviation
```

OUTPUT:
ans = 3.3786 0.0516

2.18.16   Scenario 7: Plotting the fitness function

Differs slightly from R code in that W rather than $-\log W$ is returned.

```
  function W=FITNESS(x)          % Function to evaluate fitness
  Af = 2; Bf = 2 ; As = 0.6;     % Parameter values
  pBs = [0.1,0.3,0.4,0.2];       % Vector of probabilities for Bs
  Bs = [0.1,0.12,0.14,0.2];      % Vector of Bs values
  W_ind = (Af+Bf*x)*(As-Bs*x);   % Fitness values for each Bs value
% log Fitness. Note use of "." to denote element by element multiply
  log_W = -sum(pBs.*log(W_ind));
  W = exp(-log_W);               % Send back fitness
```

Main Program:

```
  clear all;                       % Clear the workspace
  fplot(@FITNESS, [0,2.999])       % Plot. Note W =INF at x=3
  xlabel('SIZE'); ylabel('FITNESS');
```

2.18.17 Scenario 7: Finding the maximum using the calculus

Calculating the optimum using equation (2.52)

```
function D=DERIV(x)    %Function to calculate value of derivative
   Af = 2; Bf = 2 ; As = 0.6;         % Parameter values
   pBs = [0.1,0.3,0.4,0.2];         % Vector of probabilities for Bs
   Bs = [0.1,0.12,0.14,0.2];        % Vector of Bs values
% Derivative Note "." for multiplying element by element
   D = sum(pBs.*(As*Bf-Af*Bs-Bf*Bs*2*x)./((Af+Bf*x)*(As-Bs*x)));
```

Main Program:
```
   clear all;       % Clear the workspace
   fzero(@DERIV,2)   % Call fzero to find root
```

OUTPUT:
ans = 1.5457

Computing the derivative using the fitness function directly
First we get the derivative with respect to x with pBs and Bs entered as symbolic:

```
clear all;                       % Clear the workspace
Af = 2; Bf = 2 ; As = 0.6;        % Parameter values
syms x; syms pBs; syms Bs;        % Make symbolic parameters
dx = diff(pBs*log((Af+Bf*x)*(As-Bs*x)),x)   % Get differential
```

OUTPUT:
dx =pBs*(6/5-2*Bs*x-(2+2*x)*Bs)/(2+2*x)/(3/5-Bs*x)

We can now use the previous code to find the solution, except that vector notation is not used (it will supply an answer but not the correct one):

```
function D=DERIV(x)       % Function to calculate value of derivative
Af = 2; Bf = 2 ; As = 0.6;  % Parameter values
pBs = [0.1,0.3,0.4,0.2];% Vector of probabilities for Bs
Bs = [0.1,0.12,0.14,0.2];        % Vector of Bs values
D=0;   % Set D to zero and sum derivative values
for i=1:4                        % Iterate over Bs values
D = D+ pBs(i)*(6/5-2*Bs(i)*x-(2+2*x)*Bs(i))/(2+2*x)/(3/5-Bs
(i)*x);
end
```

Main Program:
```
   clear all;       % Clear the workspace
   fzero(@DERIV,2)   % Find root
```

OUTPUT:
ans   = 1.5457

2.18.18   Scenario 7: Finding the maximum using numerical methods

```
function W=FITNESS(x)      % Function to evaluate ®tness
```

Same as function used in plotting except last line is changed to return the negative of the fitness:

```
W = -exp(-log_W);          % Send back negative of ®tness
```

Main Program:

```
clear all;                 % Clear the workspace
fminsearch(@FITNESS,2)     % Call fminsearch giving 2 as starting
                             estimate
```

OUTPUT:
ans =   1.5457

2.18.19   Scenario 8: Plotting the fitness function

There are two approaches, depending on the fitness function:

Approach 1: Fitness function can be integrated
The above fitness function can be simplified for the purposes of integration by rewriting equation (2.55) as

$$\log W = c \int \log(A - Bb_s)db_s \qquad (2.97)$$

where $A = a_S(a_F + b_Fx)$ and $B = x(a_F + b_Fx)$. Now using MATLAB code

```
int('log((A-B*Bs))','Bs')
```

gives the output
ans = -1/B*log(A-B*Bs)*A+log(A-B*Bs)*Bs+1/B*A-Bs

The definite integral of equation (2.97) is readily obtained from the above using the following function:

```
function y=INTEGRAND(x)            % Function to integrate function
Af = 2; Bf = 2; As = 0.6; c=5;     % Parameter values
A=As*(Af+Bf*x);B=x*(Af+Bf*x);      % Define A and B
Bmin = 0.0; Bmax=0.2;              % Set limits of integration
% Get upper and lower values of integral
  Wmin=c*(-1/B*log(A-B*Bmin)*A+log(A-B*Bmin)*Bmin+1/B*A-Bmin);
  Wmax=c*(-1/B*log(A-B*Bmax)*A+log(A-B*Bmax)*Bmax+1/B*A-Bmax);
  y = exp(Wmax-Wmin);              % Fitness
```

Main Program:

```
clear all;                              % Clear the workspace
fplot(@INTEGRAND, [1 3]);               % Plot function
xlabel('Body size'); ylabel('Fitness'); % Add axis labels
```

Approach 2: Fitness function cannot be integrated symbolically
In this case we use the numerical integration routine quad:

```
function W=INTEGRAND(x)          % Function to integrate function
Af = 2; Bf = 2 ; As = 0.6; c=5;  % Parameter values
Bmin = 0.0; Bmax=0.2;            % Set limits of integration
syms Bs;                         % Define Bs to be symbolic
y=quad(@(Bs) c*log((Af+Bf*x)*(As−Bs*x)), Bmin, Bmax); % integrate
W=exp(y)
```

Main Program:

```
clear all;                  % Clear the workspace
fplot(@INTEGRAND, [1 3]);   % Call plotting routine
xlabel('Body size'); ylabel('Fitness');
```

2.18.20   Scenario 8: Finding the maximum using a numerical approach

Fitness is calculated using the function INTEGRAND previously used in plotting, except that the last line is changed to pass the negative of the fitness value: W = -exp(y). The main program is then

```
clear all;                    % Clear the workspace
fminsearch(@INTEGRAND,2)      % Find minimum
```

OUTPUT:
```
ans =   2.0323
```

2.18.21   Scenario 9: The derivative can also be determined using MATLAB

```
clear all       % Clear the workspace
% Designate parameters and variables as symbolic
syms Axy; syms A0; syms Bxy;
syms Cxy; syms Byx; syms Cyx;
syms x; syms y;
f = Axy*x*y-A0+Bxy*x-Cxy*x^2+Byx*y-Cyx*y^2 % Function
diff(f,x)    %Differentiate with respect to x
diff(f,y)    %Differentiate with respect to y
```

OUTPUT:
```
ans = Axy*y+Bxy-2*Cxy*x
    ans = Axy*x+Byx-2*Cyx*y
```

2.18.22   Scenario 9: Plotting the fitness function

```
clear all                     % Clear the workspace
x = linspace(1, 3, 20);       % x from 1 to 3 length 20
```

```
y = linspace(1, 3, 20);          % y from 1 to 3 length 20
[xx,yy]=meshgrid(x,y);           % Create a grid
A0=0.8; Bxy=0.8; Byx=0.8;        % parameter values
Axy=0.4; Cxy=0.4; Cyx=0.4;       % Parameter values
% Fitness values at each x y coordinate
% Note use of".".to denote vectors
zz=(Axy.*xx.*yy-A0)-(-Bxy.*xx+Cxy.*xx.^2)-(-Byx.*yy+Cyx.
*yy.^2);
subplot(2,2,1); % Divide graph sheet into 4 and plot contour in
                top left
[C,h]=contour(x,y,zz); % Create contour plot
%clabel(C,h) rotates the labels and inserts them in the contour
lines.
clabel(C,h);
xlabel('Foraging'); ylabel('Vigilance'); % Add text
subplot(2,2,2);% Divide graph sheet into 4 and plot 3D in top right
surfc(xx,yy,zz); % Plot a 3D surface
xlabel('Foraging'); ylabel('Vigilance'); zlabel('Fitness') %
Add text
```

2.18.23   Scenario 9: Finding the maximum using the calculus

Create function FUNC as in R:

```
function b=FUNC(v)       % Create same function as in R
x=v(1);y=v(2);           % Set two values
b=abs( 0.4.*y+0.8-2*0.4*x)+abs((0.4*x+0.8-2*0.4*y)); % Value
```

Now call fminsearch:

```
clear all;               % Clear the workspace
v=[1,1];                 % Initial estimates
fminsearch(@FUNC,v)      % Call fminsearch
```

OUTPUT:

```
ans =    2.0000    2.0000
```

2.18.24   Scenario 9: Finding the maximum using a numerical approach

```
function w=FITNESS(v)          % Function to evaluate fitness
A0=0.8;Bxy=0.8;Byx=0.8;        % parameter values
Axy=0.4;Cxy=0.4;Cyx=0.4;       % Parameter values
x=v(1); y=v(2);                % Set two variables
% Remember to pass minus fitness
w=-((Axy.*x.*y-A0)-(-Bxy.*x+Cxy.*x.^2)-(-Byx.*y+Cyx.*y.^2));
```

Call above function:

```
clear all;               % Clear the workspace
```

```
v=[1,1];                   % Initial values
fminsearch(@FITNESS,v)  % Call search routine
```

OUTPUT:
```
Ans =   2.0000   2.0000
```

2.18.25   Scenario 11: Plotting the fitness function

First create fitness function:
```
function w=FITNESS(x1)        % Function to evaluate fitness
% Parameter values
S1=0.005; S2 = 0.002; Fmax = 2; a = 1; N = 100; R = 400;
ExpFec1 = Fmax*(1-exp(-a*x1)); % Expected fecundity from 1st clutch
x2 = (R/N)-x1;                % Propagule size in 2nd clutch
x2 = max(x2,0);               % If x2 <0 set x2=0
ExpFec2 = Fmax*(1-exp(-a*x2)); % Expected fecundity from 2nd clutch
w = N*(S1*ExpFec1+S2*ExpFec2);   % Fitness
% Check to see if x1 is acceptable size
  Xmax = N*x1;
  if (Xmax>R)
  w = 0;                      % if x1 too big set fitness to zero
end;
```

Call plotting function:
```
clear all;                          % Clear the workspace
fplot(@FITNESS,[0,4]);              % Plot fitness function
xlabel('Propagule size'); ylabel('Fitness'); % Label axes
```

2.18.26   Scenario 11: Finding the optimum using the calculus

Using the derivative directly
```
function y=DFUNC(x)                      % Derivative function
% Parameter values
  S1 = 0.005; S2 = 0.002; a = 1; N = 100; R = 400;
  y=(S1*exp(-a*x)-S2*exp(-a*(R/N-x)));     % Return deriv value
```

Call function DFUNC with fzero to locate optimum *x*:
```
clear all;      % Clear the workspace
fzero(@DFUNC,1) % Call root-finding function with initial value at 1
```

OUTPUT:
```
ans = 2.4581
```

Getting the derivative using R or MATLAB
```
clear all;                   % Clear the workspace
```

```
S1 = 0.005; S2 = 0.002; a = 1; N = 100; R = 400; Fmax= 2;
syms x;                       % make x symbolic
y=diff(N*(S1*Fmax*(1-exp(-a*x))+S2*Fmax*(1-exp(-a*(R/N-x))))); %
Differential
x1 = vpa(solve(y),5);      % x1 to 5 decimal places
% Calculate x2 for optimum x1
x2= (R/N)-x1 ;                % Size of 2nd propagule
x1                            % print x1
x2                            % Print x2
```

OUTPUT:
```
x1 = 2.4581
        x2 = 1.5419
```

2.18.27   Scenario 11: Finding the optimum using a numerical approach

The fitness function routine is the same as used for plotting *except that we add a
final line to return minus fitness:* w=−w.
   We then use fminsearch:

```
clear all;                    % Clear the workspace
N = 100; R = 400; Fmax= 2;    % Set parameter values
x1=fminsearch(@FITNESS,1);    % Call fminsearch with initial esti-
                                 mate of 1
% Calculate x2 for optimum x1
x2= (R/N)-x1 ;                % Size of 2nd propagule
x1                            % print x1
x2                            % print x2
```

OUTPUT:
```
x1 = 2.4581
x2 = 1.5419
```

2.18.28   Scenario 12: Plotting the fitness function

Fitness function:

```
function W=FITNESS(v)      % Function to evaluate fitness
x1=v(1);                   % x1 = Propagule size in 1st clutch
x2=v(2);                   % x2 = Propagule size in 2nd clutch
% Set parameter values
N = 100;       R = 400;
S1 = 0.035;   S2 = 0.030;   S3 = 0.025;
Fmax = 2;   a = 0.1;
W1=0; W2=0; W3=0;          % Initial values
% Check if first clutch mass exceeds reserves
if N*x1>R
W = 0;                     % Propagule too large
```

```
else
% Calculate first fecundity
  W1 = N*S1*Fmax*(1-exp(-a*x1));
% Calculate size of propagules in 2nd clutch and see if reserves
exceeded
if N*(x1+x2)>R
  W = W1;            % Propagules in 2nd clutch too large
else
  W2 = N*S2*Fmax*(1-exp(-a*x2)); % Calculate 2nd fecundity
% Calculate the size of Propagules in 3rd clutch
% Note that there must be reserves remaining at this stage
  x3 = (R-N*(x1+x2))/N;
  W3 = N*S3*Fmax*(1-exp(-a*x3)); % Calculate 3rd fecundity
  W = W1+W2+W3;
end % End 2nd else
end % End 1st else
  W=-W; % Return negative of fitness
```

MATLAB code to call fitness function and make plots:

```
clear all;              % Clear the workspace
n=20;                   % Number of divisions to be made
x1 = linspace(1, 5, n); % x1 from 1 to 5 length 20
x2 = linspace(1, 5, n); % x2 from 1 to 5 length 20
z = zeros(n);           % Preallocate z matrix
% Fitness values at each x1 x2 coordinate
for i = 1:n
  for j = 1:n
    z(j,i)=-FITNESS([x1(i),x2(j)]); % Convert to positive fitness
    end
end
    subplot(2,2,1) % Divide graph sheet into 2 x 2 panels, contour top
left
    [C,h]=contour(x1,x2,z);       % Create contour plot
%clabel(C,h) rotates the labels and inserts them in the contour
lines.
    clabel(C,h);
    xlabel('x1'); ylabel('x2');   % Add text
    subplot(2,2,2)   % Divide graph sheet into 2 x 2 panels, 3D top right
    [xx,yy] = meshgrid(x1,x2);    % Create grids for 3D plot
    surfc(xx,yy,z);               % Plot 3D
    xlabel('x1'); ylabel('x2'); zlabel('Fitness')   % Add text
```

2.18.29 Scenario 12: Finding the maximum using the calculus

Using R or MATLAB to find the optima given the differential

The MATLAB code does not give any warning or error messages. First we write the fitness function:

```
  function W=FITNESS(x2)    % Function to evaluate fitness
% Differs from that used in plotting in only a single variable being
input
% Set parameter values
  N = 100;       R = 400;
  S1 = 0.035;   S2 = 0.030;   S3 = 0.025;
  Fmax = 2;   a = 0.1;
  x1 = (1/a)*log(S1/S2)+x2;     % x1 given the value of x2
  x3 = (R-N*(x1+x2))/N;         % Value of x3
if x3<0
  W=0;                          % Check that x3 exists
else
% Check if first clutch mass exceeds reserves
if N*x1 > R
  W = 0;                        % Propagule too large
else
  W1 = N*S1*Fmax*(1-exp(-a*x1));   % Calculate first fecundity
% Calculate size of propagules in 2nd clutch and see if reserves
exceeded
if N*x2 > R
    W = W1;                     % Propagules in 2nd clutch too large
else
  W2 = N*S2*Fmax*(1-exp(-a*x2));   % Calculate 2nd fecundity
% Calculate the size of Propagules in 3rd clutch
% Note that there must be reserves remaining at this stage
  W3 = N*S3*Fmax*(1-exp(-a*x3));   % Calculate 3rd fecundity
  W = W1+W2+W3;
end % End 3rd else
end % End 2nd else
end % End 1st else
  Propagules =[x1,x2,x3];              % Store sizes
  save PROPAGULE.txt Propagules -ASCII % Output sizes
  W= -W;         % Return negative of fitness
```

Main MATLAB Program:

```
  clear all;                 % Clear the workspace
% Locate optimum x2 and calculate x1 and x3
fminsearch(@FITNESS,1);        % Call fminsearch with estimate at 1
load PROPAGULE.txt             % Get optima from file
PROPAGULE                      % Print out results
```

OUTPUT:

```
PROPAGULE =   2.7705   1.2290   0.0005
```

The MATLAB output gives more or less the same answer as the R output for x_1 and x_2 but the slight differences makes a difference to the estimated value of x_3, the MATLAB estimate being larger (9.7×10^{-7} in R and 5×10^{-4} in MATLAB). Though the difference may seem large, the overall conclusion for the third propagule is that it will be very, very small.

Using R or MATLAB to do the calculus
We do not have to resort to a numerical derivative since we can use `diff` to find the absolute value of the difference between the partial derivatives as functions of x_1 and x_2:

```
clear all    % clear the work space
% Set parameter values
  N  = 100;        R = 400;
  S1  = 0.035;    S2 = 0.030;    S3 = 0.025;
  Fmax = 2;        a = 0.1;
  syms x1; syms x2;    % make x1 and x2 symbolic
% Differential with respect to x1
  dx1=diff(N*S1*Fmax*(1-exp(-a*x1))+N*S2*Fmax*(1-exp
(-a*x2))+N*S3*Fmax*(1-exp(-a*(R/N-(x1+x2)))),x1);
% Differential with respect to x2
  dx2=diff(N*S1*Fmax*(1-exp(-a*x1))+N*S2*Fmax*(1-exp
(-a*x2))+N*S3*Fmax*(1-exp(-a*(R/N-(x1+x2)))),x2);
  dx1-dx2            % output difference
```

OUTPUT:
```
ans =7/10*exp(-1/10*x1)-3/5*exp(-1/10*x2)
```
We can now use the same approach as in the R code. First define the function GRADIENT:
```
function d=GRADIENT(x1,x2)
d =abs(7/10*exp(-1/10*x1)-3/5*exp(-1/10*x2));    % Abs value of
difference
```

Next the fitness function:
```
  function W=FITNESS(x2)
% Fitness function given x2, and calling fminsearch to find x1
% Set parameter values
  N = 100;        R = 400;
  S1 = 0.035;    S2 = 0.030;    S3 = 0.025;
  Fmax = 2;    a = 0.1;
% Find value of x1 given x2 using fminsearch to set derivatives to
zero
% Must pass x2 to GRADIENT as an extra parameter
% The next line is the one that differs from the previous code
  x1 = fminsearch(@(x) GRADIENT(x,x2),1);  % find x1 using fmin-
search
```

```
% Now calculate x3 and fitness
   x3 = (R-N*(x1+x2))/N ;                    % Determine x2
if (x3 < 0)                                  % Check if x3 exists (>0)
    W=0 ;
else % Check if first clutch mass exceeds reserves
if (N*x1 > R)                                % Propagule too large
    W = 0;
else
  W1 = N*S1*Fmax*(1-exp(-a*x1));   % Calculate first fecundity
% Calculate size of propagules in 2nd clutch and see if reserves
exceeded
if (N*x2 > R)
    W = W1; %Propagules in 2nd clutch too large
else
  W2 = N*S2*Fmax*(1-exp(-a*x2));     % Calculate 2nd fecundity
% Calculate the size of Propagules in 3rd clutch
% Note that there must be reserves remaining at this stage
  W3 = N*S3*Fmax*(1-exp(-a*x3));     % Calculate 3rd fecundity
  W = W1+W2+W3;                      % Sum fitness components
end                                 % End 3rd else
end                                 % End 2nd else
end                                 % End 1st else
  Propagules =[x1,x2,x3];                % Store sizes
  save PROPAGULE.txt Propagules -ASCII   % Output sizes
  W= -W;                                 % Return -fitness
```

Finally the main program:

```
  clear all;             % Clear the workspace
% Locate optima
fminsearch(@FITNESS,1);  % Call fminsearch with estimate at 1
load PROPAGULE.txt       % Get optima from file
PROPAGULE                % Print out results
```

OUTPUT:

PROPAGULE = 2.7705   1.2290   0.0005

As with R, MATLAB gives more or less the same answer as before.

2.18.30   Scenario 12: Finding the maximum using a numerical approach

Using nlm *(R) or* fminsearch *(MATLAB)*

```
function W=FITNESS(v)           % Function to evaluate fitness
```

{ This function is the same as that used in plotting}

Main Program:

```
   clear all;                    % Clear the workspace
% MAIN PROGRAM
% Call fminsearch passing fitness function with initial estimates
   X = fminsearch(@FITNESS, [0.1,0.1]);% Store estimates in X
% Calculate x3
   R = 400; N = 100;             % Parameter values
   x3 = (R-N*(X(1)+X(2)))/N;     % x3
   vpa([X(1),X(2), x3],6)        % Output propagule sizes
```

OUTPUT:
ans =[2.77073,   1.22927,   .228709e-7]

Previous results:
ans =   2.7705   1.2291   0.0005
ans =   2.7705   1.2291   0.0005

The estimates for x_1 and x_2 are more or less consistent but the estimate for x_3 does differ, though all estimates of x_3 are very small.

The Brute force approach

Where possible, loops are to be avoided. In MATLAB this can be generally done using vectorization. However, because of the "if statements", this cannot be done simply in the present case (it is possible to avoid looping by using filters but these make very obscure code). Therefore, we shall employ a loop structure, which in this circumstance runs fast enough not to warrant a more refined approach (clear code is to be preferred unless it impedes speed excessively). The program works in a similar fashion as the R program in generating three vectors, x_1, x_2, and W and then using a MATLAB function, max, to locate the maximum value of W and the associated values of x_1 and x_2.

```
function W=FITNESS(v)      % Function to evaluate fitness
```

{ This function is the same as that used in plotting}
Main Program:

```
   clear all;              % Clear the workspace
   n=100;                  % Number of divisions to be made
   x1 = linspace(0, 5, n); % x1 from 1 to 5 length n
   x2 = linspace(0, 5, n); % x2 from 1 to 5 length n
   m = n^2;
   W = zeros(m,1); x=W;y=W; % Preallocate x,y, W vectors
% Fitness values at each x1 x2 coordinate
      row=0;                % Set index value to
% Iterate over all combinations of x1 and x2
      for i = 1:n
      for j = 1:n
      row=row+1;                         % Increment row
      x(row) = x1(i); y(row)=x2(j);      % store x1 and x2
```

```
    W(row)=-FITNESS([x1(i),x2(j)]); % Convert to positive fit-
                                               ness & store
end
end
[C,I] = max(W);          % C = max W, I = row in vectors
X1 = x(I); X2 = y(I);    % Get values of x1 and x2
% Calculate x3
R = 400; N = 100;        % Parameter values
x3 = (R-N*(X1+X2))/N;    % x3
[X1,X2,x3,C]             % print out x1, x2, x3 and Wmax
```

OUTPUT:

ans = 2.7778 1.2121 0.0101 2.3877

Using the brute force results to refine the search (replace with the following lines):

```
x1 = linspace(2.7, 2.8, n); % x1 from 1 to 5 length n
x2 = linspace(1.0, 1.3, n); % x2 from 1 to 5 length n
```

gives

ans = 2.7697 1.2303 0 2.3880

Of course the results are the same as obtain in R.

2.18.31 Scenario 13: Plotting the fitness function

The fitness function follows that given in the R code. It is possible to replace the loops doing the recursion with vectorized code using the function `filter` but the code is so obscure that I would recommend it only if there is a real saving in time, which in this case there certainly isn't (for an example of using `filter` to replace a loop see the online MathWorks support function (http://ww.mathworks.com/support/tech-notes/1100/1109.html, p. 8).

```
function W=FITNESS(x)    % Function to evaluate fitness given Alpha
G        = x(1);         % G values
Alpha    = x(2);         % Alpha value
% Set parameter values
Mj       = 0.05;         % Background mortality rate
Ma       = 0.4;          % Constant of mortality function
Agemax   = 30;           % Maximum age (arbitrary)
a        = 0.05;         % Fecundity constant
A        = 10;           % Wt increase/annum without reproduction
Aminus1  = Alpha-1;      % Year before first reproduction
S = zeros(Agemax,1);     % Pre-allocate vector for annual survival
% Growth prior to reproduction is linear
```

```
% To include cases in which growth is more complex I here use a for
loop
  Wt    = zeros(Agemax,1);    % Initialize Wt vector
  S(1)= exp(-Mj);             % Survival to age 1
% Calculate Wt and Survival from age 2 to alpha-1
for i = 2: Aminus1
  Wt(i) = Wt(i-1) + A;        % Weight
  S(i)= S(i-1)*exp(-Mj);      % Annual survival
end
% Now calculate change in wt and survival for age alpha to max age
for i = Alpha: Agemax
  Wt(i)= Wt(i-1)+A-G*Wt(i-1); % Weight
  S(i)= S(i-1)*exp(-(Mj+Ma*G)); % Annual survival
end
% Calculate W=Fitness Note "." for element by element vector multi-
plication
  W = a*sum(S(Alpha:Agemax).*Wt(Alpha:Agemax)*G);
  W = -W;        % Return negative of fitness
```

Main Program:

```
  clear all;                 % Clear the workspace
  nG = 11;                   % Number of G values
  G = linspace(0.01, 0.5, nG);    % G from 0.01 to 0.5 length nG
  nalpha = 20-3+1;           % Number of ages to consider
  alpha = linspace(3, 20, nalpha);   % x2 from 1 to 5 length 20
  z = zeros(nG,nalpha);      % Preallocate z matrix
% Fitness values at each G alpha coordinate
for i = 1:nG
  for j = 1:nalpha
    z(i,j)=-FITNESS([G(i),alpha(j)]); % Convert to positive fitness
  end
end
    subplot(2,2,1) % Divide graph sheet into 2 x 2 panels, contour
top left
    [C,h]=contour(alpha,G,z); % Create contour plot
%clabel(C,h) rotates the labels and inserts them in the contour
lines.
  clabel(C,h);
  xlabel('Alpha'); ylabel('G');    % Add text
  subplot(2,2,2) % Divide graph sheet into 2 x 2 panels, 3D top right
  [xx,yy] = meshgrid(alpha,G);     % Create grids for 3D plot
  surfc(xx,yy,z);                  % Plot 3D
  xlabel('Alpha'); ylabel('x2'); zlabel('Fitness')    % Add text
```

2.18.32   Scenario 13: Finding the maximum using a numerical approach

Brute force using many values

Because we want to calculate the optimal G for a given Alpha, we must make a slight modification to the fitness function:

Replace

```
function W=FITNESS(x)    % Function to evaluate fitness given Alpha
    G = x(1);            % G values
    Alpha = x(2);        % Alpha value
```

with

```
function W=FITNESS(G,Alpha) % Function to evaluate fitness given
                            Alpha
```

The above changes could have also been made in the plotting section. The fitness function is called by the main program:

```
  clear all;                          % Clear the workspace
% Create vector for alpha values
  nalpha = 20-3+1;                    % Number of ages to consider
  alpha = linspace(3, 20, nalpha);  % alpha vector from 1 to 5 length 20
  G = zeros(nalpha,1);               % Create vector to store best G values
  W = zeros(nalpha,1);               % Create vector to store W values
for i = 1:nalpha                     % Iterate over alpha vector values
% Find best G for this alpha by calling fminsearch
% alpha(i) is passed as a fixed parameter
  G(i) = fminsearch(@(G) FITNESS(G,alpha(i)),0.1); % Store best G
  W(i) = -FITNESS(G(i),alpha(i)); % Get W at best G for given alpha
end
% Now locate best combination and write out values
  [C,I] = max(W);                    % C = max W, I = row in vectors
  Alpha_best = alpha(I);             % Best alpha
  G_best = G(I                       % Best G
  W_best = C; );                     % W at best alpha, best G
  [Alpha_best,G_best,W_best]    % Print out best alpha, G and max W
```

OUTPUT: Ans = 8.0000 0.1345 2.6849

Brute force using iteration

The fitness function is the same as in the previous code. We also need another function which I shall call BESTG that calculates the optimal G value for consecutive pairs of Alpha. Note that this function passes back a vector.

```
% Function to get best G for consecutive pairs of alpha
  function Wdiff =BESTG(alpha)
% Results for alpha
  G1 = fminsearch(@(G) FITNESS(G,alpha),0.1);   % Store best G
  W1 = -FITNESS(G1,alpha);                       % Fitness
% Results for alpha+1
```

```
G2 = fminsearch(@(G) FITNESS(G,alpha+1),0.1); % Store best G
W2 = -FITNESS(G2,alpha+1);              % Fitness
W3 = W2-W1;                             % Diff between fitnesses
% return Wdiff, W1, G1 % G1 will eventually be the best G
Wdiff = [W3, W1, G1];
```

Main Program:

```
clear all;              % Clear the workspace
ALPHA = 5;              % Set initial alpha
DIFF = BESTG(ALPHA);  % Calculate difference between W at two alphas
while DIFF(1) > 0;      % If DIFF[1] > 0 then W still increasing
ALPHA = ALPHA+1;       % Increment alpha
DIFF = BESTG(ALPHA);   % Call BESTG and get difference
end
% Out of loop and thus ALPHA is the best
[ALPHA, DIFF(3),DIFF(2)] % Print out alpha, G, W
```

2.18.33   Scenario 14: Finding the maximum using a numerical approach

MATLAB code changes in bold:

function W=FITNESS(G,Alpha,N) % Function to evaluate fitness given Alpha
% G IS NOW A VECTOR WITH N ENTRIES
```
% Set parameter values
Mj = 0.05;              % Background mortality rate
Ma = 0.4;               % Constant of mortality function
```
Age_max = Alpha+1; % Maximum age
```
a = 0.05;               % Fecundity constant
A = 10;                 % Wt increase/annum without reproduction
A_minus_1 = Alpha-1;    % Year before first reproduction
S = zeros(Age_max,1);   % Vector of annual survival
% Growth prior to reproduction is linear
% To include cases in which growth is more complex I here use a for loop
Wt = zeros(Age_max,1);  % Initialize Wt vector
S(1) = exp(-Mj);        % Survival to age 1
% Calculate Wt and Survival from age 2 to alpha-1
for i = 2 : A_minus_1
Wt(i) = Wt(i-1) + A;    % Weight
S(i) = S(i-1)*exp(-Mj); % Annual survival
end
% Now calculate change in wt and survival for age alpha to max age
```
% Accumulate W. W is now accumulated in the loop rather than after
** W = 0;**
for J = 1:N % Iterate over the adult ages

```
   i = Alpha + J - 1;                    % Get age i = Alpha, Alpha+1
   Wt(i) = Wt(i-1) + A- G(J)*Wt(i-1);    % Wt
   S(i) = S(i-1)*exp(-(Mj+Ma*G(J)));     % Annual survival
   W = W + a*S(i)*Wt(i)*G(J);            % Cumulative fitness
end
   W= -W;                                % Return negative of fitness
```

Now function BESTG:

```
% Function to get best G for consecutive pairs of alpha
function Wdiff = BESTG(alpha)
  N = 2; % Nos of mature ages
% Results for alpha Note that G is passed two values
  G1 = fminsearch(@(G) FITNESS(G,alpha,N),[0.1,0.1]); % Store best G
  W1 = -FITNESS(G1,alpha,N);                          % Fitness
% Results for alpha+1
  G2 = fminsearch(@(G)FITNESS(G,alpha+1,N),[0.1,0.1]);%Store best G
  W2 = -FITNESS(G2,alpha+1,N);                        % Fitness
  W3 = W2-W1;          % Diff between fitnesses
% return Wdiff,W1,G1   % G1 will eventually be the best G
  Wdiff = [W3, W1, G1];
```

Main program calls BESTG:

```
clear all;          % Clear the workspace
  ALPHA = 5;        % Set initial alpha
  DIFF = BESTG(ALPHA); % Calculate difference between W at two alphas
while DIFF(1) > 0; % If DIFF[1] > 0 then W still increasing
  ALPHA = ALPHA+1;
  DIFF = BESTG(ALPHA);
end
% Out of loop and thus ALPHA is the best
% Print Alpha, Wdif, G1, G2...GN
  [ALPHA,DIFF(1),DIFF(3),DIFF(4)] %Print out alpha, G, W
```

OUTPUT: (Same as R)
Ans = 19.0000 0−0.0003 0.3497 0.4835

To increase the number of ages and hence the number of variables we alter N in function BESTG, and modify the following lines given that we wish to set N = 5 (giving 6 variables to be estimated):

```
N = 6; % Nos of mature ages
G1 = fminsearch(@(G) FITNESS(G,alpha,N),[0.1,0.1,0.1,0.1,0.1,0.1]);
G2 = fminsearch(@(G) FITNESS(G,alpha+1,N),[0.1,0.1,0.1,0.1,0.1,0.1]);
  [ALPHA,DIFF(1),DIFF(3),DIFF(4),DIFF(5),DIFF(6)] %Print out
```

The result is
ans = 18.0000 −0.0042 0.2166 0.2463 0.2917 0.3666

CHAPTER 3

Invasibility Analysis

3.1 Introduction

An alternative approach to that used in the last chapter is invasibility analysis, which consists of asking if a clone displaying an alternate life history can invade a resident population. While one could compare results for markedly different life histories, in general, invasibility analysis has been used to locate the optimal combinations of parameter values rather than qualitatively different life histories. As with the "Fisherian" optimality approach, sexual reproduction is ignored. Invasibility analysis is used extensively, and is most useful, when fitness is density-dependent and there is age- or stage-structuring in the model. The method can handle stable, cyclical, and chaotic population dynamics. In this section I first consider the general structure of age- and stage-structured models and then describe the two general approaches of invasibility analysis, namely pairwise-invasibility and multiple-invasibility analysis. For all that you ever wanted to know about matrix population models see Caswell (2002).

3.1.1 Age- or stage-structured models

Consider the life table shown in Table 3.1.

Table 3.1 Calculation of age-specific survival probabilities and fertilities for the Leslie matrix.

Age x	l_x	m_x	Post-breeding census		Pre-breeding census	
			$S_x = \frac{l_x}{l_{x-1}}$	$F_x = S_x m_x$	$S_x = \frac{l_{x+1}}{l_x}$	$F_x = S_x m_x$
0	1	0	–	–	0.8	0
1	0.80	1	0.80	0.8	0.4	0.4
2	0.20	3	0.40	1.2	0.25	0.75
3	0.05	4	0.25	1.0	0	0
4	0.00	1	0.00	0.00	–	–

Using the post-breeding census, which is an assumption for the models discussed in Chapter 2, the number of individuals entering age 1 at time $t + 1$ is given by

$$
\begin{aligned}
n_{1,t+1} &= S_1 m_1 n_{1,t} + S_2 m_2 n_{2,t} + S_3 m_3 n_{3,t} + S_4 m_4 n_{4,t} \\
&= (0.8)(1)n_{1,t} + (0.4)(3)n_{2,t} + (0.25)(4)n_{3,t} + (0)n_{4,t} \\
&= 0.8 n_{1,t} + 1.2 n_{2,t} + 1 n_{3,t} + 0 n_{4,t}
\end{aligned} \tag{3.1}
$$

where $n_{i,t}$ is the number in age class i at time t. The number surviving from t to $t + 1$ is given by

$$
\begin{aligned}
n_{2,t+1} &= S_1 n_{1,t} = 0.8 n_{1,t} \\
n_{3,t+1} &= S_2 n_{2,t} = 0.4 n_{2,t} \\
n_{4,t+1} &= S_3 n_{3,t} = 0.25 n_{3,t}
\end{aligned} \tag{3.2}
$$

This set of equations can be represented in matrix format as

$$
\begin{pmatrix} n_{1,t+1} \\ n_{2,t+1} \\ n_{3,t+1} \\ n_{4,t+1} \end{pmatrix} = \begin{pmatrix} F_1 & F_2 & F_3 & F_4 \\ S_1 & 0 & 0 & 0 \\ 0 & S_2 & 0 & 0 \\ 0 & 0 & S_3 & 0 \end{pmatrix} \begin{pmatrix} n_{1,t} \\ n_{2,t} \\ n_{3,t} \\ n_{4,t} \end{pmatrix} \tag{3.3}
$$

If a pre-breeding census is assumed, then $S_x = l_{x+1}/l_x$ (Caswell 1989, p. 12). The matrix can be written in shorthand as

$$
\mathbf{n}_{t+1} = \mathbf{A} \mathbf{n}_t \tag{3.4}
$$

The matrix $\mathbf{A}$ is known as the **Leslie matrix** after the ecologist who first introduced it into the population biology literature (Leslie 1945). The advantage of using the matrix notation is that there are well-defined rules for manipulating matrices, particularly for matrix multiplication. From an evolutionary biologist's point of view the important feature of this matrix is that the population rate of increase at a stable age distribution, λ, is given by the first **eigenvalue** of the matrix. This value is readily obtained in R or MATLAB. For example, in the life history specified by equations (3.1) and (3.2) the Leslie matrix is

$$
\mathbf{A} = \begin{pmatrix} 0.8 & 1.2 & 1.0 & 0 \\ 0.8 & 0 & 0 & 0 \\ 0 & 0.4 & 0 & 0 \\ 0 & 0 & 0.25 & 0 \end{pmatrix} \tag{3.5}
$$

which can be entered using R as

```
Leslie.matrix <- matrix(c(0.8, 1.2, 1.0,  0,
                          0.8, 0.0, 0.0,  0,
                          0.0, 0.4, 0.0,  0,
                          0.0, 0.0, 0.25, 0 ),4,4, byrow=TRUE)
```

where, for ease of writing, I have aligned the columns. The eigenvalues and eigenvectors can be obtained with the command eigen (R) or eig (MATLAB).

In R the appropriate eigenvalue can be drawn from the list with the suffix `$values[1]`. Thus the following commands in R,

```
Eigen.data <- eigen(Leslie.matrix)
Eigen.data$values[1]   # Get first eigenvalue
```

gives 1.5516.

Equation (3.3) defines the change in population size after one generation. If the initial population consists of a single gravid female the population size in the next generation is given by

$$\begin{pmatrix} n_1 \\ n_2 \\ n_3 \\ n_4 \end{pmatrix} = \begin{pmatrix} 0.8 & 1.2 & 1.0 & 0 \\ 0.8 & 0 & 0 & 0 \\ 0 & 0.4 & 0 & 0 \\ 0 & 0 & 0.25 & 0 \end{pmatrix} \begin{pmatrix} 1 \\ 0 \\ 0 \\ 0 \end{pmatrix} = \begin{pmatrix} 0.8 \\ 0.8 \\ 0 \\ 0 \end{pmatrix} \quad (3.6)$$

Matrix multiplication in R is coded by `%*%`, thus

```
n <- Leslie.matrix%*%n
```

gives the multiplication shown in equation (3.6). Progressive application of matrix multiplication produces the population projection. The following coding calculates and plots the trajectories of the individual cohorts (ages 1–4) and the total population size. Additionally, the observed rate of increase, given by N_{t+1}/N_t, and the instantaneous rate of increase, r, given by $\log_e(N_{t+1}/N_t)$ are plotted.

```
rm(list=ls()) # Clear workspace
Leslie.matrix <- matrix(c(0.8, 1.2, 1.0, 0,
                          0.8, 0.0, 0.0, 0,
                          0.0, 0.4, 0.0, 0,
                          0.0, 0.0, 0.25,0),4,4, byrow=TRUE)
Eigen.data <- eigen( Leslie.matrix)
Lambda     <- Eigen.data$values[1]   # Get first eigenvalue
Maxgen     <- 12                     # Number of generations
                                       simulation runs
n          <- c(1,0,0,0)             # Initial population
# Pre-assign matrix to hold cohort number and total population size
Pop        <- matrix(0,Maxgen,5)
Pop[1,]    <- c(n[1:4], sum(n))      # Store initial population
# Pre-assign storage for observed lambda
Obs.lambda <- matrix(0,Maxgen,5)
for ( Igen in 2:Maxgen)              # Iterate over generations
{
n <- Leslie.matrix%*%n               # Apply matrix multiplication
```

```
  Pop[Igen,1:4]<- n[1:4]            # Store cohorts
  Pop[Igen,5] <- sum(n)             # Store total population size

  Obs.lambda[Igen,] <- Pop[Igen,]/Pop[Igen-1,] # Store observed
                                                       lambda
  }                                 # End of Igen loop
# Print out observed lambda in last generation and ratio
  print(c(Obs.lambda[Maxgen], Obs.lambda[Maxgen]/Lambda))
  par(mfrow=c(2,2))                 # Make 2x2 layout of plots
  Generation <- seq(from=1, to=Maxgen)    # Vector of generation
                                                    number
# Plot population and cohort trajectories
  ymin <- min(Pop); ymax <- max(Pop) # get minimum and maximum pop
                                            sizes
  plot(   Generation,   Pop[,1],   type='l',ylim=c(ymin,ymax),
ylab='Population and cohort sizes') # Cohort 1
  for( i in 2:4) {lines(Generation, Pop[,i]) } # Cohorts 2-4
  lines(Generation, Pop[,5], lty=2) # Total population
# Plot log of population and cohort trajectories
# Log zero is undefined so remove these
  x <- matrix(Pop,length(Pop),1)    # Convert to one dimensional
                                            matrix
  ymin <- min(log(x[x!=0]))    # minimum log value
  ymax <- max(log(Pop))         # get minimum and maximum pop sizes
  plot( Generation, log(Pop[,1]), type='l', ylim=c(ymin,ymax),
ylab='log Sizes')
  for(i in 2:4) {lines(Generation, log(Pop[,i]))}
  lines(Generation, log(Pop[,5]), lty=2)     # Total population
# Plot Observed lambdas
  plot(Generation, Obs.lambda[,1], type='l', ylab='Lambda')
  for( i in 2:4) {lines(Generation, Obs.lambda[,i])}
  lines(Generation, Obs.lambda[,5], lty=2)   # Total population
# Plot observed r
  plot(Generation, log(Obs.lambda[,1]), type='l', ylab='r')
  for( i in 2:4) {lines(Generation, log(Obs.lambda[,i]))}
  lines(Generation, log(Obs.lambda[,5]), lty=2)
                                          # Total population
```

OUTPUT: (Figure 3.1)

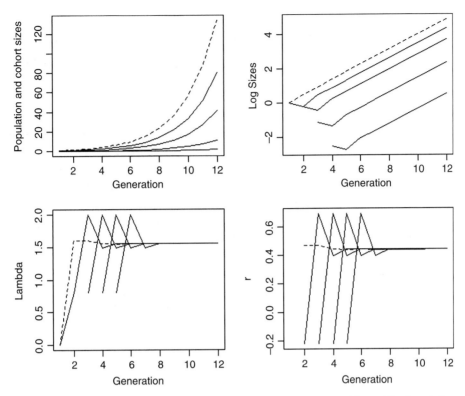

Figure 3.1 Trajectories of cohort (solid lines) and population sizes (dotted line) and the observed values of λ and r.

```
> print(c(Obs.lambda[Maxgen], Obs.lambda[Maxgen]/Lambda))
[1] 1.5516186+0i 0.9999971+0i
```

The simulation shows that the population quickly reaches a stable age distribution, shown by the linearity of the plot of log(population or cohort size) on time and the constancy of the observed λ (Figure 3.1).

3.1.2   Modeling evolution using the Leslie matrix

Because the population quickly reaches a stable age distribution and there is no density-dependence the methods presented in Chapter 2 can be used to analyse models defined by a Leslie matrix. However, because of the ease with which λ or r ($= \log_e \lambda$) is calculated from a Leslie matrix, a matrix approach can sometimes be a more easily programmed method than those used in Chapter 2. Scenario 1 gives an example of finding the optimal life history using the Leslie matrix compared to the approach used in Chapter 2.

3.1.3 Stage-structured models

In many cases a life cycle is better classified according to stages rather than ages: for example, the transition from juvenile to adult is probably more frequently dependent on passing some size-threshold than a particular age. Suppose we have a population in which maturity depends upon reaching a minimum size, after which there are two adult stages. The two adult stages differ and passage from one to another is also size dependent (e.g., in the first adult stage males might be too small to compete for territories and adopt a satellite strategy. Note that in this case the symbol F refers to reproductive success). The three transition equations are

$$
\begin{aligned}
n_{1,t+1} &= P_1 n_{1,t} + F_2 n_{2,t} + F_3 n_{3,t} \\
n_{2,t+1} &= S_1 n_{1,t} + P_2 n_{2,t} \\
n_{3,t+1} &= S_2 n_{2,t}
\end{aligned}
\tag{3.7}
$$

where P_i is the surviving proportion that remain in the ith stage and S_i is the proportion that pass from stage i and survive to the next stage. These equations can be converted into the matrix

$$
\begin{pmatrix} n_{1,t+1} \\ n_{2,t+1} \\ n_{3,t+1} \end{pmatrix}
=
\begin{pmatrix} P_1 & F_2 & F_3 \\ S_1 & P_2 & 0 \\ 0 & S_2 & 0 \end{pmatrix}
\begin{pmatrix} n_{1,t} \\ n_{2,t} \\ n_{3,t} \end{pmatrix}
\tag{3.8}
$$

There is no fundamental mathematical difference between age and stage-structured models and the latter can be analyzed using the "Fisherian" optimality approach. Difficulties arise when fitness is density-dependent, a topic to which we now turn.

3.1.4 Adding density-dependence

The Leslie matrix or its stage-based analogue can be readily modified to accommodate density-dependent effects. There are many ways that a density-dependent effect can be entered, for example, fertility might only be affected or survival or both. Only one age class might be affected or the effect spread over several or all age classes. Two common functions are the Beverton–Holt function and the Ricker function (both named after the fisheries biologists who suggested it). The Beverton–Holt function is compensatory in that it progresses smoothly to an asymptotic value, whereas the Ricker function is overcompensatory in that for some portion of the curve N_{t+1} is less than N_t. The standard forms of these two models for an unstructured population are

$$
\begin{aligned}
N_{t+1} &= N_t \frac{c_1}{1 + c_2 N_t} \quad \text{Beverton} - \text{Holt} \\
N_{t+1} &= N_t \alpha e^{-\beta N_t} \quad \text{Ricker}
\end{aligned}
\tag{3.9}
$$

The Beverton–Holt model asymptotes at an equilibrium population, whereas the Ricker model can equilibrate, cycle, or show chaotic behavior (Figure 3.2). In applying these functions the population size terms immediately adjacent to the

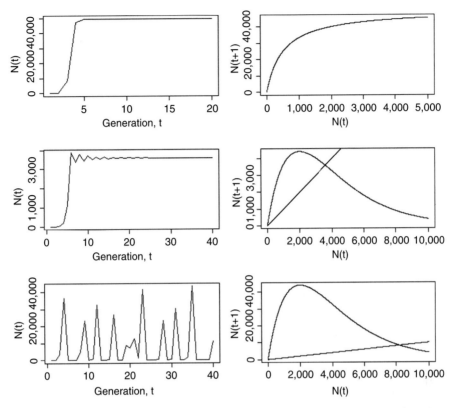

Figure 3.2 Examples of population trajectories for the Beverton–Holt (first row) and Ricker models. Depending on parameter values, the Ricker model may reach a stable equilibrium (second row), or show cyclical behavior (not shown) or chaotic behavior (third row). Plots on the right show the change in population size as a function of the previous population. The R coding to produce these plots is as follows:

```
rm(list=ls())              #  Clear workspace
par(mfrow=c(3,2))          #  Divide page into 6 panels
BH.FUNCTION        <-  function(n,c1,c2)  {c1/(1+c2*n)}
RICKER.FUNCTION  <-  function(n, ALPHA, BETA)  {ALPHA*exp
(-BETA*n)}
################### MAIN PROGRAM ##################
########## Beverton Holt function ##########
 c1  <-  100;   c2 <- 2*10^-3  # B-H parameters
# Plot N(t) on t
 Maxgen  <- 20; N.t  <- matrix(0,Maxgen); N.t[1]  <-  1
 for ( i in 2:Maxgen)
 {N.t[i] <- N.t[i-1]*BH.FUNCTION(N.t[i-1], c1,c2) }
 plot(seq(from=1, to=Maxgen), N.t, xlab = 'Generation, t', ylab
='N(t)',type='l')
# Plot N(t+1) on N(t)
 MaxN       <- 5000; N.t  <- matrix(seq(from=1, to=MaxN))
 N.tplus1  <- N.t*apply(N.t,1,BH.FUNCTION, c1,c2)
```

                                                        (cont'd)

Fig 3.2 (cont'd)

```
plot(N.t, N.tplus1, xlab = 'N(t)', ylab='N(t+1)', type='l')
##########  Ricker function  ##########
    ALPHA    <-c(6, 60);   BETA   <- .0005    # Parameter values
# Plot N(t) on t for 2 values of ALPHA
    Maxgen   <- 40
    for (j in 1:2)
{
  N.t         <- matrix(0,Maxgen,1);   N.t[1] <- 1
  for   ( i in 2:Maxgen)
  {N.t[i]<- N.t[i-1]*RICKER.FUNCTION(N.t[i-1], ALPHA[j], BETA)}
  plot(seq(from=1, to=Maxgen), N.t, xlab = 'Generation, t', ylab
='N(t)', type='l')
# Plot N(t+1) on N(t)
  MaxN  <- 10000;     N.t  <- matrix(seq(from=1, to=MaxN))
  N.tplus1  <- N.t*apply(N.t, 1, RICKER.FUNCTION, ALPHA[j],BETA)
  plot(N.t, N.tplus1, xlab='N(t)', ylab='N(t+1)', type='l')
  lines(N.t, N.t)
  } # End of j loop
```

equality sign are replaced by fertility and/or survival terms. Thus if fertility in the previously described Leslie matrix is modified by a Ricker density dependent function that affects all ages we have

$$A_t = \begin{pmatrix} 0.8\alpha e^{-\beta N_t} & 1.2\alpha e^{-\beta N_t} & 1.0\alpha e^{-\beta N_t} & 0\alpha e^{-\beta N_t} \\ 0.8 & 0 & 0 & 0 \\ 0 & 0.4 & 0 & 0 \\ 0 & 0 & 0.25 & 0 \end{pmatrix} \tag{3.10}$$

where N_t may be the total population size or some particular set of ages (see example below). How one introduces the density-dependent function is determined by the biological assumptions. Similarly, the particular density-dependent function is a function of the particular biological scenario envisaged. If one wishes to do a general analysis, both functions, with a range of parameter values, should be tried. Another suggested density-dependent function is the Usher function:

$$\frac{1}{1 + e^{aN+b}} \tag{3.11}$$

which produces a sigmoidal growth curve. Benton and Grant (1999) modified this function to produce a gradual or sudden onset of density-dependence:

$$\frac{1}{1 + e^{1.25bN}} - 50,000b \quad \text{gradual onset}$$

$$\frac{1}{1 + e^{12.5bN}} - 500,000b \quad \text{sudden onset} \tag{3.12}$$

where $b = 2 \times 10^{-5}$. None of the above equations are sacrosanct and in the absence of detailed information any function that produces a density-dependent effect might be tried. In general, the Beverton–Holt and Ricker functions do cover a wide range of behaviors and are reasonable functions to use.

A simple example of a stage structured model that includes density-dependence is that for *Tribolium spp.* proposed by Dennis et al. (1995) and further analyzed by Grant and Benton (2003). The life cycle of the beetle is divided into three stages, larval, pupal, and adult with transitions between stages governed by the following assumptions:

1. The number of larvae at time $t + 1$, L_{t+1} is determined by the number of adults at time t, A_t, the rate at which eggs are cannibalized by adults, $c_{A.eggs}$, and the rate of cannibalization by the larvae, $c_{L.eggs}$. These effects can be modeled by a Ricker function.

$$L_{t+1} = bA_t e^{-(c_{A.eggs}A_t + c_{L.eggs}L_t)} \tag{3.13}$$

where b is a constant.

2. The number of pupae that survive to time $t + 1$ is

$$P_{t+1} = L_t S_L \tag{3.14}$$

where S_L is the survival probability of non-cannibalized larvae.

3. The number of adults is a function of the number of pupae that are cannibalized by the adults (a Ricker function) and the survival of adults (S_A):

$$A_{t+1} = P_t e^{-c_{A.pupae}A_t} + A_t S_A \tag{3.15}$$

These three equations can be written in matrix form as

$$\begin{pmatrix} L_{t+1} \\ P_{t+1} \\ A_{t+1} \end{pmatrix} = \begin{pmatrix} 0 & 0 & be^{-(c_{A.eggs}A_t + c_{L.eggs}L_t)} \\ S_L & 0 & 0 \\ 0 & e^{-c_{A.pupae}A_t} & S_A \end{pmatrix} \begin{pmatrix} L_t \\ P_t \\ A_t \end{pmatrix} \tag{3.16}$$

3.1.5 Estimating fitness

If density-dependence is not a function of the trait of interest and the population is stable then an appropriate measure of fitness is R_0, which will generally be much easier to evaluate than using an invasibility approach (see Scenario 2). The operational definition of fitness for invasibility analysis is the ability of a novel clone (the invader) to invade a resident population. However, this does mean that the invader will replace the resident population as it could coexist with the resident. The fitness of the invader is the long-term growth rate of the invader population, which can be equated to the dominant Lyapunov exponent of the matrix. In most cases relevant to this book this exponent, also called the invasion exponent, has to be estimated by simulation. Two approaches for determining the equilibrium set of trait variables are pairwise invasibility analysis and multiple invasibility analysis.

3.1.6 Pairwise invasibility analysis

This is a graphical method that identifies putative Evolutionarily Stable Strategies (ESS) on a surface comprising the set of combinations of resident and invader trait values. There are four possible outcomes, diagrammed in Figures 3.3 and 3.4. The x-axis is the set of trait values for the resident and the y-axis is the same set of trait values representing the trait values of the invader. For each combination we estimate the long-term growth rate of the invader. The hypothetical long-term growth rate of the invader in the stationary resident population is given by the dominant Lyapunov exponent, called by Rand et al. (1994) the invasion exponent, ϑ:

$$\vartheta = \lim_{t \to \infty} \frac{1}{t} \ln \frac{N_t}{N_0} \tag{3.17}$$

Because of the small population size of the invader population, the invasion exponent can be estimated by assuming that the invader population will either increase or decrease exponentially (at least measured over a sufficient time period):

$$N_{t+1} = N_0 e^{r_{\text{invader}} t} = N_0 \lambda_{\text{invader}}^t$$
$$\ln N_{t+1} = \ln N_0 + t \; \ln \lambda_{\text{invader}} \tag{3.18}$$

Thus after some specified number of iterations the growth rate of the invader population, ϑ, can be estimated from a linear regression of log(invader population size) on generation.

Two contour lines are shown on the invasibility plots of Figure 3.3. Both lines denote the set of combinations at which the growth rate of the invader is zero. Obviously when the parameter value of the invader is the same as that of the resident then the invader will neither increase nor decrease: this is the $x = y$ line shown in the plots. Now consider a trait combination that lies very close to the origin but above the line of equality: at this point the growth rate of the invader is positive and it increases in frequency and eventually becomes the resident population. For a combination that lies in the upper right of the plots the growth rate of the invader is negative and it cannot penetrate the resident population. Thus at some combinations other than $x = y$ the growth rate of the invader must equal that of the resident population. The point at which this second zero isocline crosses the line of equality is the putative ESS. Several such points could exist or there could be zero isoclines that do not intersect the line of equality (e.g., see White et al. [2006]). Whether the putative ESS is a stable ESS (termed a **convergence stable ESS**) or an unstable equilibrium depends on the shape of the second zero isocline: if the slope of the second isocline is greater than 90° as measured in relation to the x and y-axes (see top plots in Figure 3.3) the intersection is an ESS, otherwise the equilibrium is unstable and subject to invasion (bottom panels of Figure 3.3). The plot on the left of Figure 3.3 shows a case in which the putative ESS is a convergence stable ESS, while that on the right shows a case in which the intersection defines an unstable equilibrium termed an **evolutionary branching**

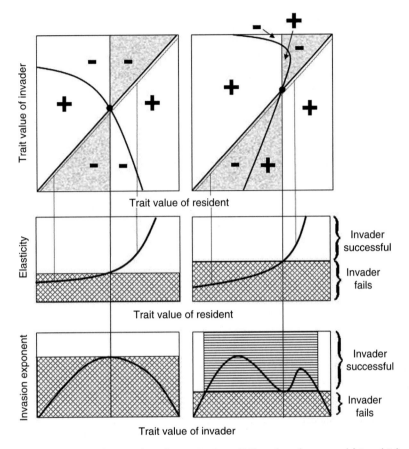

Trait value of resident

Trait value of resident

Trait value of invader

Invader successful

Invader fails

Invader successful

Invader fails

Figure 3.3 Hypothetical examples of pairwise invasibility plots (top panels) in which there is convergence but not necessarily an ESS. The panels on the left show a convergence stable ESS and those on the right show an evolutionary branching point. A "+" denotes a positive long-term growth rate of the invader population (i.e., invasion successful) and a "−" indicates a negative long-term growth rate (i.e., invasion unsuccessful). The dotted lines paralleling the x = y line indicate the values used in the elasticity analysis and the vertical dotted lines show examples of the elasticity values obtained at those points. The shaded areas indicate the zones that are relevant for plotting the invasion exponent of the invader against the putative ESS value of the resident as shown in the bottom panels. Panels below the first row show the elasticity analyses. In the middle panels the trait value of the invader is set at some fraction slightly smaller than 1 (e.g., 0.995) of the trait value of the resident. This analysis is used to determine the putative ESS value. In the bottom panels the trait value of the resident is set at the putative ESS. This analysis determines if the putative ESS value is resistant to invasion. The cross-hatched areas indicate those resident–invader combinations which lead to extinction of the invader. The horizontal hatched areas indicate trait values for which invasion occurs when the resident population is at its putative ESS. In the left-hand column there are no values for which invasion is successful when the resident population is at the putative ESS, whereas in the right-hand plot there are values for which invasion is successful.

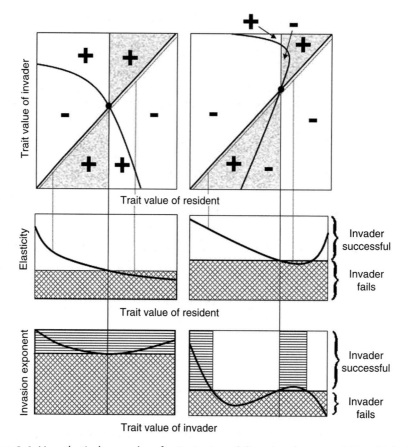

Figure 3.4 Hypothetical examples of pairwise invasibility plots (top panels) in which there is neither convergence nor a stable ESS. The panels on the right show an invasible repellor and those on the left show a Garden-of-Eden ESS. A "+" denotes a positive long-term growth rate of the invader population (i.e., invasion successful) and a "–" indicates a negative long-term growth rate (i.e., invasion unsuccessful). The dotted lines paralleling the x = y line indicate the values used in the elasticity analysis and the vertical dotted lines show examples of the elasticity values obtained at those points. The shaded areas indicate the zones that are relevant for plotting the invasion exponent of the invader against the putative ESS value of the resident as shown in the bottom panels. Panels below the first row show the elasticity analyses. In the middle panels the trait value of the invader is set at some fraction slightly smaller than 1 (e.g., 0.995) of the trait value of the resident. This analysis is used to determine the putative ESS value. In the bottom panels the trait value of the resident is set at the putative ESS. This analysis determines if the putative ESS value is resistant to invasion. The cross-hatched areas indicate those resident-invader combinations which lead to extinction of the invader. The horizontal hatched areas indicate trait values for which invasion is indicated by both the analysis of elasticity with respect to the trait value of the resident (middle panels) and with respect to the trait value of the invader (bottom panels). In both cases there are combinations from both the elasticity and invasion exponent plots for which invasion is successful.

point. In theory the ESS is not resistant to mutants and polymorphisms will occur (however, see Scenario 5 of Chapter 4, in which the "unstable" ESS of Scenario 3 of this chapter is stable when parameters are inherited according to a quantitative genetic model). The plot of elasticity versus the trait value of the resident shows that there is convergence but the invasion exponent plotted against the trait value of the invader shows that invasion is possible in the rightmost scenario. There are two other possible pairwise invasibility plots, obtained if the areas defining the positive and negative growth of the invader are reversed (Figure 3.4). In both cases the elasticity plotted against the trait value of the resident shows that there is no convergence and the invasion exponent versus the trait value of the invader shows that invasion is possible in both scenarios. The scenario on the left is termed an **invasibility repellor** and that on the right a **Garden-of-Eden ESS**.

Suppose the trait under study, say X, can reasonably range from X_{min} to X_{max}. To produce a pairwise invasibility plot we proceed as follows:

Step 1: Divide X_{min} to X_{max}. into N_{inc} increments. This set of values will be applied to residents and invaders: for example, in R

```
X.Resident <- seq(from=X.min, to=X.max, length=N.inc)
X.Invader <- X.residents
```

Step 2: Create the set of all combinations for resident and invader types. This can be done using the R function `expand.grid`

```
Combinations <- expand.grid(X.Resident, X.Invader)
```

Step 3: For each combination calculate the population growth rate of the invader entering a resident population. If this growth rate is positive then the invader trait value has a higher fitness than the resident trait value. The calculation of the invader growth rate will typically be estimated by calling some function, say `POP.DYNAMICS` that has the following elements in sequence:

a. The call to function `POP.DYNAMICS` passes the parameter value, in this case `ALPHA`, and the multiplier for the invader parameter value, in this case called `Coeff`. These two parameters could be passed as a vector of length 2 or, as done below, as separate elements.

```
POP.DYNAMICS   <- function(ALPHA, Coeff)
ALPHA.resident    <- ALPHA            # Alpha for resident
ALPHA.invader   <- ALPHA*Coeff        # Alpha for invader
```

b. Iteration of population growth of the resident population alone until it has passed any effects due to initial starting conditions (this does not necessarily mean that the population will be at equilibrium as it might exhibit cyclical or chaotic behavior or subject to environmental fluctuations). For example, suppose we run the resident-only time trace for 50 generations and the time trace after the invader is introduced for 300 generations. To hold the entire trace, which we might wish to do for later plotting, we need a matrix of 350 rows.

```
Maxgen1      <- 50    # Generations when only resident present
Maxgen2      <- 300   # Generations after invader introduced
Tot.Gen <- Maxgen1+Maxgen2 # Total number of generations
N.resident <- N.invader <- matrix(0,Tot.Gen)    # Allocate space
N.resident[1]    <- 1             # Initial number of resident
N.invader[Maxgen1] <- 1           # Initial number of invader
for (Igen in 2:Maxgen1)           # Iterate over only resident
{
  N <- N.resident[Igen-1]          # For typing convenience
  N.resident[Igen] <- DD.FUNCTION (ALPHA.resident, N, N)
} # End of resident only period
```

The density-dependent function, DD.FUNCTION, takes the parameter value, the population size of the focal type (resident or invader), and the total population size. In the present case these are the same. An example of the density dependent function, which is that used in Scenario 3, is

```
DD.FUNCTION <- function(ALPHA,N1,N2)    # Density-dependence
                                                function
{
  BETA         <- ALPHA*0.001               # Set value of beta
  N   <- N1*ALPHA*exp(-BETA*N2)      # New population size
  return(N)
}   # End  of  DD.FUNCTION
```

c. Introduction of a single invader into the resident population, which should be large so that the initial population size of the invader has no significant effect on the density-dependent effect. Note that now the call to the density-dependent function passes the total population size as the third element. Although the number of invaders should be sufficiently small that they contribute insignificantly to the density-dependence I prefer to include their number in the total population size as it seems more biologically realistic.

```
# Now  add  invader
  J  <-  Maxgen1+1         # Starting generation of this period
  for (Igen  in  J:Tot.Gen) # Iterate after introduction of invader
{
  N.tot <-  N.resident[Igen-1]+ N.invader[Igen-1] # Total
                                                popn size
  N.resident[Igen] <- DD.FUNCTION(ALPHA.resident, N.resident
[Igen-1], N.tot)
  N.invader[Igen] <- DD.FUNCTION(ALPHA.invader, N.invader
[Igen-1], N.tot)
} # End of invasion period
```

d. As noted above the hypothetical long-term growth rate of the invader in the stationary resident population is estimated by the slope of a linear regression of log (invader population size) on generation. Because of initial fluctuations in the invader population due to initial population composition, it may be necessary to ignore the first few generations (in the example coding below I ignore the first 10 generations). The number of generations that the model must be run to get an accurate estimate of the growth of the invader population will depend on the dynamics of the population – if there are fluctuations due to intrinsic population properties (e.g., a Ricker function) or environmental factors the number of generations may be large (e.g., 500) whereas if the model shows little fluctuation only 50 generations might be required. The appropriate number can be assessed by trial and error: lack of smoothness in the curves constructed from the simulated data will generally indicate an insufficient number of generations.

```
  Generation   <- seq(from=1, to=Tot.Gen) # Generation sequence
  N0    <- 10 + Maxgen1         # Starting point for regression
# Regression model
  Invasion.model <- lm(log(N.invader[N0:Tot.Gen]) ~ Generation
  [N0:Tot.Gen])
  Elasticity     <- Invasion.model$coeff[2] # Elasticity
  return(Elasticity)
} # End of POP.DYNAMICS function
```

e. The function passes the estimated growth rate of the invader to the main program. The growth rate of the invader is estimated for all combinations and the result converted into matrix form from which a contour plot can be constructed

```
  z              <- apply(Combinations,1,POP.DYNAMICS)
  z.matrix  <- matrix(z, N.inc, N.inc)    # Convert to a matrix
# Plot contours
  contour(X.Resident, X.Invader, z.matrix, xlab="Resident",
ylab="Invader")
```

Step 4: If there is an ESS there will be at least two relevant zero isoclines. The first is the line described by the equation X.Resident = X.Invader (obviously if the invader trait equals the resident trait it has the same fitness as the resident). Suppose there is a single ESS, this implies that there must be a second zero isocline that intersects the first (Figure 3.3). The two zero isoclines divide the plane into four quadrats as shown in Figure 3.3, where the shape of the second zero isocline will depend upon the details of the model.

Step 5: The putative ESS value can be read off the graph and its stability gauged from the isocline shapes.

While the above approach may demonstrate the existence of an equilibrium point it does not provide a ready means of determining the trait value. One way to examine the stability of the point and to numerically obtain its value is the elasticity approach of Grant (1997).

3.1.7 Elasticity analysis

To understand the mechanics of this method we need only consider how to estimate the putative ESS from the pairwise invasibility plot. Suppose we start at X_{min} for the resident population and set the trait value of the invader at some value slightly below that of the resident population (dotted lines in Figures 3.3 and 3.4) say 0.995 X_{min}, which is the value suggested by Benton and Grant (1999). At this point the growth rate of the invader population is negative and the invader cannot invade. We now sequentially advance the value of the resident trait value, increasing that of the invader by the same proportion of the resident value as before (the dotted lines shown in Figures 3.3 and 3.4). When the resident trait value exceeds the putative ESS value the sign of the invader growth rate changes we have passed the putative ESS point and we have fixed the ESS value within the limits set by the increments by which we increased the invader trait value (middle panels in Figures 3.3 and 3.4)

The growth rate of the invader population in the above situation is called the elasticity (see Chapter 1) of the invasion exponent to a change in the resident trait value. Provided that the elasticity is a monotonic function of the trait value, as shown in Figure 3.3, the point at which the elasticity is zero, which is the ESS value, can be found using a numerical search routine such as uniroot.

```
Optimum <- uniroot(POP.DYNAMICS, interval=c(X.min,X.max),0.995)
Best.E <- Optimum$root   # Store the optimum reproductive effort
print(Best.E)            # Print optimum E
```

As always it is good practice to use a graphical analysis to confirm the above answer:

```
# Create plot of elasticity versus E
  N.int     <- 30         # Nos of increments
# Create sequence of X from X.min to X.max in N.int increments
      X    <- matrix(seq(from=X.min, to=X.max, length=N.int),
N.int,1)
  # Create vector of elasticities using apply function
     Elasticity   <- apply(X, 1, POP.DYNAMICS, 0.995)
     plot(E, Elasticity, type='l') # Plot elasticity vs E
     lines(c(X.min,X.max), c(0,0)) # Add horizontal line at zero
```

As a final check we plot the invasion exponent of the invader (ϑ = long-term growth rate) relative to a resident population with the predicted optimum trait value. The sign of this is indicated by the shaded areas in Figures 3.3 and 3.4. If, as in the left-hand example shown in Figure 3.3, the predicted value is the ESS then all ϑ not equal to the ESS value should be negative and ϑ =0 at the ESS value. If the putative ESS is not resistant to invasion, as in the right-hand example of Figure 3.3

and the plots in Figure 3.4, the invasion exponent will not be negative for all values other than the putative ESS value (Figures 3.3, 3.4 and Scenario 6).

R CODE:

```
# Now plot Invasion exponent when resident is optimal
  Coeff              <- E/Best.E       # Coeff of invader DD function
  Invasion.exponent <- matrix(0,N.int,1) # pre-allocate space
# Iterate and calculate invasion exponent
# Note that a loop is used rather than apply because it is coefficient
  that is changing
  for (i in 1:N.int){ Invasion.exponent[i] <- POP.DYNAMICS
(Best.E, Coeff[i])
}
  plot(E, Invasion.exponent, ylab ='Invasion exponent', type='l')
  points(Best.E,0, cex=2) # Plot point at previously estimated
optimum E
```

In the scenarios that follow I have commenced the analysis by producing graphical output using pairwise invasibility analysis, but have placed on the graph the combination subsequently found with elasticity analysis.

3.1.8 Multiple invasibility analysis

An alternative approach that has been adopted is to introduce mutant clones at each generation into the population. This approach potentially permits the accumulation of multiple types in a population and thus demonstrates the existence of polymorphic populations but has the disadvantage that it is extremely computer intensive. The general approach is as follows:

1. We need to follow the sizes of cohorts with particular parameter values. There are two ways in which this can be accomplished. The first and simplest way is to turn the range of the parameter value into discrete units, for example, suppose the parameter, X, can vary from 2 to 15. This range can be divided into some specified number of intervals, say 50:

```
X <- sequence(from=2, to=15, length=50)
```

The number of individuals in each class can be placed in a separate vector, or the two can be combined into a single matrix with the class values in the first column and the numbers in the second. Suppose we commence with a single individual in the middle of the range (more or less)

```
Data      <- matrix(0, 50, 2)                   # Allocate apace
Data[,1] <- sequence(from=2, to=15, length=50) # Set X values
Data[25,2] <- 1                                 # Initial population
```

An alternate method is to generate types and follow them through time. The advantage of this alternate approach is that it permits the population to move to its ESS exactly. The disadvantage of this method is that it complicates the bookkeeping and it may be necessary at specified intervals to purge types that are in low numbers or the number of types to be kept track of will become exorbitant. This problem can be resolved in the former method by increasing the number of divisions though this will, of course, increase computational time. Because the only difference is one of bookkeeping I shall use only the former approach.

2. A density-dependent function must be specified. As an example, suppose that population size is determined by a Ricker function,

$$N_{t+1} = \alpha N_t e^{-\beta N_{\text{total}}} \tag{3.19}$$

in which there is a trade-off between the density-independent component α and the density dependent component β. This trade-off is actually specified by a positive relationship such as $\beta = 0.001\alpha$, which is used in Scenario 3. Coding for this function is as follows:

```
DD.FUNCTION<- function (X, N.total)  # Density-dependence function
{
# Set parameter values
    ALPHA <- X[1]                       # Set alpha
    N    <- X[2]                         # Population size for this
                                         alpha
    BETA <- ALPHA*0.001                  # Set value of beta
    N <- N*ALPHA*exp(-BETA*N.total)      # New cohort size
    return(N)
} # End of function
```

3. New cohort sizes are generated by using the R function `apply`, providing it with the density-dependent function, `DD.FUNCTION`:

```
N.total   <- sum(Data[,2])                      # Total population
                                                 size
Data[,2] <- apply(Data,1,DD.FUNCTION, N.total) # New population
                                                 sizes
```

4. The above is enclosed within a loop that iterates over generations. After each generation new types are introduced at a low frequency. These are generally referred to as "mutations" but this assumes a biological scenario that can be misleading. The object of the analysis is to examine the placement of the optimal trait value, should it exist, and its stability. As written, the model assumes a clonal structure, which may apply to some organisms but generally not to the ones for which the analysis is supposed

to apply. The assumption is that the results will apply in general to both clonal and sexual organisms. A comparison of Scenario 6 in this chapter with Scenario 5 of the next chapter, in which the same scenario is examined using a quantitative genetic perspective scenario, suggests that this assumption may, in some instances, be erroneous. Given this, I believe that it is better to regard the analysis not as a biological scenario but simply as a mathematical means of judging potential evolutionary history in the sense of movement to a single ESS, maintenance of polymorphisms or the existence of multiple equilibria. In the two examples presented in the subsequent scenarios I assume that a new type is introduced into the population at each generation: should this be judged too liberal, it is easy to alter the coding to make the introduction of a new type a probabilistic event (e.g., the type of "mutation" could be depend on the frequency of types already present in the population). Based on the assumption that a new type appears at each generation and is a random draw from all the possible types (this could also be changed such that the frequency distribution is, say, normal rather than uniform), coding is

```
for (Igen in 1:Maxgen)
{
  N.total   <- sum(Data[,2])                    # Total population size
  Data[,2]  <- apply(Data,1,DD.FUNCTION, N.total)   # New cohort
# Keep track of population size, mean trait value and SD of trait value
  Stats[Igen,2] <- sum(Data[,1]*Data[,2])/sum(Data[,2]) # Mean
  S             <- sum(Data[,2])                  # Popn size
  Stats[Igen,1] <- S                              # Popn size
  SX1           <- sum(Data[,1]^2*Data[,2])
  SX2           <- (sum(Data[,1]*Data[,2]))^2/S
  Stats[Igen,3] <- sqrt((SX1-SX2)/(S-1))          # SD of trait
# Introduce a mutant by picking a random integer between 1 and 50
  Mutant        <- ceiling(runif(1, min=0, max=50))
  Data[Mutant,2] <- Data[Mutant,2]+1              # Add mutant to class
} # End of Igen loop
```

In the above coding the program keeps track of the total population size, `Stats[Igen,1]`, the mean trait value, `Stats[Igen,2]`, and its standard deviation, `Stats[Igen,3]`. If there is a unique equilibrium the mean value should asymptote to this value and the standard deviation should equilibrate at a value determined by the difference between adjacent bins of the trait value (i.e., `Data[,1]`). If there are multiple equilibria the mean should fluctuate and the standard deviation should not reach a small limiting value. A plot of trait value class on population size (called a frequency polygon) is useful to provide a visual indication of the spread of the trait values.

Multiple invasibility analyses are given in Scenario 3, where there is a unique equilibrium and in Scenario 6, where the trait value fluctuates wildly.

3.2   Summary of scenarios

Scenario 1: Illustrates the use of the Leslie matrix to solve Scenario 5 of Chapter 2, in which there is no density-dependence and the population achieves a stable age distribution.

Scenario 2: Takes Scenario 1 and adds density-dependence that is independent of body size, which changes the fitness measure and thus the optimum body size.

Scenario 3: Considers a model in which population dynamics is governed by the Ricker function with a dependency between the components of the Ricker function.

Scenario 4: Gives another example of an age-structured model with density-dependence affecting the trait of interest. In this case the trait under study is the optimal reproductive effort.

Scenario 5: A stage-structured model in which the immature stage may delay moving into the adult stage. Depending on the proportion delaying maturity, the density dependent function can induce cyclical population dynamics which greatly affects the required number of generations that must be followed in the elasticity analysis.

Scenario 6: A model demonstrating the coexistence of multiple types in a population.

3.3   Scenario 1: Comparing approaches

To Illustrate and compare the approach used in Chapter 2 with that using a matrix modeling approach I shall use the example given in Scenario 5 of Chapter 2, with the change that a discrete time model rather than an integral model is used.

3.3.1   General assumptions

1. The organism is iteroparous.
2. Fecundity, F, increases with body size, x, which does not change after maturity (e.g., as in insect).
3. Survival, S, decreases with body size, x.
4. Fitness, W, is a function of fecundity and survival.

3.3.2   Mathematical assumptions

1. Maturity occurs at age 1 after which no further growth occurs.

2. Fecundity increases linearly with size at maturity, resulting in fecundity being a uniform function of age:

$$F_t = a_F + b_F x \tag{3.20}$$

3. The instantaneous rate of mortality increases linearly with the body size attained at age 1 and is constant per time unit. Under this assumption, survival to age t is given by

$$S_t = e^{-(a_s + b_s x)t} \tag{3.21}$$

4. Taking r to be the measure of fitness, the fitness function is given by the solution of the characteristic equation

$$\sum_{t=1}^{\infty} e^{-rt}(a_F + b_F x)e^{-(a_s + b_s x)t} = 1 \tag{3.22}$$

where the initial value of the summation is set at 1, as this is the age of first reproduction.

3.3.3   Solving using the methods of Chapter 2

The two exponents can be absorbed into a single term, giving

$$\sum_{t=1}^{\infty} (a_F + b_F x)e^{-(a_s + b_s x + r)t} = 1 \tag{3.23}$$

The above equation is a geometric series (see Section 2.5.2 for a discussion) and can be reduced to

$$\frac{(a_F + b_F x)e^{-(a_s + b_s x + r)}}{1 - e^{-(a_s + b_s x + r)}} = 1 \tag{3.24}$$

For convenience in the following derivation let $A = a_F + b_F x$ and $B = a_s + b_s x$ giving

$$
\begin{aligned}
\frac{Ae^{-(B+r)}}{1 - e^{-(B+r)}} &= 1 \\
Ae^{-(B+r)} &= 1 - e^{-(B+r)} \\
e^{-(B+r)}(A + 1) &= 1 \\
-(B + r) + \log_e(A + 1) &= 0 \\
r &= \log_e(A + 1) - B \\
&= \log_e(a_F + b_F x + 1) - (a_s + b_s x)
\end{aligned}
\tag{3.25}
$$

Thus we have an explicit expression for r as a function x (body size). Following the recipes given in Chapter 2 (e.g., Scenario 3, Section 2.5.2) the optimal body size is readily found. We define a function RCALC to calculate r using equation (3.25) and the call the R function optimize to locate the value of x at which fitness (r) is maximized:

```
rm(list=ls())                          # Clear workspace
RCALC <- function(x)                   # Function to calculate r
Af <-0; Bf<-16; As<-1; Bs<-0.5         # parameter values
r <- log(Af+Bf*x+1)-(As+Bs*x)          # r
return(r)                              # return value
}
# Call optimize to find best x
  optimize(f=RCALC,interval= c(0.1,3), maximum=TRUE)$maximum
```

OUTPUT:

`[1] 1.937494`

If the fitness equation (3.22) cannot be resolved into a simple function of r it may be necessary to locate r by numerical means as done in Section 2.3.5. Note that this requires that we use a finite sum. Because of the rapid decline in survival with age only about 10 age classes are necessary: however, it is advisable to try several values to ensure that the result is not altered. Here I use 50, which gives essentially the same as answer as 10. Plotting r versus x (not shown) indicates that the optimum x lies between 1 and 3. This interval is passed to `optimize`.

```
rm(list=ls())                          # Clear workspace
# Define function to sum characteristic eqn given r and x
  SUMMATION <- function(r,x)
{
  Maxage <- 50                         # Maximum age
  age     <- seq( from=1, to=Maxage)       # Vector of ages
  Af      <- 0; Bf <- 16; As <- 1 ; Bs <- 0.5 # Parameter values
  m <- rep(Af+Bf*x, times= Maxage)     # number of female offspring
  l <- exp(-(As+Bs*x)*age)             # Survival to age
  Sum     <- sum(exp(-r*age)*l*m)          # Characteristic eqn sum
  return(1-Sum)                        # Subtract 1 and return
}
# Define function to find r given x
  RCALC <- function(x){uniroot(SUMMATION, interval=c(-1,2),x)
$root}
# Calculate the best x by calling optimize, which calls RCALC
  optimize(f=RCALC,interval= c(0.1,3), maximum=TRUE)
```

OUTPUT:

`[1] 1.937458`

The result matches to three decimal places that obtained using the exact equation.

3.3.4   Solving using the eigenvalue of the Leslie matrix

The first task is to convert the life table specified by the model into a Leslie matrix. The coding is contained within the function RCALC which passes back the estimates r, calculated as the log of the first eigenvalue. This function is called by the R function `optimize`. Important points to note are

1. The age-specific survival (i.e., survival from age t to $t + 1$), $S(t)$ is given by $l(t + 1)/l(t)$, except for the last age which must be zero.

2. The top row of the Leslie matrix is not m but $m(t)S(t)$, often referred to as the fertility.

3. To create the Leslie matrix we first create a matrix that is one row and one column smaller than required and use the R function `diag` to assign the survivals. This matrix is then inserted into the required spaces of the Leslie matrix. An alternate method using a loop is also shown in the coding below.

4. The value of r is obtained by taking the log of λ. For reasons that are not clear if `log(Lambda)` is returned the R function `optimize` gives the following error message:

```
Error in optimize(RCALC, interval = c(1, 3), maximum = TRUE):
invalid function value in 'optimize'
```

However, `abs(log(Lambda))` does not produce this error, even though all values of `log(lambda)` are already positive (the same error message is generated if `Lambda` alone is returned.

5. As suggested in Chapter 2, the relationship of r to body size is plotted to check graphically that the optimum is more or less at the value given by `optimize`.

R CODE:

```
rm(list=ls())                              # Clear workspace
RCALC <- function(x) # Function to generate Lelsie matrix and
eigenvalue
{
Maxage <- 50                               # Maximum age
M       <- Maxage-   1                      # 1 less than the maximum
                                             age
age     <- seq( from=1, to=Maxage)          # vector of ages
Af      <- 0 ;Bf <- 16; As <-1 ; Bs <- 0.5  # Parameter values
m       <- rep(Af+Bf*x, times=Maxage)       # number of female
                                             offspring
l       <- exp(-(As+Bs*x)*age)              # Survival to age
S       <- matrix(0,Maxage,1)               # Pre-assign space for
                                             age-specific survival

S[1]   <- l[1]                              # Survival to age 1
# Calculate the survival from t to t+1
for ( i in 2:M) {S[i] <- l[i]/l[i-1]}
Fertility <- m*S                            # Top row of Leslie matrix
Dummy      <- matrix(0,M,M)                 # Create a temporary matrix
```

```
   diag(Dummy) <- S[1:M]                  # Assign survivals to diagonal
   Leslie.matrix <- matrix(0, Maxage, Maxage)  # Pre-assign space
   Leslie.matrix[1,] <- Fertility        # Add fertilities to top row
   Leslie.matrix[2:Maxage,1:M] <- Dummy  # Add dummy to appropriate
                                            space
# An alternate approach using a loop is shown below
#j <- 0; for (i in 2:Maxage){j <- j+1 ;Leslie.matrix[i,j] <- S
[i-1]}
   Eigen.data <- eigen(Leslie.matrix)     # Call eigen
   Lambda <- Eigen.data$values[1]         # Get first eigenvalue
   return(abs(log(Lambda)))               # Return r
}
   Optimum <- optimize(RCALC, interval= c(1,3), maximum=TRUE)
   Best.X <- Optimum$maximum                  # Optimum body size
   Best.r <- Optimum$objective                # Maximum r
# Print out results to 6 significant digits
   print(c('Best x = ', signif(Best.X, 6), 'Best r = ', signif
   (Best.r,6)))
   # Plot r.est vs x
   n      <- 50                                # Nos of increments
   x      <- matrix(seq(from=1, to=2.5, length=n))   # Values of x
   r.est  <- apply(x,1,RCALC)                  # Get values of r
   plot(x, r.est,xlab="Body size, x", ylab="r.est", type='l')
   points( Best.X, Best.r, cex=2) # Add point to graph at optimum
```

OUTPUT:
Figure not shown but same as Figure 2.5, except for added point at optimum.

```
[1] "Best x = "   "1.93751"   "Best r = " "1.49699"
```

which agrees, as expected, with the previous results. The matrix approach is somewhat simpler in its coding compared to the summation approach of the last section but not to that using the explicit function that relates r to x (equation (3.25)).

3.4 Scenario 2: Adding density-dependence

We continue with the previous model but add density-dependence and use pairwise invasibility and elasticity analyses to locate the optimum body size.

3.4.1 General assumptions

1. All assumptions given in Scenario 1 hold.
2. Population size is limited by density-dependence.

3.4.2 Mathematical assumptions

1. All assumptions given in Scenario 1 hold.
2. Population size is controlled by a Ricker density-dependent function:

$$F_t^* = F_t \alpha e^{-\beta N_t} \qquad (3.26)$$

where N_t is total population size, F_i is the density-independent component of fertility as defined by equation (3.20), and F_t^* is the density-dependent fertility.

3.4.3 Solving using R_0 as the fitness measure

Because the density-dependence does not directly affect the trait under consideration the appropriate measure of fitness is not r but R_0. The relevant equation is equation (3.24) rewritten as

$$\frac{(a_F + b_F x)e^{-(a_S + b_S x)}}{1 - e^{-(a_S + b_S x)}} = R_0 \qquad (3.27)$$

We can use the previous coding, modified for the change in function, to find the value of x that maximizes R_0 (alternatively, one could find x such that $\frac{dR_0}{dx} = 0$).

R CODE:

```
rm(list=ls())                    # Clear workspace
RCALC <- function(x)             # Function to calculate r
{
  Af <-0; Bf<-16; As<-1; Bs<-0.5  # parameter values
  A <- Af+Bf*x; B <- As+Bs*x      # For convenience
  R0 <- A*exp(-B)/(1-exp(-B))     # R0
  return(R0)                      # return value
}
# Call optimize to find best x
  optimize(f=RCALC,interval= c(0.1,3), maximum=TRUE)$maximum
```

OUTPUT:
[1] 1.682795

Although the density-dependence does not directly involve body size it changes the operational fitness measure and hence also the optimal body size. We now examine the approaches of invasibility and elasticity analyses.

3.4.4 Pairwise invasibility analysis

The program follows the pattern outlined in the introduction with minor changes. A general description of the functions follows:

1. `LESLIE <- function(x,Maxage)`: This is the same function as in the previous scenario and constructs the Leslie matrix from the relevant equations.

2. `DD.FUNCTION <- function(ALPHA, BETA, Fi, n) {Fi*ALPHA*exp (-BETA*n) }`: This passes the two density dependent parameters, the DI (density-independent) fertility coefficient and total population size, and passes back the new fertility as defined by equation (3.26). Parameter values are set at $\alpha = 1$, $\beta = 2 \times 10^{-5}$, which produces a stable equilibrium of 80782.

3. `POP.DYNAMICS <- function(X)`: X contains the body size of the resident and the body size of invader (this differs from the example in the introduction which passed the multiplier for the invader). The function calculates the growth rate of the invader. Unlike the example given in the introduction the trajectory of the resident-only population is not followed.

4. Main program: This follows the approach outlined in the introduction. The body size obtained from the elasticity analysis that follows is plotted onto the contour surface.

R CODE:

```
rm(list=ls()) # Clear workspace
LESLIE <- function(x,Maxage) # Function to generate Leslie matrix
{
  M      <- Maxage-1                   # 1 less than the maximum age
  age    <- seq( from=1, to=Maxage)        # vector of ages
  Af     <- 0 ;Bf <- 16; As <-1 ; Bs <- 0.5   # Parameter values
  m      <- rep(Af+Bf*x, times=Maxage) # number of female offspring
  l <- exp(-(As+Bs*x)*age)             # Survival to age
  S <- matrix(0,Maxage,1)        # Space for age-specific survival
  S[1] <- l[1]                         # Survival to age 1
# Calculate the survival from t to t+1
  for ( i in 2:M) {S[i] <- l[i]/l[i-1]}
  Fertility        <- m*S              # Top row of Leslie matrix
  Dummy            <- matrix(0,M,M) # Create a temporary matrix
  diag(Dummy)      <- S[1:M]            # Assign survivals to diagonal
  Leslie.matrix  <- matrix(0, Maxage, Maxage)  # Pre-assign space
  Leslie.matrix[1,] <- Fertility       # Add fertilities to top row
  Leslie.matrix[2:Maxage,1:M] <- Dummy    # Add dummy to appropriate
                                        space
  return(Leslie.matrix)
} # End of Leslie function
############## Density-dependence function ##############
  DD.FUNCTION    <-    function(ALPHA,BETA,Fi,n)    {Fi*ALPHA*exp
  (-BETA*n)}
##############Population dynamics function ##############
  POP.DYNAMICS <- function(X)
  {
  X.Resident <- X[1]    # Body size of resident population
  X.invader  <- X[2]    # Body size of invader
  ALPHA  <- 1 ; BETA <- 2*10^-5    # Density dependence parameters
  Maxage <- 50                     # Maximum age
```

```
   Resident.matrix <- LESLIE(X.Resident, Maxage) # Resident Leslie
                                                   matrix
   Invader.matrix  <- LESLIE(X.invader, Maxage) # Invader leslie
                                                   matrix
   F.resident <- Resident.matrix[1,]    # Resident DI fertility
   F.invader  <- Invader.matrix[1,]     # Invader DI fertility
   Maxgen     <- 30                      # Nos of gens to run
   n.resident <- matrix(0,Maxage,1) # Resident population vector
   n.resident[1] <- 1                   # Initial resident popn size
   for ( Igen in 2:Maxgen)              # Iterate over generations
{
  N <- sum(n.resident)                  # Total popn size
# Get DD fertility for resident population at time Igen
  Resident.matrix[1,] <- DD.FUNCTION(ALPHA, BETA, F.resident, N)
  n.resident  <- Resident.matrix%*%n.resident   # Resident popn
} # End of first Igen loop
### Introduce invader ####
  Maxgen <- 100                  # Number of generations to run
# Pre-allocate space for storage of invader population numbers
  Pop.invader     <- matrix(0,Maxgen,1)
# Pre-allocate space for invader vector
  n.invader       <- matrix(0,Maxage,1)
  n.invader[1]    <- 1                  # Initial number of invaders
  Pop.invader[1,1]  <- n.invader[1] # Store initial numbers of
                                         invaders
  for (Igen in 2:Maxgen)              # Iterate over generations
{
# Total number in population.
  N <- sum(n.resident) + sum(n.invader)
# DD fertility of resident
  Resident.matrix[1,] <- DD.FUNCTION(ALPHA, BETA, F.resident, N)
# New resident vector
  n.resident           <- Resident.matrix%*%n.resident
# DD fertility of invader
  Invader.matrix[1,] <- DD.FUNCTION(ALPHA, BETA, F.invader, N)
# New invader vector
  n.invader            <- Invader.matrix%*%n.invader
  Pop.invader[Igen]   <- sum(n.invader) # Store invader popn size
} # End of second Igen loop
# Now do linear regression of log(Pop.invader) on Generation
  Generation <- seq(from=1, to=Maxgen) # Generate generation vector
  Nstart      <- 20                      # Generations to ignore
# Linear regression
  Invasion.model <-
  lm(log(Pop.invader[Nstart:Maxgen])~Generation[Nstart:Maxgen])
```

```
# Elasticity value = regression slope
  Elasticity <- Invasion.model$coeff[2]
} # End of POP.DYNAMICS function
######################  MAIN PROGRAM  ######################
  N1             <- 30 # Nos of increments
  X.Resident  <- seq(from=1, to=3, length=N1) # Resident body sizes
  X.Invader   <- X.Resident                    # Invader body sizes
  d   <- expand.grid(X.Resident, X.Invader)   # Combinations
# Generate values at combinations
  z             <- apply(d,1,POP.DYNAMICS)
  z.matrix    <- matrix(z, N1, N1)           # Convert to a matrix
# Plot contours
contour(X.Resident,    X.Invader,z.matrix,    xlab="Resident",
ylab="Invader")
# Place circle at predicted optimal body size
  points(1.68703, 1.68703, cex=3)      # cex triples size of circle
```

OUTPUT: (Figure 3.5)

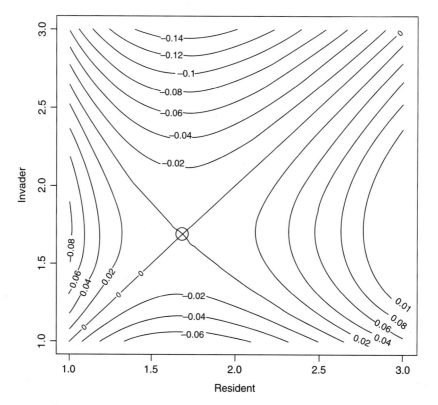

Figure 3.5 Pairwise invasibility plot for Scenario 2. The circle indicates the value obtained from the elasticity analysis.

There is a single putative ESS, which, as shown by the circle, is confirmed by the elasticity analysis described below.

3.4.5 Elasticity analysis

The program consists of the same components with the following changes

1. POP.DYNAMICS(X, Coeff): The body size of the resident and the multiplier for the invader is passed to POP.DYNAMICS. As suggested by Benton and Grant (1999), the value of the invader trait is set at 0.995 times that of the resident (Coeff = 0.995 in call to POP.DYNAMICS and hence X.invader = 0.995*X. resident). The change in population size of the invader population, Pop. invader is stored and after the specified number of generations (Maxgen) the elasticity is estimated as the slope of the linear regression of log(Pop. invader) on Generation. To avoid poor estimates due to the initial stabilization of the invader population the regression ignores the first 20 generations.

2. The optimum body size is that value at which elasticity is zero. This is estimated first by calling the R function uniroot and then visually checked by plotting elasticity versus body size and also the invasion exponent versus body size.

R CODE:

```
rm(list=ls())                 # Clear workspace
LESLIE <- function(x,Maxage)  # Function to generate Leslie
                                matrix
{
CODING SAME AS IN INVASIBILITY ANALYSIS
} # End of Leslie function
############## Density-dependence function ##############
DD.FUNCTION     <-  function(ALPHA,BETA,Fi,n)  {Fi*ALPHA*exp
(-BETA*n)}
##############Population dynamics function ##############
POP.DYNAMICS    <- function(X, Coeff)
{
X.Resident   <- X              # Body size of resident population
X.invader    <- X.Resident*Coeff      # Body size of invader
REST OF CODE SAME AS IN INVASIBILITY ANALYSIS
} # End of POP.DYNAMICS function
####################### MAIN PROGRAM ####################
par(mfrow=c(2,2))         # Divide graphics page into quarters
# Plot elasticity vs x
N.int <- 20                           # Number of increments
X <- matrix(seq(from=.5, to=3, length=N.int))   # Sequence of
                                body sizes
# Calculate elasticities for sequence
Elasticity <- apply(X,1,POP.DYNAMICS,0.995)
```

```
plot(X, Elasticity, type='l') # Plot elasticity as a function of X
lines(c(.5,3), c(0,0))        # Add horizontal line at zero
# Calculate the optimum by calling uniroot
Optimum <- uniroot(POP.DYNAMICS, interval=c(0.5,3),0.995)
Best.X  <- Optimum$root # Save optimum X
print(c("Optimum body size =",signif(Best.X,6))) # Print out value
# Now plot Invasion exponent when resident is optimal
# Note that because of order in call cannot use apply here
# Convert the X sequence to coefficients for call to POP.DYNAMICS
Coeff      <- X/Best.X
Invasion.exponent <- matrix(0,N.int,1) # Pre-allocate space
# Loop through values of X comparing to Best.X
for (i in 1:N.int){Invasion.exponent[i] <- POP.DYNAMICS(Best.X,
Coeff[i]) }
plot(X, Invasion.exponent, type='l')  # Plot invasion exponent vs x
points(Best.X, 0, cex=2)              # Plot point at predicted
                                        optimum
```

OUTPUT: (Figure 3.6)

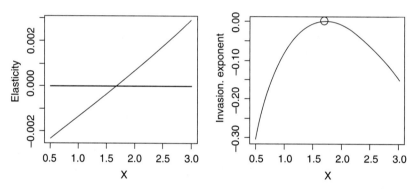

Figure 3.6 Graphical analysis of elasticity and invasion exponent as a function of body size as determined by an analysis of Scenario 2. The circle demarks the position of the predicted optimum.

[1] "Optimum body size =" "1.68703"

The results from uniroot indicate that the optimum under density-dependent regulation is smaller than in the density-independent case (Scenario 1). The plot of invasion exponent on body size confirms that the putative ESS is indeed an ESS.

3.5   Scenario 3: Functional dependence in the Ricker model

Ebenman et al. (1996) studied a stage-structured model in which selection favors stability, whereas oscillatory behavior is favored in the age-structure model studied by Greenman et al. (2005). In this model we consider how evolution will shape population dynamics by an analysis of the optimal parameter values in the Ricker model. No age or stage structure is assumed.

3.5.1 General assumptions

1. The organism is semelparous.
2. Recruitment is governed by a density-dependence function that allows for cyclical or chaotic population dynamics.
3. The parameters of the recruitment function are related such that the density-independent component is negatively related to the density-dependent component.

3.5.2 Mathematical assumptions

1. Population at time $t + 1$ is a Ricker function of the population at time t:

$$N_{t+1} = N_t \alpha e^{-\beta N_t} \tag{3.28}$$

2. The parameter α is a measure of density-independent recruitment whereas β is a measure of the density-dependent effect: increases in α increase recruitment but increases in β decrease recruitment by increasing the density-dependent component, $e^{-\beta N_t}$. Thus a positive functional relationship between α and β is indicative of a trade-off between the two recruitment components. For this scenario I shall assume the relationship

$$\beta = 0.001\alpha \tag{3.29}$$

Examples of the population dynamics for increasing values of α are shown in Figure 3.7. For low values of α the population reaches a stable equilibrium but as α is increased the dynamics first become cyclical and then chaotic.

3.5.3 Pairwise invasibility analysis

The coding follows the general pattern of that in Scenario 2, again plotting the value from the subsequent elasticity analysis on the contour plot. The DD.FUNC-TION passes back the new population size using equation (3.28).

R CODE:

```
rm(list=ls())                          # Clear memory
DD.FUNCTION <- function(ALPHA,N1,N2)   # Density-dependence
                                         function
{
  BETA <- ALPHA*0.001          # Set value of beta
  N <- N1*ALPHA*exp(-BETA*N2)  # New population size
  return(N)
} # End of DD.FUNCTION
```

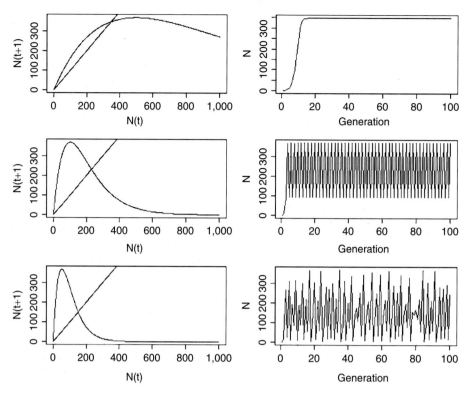

Figure 3.7 Population dynamics in the Ricker model in which $\beta = 0.001\alpha$. From top to bottom the values of α are 2, 10, and 20.

R CODING:

```
rm(list=ls())        # Clear workspace
par(mfrow=c(3,2))    # Divide graphics page into 3x2 panels
DD.FUNCTION  <- function(n,ALPHA, BETA)  {ALPHA*exp(-BETA*n)}
# main program
A   <- c(2,10,20)    # Values of alpha
for( j in 1:3)       # Iterate over values of alpha
{
 N.t       <- seq(from=0, to=1000)      # Population sizes
 ALPHA     <-A[j]                        # alpha
 BETA      <- ALPHA*0.001                # Beta
# Plot N(t+1) vs N(t)
 N            <- length(N.t)      # Nos of values of N(t)
 N.tplus1  <- matrix(0,N)         # Pre-allocate space for N(t+1)
 for ( i in 1:N)                  # Iterate over values of N
{
 N.tplus1[i]  <- N.t[i]*DD.FUNCTION(N.t[i],ALPHA,BETA)
}  # End of N(t+1) on N(t) calculation
 plot(N.t, N.tplus1, type='l', xlab='N(t)',ylab='N(t+1)')
 lines(N.t, N.t)                  # Plot the line of equality
# Plot N(t) vs t
 Maxgen      <- 100                       # Number of generations
 N           <- matrix(0, Maxgen)         # Pre-allocate space for N(t)
 N[1]        <- 1                         # Initial vale of N
 for   ( Igen in 2:Maxgen)                # Iterate over generations
{
 N[Igen]   <-  N[Igen-1]*DD.FUNCTION(N[Igen-1],ALPHA,BETA)
} # End of Igen loop
 Generation  <- seq(1,Maxgen)       # Vector of generation numbers
 plot(Generation, N, type='l')      # Plot population trajectory
} # End of j loop
```

```
#### Function specifying population dynamics ####
  POP.DYNAMICS <- function(ALPHA)
{
  ALPHA.resident <- ALPHA[1]        # Alpha for resident
  ALPHA.invader  <- ALPHA[2]        # Alpha for invader
  Maxgen1      <- 50                # Generations when only invader
                                      present
  Maxgen2      <- 300               # Generations after invader
                                      introduced
  Tot.Gen <- Maxgen1+Maxgen2        # Total number of generations
  N.resident <- N.invader <- matrix(0,Tot.Gen) # Allocate space
  N.resident[1]        <- 1         # Initial number of resident
  N.invader[Maxgen1]<- 1            # Initial number of invader
  for (Igen in 2:Maxgen1)           # Iterate over only resident
{
  N.resident[Igen]  <- DD.FUNCTION(ALPHA.resident, N.resident
[Igen-1],N.resident[Igen-1])
} # End of resident only period
# Now add invader
  J <- Maxgen1+1             # Staring generation of this period
  for (Igen in J:Tot.Gen)  # Iterate after introduction of invader
{
  N.total <- N.resident[Igen-1]+N.invader[Igen-1]   # Total popn
                                                        size
# Resident population size
  N.resident[Igen]  <- DD.FUNCTION(ALPHA.resident, N.resident
[Igen-1],N.total)
# Invader population size
  N.invader[Igen] <- DD.FUNCTION(ALPHA.invader, N.invader[Igen-
1],N.total)
} # End of invasion period
  Generation <- seq(from=1, to=Tot.Gen) # Generation sequence
  Nstart <- 10 + Maxgen1            # Starting point for regression
# Regression model
  Invasion.model  <- lm(log(N.invader[Nstart:Tot.Gen])˜ Genera-
tion[Nstart:Tot.Gen])
  Elasticity <- Invasion.model$coeff[2]    # Elasticity
return(Elasticity)
} # End of POP.DYNAMICS function
############ MAIN PROGRAM #############
  N1 <- 30 # Nos of increments
  A.Resident  <- seq(from=2, to= 4, length=N1) # Resident alpha
  A.Invader   <- A.Resident              # Invader alpha
```

```
  d        <- expand.grid(A.Resident, A.Invader)  # Combinations
# Generate values at combinations
  z        <- apply(d,1,POP.DYNAMICS)
  z. matrix <- matrix(z, N1, N1)                   # Convert to a matrix
# Plot contours
  contour(A.Resident, A.Invader,z.matrix, xlab="Resident",
  ylab="Invader")
# Place circle at predicted optimal body size
points(2.725109, 2.725109, cex=3)     # cex triples size of circle
```

OUTPUT: (Figure 3.8)

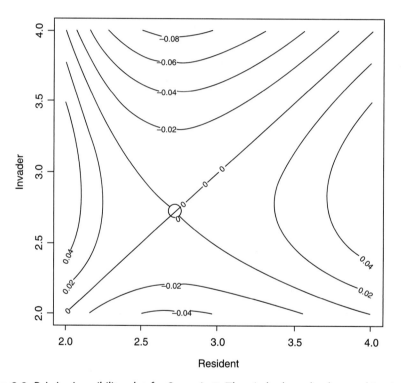

Figure 3.8 Paiwise invasibility plot for Scenario 3. The circle demarks the combination obtained from the elasticity analysis.

There is a single putative ESS which corresponds to the value obtained from the elasticity analysis described below.

3.5.4 Elasticity analysis

In addition to the two plots produced from the elasticity analysis two further plots are produced, $N(t+1)$ on $N(t)$ and $N(t)$ on t. These plots show the population dynamics as a function of the optimal value of α.

R CODE:

```
DD.FUNCTION  <-  function(ALPHA,N1,N2)  # Density-dependence
                                        function
{
BETA <- ALPHA*0.001              # Set value of beta
N <- N1*ALPHA*exp(-BETA*N2)      # New population size
return(N)
} # End of DD.FUNCTION
#### Function specifying population dynamics ####
POP.DYNAMICS <- function(ALPHA, Coeff)
{
ALPHA.resident <- ALPHA                 # Alpha for resident
ALPHA.invader <- ALPHA.resident*Coeff   # Alpha for invader
REST OF CODING SAME AS IN INVASIBILITY ANALYSIS
} # End of POP.DYNAMICS function
############## MAIN PROGRAM ##############
par(mfrow=c(2,2))             # Divide graphics page into quadrats
# Call uniroot to find optimum
minA        <-1; maxA <-10 # Limits for search
Optimum     <-    uniroot(POP.DYNAMICS,    interval=c(minA,
                                        maxA),0.995)
Best.Alpha  <- Optimum$root      # Store optimum Alpha
  print(Best.Alpha)              # Print out optimum
# Plot Elasticity vs alpha
N.int       <- 30 # Nos of intervals for plot
Alpha       <- matrix(seq(from=minA, to=maxA, length=N.int),
N.int,1)
Elasticity <- apply(Alpha,1,POP.DYNAMICS, 0.995) # Get elastici-
                                           ties
plot(Alpha, Elasticity, type='l')
lines(c(minA,maxA), c(0,0))   # Add horizontal line at zero
# Plot Invasion exponent when resident is optimal
Coeff <- Alpha/Best.Alpha      # Convert alpha to coefficient
Invasion.coeff <- matrix(0,N.int,1) # Allocate space
# Calculate invasion coefficient
for (i in 1:N.int){ Invasion.coeff[i] <- POP.DYNAMICS(Best.
                                Alpha, Coeff[i]) }
plot(Alpha, Invasion.coeff, type='l')   # Plot invasion coeff on
                                        alpha
points(Best.Alpha,0, cex=2)      # Plot optimum alpha on graph
# Plot N(t+1) on N(t) for optimum alpha
maxN      <- 1000                 # Number of N
N.t       <- seq(from=1, to=maxN) # Values of N(t)
```

```
 N.tplus1 <- matrix(0,maxN)          # Allocate space for N(t+1)
 for ( i in 1:maxN)                  # Iterate over values of N
{
 N.tplus1[i] <- DD.FUNCTION(Best.Alpha, N.t[i], N.t[i])
}    # End of i loop
 plot(N.t, N.tplus1, type='l', xlab='N(t)', ylab='N(t+1)')
# Plot N(t) on t
 N <- matrix(1,100) # Allocate space. Note reuse of N
 for (i in 2:100){N[i]<- DD.FUNCTION(Best.Alpha, N[i-1], N[i-1])}
 plot(seq(from=1, to=100), N, type='l', xlab='Generation',
ylab='Population')
```

OUTPUT: (Figure 3.9)

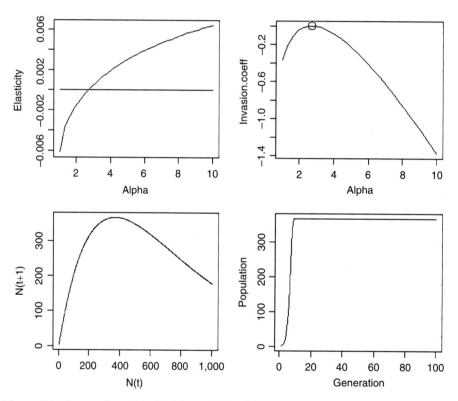

Figure 3.9 Output from the elasticity analysis of Scenario 3.

```
>  print(Best.Alpha) # Print out optimum
[1] 2.725107
```

At the optimal value of α the population reaches a stable equilibrium (Figure 3.9). Thus in this case selection favors stability.

3.5.5 Multiple invasibility analysis

The program follows the outline previously given and introduces a single random
mutant in each generation. The simulation is run for 5,000 generations.

R CODE:

```
 rm(list=ls())                            # Clear memory
  DD.FUNCTION<- function(X, N.total)      # Density-dependence
                                            function
{
# Set parameter values
  ALPHA    <- X[1]                  # Set alpha
  N        <- X[2]                  # Population size for this alpha
  BETA     <-  ALPHA*0.001     # Set value of beta
  N    <- N*ALPHA*exp(-BETA*N.total)      # New cohort size
  return(N)
} # End of function
############## MAIN PROGRAM ##############
  set.seed(10)               # Initialize the random number seed
  Maxgen  <- 5000            # Number of generations run
  Stats   <- matrix(0,Maxgen,3) # Allocate space for statistics
  MaxAlpha   <- 4            # maximum value of alpha
  Ninc       <- 50           # Number of classes for alpha
# Allocate space to store data for each generation
  Store      <- matrix(0,Maxgen, Ninc)
# Allocate space for alpha class and population size
  Data       <- matrix(0,Ninc,2)
  Data[24,2] <- 1    # Initial population size and alpha class
  ALPHA   <-  matrix(seq(from=2,  to=MaxAlpha,  length=Ninc),
Ninc,1) # Set Alpha
  Data[,1] <- ALPHA           # Place alpha in 1st column
  for (Igen in 1:Maxgen)      # Iterate over generations
{
  N.total   <- sum(Data[,2])             # Total population size
  Data[,2]  <- apply(Data,1,DD.FUNCTION, N.total)   # New cohort
  Store[Igen,]    <- Data[,2]   # Store values for this generation
# Keep track of population size, mean trait value and SD of trait
value
  Stats[Igen,2]   <- sum(Data[,1]*Data[,2])/sum(Data[,2])  # Mean
  S            <- sum(Data[,2])              # Population size
  Stats[Igen,1]   <- S                  # Population size
  SX1          <- sum(Data[,1]^2*Data[,2])
  SX2          <- (sum(Data[,1]*Data[,2]))^2/S
  Stats[Igen,3]   <- sqrt((SX1-SX2)/(S-1))  # SD of trait
```

```
# Introduce a mutant by picking a random integer between 1 and 50
  Mutant           <- ceiling(runif(1, min=0, max=50))
  Data[Mutant,2]   <- Data[Mutant,2]+1      # Add mutant to class
} # End of Igen loop
  par(mfrow=c(2,2))   # Split graphics page into quadrats
#   Plot last row of Store
  plot(ALPHA,     Store[Maxgen,],     type='l',     xlab='Alpha',
ylab='Number')
#   plot(Data.out[,1], Data.out[,2],
  Generation <- seq(from=1, to=Maxgen)
  N0           <- 1
  plot(Generation[N0:Maxgen],    Stats[N0:Maxgen,1],    ylab='Pop-
ulation size', type='l')
  plot(Generation[N0:Maxgen],   Stats[N0:Maxgen,2],   ylab='Mean',
type='l')
  plot(Generation[N0:Maxgen],   Stats[N0:Maxgen,3],   ylab='SD',
type='l')
  print(c('Mean alpha in last gen = ',Stats[Maxgen,2]))
  print(c('SD of alpha in last gen = ',Stats[Maxgen,3]))
```

OUTPUT: (Figure 3.10)

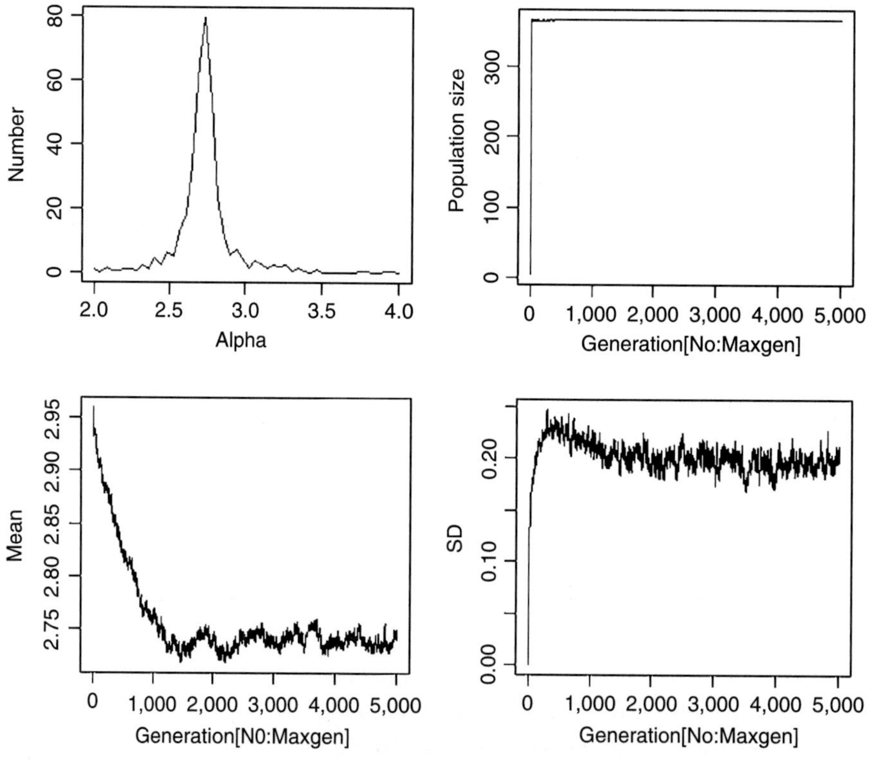

Figure 3.10 Results of multiple invasibility analysis for Scenario 3. Top panels show a frequency polygon of the distribution of α at the last generation and the population size over the simulation. The bottom row shows the change in the mean and standard deviation of α.

```
> print(c('Mean alpha in last gen = ',Stats[Maxgen,2]))
[1]  "Mean alpha in last gen =" "2.74127304258184"
> print(c('SD of alpha in last gen = ',Stats[Maxgen,3]))
[1]  "SD of alpha in last gen =" "0.198511654428470"
```

As indicated by the previous analyses, the population evolves to a single equilibrium. While there is variation about the mean value, it is not significantly different from that obtained from the elasticity analysis (2.74 in this analysis compared to 2.73 in the last).

3.6 Scenario 4: The evolution of reproductive effort

Complexity is added in this scenario by the addition of age structure and density-dependence that affects the parameter of interest, which here is reproductive effort. This scenario is taken from Benton and Grant (1999).

3.6.1 General assumptions

1. The population is composed of two age classes.
2. Fecundity increases with reproductive effort.
3. Survival decreases with reproductive effort.
4. Fecundity is a negative function of population size.

3.6.2 Mathematical assumptions

1. Fecundity, F_i, is defined as the number of offspring born to an individual that survive to the next age or stage.
2. Fecundity is the following function of reproductive effort, E, and population size:

$$F_i E \alpha e^{-\beta N} \tag{3.30}$$

where N is the total population size $(= n_1 + n_2)$.

3. Survival is governed by the relationship

$$S_i(1 - E^Z) \tag{3.31}$$

The matrix model is thus

$$\begin{bmatrix} n_{1,t+1} \\ n_{2,t+1} \end{bmatrix} = \begin{bmatrix} F_1 E \alpha e^{-\beta N} & F_2 E \alpha e^{-\beta N} \\ S_1(1 - E^Z) & S_2(1 - E^Z) \end{bmatrix} \begin{bmatrix} n_{1,t} \\ n_{2,t} \end{bmatrix} \tag{3.32}$$

The value of Z was set at 6 which matches approximately and corresponds to the mean value found in lowland birds (Benton and Grant 1999). The Ricker parameters were set at $\alpha = 1$ and $\beta = 2 \times 10^{-5}$: these parameters produce a stable population.

3.6.3 Pairwise invasibility analysis

The function DD.FUNCTION calculates the density-dependent fertilities according to equation (3.30); otherwise the program follows the same pattern as in the previous two scenarios.

R CODE:

```
  rm(list=ls())    # Clear workspace
# Density-dependent function
  DD.FUNCTION <- function(ALPHA, BETA, F.DI, Ei, n)
  {Ei*F.DI*ALPHA*exp(-BETA*n)}
# Function to calculate dynamics of invasion
  POP.DYNAMICS <- function(E)
{
  E.resident   <- E[1]              # E for resident
  E.invader    <- E[2]              # E for invader
  F.DI      <- c(4, 10)             # DI Fertilities
  S.DI      <- c(0.6,0.85)          # DI Survivals
  ALPHA   <- 1; BETA <- 2*10^-5     # DD parameter values
  z        <- 6                     # RE survival parameter value
# Preallocate space for matrices
  Resident.matrix  <- matrix(0,2,2) # Pre-assign space for matrix
  Invader.matrix   <- matrix(0,2,2) # Pre-assign space for matrix
# Apply reproductive effort to F
  Resident.matrix[1,]  <- E.resident*F.DI
  Invader.matrix[1,]   <- E.invader*F.DI
# Apply reproductive effort to S
  Resident.matrix[2,]  <- (1-E.resident^z)*S.DI
  Invader.matrix[2,]   <- (1-E.invader^z)*S.DI
# Run Maxgen generation with resident only
  Maxgen            <- 20           # Nos of generations
  n.resident        <- c(1,0)       # Initial population vector
  for ( Igen in 2:Maxgen)           # Iterate over generations
{
# Calculate the new entries
  N                 <- sum(n.resident)    # Pop size of residents
  Resident.matrix[1,]<- DD.FUNCTION(ALPHA, BETA, F.DI, E.resi-
dent, N)                                  # New Fs
  n.resident   <- Resident.matrix%*%n.resident    # New pop vector
} # End of first Igen loop
```

```
# Introduce invader
  Maxgen         <- 100                    # Set nos of generations to run
  Pop.invader   <- matrix(0,Maxgen,1)      # pre-allocate space of pop size
  Pop.invader[1,1]  <- 1                   # Initial population size
  n.invader          <- c(1,0)             # Initiate invader pop vector
  for (Igen in 2:Maxgen)                   # Iterate over generations
{
  N         <- sum(n.resident) + sum(n.invader)     # Total pop
# Apply density dependence to fertilities
  Resident.matrix[1,] <- DD.FUNCTION(ALPHA, BETA, F.DI, E.resident, N)
  Invader.matrix[1,]  <- DD.FUNCTION(ALPHA, BETA, F.DI, E.invader, N)
# Calculate new population vectors
  n.resident          <- Resident.matrix%*%n.resident
  n.invader           <- Invader.matrix%*%n.invader
  Pop.invader[Igen] <- sum(n.invader)   # Store pop size of invader
} # End of second Igen loop
  Generation      <- seq(from=1, to=Maxgen)   # Create vector of
                                                        generations
# Get growth of invader starting at generation 20
  Invasion.model <- lm(log(Pop.invader[20:Maxgen])~Generation
[20:Maxgen])
# Elasticity = slope of regression
  Elasticity      <- Invasion.model$coeff[2]
  return(Elasticity)
} # End of function
######################### MAIN PROGRAM #######################
par(mfrow=c(1,1))
N1           <- 30  # Nos of increments
E.Resident   <- seq(from=.2, to=.9, length=N1) # Resident body sizes
E.Invader    <- E.Resident                     # Invader body sizes
d     <- expand.grid(E.Resident, E.Invader)   # Combinations
# Generate values at combinations
z            <- apply(d,1,POP.DYNAMICS)
z.matrix     <- matrix(z, N1, N1)              # Convert to a matrix
# Plot contours
contour(E.Resident, E.Invader,z.matrix, xlab="Resident", ylab
="Invader")
# Place circle at predicted optimal body size
points( 0.5651338, 0.5651338, cex=3)   # cex triples size of circle
```

OUTPUT: (Figure 3.11)

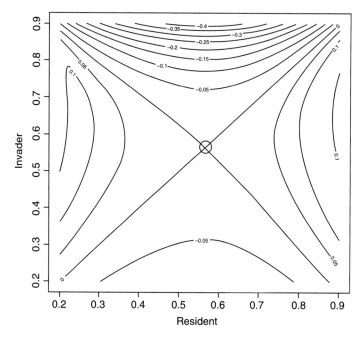

Figure 3.11 Pairwise invasibility plot for Scenario 4. The circle demarks the combination obtained from the elasticity analysis.

A single putative ESS is identified, corresponding to the predicted value from the following elasticity analysis.

3.6.4   Elasticity analysis

R CODE:

```
  rm(list=ls())    # Clear workspace
# Density-dependent function
  DD.FUNCTION    <- function(ALPHA, BETA, F.DI, Ei, n)
  {Ei*F.DI*ALPHA*exp(-BETA*n)}
# Function to calculate dynamics of invasion
  POP.DYNAMICS    <- function(E, Coeff)
{
  E.resident  <- E                  # E for resident
  E.invader   <- E*Coeff            # E for invader
  REMAINDER OF CODING AS IN INVASIBILITY ANALYSIS
} # End of function
```

```
#################### MAIN PROGRAM ####################
   par(mfrow=c(2,2))   # Divide graphics page into quarters
# Locate value at which elasticity equals zero
   Optimum      <- uniroot(POP.DYNAMICS, interval=c(0.01,0.9),0.995)
   Best.E      <- Optimum$root # Store the optimum reproductive effort
   print(Best.E)            # Print optimum E
# Create plot of elasticity vs E
   N.int      <- 30              # Nos of increments
# Create sequence of E from .1 to 0.9 in N.int increments
   E        <- matrix(seq(from=0.2, to=.9, length=N.int), N.int,1)
# Create vector of elasticities using apply function
   Elasticity  <- apply(E,1,POP.DYNAMICS, 0.995)
   plot(E, Elasticity, type='l')      # Plot elasticity vs E
   lines(c(.2,.9), c(0,0))             # Add horizontal line at zero
# Now plot Invasion exponent when resident is optimal
   Coeff       <- E/Best.E      # Coefficient of invader DD function
   Invasion.exponent  <- matrix(0,N.int,1)   # pre-allocate space
# Iterate and calculate invasion exponent
# Note that a loop is used rather than apply because it is coeffi-
cient that
# is changing
   for (i in 1:N.int){Invasion.exponent[i]      <- POP.DYNAMICS(Best.
E, Coeff[i])
   }
   plot(E, Invasion.exponent, ylab ='Invasion exponent', type='l')
   points(Best.E,0, cex=2) # Plot point at previously estimated
optimum E
```

OUTPUT: (Figure 3.12)

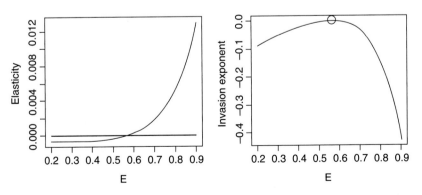

Figure 3.12 Output from elasticity analysis of Scenario 4.

```
> print (Best.E) # Print optimum E
[1] 0.5651338
```

The results indicate that under this scenario a medium reproductive effort is optimal. Benton and Grant (1999) explored a range of scenarios in which both the density-dependent function and traits affected were varied. The results are given in Table 1 of their paper: I suggest that the reader modify the above coding to replicate the results of that table.

3.7   Scenario 5: A two stage model

The primary purpose of this scenario is to illustrate the importance of correctly setting the number of generations over which the invader population growth rate is estimated. The problem is to estimate the optimal proportion of a population delaying maturity (or equivalently the proportion of immatures entering diapause or dormancy as found in many invertebrates and plants). For a detailed discussion of the model see van Dooren and Metz (1998). In this case I present the elasticity analysis first. Because the coding for multiple invasibility analysis is essentially the same as in previous scenarios, I have omitted it here.

3.7.1   General assumptions

1. The population consists of two stages with reproduction in the second stage.
2. A proportion of the first stage remains in that stage for more than one population cycle.
3. Fecundity is density dependent.

3.7.2   Mathematical assumptions

1. The proportion showing delayed maturity is P and the survival between stages is S.
2. Fecundity is determined by the Ricker function as $\alpha e^{-\beta A_t}$.

The matrix model is thus

$$\begin{bmatrix} I_{t+1} \\ A_{t+1} \end{bmatrix} = \begin{bmatrix} SP & \alpha e^{-\beta A_t} \\ S(1-P) & 0 \end{bmatrix} \begin{bmatrix} I_t \\ A_2 \end{bmatrix} \qquad (3.33)$$

Parameter values are set at $S = 0.8$, $\alpha = 18$, and $\beta = 0.01$. The dynamics of the adult population depend critically on the proportion delaying maturity. Low values of P produce cyclical behavior and larger values produce a stable equilibrium, with the time attaining the equilibrium becoming shorter as P gets bigger (Figure 3.13). As a consequence the dynamics of the resident and invader populations, both may

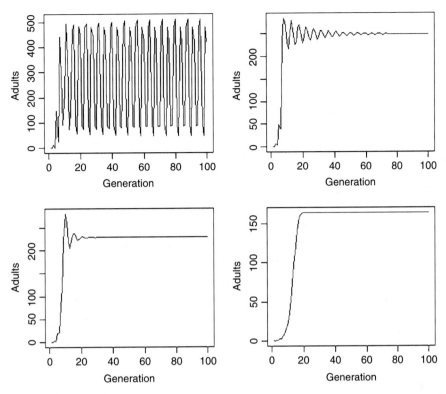

Figure 3.13 Population dynamics for the stage-dependent model of Scenario 5. Values of P from right to left and top to bottom are 0.1, 0.5, 0.7, and 0.9.

```
rm(list=ls())              # Clear workspace
par(mfrow=c(2,2))            # Divide graphics page into quarters
ALPHA    <- 18 ;  BETA    <- 0.01;  S   <- 0.8 # Parameter values
Ps         <- c(.1,.5,.7,.9)      # Values of P
for  ( Ith.P in 1:4)             # Iterate over P values
{
  P        <-  Ps[Ith.P]          # Select P value
  Stage   <- c(0,1)               # Start with one Adult
# Initialize matrix
  Stage.matrix   <- matrix(c(S*P, S*(1-P), ALPHA*exp(-BETA*Stage
[2]),0),2,2)
  Maxgen         <- 100    # Nos of generations to run simulation
  Store.Stage<-matrix(0,Maxgen,2) # Preallocate space for storage
  Store.Stage[1,]   <- Stage  # Store generation 1
  for  (Igen in 2:Maxgen)        # Iterate over generations
{
  Stage                 <- Stage.matrix%*%Stage       # New matrix
  Stage.matrix[1,2] <- ALPHA*exp(-BETA*Stage[2]) # Apply DD func-
                                                       tion
  Store.Stage[Igen,]<- Stage              # Store data
}  # End of Igen loop
  plot(seq(from=1,  to=Maxgen),  Store.Stage[,2],xlab='Genera-
tion', ylab='Adults', type='l')
}  # End of Ith.P loop
```

fluctuate, leading to uncertainty in the outcome of an invasion unless the time span is sufficiently long. Further, the variable dynamics may generate polymorphisms or multiple equilibria.

3.7.3 Elasticity analysis

Program coding follows the same pattern as in the previous scenario, except that the density dependence function is placed directly in the function POP.DYNAMICS. The line of coding shown in bold font is critical in this case.

R CODE:

```
rm(list=ls())             # Clear workspace
par(mfrow=c(1,1))         # Divide graphics page into quarters
POP.DYNAMICS <- function(P, P.invader.coeff)
{
P.resident        <- P                    # Resident delay
P.invader         <- P*P.invader.coeff  # Invader delay
ALPHA <- 18; BETA <- 0.01; S <- 0.8       # parameter values
Resident.Stage    <- c(1,1)               # Initial resident population
Invader.Stage     <- c(1,1)               # Initial invader population
# Initiate resident and invader matrices
Resident.matrix      <- matrix(c(S*P.resident, S*(1-P.resident),
ALPHA*exp(-BETA*Resident.Stage[2]),0),2,2)
Invader.matrix       <- matrix(c(S*P.invader, S*(1-P.invader),
ALPHA*exp(-BETA*Invader.Stage[2]),0),2,2)
Maxgen               <- 100   # Generations with resident alone
Store.Invader        <- matrix(0,Maxgen,2)
Store.Invader[1,]    <- Invader.Stage
for (Igen in 2:Maxgen)       # Iterate until resident is stable
{
Resident.Stage  <- Resident.matrix%*%Resident.Stage  # New matrix
Resident.matrix[1,2] <- ALPHA*exp(-BETA*Resident.Stage[2])
# DD effect
} # End of 1st Igen loop
# Now enter invader
Pop.invader   <- matrix(0,Maxgen,1)
Maxgen           <- 100   # Set number of generations for invasion
for (Igen in 1:Maxgen) # Iterate over generations after invasion
{
N <- Resident.Stage[2]+ Invader.Stage[2]# Adult population size
Resident.matrix[1,2]   <- ALPHA*exp(-BETA*N)  # Apply DD to resident
Invader.matrix[1,2]    <- ALPHA*exp(-BETA*N)  # Apply DD to invader
# New matrices
Resident.Stage    <- Resident.matrix%*%Resident.Stage
Invader.Stage     <- Invader.matrix%*%Invader.Stage
```

```
  Pop.invader[Igen] <- Invader.Stage[2]  # Store invader adult pop
} # End of 2nd Igen loop
  Generation        <- seq(from=20, to=Maxgen)    # Generation vector
# Get invasion exponent from linear regression
  Invasion.model  <-  lm(log(Pop.invader[20:Maxgen])~Generation
[20:Maxgen])
  Elasticity        <- Invasion.model$coeff[2]
  } # End of POP.DYNAMICS
################### MAIN PROGRAM ###################
  par(mfrow=c(2,2))        # Divide graphics page into 4 quadrats
# Call uniroot to find optimum
  Optimum    <- uniroot(POP.DYNAMICS, interval=c(0.1,0.6),0.995)
  Best.P     <- Optimum$root   # Store optimum P
  print(Best.P)                # Print out optimum
  N.int      <- 30             # Nos of intervals for plot
  P          <- matrix(seq(from=0.1, to=.6, length=N.int), N.int,1)
  Elasticity <- apply(P,1,POP.DYNAMICS, 0.995)
  plot(P, Elasticity, type='l')
  lines(c(.01,.9), c(0,0))     # Add horizontal line at zero
# Now plot Invasion exponent when resident is optimal
  Coeff          <- P/Best.P    # Convert P to coefficient
  Invasion.coeff <- matrix(0,N.int,1)
  for (i in 1:N.int){ Invasion.coeff[i] <- POP.DYNAMICS(Best.P,
Coeff[i])}
  plot(P, Invasion.coeff, type='l')
  points(Best.P,0, cex=2)
```

OUTPUT:
```
>  print(Best.P) # Print out optimum
[1] 0.3506968
```

The R function `uniroot` is successful in finding a root but it is quite clear from the graphical output (upper panels of Figure 3.14) that this is not the optimum. At first glance one might suppose that there are multiple ESS values, however, this variation disappears if the invader population is monitored for 2,000 generations and a single ESS value of 0.307579 is found (lower panels of Figure 3.14).

3.7.4 Pairwise invasibility analysis

Coding is omitted as it is essentially the same as in the previous two scenarios. What is important is that the plot generated after only 100 generations gives a remarkably accurate graphical estimate (Figure 3.15), as indicated by the super-imposed plot from the elasticity analysis.

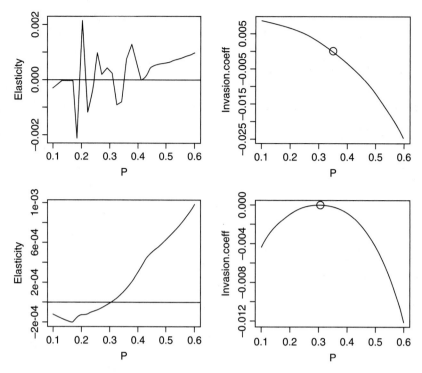

Figure 3.14 Elasticity analysis of Scenario 4. Top row shows results when invader is monitored for 100 generations and bottom row shows the results of monitoring for 2,000 generations.

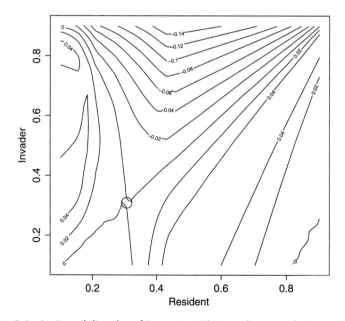

Figure 3.15 Pairwise invasibility plot of Scenario 5. The invading population was monitored for only 100 generations. Superimposed is the value (circle) predicted from the elasticity analysis run for 2,000 generations.

3.8   Scenario 6: A case in which the putative ESS is not stable

This scenario is discussed in detail in White et al. (2006). The present model is slightly modified to ensure that population size is reasonably large (>20). The results illustrate the importance of both an invasibility analysis and an elasticity analysis. The coding is essentially same as in previous scenarios.

3.8.1   General assumptions

1. Population size is governed by both density dependent and density-independent factors.
2. The density-independent components of fecundity and survival are negatively related.
3. The above function generates complex population dynamics.

3.8.2   Mathematical assumptions

1. Population size at time $t + 1$, N_{t+1}, is given by the equation

$$N_{t+1} = N_t(\alpha e^{-\beta N_t} + S_\alpha) \tag{3.34}$$

where S_α is survival as a function of α:

$$S_\alpha = \frac{(S_{max} - S_{min})\left(1 - \frac{\alpha - \alpha_{min}}{\alpha_{max} - \alpha_{min}}\right)}{1 + a\frac{\alpha - \alpha_{min}}{\alpha_{max} - \alpha_{min}}} \tag{3.35}$$

Depending on the value of α, S_α is a concave, convex, or linear function of α. In the present example parameter values are set as $S_{min} = 0$, $S_{max} = 0.9$, $\alpha_{max} = 50$, $\alpha_{min} = 1$, $a = 20$, and $\beta = 0.01$.

3.8.3   Pairwise invasibility analysis

R CODE:
```
rm(list=ls())    # Clear memory
DD.FUNCTION<-    function(ALPHA,N1,N2)  #  Density-dependence
function
{
# Set parameter values
  Amin <- 1; Amax <- 50; Bmin <- 0; Bmax <- 0.9; a <- 20; BETA <- 0.01
  AA   <- (ALPHA-Amin)/(Amax-Amin)      # For convenience
  S    <- (Bmax-Bmin)*(1-AA)/(1+a*AA)   # Survival
  N    <- N1*(ALPHA*exp(-BETA*N2)+S)    # new population
  return(N)
} # End of function
```

```
############### POP.DYNAMICS FUNCTION ###############
POP.DYNAMICS <- function(ALPHA)
{
  ALPHA.resident <- ALPHA[1]              # Resident value
  ALPHA.invader  <- ALPHA[2]              # Invader value
  Maxgen1        <- 50         # Nos of generations for resident only
  Maxgen2        <- 300        # Nos of generations after invasion
  Tot.Gen        <- Maxgen1+Maxgen2   # Total number of generations
  N.resident <- N.invader <- matrix(0,Tot.Gen)    # Allocate space
  N.resident[1]        <- 1         # Initial pop size of resident
  N.invader[Maxgen1]<- 1            # Initial pop size of invader
  for (Igen in 2:Maxgen1)          # Iterate over generations with
                                     resident only
{
  N <- N.resident[Igen-1]
  N.resident[Igen] <- DD.FUNCTION(ALPHA.resident, N, N)
} # End of 1st Igen loop
# Now add invader
  J <- Maxgen1+1                  # Starting generation
  for (Igen in J:Tot.Gen)        # Iterate over generations with invader
{
  N <- N.resident[Igen-1]+N.invader[Igen-1]   # Total pop size
  N.resident[Igen]  <-  DD.FUNCTION(ALPHA.resident, N.resident
[Igen-1], N)
  N.invader[Igen]   <- DD.FUNCTION(ALPHA.invader, N.invader[Igen-
1], N)
} # End of 2nd Igen loop
  Generation <- seq(from=1, to=Tot.Gen) # Vector of generation
                                                   numbers
  N0       <- 10+Maxgen1   # Gen at which to start regression analysis
  Invasion.model <- lm(log(N.invader[N0:Tot.Gen])~ Generation
[N0:Tot.Gen])
  Elasticity <- Invasion.model$coeff[2] # Elasticity coefficient
  return(Elasticity)
} # End of function
#################### MAIN PROGRAM ####################
  N1           <- 30 # Nos of increments
  A.Resident <- seq(from=5, to= 45, length=N1)   # Resident alphas
  A.Invader  <- A.Resident                       # Invader alphas
  d       <- expand.grid(A.Resident, A.Invader)  # Combinations
# Generate values at combinations
  z       <- apply(d,1,POP.DYNAMICS)
  z.matrix    <- matrix(z, N1, N1)               # Convert to a matrix
# Plot contours
```

```
contour(A.Resident,   A.Invader,   z.matrix,   xlab="Resident",
ylab="Invader")
# Place circle at predicted optimal alpha
points(24.21837, 24.21837, cex=3)   # cex triples size of circle
```

OUTPUT: (Figure 3.16)

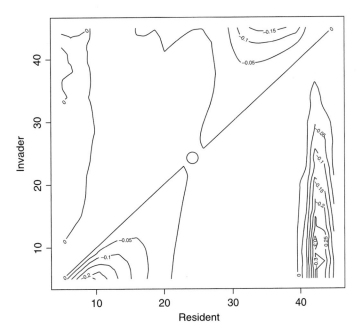

Figure 3.16 Pairwise invasibility plot for Scenario 6. The circle indicates the optimum obtained from the elasticity analysis.

There is a single putative ESS value that is at the point predicted by the elasticity analysis given below but the surface appears complex, with zero isoclines that do not intersect the $x = y$ line. Further, the one that does intersect the $x = y$ line is less than 90°, suggesting that the putative ESS is not stable (compare with the right-hand plots of Figure 3.3).

3.8.4 Elasticity analysis

R CODE:

```
  rm(list=ls())                        # Clear memory
  DD.FUNCTION <- function(ALPHA,N1,N2)  # Density-dependence
function
{
SAME AS IN INVASIBILITY ANALYSIS
} # End of function
```

```
############### POP.DYNAMICS FUNCTION ###############
POP.DYNAMICS <- function(ALPHA, Coeff)
{
  ALPHA.resident   <- ALPHA         # Resident value
  ALPHA.invader    <- ALPHA*Coeff   # Invader value
  REMAINDER THE SAME AS IN INVASIBILITY ANALYSIS
} # End of function
################### MAIN PROGRAM ###################
  par(mfrow=c(2,2))     # Divide graphics page into quadrats
# Call uniroot to find optimum
  minA       <-10; maxA <-40       # Limits of search for alpha
  Optimum    <-    uniroot(POP.DYNAMICS,    interval=c(minA,
maxA),0.995)
  Best.A       <- Optimum$root       # Store optimum Alpha
  print(Best.A)                      # Print out optimum
  N.int        <- 30                 # Nos of intervals for plot
  A   <- matrix(seq(from=minA, to=maxA, length=N.int), N.int,1)
  Elasticity  <- apply(A,1,POP.DYNAMICS, 0.995)
  plot(A, Elasticity, type='l')
  lines(c(minA, maxA), c(0,0))       # Add horizontal line at zero
# Now plot Invasion exponent when resident is optimal
  Coeff         <- A/Best.A          # Convert A to coefficient
  Invasion.coeff <- matrix(0,N.int,1) # Allocate space
# Calculate invasion coefficient
  for (i in 1:N.int){ Invasion.coeff[i] <- POP.DYNAMICS(Best.A,
Coeff[i])}
  plot(A, Invasion.coeff, type='l')   # Plot invasion coeff vs alpha
  points(Best.A,0, cex=2)            # Add predicted optimum
# Plot N(t+1) on N(t) for best model
  N <- 1000                 # Nos of data points
  N.t <- seq(from=1, to=N)         # Values of N(t)
  N.tplus1 <- matrix(0,N)          # Allocate space
# Iterate to get N(t+1) on N(t)
  for ( i in 1:N){N.tplus1[i] <- DD.FUNCTION(Best.A, N.t[i], N.t
[i])}
  plot(N.t, N.tplus1, type='l')    # Plot N(t+1) on N(t)
# Plot N(t) on t
  N      <- matrix(0,100)          # Allocate space
  N[1]   <- 1                      # Initial value of N(t)
  for (i in 2:100){N[i]<- DD.FUNCTION(Best.A, N[i-1], N[i-1])}
  plot(seq(from=1, to=100), N, type='l', xlab='Generation',
ylab='Population')
```

OUTPUT: (Figure 3.17)

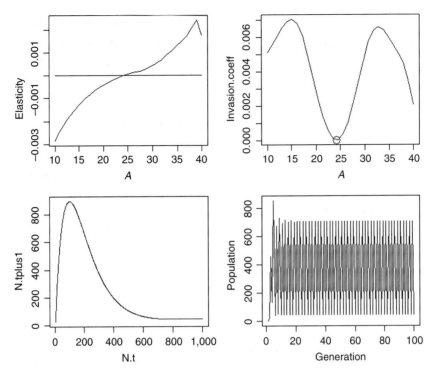

Figure 3.17 Elasticity analysis of Scenario 6.

```
>    print(Best.A) # Print out optimum
[1] 24.21837
```

The putative ESS is consistent with the pairwise invasibility analysis but the elasticity analysis does not indicate that the invasion coefficient is negative for values different from the putative ESS. In fact, the elasticity analysis suggests that invasion is highly likely. To view the population dynamics we can simply insert plot commands into the function POP.DYNAMICS (shown in bold font) and call this for the optimum α and a value for an invader.

R CODE:

```
rm(list=ls())                                 # Clear memory
  DD.FUNCTION  <- function(ALPHA,N1,N2)    # Density-dependence
function
{
SAME AS IN PREVIOUS
} # End of function
############### POP.DYNAMICS FUNCTION ###############
POP.DYNAMICS <- function(ALPHA, Coeff)
{
  ALPHA.resident     <- ALPHA            # Resident value
  ALPHA.invader      <- ALPHA*Coeff    # Invader value
  Maxgen1            <- 50    # Nos of generations for resident only
  Maxgen2            <- 300      # Nos of generations after invasion
  Tot.Gen <- Maxgen1+Maxgen2   # Total number of generations
```

```
N.resident <- N.invader <- matrix(0,Tot.Gen)    # Allocate space
N.resident[1]       <- 1          # Initial pop size of resident
N.invader[Maxgen1] <- 1           # Initial pop size of invader
for (Igen in 2:Maxgen1)    # Iterate over generations with resident
                                  only
{
  N <- N.resident[Igen-1]
  N.resident[Igen] <- DD.FUNCTION(ALPHA.resident, N, N)
} # End of 1st Igen loop
# Now add invader
  J <- Maxgen1+1          # Starting generation
  for (Igen in J:Tot.Gen)    # Iterate over generations with invader
{
  N <- N.resident[Igen-1]+N.invader[Igen-1]    # Total pop size
  N.resident[Igen]  <-  DD.FUNCTION(ALPHA.resident, N.resident
[Igen-1], N)
  N.invader[Igen]  <-  DD.FUNCTION(ALPHA.invader, N.invader[Igen-
1], N)
} # End of 2nd Igen loop
  Generation <- seq(from=1, to=Tot.Gen) # Vector of generation
                                           numbers
  plot (Generation, N.resident, xlab='Generation', ylab='Resident
N', type='l')
  plot (Generation, N.invader, xlab='Generation', ylab='Invader
N', type='l')
} # End of function
############# MAIN PROGRAM #############
  par(mfrow=c(2,2))          # Divide graphics page into quadrats
  Best.A     <- 24.21635     # Best alpha from elasticity analysis
  Invader.A <- 10            # Alpha for invader
  Coeff      <- Invader.A/Best.A  # Calculate relevant coefficient
  POP.DYNAMICS ( Best.A,Coeff)    # Call functiom
```

OUTPUT: (Figure 3.18)

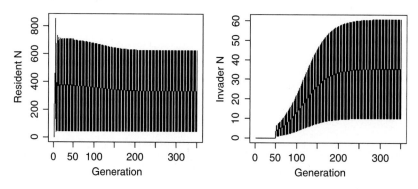

Figure 3.18 Temporal plots of resident and invader populations. Left-hand plot shows the population trajectory for the optimum α and the right-hand plot shows the population trajectory for an invader with $\alpha = 10$.

It is evident from the output that an invader with $\alpha = 10$ can invade the population but not replace the resident population. This explains the relation between the invasion coefficient and the optimum α and emphasizes the importance of elasticity analysis in conjunction with pairwise invasibility analysis.

3.8.5 Multiple invasibility analysis

The program is the same as in Scenario 6 except for: (a) it is run 10,000 generations to ensure sufficient time for equilibrium to be attained (if possible), (b) because the elasticity analysis indicated that a single equilibrium is unlikely, frequency polygons are plotted for the last three generations.

R CODE:

```
rm(list=ls())   # Clear memory
  DD.FUNCTION<- function(X, N.total)   # Density-dependence function
{
# Set parameter values
  ALPHA    <- X[1];    N <- X[2]
  Amin     <- 1; Amax <- 50; Bmin <- 0; Bmax <- 0.9; a <- 20; BETA <- 0.01
  AA       <- (ALPHA-Amin)/(Amax-Amin)       # For convenience
  S        <- (Bmax-Bmin)*(1-AA)/(1+a*AA)    # Survival
  N        <- N*(ALPHA*exp(-BETA*N.total)+S) # new population
  N        <- max(0,N)                       # N cannot be negative
  return(N)
} # End of function
############## MAIN PROGRAM ##############
  set.seed(10)              # Initialize the random number seed
  Maxgen    <- 10000        # Number of generations run
  Stats     <- matrix(0,Maxgen,3) # Allocate space for statistics
  MaxAlpha <- 50            # maximum value of alpha
  Ninc      <- 50           # Number of classes for alpha
# Allocate space to store data for each generation
  Store      <- matrix(0,Maxgen, Ninc)
# Allocate space for alpha class and population size
  Data       <- matrix(0,Ninc,2)
  Data[24,2] <- 1        # Initial population size and alpha class
  ALPHA <- matrix(seq(from=1, to=MaxAlpha, length=Ninc),Ninc,1)
# Set Alpha
  Data[,1] <- ALPHA         # Place alpha in 1st column
  for (Igen in 1:Maxgen)    # Iterate over generations
{
  N.total    <- sum(Data[,2])   # Total population size
  Data[,2]   <- apply(Data,1,DD.FUNCTION, N.total)   # New cohort
  Store[Igen,]   <- Data[,2]   # Store values for this generation
# Keep track of population size, mean trait value and SD of trait value
  Stats[Igen,2]  <- sum(Data[,1]*Data[,2])/sum(Data[,2])   # Mean
  S              <- sum(Data[,2])                  # Population size
  Stats[Igen,1]  <- S                              # Population size
```

```
 SX1              <- sum(Data[,1]^2*Data[,2])
 SX2              <- (sum(Data[,1]*Data[,2]))^2/S
 Stats[Igen,3] <- sqrt((SX1-SX2)/(S-1))    # SD of trait
# Introduce a mutant by picking a random integer between 1 and 50
 Mutant           <- ceiling(runif(1, min=0, max=50))
 Data[Mutant,2] <- Data[Mutant,2]+1      # Add mutant to class
} # End of Igen loop
 par(mfrow=c(3,2))        # Split graphics page into 3 x 2 panels
 for (Row in 9998:Maxgen) # Select rows to be plotted
{
 plot(ALPHA, Store[Row,], type='l', xlab='Alpha', ylab='Number')
} # End of frequency polygon plots
 Generation  <- seq(from=1, to=Maxgen)  # Vector of generations
 N0              <- 9900                   # Starting value for plots
 plot(Generation[N0:Maxgen], Stats[N0:Maxgen,1], ylab='Popula-
tion size',xlab='Generation', type='l')
 plot(Generation[N0:Maxgen], Stats[N0:Maxgen,2], ylab='Mean',
xlab='Generation', type='l')
 plot(Generation[N0:Maxgen], Stats[N0:Maxgen,3], ylab='SD',
xlab='Generation', type='l')
 print(c('Mean alpha in last gen = ',Stats[Maxgen,2]))
 print(c('SD of alpha in last gen = ',Stats[Maxgen,3]))
```

OUTPUT: (Figure 3.19)

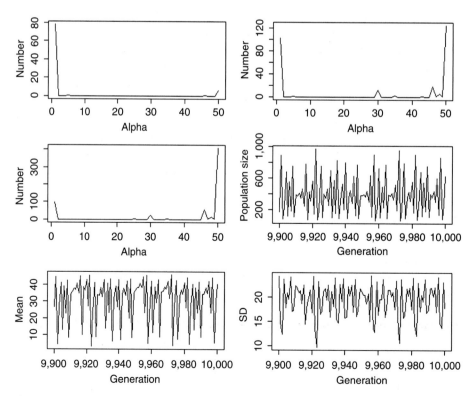

Figure 3.19 Results of multiple invasibility analysis of Scenario 6. The three frequency polygons show results for generation 9,998, 9,999 and 10,000.

```
>   print(c('Mean alpha in last gen = ',Stats[Maxgen,2]))
[1] "Mean alpha in last gen = " "40.6067676012847"
>   print(c('SD of alpha in last gen = ',Stats[Maxgen,3]))
[1] "SD of alpha in last gen = " "17.8941418836399"
```

The frequency polygon plots for the last three generations show dramatic shifts in the mean and modal values of α. As indicated by the previous analyses, the equilibrium from the pairwise invasibility analysis is highly unstable and is unlikely to be ever attained, since any small deviations set the population into extreme fluctuations. The population consists of different clones, with their frequencies changing through time.

3.9 Some exemplary papers

Katsukawa, Y., T. Katsukawa, and H. Matsuda. 2002. Indeterminate growth is selected by a trade-off between high fecundity and risk avoidance in stochastic environments. *Population Ecology* **44:265–272.**

Problem: Optimal allocation of energy to growth, survival, and reproduction when survival is temporally variable

Model type: Two age/stage

Density-dependence: None

Trade-off: Total allocation of energy to survival, growth, and reproduction fixed

Analysis: Maximization of λ

Reference scenario: Scenario 1

Ebenman, B., A. Johansson, T. Jonsson, and U. Wennergren. 1996. Evolution of stable population dynamics through natural selection. Proceedings of the Royal Society of London – Series B: *Biological Sciences* **263:1145–1151.**

Problem: Optimal combination of density-dependent parameters when population dynamics can range from a fixed equilibrium to chaotic

Model type: Two-stage

Density-dependence: Ricker function applied to maturation rate and juvenile survival

Trade-off: Maturation rate and juvenile survival

Analysis: Invasibility analysis

Reference scenario: Scenarios 3 and 5

Lalonde, R. G. and B. D. Roitberg. 2006. Chaotic dynamics can select for long-term dormancy. *American Naturalist* **168:127–131.**

Problem: The optimal dormancy when population dynamics are chaotic

Model type: Up to 13 generations of dormancy

Density-dependence: Ricker function

Trade-off: No explicit trade-off

Analysis: Multiple invasibility analysis

Reference scenario: Scenarios 3 and 6

Johst, K., M. Doebeli, and R. Brandl. 1999. Evolution of complex dynamics in spatially structured populations. Proceedings of the Royal Society of London – Series B: *Biological Sciences* **266:1147–1154.**

Problem: The optimal density-dependent and density-independent dispersal rates

Model type: One generation per time step

Density-dependence: Fecundity varies with density using an equation that can take a variety of shapes

Trade-off: No explicit trade-offs

Analysis: Multiple invasibility analysis

Reference scenario: Scenarios 3 and 6

Benton, R. A. and A. Grant. 1999. Optimal reproductive effort in stochastic, density-dependent environments. *Evolution* **53:677–688.**

Problem: Optimal reproductive effort

Model type: Two age/stage class

Density-dependence: Various

Trade-off: Various combinations of reproductive effort and survival at age with or without temporal variation

Analysis: Elasticity analysis

Reference scenario: Scenario 4

Wilbur, H. M. and V. H. W. Rudolf. 2006. Life-history evolution in uncertain environments: Bet hedging in time. *American Naturalist* **168:398–411.**

Problem: Optimal iteroparity and delayed maturity in a stochastic environment

Model type: Two-stage

Density-dependence: Ricker function applied to fertility with parameters selected to ensure a stable population in a deterministic environment

Trade-off: Adult survival and clutch size in some model variants

Analysis: Invasibility analysis

Reference scenario: Scenarios 4 and 5

White, A., J. V. Greenman, T. G. Benton, and M. Boots. 2006. Evolutionary behaviour in ecological systems with trade-offs and non-equilibrium population dynamics. *Evolutionary Ecology Research* **8:387–398.**

Problem: Optimal reproductive effort when population dynamics are complex

Model type: No explicit age structure

Density-dependence: Ricker function

Trade-off: Density-independent fecundity and survival

Analysis: Invasibility analysis

Reference scenario: Scenario 6

CHAPTER 4

Genetic Models

4.1 Introduction

The "Fisherian" optimality approach determines the optimal combination of trait values but not the evolutionary trajectory nor, in general, the variation to be expected about the optimal combination. Invasibility analysis is also primarily concerned with the Evolutionarily Stable Strategy (ESS) values; though assuming clonal inheritance, it can give insight into the temporal evolution of trait values. Whether such analyses can be extended to organisms with other modes of inheritance is not clear, though the analysis presented in Scenario 5 of this chapter suggests that caution is warranted in applying the results of invasibility analysis to sexually reproducing organisms.

There are basically three ways to implement a genetic model, which I shall refer to as (a) the population variance components approach, (b) the individual variance components approach, and (c) the individual locus approach. The first two are primarily for quantitative genetic modeling whereas the last can be used for both quantitative genetic modeling and modeling simple Mendelian inheritance (e.g., single locus). The advantages of an individual-based model (IBM) are that it is easy to incorporate complex population dynamics, frequency-dependence, and functional constraints. IBMs are, however, relatively computer-intensive (particularly individual locus models).

4.1.1 Population variance components (PVC) models

Rather than focus upon individual loci this method tackles the problem by focusing at the population level upon the variances and covariances of the traits. The phenotypic value, X, of a trait can be decomposed into the sum of genetic, G, and environmental, E, components:

$$X = G + E \tag{4.1}$$

where it is assumed that G and E are uncorrelated and normally distributed, the latter with a zero mean. The phenotypic variance, σ_P^2 is thus also composed of the sum of the genetic, σ_G^2, and the environmental, σ_E^2, variances

$$\sigma_P^2 = \sigma_G^2 + \sigma_E^2 \tag{4.2}$$

The genetic variance can itself be broken down into additive, dominance, and epistatic components, but I shall ignore the latter two, as is typically done. **Heritability** is a measure of the extent to which the resemblance between relatives is due to additive genetic effects. A simple way to estimate heritability is to regress the average trait value of offspring on the mid-parent value. Provided that there are no maternal (or paternal) effects or environmental effects due to similarity in the rearing environment within but not among families, the slope of this regression is equal to the heritability of the trait. The general definition of heritability, h^2, is the ratio of additive genetic variance to phenotypic variance:

$$h^2 = \frac{\sigma_G^2}{\sigma_P^2} \tag{4.3}$$

Heritability measures the proportion of the total variance that can be ascribed to the additive effect of genes. A zero heritability means that variation is entirely environmental whereas a heritability of one means that the variation is entirely due to the additive effects of genes. The general relationship between offspring and parents is

$$\mu_{\text{Offspring}} = (1 - h^2)\mu_{\text{Population}} + h^2\mu_{\text{Parents}} \tag{4.4}$$

where μ refers to the mean values. Under **directional selection** the mean value of parents is greater or less that of the population, depending on the direction of selection, and by rearranging equation 4.4 we get the response to the selection as

$$\mu_{\text{Offspring}} - \mu_{\text{Population}} = h^2(\mu_{\text{Parents}} - \mu_{\text{Offspring}})$$
$$R = h^2 S = \frac{\sigma_G^2}{\sigma_P^2} S \tag{4.5}$$

where S is the **selection differential**. The above equation is referred to as the **Breeder's equation**. It is frequently more convenient to write S in terms of phenotypic standard deviations:

$$S = i\sigma_P \tag{4.6}$$

where i is called the **selection intensity**,

$$i = \frac{S}{\sigma_P} = \frac{z}{P} \tag{4.7}$$

P is the proportion selected for each generation and z is the ordinate at the point of truncation. Suppose we wish to apply **truncation selection** by selecting the top P proportion of the population, the selection intensity can be calculated using the following R code:

```
Vp  <- 1                         # Phenotypic variance
P   <- 0.2                       # Proportion selected
x   <- -qnorm(P, mean = 0, sd = 1)   # x value
z   <- exp(-0.5*x^2)/(sqrt(2*pi))    # z
```

```
i   <- z/P                         # Selection intensity
S   <- i*sqrt(Vp)                  # Selection differential
```

The change per generation is a constant and hence a plot of mean trait value on generation will give a straight line (i.e., $\mu_{t+1} = \mu_t + h^2 S$).

In nature, selection is likely to be generally stabilizing rather than directional. Two functions often used for such a scenario are a quadratic fitness function and a Gaussian fitness function. Under the latter function the fitness of a trait, W, can be written as

$$W = e^{-\frac{1}{2}\left[\frac{(x-\theta)^2}{\omega}\right]}$$
(4.8)

where θ is the value at which fitness is maximized and ω is a measure of the strength of stabilizing selection, the strength of selection decreasing with increasing ω. Stabilizing selection can be incorporated into the single trait model as

$$R_t = \frac{\sigma_G^2}{\omega + \sigma_P^2}(\theta - \mu_{\text{Population},t})$$
(4.9)

Note that the response to selection is now a function of the distance from the optimum value and hence is a function of generation. Over time the population moves smoothly to the optimum value.

Extension of the above model to multiple traits requires the introduction of the correlation between traits. Correlations can arise because genes may affect several traits (called **pleiotropy**), be associated because of **linkage** or because of environmental factors. Assuming, as is generally done, that the environmental and genetic covariances are independent we can break the phenotypic covariance between traits X and Y, σ_{PXY}, into the sum of the two covariances:

$$\sigma_{PXY} = \sigma_{GXY} + \sigma_{EXY}$$
(4.10)

Noting that a correlation, r, is equal to

$$r = \frac{\sigma_{XY}}{\sigma_X \sigma_Y}$$
(4.11)

the phenotypic correlation can be obtained from the above relationship as

$$\begin{aligned} r_{PXY} &= r_G \frac{\sigma_{GX}\sigma_{GY}}{\sigma_{PX}\sigma_{PY}} + r_E \frac{\sigma_{EX}\sigma_{EY}}{\sigma_{PX}\sigma_{PY}} \\ &= r_G \sqrt{h_X^2 h_Y^2} + r_E \sqrt{(1-h_X^2)(1-h_Y^2)} \end{aligned}$$
(4.12)

For multiple traits the Breeder's equation can be expanded using matrix notation as

$$\mathbf{\Delta \bar{z}} = \mathbf{GP}^{-1}\mathbf{S}$$
(4.13)

where is $\Delta\bar{z}$ the vector of changes in trait means, $\mathbf{G}$ is the additive genetic variance–covariance matrix, $\mathbf{P}$ is the phenotypic variance–covariance matrix, $\mathbf{S}$ is the vector of selection differentials, and the -1 means the matrix inverse. For two traits, labeled 1 and 2, equation (4.13) can be written in explicit matrix format as

$$\begin{pmatrix} \Delta\bar{z}_1 \\ \Delta\bar{z}_2 \end{pmatrix} = \begin{pmatrix} \sigma_{G1}^2 & \sigma_{G12} \\ \sigma_{G21} & \sigma_{G2}^2 \end{pmatrix} \begin{pmatrix} \sigma_{P1}^2 & \sigma_{P12} \\ \sigma_{P21} & \sigma_{P2}^2 \end{pmatrix}^{-1} \begin{pmatrix} S_1 \\ S_2 \end{pmatrix} \qquad (4.14)$$

The diagonal elements of the genetic and phenotypic matrices hold the variances and the off-diagonals the covariances (note that the matrices are symmetrical and hence $\sigma_{ij} = \sigma_{ji}$). The response to directional truncation selection is the same as in the single trait model, in that both traits change by a fixed amount per generation, though in this case the amount is a function of the selection differential and the correlation between the traits.

To set the values in equation (4.14) it is generally easier to commence with the heritabilities, phenotypic variances, and correlations, and then make use of equations (4.3) and (4.12). For two traits the coding is simple: for example,

```
h2      <- c(0.2,0.4)                    # Set heritabilities
Vp      <- c(1,2)                        # Set phenotypic variances
Rp      <- 0.4                           # Set phenotypic correlation
Ra      <- 0.15                          # Set genetic correlation
Va      <- h2*Vp                         # Using h2 =Va/Vp
Covp    <- Rp*sqrt(Vp[1]*Vp[2])          # Using r = Cov/SD1SD2
Cova    <- Ra*sqrt(Va[1]*Va[2])          # Using r = Cov/SD1SD2
Gmatrix <- matrix( c(Va[1],Cova, Cova, Va[2]),2,2)   # G matrix
Pmatrix <- matrix(c(Vp[1],Covp, Covp, Vp[2]),2,2)    # P matrix
```

The environmental correlation must lie between -1 and $+1$, which is not guaranteed by the above coding. It is therefore necessary to put in a check, using equation (4.12) and stop the program if r_E falls outside the permissible limits:

```
# Check that Re is possible
Re <- (Rp-Ra*sqrt(h2[1]*h2[2]))/sqrt((1-h2[1])*(1-h2[2]))
if(abs(Re) >1 ) stop (c("problem with Re"))
```

The value of the heritability is unlikely to matter in terms of the final equilibrium but will certainly affect the time taken to reach this value, should it exist, and the variation about the value.

With more than two traits the above coding can be tedious but it can be replaced by the following more general code. Suppose we have three traits. First we construct a matrix, which I have called H2, which holds the heritabilities on the diagonal, the genetic correlations above the diagonal and the phenotypic correlations below the diagonal. We then use this matrix in conjunction with the phenotypic variances (assumed to be 1.5, 1.0, and 0.5 in the example below) to construct the necessary covariance matrices:

```
NX            <- 3                 # Number of traits
# Matrix of heritabilities and correlations.
# Values in bold are the heritabilities
# Genetic correlations are above the diagonal, phenotypic correl-
  ations below
  H2             <- matrix (c (0.4, 0.7, 0.3,
                               0.6, 0.5, 0.1,
                               0.4, 0.6, 0.3), NX, NX, byrow=TRUE)
# Construct the Phenotypic Covariance matrix
# Note that initial covariances are set to 1 (arbitrary)
  CovP         <- matrix (1, NX, NX)  # Phenotypic variances
  diag (CovP) <-c (1.5, 1.0, 0.5) # Sets diagonal elements = variances
# Establish CovA from h2 and CovP and CovE from CovA and CovP
  CovA         <- matrix (0, NX, NX)   # Allocate space
  CovE         <- matrix (0, NX, NX)   # Allocate space
  for   ( i in 1:NX)                   # Iterate over cells
{
  CovA[i,i]       <- CovP[i,i]*H2[i,i]      # = Vp*h2
  CovE[i,i]       <- CovP[i,i]-CovA[i,i]   # Variances
# Check that environmental variance is positive
  if (CovE[i,i] < 0) stop (c("Problem with CovE"))
}
# Phenotypic and genetic covariances
  N. minus. 1   <- NX-1
  for ( i in 1:N.minus.1)
{
  jj   <- i+1
  for (j in jj:NX)
{
# Phenotypic covariances
  CovP [i,j]  <- H2[j,i]*sqrt (CovP[i,i]*CovP[j,j])
  CovP[j,i]   <- CovP[i,j]
  CovA[i,j]   <- H2[i,j]*sqrt (CovA[i,i]*CovA[j,j]) #Ra*sqrt (VaxVay)
  CovA j,i]   <- CovA [i,j]
  CovE[i,j]   <- CovP [i,j]-CovA[i,j]                # By difference
  CovE[j,i]   <- CovE [i,j]
}
}
```

Stabilizing selection can be incorporated using a third matrix (Lande 1980),

$$\Delta \bar{\mathbf{z}} = \mathbf{G}(\mathbf{W} + \mathbf{P})^{-1}\mathbf{S}(\boldsymbol{\mu} - \boldsymbol{\theta}) \qquad (4.15)$$

where $\mathbf{W}$ is a positive semidefinite matrix, μ is a vector of trait means, and θ is a vector of optimal trait values. The diagonal elements of $\mathbf{W}$ are measures of the strength of stabilizing selection acting directly on the character (e.g., ω in the Gaussian fitness function, see equation (4.8)) while the off-diagonals measure the strength of **correlational selection** which is the extent to which selection acts jointly on two characters. If **W** is a semidefinite positive matrix then its eigenvalues are all nonnegative: this can be checked by the call `eigen(Wmatrix)` `$values` which will print out the eigenvalues of the matrix, here, called `Wmatrix`. Care has to be taken in programming $(\mathbf{W} + \mathbf{P})^{-1}$: the code `(W+P)^-1` takes the reciprocal of all the matrix elements, which is not the same as matrix inversion. The correct call is `solve(W+P)`.

For some species maternal effects and/or common environment may be very important and can significantly affect the evolutionary trajectory but not the final outcome. For methods of incorporating these effects in a matrix formulation see Kirkpatrick and Lande (1989) and for a summary see Roff (1997, pp. 250–257).

The above approach assumes an infinitely large population and may be difficult to implement in scenarios that contain functional constraints. An alternate approach is that of an IBMs. In this chapter two such classes are considered: individual variance components (IVC) models and the individual locus (IL) models.

4.1.2   Individual variance components (IVC) models

As noted earlier, the phenotypic value is the sum of a genetic value and an environmental value. Both components are normally distributed (or the trait can be transformed to be so), the former with some mean that varies as a result of selection and drift and the latter with a zero mean. The phenotypic value of an individual can be created by generating random normal values from normal generating functions with the appropriate means and variances. Genetic dominance can be introduced by using the theoretical contribution of the additive and dominance components given a known pedigree, but for simplicity, I shall consider only additive effects. I shall also assume that the genetic variances do not change as evolution proceeds. The extension of equation (4.1) to multiple traits simply requires a move from the normal distribution (`rnorm` in R) to the multivariate normal distribution (`mvrnorm` in R).

The advantages of the individual variance-components approach over the population-based approach are that changes in both means and the phenotypic distributions can be assessed and functional constraints (e.g., thresholds, see later) are readily accommodated. Application of the approach is straightforward for many phenotypic traits. However, there are three types of traits that require specialized treatment. For these traits, the phenotypic value as defined by the sum of the normally distributed additive genetic and environmental values is not the value of the phenotype that is actually expressed (hereafter the "realized phenotype"). The first is a class of traits known as **threshold traits** in which the realized phenotype consists of two or more discrete forms or states, examples include wing dimorphism in insects, horn dimorphism in some species of beetles, and susceptibility to disease (reviewed in Roff [1996]). The threshold model resolves the apparent paradox of polygenic determination of discrete morphs by assuming an underlying normally distributed trait called the **liability**. Individuals with liability values exceeding a critical threshold develop into one morph and those below the threshold develop into the alternate morph (Figure 1.10).

The second circumstance in which the realized phenotype is not the sum of the genetic and environmental values is when the trait has a limiting boundary, for example, fecundity cannot be less than zero. The threshold concept resolves this problem by assuming that values less than the limiting boundary have values equal to the limiting boundary, which in the case of fecundity would be zero. The phenotypic value on the underlying scale is thus continuously distributed but the realized phenotype may appear as a bimodal distribution as the mean trait value approaches the limiting boundary.

Finally, trait expression may be sex or morph-specific. For example, in most wing-dimorphic insects the development of the flight muscles is suppressed in short-winged individuals. In a simulation model, flight muscle weight would thus be set to zero in this morph. These three categories of traits are easily incorporated into an IBM.

The individual variance-components approach has been used extensively to study the performance of statistical methods for estimating genetic parameters such heritability and genetic correlations (e.g., Ronningen [1974]; Olausson and Ronningen [1975]; Roff and Preziosi [1994]; Lynch [1999]; Roff [2001]; Roff and Reale [2004]) but has been rarely used to model evolution in general. However, this approach can also be extremely useful in simulating evolutionary responses (Gilchrist 2000), and specifically, in predicting the trajectory of experimental evolution (Roff and Fairbairn 2007, 2009). By taking an individual-based modeling approach one is able to directly incorporate functional constraints, complexities of genetic architecture (such as the inclusion of threshold traits, continuously manifested traits and simple Mendel single locus models), and trait distributions that may be far from normal at the realized phenotypic level.

To implement this approach we commence in the same manner as with the population variance-components approach, namely by defining the genetic and environmental variance–covariance matrices. For a single trait we need only the genetic variance, the environmental variance, and the mean genotypic trait value: these are most easily obtained by specifying the two measurable quantities heritability and phenotypic variance. The genotypic mean is set at an arbitrary value that will generally be set close to the presumed equilibrium value. Sample coding assuming a heritability of 0.5, a phenotypic variance of 1, and a mean genotypic value of 3 follows:

```
h2    <- 0.5        # Heritability
Vp    <- 1          # Phenotypic variance
Va    <- h2*Vp      # Additive genetic variance
Ve    <- Vp-Va      # Environmental variance
SD.A  <- sqrt(Va)   # Additive genetic standard deviation
SD.E  <- sqrt(Ve)   # Environemtal standard deviation
mu    <- 3          # Mean genotypic value
```

To generate a population of size N with these parameters we first set the seed to ensure that the simulation can be repeated exactly (useful for debugging), then generate the genetic and environmental values and finally add them to get a vector of phenotypic values:

```
set.seed(10)                          # Initiate random number generator
N       <- 1000                       # Population size
G.X     <- rnorm(N, mean=mu, sd=SD.A) # Genetic values
E.X     <- rnorm(N, mean=0, sd=SD.E)  # Environmental values
P.X     <- G.X + E.X                  # Phenotypic values
```

With more than one trait the variance–covariances matrices are generated as previously described and the values are obtained from mvrnorm. A requirement for this function is that the covariance matrix is positive definite, which means that all the eigenvalues must be positive, if it is not then an error message is generated. For a two trait model this means that the correlation cannot be ±1: this is not a restriction since in this case there is actually only a single trait as each trait's genetic value bears an exact algebraic relationship to the other. To check for a matrix that is not positive definite insert the following code:

```
a <- eigen(CovA)$values    # Get eigenvalues of CovA
print(a)                   # print out
for (i in 1:NX){   if (a[i]<0) stop (c("CovA not positive
definite"))    }
a <- eigen(CovE)$values    # Get eigenvalues of CovE
print(a)
for ( i in 1:NX){   if (a[i]<0) stop (c("CovE not positive
definite"))    }
```

Assuming the previously defined parameter values for 3 traits and genetic means of 1, 2, and 3 we can generate a population of 5 individuals by

```
mu      <- c(1,2,3)                            # trait means
G.X     <- mvrnorm(n = 5, mu=mu, Sigma=CovA)   # Genetic values
E.X     <- mvrnorm(n = 5, mu=c(0,0,0), Sigma=CovE) # Get environmen-
                                                     tal values
P.X     <- G.X + E.X                           # Phenotypic values
P.X
```

which prints out

```
          [,1]       [,2]      [,3]
[1,]   0.6530183  1.814369  4.541958
[2,]   1.8563797  2.311612  2.720842
[3,]  -0.6034434  1.097827  3.708289
[4,]   2.7797293  3.360863  2.851850
[5,]   1.2532598  2.336497  3.578804
```

where the columns represent the trait values and the rows the individuals.

Having produced a population of individuals with phenotypic values it is now necessary to impose selection. Three common types of selection are stabilizing selection, rank-order selection, and threshold selection. Stabilizing selection can be incorporated using the matrix model (Jones et al. 2003)

$$W(z) = \exp\left[-\frac{1}{2}(\mathbf{z} - \theta)^{\mathrm{T}}\omega^{-1}(\mathbf{z} - \theta)\right] \qquad (4.16)$$

where $\mathbf{z}$ is a vector of trait values, θ is a column vector of trait optima, the superscript T indicates matrix transposition and ω is a matrix that describes the selection surface, the diagonal elements describing the strength of stabilizing selection (analogous to the variance of a bivariate normal distribution) and the off-diagonals the strength of correlational selection. Suppose our model consists of two traits for which there is (a) no correlational selectional and stabilizing selection with strengths 2 and 3, respectively, and (b) independent optima of 1 and 4. In the main program we define the relevant two matrices as

```
Theta       <- c(1,4)                 # This is θ
w.matrix    <- matrix(c(2,0,0,3,2,2))  # This is ω
```

The user-defined function SELECTION takes these two matrices plus a vector of phenotypic trait values, z, for a given individual and computes its fitness:

```
SELECTION <- function(z,  Theta,  w.matrix)
{
    Diff      <- z-theta
    Fitness   <- exp(-0.5*t(Diff)%*%solve(w.matrix)%*%Diff)
    return(Fitness)
}
```

The vector of fitnesses of all individuals is computed in the main program using the R function apply:

```
W   <- apply(X=P.X,  MARGIN=1, FUN=SELECTION, Theta, w.matrix)
```

In the case of rank-order selection, which is typically done in artificial selection experiments, the individuals are ranked according to some phenotypic value, which might be a particular trait or a function of several traits (referred to as index selection), and the top or bottom assigned proportion selected to be parents of the next generation. The sample coding below assumes that the smallest 25% of 100 individuals is selected based on the value of the first phenotypic trait (i.e., first column of P.X):

```
# Select the smallest 25% of individuals
    P.selected   <- 0.25   # Proportion selected
    N.Pop        <- 100    # Population size before selection
# Calculate the number selected. Must be integral
```

```
N.selected    <- round(P.selected*N.Pop)
Ranked.Data <- order(P.X[,1])# Find ranking indexes
P.X    <- P.X[Ranked.Data,]    # Reorder P.X in ascending order
```

Threshold selection is the easiest method to impose as it only requires selecting those individuals that lie above or below a threshold value (e.g., Scenarios 4 and 7). In the sample coding individuals below the threshold with respect to a phenotypic trait, T0, are assigned fitness of 0 and those above are assigned a fitness of 1:

```
SELECTION(Phenotype, T0)
{
  n<- length(Phenotype)   # Number of individuals in vector Phenotype
  W<- matrix(0,n)         # Assign all inds an initial fitness of zer0
  W[Phenotype>T0] <- 1    # Assign 1 to those above threshold
  return(W)               # Return fitnesses
}
```

The new genetic mean is calculated from the vector of fitnesses passed back to the main program. On the simple assumption of random mating and no sex differences in the trait the new genetic mean of the population is given by

$$\mu = \frac{\sum_{i=1}^{N} W_i G_i}{\sum_{i=1}^{N} W_i} \tag{4.17}$$

where W_i is the fitness of the ith individual and G_i is its genetic value. Coding for this is simply

```
mu <- sum(Fitness*G.X)/sum(Fitness)
```

If there are differences between the sexes either in trait values or selection then two vectors are required, one for each sex. The two vectors might be passed to the selection function as

```
Fitness <- SELECTION(P.Xmale,    P.Xfemale)
```

Given random mating, the new genetic mean would be

$$\mu = \frac{1}{2}\left(\frac{\sum_{i=1}^{N_{Male}} W_{i,Male} G_{i,Male}}{\sum_{i=1}^{N_{Male}} W_{i,Male}} + \frac{\sum_{i=1}^{N_{Female}} W_{i,Female} G_{i,Female}}{\sum_{i=1}^{N_{Male}} W_{i,Female}} \right) \tag{4.18}$$

4.1.3 Individual locus (IL) models

In this approach to model the evolution of traits an explicit Mendelian model is used. In the simplest case this would be a single locus with two alleles. Complexity can be introduced first by the addition of more alleles and second by the addition of more loci. In the second case one has to consider the possibility of linkage and epistasis. If the time course of the simulation is small (less than 100 generations) and the population is small (say less than a hundred) mutation will generally not have to be incorporated. For the most complex cases in which linkage and epistasis is assumed neither R nor MATLAB is generally fast enough to be useful. Epistasis can be incorporated in simple models (e.g., two locus models) but can become difficult to incorporate in models with many loci and alleleles.

The major problem with explicit Mendelian models is primarily one of book-keeping, which can be very time-consuming both in terms of creating the programs and in running them. Here I shall consider the case of modeling a quantitative trait by assuming that each trait is composed of multiple (from 2 to hundreds) of loci with two or more alleles per locus. For the simplest case of a strictly additive model individuals are explicitly modeled with their trait values determined from the sum of the allelic values plus a normally distributed environmental value with a mean of zero and a variance necessary to generate the required heritability. Genetic correlations due to pleiotropy are created by some genes affecting more than one trait. Examples are given by Mani et al. (1990), Reeve (2000), Reeve and Fairbairn (2001), and Jones et al. (2003, 2004).

To illustrate the general approach I shall consider the problem of programming a simple additive model consisting of two correlated traits, say X and Y. For simplicity, I shall ignore the two sexes but assume a diploid organism, which means that individuals are hermaphrodites (the inclusion of separate sexes only complicates the bookkeeping and for most cases does not change the answer). Genetic correlation between these two traits is caused by loci that affect both traits. Let the number of loci unique to X ("x" loci) be n_x, the number unique to Y ("y" loci) be n_y, and the number that are in common ("c" loci) be n_c. All loci are assumed unlinked and no epistasis. The trait genotypic means are then

$$\begin{aligned} \mu_X &= 2n_x\mu_x + 2n_c\mu_c \\ \mu_Y &= 2n_y\mu_y \pm 2n_c\mu_c \end{aligned} \tag{4.19}$$

where μ_k is the mean at the "k"th type of locus (x, y, c and X, Y). The $\pm$ sign is given for trait Y because the sign depends on whether the traits are positively (thus a "+" sign) or negatively correlated (thus a "−" sign). Trait genetic variances, σ_{GX}^2 and, σ_{GY}^2, are

$$\begin{aligned} \sigma_{GX}^2 &= 2n_x\sigma_x^2 + 2n_c\sigma_c^2 \\ \sigma_{GY}^2 &= 2n_y\sigma_y^2 + 2n_c\sigma_c^2 \end{aligned} \tag{4.20}$$

where σ^2_{Gk} is the variance at the "k"th type of locus (x, y, c). The only loci that contribute directly to the covariance are those that are in common. Thus for a positive correlation the genetic covariance, σ_{GXY}, is

$$
\begin{aligned}
\sigma_{GXY} &= E[(x-\mu_X)(y-\mu_y)] \\
&= E\{[(x+c) - (n_x\mu_x + n_c\mu_c)][(y+c) - (n_y\mu_y + n_c\mu_c)]\} \\
&= E[(x-n_x\mu)(y-n_y\mu_y)] + E[(x-n_x\mu_x)(c-n_c\mu_c)] + E[(y-n_y\mu_y)(c-n_c\mu_c)] + E[(c-n_c\mu_c)^2] \\
&= 0+0+0+E[(c-n_c\mu_c)^2] \\
&= 2n_c\sigma_c
\end{aligned}
$$

(4.21)

and for a negative correlation the result is simply $\sigma_{GXY} = -2n_c\sigma^2_c$

The **G** matrix is therefore

$$
\begin{pmatrix} 2n_x\sigma^2_x + 2n_c\sigma^2_c & \pm 2n_c\sigma^2_c \\ \pm 2n_c\sigma^2_c & 2n_y\sigma^2_y \pm 2n_c\sigma^2_c \end{pmatrix}
$$

(4.22)

In principle we could analyze the model using the methods outlined in Section 1. However, if we are interested in following changes in genetic variances or covariances an individual locus model is required.

To program the above model each trait consists of two matrices (one for the unique loci and one for the common loci, making three matrices in total for the two traits), where the columns correspond to the loci and the rows to individuals. Assuming a diploid organism the first half of the columns represent one set of loci and the second half the other set of loci. Suppose we take the simplest model in which there are two alleles at each locus one contributing 0 and the other 1 to the genetic value. Using equations (4.19–4.21) the parameter values are

$$
\begin{aligned}
\mu_X &= 2n_x p_x + 2n_c p_c \\
\sigma^2_{GX} &= 2n_x p_x(1-p_x) + 2n_c p_c(1-p_c) \\
\sigma_{GXY} &= \pm 2n_c p_c(1-p_c)
\end{aligned}
$$

(4.23)

with similar terms for trait Y (note that $\mu_Y = 2n_y p_y \pm 2n_c p_c$). The number of loci is assigned by the user and the initial allele frequencies are set to generate the appropriate genetic correlation. I shall assume that $n_x = n_y = n$. Given this, the genetic correlation, r_G, is

$$
r_G = \pm \frac{n_c p_c(1-p_c)}{np\left(1-p\right) + n_c p_c(1-p_c)}
$$

(4.24)

where p is the frequency of the loci unique to each trait. A simple approach to fixing p_c and p is to iterate over the range and pick a value that gives the appropriate genetic correlation. The coding below does this for $n = 30$ and $n_c = 25$. The program components are

1. A function called RG that calculates the genetic correlation given p, p_c (passed in vector P), n and n_c (passed as n and nc).

2. A function called TRAIT that calculates the trait mean given the above parameters.

3. A main program in which contour maps of genetic correlations and trait means are constructed. The data for the genetic correlations are also sorted into ascending order and printed, allowing for the selection of allele frequencies that give the appropriate genetic correlation.

R CODE:

```
rm(list=ls())      # Remove all objects from memory
RG <- function(P,n,nc){nc*P[2]*(1-P[2])/(n*P[1]*(1-P[1])+nc*P
[2]*(1-P[2]))}
TRAIT <- function(P,n,nc){2*(P[1]*n+P[2]*nc)}
   ninc     <- 20  # Number of increments in which frequency range is
                   divided
   P.unique <- seq(0.01, 0.99, length=ninc) # Loci unique to a trait
   P.common <- seq(0.01,0.99, length=ninc)   # Loci common to both
                                              traits
#   Create all combinations
   Combinations     <- expand.grid(P.unique, P.common)
   N.unique         <- 30       # Nos of unique loci per trait
   N.common         <- 25       # Nos of common loci per trait
#   Calculate Rg for all combinations
   Rg <- apply(X=Combinations, MARGIN=1, FUN=RG, N.unique, N.
common)
#   Create matrix of Rg for contour plotting
#   Columns = changing P.common, Rows = changing P.unique
   Rg.matrix <- matrix(Rg,ninc,ninc)
   par(mfrow=c(2,2))       # Divide graphics page
   contour(P.unique, P.common, Rg.matrix, xlab="Freq of unique al-
leles", ylab ="Freq of common alleles")
#   Calculate trait values
   Trait <- apply(X=Combinations, MARGIN=1, FUN=TRAIT, N.unique,
N.common)
   Trait.matrix <- matrix(Trait,ninc,ninc) # Convert to matrix
   contour(P.unique, P.common, Trait.matrix, xlab="Freq of unique
alleles", ylab ="Freq of common alleles")
   h <- cbind(Combinations, Rg, Trait) # Combine combinations and Rg
   y <- order(Rg)                      # Get order for Rg
   x <- h[y,]                          # Create an ordered set
   x                                   # Print set
```

OUTPUT: (Figure 4.1)

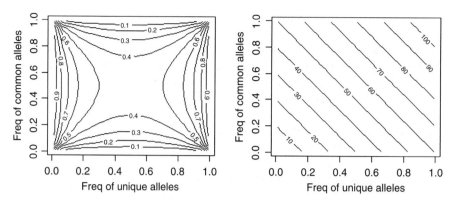

Figure 4.1 Contour plots showing the effect of varying the frequencies of unique and common alleles in an individual locus model.

The printed output is not shown. Suppose we wanted a genetic correlation of ± 0.9, given the above ranges the values from the printout closest to 0.9 are

```
 41 0.01000000 0.11315789 0.89414895    6.257895
 60 0.99000000 0.11315789 0.89414895   65.057895
341 0.01000000 0.88684211 0.89414895   44.942105
360 0.99000000 0.88684211 0.89414895  103.742105
```

Note that there are a range of combinations that give the same genetic correlation and that they result in different trait means. The particular combination chosen will likely affect the rate of change of genetic parameters such as the heritabilities and genetic correlation. Values closer to 0.9 can be found by varying the number of increments and the ranges. An alternative method is to rearrange equation (4.24) to give

$$p^2 - p + \left(\frac{1 - r_G}{r_G}\right)\left(\frac{n_c}{n}\right)p_c(1 - p_c) = 0 \qquad (4.25)$$

which can be readily solved for p, given the other parameter values. A solution is not guaranteed and so it is worthwhile to construct the contour graph to ensure that the values do permit a sensible solution. For example, from Figure 4.1 it can be seen that it is not possible to get a value of p for $r_G = 0.9$ and $p_c = 0.5$.

We get the environmental variance by rearranging the formula $h^2 = \sigma_G^2/(\sigma_G^2 + \sigma_E^2)$ to give

$$\sigma_E^2 = \frac{(1 - h^2)\sigma_G^2}{h^2} \qquad (4.26)$$

Next we need to specify the phenotypic correlation as this determines the covariance between the environmental values. To obtain the latter we first rearrange the formula relating the phenotypic correlation to the genetic and environmental correlations (equation (4.12)) to give

$$r_E = \frac{r_P - r_G\sqrt{h_X^2 h_Y^2}}{\sqrt{(1 - h_X^2)(1 - h_Y^2)}} \qquad (4.27)$$

We then rearrange the formula for the correlation to give us

$$\sigma_{EXY} = r_E \sigma_{EX} \sigma_{EY} \qquad (4.28)$$

In the following coding an additional parameter value to be assigned by the user is the total population size at each generation (set at 6 in the coding below). In the sample coding the initial allele frequencies

```
Pxy        <- 0.16        # Proportion at x or y loci
Pc         <- 0.63        # Proportion of c loci
```

are set to give a genetic correlation of about 0.5 (actual value from code = 0.5099541), given that the number of unique loci per trait is 5 and the number of loci common to both traits is 3. The allele frequencies are set in the function ASSIGN.LOCI which determines whether an allele takes the value of 0 or 1 based on a random number. For example, if $Pxy = 0.16$ then a random number that is less than 0.16 generates an allelic value of 1 whereas a random number greater than 0.16 generates an allelic of zero. Thus summing over all loci will give an expected frequency 0.16. The initial mean trait value is 5.38 for both traits (if the genetic correlation were negative the initial means would differ as per equation (4.19)).

```
rm(list=ls())                 # Remove all objects from memory
ASSIGN.LOCI <- function(G.loci,   N.Pop, P)
{
Total.loci   <-N.Pop*2*G.loci   # Total number of loci in population
Alleles   <- runif(Total.loci)    # Generate random number 0-1
Temp              <- Alleles
Alleles[Temp<P] <- 1          # Allocate to 1s
Alleles[Temp>P] <- 0          # Allocate to 0s
return(Alleles)
} # End of function
##################### Main Program #####################
set.seed(10)              # Initialize random number generator
N.Pop      <- 6           # Population size at each generation
X.loci   <- Y.loci <- 5  # Loci per gamete unique to X or Y
C.loci   <- 3            # Loci per gamete common to X and Y
h2.X      <- 0.5          # heritability of X
h2.Y      <- 0.25         # Heritability of Y
Rp        <- 0.25         # Phenotypic correlation
S         <- 1            # Sign of genetic correlation
Pxy       <- 0.16         # Proportion unique to x or y loci
Pc        <- 0.63         # Proportion of c loci
```

```
  Trait.X    <- 2*(Pxy*X.loci + Pc*C.loci)      # Mean value of X
  Trait.Y    <- 2*(Pxy*Y.loci + S*Pc*C.loci)   # Mean value of Y
# Genetic variance of iX/i and Y
  VarGX   <- 2*(X.loci*Pxy*(1-Pxy)+ C.loci*Pc*(1-Pc))
  VarGY   <- 2*(Y.loci*Pxy*(1-Pxy)+ C.loci*Pc*(1-Pc))
  CovGXY  <- 2*C.loci*Pc*(1-Pc)             # Genetic covariance
  Rg    <- S*CovGXY/sqrt(VarGX*VarGY)       # Genetic correlation
  print(c(Rg, VarGX, VarGY, Trait.X, Trait.Y)) # Print out values
# Calculate the environmental correlation
  Re <- (Rp - Rg*sqrt(h2.X*h2.Y))/sqrt((1-h2.X)*(1-h2.Y))
# Check that this Re is possible
  if (abs(Re)>1) stop (c("Re not possible"))
# Environmental Variances and Standard deviations
  Ve.X   <- (1-h2.X)*VarGX/h2.X   # Environmental variance for X
  SDe.X  <- sqrt(Ve.X)            # Environmental SD for X
  Ve.Y   < (1-h2.Y)*VarGY/h2.Y   # Environmental variance for Y
  SDe.Y  <- sqrt(Ve.Y)           # Environmental SD for Y
  CovE   <- Re*SDe.X*SDe.Y       # Environmental covariance
  Ematrix <- matrix(c(Ve.X,CovE,CovE,Ve.Y),2,2)  # Covariance
                                                    matrix
# Nos of loci in each category
  Nx.Alleles <-ASSIGN.LOCI(X.loci, N.Pop, Pxy) #Alleles unique to X
  Ny.Alleles <-ASSIGN.LOCI(Y.loci, N.Pop, Pxy) #Alleles unique to Y
  Nc.Alleles <-ASSIGN.LOCI(C.loci, N.Pop, Pc)  #Alleles common to X & Y
# Now make three matrices for loci in individuals

  G.Xmatrix <- matrix(Nx.Alleles, N.Pop, 2*X.loci)  # X composition
  G.Ymatrix <- matrix(Ny.Alleles, N.Pop, 2*Y.loci)  # Y composition
  G.Cmatrix <- matrix(Nc.Alleles, N.Pop, 2*C.loci)  # C composition
```

The above coding generates the three matrices. A sample output for G.Xmatrix is

```
       [,1] [,2] [,3] [,4] [,5] [,6] [,7] [,8] [,9] [,10]
[1,]    1    1    0    1    1    1    1    0    0    1
[2,]    1    1    1    1    1    0    1    1    1    1
[3,]    1    1    1    1    1    1    1    1    1    1
[4,]    1    1    1    1    1    1    1    1    1    1
[5,]    0    1    0    1    1    1    1    0    1    1
[6,]    1    1    1    1    1    1    1    1    1    1
```

Note that there are 6 rows, corresponding to 6 individuals, and 10 columns, corresponding to 5 diploid loci. We can get the actual genetic variances using the two R functions rowSums, which calculates the sum of the values in each row (which is the genetic value of the individual), and var, which calculates the variances among these sums:

```
# Get actual genotypic values
  G.X    <- rowSums(G.Xmatrix) + rowSums(G.Cmatrix) # X Genotypic
                                                        values
  VarGX <- var(G.X)                                 # Vg for X
  G.Y<- rowSums(G.Ymatrix) + rowSums(G.Cmatrix) # Y Genotypic values
  VarGY <- var(G.Y)                                 # Vg for Y
  print(c(VarGX, VarGY))
```

For a population size of 1,000 the output from the above code is `[1] 2.724881 2.594794`, as compared to the expected 2.7426 for both traits. To create the phenotypic values we add an environmental value to each individual. The environmental values are correlated and hence we use the function `mvrnorm` to generate an `N.Pop` x 2 matrix of environmental values the first column giving the X values and the second column giving the Y values (remember to load the library MASS):

```
# Create phenotypic values
  Env <- mvrnorm(n=N.Pop, mu=c(0,0), Sigma=Ematrix) # Environmen-
                                                        tal values
  P.X    <- G.X + Env[,1]      # Vector of X phenotypes
  P.Y    <- G.Y + Env[,2]      # Vector of Y phenotypes
  VarPX  <- var(P.X)           # Phenotypic variance of X
  VarPY  <- var(P.Y)           # Phenotypic variance of Y
```

The actual heritabilities are thus given by

```
  h2.X   <- VarGX /VarPX       # Heritability of X
  h2.Y   <- VarGY/VarPY        # Heritability of Y
  print(c(h2.X, h2.Y))         # Print results
```

For the same population of 1,000, as used above, the output is `[1] 0.4708531 0.2582277`, the expected values being 0.5 and 0.25. The correlations are readily obtained using the R function `cor`:

```
  Rg <- cor(G.X, G.Y)        # Genetic correlation
  Rp <- cor(P.X, P.Y)        # Phenotypic correlation
  print(c(Rg, Rp))
```

which gives `[1] 0.4947939 0.1973116`, where the expected values are 0.5 and 0.25, respectively.

The next process to consider is that of selection. Here I shall assume a threshold regime in which individuals with an X trait value greater than `T0` are selected. In the coding below `T0` is set at the initial mean trait value (`Trait.X`):

```
SELECTION <- function(Phenotype, Genotype, T0)   # Selection
                                                     function
{
  Selected <- Genotype[Phenotype>T0,] # Selection
  return(Selected)                # Return matrix of selected genotypes
} # End function
```

In the main program the above function is called three times to select from the three genotypic matrices according to the values of the phenotypes, in this case the X phenotype:

```
ParentX  <- SELECTION (P.X, G.Xmatrix, Trait.X) # Select from the X matrix
ParentY  <- SELECTION (P.X, G.Ymatrix, Trait.X) # Select from the Y matrix
ParentC  <- SELECTION (P.X, G.Cmatrix, Trait.X) # Select from the C matrix
ParentX  # Print selected matrix
ParentY  # Print selected matrix
ParentC  # Print selected matrix
```

In the above example selection involves only a single trait: selection on multiple traits can also be done by, for example, using sequential culling or an index. Starting with a population size of 6 (as in the coding above) the following individuals were selected:

```
> ParentX # Print selected matrix
      [,1] [,2] [,3] [,4] [,5] [,6] [,7] [,8] [,9] [,10]
[1,]   1    1    0    1    1    1    1    0    0    1
[2,]   1    1    1    1    1    0    1    1    1    1
[3,]   1    1    1    1    1    1    1    1    1    1
[4,]   1    1    1    1    1    1    1    1    1    1
[5,]   0    1    0    1    1    1    1    0    1    1
[6,]   1    1    1    1    1    1    1    1    1    1

> ParentY# Print selected matrix
      [,1] [,2] [,3] [,4] [,5] [,6] [,7] [,8] [,9] [,10]
[1,]   0    1    1    1    1    1    1    1    1    1
[2,]   0    1    1    1    0    1    1    1    1    1
[3,]   1    0    0    1    1    1    1    1    1    1
[4,]   1    1    1    1    1    1    0    1    1    1
[5,]   1    0    1    1    1    1    1    1    1    1
[6,]   1    1    1    1    1    1    0    1    1    1

> ParentC # Print selected matrix
      [,1] [,2] [,3] [,4] [,5] [,6]
[1,]   0    1    1    0    0    1
[2,]   0    0    0    0    1    0
[3,]   0    1    0    1    0    0
[4,]   0    1    0    0    0    0
[5,]   0    1    1    0    0    0
[6,]   0    0    1    1    1    0
```

The third process to consider is that of offspring production. Given that each locus is independent and of equal value (0 or 1) I shall simplify the problem of forming a gamete pool by ignoring the distinction among loci (i.e., that the first G.loci represent one set and the second half of the row represents the other set) and drawing from each individual G.loci from each category at random. For example, suppose the set of loci for an individual with 5 X loci is given by the vector

Column number	1	2	3	4	5	6	7	8	9	10
	1	0	0	0	0	1	1	0	0	0

To exactly mimic sexual reproduction we would select at random between alleles at positions 1 and 6, 2 and 7, 3 and 8, 4 and 9, 5 and 10. A simpler approach that should be adequate unless loci differ in their contributions is to select at random, without replacement, 5 alleles from the set and assign them to the gamete pool:

```
GAMETE <- function(X,  G.loci)                    # Pick loci for gamete pool
{
Y <- sample(x=X, size=G.loci, replace=FALSE) # Randomly select G.loci
return(Y)
}
```

This function is called from the main program using the R function `apply`. Note that the resulting matrix has to be transposed to conform to the correct matrix structure:

```
# Form Gamete pool
   GameteX     <- apply(ParentX, 1, GAMETE, X.loci)
   GameteX     <- t(GameteX)         # Convert to proper matrix
   GameteY     <- apply(ParentY, 1, GAMETE, Y.loci)
   GameteY     <- t(GameteY)         # Convert to proper matrix
   GameteC     <- apply(ParentC, 1, GAMETE, C.loci)
   GameteC     <- t(GameteC)         # Convert to proper matrix
```

From the gamete pool we now select 2*N.Pop gametes which are combined at random to form the next generation of individuals. To do this we first create a sequence from 1 to N.Parents, where N.Parents is the number of selected individuals. We next sample at random, with replacement, from this sequence 2*N.Pop values, which become the index values defining the gametes to be combined to give the next generation. This matrix is called S.GameteJ, where J = X, Y, or C and consists of 2*N.Pop rows and columns equal to the number of loci in the relevant category. Individuals are formed by combining the first N.Pop rows with the second set of rows.

```
   N.Parents  <- nrow(ParentX)       # Number of available parents
   n          <- seq(1, N.Parents)   # sequence 1 to N.Parents
# Get 2*N.Pop random indices with replacement
   G.Index    <- sample(x=n, size=2*N.Pop, replace=TRUE)
# Get gametes from gamete pool
  S.GameteX   <- GameteX[G.Index,]
  S.GameteY   <- GameteY[G.Index,]
  S.GameteC   <- GameteC[G.Index,]
# Next generation
```

```
n1           <- N.Pop+1
n2           <- 2*N.Pop
G.Xmatrix    <- cbind(S.GameteX[1:N.Pop,], S.GameteX[n1:n2,])
G.Ymatrix    <- cbind(S.GameteY[1:N.Pop,], S.GameteY[n1:n2,])
G.Cmatrix    <- cbind(S.GameteC[1:N.Pop,], S.GameteC[n1:n2,])
```

At this point we introduce mutation into the scenario. One method is to iterate over all loci and use a random number generator to determine if the allele at the locus changes. Such an approach is very time consuming. An alternate approach is to first generate the number of mutations occurring in this particular set of loci. Given that the probability of a mutation at a locus is very small the total number of mutations will follow a Poisson distribution:

$$P(x) = \frac{e^{-\lambda x}}{\lambda!} \tag{4.29}$$

where x is the number of mutations and λ is the mean, given as $\lambda = P_M N_{Pop} 2 n_{loci}$, in which P_M is the per locus mutation rate, N_{Pop} is the population size, and n_{loci} is the number of loci in the relevant category. The distribution of the number of mutations is given by the R function rpois and thus for each generation the number of mutations can be generated by the call

```
N.mutations <- rpois(1,lambda)
```

To select and convert alleles we pass the matrix G.Xmatrix, G.Ymatrix, or G.Cmatrix to the use function MUTATION, which does the following:

1. Convert the matrix of alleles, called X in the function, into a column vector, Temp, of length 2*N.inds*G.loci=T.loci, where G.loci is X.loci, Y. loci, or C.loci and N.inds is the number of individuals (here N.Pop):

```
Temp <- matrix(X)   # Convert X to a vector
```

2. Generate N.mutations random integers between 1 and T.loci using the uniform generator R function runif and the R function ceiling:

```
Row <- ceiling (runif (N.mutations, min=0, max=T.loci))
```

3. This set of integers represents the rows of the vectors that are affected by mutation. In principle it is possible to pick the same row twice, though this is highly unlikely given the low probability of mutation (say 10^{-4} or less). At each of these rows the value is changed, 0 to 1 or 1 to 0:

```
Temp[Row] <- (abs(Temp[Row]-1))
```

4. The vector is now converted back into a matrix and passed back to the main program:

```
X <- matrix(Temp, N.inds, 2*G.loci)
```

The complete function (where Pmut is the mutation probability) is

```
MUTATION <- function(X, Pmut, G.loci, N.inds)
{
  T.loci  <- N.inds*2*G.loci     # Total number of alleles
  lambda  <- Pmut*T.loci   # Mean number of mutations in population
  N.mutations <- rpois(1,lambda)     # Number of mutations
  Row      <- ceiling(runif(N.mutations, min=0, max=T.loci))
  Temp     <- matrix(X)                # Convert matrix to a vector
  Temp[Row] <- (abs(Temp[Row]-1))     # Change relevant row entries
  X     <- matrix(Temp, N.inds, 2*G.loci) # Convert back to a matrix
return(X)
} # End function
```

This completes a single generation of selection. Multiple generations are simulated by the appropriate inclusion of an iteration loop. The complete program is discussed in scenarios 4 and 7.

4.2 Summary of scenarios

Scenario 1: Illustration of the use of a PVC model to plot the trajectory of two traits under stabilizing selection

Scenario 2: Usage of an IVC model to solve the life history model examined in Scenario 1 of Chapter 2

Scenario 3: Demonstration of the use of an IVC model to analyze the effect of directional selection on a single trait

Scenario 4: Illustration of the use of an individual locus model to analyze the effect of directional selection on a single trait

Scenario 5: An IVC model of Scenario 3 of Chapter 3, namely density-dependent selection in the evolution of a parameter in the Ricker function

Scenario 6: Analysis of directional selection on a trade-off using an IVC model

Scenario 7: Analysis of directional selection on a trade-off using an individual locus model

4.3 Scenario 1: Stabilizing selection on two traits using a PVC model

This scenario explores the consequences of stabilizing selection acting on two traits as expressed by equation (4.15).

4.3.1   General assumptions

1. Both traits are quantitative with non-zero heritabilities.
2. Selection is stabilizing.
3. Generations do not overlap.

4.3.2   Mathematical assumptions

1. The change in trait values is governed by equation (4.15).
2. For the purposes of this example the heritabilities are set at 0.2 and 0.4, the phenotypic correlation at 0.4, the genetic correlation at 0.15, and the phenotypic variances at 1 and 2. The diagonal elements of the **W** matrix are set at 2 and 3 and the off-diagonal elements at 0, giving no correlational selection. The optimum trait values are both set at 2 and the initial trait values at 10.

4.3.3   Analysis

R CODE:

```
rm(list=ls())        # Clear workspace
h2   <- c(0.2,0.4)   # Set heritabilities
Vp   <- c(1,2)       # Set phenotypic variances
Rp   <- 0.4          # Set phenotypic correlation
Ra   <- 0.15         # Set genetic correlation
# Check that Re is possible
Re <- (Rp-Ra*sqrt(h2[1]*h2[2]))/sqrt((1-h2[1])*(1-h2[2]))
if(abs(Re) >1 )
{
  print (c("problem with Re", Re))
        stop
}
Va        <- h2*Vp                      # Using h2 =Va/Vp
Covp      <- Rp*sqrt(Vp[1]*Vp[2])       # Using r = Cov/SD1SD2
Cova      <- Ra*sqrt(Va[1]*Va[2])       # Using r = Cov/SD1SD2
Gmatrix   <- matrix( c(Va[1],Cova,Cova,Va[2]),2,2)   # G matrix
Pmatrix   <- matrix(c(Vp[1],Covp,Covp,Vp[2]),2,2)    # P matrix
Theta     <- c(2,2)                 # Optimum trait values
Maxgen    <- 100                    # Number of generations
par(mfrow=c(2,2))                   # Divide graphic page
Wmatrix   <- matrix(c(2,0,0,3), 2,2)  # Set the W matrix
Trait <- matrix(0,Maxgen,2)  # Pre-assign space for trait values
Trait[1,]   <- 10                   # Initial trait values
for (Igen in 2:Maxgen)              # Iterate over generations
{
# Delta z
  Delta.Z  <-  Gmatrix%*%solve(Wmatrix+Pmatrix)%*%(Trait[Igen-
1,]-Theta)
```

```
  Trait[Igen,] <- Trait[Igen-1,]- Delta.Z    # New trait value
}                              # End of Igen loop
# Set axis values for graphing
  min.y <- min.x <- min(Trait); max.y <- max.x <- max(Trait)
# Plot by generation
  Generation <- seq(from=1, to=Maxgen)
  plot(Generation, Trait[,1], ylim <- c(min.y, max.y), xlim=c(0,
Maxgen), ylab='Trait', type='l')
  lines(seq(from=1,to=Maxgen),Trait[,2],lty=2)
# Plot Trait 2 on Trait 1
  plot(Trait[,1], Trait[,2])
  lines(Trait[,1],Trait[,2])
print( c(Rp,Ra,Re))
eigen(Wmatrix)$values
```

OUTPUT: (Figure 4.2)

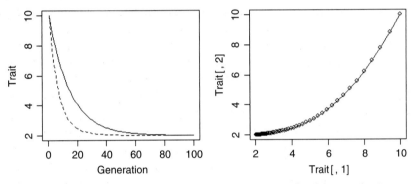

Figure 4.2 Output from Scenario 1 showing the time course of stabilizing selection on two traits (left) and their joint evolution (right).

```
> print( c(Rp,Ra,Re))
[1] 0.400000 0.150000 0.516113
> eigen(Wmatrix)$values
[1] 3 2
```

Both traits eventually reach their respective optima, although it takes quite a few generations.

4.4   Scenario 2: Stabilizing selection using an IVC model

This scenario is an individual-based quantitative genetic model of Scenario 1 of Chapter 2.

4.4.1 General assumptions

1. The organism is semelparous.
2. Fecundity, F, increases with body size, x.
3. Survival, S, decreases with body size, x.
4. Fitness, W, is a function of fecundity and survival.
5. Body size is inherited as a quantitative trait.

4.4.2 Mathematical assumptions

1. Fecundity increases linearly with body size:

$$F = a_F + b_F x \qquad (4.30)$$

where a_F and b_F are constants.

2. Survival decreases linearly with body size:

$$S = a_S - b_S x \qquad (4.31)$$

3. Fitness, W, is the expected lifetime reproductive success, R_0, given as the product of fecundity and survival:

$$
\begin{aligned}
W = R_0 &= FS \\
&= (a_F + b_F x)(a_S - b_S x) \\
&= a_F a_S - b_F b_S x^2 + (a_S b_F - a_F b_S)x
\end{aligned}
\qquad (4.32)
$$

The above equation describes a parabola that is concave down. As in the optimality analysis parameter values are set at $a_F = 0$, $b_F = 4$, $a_S = 1$, and $b_S = 0.5$. The fitness equation can now be written as

$$
\begin{aligned}
W &= 0 \times 1 - 4 \times 0.5x^2 + (1 \times 4 - 0 \times 0.5)x \\
&= -2x^2 + 4x
\end{aligned}
\qquad (4.33)
$$

which has a maximum at $x = 1$.

4.4.3 Analysis

Because it is not possible for individuals to have negative body sizes it may be necessary to either eliminate these from the population or set them at some minimal value. In the present example this possibility is highly unlikely as the optimal body size is 10 phenotypic standard deviations from zero. However, to be sure, I set all negative fecundities, which would correspond to negative body sizes, to zero, giving such individuals zero fitness. I also insert a check on survival to ensure that it is always positive. The calculation of the new genetic mean is done within the function SELECTION. The matrix X passed to SELECTION contains the phenotypic values in the first column and the genetic values in the second. The long-term mean phenotype is calculated ignoring the first 500 generations of selection.

R CODE:

```
rm(list=ls())              # Remove all objects from memory
```

```r
SELECTION <- function(X) # Function to calculate new mean value
{
  As <- 1; Bs <- 0.5; Af    <- 0; Bf <- 4       #   Parameter values
  Survival                  <- As-Bs*X[,1]      #   Survival
  Survival[Survival<0]   <- 0                    #   Check on sign
  Fecundity               <- Af+Bf*X[,1]        #   Fecundity
  Fecundity[Fecundity<0]   <- 0                  #   Check on sign
  X.Fitness            <- Survival*Fecundity  #   Fitness
  mu                   <- sum(X.Fitness*X[,2])/sum(X.Fitness)
  return(mu)
} #   End of selection function
################ Main program ################
  set.seed(100)          #   Initialize random number generator
  N          <- 100      #   Set population size
  MaxGen   <- 2000              #   Number of generations
  Output  <- matrix(0,MaxGen,2)  #   Create file for output
  h2         <- 0.5              #   Set heritability
  Vp         <- (.1)^2           #   Set Phenotypic variance
  Va         <- Vp*h2       #   Calculate Additive genetic variance
  Ve         <- Vp-Va       #   Calculate Environmental variance
  mu         <- 1.5         #   Initial trait mean genetic value
  SDa       <- sqrt(Va)         #   SD of Va
  SDe       <- sqrt(Ve)         #   SD of Ve
  for (Igen in 1:MaxGen)        #   Iterate over generations
{
# Generate Genetic and environmental values using normal distri-
  bution
  GX   <- rnorm(N, mean=mu, sd=SDa)   #   Genetic values
  EX   <- rnorm(N, mean=0, sd=SDe)    #   Environmental values
  PX   <- GX + EX                     #   Phenotypic values
# Combine phenotypic and genetic values
  X   <- cbind(PX,GX)
  Output[Igen,1]   <- Igen       #   Store generation
  Output[Igen,2]   <- mean(PX)   #   Store mean phenotype
# Calculate new mean genetic value by applying fitness criterion
  mu   <- SELECTION(X)          #   apply SELECTION
} # End of Igen loop
# Plot trajectory over generations
  plot(Output[1:MaxGen,1], Output[1:MaxGen,2], type='l',
  xlab='Generation', ylab='Trait value')
  mean(Output[500:MaxGen,2])   # Mean phenotype
  sd(Output[500:MaxGen,2])     # SD of mean
```

OUTPUT: (Figure 4.3)

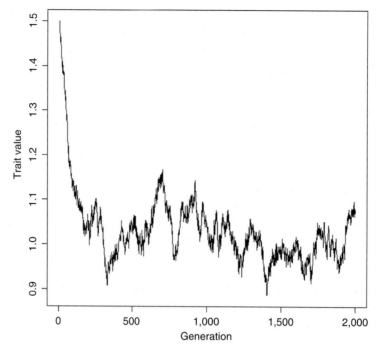

Figure 4.3 Time trace for Scenario 2.

```
> mean(Output[500:MaxGen,2])
[1] 1.017443
> sd(Output[500:MaxGen,2])
[1] 0.04910655
```

The trait value evolves toward the value predicted by the optimality approach (1) and clearly fluctuates about this value (mean ± 2SD encloses 1). Obviously the optimality approach is better for efficiently determining the equilibrium value, but gives no idea of how long this might take or how much the trait value might fluctuate. The quantitative genetic approach can address these questions and herein lies its value in the present case.

4.5   Scenario 3: Directional selection using an IVC model

In this scenario we analyze directional selection on a single trait. For the general quantitative trait the breeder's equation is adequate if the population size is large. However, for small populations there will be stochastic variation which will reduce the rate of change. Formulae to calculate the expected variance about the response to selection have been worked out for the typical cases (see Roff [1997], pp. 137–143) but an individual-based quantitative genetic model can be useful in the case of unusual modes of selection or with traits, such as threshold traits, that are not normally distributed on the expressed scale. The model examined here assumes selection on a threshold trait, but it can be easily modified to accommodate other types of traits or selection scenarios.

4.5.1 General assumptions

1. The trait under selection has two phenotypic expressions but is determined by an underlying normally distributed liability.
2. Only one morph is allowed to contribute to the next generation.

4.5.2 Mathematical assumptions

1. Males and females do not differ in the expression of the trait. They will, nevertheless, be considered separately.
2. Mating between selected individuals is at random.
3. Selected individuals do not differ in their fitness.
4. The two morphs are coded as 0 and 1, with the morph coded as 1 being that which is selected. This coding means that the morph code also corresponds to the morph fitness and the mean genetic value of the parents of the next generation is given by equation (4.18), where fitness, W, is either 0 or 1.

4.5.3 Analysis

In the present coding I have assumed that the trait is wing morph with the short-winged morph being favored (i.e., short-winged individuals are coded as 1 and long-winged individuals are coded as 0). The function SELECTION calculates the new genetic mean liability value using equation (4.18). Although not required, the phenotypic values of the liability are also passed to the selection function: this is done here so that the present coding can be more easily modified for selection on a normally distributed trait that is phenotypically expressed.

At the start of the main program the initial proportion of the two morphs is set and the required threshold value, Z.LW, calculated assuming, without loss of generality, a normal distribution with a mean of 0 and a standard deviation of 1 (use the R function qnorm). Male and female short-winged proportions are shown on the same graph with the values labeled as M or F.

R CODE:
```
rm(list=ls())                    # Remove all objects from memory
SELECTION <- function(Male, Female) # Function to calculate new
                                        mean value
{
# Mean genetic value of males, mu.M, and females, mu.F
# Col1 = Phenotypic value, col 2 = Genetic value, col 3 = Morph code
  mu.M  <- sum(Male[,3]*Male[,2])/sum(Male[,3])
  mu.F  <- sum(Female[,3]*Female[,2])/sum(Female[,3])
  mu    <- (mu.M + mu.F)/2        # New population mean
  return(mu)
}
```

```
##################### Main program #####################
  set.seed(100)              # Initialize random number generator
  N          <- 100          # Set population size
  Prop.LW <- 0.85            # Set initial proportion LW
  Z.LW  <- -qnorm(Prop.LW)   # Threshold. Values greater are LW
  MaxGen     <- 10              # Number of generations
  Output     <- matrix(0,MaxGen,4)       # Create file for output
  h2         <- 0.5           # Set heritability of liability
  Vp      <- 1               # Set Phenotypic variance
  Va      <- Vp*h2           # Calculate Additive genetic variance
  Ve      <- Vp-Va           # Calculate Environmental variance
  mu      <- 0               # Initial mean genetic liability
  SDa     <- sqrt(Va)        # SD of Va
  SDe     <- sqrt(Ve)        # SD of Ve
  for (Igen in 1:MaxGen)     # Iterate over generations
{
# Generate Genetic and environmental values using normal distribu-
  tion
  GM <- rnorm(N, mean=mu, sd=SDa) # Genetic values of males
  GF <- rnorm(N, mean=mu, sd=SDa) # Genetic values of females
  EM  <- rnorm(N, mean=0,  sd=SDe)    # Environmental values of
males
  EF <- rnorm(N, mean=0, sd=SDe)   # Environmental value of females
  PM <- GM + EM                       # Phenotypic value of males
  PF <- GF + EF                       # Phenotypic value of females
# Calculate wing morphs by comparing liability to threshold
  Male.Morph   <- matrix(1,N)      # Set all initially to SW (=1)
  Male.Morph[PM > Z.LW] <- 0       # Set LW to 0
  Female.Morph   <- matrix(1,N)    # Set all initially to SW (=1)
  Female.Morph[PF > Z.LW] <- 0     # Set LW to 0
# Combine phenotypic and genetic values
  Male     <- cbind(PM, GM, Male.Morph )
  Female  <- cbind(PF, GF, Female.Morph)
# Store data
  Output[Igen,1] <- Igen                  # Generation
  Output[Igen,2] <- mean(PM+PF)/2         # Mean liability
  Output[Igen,3] <- sum(Male.Morph)/N     # Proportion of SW males
  Output[Igen,4] <- sum(Female.Morph)/N  # Proportion of SW females
# Calculate new mean genetic value by applying fitness criterion
  mu <- SELECTION(Male,Female)
} # End of Igen loop
  par(mfrow=c(2,2))    # Divide graphics page into quadrats
# Plot proportion of SW males, and SW females over generation on same
graph
```

```
    plot(Output[,1],    Output[,3],pch="M",    xlab='Generation',
ylab='Proportion Short Wings')
    lines(Output[,1], Output[,3])              # Males
    points(Output[,1],Output[,4], pch="F")   # Females
    lines(Output[,1], Output[,4])            # Females
    plot(Output[,1],  Output[,2], xlab='Generation', ylab='Mean
liability')
    lines(Output[,1], Output[,2])
```

OUTPUT: (Figure 4.4)

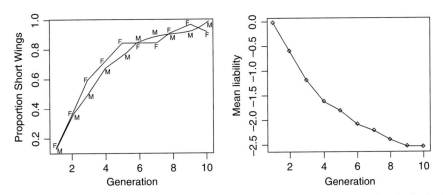

Figure 4.4 Results for Scenario 3. Response by females labeled "F" and that of males by "M."

Note that the response to selection is not constant at either the expressed level or on the underlying liability scale. The reason for this is that the selection intensity decreases as the proportion of the selected morph increases in the population. For experimental data showing this process see Roff (1990).

4.6   Scenario 4: Directional selection using an IL model

The previous scenario is here repeated using an individual locus model. The basic approach is the same as outlined in Section 1.3. This model is a simplified version of that described in Roff (1994b, 1998a, b).

4.6.1   General assumptions

1. The trait under selection has two phenotypic expressions but is determined by an underlying normally distributed liability.
2. Only one morph is allowed to contribute to the next generation.

4.6.2 Mathematical assumptions

1. Males and females do not differ in the expression of the trait. They are not separately distinguished in this model.
2. Mating between selected individuals is at random and can include selfing.
3. Selected individuals do not differ in their fitness.
4. The two morphs are coded as 0 and 1, with the morph coded as 1 being that which is selected. This coding means that the morph code also corresponds to the morph fitness and the mean genetic value of the parents of the next generation is given by equation (4.18), where fitness, W, is either 0 or 1.
5. The phenotypic value is the sum of allelic values and 100 loci, which take values of 0 or 1, plus an environmental deviation.

4.6.3 Analysis

In Section 1.3 a bivariate model was described: the coding below is a simplified version of this model. The initial population is started with a random selection of alleles but the threshold for morph expression is set to 0.85 for long-winged individuals, as in the previous scenario. Prior to the selection the population is run for 10 generations to establish an equilibrium distribution of genotypes. The switch to a selection regime is determined using an "if" statement. A more efficient method is shown in Scenario 7.

R CODE:

```
rm(list=ls()) # Clear memory
  SELECTION <- function(Morph, Genotype)
{
  Selected <- Genotype[Morph==1,] # 1=SW, 0=LW
  return(Selected)
} # End function
################ Function Mutation #################
MUTATION <- function(X, N.mutations, Total.loci, N.ind)
{
# Apply mutation by randomly selecting N.mutations
  Row  <- ceiling(runif(N.mutations, min=0, max=Total.loci))
  Temp       <- matrix(X)
  Temp[Row]  <- (abs(Temp[Row]-1))
  X          <- matrix(Temp,N.ind,N.loci)
  return(X)
} # End function
################ Function Gamete #################
GAMETE <- function(X, G.loci, N.loci)     # Pick loci for gamete
{
  Y <- sample(x=X, size=G.loci, replace=FALSE)  # Random G.loci
                                            from N.loci
  return(Y)
}
```

```
################### Main Program ####################
  set.seed(100)   # Initialize random number generator
  P          <- 0.0001         # Probability of mutation at a locus
  N.Pop      <- 1000           # Population size at each generation
  G.loci     <- 100            # Loci per gamete
  N.loci     <- G.loci*2       # Loci per individual
  Total.loci <- N.Pop*N.loci   # Total number of loci in population
  H2         <- 0.5            # Heritability
  Vg         <- 0.5*G.loci     # Additive genetic variance
  Ve         <- (1-H2)*Vg/H2   # Environmental variance
  SD.E       <- sqrt(Ve)       # Environmental SD
  Prop.LW    <- 0.85           # Set initial proportion LW
# Set Threshold value. Values greater than Z.LW are LW
  Z.LW   <- qnorm(1-Prop.LW, mean=G.loci, sd=sqrt(Vg+Ve))
# Generate matrix of individuals in which
# rows hold individuals while columns hold loci. Allelic values are
1 and 0
# Randomly generate Total.loci number of loci with values of 0 & 1
  Dl <- round(runif(Total.loci))
# Genetic composition of individuals
  Genotype     <- matrix(Dl, N.Pop, N.loci)
  Maxgen       <- 30 # Number of generations simulation runs
  Output       <- matrix(0,Maxgen,5) # Allocate space for output
  Output[,1]   <- seq(from=1, to=Maxgen) # First col=generation
  for (Igen in 1:Maxgen)                  # Iterate over generations
{
  Env.X   <- rnorm(N.Pop, mean=0, sd=SD.E)   # Environmental de-
                                                viations
# Phenotypic values of liability
  Phenotype  <- rowSums(Genotype) + Env.X
  Vg         <- var(rowSums(Genotype))    # Calculate the genetic
variance
  Vp         <- var(Phenotype)         # Phenotypic variance
  H2         <- Vg/Vp                  # heritability
  Morph      <- matrix(1,N.Pop)        # Set morphs initially to SW
  Morph[Phenotype > Z.LW] <- 0         # Change relevant individuals
                                          to LW
  Prop.SW        <- sum(Morph)/N.Pop   # Proportion SW
  Output[Igen,2] <- Prop.SW            # Store proportion SW
  Output[Igen,3] <- H2                 # Store heritability
################### Apply Selection ###################
  if (Igen < 10) # No selection until after generation 10
{
  Parents <- Genotype                        # No selection
}else
```

```
{
   Parents    <- SELECTION(Morph, Genotype)   # Apply selection
}
   N.Parents <- nrow(Parents)                      # Number of parents
# Form next Generation
# Apply Mutation
# Mean number of mutations in population
   lambda          <- P*N.Parents*N.loci
# Number of mutations using a Poisson distribution
   N.mutations    <- rpois(1,lambda)
   Output[Igen,4]   <- N.mutations # Store number of mutations this
                                    generation
# Apply function MUTATION to generate mutant loci
   Genotype    <- MUTATION(Genotype, N.mutations, Total.loci, N.Pop)
# Mating
# Produce gametes for female offspring
# Select from each row G.loci at random
# We do not distinguish individual loci
# Note that this creates a matrix of G.loci rows and N.Females
   columns
# The matrix is transposed to produce the required matrix
   Gametes    <- apply(Parents, 1, GAMETE, G.loci, N.loci)
   Gametes    <- t(Gametes) # Convert to proper matrix
# Produce N.Pop offspring by selecting at random with replacement
   Output [Igen,5]<- N.Parents
# Get N.Pop gametes from "females"
   n           <- seq(1, N.Parents)
   G.Index    <- sample(x=n, size= N.Pop, replace=TRUE)
   F.Gametes <- Gametes[G.Index,]
# Get N.Pop gametes from "males"
   G.Index    <- sample(x=n, size= N.Pop, replace=TRUE)
   M.Gametes <- Gametes[G.Index,]
# New Genotypes
   Genotype    <- cbind(F.Gametes, M.Gametes) # Combine gametes
}
par(mfrow=c(2,2)) # Divide graph page into four quadrats
plot(Output[,1], Output[,2], xlab='Generation', ylab='Propor-
tion SW', type='l')
plot(Output[,1], Output[,3], xlab='Generation', ylab='Herit-
ability',type='l')
plot(Output[,1], Output[,4], xlab='Generation', ylab='Nos of
mutations',type='l')
plot(Output[,1], Output[,5], xlab='Generation', ylab='Nos of
Parents',type='l')
```

OUTPUT: (Figure 4.5)

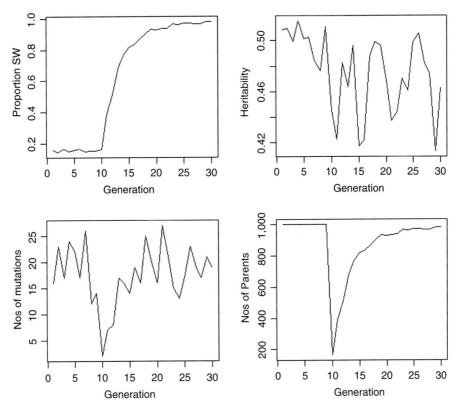

Figure 4.5 Results for Scenario 4.

The general response is the same as in Scenario 3. The primary difference is that selection leads to a loss in genetic variation, though the effect is slight and would be very hard to experimentally detect. Also note that after a brief period following the initiation of selection the population returns very close to its starting value.

4.7   Scenario 5: A quantitative genetic analysis of the Ricker model

This scenario investigates the influence of density-dependent selection in the evolution of a parameter of the Ricker function. It is an individual-based quantitative genetic model of Scenario 3 of Chapter 3.

4.7.1   General assumptions

1. The organism is semelparous.

2. Recruitment is governed by a density-dependence function that allows for cyclical or chaotic population dynamics.

3. The parameters of the recruitment function are related such that the density-independent component is negatively related to the density-dependent component.

4. These parameters are inherited.

4.7.2   Mathematical assumptions

1. Population at time $t + 1$ is a Ricker function of the population at time t:

$$N_{t+1} = N_t \alpha e^{-\beta N_t} \qquad (4.34)$$

2. The parameter α is a measure of density-independent recruitment whereas β is a measure of the density-dependent effect: increases in α increase recruitment but increases in β decrease recruitment by increasing the density-dependent component, $e^{-\beta N_t}$. Thus a positive functional relationship between α and β is indicative of a trade-off between the two recruitment components. For this scenario I shall assume the relationship

$$\beta = 0.001\alpha \qquad (4.35)$$

3. The parameter α is a quantitative genetic trait. By the previous assumption, the correlation between α and β is 1. Note that the genetic correlation could still be one but that the phenotypic value might still be influenced by a separate environmental value, in which case we would have

$$\beta = 0.001\alpha + \varepsilon \qquad (4.36)$$

where ε is a random normal variable with mean zero. For simplicity, and to maintain comparison with the clonal model of Chapter 3, I shall set $\varepsilon = 0$.

4. Fitness is the number of offspring left by each individual. Thus individual fitness, W_i, which also equates to cohort size, N_i, is

$$W_i = N_i = \alpha_i e^{-\beta_i N_{\text{Pop}}} \qquad (4.37)$$

and the new mean trait value and population size are (subscripts for generation omitted for simplicity)

$$\mu_\alpha = \frac{\sum\limits_{i=1}^{N_{\text{Pop}}} W_i G_{\alpha,i}}{\sum\limits_{i=1}^{N_{\text{Pop}}} W_i} \qquad (4.38)$$

$$N_{\text{Pop}} = \sum\limits_{i=1}^{N_{\text{Pop}}} W_i$$

where N_{Pop} is the total population size and $G_{\alpha,i}$ is the genetic value of the ith individual.

4.7.3 Analysis

The selection function SELECTION requires both the X matrix (consisting of the phenotypic and genetic values) and the total population size, N. Population size must be an integer and so is rounded to the nearest integer value. The simulation is run for 10,000 generations and the mean trait value is calculated after the first 2,000 generations, which appears to be the approximate number of generations required to achieve the equilibrium value, given the starting value, which is quite far removed from the optimal value.

R CODE:

```
rm(list=ls())                   # Remove all objects from memory
SELECTION <- function(X,N) # Function to calculate new mean value
{
BETA      <- X[,1]*0.001                    # Beta
X.Fitness <- X[,1]*exp(-BETA*N)            # Fitness
mu        <- sum(X.Fitness*X[,2])/sum(X.Fitness)  # New mu
N         <- round(sum(X.Fitness))         # Popn size
return(c(mu, N))                           # Return values
}   # End of selection function
#################### Main program ####################
set.seed(100)           # Initialize random number generator
N          <- 100       # Set population size
MaxGen     <- 10000     # Number of generations
Output     <- matrix(0,MaxGen,3)   # Create file for output
h2         <- 0.5       # Set heritability
Vp         <- .1        # Set Phenotypic variance
Va         <- Vp*h2     # Calculate Additive genetic variance
Ve         <- Vp-Va     # Calculate Environmental variance
mu         <- 10        # Trait mean genetic value
SDa        <- sqrt(Va)  # SD of Va
SDe        <- sqrt(Ve)  # SD of Ve
for (Igen in 1:MaxGen)  # Iterate over generations
{
# Generate Genetic and environmental values using normal distribution
GX  <- rnorm(N, mean=mu, sd=SDa)   # Genetic values
EX  <- rnorm(N, mean=0, sd=SDe)    # Environmental values
PX  <- GX + EX                     # Phenotypic values
# Combine phenotypic and genetic values
X                 <- cbind(PX,GX)
Output[Igen,1]    <- Igen         # Store generation
Output[Igen,2]    <- mean(PX)     # Store mean phenotype
Output[Igen,3]    <- N            # Store popn size
```

```
# Calculate new mean genetic value by applying fitness criterion
   B       <- SELECTION(X,N)
   mu      <- B[1]    # New mu
   N       <- B[2]    # New population size
}    # End of Igen loop
   par(mfrow=c(2,2)) # Divide graphics page into quadrats
   plot(Output[10:MaxGen,1],    Output[10:MaxGen,2],    type='l',
xlab='Generation', ylab='Trait value')
   plot(Output[10:MaxGen,1], Output[10:MaxGen,3],type='l',
   xlab='Generation',ylab='Population Size, N')
# Print out mean trait value and mean population size
   c(mean(Output[2000:MaxGen,2]), mean(Output[1000:MaxGen,3]))
```

OUTPUT: (Figure 4.6)

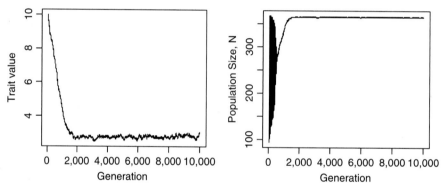

Figure 4.6 Results for Scenario 5.

```
> c(mean(Output[2000:MaxGen,2]), mean(Output[1000:MaxGen,3]))
[1] 2.752786 364.705144
```

After considerable fluctuation both the trait value (α) and population size settle
down to values more or less the same as those equilibria obtained in the invasibility and elasticity analyses (2.73 and 368 [latter not previously given]).

4.8   Scenario 6: Evolution of two traits using an IVC model

The advantage of an IBM using a variance components approach is that it readily
accommodates scenarios that are difficult to incorporate in a population variance
components approach, particularly if one is interested in the effect of small population sizes. The following scenario assumes selection on one trait that is negatively
correlated with another trait. The component that is difficult to incorporate in a
population variance components approach is that fitness is a truncated distribution.

4.8.1 General assumptions

1. Generations are non-overlapping.
2. There is a negative correlation (both genetic and phenotypic) between the two traits X and Y.
3. Fitness is equal to the value of trait X for $X > 0$. If trait X is negative fitness is zero. A simple example of this is if the realized manifestation of trait X is itself fecundity.

4.8.2 Mathematical assumptions

1. The two traits follow the usual quantitative genetic assumptions.
2. Males and females have the same phenotypic values and subject to the same selection. Thus the fitness of an individual, W_i, with trait value X_i is given by

$$\text{if } X_i > 0 \; z_i = X_i \text{ else } z_i = 0$$

$$W_i = \frac{z_i}{\sum\limits_{i=1}^{N_{Pop}} z_i} \tag{4.39}$$

where N_{Pop} is the number of individuals in the population.

3. Mating is random. Because males and females are identical in this scenario the new genetic mean of trait X, μ_{GX}, is

$$\mu_{GX} = \frac{\sum\limits_{i=1}^{N_{Pop}} W_i X_{GXi}}{\sum\limits_{i=1}^{N_{Pop}} W_i} \tag{4.40}$$

where X_{GXi} is the genetic value of the ith individual. Because of the selection on trait X, the mean genetic value of trait Y is given by

$$\mu_{GY} = \frac{\sum\limits_{i=1}^{N_{Pop}} W_i X_{GYi}}{\sum\limits_{i=1}^{N_{Pop}} W_i} \tag{4.41}$$

4.8.3 Analysis

For the purpose of illustration the heritabilities are set at 0.4 and 0.5 for X and Y, respectively. The genetic and phenotypic correlations are set at -0.8 and -0.7, respectively. From these values plus the phenotypic variances (set at 1 and 0.5) the genetic, and environmental variance–covariance matrices are calculated as described in Section 1.2. Remember to load the library MASS, which is required for the multivariate normal routine. The general flow of the program is

1. Selection function
2. Set parameter values
3. Enter loop for iterating over generations
4. Generate genetic, environmental, and phenotypic values using `mvrnorm`
5. Apply selection
6. Next generation
7. Plot results

R CODE:

```
rm(list=ls())        # Clear workspace
library(MASS)        # Load library MASS
SELECTION <- function(Trait.P, Trait.A)
{
# Determine fitness from trait X (=trait 1)
# Traits with negative value have zero fitness, e.g. zero fecundity
Fec    <- Trait.P[,1]           # Preliminary fecundities
Fec[Trait.P[,1]<00]   <- 0      # Adjust fecundity of individuals
Total.Fec   <- sum(Fec)         # Total fecundity of popn
NewX1       <- sum(Fec*Trait.A[,1])/Total.Fec   # New mean X
NewX2       <- sum(Fec*Trait.A[,2])/Total.Fec   # New mean Y
Mean.A      <- c(NewX1, NewX2)                   # Combine
return(Mean.A)
}   # End of function
###################### MAIN PROGRAM ######################
set.seed(100)        # Initialize random number generator
Npop     <- 1000     # Population size
MaxGen   <- 10       # Nos of generations for simulation
Output   <- matrix(0,MaxGen,3)    # Allocate storage for trait
################# Create initial matrices #################
# In this version the sexes are ignored
# This assumes that selection acts equally
# Give.Hmatrix is a dataframe with genetic correlations in upper
  diagonal
# heritabilities along the diagonal and phenotypic correlations in
  the lower diagonal
NX     <- 2     # Number of traits
# Matrix of heritabilities and correlations
H2     <- matrix(c(0.4,-0.8,
               -0.7, 0.5), 2,2, byrow=TRUE)
Mean.A  <- c(3, 3)    # Initial additive genetic means
Mean.E  <- c(0,0)     # Environmental means
Var.P   <- c(1, 0.5)  # Phenotypic variances
# Phenotypic Covariance matrix
# Note that initial covariances set to 1 (arbitrary)
CovP     <- matrix(1,NX,NX)    # Phenotypic variances
```

```
  diag(CovP) <- Var.P           # Diagonal elements = variances
# Establish CovA from h2 and CovP and CovE from CovA and CovP
  CovA    <- matrix(0,NX,NX)  # Allocate memory for genetic matrix
  CovE    <- matrix(0,NX,NX)  # Allocate memory for envir. matrix
for ( i in 1:NX)    # Iterate over components of (co)variance matrix
{
  CovA[i,i]   <- CovP[i,i]*H2[i,i]   # Genetic variance = Vp*h2
  CovE[i,i]   <- CovP[i,i]-CovA[i,i]   # Environmental covariances
if(CovE[i,i] < 0) stop (print(c("CovE cannot be",i,j,CovE[i,i])))
}
# Phenotypic and genetic covariances
  N.minus.1 <- NX-1
for( i in 1:N.minus.1)
{
    jj <- i+1
for(j in jj:NX)
{
  CovP[i,j] <  CovP[j,i]  <- CovP[i,j]        # Matrix symmetrical
  CovA[i,j] <-H2[i,j]*sqrt(CovA[i,i]*CovA[j,j]) # Genetic covariance
  CovA[j,i] <-CovA[i,j]                         # Matrix symmetrical
  CovE[i,j] <-CovP[i,j]-CovA[i,j]               # Environ. covariance
  CovE[j,i] <-CovE[i,j]
}  # End of j loop
}  # End of i loop
##################### Start Simulation #####################
for (Igen in 1:MaxGen)   # Iterate to MaxGen
{
# Generate additive and environmental values
  Trait.E <- mvrnorm(Npop, mu=Mean.E, Sigma=CovE)  # Environ.
  Trait.A <- mvrnorm(Npop, mu=Mean.A, Sigma=CovA) # Genetic
  Trait.P <- Trait.A + Trait.E                   # Phenotypic
# Store data
  Output[Igen,1]  <- Igen
  Output[Igen,2]  <- mean(Trait.P[,1])              # X
  Output[Igen,3]  <- mean(Trait.P[,2])              # Y
  Mean.A  <- SELECTION(Trait.P, Trait.A)      # New X and Y
} # End of Igen loop
# Plot results
  ymin <- min(Output[,2:3]); ymax <- max(Output[,2:3]) # Trait X
  plot(Output[,1], Output[,2], xlab="Generations", ylab="Trait
  X (solid) and Y (dotted)", type='l', ylim = c(ymin, ymax)) # Trait
  X on generation
  lines(Output[,1], Output[,3], lty=2)  # Trait Y on generation
```

OUTPUT: (Figure 4.7)

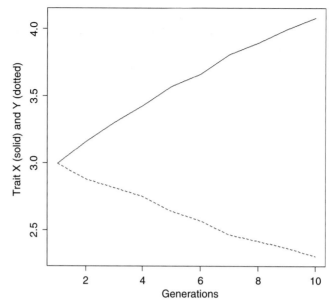

Figure 4.7 Results for Scenario 6.

The figure shows that selection on trait X increases trait X but, because of the negative correlation, trait Y declines in value.

4.9   Scenario 7: Evolution of two traits using an IL model

The general scenario is similar to Scenario 4 in which fitness is a threshold function and to Scenario 6 in which two negatively correlated traits are modeled. The basic coding follows which is similar to the one discussed in Section 1.3.

4.9.1   General assumptions

1. Generations are non-overlapping.
2. There is a negative correlation (both genetic and phenotypic) between the two traits X and Y.
3. Fitness is a threshold value, such that individuals above some threshold T0 contribute equally to the next generation whereas individuals below T0 have zero fitness.

4.9.2   Mathematical assumptions

1. Males and females do not differ in the expression of the trait. They are not separately distinguished in this model.
2. Mating between selected individuals is at random and can include selfing.
3. Selected individuals do not differ in their fitness.

4. The threshold for selection is set at the initial mean value of trait X

5. The phenotypic value is the sum of allelic values, which take values of 0 or 1, plus an environmental deviation.

6. Parameter values are as follows:

   a. Population size is 1,000.

   b. Number of unique loci is 30.

   c. Number of loci in common is 25.

   d. Initial frequency at unique loci is 0.68.

   e. Initial frequency at common loci is 0.47.

   f. Initial genetic correlation given the forgoing values is -0.488.

   g. Initial trait value of X is 64.3 and of Y is 17.3.

   h. Initial heritabilities are 0.4 and 0.5.

   i. Initial phenotypic correlation is -0.7.

4.9.3 Analysis

The general flow of the model is described in detail in Section 1.3. Simulation proceeds in the following steps:

1. Assign parameter values as given above.

2. Calculate other required parameters (e.g., r_E).

3. Set up initial genotypes using function `ASSIGN.LOCI`.

4. Set up selection threshold for required generations of selection (matrix `T0`). The threshold is set for the first generations such that there is no selection, allowing the stabilization of genotypic frequencies. After five generations the threshold is set to the initial value of X (`Trait.X`).

5. Iterate over generations. Within this loop we

   5a. Calculate genotypic values using `rowSums`

   5b. Create environmental values using `mvrnorm`

   5c. Add the environmental values to generate phenotypic values

   5d. Apply function `SELECTION`

   5e. Create the gamete pool using function `GAMETE`

   5f. Get gametes from pool and create the next generation of genotypes

   5g. Apply function `MUTATION`

6. Plot results.

R CODE:

```
rm(list=ls())                    # Remove all objects from memory
ASSIGN.LOCI <- function(G.loci, N.Pop, P)
{
```

```
    Total.loci <- N.Pop*2*G.loci      # Total number of loci in population
    Alleles <- runif(Total.loci)      # Generate random number 0-1
    Temp          <- Alleles
    Alleles[Temp<P] <- 1              # Allocate to 1s
    Alleles[Temp>P] <- 0              # Allocate to 0s
    return(Alleles)
} # End of function
###################### SELECTION ######################
SELECTION  <-  function(Phenotype, Genotype, T0)  # Selection
                                                    function
{
  Selected <- Genotype[Phenotype >T0,]  # Selection
  return(Selected)                      # Return selected genotypes
} # End function
###################### GAMETE ######################
GAMETE <- function(X, G.loci)   # Pick loci for gamete pool
{
  Y <- sample(x=X, size=G.loci, replace=FALSE) # Randomly select G.loci
  return(Y)
}
################# Function Mutation #################
MUTATION <- function(X, Pmut, G.loci, N.inds)
{
  T.loci   <- N.inds*2*G.loci
  lambda   <- Pmut*T.loci # Mean number of mutations in population
# Number of mutations using a Poisson distribution
  N.mutations <- rpois(1,lambda)
# Randomly select N.mutations rows
  Row     <- ceiling(runif(N.mutations, min=0, max=T.loci))
  Temp    <- matrix(X)                    # Convert to a vector
  Temp[Row]  <- (abs(Temp[Row]-1))        # Convert mutated rows
  X   <- matrix(Temp, N.inds, 2*G.loci)   # Convert back to matrix
  return(X)
} # End function
##################### Main Program #####################
  set.seed(10)           # Initialize random number generator
  N.Pop     <- 1000      # Population size at each generation
  X.loci <- Y.loci<- 30  # Loci per gamete unique to X
  C.loci   <- 25         # Loci per gamete common to X and Y
  h2.X     <- 0.4        # heritability of X
  h2.Y     <- 0.5        # Heritability of Y
  S        <- -1         # Sign of genetic correlation
  Rp       <- -0.7       # Phenotypic correlation
  Pxy      <- 0.68       # Proportion at x or y loci
  Pc       <- 0.47       # Proportion of c loci
  TraitX<-2*(Pxy*X.loci+Pc*C.loci) # Initial mean trait value of X
```

```
  TraitY <- 2*(Pxy*X.loci+S*Pc*C.loci) # Initial mean trait value of Y
  VarGX    <- 2*(X.loci*Pxy*(1-Pxy)+ C.loci*Pc*(1-Pc))   # Vg of X
  VarGY    <- VarGX                        # Vg of Y
  CovGXY   <- 2*C.loci*Pc*(1-Pc)           # Genetic covariance
  Rg       <- S*CovGXY/sqrt(VarGX*VarGY)   # Genetic correlation
  print(c(Rg, TraitX, TraitY))            # Print values
# Calculate the environmental correlation
  Re   <- (Rp - Rg*sqrt(h2.X*h2.Y))/sqrt((1-h2.X)*(1-h2.Y))
# Check that this Re is possible
  if (abs(Re)>1) stop (c("Re not possible"))
# Environmental Variances and Standard deviations
  Ve.X <- (1-h2.X)*VarGX/h2.X   # Environmental variance for X
  SDe.X   <- sqrt(Ve.X)         # Environmental SD for X
  Ve.Y    <- (1-h2.Y)*VarGY/h2.Y   # Environmental variance for Y
  SDe.Y   <- sqrt(Ve.Y)         # Environmental SD for Y
  CovE    <- Re*SDe.X*SDe.Y     # Environmental covariance
  Ematrix <- matrix(c(Ve.X,CovE,CovE,Ve.Y),2,2) # Covariance ma-
                                               trix

# Nos of loci in each category
  Nx.Alleles <- ASSIGN.LOCI(X.loci, N.Pop, Pxy) # Alleles unique to X
  Ny.Alleles <- ASSIGN.LOCI(Y.loci, N.Pop, Pxy) # Alleles unique to Y
  Nc.Alleles <- ASSIGN.LOCI(C.loci, N.Pop, Pc)  # Alleles common to X & Y
# Now make three matrices for loci in individuals
  G.Xmatrix  <- matrix(Nx.Alleles, N.Pop, 2*X.loci)  # X composition
  G.Ymatrix  <- matrix(Ny.Alleles, N.Pop, 2*Y.loci)  # Y composition
  G.Cmatrix  <- matrix(Nc.Alleles, N.Pop, 2*C.loci)  # C composition
################## Iterate over generations ##################
  Maxgen    <- 40            # Number of generations simulation runs
  Output    <- matrix(0, Maxgen, 9)      # Allocate space for output
  T0        <- matrix(TraitX,Maxgen,1) # Set T0 for generations
  T0[1:5]   <- -100 # Set T0 so that 1st 5 gens there is no selection
  for (Igen in 1:Maxgen)               # Iterate over generations
{
# Get actual genotypic values
  G.X <- rowSums(G.Xmatrix) + rowSums(G.Cmatrix) # X Genotypic values
  VarGX    <- var(G.X)                       # Vg for X
  G.Y <- rowSums(G.Ymatrix) + S*rowSums(G.Cmatrix) # Y Genotypic values
  VarGY    <- var(G.Y)                       # Vg for Y
# Create phenotypic values
  Env   <- mvrnorm(n=N.Pop, mu=c(0,0), Sigma=Ematrix) # Environmental
                                                        values
  P.X       <- G.X + Env[,1]    # Vector of X phenotypes
  P.Y       <- G.Y + Env[,2]    # Vector of Y phenotypes
  VarPX  <- var(P.X)            # Phenotypic variance of X
  VarPY  <- var(P.Y)            # Phenotypic variance of Y
  h2.X   <- VarGX /VarPX        # Heritability of X
```

```
   h2.Y     <- VarGY/VarPY    # Heritability of Y
   Rg       <- cor(G.X, G.Y)  # Genetic correlation
   Rp       <- cor(P.X, P.Y)  # Phenotypic correlation
# Store results
   Output[Igen,1:9] <- c(Igen, VarGX, VarGY, mean(P.X), mean(P.Y),
h2.X, h2.Y, Rg, Rp)
# Apply Selection. Note that selection here is only a function of X
   ParentX   <- SELECTION(P.X, G.Xmatrix, T0[Igen])
   ParentY   <- SELECTION(P.X, G.Ymatrix, T0[Igen])
   ParentC   <- SELECTION(P.X, G.Cmatrix, T0[Igen])
# Form Gamete pool
   GameteX   <- apply(ParentX, 1, GAMETE, X.loci)
   GameteX   <- t(GameteX) # Convert to proper matrix
   GameteY   <- apply(ParentY, 1, GAMETE, Y.loci)
   GameteY   <- t(GameteY) # Convert to proper matrix
   GameteC   <- apply(ParentC, 1, GAMETE, C.loci)
   GameteC   <- t(GameteC) # Convert to proper matrix
   N.Parents <- nrow(ParentX)      # Number of available parents
   n            <- seq(1, N.Parents) # sequence 1 to N.Parents
# Get 2*N.Pop random indices with replacement
   G.Index      <- sample(x=n, size=2*N.Pop, replace=TRUE)
# Get gametes from gamete pool
   S.GameteX   <- GameteX[G.Index,]
   S.GameteY   <- GameteY[G.Index,]
   S.GameteC   <- GameteC[G.Index,]
# Form next generation
   n1           <- N.Pop+1
   n2           <- 2*N.Pop
   G.Xmatrix   <- cbind(S.GameteX[1:N.Pop,], S.GameteX[n1:n2,])
   G.Ymatrix   <- cbind(S.GameteY[1:N.Pop,], S.GameteY[n1:n2,])
   G.Cmatrix   <- cbind(S.GameteC[1:N.Pop,], S.GameteC[n1:n2,])
# Mutations
   Pmut         <- 0.0001 # Mutation probability
   G.Xmatrix   <- MUTATION(G.Xmatrix, Pmut, X.loci, N.Pop)
   G.Ymatrix   <- MUTATION(G.Ymatrix, Pmut, Y.loci, N.Pop)
   G.Cmatrix   <- MUTATION(G.Cmatrix, Pmut, C.loci, N.Pop)
} # Next generation
   par(mfrow=c(2,2))
# Plot phenotypic value on generation
   ymin <- min(Output[,4:5]); ymax <- max(Output[,4:5]) # Limits on y
   plot( Output[,1], Output[,4], xlab='Generation', ylab='Pheno-
types', type='l', ylim=c(ymin,ymax))
   lines(Output[,1], Output[,5], lty=2)
# Plot genetic variances on generation
   ymin <- min(Output[,2:3]); ymax <- max(Output[,2:3]) # Limits on y
```

```
plot(Output[,1], Output[,2], xlab='Generation', ylab='Genetic
variances', type='l', ylim=c(ymin,ymax))
  lines(Output[,1], Output[,3], lty=2)
# Plot heritabilities on generation
  ymin <- min(Output[,6:7]); ymax <- max(Output[,6:7]) # Limits on y
  plot(  Output[,1],   Output[,6],   xlab='Generation',   ylab-
='Heritabilities', type='l', ylim=c(ymin,ymax))
  lines(Output[,1], Output[,7], lty=2)
# Plot correlations on generation
  ymin <- min(Output[,8:9]); ymax <- max(Output[,8:9]) # Limits on y
  plot(  Output[,1],   Output[,8],   xlab='Generation',   ylab-
='Correlations', type='l', ylim=c(ymin,ymax))
  lines(Output[,1], Output[,9], lty=2)
```

OUTPUT: (Figure 4.8)

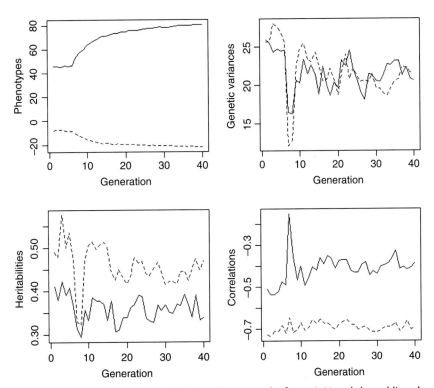

Figure 4.8 Results for Scenario 7. Solid lines shows results for trait X and dotted line shows results for trait Y, except for the plot of correlations in which case the solid line gives the genetic correlation and the dotted line the phenotypic correlation.

As in Scenario 6, selection on trait X increases trait X but decreases trait Y. There is an initial decline in the genetic variances and heritabilities followed by stabilization. The genetic correlation actually increases. Because of the threshold selection, the divergence slowly declines as the proportion of the population exceeding the threshold increases. With rank-order selection we would expect a continuous decline in the genetic variances ultimately leaving the genetic variance at mutation-selection balance.

4.10   Some exemplary papers

Via, S. and R. Lande. 1985. Genotype-environment interaction and the evolution of phenotypic plasticity. *Evolution* **39:505–522.**

Type of model: Population variance components

Characteristics: Single trait, two habitats

Object: To examine the evolution of phenotypic plasticity

Roff, D. A. and D. J. Fairbairn. 2007. Laboratory evolution of the migratory polymorphism in the sand cricket: combining physiology with quantitative genetics. *Physiological and Biochemical Zoology* **80:358–369.**

Type of model: Individual variance components

Characteristics: Three traits (one threshold), directional selection

Object: To predict the evolution of traits in a laboratory population of the cricket, *Gryllus firmus*

Roff, D. A. and D. J. Fairbairn. 2009. Modeling experimental evolution using individual-based variance-components models, in T. Garland and M. Rose (eds.), *Experimental Evolution.* **University of California Press, Berkeley, California.**

Type of Model: Individual variance components

Characteristics: Multiple examples

Object: To illustrate the use of IVC models for the analysis of experimental evolution experiments

Reeve, J. P. 2000. Predicting long-term response to selection. *Genetical Research* **75:83–94.**

Type of model: Independent locus

Characteristics: Three traits, mutation, no linkage, stabilizing, correlational and directional selection

Object: Compare predictions with a population variance component models

Jones, A. G., S. J. Arnold, and R. Borger. 2003. Stability of the G-matrix in a population experiencing pleiotropic mutation, stabilizing selection, and genetic drift. *Evolution* **57:1747–1760.**

Type of model: Independent locus

Characteristics: Two traits, mutation, stabilizing selection, no linkage

Object: To examine the stability of the *G* matrix, particularly with respect to orientation

Guillaume, F. and M. C. Whitlock. 2007. Effects of migration on the genetic covariance matrix. *Evolution* **61:2398–2409.**

Type of model: Independent locus

Characteristics: Two traits, mutation, stabilizing selection, no linkage, two populations

Object: Evolution of the *G* matrix

Boulding, E. G., T. Hay, M. Holst, S. Kamel, D. Pakes, and A. D. Tie. 2007. Modelling the genetics and demography of step cline formation: gastropod populations preyed on by experimentally introduced crabs. *Journal of Evolutionary Biology* **20:1976–1987.**

Type of model: Independent locus

Characteristics: One trait, no mutation, stabilizing selection, no linkage, clinal populations

Object: To predict the evolution of shell thickness along a cline in a snail subject to predation by crabs

CHAPTER 5

Game Theoretic Models

5.1 Introduction

Thus far, frequency-dependent interactions have been assumed not to be present, although they are undoubtedly important in nature (Clarke 1969, 1979; Endler 1986, 1988; Sherratt and Harvey 1993; Sinervo and Calsbeek 2006; Bond 2007). Putative examples of traits under frequency-dependent selection in natural populations are resource polymorphisms (Smith and Skulason 1996), mating polymorphisms (Sinervo and Lively 1996), color polymorphisms (Bond 2007), plant defenses (Núñez-Farfán et al. 2007), and blood group antigen genes (Fumagalli et al. 2009). Analysis of models involving frequency-dependence is the domain of game theory. In a general sense, game theory is concerned with interactions between individuals: The basic scenario is one in which two individuals, called the **players**, meet and interact and either suffer a loss in fitness or an increase in fitness, called in either case the **payoff**. The important element of game theory is the **Payoff matrix**, which designates the increase or decrease in fitness to each player. Analysis consists in locating the **Evolutionarily Stable Strategy** (**ESS**), which, as previously noted, is defined as that strategy (or phenotype) which if adopted by all members of a population cannot be invaded by a mutant strategy (or phenotype) (Maynard Smith 1982). In general, game theoretic models are frequency-dependent but this is not an essential element of such models. Kokko (2007) gives an example of a frequency-independent model that involves the optimal growth rate of two neighboring trees. This case is considered in detail in Scenario 1. Here I shall examine the general elements of the analysis.

5.1.1 Frequency-independent models

The scenario is one in which two trees grow sufficiently close to each other that they interfere with each other's growth. The taller tree has an advantage over the smaller one in that it potentially captures more light (i.e., overshadows the other tree). However, to increase height requires an allocation into structures other than leaves and hence this potentially decreases the light-gathering ability of the tree. Let the payoff, which in this instance equates directly to fitness, to tree A of height h_A when competing against tree B of height h_B be designated by the function $P(h_A, h_B)$. Table 5.1 shows a payoff matrix for the particular functions examined in Scenario 1, the mathematical details of which do not matter at this time. The first entry in each cell of the matrix shows the payoff to tree A for the given combination of heights and the second entry shows the payoff to tree B. The payoff matrix is symmetrical and at equilibrium both trees must be of the same height. Both trees can achieve their best common payoff when they both have zero heights. However, either tree can increase its payoff by increasing its height provided the other tree does not do likewise. Now consider the possible equilibrium of 0.333 for both trees: notice that the changes in payoffs are not symmetrically distributed about this cell, meaning that this equilibrium is not stable. In contrast, the changes in payoffs about the height 0.666 are symmetrical indicating that a stable equilibrium exists in this region. While the equilibrium value can be numerically estimated by graphically plotting the best responses for each tree when faced with a second tree of a given height (see Scenario 1 for details), it can be readily found analytically as follows:

1. Differentiate the payoff function with respect to one of the tree heights (say tree A):

$$\frac{\partial P(h_A, h_B)}{\partial h_A} \tag{5.1}$$

2. Set $h_B = h_A = h$ (because at equilibrium this must be true).
3. Find the value h at which the above differential is zero. This is the ESS.

Table 5.1 Payoff matrix for two trees growing and competing according to the model described in Scenario 1

Height of tree A	Height of tree B			
	0.000	0.333	0.666	1.000
0.000	0.62, 0.62	0.37, 0.85	0.28, 0.69	0.25, 0.00
	0	–	–	+
0.333	0.85, 0.37	0.60, 0.60	0.36, 0.62	0.27, 0.00
	+	0	–	+
0.666	0.68, 0.27	0.62, 0.36	0.44, 0.44	0.26, 0.00
	+	+	0	+
1.000	0.00, 0.25	0.00, 0.27	0.00, 0.26	0.00, 0.00
	–	–	–	0

Note: In each cell the payoff to tree A is placed first and the payoff to tree B is placed second. The sign of the difference of A minus B is shown in the table.

Source: Adapted from Kokko (2007).

5.1.2 Frequency-dependent models

A more usual scenario considered by evolutionary game theory is that in which the ESS is frequency-dependent. The "classic" example of this type of game is the Hawk-Dove game. In this scenario there are two responses to a meeting between two individuals: A hawk response is aggressive, whereas a dove response is passive or at least less aggressive. Plausible biological examples of this scenario are fights for territories, food resources, mates, or some other resource that affects fitness. The simplest payoff matrix for this situation is given in Table 5.2. A hawk interacting with a dove receives a gain in fitness of V whereas the dove receives no fitness increment (in fact it might loose fitness). Two doves interacting split the potential gain in fitness and both receive $V/2$. Two hawks interacting also split the potential fitness which is V minus an amount C that is the cost to fighting: thus the payoff to each hawk is $(V - C)/2$. It is important to remember that the payoff is not fitness but the change in fitness. Thus the fitness of an individual after an encounter is $W_0 -$ payoff, where W_0 is the initial fitness.

At one extreme a population could consists of only one type of individual that adopts a Hawk strategy at an encounter with some probability, p, and thus a Dove strategy with probability $1 - p$: such a strategy is termed a **Mixed strategy**. At the other extreme the role might be fixed in the population, there being p hawks and $1 - p$ doves. This is a **Pure strategy** because the behavior is fixed within a morph. This makes no difference to the ESS but, as is discussed below, is important in numerical analyses. At the ESS the fitness of hawks must match the fitness of doves. Assuming only a single encounter the two fitnesses, $W(Hawk)$ and $W(Dove)$ are

$$W(Hawk) = W_0 + p\frac{1}{2}(V - C) + (1 - p)V$$

$$W(Dove) = W_0 + p0 + (1 - p)\frac{1}{2}V$$

(5.2)

At equilibrium

$$W(Hawk) = W(Dove)$$

$$W_0 + p\frac{1}{2}(V - C) + (1 - p)V = W_0 + p0 + (1 - p)\frac{1}{2}V$$

$$p = \frac{V}{C}$$

Table 5.2 Payoff matrix for the Hawk-Dove game

	Hawk	Dove
Hawk	½(V–C)	V
Dove	0	½V

Note: The payoffs are those achieved by the individuals in the left-hand column when interacting with an individual along the given row.

If an equilibrium exists (i.e., $0 < p < 1$) then $V < C$, which means that the cost of fighting must exceed the gains or else the population will consist only of one type. We cannot stop here because the equilibrium might not be stable (e.g., a billiard ball balanced at the end of a cue is at equilibrium only so long as it is not moved fractionally). What we need to show is that if the proportion of hawks increased their overall fitness would decrease, and similarly, any increase in the proportion of doves would decrease their overall fitness. To do this we consider two situations:

1. Payoff in the mixed equilibrium population when a dove is encountered: from Table 5.2 this is $pV + (1 - p)\frac{1}{2}V = \frac{1}{2}V(1 + p)$. The payoff to a pure dove population is $\frac{1}{2}V$, which is clearly less than the payoff in the mixed population and hence an increase in the proportion of doves will be opposed by natural selection.

2. Payoff in a mixed population when a hawk is encountered is $p\frac{1}{2}(V - C)$ and the payoff to a pure hawk population is $\frac{1}{2}(V - C)$. Because $V < C$ the payoff to the mixed population is greater than that in a pure hawk population and hence an increase in the proportion of hawks will be opposed by natural selection.

The Hawk-Dove game exemplifies the general strategy for finding the ESS in frequency-dependent games. In some games not all possible interactions might occur: For example, in some animal species certain individuals hold territories while others act as satellites and attempt to sneak insemination of the female attracted to the territorial male. In this situation, the interactions between individuals of the same type are typically not considered. Examples of this type of scenario are Atlantic salmon, bluegill sunfish, and certain cricket species (Roff 1996). The analysis of this type of game is illustrated in Scenario 8.

As described earlier, the Hawk-Dove game is a very simple game and there are a large number of complications one could add to make the model more biologically realistic. Of particular importance for which numerical analyses may be a fruitful approach are (a) the size of the population, (b) the mode of inheritance, and (c) the number of different strategies.

5.1.3   The size of the population

In general, population size is assumed to be infinite thus eliminating stochastic variation. However, population sizes may be quite small (see table 8.3 in Roff [1997]), particularly in experimental situations. Recent theoretical work has shown that in a finite population evolution to the ESS, even if it exists for the infinite population, is not assured (Lessard 2005; Orzack and Hines 2005). Thus, it is highly advisable to study the stability of the ESS as a function of population size.

5.1.4   The mode of inheritance in two-strategy games

In Chapter 4 genetic models were used to establish the evolutionary trajectory of traits in density-dependent models. Such models are excellent also for the analysis of frequency-dependent models. For convenience of discussion, I shall use the Hawk-Dove game as a model, but the following applies to any game with two types of players. There are four possible ways in which two types might be determined:

1. There is no genetic variation in the population, the role taken by an individual being entirely probabilistic. This is a highly unlikely situation since there could be no evolution to the ESS. However, this does not preclude an entirely phenotypic analysis based on this assumption if we further assume that the genetic mechanism is not a bar to the evolution. The numerical analysis in this case can be tedious as it requires the introduction of "mutants" into the population, which can be computationally intensive. One approach would be to introduce a learning function which would allow individuals to locate their optimal behavior within the population. Harley (1981) has considered the issue of learning in this context but as discussed in Scenario 9, this approach does not seem viable for numerically locating the ESS, though it gives considerable insight into the variation expected in a population.

2. The population consists of two or more clones, each clone being either a hawk or a dove.

3. The determination of each type could be programmed by a simple Mendelian inheritance pattern such as a single locus with two alleles. The programming in this case could be quite varied: For example, we might have HH, HD, and DD being three genotypes with HH being hawk, DD being dove, and HD a mixture, or the genotypes might program a propensity to adopt one strategy. Depending on the details of the genetic model it is possible that the ESS might not be attainable (Maynard Smith 1982). Working out the equilibrium frequency given a Mendelian mode of inheritance can be difficult analytically but can be resolved numerically (see Scenarios 3 and 6).

4. The determination of each type is a function of many loci making a quantitative genetic approach appropriate. A simple quantitative genetic model that has been applied to many cases of dimorphic morphological variation and could equally well be applied to other dimorphisms is the threshold model, described in Chapter 4. In this model, we assume that there is an underlying normally distributed trait called the liability and a threshold of expression: individuals below the threshold display one morph while individuals above display the alternate morph (Figure 1.10). Under this model there is no constraint to the population achieving the ESS (e.g., Scenario 4). While it is possible to determine the equilibrium proportions using the threshold model, there is no advantage to be gained over using the more easily analyzed phenotypic model. The specific case in which this is not so is when the population is finite and one is interested in investigating the degree of population fluctuations (see Scenario 4).

5.1.5 The number of different strategies

Games with just two morphs are relatively simple but the addition of more strategies can complicate analysis. The Hawk–Dove game can be extended by introducing a third strategy, which Maynard Smith called "Bourgeois," in which the role taken depends on the circumstance: For example, if the fight is over territory, the Bourgeois strategy is be Hawk if the owner and Dove if the intruder. In the numerical example given by Maynard Smith the Bourgeois strategy is an ESS and hence the population is reduced to a single type. While the ESS of games with multiple roles might be resolved analytically, a numerical approach can be useful in checking on the result and looking for dynamical behavior such as cycles. An interesting example of a three-role game is the Rock-Paper-Scissors (R-P-S) game, which has recently been applied by Sinervo and Lively (1996) to the case of three-color morphs in the side-blotched lizard (this game is examined in detail in Scenarios 5, 6, and 7).

As with the two-role game, the analysis of the phenotypic model is relatively straightforward, although, as exemplified by the R-P-S game, there may not be a single stable equilibrium. Numerical analysis can be helpful in testing for such behaviors. Potential difficulty arises when attempting to assign a genetic model to multiple role games. The clonal model is simple and presents no difficulty in assigning roles but in any Mendelian model there are potentially a large number of ways of assigning phenotypes to genotypes. The simplest Mendelian model is one in which there is a single locus with three alleles, eventhough in this model there are three heterozygotes which have to be assigned phenotypes. Unless there is empirical data to suggest a plausible model one must question the merit of such an investigation. Even greater difficulties arise with a quantitative genetic model. The general threshold model for polymorphisms is to assign several thresholds. This model seems appropriate for cases where the morphs are actual multiples of each other, as in the case of multiple digits in guinea pigs but is harder to justify in the case of qualitatively distinct morphs. Furthermore, the range of combinations of morph types is severely restricted in the multiple threshold model and an ESS may not, in general, be possible. An alternative model is to have three separate traits that are normally distributed with the morph being "decided" by the trait with the highest value. A plausible model for this could be three hormones or other physiological products that direct development or behavior, with the expression being dictated by the largest product. A variant on this would be to have the probability of expression of a morph being a function of the relative values of the three traits. Coding for these models is given in Scenario 7.

5.2 Summary of scenarios

Scenario 1: Describes the application of the game theory approach to a frequency-independent game. competition between neighboring trees are discussed in Section 1.1.

Scenarios 2–4: In these scenarios the Hawk-Dove game is analyzed using three modes of transmission between generations: a clonal model (Scenario 2), a simple Mendelian model (Scenario 3), and a quantitative genetic model (Scenario 4).

Scenarios 5–7: Model complexity is increased by the possibility of three behaviors. The particular scenario is the R-P-S game discussed by Sinervo (2001) in relation to the interactions among lizard morphs. As in the Hawk-Dove game, three modes of transmission are considered: a clonal model (Scenario 5), a simple Mendelian model (Scenario 6), and a quantitative genetic model (Scenario 7).

Scenario 8: In the previous scenarios any morph could interact with any other morph. In some cases only a limited set of interactions might be possible: For example, with territorial and satellite behaviors the set of possible interactions may not include territorial versus territorial.

Scenario 9: Behavioral responses may change with learning. This scenario describes the coding for the model presented by Harley (1981).

5.3   Scenario 1: A frequency-independent game

Frequency-independent games are not as common as those involving frequency-dependence and are more readily solved. The illustrative example given here is taken from Kokko (2007) and considers the optimal growth strategies of two trees that interfere with each other.

5.3.1   General assumptions

1. Two trees grow sufficiently close to each other that they interfere with each other's growth.
2. Growth is positively related to the amount of leaf tissue and the amount of this that can photosynthesize.
3. The amount of leaf tissue is a function of the allocation to growth in height versus the growth in leaf tissue.
4. The proportion of leaf tissue declines as biomass is allocated to increasing plant height.
5. The amount of photosynthesis is a function of the difference in height of the trees, the larger tree being potentially capable of having greater photosynthesis per leaf.
6. Fitness is a function of the payoff matrix, being greatest for the plant with the highest payoff.

5.3.2   Mathematical assumptions

1. The proportion of leaf tissue declines monotonically with plant height, h, according to the equation

$$f(h) = 1 - h^{\alpha} \tag{5.4}$$

where α is a constant. This equation is arbitrary except that it satisfies the criteria that at zero height $f(h) = 0$ (all tissue is leaf tissue) and at maximum height ($h = 1$) $f(h) = 0$ (no allocation to leaf tissue).

2. Photosynthesis per leaf increases in the focal tree as the difference in height, Δh, increases, having a minimum at a value of P_L and a maximum at P_H

$$g(\Delta h) = P_L + \frac{P_H - P_L}{1 + e^{-5\Delta h}} \tag{5.5}$$

As with equation (5.4) the particular form of the equation is arbitrary except for satisfying the two criteria stated above and showing a sigmoidal shape.

3. Designating the two trees as A and B, the difference in height is $h_{\alpha A} - h_{\alpha B}$ and the payoff to tree A and B (P_A and P_B, respectively) is

$$P_A = (1 - h_A^{\alpha}) \left[P_L + \frac{P_H - P_L}{1 + e^{-5(h_{\alpha A} - h_{\alpha B})}} \right]$$

$$P_B = (1 - h_B^{\alpha}) \left[P_L + \frac{P_H - P_L}{1 + e^{-5(h_{\alpha B} - h_{\alpha A})}} \right] \tag{5.6}$$

Values for the constants were set at $\alpha = 3$, $P_L = 0.25$, and $P_H = 1$. These are arbitrary but reasonable.

4. Fitness is equated to the payoff.

5.3.3 Plotting the fitness curves

The first thing to note about the payoffs to A and B is that they are symmetrical. Therefore, we only have to find the optimal fitness curves for one of the trees as, by symmetry, this must be the same for the other tree, though care is needed in converting it to a form that can be plotted on the same graph. To do this we create a function for the payoff matrix and call this over a range of heights for trees A and B.

A simple way to code the problem would be to use two loops. While this is intuitively clear it is relatively slow and a faster way is to make use of the R function `expand.grid`, which takes the **x** and **y** vectors (here denoted by *Height*, because both vectors are identical) and creates a two-column matrix of all combinations. Following the calculation of the payoffs for these combinations, the vector of payoffs is converted into an $n \times n$ matrix, where n is the number of points into which *Height* has been divided. We then must find the highest payoff for each value of *Height*, which we do using the R function `order`. The first call finds the optimal response of tree B to a given height of tree A. To obtain the reverse response we simply reverse the coordinates in the call to the plotting routine.

R CODE:

```
rm(list=ls())
PAYOFF <- function(X)    # Function to calculate the payoff
{
# Set constants. Note that these could be passed to the function
  alpha <- 3; Pl <- 0.25; Ph <- 1
# Note that X[2] is the first height to ensure that payoff matrix
# corresponds to the shape shown in Table 5.1
  f   <- (1-X[2]^alpha)                    # Calculate f
  g   <- Pl + (Ph-Pl)/(1+exp(-5*(X[2]-X[1])))  # Calculate g
  Pay   <- f*g                            # Calculate payoff
  return(Pay)                             # Return payoff
}
############### Main Program ##############
  n        <-   200              # Number of divisions
  Height <- seq(0,1, length=n)    # Vector of heights for each tree
  d     <- expand.grid(Height, Height) # Create matrix of all comb-
                                          inations
  Paytemp <- apply(d,1,PAYOFF)         # Get payoff matrix for tree
  Payoff  <- matrix(Paytemp, n, n, byrow=T) # Convert to a matrix
  BestResponse <- matrix(0,n,1)        # Create a vector to take
                                         best response
  for (i in 1:n)                    # Iterate over each value of Height
{
# Get order of indexes (Highest first) for Payoffs to Tree B for a
# given Height of tree A. Get order by column200
  Index <- order(Payoff[,i], na.last=TRUE, decreasing=TRUE)
# Store best Payoff for Tree B against tree A
  BestResponse[i]   <- Height[Index[1]]
}
# Plot the best response of tree B against tree A as a solid line
  plot(Height, BestResponse, type='l', xlab='Height of tree A',
ylab='Height of tree B', xlim=c(0,1), ylim=c(0,1))
# Plot the best response of tree A against tree B as a dashed line
# Note that because of symmetry this is done by reversing the axes
  lines(BestResponse, Height, lty=2)
```

OUTPUT: (Figure 5.1)

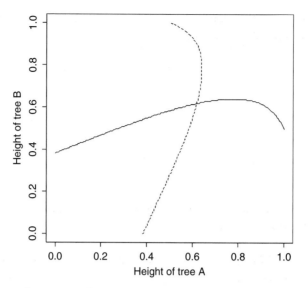

Figure 5.1 Optimal response of one tree given the height of its neighbor. The solid line shows the best response of tree B given the height of tree A. The dashed line shows the best response of tree A given the height of tree B. The ESS is at the point of intersection.

Reading from the graph, the optimum is in the region of 0.6 as previously surmised from Table 5.1. We now consider an analytical solution.

5.3.4   Finding the ESS using the calculus

5.3.4.1   Using the derivative directly

We begin by differentiating P_A with respect to h_A. To utilize the chain rule (Appendix 2) I find that it is easier to rewrite the function as

$$P_A = (1 - h_A^\alpha)\left\{P_L + (P_H - P_L)[1 + e^{-5(h_A - h_B)}]^{-1}\right\} \tag{5.7}$$

And thus

$$\frac{\partial P_A}{\partial h_A} = -\alpha h_A^{\alpha-1}\left[P_L + \frac{P_H - P_L}{1 + e^{-5(h_A - h_B)}}\right] + (1 - h_A^\alpha)(P_H - P_L)(-1)[-5e^{-5(h_A - h_B)}][1 + e^{-5(h_A - h_B)}]^{-2} \tag{5.8}$$

At equilibrium $h_A = h_B$ and hence $e^{-5(h_A - h_B)} = 1$, reducing the above equation to

$$\frac{\partial P_A}{\partial h_A} = -\alpha h_A^{\alpha-1}\left(P_L + \frac{P_H - P_L}{1 + 1}\right) + (1 - h_A^\alpha)(P_H - P_L)(-1)(-5)(1 + 1)^{-2}$$

$$= -\alpha h_A^{\alpha-1}\left(P_L + \frac{P_H - P_L}{2}\right) + (1 - h_A^\alpha)(P_H - P_L)\left(\frac{5}{4}\right) \tag{5.9}$$

Substituting values for the constants ($\alpha = 3$, $P_L = 0.25$, and $P_H = 1$) and setting $\frac{\partial P_A}{\partial h_A} = 0$ gives

$$-1.875h_A^2 + (1 - h_A^3)0.9375 = 0 \qquad (5.10)$$

which can be solved numerically using `nlm` in R.

R CODE:

```
rm(list=ls())          # Clear workspace
# Function to calculate payoff Note that we pass the absolute value
# of the payoff because nlm seeks the minimum
  PAYOFF   <- function(x) {abs(-1.875*x^2+(1-x^3)*0.9375)}
  nlm(PAYOFF, p=.5) #Call nlm to find minimum with starting guess at 0.5
```

OUTPUT:
```
$minimum      7.793257e-08
$estimate     0.618034
$gradient     0.001140648
$code         2
$iterations   5
```

This is slightly modified for display and shows that the ESS is 0.618, which agrees visually with the graphic output.

5.3.4.2 Getting the derivative using R

Obtaining the differential can be tedious but can be done either by R or MATLAB (e.g., see Scenario 1 of Chapter 2). Coding in R is a little obscure but relatively simple: we first construct a function, FUNC that takes a value w, differentiates the payoff function with respect to h_A, sets $h_B = w$, and calculates the gradient at this point (grad). The main program finds the value of h_A that is the ESS by using the R function `uniroot` to locate the value of h_A at which the derivative as defined in FUNC is zero.

R CODE:

```
rm(list=ls())          # Clear workspace
# Function to obtain the gradient at a value w
  FUNC   <- function(w)
{
# Get the derivative with respect to hA and assign to y
    y    <- deriv(~(1-hA^3)*(0.25+(1-0.25)/(1+exp(-5*(hA-hB)))),"hA")
    hA   <- w                # Set hA to w
    hB   <- w                # Set hB to w
    Z    <- eval(y)          # Evaluate the derivative at w
    grad <- attr(Z, "gradient") # Assign gradient value to grad
    return(grad)
}
########### MAIN PROGRAM #############
# Call uniroot setting limits from 0 to 1
  uniroot(FUNC, interval=c(0, 1))
```

OUTPUT:
```
$root 0.6180355
$f.root hA
  -5.215027e-06
$iter 6
$estim.prec 6.103516e-05
```

This is slightly modified for display. The ESS value is 0.618 and the estimated gradient at this value is $-5.215e-06$. The ESS was found in 6 iterations with an approximate precision of $6.104e-05$.

5.3.5   Finding the ESS using a numerical approach

The ESS can be found numerically using the same program as for plotting. The ESS occurs at the height at which the height at the best payoff for A minus the height at the best payoff for B is zero. To find this create the vector `Height-BestResponse` and find the location, say k, at which this difference is closest to zero: the height that is the ESS is `Height[k]`.

R CODE:
{First lines the same as for plotting. Can delete call to plot}

```
DIFF    <- abs(Height-BestResponse) # Make vector of absolute
                                         differences
Index   <- order(DIFF)      # Find index value for smallest DIFF
Best.Height <- Height[Index[1]]      # Find Height at Index[1]
Best.Height                          # Print out best height
```

OUTPUT:
```
[1] 0.6180905
```

5.4   Scenario 2: Hawk-Dove game: a clonal model

This game is probably the one that is most often given as an illustration of game theory. Its analytical solution is trivial for the infinite population but the consequences of a finite population are not so readily obvious. In this and the next two scenarios we shall examine how to incorporate genetic inheritance into the model and examine the consequences of both the type of inheritance and the population size.

5.4.1   General assumptions

1. The population consists of two types of clones, one which adopts a hawk behavior and another that adopts the dove behavior.

2. A hawk interacting with a dove always wins.

3. A hawk interacting with a hawk earns a negative payoff.

4. A dove interacting with a dove divides the payoff.

5. Fitness is equal to some initial quantity plus the payoff.

5.4.2 Mathematical assumptions

1. The payoff matrix is as shown in Table 5.2.

2. Population size is finite.

3. Only one interaction occurs per individual.

4. Population size is constant with the contribution to the next generation being
determined by the fitness measure

$$N_H(t+1) = \frac{N_{\text{Pop}} \sum_{i=1}^{N_H(t)} W_{H,i}}{\sum_{i=1}^{N_H(t)} W_{H,i} + \sum_{j=1}^{N_D(t)} W_{D,j}} \tag{5.11}$$

where N_{Pop} is the number of individuals in the population, $N_H(t)$ is the number
of hawks at time t, $N_D(t)$ is the number of doves at time t, $W_{H,i}$ is the fitness of the
ith hawk at time t, and $W_{D,i}$ is the fitness of the ith dove at time t.

5.4.3 Finding the ESS using a numerical approach

The important part of the coding is arranging the interaction between individuals.
The population of individuals consists of a vector called `Morph` of length `Npop`
with Hawks coded as 1 and Doves coded as 2. This arrangement allows direct
access to the payoff matrix since, for example, a Hawk interacting with a Hawk
gives the combination 1,1 which corresponds to the position in the payoff matrix.
To create a vector of opponents we randomize `Morph` assigning the outcome to
the vector `Opponent`. Thus, we have two vectors which might look as shown
below for a population of size 4 individuals. Note that this method does potentially
mean that an individual could interact with itself. This is unlikely unless the
population size is very small (as below) and it is probably not worth inserting a
check to prevent this from happening.

$$\begin{matrix} \texttt{Morph} & \texttt{Opponent} \\ \begin{bmatrix} 1 \\ 2 \\ 2 \\ 1 \end{bmatrix} & \begin{bmatrix} 2 \\ 1 \\ 1 \\ 2 \end{bmatrix} \end{matrix}$$

In the above example the payoffs to the individuals in the vector `Morph` are given
from the payoff matrix at positions 1,2:2,1:2,1:1,2. One way to do this would be to
iterate over individuals using a loop of length `Npop`. To each value we add the
initial fitness (in this case 3). A much quicker method is to iterate over all four

possible combinations of the payoff matrix and assign fitnesses based on the values of Morph and Opponent in the following way:

```
Fitness <- matrix(0,Npop,1)  # Pre-assign space for Fitness
                                       vector
# Iterate over the Payoff matrix
  for (Receiver in 1:2 )        # Individual receiving payoff
{
  for (I.Opponent in 1:2)      # Opponent
{
  Fitness[Morph==Receiver & Opponent==
    I.Opponent]<- 3 + PayoffMatrix[Receiver,I.Opponent]
} # End of I.opponent loop
} # End of Receiver loop
```

The proportion of hawks is then calculated from the sum of fitnesses for hawks over the total sum of fitnesses:

```
P.Hawk    <- sum(Fitness[Morph==1])/sum(Fitness)
```

The above operations are placed in a separate function called FITNESS. The remainder of the program is straightforward bookkeeping. The payoff matrix is set such that the optimum proportion is 0.2 hawks with the initial fitness being 3. The number in the population is set at 100 and the initial proportion of hawks is set at 0.5. To see if the proportion of hawks converges to the correct value, the observed proportion after generation 20 is tested against the expected proportion of 0.8 using a *t*-test. (Strictly, an arcsine-square-root transformation should be used, but in this model and the subsequent models there is no qualitative difference and the *t*-test on the raw data is useful in that it gives the 95% confidence limits.)

R CODE:

```
rm(list=ls())        # Remove all objects from memory
# Function to calculate new proportion of Hawks
  FITNESS <- function(Morph, Npop, PayoffMatrix)
{
# Match males up to find fitness for each male
# Create a randomized vector of opponents
  Opponent <- sample(Morph)
  Fitness <- matrix(0,Npop,1) # Preassign space for Fitness vector
# Iterate over the Payoff matrix
  for (Receiver in 1:2 ) # Individual receiving payoff
{
  for (I.Opponent in 1:2) # Opponent
{
  Fitness[Morph==Receiver & Opponent==
  I.Opponent]<- 3 + PayoffMatrix[Receiver,I.Opponent]
```

```
} # End of I.opponent loop
} # End of Receiver loop
# Now calculate the relative fitness of hawks = New proportion of Hawks
P.Hawk <- sum(Fitness[Morph==1])/sum(Fitness) # Mean fitness of Hawk males
  return(P.Hawk)
}
###################### Main program #####################
  set.seed(100)          # Initialize random number generator
  Npop      <- 100       # Set population size
  MaxGen    <- 100       # Number of generations
  Output    <- matrix(0,MaxGen,2)   # Create file for output
  P.Hawk    <- 0.5                  # Initial proportion of Hawks
  Nos.of.Hawks <- Npop*P.Hawk       # Initial number of Hawks
# Set up morph vector initially with all doves
  Morph     <- matrix(2,Npop,1)
# Convert first Nos.of.Hawks rows to Hawks
  Morph[1:Nos.of.Hawks] <- 1
  PayoffMatrix <- matrix(c(-1,0,8,4),2,2) # Set up fitness matrix
# Calculate theoretical frequency
  a <- PayoffMatrix[1,1]
  b <- PayoffMatrix[1,2]
  c <- PayoffMatrix[2,1]
  d <- PayoffMatrix[2,2]
  P.Hawks <- (b-d)/(b+c-a-d)
  for (Igen in 1:MaxGen)       # Iterate over generations
{
  Output[Igen,1]    <- Igen   # Store Generation number in 1st column
# Calculate the proportion of each type
  Nos.of.Hawks      <- length(Morph[Morph==1]) # Number of hawks
  Output[Igen,2]    <- Nos.of.Hawks/Npop       # Proportion of Hawks
# Calculate new proportion of hawks by applying fitness criterion
  P.Hawk            <- FITNESS(Morph, Npop, PayoffMatrix)
# Calculate the new population, making sure Nos.of.Hawks is an
    integer
  Nos.of.Hawks           <- round(Npop*P.Hawk)
  Morph[1:Npop,1]        <- 2 # Initially set rows to Dove
  Morph[1:Nos.of.Hawks,1] <- 1 # Convert first Nos.of.Hawks rows
                                to hawks
} # End of Igen loop
# Plot Output
  plot(Output[,1],   Output[,2],type='l',   xlab='Generation',
ylab='Proportion of hawks')
  lines(Output[,1],  rep(P.Hawks,MaxGen))    # Plot theoretical
                                               expectation
# Do t test on proportion after generation 20 to see if it conforms
```

```
# to the expected value
print(c(mean(Output[20:MaxGen,2]),    sd(Output[20:MaxGen,2]),
P.Hawks))
t.test(Output[20:MaxGen,2], mu=P.Hawks)   # Test for variation
from P.Hawks
```

OUTPUT: (Figure 5.2)

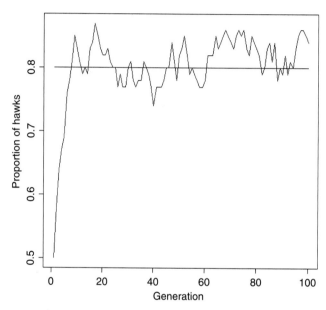

Figure 5.2 Proportion of hawks in a population in which inheritance is clonal and the ESS predicted proportion is 0.8 hawks (Scenario 2).

```
     Mean proportion     SD          Predicted
[1]   0.81160494   0.02938779   0.80000000
>    t.test(Output[20:MaxGen,2], mu=P.Hawks)   # Test for variation
from P.Hawks
  One Sample t-test
data: Output[20:MaxGen, 2]
t = 3.554, df = 80, p-value = 0.0006401
alternative hypothesis: true mean is not equal to 0.8
95 percent confidence interval:
  0.8051068   0.8181031
```

The proportion of hawks quickly rises and bounces around its expected value though the t-test indicates that it is significantly different from the predicted value. This is a consequence of the finite size and the conversion from the proportion to the number of hawks each generation. To demonstrate this we can increase the population size, which should eliminate this effect. Increasing the population size to 1,000 does in fact show the following:

```
[1] 0.80160494   0.01044232   0.80000000
>   t.test(Output[20:MaxGen,2], mu=P.Hawks)   # Test for variation
                                                 from P.Hawks

    One Sample t-test
data: Output[20:MaxGen, 2]
t = 1.3833, df = 80, p-value = 0.1704
alternative hypothesis: true mean is not equal to 0.8
95 percent confidence interval:
0.799296 0.803914
```

5.5   Scenario 3: Hawk-Dove game: a simple Mendelian model

This scenario is the same as the previous one except that the morph is determined by a single locus with two alleles. The immediate issue in such a model is the decision on what morph are heterozygotes. For this illustration I shall assume that heterozygotes are hawks: Alternate scenarios would have heterozygotes being all doves or heterozygotes being hawk or dove with some fixed probability.

5.5.1   General assumptions

1. The population consists of two morphs, one which adopts a hawk behavior and another that adopts the dove behavior.
2. Morph is determined by a single locus with two alleles, H and D.
3. The results of interactions are as specified in Scenario 2.
4. Fitness is equal to some initial quantity plus the payoff.

5.5.2   Mathematical assumptions

1. The payoff matrix is as shown in Table 5.2.
2. Population size is finite.
3. Only one interaction occurs per individual.
4. Genotypes HH and HD are hawks, whereas genotype DD is dove.
5. Population size is constant.
6. The contribution to the next generation is determined by the relative fitnesses as described below.

5.5.3   A graphical analysis

For this analysis we want to plot the change in one generation in the proportion of hawks (and possibly the allele frequency) as a function of this value. A potentially stable equilibrium is indicated by the curve crossing the zero line such that increases in the proportion lead to a decrease in the next generation after this point but an increase below it. It is possible to work out an exact analysis of this using the genotype frequencies and taking into account the relationship between genotype and phenotype. Such an analysis is specific to the given model and does not extend readily to other models. Here I shall present a more computer-intensive method that extends very easily to other Mendelian models (e.g., the R-P-S model described in Scenario 6) and is the basis for the model that follows the change in proportions over time. The essential element in the analysis is the use of an individual-based population model.

We calculate the number of H and D alleles using

$$
\begin{aligned}
n_{\mathrm{H}}(t+1) &= 2\sum_{i=1}^{n_{\mathrm{HH}}(t)} W_{\mathrm{HH},i} + \sum_{i=1}^{n_{\mathrm{HD}}(t)} W_{\mathrm{HD},i} \\
n_{\mathrm{D}}(t+1) &= 2\sum_{i=1}^{n_{\mathrm{DD}}(t)} W_{\mathrm{DD},i} + \sum_{i=1}^{n_{\mathrm{HD}}(t)} W_{\mathrm{HD},i}
\end{aligned}
\tag{5.12}
$$

where $n_{\mathrm{H}}(t+1)$ is the number of H alleles at time $t+1$, $n_{\mathrm{D}}(t+1)$ is the number of D alleles at time $t+1$, $W_{\mathrm{HH},i}$ is the fitness of the ith HH genotype, $W_{\mathrm{HD},i}$ is the fitness of the ith heterozygote, $W_{\mathrm{DD},i}$ is the fitness of the ith DD genotype, $n_{\mathrm{HH}}(t)$ is the number of HH genotypes at time t, $n_{\mathrm{HD}}(t)$ is the number of HD genotypes at time t, and $n_{\mathrm{DD}}(t)$ is the number of DD genotypes at time t. The frequency of H alleles, $p_{\mathrm{H}}(t+1)$, is given by

$$
p_{\mathrm{H}}(t+1) = \frac{n_{\mathrm{H}}(t+1)}{n_{\mathrm{H}}(t+1) + n_{\mathrm{D}}(t+1)}
\tag{5.13}
$$

Assuming random mating the frequency of the three genotypes is given by the Hardy–Weinberg formulae:

$$
\begin{aligned}
p_{\mathrm{HH}}(t+1) &= p_{\mathrm{H}}(t+1)^2 \\
P_{\mathrm{HD}}(t+1) &= 2p_{\mathrm{H}}(t+1)[1 - p_{\mathrm{H}}(t+1)] \\
P_{\mathrm{DD}}(t+1) &= [1 - p_{\mathrm{H}}(t+1)]^2
\end{aligned}
\tag{5.14}
$$

An important assumption in the above formulation is that the vector of morphs represents both males and females and that the payoff matrix for male versus male, female versus female, and male versus female are the same.

The R coding is very similar to that of Scenario 2. The calculation of the fitnesses of the two morphs is done exactly as before. Importantly, the vector `Morph` is constructed such that the first n_{HH} rows are the HH genotypes, the subsequent n_{HD} rows are heterozygotes, and the final n_{DD} rows are the DD genotypes: Thus the first $n_{\mathrm{HH}}+n_{\mathrm{HD}}$ rows are hawks. This allows us to easily compute the summed fitnesses of the H and D alleles using equation (5.12). The proportion of H alleles is then passed from the function FITNESS back to the main program. As shown in the R-P-S game (Scenario 6) this model can easily be extended to more complex Mendelian models. It is most convenient to iterate over the frequency of the hawk allele and then convert this to the proportion of hawks for plotting. The present coding also plots the frequency of the H allele on the same graph.

Because we are using a finite population model there is stochastic variation in the change in the proportion. While this can be reduced by increasing the size of the population the increase in computer time can become irksome. An alternative method, employed here, is to use a modest population size (2,000) and use a curve-fitting routine to obtain a refined function. A suitable method is the R function smooth.spline.

R CODE:

```
  rm(list=ls())        # Remove all objects from memory
# Function to calculate new frequency of H allele
  FITNESS <- function(Morph, PayoffMatrix, HH, HD, Npop)
{
# HH = number of HH genotypes HD = Number of Heterozygotes
# Npop = Population size
# Match males up to find fitness for each male
# Create a randomized vector of opponents
  Opponent    <- sample(Morph)
Fitness       <- matrix(0,Npop,1) # Pre-assign space to Fitness
# Iterate over the Payoff matrix
  for (Receiver in 1:2 ) # Individual receiving payoff
{
  for (I.Opponent in 1:2) # Opponent
{
  Fitness[Morph==Receiver & Opponent==
  I.Opponent]<- 3 + PayoffMatrix[Receiver,I.Opponent]
}} # End of the two loops
# Now we know that 1-HH are hawks
# Calculate range for heterozygotes
  n1        <- HH+1          # Starting row of heterozygotes
  n2        <- n1+HD-1       # Ending row of heterozygotes
# Number of H alleles
  H.alleles  <- 2*sum(Fitness[1:HH]) + sum(Fitness[n1:n2])
  n3             <- n2+1      # Starting row of DD homozygotes
# Number of D alleles
  D.alleles <- sum(Fitness[n1:n2]) + 2*sum(Fitness[n3:Npop])
  Prop.H    <- H.alleles/(H.alleles + D.alleles) # Proportion H
                                                 alleles
            return(Prop.H)
} # End of function
##################### Main program #####################
  set.seed(100)           # Initialize random number generator
  Npop   <- 2000          # Set population size
  Morph  <- matrix(2,Npop,1)   # Set up matrix initially with doves
  MaxProp <- 100              # Nos of divisions for proportions
  Data    <- matrix(0,MaxProp,4)     # Create file for output
```

```
# Col 1=Prop.H, col 2=Delta Prop.H, col3=P.Hawks, 3=Delta P.Hawks
  PayoffMatrix <- matrix(c(-1,0,8,4),2,2) # Set up Payoff matrix
# Calculate theoretical frequency
  a   <- PayoffMatrix[1,1]
  b   <- PayoffMatrix[1,2]
  c   <- PayoffMatrix[2,1]
  d   <- PayoffMatrix[2,2]
  P.Hawks   <- (b-d)/(b+c-a-d)     # Expected proportion of hawks
  Data[,1] <- seq(from=0.01, to=0.95, length=MaxProp)   # Propn of H
                                                              allele
   for (Prop in 1:MaxProp)      # Iterate over Proportions
{
# Calculate the number of each genotype as integers
  Prop.H <- Data[Prop,1]              # Get Proportion of H allele
  HH <- round(Prop.H^2*Npop)          # Number of HH genotypes
  HD <- round(2*Prop.H*(1-Prop.H)*Npop)# Number of HD genotypes
  Morph[1:Npop]    <- 2           # Set initially to doves
  Nos.of.Hawks     <- HH + HD   # Assuming that HD is a Hawk
  Morph[1:Nos.of.Hawks] <- 1  # Set rows 1 to Nos.of.Hawks to hawks
  Nos.of.Hawks <- sum(Morph[Morph==1])   # The nos of Hawks
# Calculate new proportion of H allele by applying fitness criterion
  New.Prop.H <- FITNESS(Morph, PayoffMatrix, HH, HD, Npop)
  Data[Prop,2] <- New.Prop.H - Prop.H  # Change in propn of H allele
  Data[Prop,3] <- Prop.H^2+ 2*Prop.H*(1-Prop.H)  # P.Hawks
  New.Hawks <- New.Prop.H^2+ 2*New.Prop.H*(1-New.Prop.H)# New P.Hawks
  Data[Prop,4] <- New.Hawks - Data[Prop,3]       # Delta P.Hawks
} # End of Prop loop
# Plot Change in proportions as a function of P.Hawks
  Ymax <- max(Data[,2],Data[,4])   # Maximum Y value
  Ymin <- min(Data[,2],Data[,4])   # Minimum Y value
# Plot Change in Proportion of H allele
  plot(Data[,1],   Data[,2],   type='l',lty=2,   xlab='Initial
Proportion (P or P.Hawks)', ylab='Change (in P or P.Hawks)',
ylim=c(Ymin,Ymax))
   lines(Data[,3], Data[,4], type='l') # Plot change in proportion
                                              of Hawks
   lines(Data[,1], rep(0,MaxProp))    # Plot theoretical ESS as
                                              horizontal line
   points(P.Hawks, 0, pch="X", cex=2)   # Plot X at ESS. cex sets size
                                              of X
# Apply smooth spline to smooth out curves
   lines(smooth.spline(Data[,1],Data[,2]))
   lines(smooth.spline(Data[,3],Data[,4]))
```

OUTPUT: (Figure 5.3)

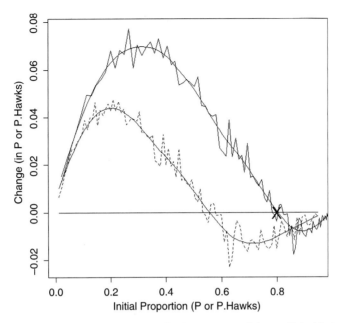

Figure 5.3 Change after one generation in the proportion of the H allele (dashed line) and proportion of hawks (solid line) as a function of the initial proportion. The X marks the theoretical ESS and the solid horizontal line the value of no change. The smooth solid lines are the smoothed functions fitted using the R routine smooth.spline.

Figure 5.3 shows that there is a potentially stable equilibrium at a hawk proportion of 0.8.

5.5.4 Finding the ESS using a numerical approach

The program is much the same as in the previous section, the primary difference being that iterations are over generations rather than initial proportions. At the end of the simulation deviations from the expected proportion of hawks is tested using a simple one-sample t-test.

R CODE:

```
  rm(list=ls())        # Remove all objects from memory
# Function to calculate new frequency of H allele
  FITNESS <- function(Morph, PayoffMatrix, HH, HD, Npop)
{
CODING FOR THIS FUNCTION IS THE SAME AS IN THE PREVIOUS SECTION
}
```

```
##################### Main program #####################
  set.seed(100)          # Initialize random number generator
  Npop   <- 100          # Set population size
  MaxGen <- 100          # Number of generations
  Output <- matrix(0,MaxGen,2) # Create file for output
  Prop.H <- 0.5              # Initial Propn of H alleles in popn
  Morph  <- matrix(2,Npop,1)   # Set up matrix initially with doves
  PayoffMatrix <- matrix(c(-1,0,8,4),2,2)   # Set up Payoff matrix
# Calculate theoretical frequency
  a <- PayoffMatrix[1,1]
  b <- PayoffMatrix[1,2]
  c <- PayoffMatrix[2,1]
  d <- PayoffMatrix[2,2]
  P.Hawks <- (b-d)/(b+c-a-d)   # Expected proportion of hawks
  for (Igen in 1:MaxGen)       # Iterate over generations
{
# Calculate the number of each genotype as integers
  HH <- round(Prop.H^2*Npop)              # Number of HH genotypes
  HD <- round(2*Prop.H*(1-Prop.H)*Npop)  # Number of HD genotypes
  Morph[1:Npop]  <- 2           # Set initially to doves
  Nos.of.Hawks   <- HH + HD      # Assuming that HD is a Hawk
  Morph[1:Nos.of.Hawks] <- 1 # Set rows 1 to Nos.of.Hawks to hawks
  Output[Igen,1]           <- Igen  # Store generation number
# Calculate and store the proportion of Hawks
  Nos.of.Hawks         <- sum(Morph[Morph==1])
  Output[Igen,2]     <- Nos.of.Hawks/Npop   # Proportion of Hawks
# Calculate new proportion of H allele by applying fitness criterion
  Prop.H <- FITNESS(Morph, PayoffMatrix, HH, HD, Npop)
} # End of Igen loop
# Plot time trace
  plot(Output[,1],  Output[,2],  type='l',  xlab='Generation',
ylab='Proportion of hawks')
  lines(Output[,1], rep(P.Hawks,MaxGen)) # Plot theoretical ex-
pectation
# Print out mean proportion hawks, SD and expected proportion
# starting at gen 20
  print(c(mean(Output[20:MaxGen,2]),  sd(Output[20:MaxGen,2]),
P.Hawks))
# t test against expected proportion
   t.test(Output[20:MaxGen,2], mu=P.Hawks)
```

OUTPUT: (Figure 5.4)

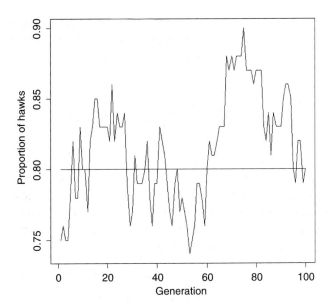

Figure 5.4 Proportion of hawks in a population in which inheritance is due to a single locus with two alleles, H and D, where HH and HD genotypes are hawks. The ESS predicted proportion is 0.8 hawks.

```
   Mean proportion    SD       Predicted
[1]   0.81814815  0.03808251  0.80000000
> t.test(Output[20:MaxGen,2],mu=P.Hawks)
   One Sample t-test
data: Output[20:MaxGen, 2]
t = 4.2889, df = 80, p-value = 4.98e-05
alternative hypothesis: true mean is not equal to 0.8
95 percent confidence interval:
0.8097274  0.8265689
```

As before, the population approaches the predicted ESS but is significantly different (with or without a transformation). The degree of fluctuation is also greater (SD of 0.029 for the clonal model and 0.038 for the Mendelian model). Increasing the population size to 1,000 decreases to nonsignificance the discrepancy between predicted and observed proportion.

```
[1]   0.80092593  0.01181289  0.80000000
> # t test against expected proportion
> t.test(Output[20:MaxGen,2],mu=P.Hawks)
   One Sample t-test
data: Output[20:MaxGen, 2]
```

```
t = 0.7054, df = 80, p-value = 0.4826
alternative hypothesis: true mean is not equal to 0.8
95 percent confidence interval:
0.7983139   0.8035380
```

By successive increases in population size one can see that the fluctuations decrease and that in an infinite population fluctuations about the equilibrium would cease.

5.6   Scenario 4: Hawk-Dove game: a quantitative genetic model

The formulation for this model follows that of the quantitative model described in Chapter 3 (individual variance components models).

5.6.1   General assumptions

1. The population consists of two morphs, one that adopts a hawk behavior and another that adopts the dove behavior.
2. Morph is determined by the action of multiple genes.
3. The results of interactions are as specified in Scenario 4.
4. Fitness is equal to some initial quantity plus the payoff.

5.6.2   Mathematical assumptions

1. The payoff matrix is as shown in Table 5.2.
2. Population size is finite.
3. Only one interaction occurs per individual.
4. Morph is determined by the threshold model of quantitative genetics (described below).
5. Interactions occur only between males and females mate randomly with males (only a simple adjustment, described below, is required to convert the model into one in which both males and females interact, as assumed in the Mendelian model).
6. Population size is constant.
7. The genetic mean values of males and females, $\bar{\mu}_{\mathrm{M}}$ and $\bar{\mu}_{\mathrm{F}}$, respectively are

$$\bar{\mu}_{\mathrm{M}}(t+1) = \frac{\sum_{i=1}^{N} W_i(t)\mu_{\mathrm{M},i}(t)}{\sum_{i=1}^{N} W_i(t)} \qquad \bar{\mu}_{\mathrm{F}}(t+1) = \bar{\mu}(t) \qquad (5.15)$$

where $W_i(t)$ is the fitness of the ith male at time t and N is the number of males. The mean genetic value of males is weighted by the fitnesses whereas, because the females are not under direct selection, the mean female value is equal to the population mean $\bar{\mu}$.

8. The population mean is the average of the male and female genetic values:

$$\bar{\mu}(t+1) = \frac{1}{2}[\bar{\mu}_M(t) + \bar{\mu}_F(t)] \tag{5.16}$$

5.6.3 A graphical analysis

The same approach as in the previous graphical analysis is used. In this case, a larger population size (10,000 rather than 2,000) was required to reduce fluctuations but as the program runs faster this is not a significant problem.

Hawk and dove behavior is assumed to be controlled by an underlying normally distributed trait called the liability. Individuals with liabilities greater than a threshold display hawk behavior, whereas those below the threshold display dove behavior. This designation is entirely arbitrary and has no effect on the model behavior. Without loss of generality we can also assume that the phenotypic variance of the liability is 1 and that the threshold, T_0, is set by the initial proportion of hawks, P_H, given a mean population liability of zero: thus we need to find T_0 such that

$$P_H = \frac{1}{\sqrt{2\pi}} \int_{T_0}^{\infty} e^{-\frac{1}{2}x^2} dx \tag{5.17}$$

In R this can be found by calling the R function `qnorm`:

```
T.zero <-qnorm(P.Hawk)
```

where `P.Hawk` is the initial proportion of hawks, here set at 0.5. The additive genetic variance of the liability, `Va`, is determined from the user-assigned heritability, `h2` (here 0.5), and phenotypic variance, `Vp` (1, as noted above):

```
Va <- Vp*h2
```

The environmental variance is the difference between `Vp` and `Va`

```
Ve <- Vp-Va
```

The genetic value of an individual is determined by drawing a random normal variate, with males and females considered separately (vectors GM and GF, respectively):

```
GM      <- rnorm(N, mean=mu, sd=Sda)   # Genetic values of males
GF      <- rnorm(N, mean=mu, sd=Sda)   # Genetic values of females
```

where `N` is the number of males and the number of females, `mu` is the population mean, changing under selection, and `Sda` is the additive genetic standard deviation. The above code assumes no sex-linkage and random mating. The environmental deviations are constructed by drawing random normal variates from a normal distribution with a mean of zero and an environmental standard deviation (SDe <- sqrt(Ve)). The phenotypic values of the male liabilities are the sums of the additive and environmental values. Because females do not take a behavioral role it is not necessary to consider their phenotypic values. The observed phenotypic morph of the males is determined from the phenotypic liability value and the threshold: phenotypic liabilities greater than the threshold become hawks and those below become doves:

```
PM.Morph[PM > T.zero]    <- 1        # Hawks
PM.Morph[PM <= T.zero ]  <- 2        # Doves
```

In accordance with the previous Hawk-Dove models, a separate function FITNESS is used to compute the fitnesses from the randomized set of pairwise interactions and the payoff matrix. The mean genetic value of the next generation is then computed as described above. If one wished to assume both males and females interact as in the clonal model then one could simply drop the female vector, regard the "male" vector as the vector of males and females, and calculate the next generation from the mean "male" genetic values (i.e., replace mu <- (mu.M + mu.F)/2 with mu <- mu.M). Once the new mean, mu, is computed and passed back to the main program it is used to calculate the new proportion of hawks, which in R is given by

```
1-pnorm (q=T.zero, mean=mu, sd=1)
```

The change in the proportion of hawks is computed by subtraction and stored. Finally, the functions are plotted as previously.

R CODE:

```
rm(list=ls())        # Remove all objects from memory
# Function to calculate new mean value
  FITNESS <- function(GM, GF, PM.Morph, PayoffMatrix, N)
{
# Match males up to find fitness for each male
# Create a randomized vector of opponents
  Opponent <- sample(PM.Morph)
  Fitness  <- matrix(0,N,1)
# Iterate over the Payoff matrix
  for (Receiver in 1:2 )   # Individual receiving payoff
{
  for (I.Opponent in 1:2) # Opponent
{
  Fitness[PM.Morph==Receiver & Opponent==
  I.Opponent]<- 3 + PayoffMatrix[Receiver,I.Opponent]
}} # End Of two loops
```

```
  mu.M <- sum(Fitness*GM)/sum(Fitness) # Mean genetic value of males
  mu.F   <- mean(GF)                   # Mean genetic value of females
  mu     <- (mu.M + mu.F)/2            # New population mean
  return(mu)
}
######################Main program#######################
  set.seed(100)              # Initialize random number generator
  N       <- 10000            # Set population size
  PM.Morph <- matrix(0,N,1)   # Create file for male phenotypes
  h2      <- 0.5              # Set heritability
  Vp      <- 1               # Set Phenotypic variance
  Va      <- Vp*h2            # Calculate Additive genetic variance
  Ve      <- Vp-Va            # Calculate Environmental variance
  mu      <- 0               # Trait mean value
# Note that mu is both the genetic mean and the phenotypic mean
# because the mean environmental value is by definition zero
  SDa     <- sqrt(Va)     # SD of Va
  SDe     <- sqrt(Ve)     # SD of Ve
  PayoffMatrix <- matrix(c(-1,0,8,4),2,2) # Set up Payoff matrix
# Calculate theoretical frequency
  a <- PayoffMatrix[1,1]
  b <- PayoffMatrix[1,2]
  c <- PayoffMatrix[2,1]
  d <- PayoffMatrix[2,2]
  P.Hawks   <- (b-d)/(b+c-a-d)
  MaxProp   <- 20            # Nos of divisions for proportions
  Data      <- matrix(0,MaxProp,2)   # Create file for output
  Data[,1]  <- seq(from=0.01, to=0.95, length=MaxProp) # Propn of
                                                          Hawks
  for (Prop in 1:MaxProp)        # Iterate over Proportions
{
  P.Hawk   <- Data[Prop,1]      ``````# Initial proportion of Hawks
  T.zero   <- -qnorm(P.Hawk, mean=0, sd=1) #Threshold. Hawks>T.zero
# Generate Genetic and environmental values using normal distribu-
  tion
  mu <- 0
  GM <- rnorm(N, mean=mu, sd=SDa) # Genetic values of males
  GF <- rnorm(N, mean=mu, sd=SDa) # Genetic values of females
  EM <- rnorm(N, mean=0, sd=SDe)  # Environmental values of males
  PM <- GM + EM                   # Phenotypic value of males
# Combine phenotypic and genetic values
  PM.Morph[PM > T.zero]    <- 1   # Hawks
  PM.Morph[PM <= T.zero ]  <- 2   # Doves
```

```
# Calculate the proportion of each type
  Nos.of.Hawks           <- sum(PM.Morph[PM.Morph==1])
# Calculate new mean genetic value by applying fitness criterion
  mu <- FITNESS(GM, GF, PM.Morph, PayoffMatrix, N)
# Store change in proportion
  Data[Prop,2] <- 1-pnorm(q=T.zero, mean=mu, sd=1)-Data[Prop,1]
} # End of Prop loop
# Plot Change in Proportion of Hawks
  plot(Data[,1], Data[,2], type='l',lty=2, xlab='Initial propor-
tion of Hawks', ylab='Change in proportion of Hawks')
  lines(Data[,1], rep(0,MaxProp)) # Plot theoretical ESS as hori-
zontal line
  points(P.Hawks, 0, pch="X", cex=2) # Plot X at ESS. cex sets size of X
# Apply smooth spline to smooth out curves
  lines(smooth.spline(Data[,1],Data[,2]))
```

OUTPUT: (Figure 5.5)

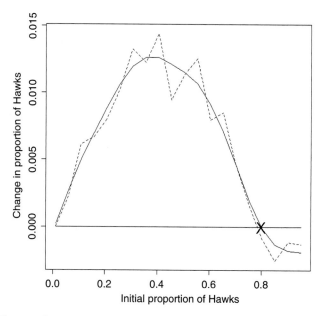

Figure 5.5 Change after one generation in the proportion of hawks (dashed line) as a function of the initial proportion in the quantitative genetic model (Scenario 6). The X marks the theoretical ESS and the solid horizontal line the value of no change. The smooth solid line is the smoothed functions fitted using the R routine smooth.spline.

The results are plotted in Figure 5.5. There is a predicted equilibrium at 0.8, which is that expected from the general phenotypic analysis.

5.6.4 Finding the ESS using a numerical approach

Because the population takes longer to reach an equilibrium than in the previous models, the simulation is run for 200 generations and mean proportion of hawks are calculated from generation 100. Population size is set at 100. The program is changed so that the model is iterated over generations rather than varying initial proportions.

R CODE:

```
  rm(list=ls())      # Remove all objects from memory
# Function to calculate new mean value
  FITNESS <- function(GM, GF, PM.Morph, PayoffMatrix, N)
{
  CODING THE SAME AS IN PREVIOUS SECTION
}
###################### Main program ######################
  set.seed(100)       # Initialize random number generator
  N          <- 100            # Set population size
  PM.Morph  <- matrix(0,N,1)   # Create file for male phenotypes
  P.Hawk    <- 0.5             # Initial proportion of Hawks
  T.zero    <- -qnorm(P.Hawk)  # Threshold. Hawks > T.zero
  h2        <- 0.5             # Set heritability
  Vp        <- 1               # Set Phenotypic variance
  Va        <- Vp*h2   # Calculate Additive genetic variance
  Ve        <- Vp-Va   # Calculate Environmental variance
  mu        <- 0       # Trait mean value
# Note that mu is both the genetic mean and the phenotypic mean
# because the mean environmental value is by definition zero
  SDa    <- sqrt(Va)     # SD of Va
  SDe    <- sqrt(Ve)     # SD of Ve
  PayoffMatrix <- matrix(c(-1,0,8,4),2,2)   # Set up Payoff matrix
# Calculate theoretical frequency
  a <- PayoffMatrix[1,1]
  b <- PayoffMatrix[1,2]
  c <- PayoffMatrix[2,1]
  d <- PayoffMatrix[2,2]
  P.Hawks <- (b-d)/(b+c-a-d)
  MaxGen  <- 200                # Number of generations
  Output  <- matrix(0,MaxGen,2) # Create file for output
  for (Igen in 1:MaxGen)        # Iterate over generations
```

```
{
# Generate Genetic and environmental values using normal distribution
  GM  <- rnorm(N, mean=mu, sd=SDa) # Genetic values of males
  GF  <- rnorm(N, mean=mu, sd=SDa) # Genetic values of females
  EM  <- rnorm(N, mean=0, sd=SDe)  # Environmental values of males
  PM  <- GM + EM                   # Phenotypic value of males
# Combine phenotypic and genetic values
  PM.Morph[PM > T.zero]    <- 1       # Hawks
  PM.Morph[PM <= T.zero ]  <- 2       # Doves
  Output[Igen,1]           <- Igen  # Initial generation
# Calculate the proportion of each type
  Nos.of.Hawks       <- sum(PM.Morph[PM.Morph==1])
  Output[Igen,2]     <- Nos.of.Hawks/N   # Proportion of Hawks
# Calculate new mean genetic value by applying fitness criterion
  mu     <- FITNESS(GM, GF, PM.Morph, PayoffMatrix, N)
} # End of Igen loop
  Start <- 100 # Starting row for calculating mean proportion
  plot(Output[,1],   Output[,2],type='l',   xlab='Generation',
ylab='Proportion of hawks')
lines(Output[,1], rep(P.Hawks,MaxGen)) # Plot theoretical expectation
  print(c(mean(Output[Start:MaxGen,2]),   sd(Output[Start:Max-
Gen,2]), P.Hawks)) # Mean proportion, SD, Expected proportion
  t.test(Output[Start:MaxGen,2], mu=P.Hawks)
```

OUTPUT: (Figure 5.6)

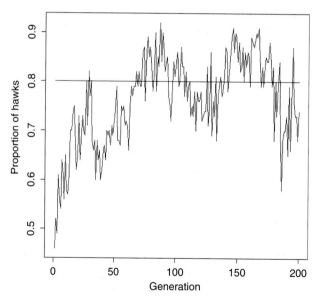

Figure 5.6 Proportion of hawks in a population in which behavior is a quantitative genetic trait (Scenario 6). The solid line shows the predicted ESS, which is 0.8 hawks.

Mean proportion   SD   Predicted

```
[1]   0.79544554   0.06787525   0.80000000
> t.test(Output[Start:MaxGen,2], mu=P.Hawks)
  One Sample t-test
data: Output[Start:MaxGen, 2]
t = -0.6744, df = 100, p-value = 0.5016
alternative hypothesis: true mean is not equal to 0.8
95 percent confidence interval:
0.7820461 0.8088450
```

There is no significant difference between the observed mean and the predicted ESS after 100 generations. However, the fluctuations are considerably larger than in either the clonal or Mendelian models (0.029, 0.038, and 0.068 for the clonal, simple Mendelian, and quantitative genetic models, respectively). The increased fluctuations are due in part to the heritability (the larger the heritability the greater the fluctuations). Changing the model such that males and females interact increases the fluctuations. Increasing population size decreases the fluctuations.

5.7   Scenario 5: Rock-Paper-Scissors: a clonal model

The R-P-S game is an excellent example of a multiple-strategy game. It is also relevant because it has recently been invoked to explain the fluctuations of the tricolor morphs of male side-blotched lizards (*Uta stansburiana*; Sinervo and Lively 1996). Males with orange throats are the most aggressive and defend large territories. Males with dark blue throats are less aggressive and defend smaller territories while males with yellow-striped throats do not defend territories but attempt to sneak copulations. According to Sinervo (2001), the large territories of the orange-throated males can be invaded by the sneaker (yellow-striped males), the orange-throated males oust the less aggressive blue-throated males but these latter males can resist the incursions of the yellow-striped males. Sinervo (2001) has examined the behavior of this model using a clonal model and ones with simple Mendelian determination. We shall consider simple versions of the game using a clonal model, a simple Mendelian model (Scenario 6), and a quantitative genetic model (Scenario 7). At first glance we might expect an ESS at 1/3, 1/3, and 1/3. However, if contests between like individuals result in a loss or the trait is genetically polymorpic, then there may be no stable ESS but fluctuations in each morph proportion (Maynard Smith 1982). For this reason numerical solutions will generally be required.

5.7.1   General assumptions

1. The population consists of three types of clones, one which adopts a "Rock" behavior, another which adopts a "Paper" behavior, and yet another that adopts a "Scissors" behavior.

2. The payoffs are symmetrical, a numerical example of which is given in Table 5.3. As per Maynard Smith (1982) I assume that an interaction between two players of the same morph incurs a fitness deficit of ε.
3. Fitness is equal to some initial quantity plus the payoff.

5.7.2 Mathematical assumptions

1. The payoff matrix is as shown in Table 5.3 with $\varepsilon = 0.1$.
2. Population size is finite.
3. Only one interaction occurs per individual.
4. Population size is constant with the contribution to the next generation being determined by the relative fitnesses. Thus the number of "Rock" individuals in the next generation is given by

$$N_R(t+1) = \frac{N_{Pop}\sum_{i=1}^{N_R(t)}W_{R,i}}{\sum_{i=1}^{N_R(t)}W_{R,i} + \sum_{j=1}^{N_P(t)}W_{P,j} + \sum_{k=1}^{N_S(t)}W_{S,k}} \tag{5.18}$$

where N_{Pop} is the number of individuals in the population, $N_R(t)$ is the number of "Rocks" at time t, $N_P(t)$ is the number of "Papers" at time t, $N_S(t)$ is the number of "Scissors" at time t, $W_{R,i}$ is the fitness of the ith "Rock" at time t, $W_{P,j}$ is the fitness of the jth "Paper" at time t, and $W_{S,k}$ is the fitness of the kth "Scissors" at time t.

5.7.3 Finding the ESS using a numerical approach

The general approach is the same as the two-strategy clonal model. The payoff matrix is increased to a 3×3 matrix and the initial fitness is set to 5 (values were chosen arbitrarily to illustrate the model behavior). In the Hawk-Dove game the morphs were designated 1 and 2; here the three morphs are designated 1, 2, and 3 to access the payoff matrix. To approach a deterministic solution population size is set 1,000 individuals and the model run for 1,000 generations, which preliminary runs showed was sufficient to demonstrate the model's behavior. The initial proportions were set at 0.33 the ESS values. Approximate equilibrium was obtained at about generation 400 and so the mean proportion of each morph was calculated from this point. Four different plots are output:

Table 5.3 Payoff matrix for the R-P- game

	Rock	Paper	Scissors
Rock	$-\varepsilon$	1	-1
Paper	-1	$-\varepsilon$	1
Scissors	1	-1	$-\varepsilon$

Note: The payoffs are those achieved by the individuals in the left-hand column when interacting with an individual along the given row.
Source: Adapted from Maynard Smith (1982).

1. The proportion of each morph versus generation. If plotted on the same scale the individual time traces are difficult to discern. For clarity, I added 0.25 and 0.55 to the scissors and papers, respectively; thus the proportions are actually Propn + 0.00, Propn + 0.25, and Propn + 0.55, as indicated by the *y*-axis label. The "predicted" (only in the long-term sense since we expect instability) ESS values (0.333, increased by 0.25 and 0.55 for scissors and papers to account for the amount added to these) are also plotted.

2. A phase plot of scissors on rock starting with generation 400, the generation at which the proportions appear to oscillate about a constant average value.

3. Two phase plots of the other two combinations of pairwise proportions, plotting from generation 1 to show the full temporal dynamics.

R CODE:

```
rm(list=ls())          # Remove all objects from memory
# Function to calculate new fitness values and morph proportions
   FITNESS <- function(Morph, PayoffMatrix, Npop)
{
# Match individuals up to find fitness for each male
   Opponent <- sample(Morph)   # Create a randomized vector of opponents
   Fitness <- matrix(0,Npop,1)  # Allocate space for fitness vector
# Iterate over the Payoff matrix
# Individual receiving payoff 1=Rock 2 = Scissors 3=Paper
   for (Receiver in 1:3 )
{
   for (I.Opponent in 1:3)    # Opponent 1=Rock 2 = Scissors 3=Paper
{
   Fitness[Morph==Receiver & Opponent==
   I.Opponent] <- 5 + PayoffMatrix[Receiver,I.Opponent]
}}
# Mean fitness of Rocks
   Prop.Rocks     <- sum(Fitness[Morph==1])/sum(Fitness)
# Mean fitness of Scissors
   Prop.Scissors  <- sum(Fitness[Morph==2])/sum(Fitness)
return(c(Prop.Rocks, Prop.Scissors))
}
################## Main program ####################
   set.seed(100)              # Initialize random number generator
   Npop       <- 1000                   # Set population size
   MaxGen     <- 1000                   # Number of generations
   Output     <- matrix(0,MaxGen,4)     # Create file for output
# Set up threshold values for Rocks and Scissors
   Prop.Rocks     <- 0.33               # Initial proportion Rocks
   Nos.of.Rocks   <- Prop.Rocks*Npop # Nos of rocks
```

```r
    Prop.Scissors <- 0.33              # Initial proportion Scissors
    Nos.of.Scissors  <- Prop.Scissors*Npop   # Nos of Scissors
# Set up morph vector initially with all Papers (=3s)
    Morph           <- matrix(3,Npop,1)
# Set up fitness matrix. Note column-wise fill
    Epsilon          <- 0.1   # Deficit when the same morph types in-
                                teract
    PayoffMatrix  <- matrix(c(-Epsilon,-1,1,1,-Epsilon,-1,-1,1,-
Epsilon),3,3)
    for (Igen in 1:MaxGen)      # Iterate over generations
{
    Output[Igen,1]   <- Igen   # Store Generation number (1st column)
# Calculate the proportion of each type
    Morph[1:Npop]     <- 3       # First put 3 in all rows
# Convert first Nos.of.Rocks rows to Rocks
    Morph[1:Nos.of.Rocks] <- 1
# Fill in rows corresponding to Scissors
    n1        <- Nos.of.Rocks+1
    n2        <- n1+ Nos.of.Scissors
    Morph[n1:n2]    <- 2
    Nos.of.Rocks   <- length(Morph[Morph==1])   # Number of Rocks
    Nos.of.Scissors <- length(Morph[Morph==2]) # Number of Scissors
    Nos.of.Papers   <- length(Morph[Morph==3]) # Number of Papers
    Output[Igen,2] <- Nos.of.Rocks/Npop      # Proportion of Rocks
    Output[Igen,3] <- Nos.of.Scissors/Npop # Proportion of Scissors
    Output[Igen,4] <- Nos.of.Papers/Npop   # Proportion of Papers
# Calculate new proportion of each morph by applying fitness criterion
    Propns          <- FITNESS(Morph,PayoffMatrix,Npop)
    Nos.of.Rocks   <- round(Npop*Propns[1])   # Nos.of.Rocks is an
                                                integer
    Nos.of.Scissors  <- round(Npop*Propns[2]) # Nos.of.Scissors is
                                                an integer
} # End of Igen loop
    par(mfrow=c(2,2))   # 4 plots per page
    plot(Output[,1],   Output[,2],type='l',   xlab='Generation',
ylab='Propns (+X)',ylim=c(0.0,1.0))  # Plot Rocks
    lines( Output[,1], Output[,3]+0.25) # Add Scissors+0.25 to plot
    lines( Output[,1], Output[,4]+0.55) # Add Papers+0.55 to plot
# Add predicted lines to plots
    lines(Output[,1], rep(0.3333,MaxGen))     # Predicted Rocks
    lines(Output[,1], rep(0.3333+0.25,MaxGen)) # Predicted Scissors
    lines(Output[,1], rep(0.3333+0.55,MaxGen)) # Predicted Papers
```

```
# Phase plots showing proportion of two morphs
  plot (Output[400:MaxGen,2],Output[400:MaxGen,3],type='l',
xlab='Rocks',
ylab='Scissors')
  plot (Output[,2],Output[,4],type='l',xlab='Rocks',ylab='Papers')
  plot (Output[,3],Output[,4],type='l',xlab='Scissors',ylab='Papers')
  print(' Mean proportions (R,P,S) from Generation 400 to MaxGen')
# Print mean proportions starting at generation 400
  print(' Mean proportions (R,P,S) from Generation 400 to MaxGen')
  c(mean(Output[400:MaxGen,2]),mean(Output[400:MaxGen,3]),
mean(Output[400:MaxGen,4]))
```

OUTPUT: (Figure 5.7)

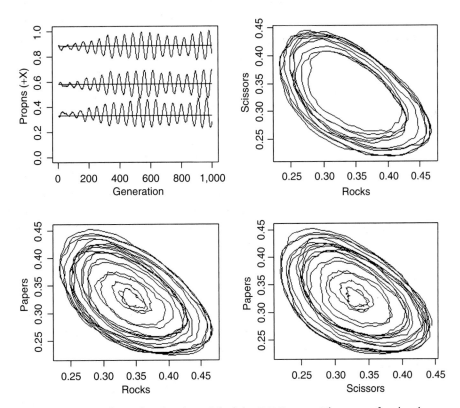

Figure 5.7 Output from the clonal model of the R-P-S game. The traces for the three proportions over time have been separated by adding 0.25 to scissors (middle trace) and 0.55 to papers (top trace). Predicted ESS values are shown as the horizontal lines (ESS = 0.333 but increased for display purposes by 0.25 and 0.55 for scissors and papers, respectively). The phase plot for rocks versus scissors starts at generation 400, whereas the other two start at generation zero.

```
[1] "Mean proportions (R,P,S) from Generation 400 to MaxGen"
[1] 0.3427022 0.3290266 0.3282712
```

After approximately 400 generations the morphs appear to fluctuate about a long-term mean of 1/3 for each morph, though it is not clear if the fluctuations are complex cycles or chaotic. Increasing ε to 0.5 does appear to produce chaotic behavior but with a very small amplitude (approximately 0.32–0.35).

5.8   Scenario 6: Rock-Paper-Scissors: a simple Mendelian model

Here we shall consider the simplest possible model, namely one in which there is a single locus with three alleles, designated R, P, and S. See Sinervo (2001) for other simple Mendelian models.

5.8.1   General assumptions

These assumptions are the same as given in Scenario 5.

5.8.2   Mathematical assumptions

1. The payoff matrix is shown in Table 5.3 with $\varepsilon = 0.1$.
2. Population size is finite.
3. Only one interaction occurs per individual.
4. Morph is determined by a single locus with three alleles, designated R, P, and S.
5. Genotype is translated into phenotype as follows: RR = "Rock," PP = "Paper," and SS = "Scissors." There are a large number of ways in which heterozygotes could be classified. I have selected a simple dominance model in which RS and RP are "Rock" phenotypes and SP is the "Scissors" phenotype.
6. Mating is at random and genotypes at each generation are determined from the Hardy–Weinberg proportions. For simplicity males and females are not distinguished, meaning that the fitnesses apply equally to each sex. In the lizard case it might be more proper to assume that the R-P-S fitnesses apply to the males and that the female allele fitnesses are equal. This would require separate coding for males and females. Because this is a simple bookkeeping chore, for clarity, I omit this possibility here.
7. Population size is constant with the contribution to the next generation being determined by the relative fitnesses. Thus, the total absolute fitness of each allele is

$$W_R(t+1) = 2\sum_{i=1}^{N_{RR}}W_{RR,i}(t) + \sum_{j=1}^{N_{RS}}W_{RS,j}(t) + \sum_{k=1}^{N_{RP}}W_{RP,k}(t)$$

$$W_P(t+1) = 2\sum_{i=1}^{N_{PP}}W_{PP,i}(t) + \sum_{j=1}^{N_{RP}}W_{RP,j}(t) + \sum_{k=1}^{N_{PS}}W_{PS,k}(t) \qquad (5.19)$$

$$W_S(t+1) = 2\sum_{i=1}^{N_{SS}}W_{SS,i}(t) + \sum_{j=1}^{N_{RS}}W_{RS,j}(t) + \sum_{k=1}^{N_{PS}}W_{PS,k}(t)$$

where W_R, W_P, and W_S are the fitnesses of R, P, and S alleles, respectively. Note that the homozygotes contribute two alleles but the heterozygotes contribute only one allele to each of the relevant two allele fitnesses. The proportion of R alleles, for example, is thus

$$P_R(t+1) = \frac{W_R(t+1)}{W_R(t+1) + W_P(t+1) + W_S(t+1)} \qquad (5.20)$$

5.8.3 A graphical analysis

At equilibrium we expect that the proportions of the three morphs should be equal, though the frequency of the three alleles will depend upon the genotype to phenotype map. In the graphical analysis of the Mendelian Hawk-Dove model we varied the allele frequency and calculated the change after one generation. In the present case we vary two frequencies, here (arbitrarily) R and S compute the changes in the allele and morph frequencies. The three zero isoclines are plotted and the equilibrium frequencies are obtained from the common point of intersection: should no point exist there can be no stable equilibrium.

The integral number of each genotype is calculated from the Hardy-Weinberg formula and for clarity designated initially by their genotype codes (e.g., RR is the number of RR genotypes). These calculations are done in the function GENOTYPE, which passes back both the numbers of each genotype and the proportions of rocks, papers, and scissors.

These numbers are then placed in the vector

```
Genotypes <- c(RR, RS, RP, SS, SP, PP)
```

As noted earlier, the rock phenotype is RR, RS, and RP while the scissors phenotype is RP and SP. We now construct a vector of morphs where the first RR + RS + RP rows are rocks (= 1), the next RS + RP rows are scissors (= 2), and the last PP rows are papers (= 3). The fitnesses of these morphs can now be calculated using the same FITNESS function as in the earlier model. In this function we must calculate the fitnesses of the alleles. This is easily done using the numbers given by the vector Genotypes, because we have allocated the genotypes in a stacked fashion of RR, RS, RP, SS, SP, and PP. After calculating the fitnesses the proportions are calculated as per equation (5.20).

The set of combinations of R and S are generated using the R function `expand.grid`. Because we require the storage of three different values it is most convenient to iterate over these combinations rather than using the `apply` function. Combinations that are not physically possible (total proportion exceeding 1) are skipped. The three resulting vectors are converted into a matrix for contour plotting and the three zero isoclines of allele frequencies (use `levels=0` in call to contour function) are plotted on the same plot (after the first plot add `draw-labels=FALSE` to the call to the contour function). The calculation of the contours for the proportions of rocks, papers, and scissors is a little trickier because we have to convert the allele frequencies into morph frequencies. To do this we make use of the R function `contourLines`, which calculates the set of *x,y* coordinates for the user-specified contour lines. In this case we want only the zero contours (so pass `levels=0`). First we obtain the relevant coordinates for the matrix **X** (say), which has dimensions `Proportion` by `Proportion`:

```
Data <-contourLines(Proportion, Proportion, X, levels=0)
```

The object `Data` is a list from which we must extract the relevant vectors. This is done using the R function `unlist`. An added complication is that `contourLines` might construct several zero isocline combinations: each set has to be extracted separately. Once this is done the isocline can be plotted using the *x,y* coordinates. This is done in the user-supplied function `ISOCLINE`.

R CODE:

```
  rm(list=ls())       # Remove all objects from memory
# Function to calculate new proportions
  FITNESS <- function(Morph, PayoffMatrix, Genotypes)
{
# To take account of integer values Npop is recalculated here
  Npop     <- sum(Genotypes)
# Match individuals up to find fitness for each
# Create a randomized vector of opponents
  Opponent <- sample(Morph)
  Fitness  <- matrix(0,Npop,1) # Allocate space for Fitness vector
# Iterate over the Payoff matrix
  for (Receiver in 1:3 ) # Ind receiving payoff 1=Rock 2 = Scissors
                         3=Paper
{
  for (I.Opponent in 1:3) # Opponent 1=Rock 2 = Scissors 3=Paper
  {
  Fitness[Morph==Receiver & Opponent==
  I.Opponent]<- 5 + PayoffMatrix[Receiver,I.Opponent]
}}
# Calculate ranges for genotypes to count alleles
  n0   <- Genotypes[1]        # Nos of RR. This is for completness
  n1   <- n0+1                # Starting row of RS
```

```
    n2    <- n1+Genotypes[2]-1  # Ending row of RS
    n3    <- n2+1                # Starting row of RP
    n4    <- n3+Genotypes[3]-1  # Ending row of RP
# Sum R alleles      RR      RS       RP
  R.alleles   <-  2*sum(Fitness[1:n0])+sum(Fitness[n1:n2])+sum
(Fitness[n3:n4])
# Number of S alleles
  R.alleles   <-  2*sum(Fitness[1:n0])+sum(Fitness[n1:n2])+sum
(Fitness[n3:n4])
# Number of S alleles
    n5    <- n4+1                # Starting row of SS
    n6    <- n5+Genotypes[4]-1  # Ending row of SS
    n7    <- n6+1               # Staring row of SP
    n8    <- n7+Genotypes[5]-1  # Ending row of SP
# Sum S alleles      SS      RS      SP
  S.alleles   <-  2*sum(Fitness[n5:n6])+sum(Fitness[n1:n2])+sum
(Fitness[n7:n8])
# Number of P alleles
    n9 <- n8+1          # Starting row of PP
# Number of P alleles  PP     RP     SP
  P.alleles   <-  2*sum(Fitness[n9:Npop])+sum(Fitness[n3:n4])+
sum(Fitness[n7:n8])
# Proportion of each allele
  Prop.R <- R.alleles/(R.alleles + S.alleles + P.alleles) # Propn R
                                                           allele
  Prop.S <- S.alleles/(R.alleles + S.alleles + P.alleles)  # Propn S
                                                           allele
  Prop.P <- P.alleles/(R.alleles + S.alleles + P.alleles) # Propn P
                                                           allele
  return(c(Prop.R, Prop.S, Prop.P))   # Return proportion of alleles
} # End of function
##################### FUNCTION GENOTYPE ####################
GENOTYPE <- function(Prop.R, Prop.S, Prop.P, Npop)
{
# Calculate the genotypes
# First all genotypes that have Rock phenotype
  RR <- round(Prop.R^2*Npop)          # Number of RR genotypes
  RS <- round(2*Prop.R*Prop.S*Npop)   # Number of RS genotypes
  RP <- round(2*Prop.R*Prop.P*Npop)   # Number of RP genotypes
# Genotypes that have Scissors phenotype
  SS <- round(Prop.S^2*Npop)          # Number of SS genotypes
  SP <- round(2*Prop.S*Prop.P*Npop)   # Number of SP genotypes
# Genotypes that have Paper phenotype
  PP <- round(Prop.P^2*Npop)     # Number of PP genotypes
  N  <- RR+RS+RP+SS+SP+PP         # To account for rounding effects
```

```
  P.Rocks      <- (RR+RS+RP)/N  # Proportion of Rocks
  P.Scissors  <- (SS+SP)/N      # Proportion of Scissors
  P.Paper      <- PP/N           # Proportion of Paper
  return( c(RR, RS, RP, SS, SP, PP, P.Rocks, P.Scissors, P.Paper))
}   # End of function
##################### FUNCTION ISOCLINE ####################
ISOCLINE <- function(X, ADD, LTY) # Function to plot zero isoclines
{
# X is the matrix of changes in proportion
# ADD is a flag. ADD=0 tells function to start a new plot
# LTY is the type of line to be drawn
# Call R function contourLines to get xy coordinates of zero isoclines
  Data   <- contourLines(Proportion, Proportion, X, levels=0)
  b        <- data.frame(unlist(Data)) # Unlist Data and convert to a
data frame
  N.zeros <- length(b[b==0])   # Number of zero isoclines
for ( i in 1:N.zeros)              # Iterate over isoclines
{
  Prop.R       <- Data[[i]]$x         # Proportion R allele
  Prop.S       <- Data[[i]]$y         # Proportion S allele
  Prop.P       <- 1- Prop.R - Prop.S  # Proportion P allele
  RR          <- Prop.R^2            # Frequency of RR genotypes
  RS          <- 2*Prop.R*Prop.S     # Frequency of RS genotypes
  RP          <- 2*Prop.R*Prop.P     # Frequencyof RP genotypes
  P.Rocks     <- RR+RS+RP            # Proportion of Rocks
  SS          <- Prop.S^2            # Frequency of SS genotypes
  SP          <- 2*Prop.S*Prop.P     # Frequency of SP genotypes
  P.Scissors  <- SS+SP               # Proportion of Scissors
# Plot lines (Have to check if new plot is requested)
if(i==1   &&   ADD==0)   {plot(P.Rocks,P.Scissors,   type='l',
xlab="Proportion  of  Rock",  ylab="Proportion  of  Scissors",
xlim=c(0,1),  ylim=c(0,1),lty=LTY) }
else{ lines(P.Rocks,P.Scissors, lty=LTY) }
}
} # end of function
#################### MAIN PROGRAM ###################
  set.seed(100)             # Initialize random number generator
  Npop     <- 2000          # Set population size
# Create a sequence of proportions for the two R and S alleles
  Nos.P    <- 30             # Number of divisions
  Proportion   <- seq(from=0.01, to=0.95, length=Nos.P)
```

```
# Use expand.grid to generate all possible combinations
  RxS            <- expand.grid(Proportion, Proportion)
  Data.Rocks  <- matrix(9,Nos.P*Nos.P,1) # Allocate space for R
                                                output
  Data.Scissors <- Data.Rocks       # Allocate space for S output
  Data.Paper   <- Data.Rocks       # Allocate space for P output
  Morph          <- matrix(0,Npop,1) # Allocate space for Phenotype
                                                vector
# Set up fitness matrix. Note column-wise fill
  Epsilon       <- 0.1 # Deficit when the same morph types interact
  PayoffMatrix  <- matrix(c(-Epsilon,-1,1,1,-Epsilon,-1,-1,1,
-Epsilon),3,3)
# Iterate over all possible combinations
  Total.Combinations <- Nos.P*Nos.P   # Total number of combinations
  for (Ith.comb in 1:Total.Combinations)
{
  Prop.R <- RxS[Ith.comb,1]       # Proportion of R allele
  Prop.S <- RxS[Ith.comb,2]       # Proportion of S allele
  Prop.P <- 1-Prop.R-Prop.S       # Proportion of P allele
  Total  <- Prop.R+Prop.S+Prop.P  # Sum of proportions
  if(Total > 0) # Check that combination is permissable
{
  D1 <- GENOTYPE(Prop.R, Prop.S, Prop.P, Npop) # Calculate the
                                                genotypes
  Genotypes       <- D1[1:6]       # Numbers of each genotype
  Prop.Morphs     <- D1[7:9]       # Proportions of each morph
  Morph[1:Npop]   <- 3             # Set initially to Paper
  Nos.of.Rocks    <- sum(Genotypes[1:3])    # RR+RS+RP
  Nos.of.Scissors <- sum(Genotypes[4:5])    # SS+SP
  Nos.of.Papers   <- Genotypes[6]       # PP genotype
  Morph[1:Nos.of.Rocks] <- 1    # Set rows 1 to Nos.of.Rocks to Rocks
  n1            <- Nos.of.Rocks+1       # Starting row for Scissors
  n2            <- n1+Nos.of.Scissors-1 # Ending row for Scissors
  Morph[n1:n2]  <- 2             # Set these rows to Scissors (=2)
# Calculate new proportions by applying fitness criterion
  Propns   <- FITNESS(Morph,PayoffMatrix,Genotypes)
  D2   <- GENOTYPE(Propns[1], Propns[2], Propns[3], Npop)
  Data.Rocks[Ith.comb] <- D1[7]-D2[7] # Change in proportion of
                                                Rocks
  Data.Scissors[Ith.comb]  <- D1[8]-D2[8]  # Change in propor-
                                                tion of Scissors
  Data.Paper[Ith.comb]     <- D1[9]-D2[9]  # Change in propor-
                                                tion of Paper
```

```
} # End of if statement
} # End of Ith.comb loop
# Convert vectors to matrices Note that fill is by column not row
  Delta.Rocks    <- matrix(Data.Rocks, Nos.P, Nos.P, byrow=F)
  Delta.Scissors <- matrix(Data.Scissors, Nos.P, Nos.P, byrow=F)
  Delta.Paper    <- matrix(Data.Paper, Nos.P, Nos.P, byrow=F)
  par(mfrow=c(2,2))   # 4 plots per page
# Plot zero isoclines for alellic frequencies
  contour(Proportion, Proportion, Delta.Rocks, xlab="Proportion
of R allele", ylab="Proportion of S allele", levels=0, drawla-
bels=FALSE)
  contour(Proportion,     Proportion,     Delta.Scissors,lty=2,
levels=0, add=TRUE, drawlabels=FALSE)
  contour(Proportion, Proportion, Delta.Paper, lty=3, levels=0,
add=TRUE, drawlabels=FALSE)
# Get zero isoclines for proportion of each morph
  ISOCLINE(Delta.Rocks, 0, 1)        # Plot Rock zero isocline
  ISOCLINE(Delta.Scissors, 1, 2)     # Plot Scissors zero isocline
  ISOCLINE(Delta.Paper, 1, 3)        # Plot Paper zero isocline
  points(0.333,0.333, cex=2)         # Add predicted ESS. cex = large
                                       symbol
```

OUTPUT: (Figure 5.8)

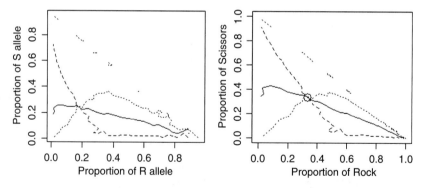

Figure 5.8 Zero isoclines for the R-P-S Mendelian model (Scenario 6): solid line, rock; dashed line, scissors; and dotted line, paper. The broken line at 45° can be ignored. The predicted ESS is indicated by the circle in the right-hand plot.

The graphical output shows that an equilibrium is possible. Note that the allele frequencies differ from each other, as expected from the genotype–phenotype map.

5.8.4 Finding the ESS using a numerical approach

R CODE:

```
rm(list=ls())        # Remove all objects from memory
# Function to calculate new proportions
  FITNESS <- function(Morph,PayoffMatrix,Npop,Genotypes)
{
SAME AS PREVIOUS CODING
}
GENOTYPE <- function(Prop.R, Prop.S, Prop.P, Npop)
{
SAME AS PREVIOUS CODING
}
################### Main program ###################
  set.seed(100)              # Initialize random number generator
  Npop       <- 2000                  # Set population size
  MaxGen     <- 2000            )    # Number of generations
  Output     <- matrix(0,MaxGen,7) # Create file for output
  Prop.R     <- 0.33                 # Proportion Rocks
  Prop.S     <- 0.33                 # Proportion Scissors
  Prop.P     <- 1-Prop.R-Prop.S    # Proportion Papers
  Morph      <- matrix(0,Npop,1)  # Allocate space for Phenotype
vector
# Set up fitness matrix. Note column-wise fill
  Epsilon      <- 0.1 # Deficit when the same morph types interact
  PayoffMatrix   <- matrix(c(-Epsilon,-1,1,1,-Epsilon,-1,-1,1,
-Epsilon),3,3)
  for (Igen in 1:MaxGen)       # Iterate over generations
{
    D1 <- GENOTYPE(Prop.R, Prop.S, Prop.P, Npop)    # Calculate the
                                                 genotypes
  Genotypes       <- D1[1:6]       # Numbers of each genotype
  Prop.Morphs     <- D1[7:9]       # Proportions of each morph
  Morph[1:Npop]  <- 3              # Set initially to Paper
  Nos.of.Rocks      <- sum(Genotypes[1:3])   # RR+RS+RP
  Nos.of.Scissors   <- sum(Genotypes[4:5])   # SS+SP
  Nos.of.Papers     <- Genotypes[6]          # PP genotype
  Morph[1:Nos.of.Rocks] <- 1 # Set rows 1 to Nos.of.Rocks to Rocks
  n1        <- Nos.of.Rocks+1          # Starting row for Scissors
  n2        <- n1+Nos.of.Scissors-1  # Ending row for Scissors
  Morph[n1:n2]   <- 2             # Set these rows to Scissors(=2)
  Output[Igen,1] <- Igen         # Store Generation number
  N            <- sum(Genotypes)    # To avoid rounding problems
```

```
  Output[Igen,2]    <- Nos.of.Rocks/N       # Proportion of Rocks
  Output[Igen,3]    <- Nos.of.Scissors/N   # Proportion of Scissors
  Output[Igen,4]    <- Nos.of.Papers/N  # Proportion of Papers
  Output[Igen,5]    <- Prop.R             # Frequency of allele R
  Output[Igen,6]    <- Prop.S             # Frequency of allele S
  Output[Igen,7]    <- Prop.P             # Frequency of allele P
# Calculate new proportion of Rocks by applying fitness criterion
  Propns        <- FITNESS(Morph,PayoffMatrix,Genotypes)
  Prop.R        <- Propns[1]       # Frequency of allele R
  Prop.S        <- Propns[2]       # Frequency of allele R
  Prop.P        <- Propns[3]       # Frequency of allele R
} # End of Igen loop
  par(mfrow=c(2,2))   # 4 plots per page
  plot(Output[,1], Output[,2], type='l', xlab='Generation',
ylab='Morph Proportions + X', ylim=c(0.0,1.8)) # Plot Rocks
  lines(Output[,1], Output[,3]+0.5, lty=2)  # Add Scissors to plot
  lines(Output[,1], Output[,4]+1.0, lty=3)  # Add Papers to plot
# Add predicted line to plots
  lines(Output[,1], rep(0.3333,MaxGen))      # "Predicted" ESS
  lines(Output[,1], rep(0.3333+0.5,MaxGen)) # "Predicted" ESS
  lines(Output[,1], rep(0.3333+1,MaxGen))    # "Predicted" ESS
# Plot Allele frquencies
    plot(Output[,1], Output[,5], type='l', xlab='Generation',
ylab='Allele Proportions', ylim=c(0.0,1))  # Plot Rocks
  lines(Output[,1], Output[,6], lty=2)    # Add Scissors to plot
  lines(Output[,1], Output[,7], lty=3)    # Add Papers to plot
# Phase plots showing proportion of two morphs
  plot(Output[,2],Output[,3],type='l', xlab='Rocks', ylab='S-
cissors')
  plot(Output[,2],Output[,4],type='l', xlab='Rocks', ylab='Pa-
pers')
# plot(Output[,3],Output[,4],type='l', xlab='Scissors', ylab='
Papers')
# Print mean proportions starting at generation 400
  print(' Mean proportions (R,P,S) from Generation 400 to MaxGen')
  c(mean(Output[400:MaxGen,2]),mean(Output[400:MaxGen,3]),
mean(Output[400:MaxGen,4]))
  print(' Mean allele freqs (R,P,S) from Generation 400 to MaxGen')
  c(mean(Output[400:MaxGen,5]),mean(Output[400:MaxGen,6]),
mean(Output[400:MaxGen,7]))
```

OUTPUT: (Figure 5.9)

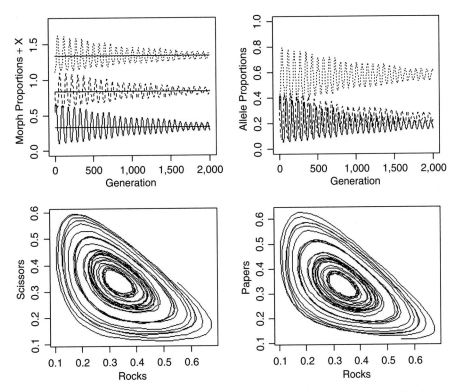

Figure 5.9 Output from the Mendelian model of the R-P-S game. The traces for the three proportions over time have been separated by adding 0.5 to the scissors (middle trace) and 1.0 to papers (top trace). Predicted ESS values are shown as the horizontal lines (ESS = 0.333 but increased for display purposes by 0.5 and 1.0 for scissors and papers, respectively). Allele proportions have not been separated. The two phase plots start at generation zero.

```
[1] "Mean proportions (R,P,S) from Generation 400 to MaxGen"
[1] 0.33980440.32908460.3311111
[1] "Mean allele freqs (R,P,S) from Generation 400 to MaxGen"
[1] 0.18938080.23929430.5713249
```

Both the allelic and morph frequencies show damped cyclic trajectories, with means being as indicated from the earlier graphical analysis (see Figure 5.9). The proportion of each morph oscillates about 1/3 but the allelic frequencies fluctuate about 0.19 (R), 0.24 (S), and 0.57 (P).

5.9   Scenario 7: Rock-Paper-Scissors: a quantitative genetic model

Although one might imagine this to be a more difficult model to code than the Mendelian model it actually turns out to be somewhat simpler. As with the Mendelian model, there are a number of ways in which genotype can translate into phenotype. I shall assume here a simple model in which the three morphs are determined by three different traits that are uncorrelated.

5.9.1 General assumptions

These are the same as that of Scenario 5.

5.9.2 Mathematical assumptions

1. The payoff matrix is as shown in Table 5.3. In this case when $\varepsilon = 0.1$ the model was completely unstable, one of the morphs eventually reaching 100%, which one depending on chance (i.e., initial starting conditions such as the random number generator). More interesting behavior was found with $\varepsilon = 0.5$ and so this is what is used here. However, it is important to note that analyses need to consider a range of values in order to arrive at generalities.

2. Population size is finite and constant.

3. Only one interaction occurs per individual.

4. Morph is determined by a polygenetic system in the following manner: There are three uncorrelated traits, each of which is a standard quantitative trait (i.e., normally distributed). The trait R_U underlies the rock morph, the trait S_U underlies the scissors morph, and the trait P_U underlies the paper morph. The morph that is phenotypically expressed is that with the highest value: a plausible biological scenario for this could be the action of three hormones.

5. Mating is at random and genotypes at each generation are determined from the multivariate normal distribution of genetic and environmental values (see Chapter 5 for details of the quantitative genetic model). As with the previous model, for simplicity, males and females are not distinguished, meaning that the fitnesses apply equally to each sex. In the lizard case it might be more proper to assume that the R-P-S fitnesses apply to the males and that the female allele fitnesses are equal. This would require separate coding for males and females (see the Hawk-Dove model for how this can be implemented).

6. The mean genetic value of the next generation is determined from the weighted (by fitness) average of the previous genetic values. Thus the mean genetic value of rock, $\bar{R}_{U,A}$, is

$$\bar{R}_{UA}(t+1) = \frac{\sum_{i=1}^{N_{Pop}} W_i(t) G_i(t)}{\sum_{i=1}^{N_{Pop}} W_i(t)} \qquad (5.21)$$

where $W_i(t)$ is the fitness of the ith phenotype at generation t, $G_i(t)$ is the genetic value of the ith phenotype at generation t, and N_{Pop} is the population size.

5.9.3 A graphical analysis

A graphical analysis is not worthwhile in this case. There are three traits which can vary, in principle, over an infinite range. Equilibrium is expected whenever the means of all three traits are the same. There is no simple way to graphically display the result varying over the three parameter space. Therefore, we proceed directly to the analysis over time.

5.9.4 Finding the ESS using a numerical approach

The initial variance–covariance matrices are determined by first creating the matrix H2 that contains the heritability of the three traits (here 0.5) along the diagonal, the correlations (here 0) on the off-diagonals:

$$\text{H2} = \begin{bmatrix} 0.5 & 0 & 0 \\ 0 & 0.5 & 0 \\ 0 & 0 & 0.5 \end{bmatrix} \tag{5.22}$$

which in R code is given by

```
H2 <- matrix(c(0.5, 0, 0, 0, 0.5, 0, 0, 0, 0.5), 3, 3)
```

Without loss of generality, the phenotypic variances are set at 1. The mean environmental values are, by definition, equal to zero throughout the simulation. Initially, the mean additive genetic values are set to zero; these change as a result of selection. The diagonal elements of the covariance matrices are the variances: hence for the phenotypic variance–covariance matrix, CovP, we have

```
diag(CovP) <- c(vars[1], vars[2], vars[3])
```

where vars[1] <- vars[2] <- vars[3] <- 1.

The additive genetic variances, V_A, are obtained from the formula $V_A = V_P h^2$, where V_P is the phenotypic variance and h^2 is the heritability. The environmental variance, V_E, is the difference between the phenotypic and genetic variances $V_E = V_A - V_P$. It is necessary to put a check in the coding since V_E must be positive. In R we can code this as

```
for ( i in 1:NX) # Iterate over traits
{
CovA[i,i] <- CovP[i,i]*H2[i,i]     # = Vp*h2
CovE[i,i] <- CovP[i,i]-CovA[i,i]   # Environmental Variance
if(CovE[i,i] < 0) stop(print(c("CovE cannot be",i,j,CovE[i,i])))
} # end of i 1:NX loop
```

The covariances (off-diagonal elements) of the phenotypic and genetic covariance matrices are obtained from the relationship $\text{Cov}_{XY} = r_{XY} V_X V_Y$, where X and Y are the two traits and r is the correlation. The environmental covariance is obtained by subtraction: coding in R is

```
N.minus.1 <- NX-1
for( i in 1:N.minus.1)
{
jj          <- i+1
for(j in jj:NX)
```

```
{
  CovP[i,j]  <- H2[j,i]*sqrt(CovP[i,i]*CovP[j,j])  # Phenotypic
                                                      covariance
  CovP[j,i] <- CovP[i,j]                # Phenotypic covariance
  CovA[i,j]<- H2[i,j]*sqrt(CovA[i,i]*CovA[j,j])# Genetic covariance
  CovA[j,i]  <- CovA[i,j]               # Genetic covariance
  CovE[i,j]  <- CovP[i,j]-CovA[i,j] # Environmental covariance
  CovE[j,i]  <- CovE[i,j]               # Environmental covariance
} # End of j jj:NX loop
} # End of i 1:N.minus.1 loop
```

Covariances can be negative and hence no check is required in this case. Note that these calculations have to be done only once. We now enter the loop that iterates over generations. At each generation we use the multivariate random normal generator mvrnorm to create matrices (size $N_{Pop} \times 3$) of environmental and genetic values (remember to load the library MASS for access to this function). These are added together to get the phenotypic values:

```
Trait.E <- mvrnorm(Npop, mu=Mean.E, Sigma=CovE) # Envir. value
Trait.A <- mvrnorm(Npop, mu=Mean.A, Sigma=CovA) # Genetic value
Trait.P <- Trait.A + Trait.E               # Phenotype
```

These phenotypic values are those of the underlying traits (to be coded as previously with Rock = 1, Scissors = 2, and Paper = 3). To obtain the expressed morph we have to find the trait for each individual that has the highest value. I have done this here by a sequence of comparisons, which may not be the fastest solution but it is the clearest: so, for example

```
Morph[Trait.P[,1]>Trait.P[,2]&Trait.P[,1]>Trait.P[,3]] <-1#Rock
```
The new mean genetic values are obtained by calling the function FITNESS, which computes the fitnesses in the same manner as in the previous models. Finally, the new means are calculated using equation (5.21): the new mean for the underlying Rock trait, mu.X1, is computed as

```
mu.X1 <- sum(Fitness*Trait.A[,1])/sum(Fitness) # Mean Rock
```

with similar coding for the other two traits.

R CODE:

```
  rm(list=ls())        # Remove all objects from memory
  library(MASS)        #  Make sure MASS library is loaded
  FITNESS  <- function(Morph, Trait.A, Npop, PayoffMatrix)
{
  Opponent <- sample(Morph)     #  Create a randomized vector of
                                    opponents
  Fitness  <- matrix(0,Npop,1)  #  Allocate space for fitnesses
# Iterate over the Payoff matrix
  for (Receiver in 1:3 )   #  Ind receiving payoff 1=Rock 2 = Scis-
                              sors 3=Paper
```

```
{
  for (I.Opponent in 1:3)  #  Opponent 1=Rock 2 = Scissors 3=Paper
{

  Fitness[Morph==Receiver  &  Opponent==
  I.Opponent]<- 3  +    PayoffMatrix[Receiver,I.Opponent]
  }}  #  End of loops
# Calculate mean genetic values
  mu.X1  <- sum(Fitness*Trait.A[,1])/sum(Fitness) #  Mean Rock
  mu.X2  <- sum(Fitness*Trait.A[,2])/sum(Fitness)  #  Mean Scissors
  mu.X3  <- sum(Fitness*Trait.A[,3])/sum(Fitness) #  Mean Paper
  return(c(mu.X1,mu.X2,mu.X3)) #  Return new mean genetic values
}
#########################MAIN PROGRAM#########################
  set.seed(10)  #  Set seed for random number generator
  Npop     <- 500              #  Population size
  MaxGen  <- 1000              #  maximum number of generations
  Output  <- matrix(0,MaxGen,4)  #  Allocate space for output
  NX       <- 3                #  Number of traits
# Matrix of heritabilities and correlations all h2=0.5, all r=0
  H2       <- matrix(c(0.5, 0, 0, 0, 0.5, 0, 0, 0,0.5), 3,3)
  mu       <- c(0,0,0)  #  Genetic means. Set initially to zero
  vars     <- c(1,1,1)  #  Variances. Set and remain at 1
  Mean.A  <-c(mu[1], mu[2], mu[3]) # Initial Additive genetic means
  Mean.E  <- c(0,0,0)              #  Environmental means
# Phenotypic Covariance matrix
# Note that initial covariances are set to 1 (arbitrary)
  CovP     <- matrix(1,NX,NX)     #  Phenotypic variances
# Set diagonal elements = variances
  diag(CovP)<- c(vars[1], vars[2], vars[3])
# Establish CovA from h2 and CovP and CovE from CovA and CovP
  CovA      <- matrix(0, NX, NX)    #  Allocate space for CovA
  CovE      <- matrix(0, NX, NX)    #  Allocate space for CovE
# Calculate environmental and genetic variances
  for ( i in 1:NX)  #  Iterate over traits
{

  CovA[i,i]  <- CovP[i,i]*H2[i,i]    #  = Vp*h2
  CovE[i,i]  <- CovP[i,i]-CovA[i,i]  #  Environmental Variance
  if(CovE[i,i] <0)  stop  (print(c("CovE cannot be",i,j,CovE[i,i])))
}  #  end of i 1:NX loop
# Calculate phenotypic, environmental and genetic covariances
  N.minus.1 <- NX-1
    for( i in   1:N.minus.1)
{

    jj         <- i+1
    for(j in jj:NX)
{

  CovP[i,j]  <-  H2[j,i]*sqrt(CovP[i,i]*CovP[j,j])    #  Phenotypic
                                                      covariance
```

```
    CovP[j,i]  <-   CovP[i,j]                  #  Phenotypic covariance
    CovA[i,j]  <-   H2[i,j]*sqrt(CovA[i,i]*CovA[j,j]) # Genetic co-
                                                             variance
    CovA[j,i]  <-   CovA[i,j]                  #  Genetic covariance
    CovE[i,j]  <-   CovP[i,j]-CovA[i,j]  #  Environmental covariance
    CovE[j,i]  <-   CovE[i,j]                  #  Environmental covariance
}  #  End of j jj:NX loop
}  #  End of i 1:N.minus.1 loop
    Epsilon  <-0.5  #  Decrement in fitness for same morph interaction
# Set up fitness matrix. Note column-wise fill
    PayoffMatrix  <- matrix(c(-Epsilon,-1,1,1,-Epsilon,-1,-1,1,-Epsi-
lon),3,3)
    Morph  <-matrix(3,Npop,1)    #  Set up initial morphs as all Paper
    for  (Igen in 1:MaxGen)       #  Iterate over generations
{
    Output[Igen,1]  <-  Igen      #  Store generation
# Generate additive and environmental values by calling mvrorm
    Trait.E  <-  mvrnorm(Npop, mu=Mean.E, Sigma=CovE)    # Envir. value
    Trait.A  <-  mvrnorm(Npop, mu=Mean.A, Sigma=CovA) # Genetic value
    Trait.P <-  Trait.A + Trait.E                 # Phenotype
# Determine morphs from trait with maximum value
    Morph[Trait.P[,1]>Trait.P[,2]&Trait.P[,1]>Trait.P[,3]] <-1 # Rock
    Morph[Trait.P[,1]>Trait.P[,2]&Trait.P[,1]<Trait.P[,3]] <-3 # Paper
    Morph[Trait.P[,1]<Trait.P[,2]&Trait.P[,1]>Trait.P[,3]] <-2 # Scis-
                                                                   sors
    Morph[Trait.P[,2]>Trait.P[,1]&Trait.P[,2]>Trait.P[,3]] <-2 # Scis-
                                                                   sors
    Morph[Trait.P[,2]>Trait.P[,1]&Trait.P[,2]<Trait.P[,3]] <-3 # Paper
    Morph[Trait.P[,2]<Trait.P[,1]&Trait.P[,2]>Trait.P[,3]] <-1 # Rock
    Morph[Trait.P[,3]>Trait.P[,1]&Trait.P[,3]>Trait.P[,2]] <- 3
                                                              # Paper
    Morph[Trait.P[,3]>Trait.P[,1] & Trait.P[,3]<Trait.P[,2]] <- 2
                                                              # Scissors
    Morph[Trait.P[,3]<Trait.P[,1] & Trait.P[,3]>Trait.P[,2]] <-1 # Rock
    Nos.of.Rocks   <- length(Morph[Morph==1])  # Number of Rocks
    Nos.of.Scissors <-  length(Morph[Morph==2])   # Number of Scissors
    Nos.of.Papers  <-  length(Morph[Morph==3])  # Number of Papers
    Output[Igen,2] <-  Nos.of.Rocks/Npop         # Proportion of Rocks
    Output[Igen,3] <-  Nos.of.Scissors/Npop # Proportion of Scissors
    Output[Igen,4] <-  Nos.of.Papers/Npop   # Proportion of Papers
# Apply selection
    Mean.A  <- FITNESS(Morph, Trait.A, Npop, PayoffMatrix)
}  #  End of generation loop
    par(mfrow=c(2,2))  #  4 plots per page
    plot(Output[,1], Output[,2], type='l', xlab='Generation', ylab='-
Propn +
X', ylim=c(0,2))                             #  Plot Rocks
    lines( Output[,1],  Output[,3]+0.5)    #  Plot Scissors + 0.5
```

```
  lines( Output[,1],  Output[,4]+1.0)        #  Plot Papers + 1
# Add "predicted" lines to plots
  lines(Output[,1], rep(0.3333,MaxGen))       #  Predicted Rocks
  lines(Output[,1], rep(0.3333+0.5,MaxGen))   #  Predicted Scissors
  lines(Output[,1], rep(0.3333+1.0,MaxGen))   #  Predicted Papers
# Phase plots
  plot(Output[400:MaxGen,2],  Output[400:MaxGen,3],   type='l',
xlab='Rocks', ylab='Scissors')
  plot(Output[,2],Output[,4],type='l',  xlab='Rocks', ylab='Pa-
pers')
  plot(Output[,3],Output[,4],type='l',  xlab='Scissors', ylab='-
Papers')
# Print mean proportions starting at generation 400
  print(' Mean proportions (R,P,S) from Generation 400 to MaxGen')
  c(mean(Output[400:MaxGen,2]),mean(Output[400:MaxGen,3]),
mean(Output[400:MaxGen,4]))
```

OUTPUT: (Figure 5.10)

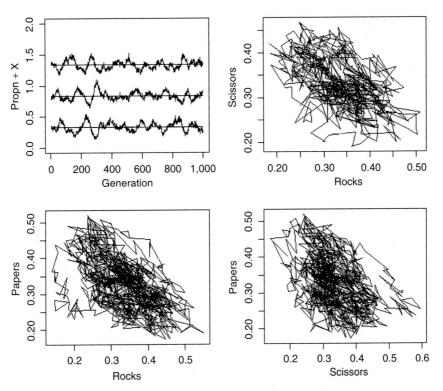

Figure 5.10 Output from the quantitative genetic model of the R-P-S game (Scenario 7). The traces for the three proportions over time have been separated by adding 0.5 to the scissors (middle trace) and 1.0 to papers (top trace). "Predicted" ESS values are shown as the horizontal lines (ESS = 0.333 but increased for display purposes by 0.5 and 1.0 for scissors and papers, respectively). The phase plot for rocks versus scissors starts at generation 400, whereas the other two start at generation zero.

```
[1] " Mean proportions (R,P,S) from Generation 400 to MaxGen"
[1] 0.3366489 0.3304027 0.3329484
```

The proportions show what appear to be small but chaotic fluctuations about 1/3. Unlike the case of $\varepsilon = 0.1$, where the fluctuations increase over time leading to monomorphism (the three underlying traits remain but one has such a high value that the others are never expressed), there appears to be persistence of all three morphs.

5.10   Scenario 8: Frequency-dependence with limited interactions

In the forgoing scenarios it was assumed that all interactions were possible, but in some cases interactions may be limited to specific combinations. A plausible example of this is the situation in which there are territorial and satellite males. In a simple model territorial males might not interact with other territorial males whereas there will obviously be interactions between satellite males and territorial males and between satellite males. I present here a very simple model for this scenario: further complexity to the model can be added using the approaches outlined in the previous scenarios.

5.10.1   General assumptions

1. A population consists of territorial and satellite males, the latter attempting to sneak copulations rather than defending a territory. A population can consist of only territorial males but not solely satellite males.

2. Territorial males do not interact with each other but satellite males interact with territorial males and other satellite males.

3. Territorial males are more successful at obtaining mates but suffer a reduction in fitness as a consequence of some other factor. For example, territorial males of certain cricket species are subject to parasitism by an acoustically orienting fly (Cade 1975, 1984) and territorial males of some fish species must delay maturity to achieve a size at which they are able to defend a territory.

4. The fitness of a satellite male is reduced by the presence of other satellite males attached to the "focal" territorial male.

5. The fitness of a territorial male is reduced by the presence of satellite males.

5.10.2   Mathematical assumptions

1. The fitness of a territorial male without satellite males is 1.

2. The fitness of a territorial male with satellite males is 0.8 (or some other user-defined value less than 1). The total fitness of all territorial males at generation t, $W_{T,t}$, is thus

$$W_{T,t} = (N_{T,t} - N_{T,S,t}) + 0.8N_{T,S,t} \qquad (5.23)$$

where $N_{T,t}$ is the number of territorial males and $N_{T,S}$ is the number of territorial males with satellite males.

3. The fitness of a satellite male is a decreasing function of the number of satellite males, $N_{S,t}$, attached to a given male. In the present model I use the simple function $5/N_{S,t}$, meaning that the fitness accruing to all $N_{S,t}$ males is $5/N_{S,t}$, not that each satellite male achieves this fitness. The total fitness of satellite males at generation t, $W_{S,t}$, is

$$W_{S,t} = \sum_{i=1}^{N_{S,t}} f_{i,t} \frac{5}{i} \qquad (5.24)$$

where $f_{i,t}$ is the frequency of occurrences of territorial males with i satellite males. Note that a single satellite male has a greater fitness than a territorial male (in fact, in this model a group of up to 5 satellite males have a fitness that is greater or equal to that of a territorial male): if this were not the case then the satellite male strategy could not invade the population. However, a satellite male has zero fitness in the absence of territorial males.

4. Satellite males are distributed at random among the territorial males. Under this scenario the probability of a satellite male being assigned to a given territorial male is $1/N_T$ and the number of satellites per territorial male follows a binomial distribution: thus the probability, P_S, of S satellites on around a male is

$$P_S = {}^{N_S}C_S p^s (1-p)^{N_S - S} \qquad (5.25)$$

where $p = 1/N_T$. Note that, in principle, a single territorial male could have all N_S satellite males around him. An alternate scenario would be to have satellite males equally distributed, an ideal free distribution, given equality among territorial males. This latter assumption greatly simplifies the analysis but may not be as realistic as the former and we shall examine both.

5. The proportion of territorial males in the next generation, $P_{T,t+1}$, is proportional to the two fitnesses:

$$P_{T,t+1} = \frac{W_{T,t}}{W_{T,t} + W_{S,t}} \qquad (5.26)$$

5.10.3 Finding the ESS analytically

Assuming that each territorial male receives the same number of satellites and the proportion of territorial males at generation t is ρ_t, the two fitnesses are

$$W_{T,t+1} = 0.8N_{T,t} = 0.8\rho_t N_t$$

$$W_{S,t+1} = N_{T,t} \frac{5}{N_{S,t}/N_{T,t}} = N_{T,t}^2 \frac{5}{N_{S,t}} = \rho_t^2 N_t^2 \frac{5}{(1-\rho_t)N_t} = \frac{5\rho_t^2 N_t}{(1-\rho_t)} \tag{5.27}$$

where N_t is the total population size at time t. The change in the proportion of territorial males is equal to

$$\Delta\rho_{t+1,t} = \rho_t - \frac{W_{T,t+1}}{W_{T,t+1} + W_{S,t+1}} \tag{5.28}$$

At equilibrium $\Delta\rho_{t+1,t} = 0$. Substituting the relevant fitnesses from equation (5.27) into equation (5.28) gives

$$\Delta\rho_{t+1,t} = \rho_t - \frac{0.8\rho_t N_t}{0.8\rho_t N_t + \dfrac{5\rho_t^2 N_t}{(1-\rho_t)}} = \rho_t - \frac{0.8}{0.8 + \dfrac{5\rho_t}{1-\rho_t}}$$

$$= \rho_t - \frac{0.8(1-\rho_t)}{0.8(1-\rho_t) + 5\rho_t} \tag{5.29}$$

$$= \frac{\rho_t^2(5-0.8) + (2)(0.8)\rho_t - 0.8}{0.8(1-\rho_t) + 5\rho_t}$$

The equilibrium value is found by setting the numerator equal to zero. This is a simple quadratic equation for which the solution is

$$\rho = \frac{-b \pm \sqrt{b^2 - 4ac}}{2a} \tag{5.30}$$

where $a = 5 - 0.8$, $b = (2)(0.8)$, and $c = -0.8$. The solution can be obtained from the R coding

```
a    <-  5-0.8; b  <- 2*0.8;  c  <-  -0.8
p1  <-  (-b-sqrt(b^2  -  4*a*c))/(2*a)
p2  <-  (-b+sqrt(b^2  -  4*a*c))/(2*a)
print(c(p1, p2))
```

which gives the output as $-0.6666667\ 0.2857143$. The first solution is clearly not physically possible, leaving the only equilibrium to be 28.57% territorial males.

Solving equation (5.29) is tedious and errors are likely to occur: thus it is good practice to also calculate the equilibrium directly from equation (5.28). The R function `uniroot` can be used to locate the equilibrium value: for good measure we also plot $\Delta\rho$ as a function of ρ (either the `apply` function or a loop could be used, both are given in the sample code below). Note that we have to designate a population size: from the above analysis the actual size should be of no consequence, which can be verified by running the model with various values (it is clear from the coding that population size could be factored out).

R CODE:

```
rm(list=ls())              #  Remove all objects from memory
FUNC  <-  function(P.T) # Function to calculate the change in rho
{
  N           <-  1000        # Population size
  N.T         <- P.T*N        # Number of territorial males
  N.S         <- (1-P.T)*N    # Number of satellite males
  N.S.per.T   <- N.S/N.T      # Satellite males per territori-
                                al male
  Sat.Fitness <- 5/N.S.per.T    # Fitness of satellite
  F.S         <- N.T*Sat.Fitness  # Total Fitness of satellites
  F.T         <- 0.8*N.T          # Total Fitness of territorials
  Delta       <- P.T - F.T/(F.T+F.S)  # Change in rho
  return(Delta)
}
#################### MAIN PROGRAM ####################
# First plot change in rho against rho
  P  <-matrix(seq(from=0.01, to=0.99, length=20),20,1) #  Propn sa-
                                                       tellites
# Using a loop
# FF  <-  matrix(0,20,1): for (i in 1:20){FF[i]  <-  FUNC(P[i])}
  FF  <-  apply(P,1,FUNC)    #  Using the apply function
# Plot the change in rho against rho
  plot(P,FF, xlab='Proportion territorial males, rho', ylab='-
Change in rho')
  lines(c(0,1),c(0,0))     #  Draw a horizontal line at zero
  uniroot(FUNC,interval=c(.01,.99))$root  #  Get solution using
                                             uniroot
```

OUTPUT:

`[1] 0.2857115`

The above output agrees with the quadratic solution and the graphical output (not shown) shows a single zero value at about this point. Thus we can be assured that our analysis is correct.

We shall now consider the slightly more complex problem of variation in the numbers per satellite male. As indicated by equation (5.25), to obtain the assumed distribution of satellites per territorial male we need to calculate the binomial probabilities, which can be done using the R function dbinom. It is most convenient to set this up as a user-supplied function, here called BINOM, to be called by the apply function (an alternative method using a loop is also given in the code below). There is a not-so-obvious correction that has to be made to the binomial probabilities. First we calculate the proportion of territorial males that do not have satellites, which is given by the simple binomial probability

$$P_0 = {}^{N_S}C_0 p^0 (1-p)^{N_S-0} = (1-p)^{N_S} \tag{5.31}$$

The R code to do this is

```
probty <-  1/N.T               ``   # Probability for binomial model
P.zero <-  dbinom(x=0, size=N.S, probty) # Probty of no satellites
```

where `N.T` is the number of territorial males and `N.S` is the number of satellite males.

Now we calculate the probability that males with satellites have 1, 2, 3, etc. or N_S satellites: this set of probabilities is required to determine the fitness of the satellite males. Thus we have to exclude the zero probability from our calculations (i.e., we are dealing with a truncated distribution). Probabilities must add up to 1 and hence to achieve this for our truncated distribution we divide throughout by the sum of the binomial probabilities from 1 to N_S, which is done by dividing $1 - P_0$

$$P_S = \frac{{}^{N_S}C_S p^S (1-p)^{N_S-S}}{1-P_0} \tag{5.32}$$

where for convenience, and hopefully without causing confusion, I have retained the same symbol, P_S, for the probability. The fitnessess of the two types of males is thus

$$W_{T,t+1} = P_0 N_{T,t} + 0.8(1-P_0)N_{T,t}$$
$$W_{S,t+1} = (N_{T,t} - N_{T,S,t})\sum_{i=1}^{N_{S,t}} \frac{C_i p^i (1-p)^{N_S-i}}{1 p_0} \frac{5}{i} \tag{5.33}$$

The coding for the fitness of satellites (with explanation following) is

```
Sat.nos      <- matrix(seq(from=1, to=N.S), N.S, 1 )
Prob.x       <- apply(Sat.nos,1, BINOM, N.S, probty)
Sat.Fitness  <- 5/Sat.nos
Freq         <- (Prob.x*(N.T-N.T.zero))/(1-P.zero)
F.S          <- sum(Freq*Sat.Fitness)
```

The sequence of operations by line is

1. Generate a vector of the sequence 1 through `N.S` to be used by the R function `apply` as the vector of index values
2. Use the `apply` function to generate the binomial probabilities
3. Calculate the vector of fitness values for each grouping of satellite males
4. Calculate the "corrected" probability of each grouping and multiply by the number of territorial males with satellites
5. Sum the above to obtain the total fitness of satellite males
6. Putting this all together we have

R CODE:

```
rm(list=ls())              #  Remove all objects from memory
#  Set up a function for the binomial
BINOM  <-  function(x, NN, probty){dbinom(x, size=NN, probty)}
FUNC   <-  function(P.T) # Function to calculate the change in rho
{
  N           <-  1000          #  Population size
  N.T         <- round(P.T*N)   #  Integer number of territorials
  N.S  <- N-N.T                 #  Number of satellites
  probty <-  1/N.T              #  Probability for binomial model
  P.zero  <-  dbinom(x=0, size=N.S, probty)  # Probty of no satellites
N.T.zero <-  N.T*P.zero   #  Nos of territorials without satellites
#  Iterate over all territorial male counts > 0
#  Line below shows how to do it using a loop
#Prob.x  <-  matrix(0, N.S,1);for (x in 1:N.S){ Prob.x[x]  <-
dbinom(x, size=N.S, probty) }
# Better approach is to use the apply function
# Generate a vector with number of satellites per territorial 1...N.S
  Sat.nos      <- matrix(seq(from=1, to=N.S), N.S, 1 )
# Probability of 1,2,3..N.S satellites
  Prob.x <- apply(Sat.nos,1, BINOM, N.S, probty)
# Fitness of satellite for each number per territorial
  Sat.Fitness <- 5/Sat.nos
# Frequency distribution of satellites per territorial
  Freq <- (Prob.x*(N.T-N.T.zero))/(1-P.zero)
  F.S   <- sum(Freq*Sat.Fitness)         # Fitness of satellites
  F.T   <- (1*N.T*P.zero + 0.8*N.T*(1-P.zero)) # Fitness of territorials
  Delta <- P.T - F.T/(F.T+F.S) # Change in proportion of territial
                               males
  return(Delta)
}
################### MAIN PROGRAM ###################
{ SAME AS IN PREVIOUS PROGRAM}
```

OUTPUT:

[1] 0.27029

The ESS, supported by the graphical output (not shown), is predicted to be 27.03% territorial males. This result is quite close to that obtained from the simpler model in which an equal number of satellites per males was assumed. Before tackling complex models it is advisable to begin with simple models. This not only makes initial analysis easier but also serves to indicate whether the added complexity is an important addition. In this case there is comparatively little difference between the two models.

5.10.4   Finding the ESS using a numerical approach

Analysis of the binomial model is "tricky" in the sense that if one does not realize that a truncated distribution is required the wrong solution is obtained. A numerical analysis can circumvent this problem by providing a more direct calculation. As with the two previous scenarios the numerical approach uses an individual-based modeling approach. The crux of the problem is to assign the N.S satellite males to the N.T number of territorial males. This is done as follows:

1. Generate a vector of integers from 1 to N.T:

$$X \quad \text{<- seq(from=1, to=N.T)}$$

This sequence of integers represents the population of territorial males, each given a unique number.

2. Pick at random with replacement N.S integers from the range 1 to N.T:

$$\text{Matches <- sample(X, N.S, replace=TRUE)}$$

These numbers represent the territorial males assigned to each satellite male. For example, suppose the integer 4 occurs 3 times: this means that territorial male number 4 has 3 satellite males.

3. Use the R function `table` to tabulate the number of times territorial males with satellites occur. Store the resulting list in an object we shall call TABLE:

$$\text{TABLE <- table(Matches)}$$

As an example, consider the following result for a population size of 20 with 65% territorial males (= 13 individuals):

$$\text{print(TABLE)}$$

Matches

1 2 5 7 9 10

1 1 1 1 1 2

The above output shows that territorial males labeled 1, 2, 5, 7, 9, and 10 received satellites, with the first 5 males receiving a single satellite while the last male received 2 satellites.

4. Convert the list entries (e.g., 1 1 1 1 1 2 in the above) into a vector:

$$\text{TABLE.MATRIX <- matrix(TABLE,,1)}$$

5. Calculate the total fitness of satellites, W.S, by summing over the above matrix, applying the fitness formula for the satellites per territorial male, as given by

equation (5.24). Note that the frequency $f_{i,t}$ does not apply in this case because each individual is kept separate.

```
W.S <- sum(5/TABLE.MATRIX)
```

6. Calculate the total fitness of territorial males. First we must calculate the number of territorial males that receive satellites, N.T.S, which is simply obtained by the number of entries in the list TABLE (or vector TABLE. MATRIX):

```
N.T.S <- length(TABLE)
```

Total fitness of territorial males is given by equation (5.23).

R CODE:

```
rm(list=ls())       # Remove all objects from memory
# Function to calculate the fitness of satellite and territorial
  males
  FITNESS <- function(P.T, Npop )
{
  N.T  <- round(Npop*P.T)      # Integral nos of territorial males
  N.S  <- Npop - N.T           # Nos of satellite males
  X    <- seq(from=1, to=N.T) # Label Territorial males
# Draw at random with replacement N.S integers of vector X. This
  represents
# the territorial males assigned to the satellite males
  Matches <- sample(X, N.S, replace=TRUE)
# Now have to find out how many satellites for each territorial
# Use function table to find number of satellites of territorial
  males
  TABLE <- table(Matches)
# Get number of satellite matings = number of picked territorial
  males
  N.T.S <- length(TABLE)
  TABLE <- matrix(TABLE,,1) # Convert TABLE to vector
  W.S  <- sum(5/TABLE)       # Calculate total fitness of satel-
                               lite males
  W.T  <- (N.T-N.T.S)*1 + N.T.S*0.8  # Total fitness of territori-
                               al males
  W    <- W.T + W.S # Total fitness
  P.T <- W.T/W      # Frequency of Territorial males
  return(P.T)       # Return frequency of territorial males
```

```
}
######################### MAIN PROGRAM ######################
  set.seed(1000)      # Set seed for random number generator
  Npop     <- 1000    # Population size
  P.T      <- 0.25    # Initial proportion of territorial males
  Maxgen   <- 100     # Number of generations simulation runs
  Output <- matrix(0,Maxgen,2) # Pre-assign space for output
  Output[,1] <- seq(from=1, to=Maxgen) # Store generation number
for ( Igen in 1: Maxgen) # Iterate over generations
{
# Call function FITNESS to find new proportion of territorial males
  P.T <- FITNESS(P.T, Npop)
  Output[Igen,2] <- P.T # Store result
} # End of Igen loop
# Plot frequency of territorial males against generation number
  plot(Output[,1],  Output[,2],  type='l',  xlab='Generation',
ylab='Proportion Territorials') # Plot output
  mean(Output[40:Maxgen,2]) # Mean frequency averaged from gener-
                                   ation 40
```

OUTPUT: (Figure 5.11)

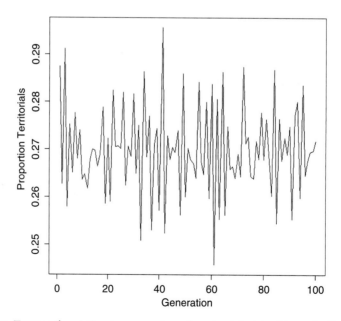

Figure 5.11 Temporal variation in proportion of territorial males (Scenario 8).

[1] 0.2696347

The frequency of territorial males fluctuates approximately between 0.29 and 0.25 with a mean of 0.27, matching the result expected from the analytical solution. The mean percentage of territorial males does not depend on the population size, but the fluctuations decrease with population size. One advantage of this modeling approach is that it becomes relatively easy to incorporate different constraints on the distribution of territorial males and the possibility of dynamical choices by the satellites.

5.11   Scenario 9: Learning the ESS

The previous scenarios assumed that individuals do not learn. However, in many cases the response of an individual is conditioned on previous experience. Thus the introduction of a learning function enhances realism, at least for some scenarios. We might also ask if this approach is a useful method to determine the optimal ESS. To illustrate the approach I shall use the learning model of Harley (1981) in the context of the Hawk-Dove game.

5.11.1   General assumptions

1. The population consists of individuals that adopt a hawk or dove behavior with a probability that is contingent on previous experience.
2. The payoff matrix resembles that given in Table 5.2 in as much as the relative magnitudes are the same but the absolute values are not constrained by the formulae given in Table 5.2. Thus a dove interacting with a hawk may receive some positive payoff. Similarly, a dove interacting with a dove receives an amount that is intermediate between the payoffs that doves receive interacting with a hawk (rather than equal to $V/2$).
3. Fitness is equated with the payoff.

5.11.2   Mathematical assumptions

1. The payoff matrix is

	H	D
H	0	18
D	12	15

2. Population size is finite.

3. An individual experiences a sequence of interactions and uses the Relative Payoff Sum (RPS) learning rule to determine its behavior at each interaction. This rule, suggested by Harley (1981), is based on the following general rule. Adjust the frequency of adopting a given behavior according to the cumulative amount received from this behavior relative to the total cumulative payoff. An additional

factor added to this rule is a "memory" factor, m, such that the most recent payoffs have greater weight. Letting the probability of adopting behavior i at interaction t be $P_i(t)$ then at the first encounter adopt this behavior according to the rule

$$P_i(t) = \frac{r_i}{\sum_{j=1}^{n} r_j} \tag{5.34}$$

where r_i is the "residual" value associated with behavior i and there are n possible behaviors (2 in the case of hawk and dove). In the absence of any information one might expect all residuals to be equal and thus at the first interaction each behavior has the same probability of being adopted. At each interaction the probability is modified according to the accumulating payoffs

$$P_i(t) = \frac{r_i + \sum_{\tau=1}^{t-1} m^{t-\tau-1} \text{Payoff}_i(\tau)}{\sum_{j=1}^{n} [r_j + \sum_{\tau=1}^{t-1} m^{t-\tau-1} \text{Payoff}_j(\tau)]} \tag{5.35}$$

The summation in the numerator is the value of adopting behavior i over the time interval elapsed weighted by the memory factor, m. The denominator is the sum over all behaviors.

5.11.3 Finding the ESS using a numerical approach

For convenience I shall label the hawk behavior as 1 and dove behavior as 2. Thus equation can be written for the probability of adopting the hawk behavior as

$$\begin{aligned} P_1(t) &= \frac{r_1 + \sum_{\tau=1}^{t-1} m^{t-\tau-1} \text{Payoff}_1(\tau)}{r_1 + \sum_{\tau=1}^{t-1} m^{t-\tau-1} \text{Payoff}_1(\tau) + r_2 + \sum_{\tau=1}^{t-1} m^{t-\tau-1} \text{Payoff}_2(\tau)} \\ &= \frac{r + \sum_{\tau=1}^{t-1} m^{t-\tau-1} \text{Payoff}_0(\tau)}{2r + \sum_{\tau=1}^{t-1} m^{t-\tau-1} \text{Payoff}_1(\tau) + \sum_{\tau=1}^{t-1} m^{t-\tau-1} \text{Payoff}_2(\tau)} \end{aligned} \tag{5.36}$$

where I have assumed that the residual values are equal ($r_1 = r_2 = r$).

At equilibrium the average probability of adopting the dove behavior should be such that the expected payoff equals that from adopting the hawk behavior. Following the protocol set out in Section 5.1.2 this can be shown to be achieved when $P_0(t) = (18 - 15)/(18 + 12 - 0 - 15) = 0.2$.

5.11.3.1 Coding $P_0(t)$

Although equation 5.36 looks rather formidable it is not difficult to program. First we consider the history for a single individual which is contained in a matrix called `Payoff` of dimensions `Trial` × 2 in which the payoffs for being a hawk are stored in column 1 and the payoffs for being a dove are stored in column 2 and the number of rows (`Trial`) is equal to the number of interactions (= t in the above equation). For each trial one entry must be zero as an individual can only adopt a single behavior. The matrix `Payoff` is initiated with zeros in every entry and then modified as a behavior is adopted. Thus the first 10 trials for an individual could be (comments attached are not in the matrix)

> Payoff[1:10]

```
    [,1] [,2]
[1,] 18  0   Hawk behavior adopted and individual interacts with a Dove
[2,] 0   0   Hawk behavior adopted and individual interacts with another Hawk
[3,] 0   0   Hawk behavior adopted and individual interacts with another Hawk
[4,] 18  0   Hawk behavior adopted and individual interacts with a Dove
[5,] 18  0   Hawk behavior adopted and individual interacts with a Dove
[6,] 0   12  Dove behavior adopted and individual interacts with a Hawk
[7,] 18  0   Hawk behavior adopted and individual interacts with a Dove
[8,] 0   15  Dove behavior adopted and individual interacts with another Dove
[9,] 0   0   Hawk behavior adopted and individual interacts with another Hawk
[10,]0   12  Dove behavior adopted and individual interacts with a Hawk
```

Equation (5.36) can now be coded as

```
Hawk <- 0; Dove <- 0    # Set sums initially to zero
MaxT <- Trial-1         # Set t-1
for (Time in 1: MaxT)   # Iterate from 1 to t-1
{
Hawk <- Hawk + m^(Trial-Time-1)*Payoff[Time,1]   # Hawk sum
Dove <- Dove + m^(Trial-Time-1)*Payoff[Time,2]   # Dove sum
}
P1.t <- (r + Hawk)/(2*r + Hawk + Dove)
```

To find the mean probability we must iterate over a number of individuals, say Npop = 30. Thus we modify the above to accommodate Npop individuals:

```
MaxT <- Trial-1         # Set t-1
for (Ind in 1:Npop)     # Iterate over individuals
{
Hawk <- 0; Dove <- 0    # Set sums initially to zero
for (Time in 1: MaxT)   # Iterate from 1 to t-1
{
Hawk <- Hawk + m^(Trial-Time-1)*Payoff[Time,1,Ind] # Hawk sum
Dove <- Dove + m^(Trial-Time-1)*Payoff[Time,2,Ind] # Dove sum
} # End of Time loop
P1.t[Ind] <- (r + Hawk)/(2*r + Hawk + Dove)
} # End of Individual loop
```

The primary changes to the coding are (a) making the payoff matrix into an array in which the third dimension stores the individual number, and (b) storing the probability in a vector (P1.t[Ind]). It is possible to replace the Ind loop with the `apply` function but the coding gets a little more obscure and there does not appear to be a significant saving in time.

5.11.3.2   Determining the behavior adopted at a trial

The next step is to determine the entries for the payoff array. To do this we must first assign the behavior adopted at any given trial. For this purpose we create a function called MORPH, passing to it the vector of probabilities for the population and the population size. Within this function three steps are followed:

1. Create a vector `Morph` of length `Npop` in which all individuals are assigned the dove behavior, which is coded as 2.
2. Generate a vector of `Npop` uniform random numbers lying between 0 and 1.
3. If individual = `Ind` receives a random number less than `P1.t[Ind]`, then it is given a value of 1 denoting that it has adopted the hawk behavior.

```
MORPH <- function(P1.t, Npop) # Function to determine behaviors
{
# Set up morph vector initially with all doves
  Morph        <- rep(2,Npop)
# Calculate behavior adopted by using random number generator
  Flag         <- runif(Npop, min=0, max=1)
# Values of Flag < P1.t become Hawks
  Morph[P1.t > Flag] <- 1
return( Morph)
} # End of function
```

5.11.3.3   Calculating the payoffs

The same procedure as used in the other Hawk-Dove models can be used for this. First, in the main program, we create the payoff matrix

```
PayoffMatrix <- matrix(c(0,12,18,15),2,2) # Set up payoff matrix
                                              for P=0.2
```

After determining the behaviors adopted by the individuals (i.e., the matrix Morph) we pass this to the previously described function FITNESS (see Scenario 2) which calculates the fitnesses:

```
FITNESS <- function(Morph, PayoffMatrix, Npop) # Function to gen-
                                                 erate payoffs
{
# Match males up to find fitness for each male
# Create a randomized vector of opponents
  Opponent   <- sample(Morph)
```

```
# Iterate over the Payoff matrix
  Fitness      <- rep(0,Npop)  # Assign space for fitness
  for (Receiver in 1:2 )       # Individual receiving payoff
{
  for (I.Opponent in 1:2)      # Opponent
{

  Fitness[Morph==Receiver & Opponent==I.Opponent]<- PayoffMatrix
[Receiver,I.Opponent]
} # End of I.opponent loop
} # End of Receiver loop
  return(Fitness)
} # End of function
```

5.11.3.4 The main program

To calculate the preceding we need to keep track of the entire behavioral history of each individual and for the final output the mean probability of adopting the Hawk behavior. This is a simple bookkeeping problem but care should be taken to ensure correct indexing. Parameter values were set at the values used by Harley (1981). After setting up the parameter values and preassigning space for the various matrices the results for the first trial are calculated and then the remaining trials addressed using a loop. The coding for the main program is

```
####################### MAIN PROGRAM #######################
  set.seed(100)           # Initialize random number generator
  Npop        <- 30       # Set population size
  MaxTrial    <- 200      # Number of generations
  r           <- 14.4     # Residual value
  m           <- 0.99     # Memory coefficient
# Set up a matrix for the output
# Rows = trial number Col 1 = trial number, Cols 2- Npop+1 = Indivi-
  duals
  Nplus1      <- Npop+1                    # Extra col for trial number
  Output      <- matrix(0,MaxTrial,Nplus1)# Create file for output
  P1.t        <- matrix(0.5,Npop,1)   # Vector of Learned Probabil-
                                          ities
  Mean.P1.t <- matrix(0,MaxTrial,1)   # matrix for Mean of Pi(t)
# Set up array for payoffs
# 1st dimension = trial, 2nd dimension = Behavior, 3rd dimension =
  Individual
  Payoff <- array(0, c(MaxTrial,2,Npop))     # Array of payoffs
  PayoffMatrix <-matrix(c(0,12,18,15),2,2) # Set up payoff matrix
                                          P=0.2
############## Calculate Payoffs for first trial ##############
  Output[1,1] <- 1     # Store Trial number in first column
  Output[1,2:Nplus1] <-P1.t  # Store Probability for each individual
  Morph <-MORPH(P1.t, Npop)  # Call function to determine behaviors
```

```
  Fitness <- FITNESS(Morph, PayoffMatrix, Npop) # Determine payoffs
# Move Payoffs into Payoff matrix
  for ( Ind in 1:Npop)      # Iterate over individuals
{
Payoff[1, Morph[Ind], Ind] <- Fitness[Ind] # Store fitnesses in
                                                      array
} # End of Ind loop
  Mean.P1.t[1] <- mean(P1.t)     # Save mean Pi(t)
###################### Subsequent Trials ######################
  for (Trial in 2:MaxTrial)  # Iterate over trials
{
  Morph <- MORPH(P1.t, Npop)  # Call function to determine behaviors
  Fitness <- FITNESS(Morph, PayoffMatrix, Npop) # Determine payoffs
  MaxT <- Trial-1          # Set t-1
  for ( Ind in 1:Npop)        # Iterate over individuals
{
Payoff[Trial, Morph[Ind], Ind] <- Fitness[Ind] # Pass payoffs to
                                                      array
}                            # End of Ind loop
# Calculate the new P1.t
  for (Ind in 1:Npop)        # Iterate over individuals
{
  Hawk <- 0;    Dove <- 0   # Set sums initially to zero
  for (Time in 1: MaxT)      # Iterate from 1 to t-1
{
  Hawk <- Hawk + m^(Trial-Time-1)*Payoff[Time,1,Ind] # Hawk sum
  Dove <- Dove + m^(Trial-Time-1)*Payoff[Time,2,Ind] # Dove sum
} # End of Time loop
  P1.t[Ind] <- (r + Hawk)/(2*r + Hawk + Dove)
} # End of Individual loop
# Store Data
  Output[Trial,1] <- Trial # Store Generation number in 1st column
  Output[Trial,2:Nplus1] <- P1.t # Store Probability for each individual
  Mean.P1.t[Trial] <- mean(P1.t) # Store mean Pi(t)
} # End of Trial loop
###### Plot Output ######
# Plot first individual
  plot(Output[,1], Output[,2],type='l', xlab='Trial  number',
ylab='Hawk P1.t', ylim =c(0,1))
for (i in 3: Nplus1) # Plot all remaining individuals
{
  lines(Output[,1], Output[,i],type='l')
}
  points(Output[,1], Mean.P1.t) # Plot trajectory of mean probty
                                of hawk
```

OUTPUT: (Figure 5.12)

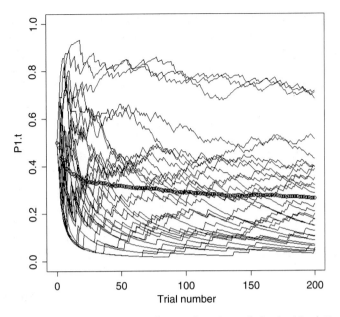

Figure 5.12 Individual trajectories using the RPS learning rule in the Hawk-Dove game (Scenario 9). The series of circles shows the mean value of P1(t).

The results from the above program are shown in Figure 5.12. As noted by Harley (1981) there is an enormous variation among individuals and approach to the expected mean value is extremely slow. The importance of this type of simulation is that it shows how difficult it may be to experimentally test predictions of game theory if learning is involved or sample sizes are relatively small.

5.12   Some exemplary papers

O'Brien, E. E. and J.S Brown. 2008. Games roots play: effects of soil volume and nutrients. *Journal of Ecology* **96:438–446.**

Problem: To find the ESS for root production for two plants growing within each others area of nutrient extraction.

Approach: The situation that is a variant of Scenario 1. The solution is approached using the calculus but the resulting equation has to be solved numerically.

Ruxton, G. D. and M. Broom. 1999. Evolution of kleptoparasitism as a war of attrition. *Journal of Evolutionary Biology* **12:755–759.**

Problem: The evolution of kleptoparasitism (defined as the stealing of resources gathered by another individual).

Approach: The "war of attrition" framework. Results are derived analytically by keeping assumptions simple and somewhat restrictive. As noted by the authors, it could be of considerable interest and biological significance to use an individual-based model to examine the consequences of variation among individuals. The approaches used in Scenarios 2–7 could be readily adopted for this purpose.

Servedio, M. R. and M. E. Hauber. 2006. To eject or to abandon? Life history traits of hosts and parasites interact to influence the fitness payoffs of alternative anti-parasite strategies. *Journal of Evolutionary Biology* 19:1585–1594.

Problem: Under what conditions is the fitness payoff of egg ejection greater than nest abandonment?

Approach: Single generation model based on a normal distribution of phenotypes. The appendix gives a detailed account of the necessary equations. The results are determined numerically. As noted by the authors, the model does not consider the possibility of both behaviors in the population. This deficiency could be remedied using an individual-based model as described in Scenarios 2 –7.

Eadie, J. M. and J. M. Fryxell. 1992. Density dependence, frequency-dependence, and alternative nesting strategies in goldeneyes. *American Naturalist* 140:621–641.

Problem: Influence of frequency- and density-dependence on the evolution of alternative nesting behaviors (brood parasitism females and parental females) in the goldeneye.

Approach: Analytical solutions of frequency- and density-dependence are taken separately followed by a simulation incorporating both effects. In the simulation clonal inheritance is implicitly assumed with each female producing daughters that have the same behavior as their mother. The model shows that both behaviors can be maintained in the population. Results compare favorably with the observed data on goldeneyes.

Sinervo, B. 2001. Runaway social games, genetic cycles driven by alternative male and female strategies, and the origin of morphs. *Genetica* 112–113:417–443.

Problem: To explain the persistence of three alternative male strategies in various lizard species (notably *Uta stansburiana*).

Approach: Simulation models using either clonal or simple Mendelian models of inheritance. The models are analogous to the R-P-S models discussed in this chapter. The results are compared to the observed dynamics of lizard populations.

Wakano, J. Y. and Y. Ihara. 2005. Evolution of male parental care and female multiple mating: Game-theoretical and two-locus diploid models. *American Naturalist* 166:E32–E44.

Problem: The evolution of male parental care and female multiple mating.

Approach: An analytical solution is derived for the case of clonal inheritance and simulation used to analyze an individual-based model in which inheritance was determined by a two-allelic, two-locus model. Under some parameter combinations predictions of the two models differed significantly.

Beauchamp, G. U. Y. 2000. Learning rules for social foragers: implications for the producer-scrounger game and ideal free distribution theory. *Journal of Theoretical Biology* **207:21–35.**

Problem: To determine the ability of various learning rules to predict the behavior of social foragers under two types of scenarios: a producer-scrounger game and an ideal free distribution game.

Approach: Simulation of various learning rules in the two scenarios. The ESS was located numerically by varying the probability of displaying a behavior. By introducing a mutant using a different learning rule the stability of the ESS was examined.

CHAPTER 6

Dynamic Programming

6.1   Introduction

Many, if not most, traits display phenotypic plasticity, that is, the phenotypic expression of the trait is contingent on the environment. In some cases, such as adult morphology, the development of the trait is determined in part by the environment but does not vary once the trait is established. On the other hand, other traits, particularly behavioral traits, may be extremely labile. For example, foraging, oviposition, migration, and parental allocation decisions are all traits that are typically state-dependent. The techniques presented in Chapter 2 may be used to analyze such models in some cases (e.g., Scenario 12, which examined the relationship between propagule size and age), but more frequently a dynamic programming approach is required, or is at least more efficient. For detailed discussions on dynamic programming, see Mangel and Clark (1988), Houston and McNamara (1999), and Clark and Mangel (2000). To illustrate the method I shall use the patch-foraging model described by Mangel and Clark (1988). As in the previous chapters I shall set the scenario both in general terms and then with specific mathematical functions. MATLAB code is provided at the end of the chapter.

6.1.1   General assumptions in the patch-foraging model

1. The habitat is divided into a number of patches.
2. The animal in question forages among the patches for food or some other fitness-related resource.
3. Patches vary in quality and hence the benefits obtained by the animal vary with patch type.
4. There is a metabolic cost to foraging.
5. Independent of the metabolic cost there is a probability of dieing from some external cause such as a predator or inclement weather conditions. This probability may vary among patches.
6. Fitness is measured as the probability of being alive at the end of some time interval (e.g., in a small terrestrial vertebrate this may be the summer period, the end of the season being the time at which hibernation is entered).

6.1.2   Mathematical assumptions in the patch-foraging model

1. There are three types of patches, which vary with respect to

   a. Benefits of the resource, $Benefit_i$, if found

   b. Probability of obtaining the benefit (e.g., food), $Pbenefit_i$

   c. Probability of mortality, $Pmortality_i$

2. The cost to foraging, $Cost$, is fixed and independent of patch type.

3. There is a minimum state, $Xcritical$, at or below which the animal cannot survive. The minimum state at which an animal can survive is $Xmin$.

4. There is limit to the state (e.g., space for storing the resource is limiting), $Xmax$.

5. Fitness is equal to the maximum probability of surviving until time T, the end of the season (or some other designated point).

6.1.3   A first look at the model

Specific values for the parameters defined above are $Xcritical = 3$, $Xmax = 10$, and for each patch:

Patch type	Benefit	Pbenefit	Pmortality	Cost
1	0	0.0	0.000	1
2	3	0.4	0.004	1
3	5	0.6	0.020	1

Patch 1 is empty of resources but is a safe haven from sources of mortality other than that of dieing because the animal's state is at or below $Xcritical$. In contrast, patch 3 is relatively rich in resources but there is also a relatively high probability of dieing. We can define two transition states, depending on whether the resource is located:

Resource found in patch:

$$X_{t+1} = X_t - Cost + Benefit, \quad \text{if } X_{t+1} > Xmax \quad \text{then } X_{t+1} = Xmax$$
$$\text{OR}$$
$$\text{if } X_{t+1} \leq Xcritical \quad \text{then} \quad \text{animal} \quad \text{dies}$$

Resource not found in patch:

$$X_{t+1} = X_t - Cost, \quad \text{if } X_{t+1} \leq Xcritical \text{ then animal dies}$$

Given some starting state we ask "What is the set of decisions that will maximize the probability of the animal reaching the end of the period?" Because there are three patches and each patch has itself two states (resource found or resource not found), there are an extremely large number of possible paths from the start to the end, most of which will be suboptimal. In mathematical notation we can state the problem as follows:

$$F(x, T) = \max \text{ Pr (survive from } t \text{ to } T | X_t = x) \tag{0.1}$$

which can be stated in words as "Maximize the probability of surviving from t until T given that the state of the animal at time t ($= X_t$), is equal to x" (throughout this chapter X will refer to the state variable while x will refer to a particular value of the state variable). Now we do know what the final state should be, namely survival and hence we can write down the value of $F(x, T)$ as

$$F(x, T) = \begin{cases} 1 & \text{if } x > Xcritical \\ 0 & \text{if } x \leq Xcritical \end{cases} \qquad (0.2)$$

that is, the probability of being alive at time T is certain if the animal's state exceeds the lower critical value and is zero if it falls below that value. At time $T - 1$ the animal must pick a patch that maximizes its probability of being alive at the end of the next (last) interval.

Suppose at time $T - 1$ the animal is in state $X_{T-1} = x = 4$: there are six scenarios we have to analyze.

Patch	X_t+1		Probablity		Probability of Survival
	Benefit	No Benefit	Pbenefit	1−Pbenefit	
Patch 1	4 − 1 + 0 = 3	4 − 1 = 3	0.0	1.0	0 because $X_t + 1 \leq Xcritical$
Patch 2	4 − 1 + 3 = 6	4 − 1 = 3	0.4	0.6	(0.996)(0.4 + 0) = 0.3984
Patch 3	4 − 1 + 5 = 8	4 − 1 = 3	0.6	0.4	(0.98)(0.6 + 0) = 0.588

The animal should choose patch 3 to maximize its survival probability. Note that this does not guarantee its survival. Suppose the animal is in state $X_{T-1} = x = 5$:

Patch	X_t+1		Probablity		Probability of Survival
	Benefit	No Benefit	Pbenefit	1−Pbenefit	
Patch 1	5 − 1 + 0 = 4	5 − 1 = 4	0.0	1.0	(1)(0+1)=1
Patch 2	5 − 1 + 3 = 7	5 − 1 = 4	0.4	0.6	(0.996)(0.4+0.6)=0.996
Patch 3	5 − 1 + 5 = 9	5 − 1 = 4	0.6	0.4	(0.98)(0.6 + 0.4) = 0.98

The appropriate patch is now patch 1, because, although the animal does not accumulate any resources, it has a 100% probability of surviving to T. In fact, provided that the animal's state exceeds 4, the best choice will always be patch 1 in this time interval. Of course, survival may not be the only consideration: for example, the amount of resources accumulated by T may also be important (we consider this in Scenario 1).

To begin the process with survival as our fitness criterion we note, as given above, that for all final values of x from $Xmin$ to $Xmax$, where $Xmin = Xcritical + 1$,

$$F(x, T) = 1 \qquad (6.3)$$

that is, we are only interested in those individuals that are alive at the end of the time period.

We now step back one time unit and consider the survival from time $T - 1$ to T for a particular value of x at time $T - 1$ (say x). Depending on whether the animal finds food or not the value of x will change to x_{Food} or x_{NoFood}, the particular values depending on the patch: let these survivals be designated as $S(x_{Food}, i, T - 1)$ and $S(x_{NoFood}, i, T - 1)$, where i is the patch number. Fitness for each patch, $W(x, i, T - 1)$ is then given by

$$W(x, i, T - 1) = (1 - Pmortality)[S(x_{Food}, i, T - 1)F(x_{Food}, T - 1) \\ + S(x_{NoFood}, i, T - 1)F(x_{NoFood}, T - 1)] \tag{6.4}$$

The $(1 - Pmortality)$ is the probability of survival, irrespective of the patch. There are now k fitness values, of which we choose the largest, the associated patch being the optimal patch choice. The value of $F(x, T - 1)$ is given by

$$F(x, T - 1) = \max\{W(x, 1, T - 1), W(x, 2, T - 1), W(x, 3, T - 1)\} \tag{6.5}$$

The above algorithm can be repeated for all possible values of the penultimate state, which in this case are unit steps from $x = 4$ to $x = 10$. Thus we arrive at the optimal set of decisions in the last period for all possible states the animal can be in at the start of this period.

We now have the best decision for the last time period and the probability of survival from this period to the end. At this point we can move one step backward and calculate the best decision for this period. The process is repeated until the first time period is arrived at. Going backward in this way we build up a **decision matrix** in which the columns give the state (*Xmin* to *Xmax*) and the rows give the time. Such a matrix is shown in Table 6.1, with the bottom half of the table showing $F(x, t)$ (i.e., the probability of surviving from t to T given the optimal path). To see how this matrix can be used let us assume that the animal commences in state 7. In the first time period the animal should select patch 3 which, if the animal survives, will change its state from 7 to $7 - 1 + 5 = 13$, if resources are found or from 7 to $7 - 1 = 6$ if resources are not found. In the first case, the total accumulated exceeds the capacity of the animal and so its state is set to its maximum of 10 and in the next time interval the animal selects patch 1. In the second case (no resources found) the animal selects patch 2.

6.1.4 An algorithm for constructing the decision matrix

The example outlined above is a simple but general example of the type of model for which dynamic programming is appropriate. The following algorithm can be modified, as shown in later examples, to deal with most dynamic programming problems. For convenience the program is divided into the main program and three functions, called FITNESS, OVER.PATCHES and OVER.STATES. FITNESS calculates the survival probability (fitness) for a given state in a given patch. The other two functions iterate over patches, where patches may be physical or

Table 6.1 Decision matrix (top) and probability of survival, F(x,t,T) (bottom) for foraging model

Time	State (Shown along bottom row)						
	[,1]	[,2]	[,3]	[,4]	[,5]	[,6]	[,7]
[1,]	3	3	3	3	2	2	1
[2,]	3	3	3	3	2	2	1
[3,]	3	3	3	3	2	2	1
[4,]	3	3	3	3	2	2	1
[5,]	3	3	3	3	2	2	1
[6,]	3	3	3	3	2	2	1
[7,]	3	3	3	3	2	2	1
[8,]	3	3	3	3	2	2	1
[9,]	3	3	3	3	2	2	1
[10,]	3	3	3	3	2	2	1
[11,]	3	3	3	3	2	2	1
[12,]	3	3	3	3	2	2	1
[13,]	3	3	3	3	2	2	2
[14,]	3	3	3	3	2	2	1
[15,]	3	3	3	3	2	1	1
[16,]	3	3	3	3	1	1	1
[17,]	3	3	3	1	1	1	1
[18,]	3	3	1	1	1	1	1
[19,]	3	1	1	1	1	1	1
[20,]	4	5	6	7	8	9	10
	[,1]	[,2]	[,3]	[,4]	[,5]	[,6]	[,7]
[1,]	0.514	0.724	0.812	0.846	0.866	0.878	0.886
[2,]	0.518	0.73	0.819	0.854	0.874	0.886	0.893
[3,]	0.523	0.737	0.826	0.861	0.881	0.893	0.901
[4,]	0.527	0.743	0.833	0.869	0.889	0.901	0.909
[5,]	0.532	0.75	0.84	0.876	0.897	0.909	0.917
[6,]	0.537	0.756	0.848	0.884	0.904	0.917	0.925
[7,]	0.541	0.763	0.854	0.891	0.912	0.925	0.933
[8,]	0.546	0.769	0.863	0.9	0.921	0.933	0.941
[9,]	0.55	0.776	0.871	0.908	0.928	0.941	0.95
[10,]	0.556	0.784	0.878	0.914	0.935	0.95	0.959
[11,]	0.561	0.79	0.884	0.921	0.945	0.959	0.966
[12,]	0.566	0.794	0.888	0.933	0.955	0.966	0.974
[13,]	0.566	0.794	0.909	0.944	0.963	0.974	0.98
[14,]	0.566	0.818	0.909	0.944	0.963	0.974	1
[15,]	0.588	0.818	0.909	0.944	0.963	1	1
[16,]	0.588	0.818	0.909	0.944	1	1	1

(continued)

Table 6.1 (Continued)

Time	[,1]	[,2]	[,3]	[,4]	State (Shown along bottom row) [,5]	[,6]	[,7]
[17,]	0.588	0.818	0.909	1	1	1	1
[18,]	0.588	0.818	1	1	1	1	1
[19,]	0.588	1	1	1	1	1	1
[20,]	4	5	6	7	8	9	10

Note: Output from R is slightly modified for display purposes.

particular decisions such as "forage" or "not forage" (see Scenario 2), and states, respectively.

The most complex part of the program is the bookkeeping of the survival probabilities. To do this we first create a matrix called F.vectors that consists of two columns with the number of rows typically being equal to the number of states to be analyzed. In the present case, the state variable ranges from 3 (= dead) to 10 (*Xmax*) and it is most convenient here to create the matrix with the number of rows going from 1 to *Xmax*. The reason for this is that the row number then corresponds to the state and indexing is simple (I consider the case later where the states cannot be so easily indexed, because they are not integers). The first column of the matrix contains the values of $F(x, t)$ and the second contains the values of $F(x, t + 1)$: Another way to look at it is that the second column contains the values used in the calculations and the first column contains the updated values, which are then passed into the second column once all the states have been processed (the apparent "backward" nature of the indexing is because we are going backward in time). Initially, all entries in the first column are set to zero, while in the second column rows 1 to *Xcritical* are set to zero and the remaining rows to 1, which is the terminal fitness value. Entries in this matrix are changed as the program runs.

The program iterates over time commencing with the last interval: this is accomplished using a while loop:

```
Horizon      <- 20           # Number of time steps
Time         <- Horizon      # Initialize Time
while ( Time > 1)
{
Time         <- Time - 1     # Decrement Time by 1 unit
```

Lines of coding
```
} # End of Time loop
```

At each value of Time the following steps are made:

Step 1: Call function OVER.STATES to iterate through values of state variables. The first state is *Xmin*.

Step 2: Call function OVER.PATCHES to iterate through patch types. The first patch type is patch 1.

Step 3: Call function FITNESS to calculate the fitness (= survival) in the selected patch (presently patch 1) given the selected state (presently *Xmin*). First we calculate the two new states the animal can achieve, which are labeled X.Food and X.NoFood, corresponding, respectively, to the situations in which the resource is found and that in which it is not found. As a general approach we first write down an **Outcome Chart** that details the various outcomes ("−" indicates that this condition is not applicable):

Food found	x > *Xcritical*	Survives	*x*
Yes	—	Yes	$\min(x - Cost + Benefit_i, Xmax)$
No	Yes	Yes	$x - Cost$
No	Yes	No	Set at *Xcritical*
No	No	-	Set at *Xcritical*

The "tricky" part now is to calculate the probability that the animal survives from this time to the end. At the start of the analysis we are at the end of the time period and hence we know that this has a probability of one, which is what the second column of F.vectors contains (except for rows below *Xmin*, which are zero since animals in these states are dead). The survival probability for an animal in state X.Food is thus equal to the probability at F.vectors[X.Food, 2], that is, the row that corresponds to state X.Food. Similarly, the survival probability for an animal in state X.NoFood is equal to the probability at F.vectors[X.No-Food, 2], that is, the row that corresponds to state X.NoFood. Both of these will initially be 1. In symbolism, survival if patch *i* is chosen is given as

$$W(x, i, t - 1) = (1 - Pmortality_i)[Pbenefit_i F(x_{Food}, t) + (1 - Pbenefit_i)F(x_{NoFood}, t)]$$

$$(6.6)$$

In R code survival is given by

```
Term1   <- Pbenefit*F.vectors[X.Food,2]          #  If food is found
Term2   <- (1-Pbenefit)*F.vectors[X.NoFood,2]    #  If food is not found
W       <- (1 - Pmortality) * (Term1 + Term2)    #  Survival in patch
```

Note that the survival is the probability of surviving this time increment multiplied by the probability of surviving from then to *T* given the optimal patch choice.

Step 4: Fitness is passed back to OVER.PATCHES where it is stored in a vector called RHS. The row number of this vector corresponds to the patch type and the value stored is the fitness (survival).

Step 5: The next patch type is selected and Steps 3 and 4 repeated.

Step 6: After the fitnesses of all patch types have been calculatedthe patch giving the highest fitness is selected. The optimal patch value is the value of i that gives the maximum value of $W(x, i, t-1)$:

$$F(x, t-1) = \max\{W(x, 1, t-1), W(x, 2, t-1), W(x, 3, t-1)\} \qquad (6.7)$$

If there were k patches then the choice would be among the k survivals. The R code is

```
# Now find optimal patch. Best row is in Best[1]
Best          <- order(RHS, na.last=TRUE, decreasing=TRUE)
Best.Patch  <- Best[1]
```

The "best" survival is stored in the cell of the first column of the appropriate row of `F.vectors`, that is `F.vectors[X,1]  <-   RHS[Best[1]]`.

Step 7: We now pass back the modified matrix `F.vectors`, the modified value of `F.vectors[X,1]`, and the best patch number, `Best.Patch`, back to OVER. STATES. This is done by concatenating `F.vectors[X,1]` and `Best.Patch` together to form a 1×2 matrix called `Temp` and then concatenating `F.vectors` and `Temp` together:

```
# Concatenate F(x,t,T) and the optimal patch number
Temp   <- c(F.vectors[X,1], Best.Patch)
# Add Temp to bottom of F.vectors and rename to Temp
Temp   <- rbind(F.vectors, Temp)
return (Temp)
```

Step 8: `Temp` is passed back to OVER.STATES (where it is also called `Temp`, but this is arbitrary), where `F.vectors` is updated and the optimal patch number and survival are stored in a two-column matrix called `Store`. Note that the updating of `F.vectors` does not affect further calls to OVER.PATCHES, because only the second column of `F.vectors` is used. The first column is being used to store the values to be used in the next iteration of `Time`.

Step 9: Another state is selected, which now would be *Xmin* + 1 and Steps 2–8 are repeated.

Step 10: After all state values have been examined `F.vectors` and `Store` are concatenated into a four-column matrix called `Temp`, the first two columns containing `F.vectors`, the third column *F(x, t)*, the survival, and the fourth column the best patch number. `Temp` is passed back to the main program.

Step 11: To store the values of *F(x, t)*, and the best patch number two matrices, named `FxtT` and `Best.patch`, respectively, were created at the start of the main program. Each matrix consists of `Horizon` number of rows (20 here) and *Xmax* columns. Thus, rows correspond to time and columns to states. The first *Xcritical* columns are redundant as they are never used. However, setting up the matrices in this manner is convenient because columns then correspond to state values. The values from OVER.STATES are passed back into a matrix called `Temp`, which is then disassembled into the components corresponding to `F.vectors` (called `TempF`), survival, and the best patch. The values in the second column of F.vectors are updated using the values in the first column of `TempF`. This updating means that in the new round the survival probability calculated in FITNESS is the survival from time t to time T (=`Horizon`) given the optimal choice of patches. The lines of coding are

```
# Extract F.vectors
TempF <- Temp[,1:2]
# Update F1
for ( J in Xmin: Xmax)   { F.vectors[J,2] <- TempF[J,1]}
# Store results
Best.Patch[Time,]                    <- Temp[,4]
FxtT[Time,]                          <- Temp[,3]
```

Step 12: Delete one unit from `Time` and repeat all previous steps. Once Time is less than one we exit the `while` loop and print out the two matrices, as shown in Table 3.1.

The complete coding in R and MATLAB is given below (note that the coding here, and throughout this chapter, is very similar and differs primarily as a consequence of syntax or the name of the built-in functions).

R CODE:

```
rm(list=ls()) # Remove all objects from memory
# Function to calculate fitness when organism is in state X
   FITNESS    <- function(X, Xcritical, Xmax, Xmin, Cost, Benefit,
Pbenefit, Pmortality, F.vectors)
   {
# State in patch if forager finds food
   X.Food     <- X - Cost + Benefit
# If X.Food greater than Xmax then X.Food must be set to Xmax
   X.Food     <- min(X.Food, Xmax)
# If X.Food less than or equal to Xcritical then set to Xcritical
   X.Food     <- max( X.Food, Xcritical)
# State in patch if forager does not find food
   X.NoFood   <- X - Cost
# If X.NoFood is less than Xcritical set X.NoFood to Xcritical
   X.NoFood   <- max(X.NoFood, Xcritical)
   Term1      <- Pbenefit*F.vectors[X.Food,2] # If food is found
   Term2      <- (1-Pbenefit)*F.vectors[X.NoFood,2] # If food is
                                                       not found
   W          <- (1-Pmortality)*(Term1+Term2) # Survival in patch
   return(W)                                  # Return Fitness
} # End of function
#.............................................................
# Function to iterate over patches
   OVER.PATCHES <- function(X, F.vectors, Xcritical,Xmax, Xmin,
Npatch, Cost, Benefit, Pbenefit, Pmortality)
```

```
   for (i in 1: Npatch)          # Cycle over patches
{
# Call Fitness function
   RHS[i] <- FITNESS(X, Xcritical, Xmax, Xmin, Cost, Benefit[i],
Pbenefit[i], Pmortality[i], F.vectors)
} # End of i loop
# Now find optimal patch Best row is in Best[1]
   Best              <- order(RHS, na.last=TRUE, decreasing=TRUE)
   F.vectors[X,1]    <- RHS[Best[1]]
   Best.Patch        <- Best[1]
# Concatenate F(x,t) and the optimal patch number
   Temp              <- c(F.vectors[X,1], Best.Patch)
# Add Temp to bottom of F.vectors and rename to Temp
   Temp              <- rbind(F.vectors, Temp)
return (Temp)
} # End of function
#................................................................
# Function to iterate over states of X
   OVER.STATES <- function(F.vectors, Xcritical, Xmax, Xmin,
Npatch, Cost, Benefit, Pbenefit, Pmortality)
{
   Store   <- matrix(0,Xmax,2) # Create matrix for output
   for ( X in Xmin : Xmax)         # Iterate over states of X
{
# For given X call Over.Patches to determine F(x,t) and best patch
   Temp     <- OVER.PATCHES(X, F.vectors, Xcritical, Xmax, Xmin,
Npatch, Cost, Benefit, Pbenefit, Pmortality)
# Extract components. Last row is F(x,t) and best patch
   n            <- nrow(Temp)-1
   F.vectors <- Temp[1:n,]
   Store[X,]  <- Temp[n+1,]                # Save F(x,t) and best patch
} # End of X loop
# Add Store values to end of F.vectors for pass back to main program
   Temp         <- cbind(F.vectors, Store) # Combined by columns
   return(Temp)                            # Return F.vectors and Store
} # End of function
#................................................................
# MAIN PROGRAM
# Initialize parameters
   Xmax         <- 10                # Maximum value of X
   Xcritical    <- 3                 # Value of X at which death occurs
   Xmin         <- Xcritical+1       # Smallest value of X allowed
   Cost         <- 1                 # Cost per period
   Pmortality  <- c(0, 0.004, 0.02) # Probability of mortality
   Pbenefit     <- c(1, 0.4, 0.6)    # Probability of finding food
{
   RHS <- matrix(0,Npatch,1)   # Pre-allocate Right Hand Side of equn
```

```
  Benefit        <- c(0, 3, 5)         # Benefit if food is discovered
  Npatch         <- 3                  # Number of patches
  Horizon        <- 20                 # Number of time steps
# Set up matrix for fitnesses
# Column 1 is F(x, t). Column 2 is F(x,t+1)
  F.vectors <- matrix(0, Xmax,2)       # Set all values to zero
  F.vectors[Xmin:Xmax,2] <- 1          # Set values > Xmin equal 1
# Create matrices for output
  FxtT           <- matrix(0,Horizon,Xmax)   # F(x,t)
  Best.Patch     <- matrix(0,Horizon,Xmax)   # Best patch number
# Start iterations
  Time           <- Horizon            # Initialize Time
  while ( Time   > 1)
{
  Time           <- Time -1            # Decrement Time by 1 unit
# Call OVER.STATES to get best values for this time step
  Temp           <- OVER.STATES(F.vectors, Xcritical, Xmax, Xmin,
Npatch, Cost, Benefit, Pbenefit, Pmortality)
# Extract F.vectors
  TempF          <- Temp[,1:2]
# Update F1
  for ( J in Xmin: Xmax) { F.vectors[J,2] <- TempF[J,1] }
# Store results
  Best.Patch[Time,] <- Temp[,4]
  FxtT[Time,]       <- Temp[,3]
}   # End of Time loop
# Output information. For display add states (=wts) to last row of
matrices
  X                        <- seq(from=1, to=Xmax)
  Best.Patch[Horizon,] <- X
  FxtT[Horizon,]       <- X
  Best.Patch[,Xmin:Xmax]      # Print Decision matrix
  signif(FxtT[,Xmin:Xmax],3)  # Print Fxt of Decision matrix: 3
                                sig places
```

OUTPUT:
See Table 6.1.

MATLAB CODE: See Section 6.9.1.

6.1.5 Using the decision matrix: individual prediction

From Table 6.1 it can be seen that an animal that starts in a low state is forced to take risks, whereas an animal that starts in a high state plays it safe. This behavior is intuitively obvious but it is not obvious what parameter values will induce the different behaviors: the decision matrix makes this clear. Most importantly, dynamic programming can show what behaviors will never be favored given a set of parameter values and also the pattern of changes. The pattern of changes in the present example is, as noted, intuitively obvious but, as further examples will show, this is not always the case.

Having created the decision matrix we would now want to explore the actual sequence of behaviors. To do this we run the model forward, as shown by the coding given below. There are two instances in which a probability has to be evaluated: Pmortality and Pbenefit. In each case, a random number between 0 and 1 is generated: If the value of this number is less than the value of the parameter, then the action specified by the parameter is taken. For example, suppose Pmortality = 0.02 and the random number generated equals 0.01: in this case the animal dies. Now suppose the random number generated equals 0.4: in this case the animal survives.

R CODE:

The coding assumes that the decision matrix has been generated. It is only necessary to generate the matrix once by running the previous program. Provided the command to clear the workspace is not issued the matrix will remain in memory and the following program or variations can be run successively:

```
# Initialize parameters
  set.seed(10)                        # Set random number seed
  Xmax          <- 10                 # Maximum value of X
  Xcritical     <- 3                  # Value of X at which death occurs
  Xmin          <- Xcritical+1        # Smallest value of X allowed
  Cost          <- 1                  # Cost per period
  Pmortality <- c(0, 0.004, 0.02)     # Probability of mortality
  Pbenefit      <- c(1, 0.4, 0.6)     # Probability of finding food
  Benefit       <- c(0, 3, 5)         # Benefit if food is discovered
  Npatch        <- 3                  # Number of patches
  Horizon       <- 15                 # Number of time steps
  Output        <- matrix(0,Horizon,10)   # Matrix to hold output
  Time          <- seq(1, Horizon)    # Values for x axis in plot
  par(mfrow=c(5,2))                   # Divide graph page into 5x2 panels
  for (Replicate in 1: 10)            # Iterate over 10 replicates
{
  X             <- 4                  # Animal starts in state 4
  for (i in 1:Horizon)               # Iterate over time
{
  if(X > Xcritical)                   # Check that animal still alive
{
  Patch <- Best.Patch[i,X]            # Select patch
# Check if animal survives predation
# Generate random number
```

```
   if(runif(1) < Pmortality[Patch]) print("Dead from predator")
# Now find new weight
# Set multiplier to zero, which corresponds to no food found
   Index <- 0
   if (runif(1) < Pbenefit[Patch]) Index <- 1 # food is discovered
   X <- X - Cost + Benefit[Patch]*Index
# If X greater than Xmax then X must be set to Xmax
   X <- min(X, Xmax)
# If X less than X then animal dies
   if ( X< Xmin) print ("Dead from starvation")
   Output[i,Replicate] <- Patch # Store data
} # End of if (X > Xcritical)
} # End of time loop
   plot(Time, Output[,Replicate], type='l', ylab='Patch selected')
} # End of replicate loop
```

OUTPUT: (Figure 6.1)

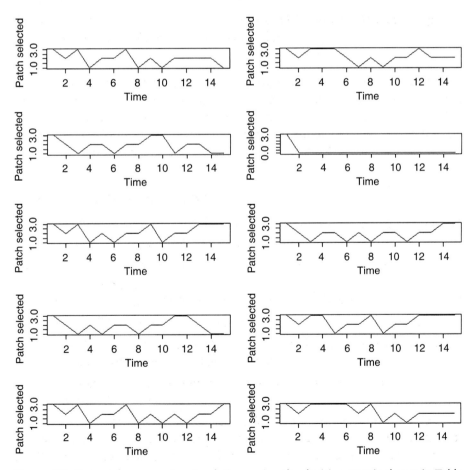

Figure 6.1 Output from running simulations using the decision matrix shown in Table 6.1, with a starting initial state of $X = 4$.

In one case the animal died from starvation by the second time unit, but in all other cases the animal survived the full period. There is considerable movement between patch types, which could not be predicted without the dynamic program solution.

MATLAB CODE: See Section 6.9.2.

6.1.6   Using the decision matrix: expected state

The traces shown in Figure 6.1 might indicate the outcome of an experiment in which one is individual is followed 10 times or 10 individuals are followed once. To ascertain the distribution of states we could run this program many times using different starting inputs. However, we can more readily compute the expected distribution of states using the following approach: We begin by asking "Given that an animal is in state z at $t - 1$, what is the probability that following the optimal behavior it moves into state x at time t?" Mangel and Clark (1988) refer to this as the **transition density** and using their mathematical symbolism it is written as $w(x, t|z)$. Next we can calculate the probability that the animal will be in state x at time t, $P(x, t)$, by summing over all z values weighted by their representation in the initial population (i.e., time $t - 1$): in the notation of Mangel and Clark

$$P(x, t) = \sum_z w(x, t|z)P(z, t - 1) \tag{6.8}$$

If there is only a single animal or all animals commence in the same state, say z^*, then $P(z, t - 1) = P(z^*, t - 1) = 1$.

To calculate the transition density matrix we proceed as follows: Using the decision matrix we select x given z: for each transition, provided z is greater than $Xcritical$, there are four possible outcomes, with the subscript i designating the best choice from the decision matrix (Table 6.2). To calculate the transition density matrix we begin with an $N \times N$ matrix, where N is the number of possible states (in this case N would be $Xmax - Xcritical + 1$), filled with zeros. If an animal does not survive, then its state is set at $Xcritical$ and the probability inserted in this cell. Next we iterate across all possible values of z (i.e., $Xmin \le z \le Xmax$) and for

Table 6.2 Transition densities for the simple foraging model

Food found	x >Xcritical	Survives	x	$w(x,t|z)$
Yes	—	Yes	min(z − Cost + Benefit$_i$, Xmax)	$(1 - Pmortality_i)Pbenefit_i$
No	Yes	Yes	z − Cost	$(1 - Pmortality_i)(1 - Pbenefit_i)$
No	Yes	No	Set at Xcritical	$Pmortality_i$
No	No	—	Set at Xcritical	$Pmortality_i + (1 - Pmortality_i)(1 - Pbenefit_i)$

Note: The source of mortality may be anything other than being less than Xcritical.

each value of z we calculate $w(x, t|z)$ using the rules given in Table 6.2. Note that we enter the decision matrix at the appropriate time, because the transition density function is a function of the current state.

R CODE:

Because *Xcritical* is close to zero it is convenient to make the transition density matrix here go from zero to *Xmax*, thus making each row and column correspond to the value of *x*, as in the decision matrix. In the program below the rows correspond to *z* and the columns to *x*. Because we want to use the decision matrix, the workspace is not cleared. The decision matrix program is first run and then the following:

```
# Set initial parameter values
  Xmax          <- 10                  # Maximum value of state
  Xcritical     <- 3                   # Critical value of state
  Xmin          <- Xcritical+1         # Lowest value of state
  Cost          <- 1                   # Metabolic cost
  Time          <- 2                   # Current state to be considered
  Npatch        <- 3                   # Npatch is number of patches
  Pmortality    <- c(0, 0.004, 0.02)   # Probability of mortality Beta
  Pbenefit      <- c(1, 0.4, 0.6)      # Probability of finding food
                                         Lambda
  Benefit       <- c(0, 3, 5)          # Benefit if food is discovered Y
# Set transition density matrix to zero
  Trans.density <- matrix(0, Xmax, Xmax)
# Step 1 Cycle over all values of z from Xmin to Xmax
  for ( z in Xmin : Xmax) # Iterate over states
{
# Select the best patch from the Decision matrix at row Time
  K <- Best.Patch[Time,z] # Decision matrix is called Best.Patch
# Calculate w(x,t|z)
# Found food and survives predator
  x <- min(z - Cost + Benefit[K], Xmax)
# Assign probability
  Trans.density[z,x]<- (1-Pmortality[K])*Pbenefit[K]
# Food not found
  x <- z - Cost
# State exceeds the critical value
  if(x > Xcritical)
{
# Animal survives
  Trans.density[z,x]<- (1-Pmortality[K])*(1-Pbenefit[K])
# Animal does not survive
  Trans.density[z,Xcritical]<- Pmortality[K]
} # end of if statement
# State is less than critical
```

```
    else{          # Note that in R the { immediately follows else
Trans.density[z,Xcritical]<- Pmortality[K]+(1-Pmortality[K])*
(1-Pbenefit[K])
} # End of else statement
} # end of z loop
  Trans.density # Write out matrix
```

OUTPUT: (Table 6.3)

Table 6.3 Transition density matrix for foraging model at time t = 2

Values of z	[,1]	[,2]	[,3]	[,4]	[,5]	[,6]	[,7]	[,8]	[,9]	[,10]
					Values of x					
[1,]	0	0	0	0	0	0	0	0	0	0
[2,]	0	0	0	0	0	0	0	0	0	0
[3,]	0	0	0	0	0	0	0	0	0	0
[4,]	0	0	0.412	0	0	0	0	0.588	0	0
[5,]	0	0	0.02	0.392	0	0	0	0	0.588	0
[6,]	0	0	0.02	0	0.392	0	0	0	0	0.588
[7,]	0	0	0.02	0	0	0.392	0	0	0	0.588
[8,]	0	0	0.004	0	0	0	0.5976	0	0	0.3984
[9,]	0	0	0.004	0	0	0	0	0.5976	0	0.3984
[10,]	0	0	0	0	0	0	0	0	0	0

Note: Each cell gives the probability, given that an animal is in state z at time t −1, that by following the optimal behavior it moves into state x at time t. Output from R program is slightly modified for display purposes.

For this particular example the transition density matrix remains the same for all times less than 13. Consider an animal (or population) commencing in state 4: it will move to state 8 with a probability of 0.588 (or 58.8% of the population will be in state 8), while there is a 0.412 probability that the animal will die (arbitrarily set into state 3, Xcritical, which ensures no further progress). For an animal commencing in state 5 there is 0.02 probability of dieing, a 0.392 probability of passing into state 4, and a 0.588 probability of passing into state 9 (Table 6.3).

MATLAB CODE: See Section 6.9.3.

6.1.7   Using the decision and transition density matrices to get expected choices

The forgoing analyses determine the expected state an animal (or population) will be in after some time steps. Of particular interest is the distribution of choices, as this is what an experimenter will likely measure. To illustrate how these values are calculated let us assume that at time $t = 2$ our population is distributed among the states, from $x = 4$ to $x = 9$ as follows: 0.1, 0.1, 0.2, 0.3, 0.2, and 0.1, respectively.

Calculations are shown in Table 6.4. The optimal patch choice ("Best Patch" in Table 6.4) for each state is obtained from the decision matrix (Table 6.1) and the transition probabilities ($P(x, t)$ in Table 6.4) are obtained from the transition density matrix (Table 6.3). In the present example two patches are expected to be chosen, patches 2 and 3. Assuming that animals that die are not counted (if they are counted then column $x = 3$ is included in subsequent calculations) the predicted proportions are calculated by summing across rows from $x = 4$ to $x = 10$, multiplying each cell by $P(z, t - 1)$ as shown in the penultimate column of Table 6.4, and then correcting for the loss of animals by dividing by the sum of this column, as shown in the last column of Table 6.4. Finally, the proportion in each patch is calculated by summing the probabilities for the individual patches. Thus, in the present example 68.4% of animals are expected to be found in patch 3 and 31.6% in patch 2.

6.1.8   Adjusting state values to correspond to index values

In the example considered the state values corresponded to the index values, namely the positions in the relevant matrices (thus $Xcritical = 3$ is both the critical value and the cell index). This will generally not be the case and we have to transform between state and index values. An example is shown in Table 6.5: the lowest state (0.1–0.3 with midpoint 0.2) is assumed to be the "dead" state, that is, $Xcritical$. The lowest state we assign to the first index (1) and then increment in unit steps, the index value is then determined from

$$Index = 1 + \frac{x - Xcritical}{Xinc} \tag{6.9}$$

where $Xinc$ is the increment (0.2 in Table 6.5). Conversion from the index value to state X is obviously

$$x = (Index - 1) * Xinc + Xcritical \tag{6.10}$$

Examples of the use of these transformations are given in Scenarios 3–5.

6.1.9   Linear interpolation to adjust for non-integer state variables

Dynamic programming works with discrete values but state variables may change by amounts not equal to the assigned interval as described in the previous section. For example, suppose the increments are 1 and states $x = 5$ and $x = 6$ correspond to index values 6 and 7 (because the first cell is reserved for $Xcritical$) but for some value of x with index value I the new state variable is 5.36, meaning that the fitness lies between $F(6, t)$ and $F(7, t)$. To estimate $F(x, t)$ we can use linear interpolation (Figure 6.2; Mangel, personal communication). To derive the formula we translate the origin of the x-axis to x_I and the y-axis to $F(x_I, t)$ giving the slope of the linear interpolation to be (Figure 6.2)

$$F(x_{I+1}, t) - F(x_I, t) \tag{6.11}$$

Table 6.4 Calculating the expected distribution of patch choice for the foraging model at time $t = 2$

| State, z | Proportion, $P(z, t-1)$ | Best Patch | Probability of $x = P(x, t)$ | | | | | | | | Predicted proportion[a] |
			3	4	5	6	7	8	9	10	$\sum_{x=4}^{10} P(x, t)P(z, t-1)$	
4	0.1	3	0.412	0	0	0	0	0.588	0	0	0.059	0.062
5	0.1	3	0.020	0.392	0	0	0	0	0.588	0	0.098	0.104
6	0.2	3	0.020	0	0.392	0	0	0	0	0.588	0.196	0.207
7	0.3	3	0.020	0	0	0.392	0	0	0	0.588	0.294	0.311
8	0.2	2	0.004	0	0	0	0.5976	0	0	0.3984	0.199	0.211
9	0.1	2	0.004	0	0	0	0	0.5976	0	0.3984	0.100	0.105
											0.946	1.000

Note: The column $x = 3$ is ignored because animals in this category do not survive.

[a]Predicted proportion = value in preceding cell divided by the sum of the preceding column (0.946), that is, $0.07 = 0.059/0.946$.
The predicted proportion in patch 3 is $0.062 + 0.104 + 0.207 + 0.311 = 0.684$.
The predicted proportion in patch 2 is $0.211 + 0.105 = 0.316$.

Table 6.5 Example of a non-integer state distribution and its conversion to an integer index

State interval	Midpoint = State	Index	Converting state to index
0.1–0.3	0.2	1	1+(0.2−0.2)/0.2=1
0.3–0.5	0.4	2	1+(0.4−0.2)/0.2=2
0.5–0.7	0.6	3	1+(0.6−0.2)/0.2=3
0.7–0.9	0.8	4	1+(0.8−0.2)/0.2=4
0.9–1.1	1.0	5	1+(1.0−0.2)/0.2=5

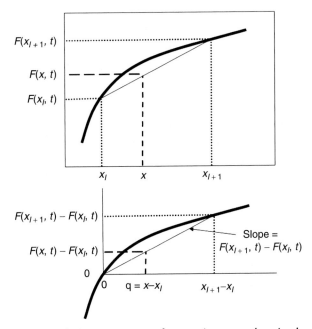

Figure 6.2 Linear interpolation to account for non-integer values in the state variable. The value of $F(x, t, T)$ is approximated by a straight line drawn through the two enclosing integer values of the state variable.

where I is the lower integer value and x_I is the values of x for index value I. The new value of x is $x - x_I = q$. The value of $F(x, t)$ with respect to the new origin is simply

$$[F(x_{I+1}, t) - F(x_I, t)]q \tag{6.12}$$

And to translate back to the original scale we add $F(x_I, t)$ to give

$$F(x, t) \approx [F(x_{I+1}, t) - F(x_I, t)]q + F(x_I, t) = qF(x_{I+1}, t) + (1 - q)F(x_I, t) \tag{6.13}$$

Examples of this are given in Scenarios 3 and 5. The above formula is problematic when $x_I = Xmax$, because in this case x_{I+1} is greater than $Xmax$ and will cause a "subscript too large" error, even though q_x is zero, and hence this term does not contribute. To resolve this, insert a test such as $x_{I+1} = \min(x_{I+1}, Xmax)$.

The interpolation formula can be extended to two state variables, x and y:

$$F(x_I, y_J, t) \approx q_x q_y F(x_{I+1}, y_{J+1}, t) + q_x(1 - q_y)F(x_{I+1}, y_J, t) +$$
$$(1 - q_x)q_y F(x_I, y_{J+1}, t) + (1 - q_x)(1 - q_y)F(x_I, y_J, t)$$

(6.14)

where $q_x = x - x_I$ and $q_y = y - y_I$.

We now consider five scenarios showing how the basic patch-foraging model can be modified to fit a range of biological situations.

6.2 Summary of scenarios

Scenario 1: In this scenario the fitness measure is changed from survival to the accumulated value of some state variable, such as energy store, at the end of the time period.

Scenario 2: The basic scenario considered in Chapter 1 is based on foraging among patches. In the second scenario I show how "patches" can be considered simply as "options" and hence how the basic scenario can be readily expanded.

Scenario 3: In the previous scenarios there were unique choices at each step, the state variable could be directly related to its position in the relevant vector and took integer values. In this scenario the problem of equivalent choices is considered and the concepts of indexing and interpolation are illustrated.

Scenario 4: The state variable in all the above scenarios increased over time (e.g., accumulation of resources). In many cases fitness may be equated to the number of eggs laid over the time period, in which case the state variable decreases over time. This circumstance is illustrated using host choice in parasitoid wasps.

Scenario 5: This scenario considers the problem of solving for two state variables, in this case egg size and number.

6.3 Scenario 1: A different terminal fitness

In the patch-foraging model examined above it was assumed that fitness was equal to survival at the terminal period. In many cases fitness will depend not simply upon survival but also upon the accumulation of resources, which might be used to survive the following period or invested in offspring.

6.3.1 General assumptions

Assumptions 1–5 are the same as previously given.
6. Fitness is a function of the state variable at the end of some time interval (e.g., in a small terrestrial vertebrate this may be the summer period, the end of the season being the time at which hibernation is entered, or it could be the reproductive episode).

6.3.2 Mathematical assumptions

Assumptions 1–5 are the same as previously given.
6. Fitness is equal to the expected value of the state variable at time T.

6.3.3 Outcome chart and expected lifetime fitness function

This is exactly the same as previously given.

6.3.4 Calculating the decision matrix

At time T we assume that the animal is alive and hence its fitness according to assumption 6 above is equal to the value of the state variable. Thus the only change we have to make to the coding in R is to adjust the terminal fitness function from

```
F.vectors[Xmin:Xmax,2] <- 1
```

to

```
F.vectors[Xmin:Xmax,2] <- seq(from=Xmin, to=Xmax)
```

or in MATLAB

```
F_vectors[Xmin:Xmax,2] = 1
```

to

```
F_vectors[Xmin:Xmax,2] = Xmin:Xmax
```

that is, the terminal fitness is now equal to the state variable, X. This principle is quite general and enables the previous coding to be used for any number of terminal fitness definitions. The effect of changing the fitness definition in this instance is to change the decisions for animals late in the season and already of high value (Table 6.6).

6.4 Scenario 2: To forage or not to forage when patches become options

This example illustrates how the basic patch-foraging model can be modified to fit a scenario in which "patches" are equated to options. The scenario is based on Kokko (2007), who presents MATLAB coding to analyze the model: For the interested reader I suggest comparing the two approaches, simply to see how the same result can be obtained by visually very different coding. The general scenario is that of a bird that must gather resources during a given period, say a winter day, to survive the following period, say the winter night.

6.4.1 General assumptions

1. During the day the bird can decide to forage or remain sedentary during any given period.

2. A non-foraging bird risks losing condition.

Table 6.6 Decision matrices for foraging model with different fitness criteria (survival vs. expected state value, the fitness criteria considered in Scenario 1)

Time	State (Shown along bottom row)						
	[,1]	[,2]	[,3]	[,4]	[,5]	[,6]	[,7]
[1,]	3	3	3	3	2	2	1
[2,]	3	3	3	3	2	2	1
[3,]	3	3	3	3	2	2	1
[4,]	3	3	3	3	2	2	1
[5,]	3	3	3	3	2	2	1
[6,]	3	3	3	3	2	2	1
[7,]	3	3	3	3	2	2	1
[8,]	3	3	3	3	2	2	1
[9,]	3	3	3	3	2	2	1
[10,]	3	3	3	3	2	2	1
[11,]	3	3	3	3	2	2	1
[12,]	3	3	3	3	2	2	1
[13,]	3	3	3	3	2	2	2
[14,]	3	3	3	3	2	2	1
[15,]	3	3	3	3	2	1,2	1
[16,]	3	3	3	3	1,2	1,2	1,2
[17,]	3	3	3	1,3	1,2	1,2	1,2
[18,]	3	3	1,3	1,3	1,3	1,3	1,2
[19,]	3	1,3	1,3	1,3	1,3	1,3	1,3
[20,]	**4**	**5**	**6**	**7**	**8**	**9**	**10**

Note: Where decisions differ, the second fitness criterion is given second.

3. A foraging bird faces a predation risk that is a function of its condition, well-fed birds being more susceptible.

4. Fitness is a function of condition at the end of the period (day).

6.4.2 Mathematical assumptions

1. The condition of a bird ranges in unit increments from 1 to 7.

2. A bird in condition 1 is dead.

3. A non-foraging bird losing one unit of condition with some fixed probability, *Ploss*.

4. A foraging bird gains one unit of condition with some fixed probability, *Pgain*.

5. A foraging bird suffers a mortality probability from predators at a rate that is a linear function of condition:

$$Pmortality = a + bx \tag{6.15}$$

where mortality at $X = 2$ is 0 and *Pmax* at $x = Xmax$, the constants a and b being determined accordingly.

6. A non-foraging bird is not susceptible to predators.

7. Fitness is the expected state value (i.e., condition) at the end of the day.

6.4.3 Outcome chart and expected lifetime fitness function

Although, at first glance, this model may not appear to resemble the patch-foraging model it is actually mathematically equivalent. First, we note that a "patch" in this scenario is simply the decision to "not forage" (patch 1) or to "forage" (patch 2). Second, the benefits in the previous foraging model are represented here by the loss or gain condition. Thus we can write the model using the same outline as in the patch-foraging model.

Patch type	Benefit	Pbenefit	Pmortality	Cost
1 = "Not forage"	−1	Ploss	0	Not applicable
2 = "Forage"	1	Pgain	a + bx	Not applicable

The outcome chart can thus be written as ("—" indicates that this condition is not applicable).

Forage	x >Xcritical	Survives	x
Yes	—	Yes	$\min(x + Benefit_i, Xmax)$
Yes	—	No	Set at Xcritical
No	Yes	—	$x + Benefit_i$
No	No	—	Set at Xcritical

The expected lifetime fitness function is the same as the patch-foraging model minus the *Cost* component.

6.4.4 Calculating the decision matrix

The changes to the program are shown in **bold** font. The most significant change is the addition of the state-dependent mortality function. To code this function we construct a matrix of two rows and *Xmax* columns. Row 1 contains the probability of being depredated if not foraging, which is zero for all values of x, coded by

$$\textbf{Pnoforage <- rep(0,Xmax)}$$

Row 2 contains the probability of being depredated if foraging. It is zero in column 1, because that corresponds to dead animals. According to assumption 5 it is zero in column 2, the minimum condition, and *Pmax* in column 7. To construct this function we make use of the seq function:

```
    Pforage <- c(0,seq(from=Pmin, to=Pmax, length=Xmax-1))
```

We then bind the two vectors together to form the predation matrix:

```
        Pmortality <- rbind(Pnoforage,Pforage)
```

The probability of mortality is then passed to the fitness function as **Pmortality [i,X]**.

Other changes consist of ignoring the parameter Cost (we could have deleted it from the program but as it is not used there is no harm in leaving it in the program) and resetting the initial values. Here we set *Ploss* = 0.4 and *Pgain* = 0.8 using the vector **Pbenefit**:

```
  Pbenefit    <- c(0.4,0.8)        # Probability of "Benefit"
  Benefit     <- c(-1,1)           # "Benefit"
```

Finally, as in Scenario 1, we set the terminal fitness to be equal to the expected state value:

```
       F.vectors[Xmin:Xmax,2] <- seq(from = Xmin, to = Xmax)
```

The program is thus

R CODE:

```
rm(list=ls()) # Remove all objects from memory
# Function to calculate fitness when organism is in state X
  FITNESS <- function(X, Xcritical, Xmax, Xmin, Cost, Benefit,
  Pbenefit, Pmortality, F.vectors)
{
# Benefit gained
# State in patch if "Benefit" gained. Note that "Benefit" can be -1
  X.Food       <- X + Benefit # Note that Cost is omitted
# If X.Food greater than Xmax then X.Food must be set to Xmax
  X.Food       <- min(X.Food, Xmax)
# If X.Food less than or equal to Xcritical then set to Xcritical
  X.Food       <- max(X.Food, Xcritical)
# State in patch if forager does not gain "Benefit"
  X.NoFood     <- X           # Note that Cost is omitted
# If X.NoFood is less than Xcritical set X.NoFood to Xcritical
  X.NoFood   <- max(X.NoFood, Xcritical)
# Now gather terms together
  Term1 <- Pbenefit*F.vectors[X.Food,2]      # If benefit gained
  Term2 <- (1-Pbenefit)*F.vectors[X.NoFood,2] # If no benefit
                                                     gained
  W       <- (1 - Pmortality)*(Term1 + Term2)    # Fitness in patch
  return(W)                                       # Return Fitness
} # End of function
#................................................................
# Function to iterate over patches
OVER.PATCHES <- function(X, F.vectors, Xcritical,Xmax, Xmin,
Npatch, Cost, Benefit, Pbenefit, Pmortality)
```

```
{
  RHS <- matrix(0,Npatch,1) # Set matrix for Right Hand Side of equn
  for (i in 1: Npatch)       # Cycle over patches
{
# Call Fitness function. Note that mortality a function of patch and X
RHS[i]   <-   FITNESS(X, Xcritical, Xmax, Xmin, Cost, Benefit[i],
Pbenefit[i], Pmortality[i,X], F.vectors)
} # End of i loop
# Now find optimal patch Best row is in Best[1]
  Best             <- order(RHS, na.last=TRUE, decreasing=TRUE)
  F.vectors[X,1]   <- RHS[Best[1]]
  Best.Patch       <- Best[1]
# Concatenate F(x,t,T) and the optimal patch number
  Temp             <- c(F.vectors[X,1], Best.Patch)
# Add Temp to bottom of F.vectors and rename to Temp
  Temp             <- rbind(F.vectors, Temp)
  return (Temp)
} # End of function
#.............................................................
# Function to iterate over states of X
OVER.STATES <- function(F.vectors, Xcritical, Xmax, Xmin, Npatch,
Cost, Benefit, Pbenefit, Pmortality)
{
```

These lines are the same as in the patch-foraging model:

```
} # End of function
#.............................................................
# MAIN PROGRAM
# Initialize parameters
  Xmax        <- 7            # Maximum value of X
  Xcritical   <-1             # Value of X at which death occurs
  Xmin        <- Xcritical+1  # Smallest value of X allowed
  Cost        <- 0.0          # Dummy not required but kept
# Probability of mortality if foraging
  Pmin        <- 0
  Pmax        <- 0.01
# Create mortality function. Make Pmin at state 2
# Probability of mortality if not foraging
  Pnoforage   <- rep(0,Xmax)
# Foraging mortality
  Pforage     <- c(0,seq(from=Pmin, to=Pmax, length=Xmax-1))
  Pmortality  <- rbind(Pnoforage,Pforage) # Mortality function
# Probability of foraging
  Pbenefit    <- c(0.4,0.8)    # Probability of "Benefit"
  Benefit     <- c(-1,1)       # "Benefit"
  Npatch      <- 2       # Number of patches = resting or foraging
```

```
Horizon        <- 6                 # Number of time steps
# Set up matrix for fitnesses
# Column 1 is F(x,t+1). Column 2 is F(x,t)
  F.vectors <- matrix(0, Xmax,2)
  F.vectors[Xmin:Xmax,2] <- seq(from=Xmin, to=Xmax) # Final wts
# Create matrices for output
  FxtT           <- matrix(0,Horizon,Xmax)  # F(x,t,T)
  Best.Patch     <- matrix(0,Horizon,Xmax)  # Best patch number
# Start iterations
  Time           <- Horizon              # Initialize Time
  while ( Time > 1)
{
  Time       <- Time -1         # Decrement Time by 1 unit
# Call OVER.STATES to get best values for this time step
  Temp       <- OVER.STATES(F.vectors, Xcritical, Xmax, Xmin,
Npatch, Cost, Benefit, Pbenefit, Pmortality)
# Extract F.vectors
TempF <- Temp[,1:2]
# Update F1
  for    ( J in Xmin: Xmax)         { F.vectors[J,2] <- TempF[J,1] }
# Store results
Best.Patch[Time,]    <- Temp[,4]
FxtT[Time,]          <- Temp[,3]
} # End of Time loop
# Output information. For display add wts to last row of matrices
X                     <- seq(from=1, to=Xmax)
  Best.Patch[Horizon,] <- X
  FxtT[Horizon,]       <- X
  Best.Patch[,Xmin:Xmax]     # Print Decision matrix
  signif(FxtT[,Xmin:Xmax],3) # Print Fxt of Decision matrix: 3 sig
                             places
```

OUTPUT:

Table 6.7 Decision matrix for the daily foraging model (Scenario 3)

Time	State (Shown along bottom row)					
	[,1]	[,2]	[,3]	[,4]	[,5]	[,6]
[1,]	2	2	2	2	1	1
[2,]	2	2	2	2	2	1
[3,]	2	2	2	2	2	1
[4,]	2	2	2	2	2	2
[5,]	2	2	2	2	2	2
[6,]	2	3	4	5	6	7

Note: Decision "1" means do not forage, whereas decision "2" means forage.

The decision matrix is shown in Table 6.7. Birds beginning in states 2–5 forage throughout the day but birds in state 6 do not forage in the first period and birds in state 7 do not forage for the first three periods.

MATLAB CODE: See Section 6.9.4.

6.5   Scenario 3: Testing for equivalent choices, indexing, and interpolation

Thus far we have assumed that among the choices at each time step that there will be one that is superior to all others. However, it is possible that two or more choices may be equivalent in which case the programmer must decide if there is a method to resolve the tie or if indeed the choice is simply made by "tossing a coin." The present scenario is taken from chapter 3 of Mangel and Clark (1988). The object of the analysis is to determine the circumstances in which it would profit animals to hunt in packs rather than singly. The specific case studied by Mangel and Clark was that of lions hunting Thomson's gazelle or zebra. Parameters used here are for Thomson's gazelle. The scenario can be placed within the framework of the patch-foraging model by noting that patches can be equated with pack (= pride in lions) size (i.e., a group of size 2 is a "patch" of value 2). In addition to the question of equivalence of choices, this scenario introduces two other new components: the transformation between index value and state variable value; the use of interpolation to estimate fitness when the index value of the state variable is not an integer.

6.5.1   General assumptions

1. The animal can hunt singly or in packs, changing pack size at each time increment.
2. Each animal has a daily food requirement.
3. An animal whose gut contents fall below a critical value dies.
4. Food within the pack is shared equally.
5. Capture probability increases with the size of the pack (possibly to a limit).
6. Fitness is a function of the probability of surviving some specified time interval.

6.5.2   Mathematical assumptions

1. Pack (patch) size varies from 1 to N.
2. Each prey animal is of a fixed size, Y.
3. The daily food requirement per individual is the same, irrespective of pack size.
4. The probability of making a kill, p_i, is a function of pack size, i.

5. Up to three kills can be made per day: designate the number of kills as k, where $k = 0$, 1, 2, and 3.

6. The probability of each kill is independent and hence the number of kills per day is a binomial variable:

$$P\left(Z = \frac{kY}{i}\right) = Pkill_{i,k} = \binom{3}{k} p_i^k (1 - p_i)^{3-k} \tag{6.16}$$

where Z is the amount per individual per day.

7. An animal whose gut contents fall to or below $Xcritical$ (i.e., $x \leq Xcritical$) is dead.

8. Gut capacity has a maximum value of $Xmax$.

9. Fitness is the survival probability to the end of some specified time interval, T.

6.5.3 Outcome chart and expected lifetime fitness function

To equate this scenario with the patch-foraging model, we note that pack size is equivalent to patch identity and thus for each pack size, i, and kill number, k:

Kill made	$x > Xcritical$	Survives	X
Yes	—	Yes	min($x - Cost + Benefit_{i,k}$, $Xmax$)
No	Yes	Yes	$x - Cost$
No	Yes	No	Set at $Xcritical$
No	No	—	Set at $Xcritical$

Benefit is a function of pack size and number of kills. We require two matrices, one for the benefits and one for the probability, in which the rows correspond to pack size and the columns to kills. For simplicity, we shall set pack size from 1 to 4. The probabilities of a kill in relation to these pack sizes are 0.15, 0.31, 0.33, and 0.33, respectively. Prey size is set at 11.25 kg.

R CODE:

```
rm(list=ls())              # Remove all objects from memory
Benefit   <- matrix(0,4,4)  # Rows = pack size, Columns = number
                              of kills+1
Pbenefit  <- matrix(0,4,4)  # Rows = pack size, Columns = number
                              of kills+1
Pi        <- c(0.15, 0.31, 0.33, 0.33) # Probability of single
                                         kill for pack size
Y         <- 11.25          # Size of single prey
k         <- c(0,1,2,3)     # Number of kills
for ( PackSize in 1:4)      # Iterate over pack sizes
{
# Calculate binomial probabilities using function dbinom
  Pbenefit[PackSize,]    <- dbinom(x=k, size=3, prob=Pi[Pack-
Size])
```

```
# Calculate benefits
  Benefit[PackSize, 2:4]   <- k[2:4]*Y/PackSize
}
  Benefit          # Print out Benefit matrix
  Pbenefit         # Print out Probability matrix
```

OUTPUT: (Table 6.8)

Table 6.8 Matrices showing benefits and probability of benefits as a function of pack size

Pack Size	Number of kills + 1				Probablity			
	[,1]	[,2]	[,3]	[,4]	[,1]	[,2]	[,3]	[,4]
[1,]	0.00	11.25	22.5	33.75	0.6141	0.3251	0.0574	0.0034
[2,]	0.00	5.625	11.25	16.875	0.3285	0.4428	0.1989	0.0298
[3,]	0.00	3.75	7.5	11.25	0.3008	0.4444	0.2189	0.0359
[4,]	0.00	2.8125	5.625	8.4375	0.3008	0.4444	0.2189	0.0359

Note: R output is slightly modified for clarity.

The MATLAB coding is given in the coding for the entire program (see section 6.9.5).

The value of *Xcritical* is assumed to be zero, that is, animals with no gut contents have starved to death. This presents a minor difficulty in coding as now the index value does not correspond to the state value. In this case, given that *Xmax* = 30, we could simply raise *Xcritical* to 1. However, to illustrate the general approach we shall here retain *Xcritical* = 0 and use the method of index adjustment previously given. The parameter Xmin is replaced by Xinc, which is used to translate from *x* to the index value. Note that the maximum value of the index, Max.Index, is passed to function OVER.STATES.

A second complication is that changes in *x* do not follow unit steps: I shall follow the suggestion of Mangel and Clark (1988) and use linear interpolation as discussed above and graphically illustrated in Figure 6.2. The coding for this is given in the function FITNESS. The parameter Pmortality has been deleted as it is not used.

Survival (= fitness) for each pack size is given by

$$W(x, i, t - 1) = \sum_{k=0}^{3} Pbenefit_{i,k} F(x, t) \tag{6.17}$$

and the optimal pack size is that pack size which maximizes survival, the fitness being

$$F(x, t - 1) = \max\{W(x, 0, t), W(x, 1, t), \dots, W(x, 4, t)\} \tag{6.18}$$

The final complication is that there may be several pack sizes that give the same fitness. I shall not here consider whether there is a biologically reasonable way to resolve this question but deal with the problem of locating those transitions where this occurs. At the start of the simulation we create a matrix called CHOICES that holds a flag indicating whether there are several equivalent choices: arbitrarily I designate 0 to indicate only one choice and 1 to indicate more than one equivalent choice. At the commencement of the simulation all cells are set to 0. The actual test for equivalent choices is done in the function OVER.PATCHES. The matrix passed back from this function has two columns and so we create a 1×2 vector called Choice that consists of two zeros:

$$\texttt{Choice <- c(0,0)}$$

one of these simply being a dummy to permit concatenation. Next we test if the fitnesses in the first two rows of the sorted values are the same and if they are the same we set the values in Choice to ones:

```
if(RHS[Best[1]]==RHS[Best[2]]) Choice <- c(1,1)
```

This vector is then added to the bottom of the matrix Temp that is passed back to OVER.STATES:

```
Temp <- rbind(Temp,Choice)
```

The data are then extracted, passed back to the main program, and stored in CHOICES.

6.5.4 Calculating the decision matrix

R CODE:
```
  rm(list=ls())        # Remove all objects from memory
# Function to calculate fitness when organism is in state X
  FITNESS <- function(X, Xcritical, Xmax, Xinc, Cost, Benefit,
Pbenefit, F.vectors)
{
# Note that the state value X is passed
# Note also that in this function Benefit and Pbenefit are vectors
# Iterate over the four kill values (0,1,2,3)
  Max.Index <- 1 + (Xmax-Xcritical)/Xinc # Get maximum index value
  W        <-0        # Set Fitness to zero
  Xstore   <- X       # Set X to Xstore to preserve value through loop
  for (I.Kill in 1:4)    # Begin loop
{
  X    <- Xstore - Cost + Benefit[I.Kill] # Calculate new state
                                            value
# If X greater than Xmax then X must be set to Xmax
  X    <- min(X, Xmax)
# If X less than or equal to Xcritical then set to Xcritical
  X    <- max(X, Xcritical)
# Convert to Index value
```

```
   Index <- 1+(X-Xcritical)/Xinc
# Index value probably not an integer
# So consider two integer values on either size of X
   Index.lower    <- floor(Index)              # Choose lower integer
   Index.upper    <- Index.lower + 1           # Upper integer
# Must stop index exceeding Max.Index. Not that Qx=0 in this case
   Index.upper    <- min(Index.upper, Max.Index)
   Qx <- X - floor(X)                 # qx for linear interpolation
   W <- W + Pbenefit[I.Kill]*(Qx*F.vectors[Index.upper,2]+(1-Qx)
*F.vectors[Index.lower,2])
} # End of I.Kill loop
   return(W)                       # Return Fitness
} # End of function
#...............................................................
# Function to iterate over patches i.e. over PACKS
OVER.PATCHES <- function(X, F.vectors, Xcritical,Xmax, Xinc,
Npatch, Cost, Benefit, Pbenefit)
{
   RHS <- matrix(0,Npatch,1)           # Set matrix for Right Hand
                                             Side of eqn

   for (i in 1: Npatch)               # Cycle over patches = pack
                                         sizes

{
# Call Fitness function. Pass Benefit and Pbenefit as vectors
RHS[i] <- FITNESS(X, Xcritical, Xmax, Xinc, Cost, Benefit[i,],
Pbenefit[i,], F.vectors)
} # End of i loop
# Now find optimal patch Best row is in Best[1]
   Best        <- order(RHS, na.last=TRUE, decreasing=TRUE)
   Index       <- 1+(X-Xcritical)/Xinc     # Get Index value
   F.vectors[Index,1]<- RHS[Best[1]]         # Get best W = F(x,t,T)
# Get best patch (=pack). Remember to convert from index value
   Best.Patch       <- Best[1]
# Concatenate F(x,t) and the optimal patch (=pack) number
   Temp        <- c(F.vectors[Index,1], Best.Patch)
# Add Temp to bottom of F.vectors and rename to Temp
   Temp        <- rbind(F.vectors, Temp)
# Create 1x2 vector to hold decision on more than one choice
# We only need one cell but it is convenient to use 2 for concatena-
   tion onto Temp, as indicated below
# Set Choice to zero
   Choice       <- c(0,0)
   if(RHS[Best[1]]==RHS[Best[2]]) Choice <- c(1,1) # Equal
                                              fitnesses
```

```
    Temp <- rbind(Temp,Choice) # Bind to bottom of matrix
    return (Temp)
} # End of function
#..........................................................
# Function to iterate over states of X
OVER.STATES <- function(F.vectors, Xcritical, Xmax, Xinc, Npatch,
Cost, Benefit, Pbenefit, Max.Index)
{
Store    <- matrix(0,Max.Index,3)    # Create matrix for output
  for ( Index in 2 : Max.Index)              # Iterate over states of X
{
# For given X call Over.Patches to determine F(x,t) and best patch
    X        <- (Index-1)*Xinc + Xcritical
Temp       <- OVER.PATCHES(X, F.vectors, Xcritical, Xmax, Xinc,
Npatch, Cost, Benefit, Pbenefit)
# Extract components. Penultimate row is F(x,t,T) and best patch
    n               <- nrow(Temp)-2
    F.vectors       <- Temp[1:n,]
    Store[Index,1:2]  <- Temp[n+1,] # Save F(x,t,T) and best patch
    Store[Index,3]    <- Temp[n+2,1] # Save Flag for several choices
} # End of X loop
# Add Store values to end of F.vectors for pass back to main program
    Temp       <- cbind(F.vectors, Store) # Combined by columns
    return(Temp)           # Return F.vectors and Store
} # End of function
#..........................................................
# MAIN PROGRAM
# Initialize parameters
    Xmax           <- 30            # Maximum value of X = gut capacity
    Xcritical      <- 0             # Value of X at which death occurs
    Xinc           <- 1             # Increment in state variable
    Max.Index <- 1 + (Xmax-Xcritical)/Xinc    # Maximum index value
    Cost           <- 6            # Cost = Daily food requirement
    Npatch         <- 4            # Number of patches= packs
# Calculate benefit as a function of pack size (rows)
# and number of kills (columns)
    Benefit        <- matrix(0,4,4)          # Rows = pack size, Columns
                                             = number of kills+1
    Pbenefit       <- matrix(0,4,4)        # Rows = pack size, Columns =
                                           number of kills+1
# Probability of single kill for pack size
    Pi       <- c(0.15, 0.31, 0.33, 0.33)
    Y        <- 11.25              # Size of single prey
```

```
  k          <- c(0,1,2,3)        # Number of kills
  for ( PackSize in 1:4)          # Iterate over pack sizes
{
# Calculate binomial probabilities using function dbinom
  Pbenefit[PackSize,]          <-  dbinom(x=k,  size=3,  prob=Pi
[PackSize])
# Calculate benefits = amount per individual
  Benefit[PackSize, 2:4]     <- Y*k[2:4]/PackSize
}
  Horizon     <- 31              # Number of time steps
# Set up matrix for fitnesses
# Column 1 is F(x, t). Column 2 is F(x, t+1)
  F.vectors                  <- matrix(0, Max.Index,2)
  F.vectors[2:Max.Index,2]  <- 1       # Cell 1,2 = 0 = Dead
# Create matrices for output
  FxtT         <- matrix(0,Horizon,Max.Index)    # F(x,t,T)
  Best.Patch   <- matrix(0,Horizon,Max.Index)    # Best patch
                                                      number
# Matrix for flag indicating multiple equivalent choices
# 0 = only one choice, 1 = more than one choice
  CHOICES      <- matrix(0,Horizon,Max.Index)
# Start iterations
  Time         <- Horizon        # Initialize Time
  while ( Time > 1)
{
  Time       <- Time - 1         # Decrement Time by 1 unit
# Call OVER.STATES to get best values for this time step
  Temp       <- OVER.STATES(F.vectors, Xcritical, Xmax, Xinc,
Npatch, Cost, Benefit, Pbenefit, Max.Index)
# Extract F.vectors
  TempF <- Temp[,1:2]
# Update F1
  for  ( J in 2: Max.Index)   { F.vectors[J,2] <- TempF[J,1]}
# Store results
  Best.Patch[Time,]        <- Temp[,4]
  FxtT[Time,]              <- Temp[,3]
  CHOICES[Time,]           <- Temp[,5]
} # End of Time loop
# Output information. For display add states to last row of matrices
# Note that state variable conversion from index value
  Index                    <- seq(from=1, to=Max.Index)
  Best.Patch[Horizon,]     <- (Index-1)*Xinc+Xcritical
  FxtT[Horizon,]           <- (Index-1)*Xinc+Xcritical
  Best.Patch[,1:Max.Index]       # Print Decision matrix
```

```
    signif(FxtT[,1:Max.Index],3)         # Print Fxt of Decision
                                            matrix: 3 sig places
    CHOICES[,1:Max.Index]       # Print matrix indicating choice flag
# Plot data
    y         <- Best.Patch[Horizon,2:Max.Index]
    x         <- seq(from=1, to=Horizon-1)
    par(mfrow=c(2,2))
    persp(x,   y,   Best.Patch[1:30,2:Max.Index],   xlab='Time',
ylab='x = Gut contents', zlab='Optimal Pack size', theta=20,
ph=25, lwd=1) # 3D plot
    image(x, y, Best.Patch[1:30,2:Max.Index], col=terrain.colors
(50), xlab='Time', ylab='x = Gut contents', las=1) # Colored grid
    image(x,   y,   CHOICES[1:30,2:Max.Index],   col=terrain.colors
(50), xlab='Time', ylab='x = Gut contents', las=1) # Colored grid
```

OUTPUT: (Figure 6.3)

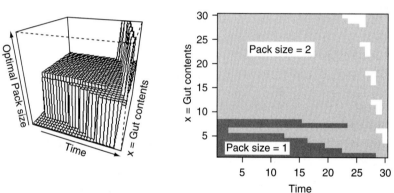

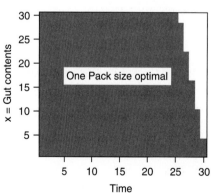

Figure 6.3 Results for Scenario 3: Top shows two graphical representation of the decision matrix (unlabeled color = optimal pack size of 3) and bottom a visualization of the choice matrix (unlabeled color = more than one optimal choice).

The decision matrix, the matrix of fitnesses, and the matrix indicating the presence of multiple equivalent choices are printed out but not shown here. Figure 6.3 shows two visualizations of the decision matrix and a visualization of the matrix CHOICE. Over most of state space a pack size of 2 is optimal. The number of cases in which there are multiple equivalent choices increase with the state value and the approach of the end of the time span.

MATLAB CODE: see Section 6.9.5

6.6 Scenario 4: Host choice in parasitoids: fitness decreases with time

A frequent use of dynamic programming is to examine oviposition behavior in organisms such as parasitoids that lay clutch sizes that depend upon host or patch quality. The important change in this scenario compared to the previous ones is that the value of the state variable increases as we move toward $t = 1$, rather than decreasing.

6.6.1 General assumptions

1. The animal commences the time period with some fixed quantity of eggs, as occurs, for example, in some Lepidoptera. In general, animals can be classified into capital breeders that use only, or primarily, resources gathered prior to maturity and income breeders that garner resources for reproduction after maturity. The present model applies to capital breeders, though it can easily be adapted for income breeders.
2. Patches or hosts vary in quality.
3. The survival and growth of larvae depend on the number in the clutch and host quality.
4. Variation in host quality can be detected by the ovipositing females.
5. Survival of the female may or may not change over time. For computational simplicity, we assume that the sequence of events is that egg-laying precedes the determination of survival over the time period.
6. Only one host at most is encountered per time interval.
7. Hosts already with eggs are not encountered.
8. Fitness is a function of the number of offspring.

6.6.2 Mathematical assumptions

1. There are four types of host.
2. The single host fitness can be modeled by a cubic function:

$$Benefit_{i,n} = a_i + b_i n + c_i n^2 + d_i n^3 \qquad\qquad (6.19)$$

where n is the number of eggs laid on a host, the subscript i refers to host type, and the coefficients vary according to host type. In this case we have not explicitly defined fitness in relation to the components of offspring survival and future reproduction, but have absorbed these into a single function empirically derived by Charnov and Skinner (1984) for the parasitoid wasp *Nasonia vitipennis*. An important feature of this function is that it has an intermediate optimum, but the fitness curve for host type 1 is clearly incorrect and derives from the fact that the model is extended beyond the observed range (Figure 6.4). It will never be optimal to increase clutch size beyond the local maximum (see below for

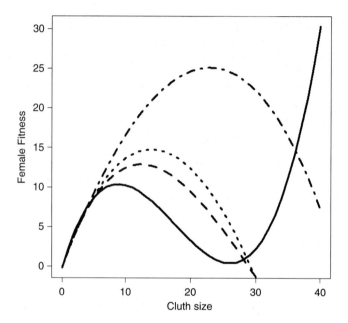

Figure 6.4 Fitness increments on each type of host parasitized by the wasp *Nasonia vitipennis* modeled by a cubic function. Coefficients from Table 4.1 of Mangel and Clark (1988). Coding to generate Benefits matrix and plot data prior to setting values greater than n^* (the single host maximum) to zero. Because zero occupies the first column we apply an index transformation.

```
rm(list=ls())  # Remove all objects from memory
Xmax                <- 40          # Maximum value of X = eggs
Xcritical           <- 0           # Lowest value of X = 0 eggs
Xinc                <- 1           # Increment in state variable
Max.Index           <- 1 + (Xmax-Xcritical)/Xinc # Max Index value
#  Create host coefficient matrix from which to get Benefits
Host.coeff          <- matrix(0,4,4)
Host.coeff[1,]      <- c(-0.2302, 2.7021, -0.2044, 0.0039)
Host.coeff[2,]      <- c(-0.1444, 2.2997, -0.1170, 0.0013)
```

derivation) and hence all values greater than this can be set to zero (coding given in figure caption). A plausible model for this type of function (i.e., single maximum) is that offspring survival and body size, which controls future fecundity, decreases with clutch size but, because fitness is equal to clutch size times, the expected fecundity of each offspring, fitness initially increases with clutch size. The optimum clutch size for a single clutch can be obtained from the calculus

$$\frac{dBenefit_{i,n}}{dn} = b_i + 2c_i n + 3d_i n^2 \qquad (6.20)$$

The optimum clutch size is then found by setting $dBenefit_{i,n}/dn = 0$ and solving the resultant quadratic (see Scenario 1 of Chapter 2), say n^*. It will never be optimal for a female to lay more eggs than n^*, but it could be optimal to lay fewer eggs if the host is of poor quality and the female is likely to find higher quality hosts in the future. As noted above, to avoid the unreal behavior of at least one of the single host fit we set values greater than n^* equal to zero.

3. The probability of encountering a host is constant but different for each host, designated as $Pbenefit_i$, where i is the ith host type. Thus the probability of not encountering a host, P_0, is

```
Host.coeff[3,]     <- c(-0.1048, 2.2097, -0.0878, 0.0004222)
Host.coeff[4,]     <- c(-0.0524, 2.0394, -0.0339, -0.0003111)
#  Calculate benefit as a function of
#  clutch size (rows) and Host type (columns)
Clutch             <- seq(from = 0, to = Xmax)
Benefit            <- matrix(0, Max.Index, 4)   #  Zero to Xmax
   for  (I.Host in 1:4) # Iterate over host types
{
  Benefit[,I.Host]    <-  Host.coeff[I.Host,1]  +  Host.coeff[I.
Host,2]*Clutch + Host.coeff[I.Host,3]*Clutch^2 + Host.coeff[I.
Host,4]*Clutch^3
}
#  Plot data
   plot(Clutch, Benefit[,1],type='l', xlab='Clutch size',ylab="-
Female Fitness", las=1, lwd=4)
#  lwd = line width, lty = line type,1=solid, 2=dashed, 3=dotted,
    4=dotdash,
   for  (i  in  2:4){lines(Clutch,  Benefit[,i],type='l',   lwd=4,
lty=i)}
   SHM   <- c(9,12,14,23)   #  Set single host maximum. See text for
                        derivation
#  Make all values  >  than SHM=0. Note that we use 1 because of zero
    class
   for  (i in 1:4){Benefit[(SHM[i]+1):Max.Index,i]  <- 0}
```

$$P_0 = 1 - \sum_{i=1}^{4} Pbenefit_i \qquad (6.21)$$

4. We shall assume a constant mortality per unit time, $Pmortality = 0.01$. At the end of the season no further eggs can be laid, meaning that the female is, from the point of view of natural selection, dead. For computational simplicity we shall use $Psurvival = 1 - Pmortality$. Thus

$$Psurvival = \begin{cases} 0.99 & \text{for } t < T-1 \\ 0.00 & \text{for } t = T-1 \end{cases} \qquad (6.22)$$

5. Overall fitness is the sum of the fitness increments obtained from each host.

6.6.3 Outcome chart and expected lifetime fitness function

The important feature of this model that differentiates it from previous models is that the value of the state variable increases as we move toward $t = 1$, rather than decreasing. Because no eggs are laid beyond time T, the terminal fitness is $F(x, T) = 0$. Because eggs are laid prior to the calculation of survival, even if the female does not survive, the state variable takes a positive value. Thus at each time step there are two possible outcomes, a host is found or a host is not found:

Host found	Survives	X
Yes	Yes	x-Benefit$_{i,n}$
Yes	No	x-Benefit$_{i,n}$
No	Yes	X
No	No	X

From the above, we have that fitness at time $t - 1$ is made up of two functions, f and g:

$$F(x, t-1) = f(\text{No host encountered}) + g(\text{Host encountered}) \qquad (6.23)$$

The function for "No host encountered" is

$$f(\text{No host encountered}) = 0.99 P_0 F(x, t) \qquad (6.24)$$

The function for "Host encountered" is more complicated. The fitness increment for each combination of host type i and clutch size, c, where c varies from 0 to x, is

$$F_{i,c} = Benefit_{i,c} + 0.99 * F(x - c, t) \qquad (6.25)$$

that is, the benefit from the present clutch plus the fitness expected from the remaining eggs $(x - c)$. Note that this particular formulation requires estimating $F(0, t)$, which means that we have to use an index transformation in the coding, as done in the last scenario. From the series generated by equation (6.25) we obviously choose the maximum value: thus for the ith host and $x = 4$, we pick

$$F_{i,\max} = \max\{F_{i,0}, F_{i,1}, F_{i,2}, F_{i,3}, F_{i,4}\} \qquad (6.26)$$

The expected maximum fitness increment over all host types is then given by

$$g(\text{Host encountered}) = \sum_{i=1}^{4} Pbenefit_i F_{i,\max} \qquad (6.27)$$

and $F(x, t-1)$ is thus

$$F(x, t-1) = 0.99 P_0 F(x, t) + \sum_{i=1}^{4} Pbenefit_i F_{i,\max} \qquad (6.28)$$

Mangel and Clark (1988) make the following predictions for this scenario:

Prediction 1: For a fixed number of remaining eggs, older insects should lay larger clutches than younger insects. The rationale for this prediction is that older insects are closer to the end of the duration and hence their expected future fitness is reduced relative to younger females, thereby making present allocation a higher contribution to overall fitness.

Prediction 2: It also follows from the preceding rationale that older insects are more likely to choose inferior hosts.

Prediction 3: Because of differing host encounters there will be a distribution of clutch sizes at any given time.

Prediction 4: As the per period survival decreases, larger clutches will be observed. This follows from the fact that survival discounts future reproduction (i.e., $Psurvival * F(x-c, t)$).

Prediction 2 is not directly addressed by this model, because females only locate one type of host at a time. Prediction 3 is not directly addressed by the decision matrix but can be addressed using the decision matrix and simulating the behavior of individual females, as described below.

6.6.4 Calculating the decision matrix

It is more convenient to place the calculations of fitness directly into the function OVER.PATCHES, which iterates over host types. Rather than storing all cases in which there are multiple choices of the greatest fitness, the program simply prints out when these occur: in this example no such cases occur (such cases are more likely to occur when survival is the fitness criterion). Except for these two changes, the basic program is the same as the patch-foraging model. (Because the state variable, number of eggs, is an integer and varies in unit steps, no interpolation is required.) While one could calculate the single host fitness functions using the cubic functions within OVER.PATCHES it is more efficient to calculate a *Benefits* matrix as given in Figure 6.3 and pass this matrix. The decision matrix gives the optimal clutch size but what is likely to be of greater interest is the decision matrix for each host type, as it is this that is required to address Predictions 1 and 4. The decision matrix for a single host type can be obtained very easily by storing this value in place of the overall clutch size, that is, to get the decision matrix for host type 3 use (in OVER.PATCHES)

```
Temp <- c(F.vectors[Index,1], Best.Clutch[3])
```

To output the decision matrix for all host types simultaneously requires more complicated bookkeeping that I leave to the reader. (Given how quickly the program runs one can simply run the model four times, changing the index value of Best.Clutch[3] or use the approach given in Scenario 5.) To illustrate the validity of Predictions 1 and 2, I stored the output for the $x = 40$ column of the decision matrix for host type 3 and ran the model with three values of *Psurvival*: 0.99, 0.90, and 0.80. I then plotted the results using SigmaPlot.

R CODE:

```
   rm(list=ls())      # Remove all objects from memory
# Set up path for output of text files
   setwd("C:/Documents and Settings/Derek Roff/My Documents/ Mod-
elling Evolution/DYNAMIC PROGRAMMING")  # This will have to be
changed for specific paths
# Function to iterate over patches i.e. over Hosts
   OVER.PATCHES <- function(X, F.vectors, Xcritical, Xmax, Xinc,
Npatch, Benefit, Pbenefit, Psurvival)
{
# Create matrix for storing best clutch size for each host type
   Best.Clutch       <- matrix(0,Npatch)
   Index       <- 1 + (X-Xcritical)/Xinc # Index for X is X+1
# Vector of clutch sizes to Index-1
   Clutch       <- seq(from =1, to = Index-1)
# Start fitness accumulation with component for case of not finding
   a host
   W       <- Psurvival*(1-sum(Pbenefit))*F.vectors[Index,2]
   for (i in 1: Npatch)        # Cycle over patches = Hosts
{
# Calculate "partial" fitness, W.partial for each clutch size
   W.partial <- Benefit[2:Index,i] + Psurvival*F.vectors[Index-
Clutch,2]
# Find largest W.partial and hence best clutch size
   Best       <- order(W.partial, na.last=TRUE, decreasing=TRUE)
   Best.Clutch[i]       <- Best[1] # Store value of best clutch for
                                    host i
```

```
# Increment fitness
  W               <- W + Pbenefit[i]*W.partial[Best[1]]
# Test for several equal optimal choices
# Only examine W.partial that contain more than one entry
if(length(W.partial)>1 & W.partial[Best[1]]==W.partial[Best[2]])
{print ("Several possible equal choices")}
} # End of i loop
  F.vectors[Index,1] <- W # Update F(x,t)
# Concatenate F(x,t,T) and the optimal clutch values for host type 2
  Temp         <- c(F.vectors[Index,1], Best.Clutch[2])
# Add Temp to bottom of F.vectors and rename to Temp
  Temp         <- rbind(F.vectors, Temp)
  return (Temp)
} # End of function
#.............................................................
# Function to iterate over states of X
  OVER.STATES  <-  function(F.vectors, Xcritical, Xmax, Xinc,
Npatch, Benefit, Pbenefit, Psurvival, Max.Index)
{
  Store <- matrix(0,Max.Index,2)    # Create matrix for output
  for ( Index in 2 : Max.Index)        # Iterate over states of X
{
# For given X call Over.Patches to determine F(x,t,T) and best patch
  X            <- (Index-1)*Xinc + Xcritical
  Temp         <- OVER.PATCHES(X, F.vectors, Xcritical, Xmax, Xinc,
Npatch, Benefit, Pbenefit, Psurvival)
# Extract components. Last row is F(x,t) and best clutch size for
  host 2
  n               <- nrow(Temp)-1
  F.vectors       <- Temp[1:n,]
  Store[Index,]   <- Temp[n+1,] # Save F(x,t,T) and best clutch
                                       size
} # End of X loop
# Add Store values to end of F.vectors for pass back to main program
  Temp         <- cbind(F.vectors, Store) # Combined by columns
  return(Temp)                           #  Return  F.vectors  and
Store
} # End of function
```

```
#...........................................................................
# MAIN PROGRAM
# Initialize parameters
  Xmax              <- 40         # Maximum value of X = eggs
  Xcritical         <- 0          # Lowest value of X = 0 eggs
  Xinc              <- 1          # Increment in state variable
  Max.Index         <- 1 + (Xmax-Xcritical)/Xinc # Max Index value
  Psurvival         <- 0.99       # Survival probty per time increment
  Npatch            <- 4          # Number of patches = hosts
# Create host coefficient matrix from which to get Benefits
  Host.coeff              <- matrix(0,4,4)
  Host.coeff[1,]          <- c(-0.2302, 2.7021, -0.2044, 0.0039)
  Host.coeff[2,]          <- c(-0.1444, 2.2997, -0.1170, 0.0013)
  Host.coeff[3,]          <- c(-0.1048, 2.2097, -0.0878, 0.0004222)
  Host.coeff[4,]          <- c(-0.0524, 2.0394, -0.0339, -0.0003111)
# Calculate benefit as a function of
# clutch size (rows) and Host type (columns)
  Clutch                  <- seq(from = 0, to = Xmax)
  Benefit                 <- matrix(0, Xmax+1, 4) # Zero to Xmax
  for (I.Host in 1:4)     # Iterate over host types
{
  Benefit[,I.Host]     <- Host.coeff[I.Host,1] + Host.coeff[I.
Host,2]*Clutch + Host.coeff[I.Host,3]*Clutch^2 + Host.coeff[I.
Host,4]*Clutch^3
}
  Benefit[1,]             <- 0              # Reset first row to zero
  SHM <- c(9,12,14,23) # Set single host maximum. See text for deri-
                          vation
# Make all values > than SHM=0. Note that we use 2 because of zero
  class
  for (i in 1:4){Benefit[(SHM[i]+2):Max.Index,i] <- 0}
# Probability of encountering host type
  Pbenefit                <- c(0.05, 0.05, 0.1, 0.8)
  Horizon                 <- 21            # Number of time steps
# Set up matrix for fitnesses
# Column 1 is F(x, t). Column 2 is F(x, t+1) Both are zero
  F.vectors               <- matrix(0, Max.Index,2)
# Create matrices for output
  FxtT              <- matrix(0,Horizon,Max.Index)        # F(x,t,T)
# Best clutch size for host 2
  Best.Patch        <- matrix(0,Horizon,Max.Index)
```

```
# Start iterations
  Time                <- Horizon              # Initialize Time
  while ( Time > 1)
{
  Time                <- Time -1              # Decrement Time by 1 unit
# Call OVER.STATES to get best values for this time step
  Temp                <- OVER.STATES(F.vectors, Xcritical, Xmax,
Xinc, Npatch, Benefit, Pbenefit, Psurvival, Max.Index)
# Extract F.vectors
  TempF               <- Temp[,1:2]
# Update F1
  for ( J in 2: Max.Index)    {F.vectors[J,2]    <- TempF[J,1]}
# Store results
  Best.Patch[Time,]<- Temp[,4]
  FxtT[Time,]         <- Temp[,3]
} # End of Time loop
# Output information. For display add states to last row of matrices
  Index                     <- seq(from=1, to=Max.Index)
  Best.Patch[Horizon,]      <- (Index-1)*Xinc+Xcritical
  FxtT[Horizon,]            <-(Index-1)*Xinc+Xcritical
  Best.Patch[,1:Max.Index]       # Print Decision matrix
  signif(FxtT[,1:Max.Index],3)    # Print Fxt of Decision matrix:
                                  3 sig places
# Plot data as 3d plot and colored grid
  y            <- Best.Patch[Horizon,2:Max.Index]
  x            <- seq(from=1, to=Horizon-1)
  par(mfrow=c(2,2))
  persp(x,   y,   Best.Patch[1:20,2:Max.Index],   xlab='Time',
ylab='x', zlab='Optimal clutch size', theta=20, ph=25, lwd=1) #
3D plot
  image(x,  y,  Best.Patch[1:20,2:Max.Index], col=terrain.colors
(50), xlab='Time', ylab='x', las=1) # Colored grid
# Output text file for future plotting to test predictions
  DATA       <- cbind(x, Best.Patch[1:Horizon-1,41])
  DATA       <- t(DATA)
  write(DATA,file="OVIPOSITION.txt",nc=2)
```

OUTPUT: (Figure 6.5)

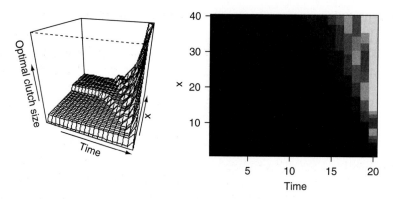

Figure 6.5 Results for Scenario 4: Top shows two graphical representation of the decision matrix and bottom a reduced decision matrix for host type 3.

	State variable, x											
Time	1	2	3	4	5	10	15	20	25	30	35	40
1	1	1	2	2	2	2	2	2	3	3	3	3
2	1	1	2	2	2	2	2	2	3	3	3	3
3	1	1	2	2	2	2	2	2	3	3	3	3
4	1	1	2	2	2	2	2	2	3	3	3	3
5	1	1	2	2	2	2	2	2	3	3	3	3
6	1	1	2	2	2	2	2	2	3	3	3	3
7	1	1	2	2	2	2	2	2	3	3	3	3
8	1	1	2	2	2	2	2	2	3	3	3	3
9	1	1	2	2	2	2	2	2	3	3	3	3
10	1	1	2	2	2	2	2	2	3	3	3	3
11	1	1	2	2	2	2	2	2	3	3	3	3
12	1	1	2	2	2	2	2	2	3	3	3	4
13	1	1	2	2	2	2	2	3	3	3	4	4
14	1	1	2	2	2	2	2	3	3	3	4	4
15	1	1	2	2	2	2	2	3	3	4	4	5
16	1	1	2	2	2	2	3	3	4	4	5	6
17	1	1	2	2	2	2	3	4	5	6	6	7
18	1	1	2	2	2	3	4	5	6	7	9	10
19	1	1	2	2	2	4	6	8	10	11	13	14
20	1	2	3	4	5	10	14	14	14	14	14	14

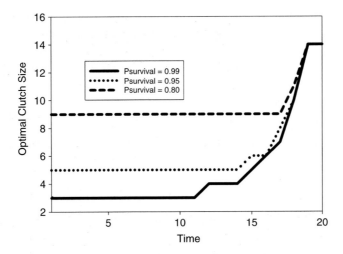

Figure 6.6 Effect of varying *Psurvival* on the optimal clutch size for host type 3 given *x* = 40. Plot generated using SigmaPlot.

The decision matrix is printed out but not shown here. Figure 6.5 shows a reduced version of this matrix for host type 3 along with two visualizations of the complete matrix. The most striking point is that, as predicted (Prediction 1), the optimal clutch size increases with age. Figure 6.6 shows the effect of varying *Psurvival*: as predicted (Prediction 3), the optimum clutch size increases as survival per unit time decreases.

MATLAB CODE: See Section 6.9.6.

6.6.5   Using the decision matrix: individual prediction

Although the distribution of clutch sizes over time can be calculated using the transition density matrix the construction is very tedious in comparison to using the individual prediction approach. By running a large number of individuals (e.g., 1,000–10,000) the resulting distribution will closely approximate the expected distribution. To obtain the decision matrix for all four hosts the preceding program was run four times and the decision matrices dumped as text files labeled

`DM1.txt`, `DM2.txt`, `DM3.txt` and `DM4.txt`, the appropriate coding being

```
DATA <- Best.Patch[1:Horizon-1,2:41]
DATA <- t(DATA)
write(DATA, file="DM4.txt",nc=40)
```

The four files were read back and placed into an array called `DM` in which the dimensions represent *x*, time, and host type. At each iteration over individual and time a host type has to be allocated based on its probability of occurrence (*Pbenefit*). To do this we proceed as follows:

Step 1: Multiply all probabilities by a common factor so that they are integers. In the present case the set of probabilities are 0.05, 0.05, 0.1, and 0.8, and hence the appropriate multiplier is 100, giving 5, 5, 10, and 80, respectively. Create a vector with these numbers:

```
Times <- c(5,5,10,80).
```

Step 2: Create a vector, Host.Type, in which there are 5 "1"s, 5 "2"s, 10 "3"s, and 80 "4"s:

```
Host.Type  <- c(rep(1,Times[1]), rep(2,Times[2]), rep(3,Times
[3]), rep(4,Times[4]))
```

Step 3: For each individual create a vector of length Horizon (the total number of time increments) of random integers between 1 and 100:

```
Host <- ceiling(100*runif(Horizon))
```

Step 4: The host type chosen at time interval *i* is Host.Type[Host[i]]. The probability of occurrence is equal to the probabilities given by Pbenefit. Survival is computed by generating a vector of (length = Horizon) random numbers between 0 and 1: values greater than 0.99 indicate that the female dies in that time period and are set to zero, all other values then being set to 1:

```
Survival <- runif(Horizon) # Vector of survival probabilities
Survival[Survival>Psurvival] <- 0
Survival[Survival!=0] <- 1 # Set all other values to 1
```

The initial distribution of egg complement (*x*) is set as a normal distribution with mean 20 and standard deviation of 5, and converted to integer values:

```
x.init <- ceiling(rnorm(N.Ind, mean=20, sd=5))
```

Because clutch sizes are integral, the results are plotted using the bar graph routine rather than the histogram routine.

R CODE:

```
rm(list=ls()) # Remove all objects from memory
setwd("C:/Documents and Settings/Derek Roff/My Documents/Mod-
elling Evolution/DYNAMIC PROGRAMMING")
Xmax    <- 40                           # Maximum value of X = eggs
DM1     <- read.table(file="DM1.txt") # Cols = x rows=time
DM2     <- read.table(file="DM2.txt")
DM3     <- read.table(file="DM3.txt")
DM4     <- read.table(file="DM4.txt")
# Create an array for Decision matrix
DM          <- array(0,c(20,Xmax,4))     # time, state, host
for (i in 1:20)
{
for ( j in 1:Xmax)
```

```
{
  DM[i,j,1] <- DM1[i,j]; DM[i,j,2] <- DM2[i,j]
  DM[i,j,3] <- DM3[i,j];DM[i,j,4] <- DM4[i,j]
}}
# Probability of encountering host type
  Pbenefit     <- c(0.05, 0.05, 0.1, 0.8)
  Times        <- c(5,5,10,80)
# Create Vector for Host type probability
  Host.Type    <-      c(rep(1,Times[1]),rep(2,Times[2]),rep(3,
Times[3]), rep(4,Times[4]))
  Psurvival    <- 0.99  # Survival probability per time increment
  Horizon      <- 10       # Number of time steps
  set.seed(10)            # Initialise random number generator
  N.Ind   <- 1000         # Number of individuals
  Output  <- matrix(0,N.Ind,Horizon)  # Allocate space for output
# Generate initial values of x from normal distribution
  x.init <- ceiling(rnorm(N.Ind, mean=20, sd=5))
  for (Ind in 1:N.Ind) # Iterate over individuals
{
# Generate vectors for choosing the Host type and probability of
  survival
  Host  <- ceiling(100*runif(Horizon))     # Vector of host types
  Survival  <- runif(Horizon)   # Vector of survival probabilities
# Set all values of Survival > Psurvival = 0
  Survival[Survival>Psurvival] <- 0
  Survival[Survival!=0] <- 1       # Set all other values to 1
  x       <- x.init[Ind]           # Initial value of x
  for (Time in 1:Horizon)          # Iterate over time periods
{
if ( x>0) # If eggs remaining calculate clutch size using DM
{
  Clutch.Size          <- DM[Time,x,Host.Type[Host[Time]]]
  Output[Ind,Time]     <- Clutch.Size # Store clutch size
# Compute new value of x
  x <- x-Clutch.Size
}
  x <- x*Survival[Time]        # Set x=0 if female does not survive
} # end of Time loop
} # End of Ind loop
par(mfcol=c(5,2)) # Set graphics page to 5 rows and 2 columns
# Iterate over time and plot bar graphs of clutch size
for (i in 1:10)
{
  Data   <- Output[,i]; Data <- Data[Data>0] # Eliminate zeroes
  xbar   <- mean(Data)        # Mean clutch size
```

```
  print(c(i, mean(Data)))       # Time, Output mean clutch size
  Data    <- table(Data)        # Tabulate data
# Plot data using a bar graph, because x is integral
  barplot(Data, xlab="Clutch Size", space=0, xlim=c(0,5), main =
paste("Time = ",i), col=1)
}
```

OUTPUT: (Figure 6.7)

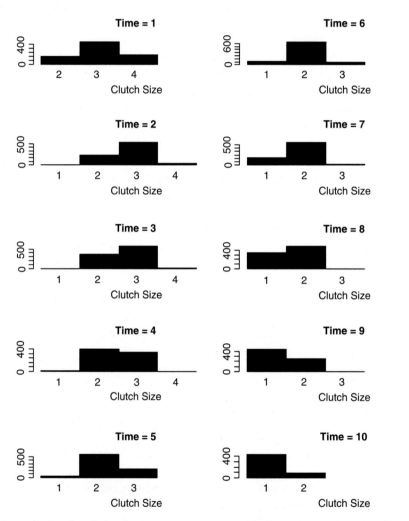

Figure 6.7 Bar graphs of clutch size over time using the decision matrix to predict oviposition behavior.

```
[1]   1.000000   3.036
[1]   2.000000   2.774619
[1]   3.000000   2.626927
[1]   4.000000   2.444906
[1]   5.000000   2.216842
[1]   6.000000   1.965921
[1]   7.000000   1.779978
[1]   8.000000   1.588661
[1]   9.000000   1.362360
[1]  10.00000    1.172745
```

The bar graphs (Figure 6.7) show an initial variation for clutch sizes from 2–4, with a diminishing of the mean size over time (see means above). This reduction is due to the female running out of eggs. If females were prevented from laying eggs, we would expect that the mean clutch size would increase. To test this prediction I commenced the simulation at time 16, essentially preventing the simulated females from laying any eggs until this time. The mean clutch sizes still show the same decrease over time (4.64, 4.38, 4.16, 3.85, and 3.55), but the proportion of females laying larger clutches increases (e.g., at $t = 16$ no females lay a clutch size of 9 eggs but some do so at $t = 30$, Figure 6.8). For a fuller discussion of this model see Mangel and Clark (1988, chapter 4).

MATLAB CODE: See Section 6.9.7.

6.7   Scenario 5: Optimizing egg and clutch size: dealing with two state variables

Thus far we have assumed only a single state variable: however, there may be many circumstances in which there are multiple state variables. In this scenario we shall examine an extension of the previous scenario in which fitness depends upon both egg size and egg number. To better focus upon the method of dealing with two state variables the previous scenario is somewhat simplified.

6.7.1   General assumptions

1. The animal commences the time period with some fixed quantity of resources that can be divided into clutches and eggs of different sizes. Thus although we have two state variables, egg size, and clutch size, these can be combined operationally into a single variable, reproductive biomass X.

2. Patches or hosts vary in quality.

3. The survival and growth of larvae depend on the number in the clutch, egg size, and host quality.

4. Variation in host quality can be detected by the ovipositing females.

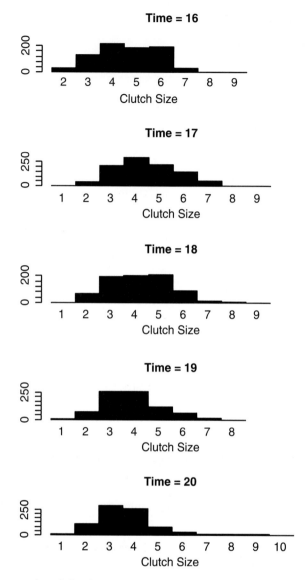

Figure 6.8 Bar graphs of clutch size over time using the decision matrix to predict oviposition behavior when females are not allowed to oviposit until $t = 16$.

5. Survival of the female may or may not change over time. For computational simplicity, I shall assume that the sequence of events is that egg-laying precedes the determination of survival over the time period.

6. One host is encountered per time interval.

7. Hosts already with eggs are not encountered.

8. Fitness is a function of the number and size of offspring.

6.7.2 Mathematical assumptions

1. There are two types of host.
2. The amount of reproductive biomass available at time t is B_t which is equal to the product of egg size and clutch size,

$$x_t = x_E x_C \tag{6.29}$$

where x_E is the egg size and x_C is the clutch size.

3. The single host fitness can be modeled by the function

$$Benefit_{i,E,C} = W_{max,i} - \sqrt{a_{E,i}(x_E - b_{E,i})^2 + a_{C,i}(x_C - b_{C,i})^2} \tag{6.30}$$

where the subscript i refers to host type and the coefficients $W_{max,i}, a_{E,i}, a_{C,i}, b_{E,i}, b_{C,i}$ vary according to host type. The maximum benefit on host type i is $W_{max,i}$ and is obtained when egg size equals $b_{E,i}$ and clutch size is $b_{c,i}$. Parameter values used in this example are

Host	W_{max}	a_E	a_C	b_E	b_C
1	10	100	1	2	5
2	20	100	1	1	10

Thus on host type 1 the single host optimum is a larger egg size but smaller clutch size than is optimal on host type 2 (Figure 6.9). The parameter space (i.e., combination space) over which fitness is positive is small on host type 1 but relatively large on host type 2.

4. A host is encountered during each time step: the probability of encountering host type 1 is $P_1 = 0.5$ and hence the probability of encountering host type 2 is $P_2 = 1 - P_1 = 0.5$.

5. We shall assume a constant mortality per unit time, $Pmortality = 0.1$. At the end of the season no further eggs can be laid, meaning that the female is, from the point of view of natural selection, dead. For computational simplicity we shall use $Psurvival = 1 - Pmortality$. Thus

$$Psurvival = \begin{cases} 0.90 & \text{for } t < T - 1 \\ 0.00 & \text{for } t = T - 1 \end{cases} \tag{6.31}$$

6. Overall fitness is the sum of the fitness increments obtained from each host.

6.7.3 Outcome chart and expected lifetime fitness function

As in the previous example, an important feature of this model that differentiates it from Scenarios 1–3 is that the value of the state variable increases as we move toward $t = 1$, rather than decreasing. Because no eggs are laid beyond time T, the terminal fitness is $F(x, T) = 0$. Because eggs are laid prior to the calculation of

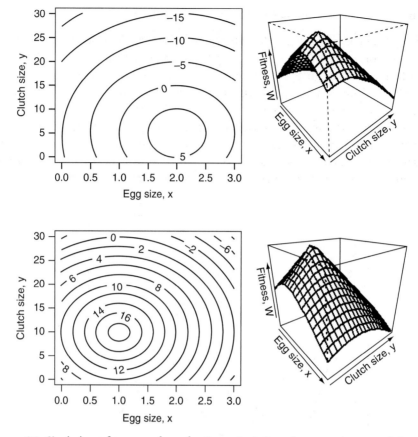

Figure 6.9 Single host fitness surfaces for Scenario 5. R code to produce graph is

```
rm(list=ls()) # Remove all objects from memory
# Function to calculate fitness, passing parameters to it
    FITNESS   <- function(X, Wmax, Xegg, Xclutch, ax, ay)
{
    W     <- Wmax-sqrt(ax*(X[1]-Xegg)^2 + ay*(X[2]-Xclutch)^2)
}
# MAIN PROGRAM
# Parameter values
Wmax   <- c(10,20); Xegg   <- c(2,1); Xclutch   <- c(5,10); ax   <-
100; ay   <- 1
n   <- 20    # Number of intervals for egg and clutch sizes
x   <- seq(from=0, to=3, length=n)   # Generate egg sizes
y   <- seq(from=0, to=30, length=n) # Generate clutch size
d   <- expand.grid(x,y)              # Expand to all combinations
# Set plotting page to put graphs side by side and not distorted
# Make plotting surface consist of four panels
    par(mfrow=c(2,2))
for   ( i in 1:2)
```

survival, even if the female does not survive, the state variable takes a positive value. Thus at each time step there is only one possible outcome, a host is found.

Host found	Survives	X
Yes	Yes	x-Beniftit$_{iE,C}$
Yes	No	x-Beniftit$_{iE,C}$

Because the model assumes that a host is encountered each time step the fitness function is somewhat simpler than in the previous scenario. The fitness increment for each combination of host type i, egg size $x_{E,i}$, and clutch size $x_{C,i}$ is

$$F_{i,E,C} = Benefit_{i,E,C} + 0.90 * F(x - x_{E,i}x_{C,i}, t) \quad (6.32)$$

The term $x - x_{E,i}x_{C,i}$ is unlikely to be an index and hence interpolation is necessary. Note that the egg–clutch size combinations are restricted to those values less than or equal to x_i, the size of the state variable at time i. Clutch sizes must be integer, but egg sizes are continuous. For each clutch size we find the egg size that maximizes $F_{i,E,C}$ and then compare different clutch sizes to get the global maximum, $F_{i,max}$. Fitness for state variable x at time $t - 1$ is given by

$$F(x, t - 1) = P_1 F_{1,max} + (1 - P_1)F_{2,max} \quad (6.33)$$

6.7.4 Calculating the decision matrix

Unlike the previous scenario it is better to place the calculation of fitness in a separate function called FITNESS, as was done in Scenarios 1–3. Two features of note in the programming of this scenario is the relatively extensive bookkeeping that is necessary and the use of interpolation. While it could be possible to place the output in a single array I prefer to make separate matrices, because the coding is clearer. The program runs in the following sequence:

Step 1: Input parameter values and the 7 matrices for storing the following output: the state value (FxtT), the optimal clutch sizes for the two hosts (Best.

```
{
# Create a vector of fitness values for all combinations
Wtemp   <- apply(d,1,FITNESS,Wmax[i],Xegg[i],Xclutch[i],ax,ay)
# Convert into matrix
   W   <- matrix(Wtemp,n,n,byrow=F)
# Plot contour. las=orientation of axis labels
# lwd= line width, labcex=size of contour labels
contour(x,y,W, xlab='Egg size, x', ylab='Clutch size,y', las=1,
lwd=3, labcex=1)
#Plot perspective plot
persp(x,y,W,xlab='Egg size, x', ylab='Clutch size, y', zlab='Fit-
ness, W',theta = 50, phi = 25,lwd=2) }
```

Clutch1, Best.Clutch2), the optimal egg sizes for the two hosts (Best.Egg1, Best.Egg2), and two matrices indicating whether there are at least two choices of maximal fitness for a given host type (Choice.H1, Choice.H2, 1 will signify a single optimum and 2 that there are at least two optima).

Step 2: Iterate over time.

Step 3: Call the function OVER.STATES to iterate over values of the state variable. This function is the same as in the previous scenario except that the number of columns in the storage matrix Store is increased to 7 to hold the increased number of output variables.

Step 4: Call the function OVER.PATCHES to calculate the optimum decision over host types for the given value of the state variable. Iterate over each host (patch) and for each do the following.

Step 5: Create a 3 × 11 matrix to store the fitness for the optimum egg size at a given clutch size.

Step 6: Iterate over clutch sizes from 1 to 11.

Step 7: Pass the function FITNESS to optimize to find the optimal egg size.

Step 8. In FITNESS the following steps are applied:
    Step 8a: Calculate the reproductive biomass for this combination (=Biomass).
    Step 8b: Check that this is a permissible biomass in that it is less than the present value of the state variable X. If this test is not passed then set fitness W to zero and return.
    Step 8c: If step 8b is passed first calculate $F(x, t)$. Because the index value of Biomass may not be an integer interpolation is used, the interpolated value being designated Fxt.interpolated.
    Step 8d: Calculate the fitness on the given host using equation (6.30). Set to zero if negative.
    Step 8e: Calculate fitness using equation (6.32) and return.

Step 9: Store fitness, clutch size, and egg size in W.host.

Step 10: After iteration over clutch sizes is completed find the combination with the highest fitness. Store in Best.in.Patch. Test if "second-best" combination has the same fitness as the "best": if so store result as 2 in matrix Choice.Flag.

Step 11: After iterating over both hosts calculate the fitness using equation (6.33).

Step 12: Concatenate the vector F.vectors with the relvant output information and pass back to OVER.STATES where it is stored and a new state value is passed to OVER.PATCHES.

Step 13: After iterating over patches, state values, and time, output matrices.

R CODE:
To ensure that "interesting" results were obtained I set the state variable, reproductive biomass, within a range, 1–10, over which the egg–clutch size

combinations for a single host cannot be achieved (a useful method of testing that the model is performing correctly is to set the state variable so high that the optimum combinations for the two hosts can be achieved).

```
rm(list=ls()) # Remove all objects from memory
FITNESS <- function (Egg, Clutch, X, F.vectors, Xcritical, Xmax,
Xinc, Psurvival, Wmax, A, Xegg, Xclutch, Ith.Patch)
{
  W                <- 0           # Set fitness to zero
  Biomass          <- Clutch*Egg  # Biomass of clutch/Egg size
                                    combination
  if ( Biomass < X)               # Continue only if Biomass < X
{
  Max.Index        <- 1 + (Xmax-Xcritical)/Xinc # Get maximum index
                                                  value
# Index value for biomass
  Index            <- 1+(Biomass-Xcritical)/Xinc
# Get fitness at lower and upper integer value of Biomass
  Index.lower      <- floor(Index)
  Index.upper      <- Index.lower + 1
# Must stop index exceeding Max.Index. Note that Qx = 0 in this case
  Index.upper      <- min(Index.upper, Max.Index)
  Qx               <- Biomass - floor(Biomass)
  Fxt.lower        <- F.vectors[Index.lower,2]
# Get fitness at upper integer value of
  Fxt.upper        <- F.vectors[Index.upper,2]
  Fxt.interpolated <- Qx*Fxt.upper + (1-Qx)*Fxt.lower # Iterpolated
                                                        value
# Calculate the fitness for this particular egg-clutch size combi-
  nation
  W <- Wmax[Ith.Patch]-sqrt(A[1]*(Egg-Xegg[Ith.Patch])^2+A[2]*
(Clutch-Xclutch[Ith.Patch])^2)
  W <- max(0, W) # Set to zero if negative
  W <- W + Psurvival*Fxt.interpolated # Fitness
  W <- max(0, W) # Set to zero if negative
} # End of if
  return(W)
} # End of function
#.............................................................
# Function to iterate over patches i.e. over Hosts
OVER.PATCHES <- function(X, F.vectors, Xcritical, Xmax, Xinc,
Npatch, Psurvival, Wmax, A, Xegg, Xclutch,P1)
{
# X is the total biomass available Get index value for X
  Index <- 1+(X-Xcritical)/Xinc
```

```
# Allocate storage of best combinations for each patch
# Columns will contain
# Fitness, Clutch, Egg
  Choice.Flag    <- matrix(0,2)      # Store information on
                                        number of choices
  Best.in.Patch  <- matrix(0,2,3)    # Allocate storage for Best
                                        Decision
# Iterate over patches
  for ( Ith.Patch in 1:Npatch)       # Iterate over the two hosts (=
                                       patches)
{
# Make a matrix called W.host with the following 3 columns:
# Fitness, Egg size, Clutch size
  W.host        <- matrix(0,11,3)
  for ( Clutch in 1:11)              # Iterate over clutch size
{
  W.host[Clutch,2]        <- Clutch # Store clutch size
# Call optimize to find best egg size
B <- optimize(f =FITNESS, interval =c(0.01,3),Clutch, X,F.vec-
tors, Xcritical, Xmax, Xinc, Psurvival, Wmax, A, Xegg, Xclutch,
Ith.Patch, maximum=TRUE)
  W.host[Clutch,1]    <- B$objective        # Fitness
  W.host[Clutch,3]    <- B$maximum          # Egg size
} # End of clutch size loop
# Get best combination for this host
  R             <- W.host[,1]
  Best          <- order(R, na.last=TRUE, decreasing=TRUE)
  Best.in.Patch[Ith.Patch,]  <-  W.host[Best[1],]  # Store best
                                                     choice
# Test for several equal optimal choices
  if(W.host[Best[1],1]==W.host[Best[2],1])Choice.Flag[Ith.
Patch] <- 2
} # Next host
# Overall fitness
  W <- P1*Best.in.Patch[1,1] +(1-P1)*Best.in.Patch[2,1]
  F.vectors[Index,1]<- W # Update F(x,t,T)
# Concatenate F(x,t) and the optimal egg and clutch values for both
  hosts
# We add to the bottom of the two column matrix F.vectors the
  # following
# F.vectors[Index,1], 1 The second entry is simply a dummy variable
# Best.in.Patch[1,2] Best.in.Patch[1,3] # Host 1 Egg size Clutch
  size
# Best.in.Patch[2,2] Best.in.Patch[2,3] # Host 2 Egg size Clutch
  size
```

```
# Choice.Flag[1:2] # Flag for multiple optima
  Temp1 <- c(F.vectors[Index,1], 1)
  Temp2 <- c( Best.in.Patch[1,2], Best.in.Patch[1,3])
  Temp3 <- c( Best.in.Patch[2,2], Best.in.Patch[2,3])
# Add Temp1, Temp2, Temp3 & Choice to bottom of F.vectors and rename
  to Temp
  Temp <- rbind(F.vectors, Temp1, Temp2, Temp3, Choice.Flag[1:2])
  return (Temp)
} # End of function
#..................................................................
# Function to iterate over states of X
  OVER.STATES <- function(F.vectors, Xcritical, Xmax, Xinc,
  Npatch, Psurvival, Max.Index, Wmax, A, Xegg, Xclutch, P1)
{
# Create matrix for output. Note that we use seven columns
  Store <- matrix(0, Max.Index,7)
# Iterate over X = Biomass X[1] is zero so skip
  for ( Index in 2 : Max.Index) # Iterate over states of X
{
# For given X call Over.Patches to determine F(x,t) and best patch
  X <- (Index-1)*Xinc + Xcritical
  Temp <- OVER.PATCHES(X, F.vectors, Xcritical, Xmax, Xinc,
  Npatch, Psurvival,Wmax, A, Xegg, Xclutch, P1)
# Extract components. Last row-2 is F(x,t) and dummy variable
# Last row-1 is best clutch and egg size for host type 1
# Last row is best clutch and egg size for host type 2
# Last row is flage indicating multiple equal choices
  n <- nrow(Temp)-4
  F.vectors<- Temp[1:n,] # Extracting F.vectors
# Add the seven output values (omit dummy) to storage
  Store[Index,] <- c(Temp[n+1,1], Temp[n+2,1:2], Temp[n+3,1:2],
  Temp[n+4, 1:2])
} # End of X loop
# Add Store values to end of F.vectors for pass back to main program
  Temp <- cbind(F.vectors, Store) # Combined by columns
  return(Temp) # Return F.vectors and Store
} # End of function
#...................................................................
# MAIN PROGRAM
# Initialize parameters
# Create the state variable (X=reproductive biomass)
  Xmax <- 10; Xcritical <- 0; Xinc <- 1
  Max.Index <- 1 + (Xmax-Xcritical)/Xinc
# Parameter values on the two hosts
  Wmax <- c(10, 20)        # Maximum fitness
```

```
   A <- c(100, 1)          # a coefficients
   Xegg <- c( 2, 1)        # "optimum" egg size
   Xclutch <- c(5, 10)     # "Optimum" clutch size
   P1 <- 0.5               # Probability of host 1
   Psurvival <- 0.90       # Survival probability per time increment
   Npatch <- 2             # Number of patches= hosts
   Horizon <- 10           # Number of time steps
# Set up matrix for fitnesses
# Column 1 is temporary F(x, t+1). Column 2 is F(x, t+1) Both are
  zero
   F.vectors <- matrix(0, Max.Index,2)
# Create matrices for output
   FxtT <- matrix(0,Horizon,Max.Index) # F(x,t)
   Best.Clutch1 <- matrix(0,Horizon,Max.Index) # Best clutch size
                                         for host 1
   Best.Clutch2 <- matrix(0,Horizon,Max.Index) # Best clutch size
                                         for host 2
   Best.Egg1 <- matrix(0,Horizon,Max.Index) # Best egg size for host 1
   Best.Egg2 <- matrix(0,Horizon,Max.Index) # Best egg size for host 2
   Choice.H1 <- matrix(1,Horizon,Max.Index) # 1 or 2 choices for
                                         host type 1
   Choice.H2 <- matrix(1,Horizon,Max.Index) # 1 or 2 choices for
                                         host type 2
# Start iterations
   Time <- Horizon         # Initialize Time
   while ( Time > 1)
{
   Time <- Time - 1        # Decrement Time by 1 unit
# Call OVER.STATES to get best values for this time step
   Temp <- OVER.STATES(F.vectors, Xcritical, Xmax, Xinc, Npatch,
   Psurvival, Max.Index, Wmax, A, Xegg, Xclutch, P1)
# Extract F.vectors
   TempF <- Temp[,1:2]
# Update F1
   for ( J in 2:Max.Index) { F.vectors[J,2] <- TempF[J,1]}
# Store results
   FxtT[Time,]           <- Temp[,3]
   Best.Clutch1[Time,] <- Temp[,4]
   Best.Egg1[Time,]    <- Temp[,5]
   Best.Clutch2[Time,] <- Temp[,6]
   Best.Egg2[Time,]    <- Temp[,7]
   Choice.H1[Time,]    <- Temp[,8]
   Choice.H2[Time,]    <- Temp[,9]
} # End of Time loop
# Output information. For display add states to last row of matrices
```

```
Index <- seq(from=1, to=Max.Index)
FxtT[Horizon,] <- (Index-1)*Xinc+Xcritical
Best.Clutch1[Horizon,] <- (Index-1)*Xinc+Xcritical
Best.Clutch2[Horizon,] <- (Index-1)*Xinc+Xcritical
Best.Egg1[Horizon,] <- (Index-1)*Xinc+Xcritical
Best.Egg2[Horizon,] <- (Index-1)*Xinc+Xcritical
Choice.H1[Horizon,] <- (Index-1)*Xinc+Xcritical
Choice.H2[Horizon,] <- (Index-1)*Xinc+Xcritical
# Print Best clutch, best egg choice flag and decision matrix
Best.Clutch1[,1:Max.Index]        # Best clutch on host 1
Best.Clutch2[,1:Max.Index]        # Best clutch on host 2
signif(Best.Egg1[,1:Max.Index],3) # Best egg on host 1
signif(Best.Egg2[,1:Max.Index],3) # Best egg on host 2
Choice.H1[,1:Max.Index]           # 1=only 1 choice 2 =1+
Choice.H2[,1:Max.Index]           # 1=only 1 choice 2 =1+
signif(FxtT[,1:Max.Index],3)      # Print Fxt of Decision
                                    matrix: 3 sig places
```

OUTPUT:
The optimum egg–clutch size combinations are shown in Table 6.9. Multiple optima occur only at the very lowest value of reproductive biomass. Variation in clutch size is evident across reproductive biomass but not over the time period. Egg size varies primarily with reproductive biomass but not time. When reproductive biomass is relatively low the optimum egg size tends to be larger than the single host optimum (cf. Figure 6.9).

MATLAB CODE: See Section 6.9.8.

6.8 Some exemplary papers

Harris, W. E. and J. R. Lucas. 2002. A state-based model of sperm allocation in a group-breeding salamander. *Behavioral Ecology* **13:705–712.**

Question: How should males of the small-mouthed salamander allocate spermatophores in the face of competitors and a variable number of females?

State variable: Number of spermatophores a male has available at any time during the breeding season. Spermatophore number is set at the start of the breeding season.

Fitness: Maximization of reproductive success = Number of clutches fertilized
Terminal fitness: $F(x, T) = 0$

Forward simulation: Yes

Experimental test: Yes

Table 6.9 Optimal clutch and egg sizes as a function of reproductive biomass and time (bold italic) on the two types of host modeled in Scenario 5

Optimum clutch size on host 1

X=Time	1	2	3	4	5	6	7	8	9	10
1	1	1	2	2	3	3	4	4	4	5
2	1	1	2	2	3	3	4	4	4	5
3	1	1	2	2	3	3	4	4	4	5
4	1	1	2	2	3	3	4	4	4	5
5	1	1	2	2	3	3	4	4	4	5
6	1	1	2	2	3	3	4	4	4	5
7	1	1	2	2	2	3	3	4	4	5
8	1	1	1	2	2	3	3	4	4	5
9	1	1	1	2	2	3	3	4	4	5

Optimum clutch size on host 2

X=Time	1	2	3	4	5	6	7	8	9	10
1	1	1	2	3	4	5	6	6	7	8
2	1	1	2	3	4	5	6	6	7	8
3	1	1	2	3	4	5	6	6	7	8
4	1	1	2	3	4	5	6	6	7	8
5	1	1	2	3	4	5	6	6	7	8
6	1	1	2	3	4	5	6	6	7	8
7	1	1	2	3	4	5	6	6	7	8
8	1	1	2	3	4	5	6	6	7	8
9	1	1	2	3	4	5	6	6	7	8

Optimum egg size on host 1

X=Time	1	2	3	4	5	6	7	8	9	10
1	3	2	1.5	2	1.67	2	1.75	2	2.04	2
2	3	2	1.5	2	1.67	2	1.75	2	2.04	2
3	3	2	1.5	2	1.67	2	1.75	2	2.04	2
4	3	2	1.5	2	1.67	2	1.75	2	2.04	2
5	3	2	1.5	2	1.67	2	1.75	2	2.04	2
6	3	2	1.5	2	1.67	2	1.75	2	2.04	2
7	3	2	1.5	2	2.05	2	2.04	2	2.03	2
8	3	2	2.02	2	2.03	2	2.03	2	2.02	2
9	3	2	2	2	2	2	2	2	2	2

Optimum egg size on host 2

X=Time	1	2	3	4	5	6	7	8	9	10
1	3	2	1.5	1.33	1.25	1.2	1.17	1.33	1.26	1.25
2	3	2	1.5	1.33	1.25	1.2	1.17	1.33	1.26	1.25
3	3	2	1.5	1.33	1.25	1.2	1.17	1.33	1.26	1.25
4	3	2	1.5	1.33	1.25	1.2	1.17	1.33	1.25	1.25
5	3	2	1.5	1.33	1.25	1.2	1.17	1.33	1.25	1.25
6	3	2	1.5	1.33	1.24	1.2	1.17	1.33	1.24	1.25
7	3	2	1.5	1.33	1.2	1.2	1.17	1.33	1.22	1.25
8	3	2	1.45	1.33	1.2	1.2	1.17	1.24	1.16	1.25
9	3	2	1.07	1.2	1.11	1	1	1.11	1.1	1.21

Note: Combinations in which simulation gave more than one optimal choice are shown in bold font.

Peterson, J. H., B. D. Roitberg, and R. C. Ydenberg. 2007. When nesting involves two sequential, mutually exclusive activities: what's a mother to do?. *Evolutionary Ecology Research* **9:1187–1197.**

Question: When should hymenopteran parents stop provisioning the current nest and decide whether to seal the entrance to the nest?

State variables: (a) Current pollen value collected and (b) current nest value

Fitness: Number of copies of alleles passed on (sons are haploid, females diploid).

Terminal fitness: $F(x_1, x_2, T) = 0$

Forward simulation: No

Experimental test: No

Kerkhoff, A. J. 2004. Expectation, explanation and masting. *Evolutionary Ecology Research* **6:1003–1020.**

Question: How should trees allocate energy to growth and reproduction?
State variables: (a) Mass and (b) stored reserves
Fitness: Total lifetime reproductive output
Terminal fitness: $F(x_1, x_2, T) = 0$
Forward simulation: Yes
Experimental test: No

Lessells, C. M. 2005. Why are males bad for females? Models for the evolution of damaging male mating behavior. *American Naturalist* **165:S46–S63.**

Question: Given that a male damages a female during mating, which reduces her survival, what is the optimal female age-specific behavior (mate or do not mate; oviposition rate)?

State variable: Level of damage

Fitness: Lifetime egg production

Terminal fitness: $F(x, T) = 0$

Forward simulation: Yes
Experimental test: No

Weber, T. P., B. J. Ens, and A. I. Houston. 1998. Optimal avian migration: A dynamic model of fuel stores and site use. *Evolutionary Ecology* **12:377–401.**

Question: What is the optimal decision (stay or depart) for a migrating bird at location i at time t?

State variable: Amount of fuel as a percentage of lean body mass

Fitness: Function of amount of fuel at final arrival, $R(x)$, arrival time $K(t)$, and a constant, B

Terminal fitness: $R(x)K(T) + B$

Forward simulation: Yes

Experimental test: No

Galvani, A. and R. Johnstone. 1998. Sperm allocation in an uncertain world. *Behavioral Ecology and Sociobiology* 44:161–168.

Question: What is the optimal allocation of sperm when females of varying quality are encountered at random?

State variable: (*a*) Quantity of sperm and (*b*) female quality

Fitness: Cumulative payoff function that for each allocation decision depends on sperm quantity and female quality

Terminal fitness: $F(x_1, x_2, T) = 0$

Forward simulation: Yes

Experimental test: No

Wajnberg, E., P. Bernhard, F. Hamelin, and G. Boivin. 2006. Optimal patch time allocation for time-limited foragers. *Behavioral Ecology and Sociobiology* 60:1–10.

Question: What is the relationship between patch residence time and age for a parasitoid searching for host on which to oviposit?

State variable: Age

Fitness: Accumulated number of offspring

Terminal fitness: $F(x, T) = 0$

Forward simulation: Yes

Experimental test: Yes

6.9   MATLAB code

6.9.1   An algorithm for constructing the decision matrix

```
Function to calculate fitness when organism is in state X
function W =FITNESS(X, Xcritical, Xmax, Xmin, Cost, Benefit, Pbe-
nefit, Pmortality, F_vectors)
% State in patch if forager finds food
  X_Food = X - Cost + Benefit;
% If X_Food greater than Xmax then X_Food must be set to Xmax
  X_Food = min(X_Food, Xmax);
% If X_Food less than or equal to Xcritical then set to Xcritical
  X_Food = max( X_Food, Xcritical);
% State in patch if forager does not find food
  X_NoFood = X - Cost;
% If X_NoFood is less than Xcritical set X_NoFood to Xcritical
  X_NoFood = max(X_NoFood, Xcritical);
  Term1 = Pbenefit*F_vectors(X_Food,2); % If food is found
  Term2 = (1-Pbenefit)*F_vectors(X_NoFood,2); % If food is not found
  W = (1 - Pmortality)*(Term1 + Term2); % Survival in patch
% End of function
```

```
% .....................................................................
% Function to iterate over patches
function Temp = OVER_PATCHES(X, F_vectors, Xcritical,Xmax, Xmin,
Npatch, Cost, Benefit, Pbenefit, Pmortality)
  RHS = zeros(Npatch); % Pre-allocate matrix for Right Hand Side of
                              equn
  for i = 1: Npatch; % Cycle over patches
% Call Fitness function
  RHS(i) = FITNESS(X, Xcritical, Xmax, Xmin, Cost, Benefit(i),
  Pbenefit(i), Pmortality(i), F_vectors);
end % End of i loop
  % Now find optimal patch C=Highest RHS, I=Row=patch number
  [C,I] = max(RHS);
  F_vectors(X,1) = C(1);
  Best_Patch = I(1);
% Concatenate F(x,t,T) and the optimal patch number
  Temp = [F_vectors(X,1), Best_Patch];
% Add Temp to bottom of F.vectors and rename to Temp
  Temp = vertcat(F_vectors, Temp);
% End of function
% .....................................................................
% Function to iterate over states of X
function  Temp=OVER_STATES(F_vectors, Xcritical, Xmax, Xmin,
Npatch, Cost, Benefit, Pbenefit, Pmortality)
  Store = zeros(Xmax,2); % Create matrix for output
  for X = Xmin : Xmax % Iterate over states of X
% For given X call Over_Patches to determine F(x,t) and best patch
  Temp = OVER_PATCHES(X, F_vectors, Xcritical, Xmax, Xmin,
  Npatch, Cost, Benefit, Pbenefit, Pmortality);
% Extract components_ Last row is F(x,t) and best patch
  n = size(Temp,1)-1;
  F_vectors = Temp(1:n,1:2);
  Store(X,1:2) = Temp(n+1,1:2); % Save F(x,t,T) and best patch
  end % End of X loop
% Add Store values to end of F_vectors for pass back to main program
  Temp = horzcat(F_vectors, Store); % Combined by columns
% End of function
% .....................................................................
% MAIN PROGRAM
% Initialize parameters
  Xmax = 10 ;                    % Maximum value of X
  Xcritical = 3;                 % Value of X at which death occurs
  Xmin = Xcritical+1;            % Smallest value of X allowed
  Cost = 1; % Cost per period
  Pmortality = [0, 0.004, 0.02]; % Probability of mortality
```

```
    Pbenefit = [1, 0.4, 0.6];        % Probability of finding food
    Benefit = [0, 3, 5];             % Benefit if food is discovered
    Npatch = 3;                      % Number of patches
    Horizon = 20;                    % Number of time steps
% Set up matrix for fitnesses
% Column 1 is F(x, t+1)_ Column 2 is F(x, t)
    F_vectors = zeros(Xmax,2);
    F_vectors(Xmin:Xmax,2) = 1;
% Create matrices for output
    FxtT = zeros(Horizon,Xmax);          % F(x,t,T)
    Best_Patch = zeros(Horizon,Xmax); % Best patch number
% Start iterations
    Time = Horizon;                      % Initialize Time
    while ( Time > 1);
    Time = Time -1;                      % Decrement Time by 1 unit
% Call OVER_STATES to get best values for this time step
    Temp = OVER_STATES(F_vectors, Xcritical, Xmax, Xmin, Npatch,
    Cost, Benefit, Pbenefit, Pmortality);
% Extract F_vectors
    TempF = Temp(:,1:2);
% Update F1
    for J = Xmin: Xmax
    F_vectors(J,2) = TempF(J,1);
    end                                  % End of J loop
% Store results
    Best_Patch(Time,:) = Temp(:,4);
    FxtT(Time,:) = Temp(:,3);
    end                                  % End of Time loop
% Output information_ For display add wts to last row of matrices
    X = 1: Xmax;
    Best_Patch(Horizon,:) = X;
    FxtT(Horizon,:) = X;
    Best_Patch(:,Xmin:Xmax)    % Print Decision matrix
    vpa(FxtT(:,Xmin:Xmax),3) % Print Fxt of Decision matrix: 3 sig
    places
```

6.9.2   Using the decision matrix: individual prediction

Because the random number generator is not the same, the output will not be exactly the same as for the R output. As with the R coding the decision matrix is first generated by running the previous program and then the following (do not issue a clear all command):

```
% Initialize parameters
    rand('twister',10);              % Set random number seed
```

```
Xmax                = 10;          % Maximum value of X
Xcritical           = 3;           % Value of X at which death occurs
Xmin                = Xcritical+1; % Smallest value of X allowed
Cost                = 1;           % Cost per period
Pmortality          = [0, 0.004, 0.0]; % Probability of mortality
Pbenefit            = [1, 0.4, 0.6]; % Probability of finding food
Benefit             = [0, 3, 5];   % Benefit if food is discovered
Npatch              = 3;           % Number of patches
Horizon             = 15;          % Number of time steps
Output              = zeros(Horizon,10);% Matrix to hold output
Time                = 1: Horizon;  % Values for x axis in plot
for Replicate       = 1: 10;       % Iterate over 10 replicates
X                   = 4;           % Animal starts in state 4
for i               = 1:Horizon;   % Iterate over time
if(X > Xcritical);                 % Check that animal still alive
Patch               = Best_Patch(i,X); % Select patch
% Check if animal survives predation
% Generate random number
if rand(1) < Pmortality(Patch)
'Dead from predator at Replicate and time = '
[Replicate, i]
end % end if
% Now find new weight
% Set multiplier to zero, which corresponds to no food found
Index                         = 0;
if rand(1) < Pbenefit(Patch)
Index                         = 1; % food is discovered
end % end if
X                             = X - Cost + Benefit(Patch)*Index;
% If X greater than Xmax then X must be set to Xmax
X                             = min(X, Xmax);
% If X less than X then animal dies
if ( X< Xmin)
'Dead from starvation at Replicate and time            ='
[Replicate, i]
end % end if
Output(i,Replicate)                       = Patch; % Store data
end % End of if(X > Xcritical)
end % End of time loop
% subplot divides the current figure into rectangular panes that
are
% numbered row-wise. Each pane contains an axes object.
% Subsequent plots are output to the current pane.
subplot(5,2,Replicate); % Divide graph page into 5x2 panels
plot(Time, Output(:,Replicate))
```

```
xlabel('Time'); ylabel('Patch selected')
axis([0 15 0 4])
end % End of replicate loop
```

6.9.3 Using the decision matrix: expected state

```
% Initialize parameters
  Xmax = 10; % Maximum value of X
  Xcritical = 3; % Value of X at which death occurs
  Xmin = Xcritical+1; % Smallest value of X allowed
  Cost = 1; % Cost per period
  Time = 2; % Current state to be considered
  Pmortality = [0, 0.004, 0.02]; % Probability of mortality
  Pbenefit = [1, 0.4, 0.6]; % Probability of finding food
  Benefit = [0, 3, 5]; % Benefit if food is discovered
% Set transition density matrix to zero
  Trans_density = zeros(Xmax, Xmax);
% Step 1 Cycle over all values of z from Xmin to Xmax
  for z = Xmin : Xmax % Iterate over states
% Select the best patch from the Decision matrix at row Time
  K = Best_Patch(Time,z); % Decision matrix is called Best_Patch
% Calculate w(x,t|z)
% Found food and survives predator
  x = min(z - Cost + Benefit(K), Xmax);
% Assign probability
  Trans_density(z,x) = (1-Pmortality(K))*Pbenefit(K);
% Food not found
  x = z - Cost;
% State exceeds the critical value
  if x > Xcritical
% Animal survives
  Trans_density(z,x) = (1-Pmortality(K))*(1-Pbenefit(K));
% Animal does not survive
  Trans_density(z,Xcritical) = Pmortality(K);
% State is less than critical
  else
  Trans_density(z,Xcritical) = Pmortality(K)+(1-Pmortality(K))
  *(1-Pbenefit(K)); % All one line
  end % End of if
  end % end of z loop
  Trans_density % Write out matrix
```

6.9.4 Scenario 2: Calculating the decision matrix

```
% Function to calculate fitness when organism is in state X
  function W =FITNESS(X, Xcritical, Xmax, Xmin, Cost, Benefit,
  Pbenefit, Pmortality, F_vectors)
% State in patch if forager finds food
  X_Food = X + Benefit; % Eliminate Cost
% If X_Food greater than Xmax then X_Food must be set to Xmax
  X_Food = min(X_Food, Xmax);
% If X_Food less than or equal to Xcritical then set to Xcritical
  X_Food = max( X_Food, Xcritical);
% State in patch if forager does not find food
  X_NoFood = X; % Eliminate Cost
% If X_NoFood is less than Xcritical set X_NoFood to Xcritical
  X_NoFood = max(X_NoFood, Xcritical);
  Term1 = Pbenefit*F_vectors(X_Food,2); % If food is found
  Term2 = (1-Pbenefit)*F_vectors(X_NoFood,2); % If food is not
                                          found
  W = (1 - Pmortality)*(Term1 + Term2); % Survival in patch
% End of function
% .................................................................
% Function to iterate over patches
  function Temp = OVER_PATCHES(X, F_vectors, Xcritical,Xmax,
  Xmin, Npatch, Cost, Benefit, Pbenefit, Pmortality)
  RHS = zeros(Npatch,1); % Pre-allocate matrix for Right Hand Side
                      of eqn
  for i = 1: Npatch; % Cycle over patches
% Call Fitness function
  RHS(i) = FITNESS(X, Xcritical, Xmax, Xmin, Cost, Benefit(i),
  Pbenefit(i), Pmortality(i,X), F_vectors);
  end % End of i loop
% Now find optimal patch C=Highest RHS, I=Row=patch number
  [C,I] = max(RHS);
  F_vectors(X,1) = C;
  Best_Patch = I;
% Concatenate F(x,t) and the optimal patch number
  Temp = [F_vectors(X,1), Best_Patch];
% Add Temp to bottom of F.vectors and rename to Temp
  Temp = vertcat(F_vectors, Temp);
% End of function
% .................................................................
% Function to iterate over states of X
  function Temp=OVER_STATES(F_vectors, Xcritical, Xmax, Xmin,
  Npatch, Cost, Benefit, Pbenefit, Pmortality)
```

These lines remain the same as in the patch-foraging model:

```
% End of function
% ...........................................................................
% MAIN PROGRAM
% Initialize parameters
  Xmax = 7; % Maximum value of X
  Xcritical = 1; % Value of X at which death occurs
  Xmin = Xcritical+1; % Smallest value of X allowed
  Cost = 0; % Not required but kept
% Probability of mortality if foraging
  Pmin = 0;
  Pmax = 0.01;
% Create mortality function. Make Pmin at state 2
% Probability of mortality if not foraging
  Pnoforage = zeros(1,Xmax);
% Foraging mortality
  Pforage = [0, linspace(Pmin, Pmax, Xmax-1)];
  Pmortality = vertcat(Pnoforage,Pforage); % Mortality function
% Probability of foraging
  Pbenefit = [0.4,0.8]; % Probability of "Benefit"
  Benefit = [-1, 1]; % "Benefit"
  Npatch = 2; % Number of patches = resting or foraging
  Horizon = 6; % Number of time steps
% Set up matrix for fitnesses
% Column 1 is F(x, t)_ Column 2 is F(x, t+1)
  F_vectors = zeros(Xmax,2);
  F_vectors(Xmin:Xmax,2) = Xmin:Xmax; % Final wts
% Create matrices for output
  FxtT = zeros(Horizon,Xmax); % F(x,t,T)
  Best_Patch = zeros(Horizon,Xmax); % Best patch number
% Start iterations
  Time = Horizon; % Initialize Time
  while ( Time > 1);
  Time = Time -1; % Decrement Time by 1 unit
% Call OVER_STATES to get best values for this time step
  Temp = OVER_STATES(F_vectors, Xcritical, Xmax, Xmin, Npatch,
  Cost, Benefit, Pbenefit, Pmortality);
% Extract F_vectors
  TempF = Temp(:,1:2);
% Update F1
  for J = Xmin: Xmax
  F_vectors(J,2) = TempF(J,1);
  end % End of J loop
% Store results
```

```
 Best_Patch(Time,:) = Temp(:,4);
 FxtT(Time,:) = Temp(:,3);
 end % End of Time loop
% Output information_ For display add wts to last row of matrices
 X = 1: Xmax;
 Best_Patch(Horizon,:) = X;
 FxtT(Horizon,:) = X;
 Best_Patch(:,Xmin:Xmax) % Print Decision matrix
 vpa(FxtT(:,Xmin:Xmax),3) % Print Fxt of Decision matrix: 3 sig
                           places
```

6.9.5   Scenario 3: Calculating the decision matrix

```
% Function to calculate fitness when organism is in state X
 function W=FITNESS(X, Xcritical, Xmax, Xinc, Cost, Benefit,
 Pbenefit, F_vectors)
% Note that the state value X is passed
% Note also that in this function Benefit and Pbenefit are vectors
% Iterate over the four kill values (0,1,2,3)
 Max_Index = 1+(Xmax-Xcritical)/Xinc; % Get maximum index value
 W = 0; % Set Fitness to zero
 Xstore = X; % Set X to Xstore to preserve value through loop
 for I_Kill = 1:4 % Begin loop
 X = Xstore - Cost + Benefit(I_Kill); % Calculate new state value
% If X greater than Xmax then X must be set to Xmax
 X = min(X, Xmax);
% If X less than or equal to Xcritical then set to Xcritical
 X = max(X, Xcritical);
% Convert to Index value
 Index = 1+(X-Xcritical)/Xinc;
% Index value probably not an integer
% So consider two integer values on either size of X
 Index_lower = floor(Index); % Choose lower integer
 Index_upper = Index_lower + 1; % Upper integer
% Must stop index exceeding Max.Index. Note that Qx=0 in this case
 Index_upper = min(Index_upper, Max_Index);
 Qx = X - Floor(X) % qx for intepolation
 W = W + Pbenefit(I_Kill)*(Qx*F_vectors(Index_upper,2)+(1-Qx)
 *F_vectors(Index_lower,2));
 end % End of I.Kill loop
% End of function ..................................................
% Function to iterate over patches i.e. over PACKS
 function Temp= OVER_PATCHES(X, F_vectors, Xcritical, Xmax,
 Xinc, Npatch, Cost, Benefit, Pbenefit)
```

```
RHS = zeros(Npatch,1); % Set matrix for Right Hand Side of eqn
for i = 1: Npatch % Cycle over patches = pack sizes
% Call Fitness function. Pass Benefit and Pbenefit as vectors
RHS(i) = FITNESS(X, Xcritical, Xmax, Xinc, Cost, Benefit(i,:),
Pbenefit(i,:), F_vectors);
end % End of i loop
% Now find optimal patch Sorted_RHS(1)=Highest RHS, I=Row=patch
number
[Sorted_RHS,I] = sort(RHS, 'descend'); % Sorts into descending
                                col
Index = 1+(X-Xcritical)/Xinc; % Get Index value
F_vectors(Index,1) = Sorted_RHS(1);
Best_Patch = I(1);
% Concatenate F(x,t,T) and the optimal patch number
Temp = [F_vectors(Index,1), Best_Patch];
% Add Temp to bottom of F.vectors and rename to Temp
Temp = vertcat(F_vectors, Temp);
% Create 1x2 vector to hold decision on more than one choice
% We only need one cell but it is convenient to use 2 for concatena-
tion
% onto Temp, as indicated below
Choice =[0,0];
if Sorted_RHS(1)== Sorted_RHS(2) % Equal fitnesses
Choice = [1,1]; % Equal fitnesses
end
Temp = vertcat(Temp, Choice);
% End of function
%.............................................................
% Function to iterate over states of X
function Temp=OVER_STATES(F_vectors, Xcritical, Xmax, Xinc,
Npatch, Cost, Benefit, Pbenefit, Max_Index)
Store = zeros(Max_Index,3); % Create matrix for output
for Index = 2 : Max_Index % Iterate over states of X
% For given X call Over_Patches to determine F(x,t,T) and best patch
X = (Index-1)*Xinc + Xcritical;
Temp = OVER_PATCHES(X, F_vectors, Xcritical, Xmax, Xinc,
Npatch, Cost, Benefit, Pbenefit);
% Extract components_ Penultimate row is F(x,t,T) and best patch
n = size(Temp,1)-2;
F_vectors = Temp(1:n,1:2);
Store(Index,1:2) = Temp(n+1,1:2); % Save F(x,t,T) and best patch
Store(Index,3) = Temp(n+2,1); % Save flag indicating choices
end % End of X loop
% Add Store values to end of F_vectors for pass back to main program
Temp = horzcat(F_vectors, Store); % Combined by columns
```

```
% End of function
%..................................................................
  clear all % Empty workspace
% MAIN PROGRAM
% Initialize parameters
  Xmax = 30; % Maximum value of X = gut capacity
  Xcritical = 0; % Value of X at which death occurs
  Xinc = 1; % Increment in state variable
  Max_Index = 1 + (Xmax-Xcritical)/Xinc; % Maximum index value
  Cost = 6; % Cost = Daily food requirement
  Npatch = 4; % Number of patches= packs
% Calculate benefit as a function of pack size (rows)
% and number of kills (columns)
  Benefit = zeros(4,4); % Rows = pack size, Columns = number of
  kills+1
  Pbenefit = zeros(4,4); % Rows = pack size, Columns = number of
                          kills+1
% Probability of single kill for pack size
  Pi = [0.15, 0.31, 0.33, 0.33];
  Y = 11.25; % Size of single prey
  k = [0,1,2,3]; % Number of kills
  for PackSize = 1:4 % Iterate over pack sizes
% Calculate binomial probabilities using function binopdf
  Pbenefit(PackSize,:) = binopdf(k, 3, Pi(PackSize));
% Calculate benefits = amount per individual
  Benefit(PackSize, 2:4) = Y*k(2:4)/PackSize;
  end % End PackSize loop
  Horizon = 31; % Number of time steps
% Set up matrix for fitnesses
% Column 1 is F(x, t). Column 2 is F(x, t+1)
  F_vectors = zeros(Max_Index,2);
  F_vectors(2:Max_Index,2) = 1; % Cell 1,2 = 0 = Dead
% Create matrices for output
  FxtT = zeros(Horizon,Max_Index); % F(x,t,T)
  Best_Patch = zeros(Horizon,Max_Index); % Best patch number
  CHOICES = zeros(Horizon,Max_Index); % Flag for choices
% Start iterations
  Time = Horizon; % Initialize Time
  while ( Time > 1)
  Time = Time - 1; % Decrement Time by 1 unit
% Call OVER.STATES to get best values for this time step
  Temp = OVER_STATES(F_vectors, Xcritical, Xmax, Xinc, Npatch,
  Cost, Benefit, Pbenefit, Max_Index);
% Extract F.vectors
  TempF = Temp(:,1:2);
```

```
% Update F1
  for J = 2: Max_Index
  F_vectors(J,2) = TempF(J,1);
  end % End J loop
% Store results
  Best_Patch(Time,:) = Temp(:,4);
  FxtT(Time,:) = Temp(:,3);
  CHOICES(Time,:) = Temp(:,5);
  end % End of Time loop
% Output information. For display add states to last row of matrices
% Note that state variable conversion from index value
  Index = 1 :Max_Index;
  Best_Patch(Horizon,:) = (Index-1)*Xinc+Xcritical;
  FxtT(Horizon,:) = (Index-1)*Xinc+Xcritical;
  Best_Patch(:,1:Max_Index)    % Print Decision matrix
  vpa(FxtT(:,1:Max_Index),3) % Print Fxt of Decision matrix: 3 sig
                                places
  CHOICES(:,1:Max_Index)       % Print out matrix for choice flag
  % Plot results
  % Note that the orientation of the plots different from the R plot
  y = Best_Patch(Horizon,2:Max_Index);
  x = 1:Horizon-1 ;
  [xx,yy] = meshgrid(x,y); % Create grid for 3D plot
  subplot(2,2,1);            % 4x4 grid with 3D plot in top left
  surfc(xx, yy, Best_Patch(1:30,2:Max_Index)) % 3D plot
% Add labels
  ylabel('Time'); xlabel('x = Gut contents'); zlabel('Optimal
  Pack size');
  subplot(2,2,2); % 4x4 grid with plot in top right
  image(x,y,Best_Patch(1:30,2:Max_Index)) % Image plot
  xlabel('x = Gut contents'); ylabel('y = Time'); % Labels
  subplot(2,2,3); % 4x4 grid with plot in bottom left
  image(x,y,CHOICES(1:30,2:Max_Index)+1) % image plot of choice
  flag
  colormap(flag); % Set color map
  xlabel('x = Gut contents'); ylabel('Time'); % Labels
```

Interestingly, the MATLAB output gives a different decision for those cases in which there are multiple equivalent choices: this is a result of the sort routines handling ties differently. In those cases in which at least two choices are optimal, the R program specifies a pack size of 2, whereas the MATLAB program specifies a pack size of 1.

6.9.6   Scenario 4: Calculating the decision matrix

Before running the program, make sure that the current directory is set for the place you want the output to go.

```
% Function to iterate over patches i_e_ over Hosts
   function Temp=OVER_PATCHES(X, F_vectors, Xcritical, Xmax,
   Xinc, Npatch, Benefit, Pbenefit, Psurvival)
% Create zeros for storing best clutch size for each host type
   Best_Clutch = zeros(Npatch,1);
   Index = 1 + (X-Xcritical)/Xinc; % Index for X is X+1
% Vector of clutch sizes to Index-1
   Clutch = 1:Index-1;
% Start fitness accumulation with component for case of not finding
a host
   W = Psurvival*(1-sum(Pbenefit))*F_vectors(Index,2);
   for i = 1: Npatch % Cycle over patches = Hosts
   W_partial = Benefit(2:Index,i) + Psurvival*F_vectors(Index-
   Clutch,2);
% Find largest W_partial and hence best clutch size
% Use sort because we need to inspect best two
   [Sorted_Clutch,I] = sort(W_partial, 'descend'); % Sorts into
   descending col
   Best_Clutch(i) = I(1); % Store value of best clutch for host i
% Increment fitness
   W = W + Pbenefit(i)*Sorted_Clutch(1);
% Test for several equal optimal choices
% Only examine W_partial that contain more than one entry
   if length(W_partial) >1 && Sorted_Clutch(1) == Sorted_Clutch(2)
     'Several possible equal choices'
   end % End if construct
   end % End of i loop
     F_vectors(Index,1) = W;     % Update F(x,t,T) ;
% Concatenate F(x,t) and the optimal clutch values for host type 2
   Temp     = [F_vectors(Index,1), Best_Clutch(3)];
% Add Temp to bottom of F_vectors and rename to Temp
   Temp     = vertcat(F_vectors, Temp);
% End of function
%...............................................................
% Function to iterate over states of X
   function Temp =OVER_STATES(F_vectors, Xcritical, Xmax, Xinc,
   Npatch, Benefit, Pbenefit, Psurvival, Max_Index)
     Store = zeros(Max_Index,2); % Create zeros for output
   for Index = 2 : Max_Index % Iterate over states of X
% For given X call Over_Patches to determine F(x,t) and best patch
     X   = (Index-1)*Xinc + Xcritical;
```

```
  Temp  =  OVER_PATCHES(X,  F_vectors,  Xcritical,  Xmax,  Xinc,
  Npatch, Benefit, Pbenefit, Psurvival);
% Extract components_ Last row is F(x,t,T) and best clutch size for
host 2
   n  = size(Temp,1)-1;
  F_vectors = Temp(1:n,:);
    Store(Index,1:2)  = Temp(n+1,1:2);  % Save  F(x,t,T)  and best
    clutch size
  end % End of X loop
% Add Store values to end of F_vectors for pass back to main program
  Temp = horzcat(F_vectors, Store); % Combined by columns
% End of function
%...........................................................................
% MAIN PROGRAM
  clear all
% Initialize parameters
  Xmax      = 40;      % Maximum value of X = eggs
  Xcritical = 0; % Lowest value of X = 0 eggs
  Xinc      = 1;      % Increment in state variable
  Max_Index    = 1 + (Xmax-Xcritical)/Xinc; % Max Index value
  Psurvival    = 0.99;    % Survival probty per time increment
  Npatch = 4; % Number of patches= hosts
% Create host coefficient zeros from which to get Benefits
  Host_coeff     = zeros(4,4);
  Host_coeff(1,1:4) = [-0.2302, 2.7021, -0.2044, 0.0039];
  Host_coeff(2,1:4) = [-0.1444, 2.2997, -0.1170, 0.0013];
  Host_coeff(3,1:4) = [-0.1048, 2.2097, -0.0878, 0.0004222];
  Host_coeff(4,1:4) = [-0.0524, 2.0394, -0.0339, -0.0003111];
% Calculate benefit as a function of
% clutch size (rows) and Host type (columns)
  Clutch  = 0:Xmax;      % Create sequence from 0 to Xmax
  Max      = Xmax+1;      % Number of rows
  Benefit = zeros(Xmax+1, 4); % Zero to Xmax
  for I_Host = 1:4 % Iterate over host types
  for I_Clutch = 1:Max
  Benefit(I_Clutch,I_Host) = Host_coeff(I_Host,1) + Host_coeff
  (I_Host,2)*Clutch(I_Clutch)  +  Host_coeff(I_Host,3)*Clutch
  (I_Clutch)^2 + Host_coeff(I_Host,4)*Clutch(I_Clutch)^3;
  end % end clutch loop
  end % End Benefit loop
  Benefit(1,:)    = 0; % Reset first row to zero
  SHM=[9,12,14,23]; % Set single host maximum_ See text for derivation
% Make all values > than SHM=0_ Note that we use 2 because of zero
class
  for i = 1:4
```

```
      Benefit((SHM(i)+2):Max_Index,i) = 0;
      end % End I loop
% Probability of encountering host type
   Pbenefit    = [0.05, 0.05, 0.1, 0.8];
   Horizon    = 21;             % Number of time steps
% Set up zeros for fitnesses
% Column 1 is F(x, t)_ Column 2 is F(x, t+1) Both are zero
   F_vectors = zeros(Max_Index,2) ;
% Create matrices for output
   FxtT = zeros(Horizon,Max_Index) ; % F(x,t)
% Best clutch size for host 2
   Best_Patch = zeros(Horizon,Max_Index);
% Start iterations
   Time   = Horizon;        % Initialize Time
   while ( Time > 1)
   Time   = Time -1;        % Decrement Time by 1 unit
% Call OVER_STATES to get best values for this time step
   Temp = OVER_STATES(F_vectors, Xcritical, Xmax, Xinc, Npatch,
   Benefit, Pbenefit, Psurvival, Max_Index);
% Extract F_vectors
   TempF   = Temp(:,1:2);
% Update F1
   for J = 2: Max_Index
   F_vectors(J,2) = TempF(J,1);
   end % End of J loop
% Store results
   Best_Patch(Time,1:Max_Index)  = Temp(:,4);
   FxtT(Time,:)       = Temp(:,3);
   end % End of Time loop
% Output information_ For display add states to last row of matrices
   Index  = 1:Max_Index;
   Best_Patch(Horizon,:) = (Index-1)*Xinc+Xcritical;
   FxtT(Horizon,:)    = (Index-1)*Xinc+Xcritical;
   Best_Patch(:,1:Max_Index)  % Print Decision zeros
   vpa(FxtT(:,1:Max_Index),3)% Print Fxt of Decision zeros: 3 sig
places
   x    = Best_Patch(Horizon,2:Max_Index);
   y = 1:Horizon-1 ;
   [xx,yy] = meshgrid(x,y); % Create grid for 3D plot
   subplot(2,2,1); % Divide page into four an plot in top left
   surfc(xx, yy, Best_Patch(1:20,2:Max_Index)) % 3D plot
% Add labels
   ylabel('Time'); xlabel('x = Eggs'); zlabel('Optimal Clutch
   size');
   subplot(2,2,2) ; % 4x4 grid with plot in top right
```

```
   image(x,y,Best_Patch(1:20,2:Max_Index)) % Image plot
   xlabel('x = Eggs');ylabel=('Time'); % labels
   colormap(flag); % Set color map
% Get components of Decision matrix for saving
   Data =Best_Patch(1:Horizon-1,2:41);
   save oviposition.txt Data -ASCII    % Save to text file
```

6.9.7 Scenario 4: Using the decision matrix: individual prediction

```
clear all; % Remove all objects from memory
   Xmax = 40;    % Maximum value of X = eggs
   load DM1.txt    % Cols = x rows=time
   load DM2.txt
   load DM3.txt
   load DM4.txt
% Create an array for Decision matrix
   DM = zeros(20,Xmax,4); % time, state, host
for i = 1:20
for j = 1:Xmax
   DM(i,j,1) = DM1(i,j); DM(i,j,2) = DM2(i,j);
   DM(i,j,3) = DM3(i,j);DM(i,j,4) = DM4(i,j);
end % end i loop
end % end j loop
% Probability of encountering host type
   Pbenefit   = [0.05, 0.05, 0.1, 0.8];
   Times      = [5,5,10,80];
% Create Vector for Host type probability
   Host_Type  =    vertcat(ones(Times(1),1),2*ones(Times(2),1),
3*ones(Times(3),1), 4*ones(Times(4),1));
   Psurvival  = 0.99;   % Survival probability per time increment
   Horizon    = 10;      % Number of time steps
   rand('twister',10)    % Initialise random number generator
   N_Ind   = 1000;    % Number of individuals
   Output  = zeros(N_Ind,Horizon,1);% Allocate space for output
% Generate initial values of x from normal distribution
x_init = ceil(random('Normal', 20,5, N_Ind,1));
for Ind = 1:N_Ind    % Iterate over individuals
% Generate vectors for choosing the Host type and probability of
survival
   Host     = ceil(100*rand(Horizon,1)); % Vector of host types
   Survival = rand(Horizon,1); % Vector of survival probabilities
% Set all values of Survival > Psurvival = 0
   Survival(Survival>Psurvival) = 0;
   Survival(Survival~=0) = 1; % Set all other values to 1
```

```
x      = x_init(Ind);     % Initial value of x
for Time = 1:Horizon % Iterate over time periods
if(x>0) % If eggs remaining calculate clutch size using DM
  Clutch_Size    = DM(Time,x,Host_Type(Host(Time)));
  Output(Ind,Time) = Clutch_Size;    % Store clutch size
  x      = x-Clutch_Size; % Compute new value of x
end % End of if
  x = x*Survival(Time);     % Set x=0 if female does not survive
end % end of Time loop
end % End of Ind loop
% Iterate over time and plot bar graphs of clutch size
% Set up vector to plot by columns
  Plot_position = [1,3,5,7,9,2,4,6,8,10];
  Mean_Clutch = zeros(10,2); % Allocate space for mean clutch size
  for i = 1:10
% Set graphics page to 5 rows and 2 columns
subplot(5,2,Plot_position(i))
Data = Output(:,i); Data = Data(Data>0);% Eliminate zeroes
xbar = mean(Data);     % Mean clutch size
Mean_Clutch(i,:)=[i, mean(Data)]; % Time, Output mean clutch size
Data = tabulate(Data);     % Tabulate data
bar(Data(:,1), Data(:,2))    % Draw bar plots
xlabel('Clutch size') % X label
end                    % end of i loop
Mean_Clutch       % Output data
```

6.9.8   Scenario 5: Calculating the decision matrix

```
function W=FITNESS( Egg, Clutch, X, F_vectors, Xcritical, Xmax,
Xinc, Psurvival, Wmax, A, Xegg, Xclutch, Ith_Patch)
W            = 0;     % Set fitness to zero
Biomass = Clutch*Egg; % Biomass of clutch/Egg size combination
if( Biomass < X)       % Continue only if Biomass < X
Max_Index = 1 + (Xmax-Xcritical)/Xinc; % Get maximum index value
% Index value for biomass
  Index        = 1+(Biomass-Xcritical)/Xinc;
% Get fitness at lower and upper integer value of Biomass
  Index_lower    = floor(Index);
  Index_upper    = Index_lower + 1;
% Must stop index exceeding Max_Index_ Note that Qx = 0 in this case
  Index_upper    = min(Index_upper, Max_Index);
  Qx            = Biomass - floor(Biomass);
  Fxt_lower    = F_vectors(Index_lower,2);
% Get fitness at upper integer value
```

```
  Fxt_upper       = F_vectors(Index_upper,2);
  Fxt_interpolated = Qx*Fxt_upper + (1-Qx)*Fxt_lower; % Iterpo-
  lated value
% Calculate the fitness for this particular egg-clutch size combi-
nation
  W = Wmax(Ith_Patch)-sqrt(A(1)*(Egg-Xegg(Ith_Patch))^2 + A(2)*
(Clutch-Xclutch(Ith_Patch))^2);
  W = max(0, W); % Set to zero if negative
  W = W + Psurvival*Fxt_interpolated; % Fitness
  W = max(0, W); % Set to zero if negative
end % End of if
  W = -W; % Make Fitness negative for fminbnd function
% _____

  function Temp=OVER_PATCHES(X, F_vectors, Xcritical, Xmax,
  Xinc, Npatch, Psurvival, Wmax, A, Xegg, Xclutch,P1)
% Function to iterate over patches i_e_ over Hosts
  Index       = 1+(X-Xcritical)/Xinc;
% Allocate storage of best combinations for each patch
% Columns will contain
% Fitness, Clutch, Egg
  Choice_Flag = zeros(2,1);  % Store information on number of
                              choices
  Best_in_Patch = zeros(2,3); % Allocate storage for Best Decision
% Iterate over patches
  for Ith_Patch = 1:Npatch % Iterate over the two hosts (= patches)
% Make a matrix called W_host with the following 3 columns:
% Fitness, Egg size, Clutch size
  W_host      = zeros(11,3);
  for Clutch = 1:11 % Iterate over clutch size
  W_host(Clutch,2) = Clutch;      % Store clutch size
% Call fminbnd to find best egg size Note that this is finding a
minimum
  x = fminbnd(@(x) FITNESS(x,Clutch, X,F_vectors, Xcritical,
  Xmax, Xinc, Psurvival, Wmax, A, Xegg, Xclutch,Ith_Patch),0.01,3);
  W_host(Clutch,1) = -FITNESS(x,Clutch, X,F_vectors, Xcritical,
  Xmax, Xinc, Psurvival, Wmax, A, Xegg, Xclutch,Ith_Patch); %Fitness
W_host(Clutch,3) = x;       % Egg size
end % End of clutch size loop
% Get best combination for this host
% Use sort because we need to inspect best two
R       = W_host(:,1);
  [Sorted_W_host,I]=sort(R, 'descend'); %Sorts into descending col
  Best_in_Patch(Ith_Patch,:) = W_host(I(1),:);  % Store best
  choice
% Test for several equal optimal choices
```

```
  if(W_host(I(1),1)==W_host(I(2),1))
  Choice_Flag(Ith_Patch) = 2;
  end % end if
  end % Next host
% Overall fitness
  W  = P1*Best_in_Patch(1,1) +(1-P1)*Best_in_Patch(2,1);
  F_vectors(Index,1)= W ;        % Update F(x,t,T)
% Concatenate F(x,t) and the optimal egg and clutch values for both
hosts
% We add to the bottom of the two column matrix F_vectors the follow-
ing
% F_vectors(Index,1), 1 The second entry is simply a dummy variable
% Best_in_Patch(1,2) Best_in_Patch(1,3) % Host 1 Egg size Clutch
size
% Best_in_Patch(2,2) Best_in_Patch(2,3) % Host 2 Egg size Clutch
size
% Choice_Flag(1:2)            % Flag for multiple optima
  Temp1    = horzcat(F_vectors(Index,1), 1);
  Temp2    = horzcat( Best_in_Patch(1,2), Best_in_Patch(1,3));
  Temp3    = horzcat( Best_in_Patch(2,2), Best_in_Patch(2,3));
% Add Temp1, Temp2, Temp3 & Choice to bottom of F_vectors and rename
to Temp
  Choice   = Choice_Flag' % Convert into column matrix
  Temp = vertcat(F_vectors, Temp1, Temp2, Temp3, Choice);
% End of function
%──────────────────────────────────────────────
  function Temp=OVER_STATES(F_vectors, Xcritical, Xmax, Xinc,
  Npatch, Psurvival, Max_Index, Wmax, A, Xegg, Xclutch, P1)
% Function to iterate over states of X
% Create matrix for output. Note that we use seven columns
  Store    = zeros(Max_Index,7);
% Iterate over X = Biomass X(1) is zero so skip
  for Index = 2 : Max_Index % Iterate over states of X
% For given X call Over_Patches to determine F(x,t) and best patch
  X   = (Index-1)*Xinc + Xcritical;
  Temp   = OVER_PATCHES(X, F_vectors, Xcritical, Xmax, Xinc,
  Npatch, Psurvival,Wmax, A, Xegg, Xclutch, P1);
% Extract components_ Last row-2 is F(x,t) and dummy variable
% Last row-1 is best clutch and egg size for host type 1
% Last row is best clutch and egg size for host type 2
% Last row is flage indicating multiple equal choices
  n    = size(Temp,1)-4;
  F_vectors = Temp(1:n,:);    % Extracting F_vectors
% Add the seven output values (omit dummy) to storage
```

```
    Store(Index,:)  =  horzcat(Temp(n+1,1),  Temp(n+2,1:2),  Temp
    (n+3,1:2), Temp(n+4, 1:2));
end % End of X loop
% Add Store values to end of F_vectors for pass back to main program
    Temp      = horzcat(F_vectors, Store); % Combined by columns
% End of function
%─────────────────────────────────────────────────────
% MAIN PROGRAM
    clear all       % Remove all objects from memory
% Initialize parameters
% Create the state variable (X=reproductive biomass)
    Xmax          = 10; Xcritical = 0; Xinc = 1;
    Max_Index     = 1 + (Xmax-Xcritical)/Xinc;
% Parameter values on the two hosts
    Wmax      = [10, 20]; % Maximum fitness
    A         = [100, 1]; % a coefficients
    Xegg      = [2, 1]; % "optimum" egg size
    Xclutch   = [5, 10]; % "Optimum" clutch size
    P1        = 0.5;    % Probability of host 1
    Psurvival= 0.90;   % Survival probability per time increment
    Npatch    = 2;      % Number of patches= hosts
    Horizon   = 10;     % Number of time steps
% Set up matrix for fitnesses
% Column 1 is temporary F(x, t)_ Column 2 is F(x, t+1) Both are zero
    F_vectors    = zeros(Max_Index,2) ;
% Create matrices for output
    FxtT        = zeros(Horizon,Max_Index);% F(x,t)
    Best_Clutch1 = zeros(Horizon,Max_Index);% Best clutch size
                                             for host 1
    Best_Clutch2 = zeros(Horizon,Max_Index);% Best clutch size for
                                             host 2
    Best_Egg1    = zeros(Horizon,Max_Index);% Best egg size for
                                             host 1
    Best_Egg2    = zeros(Horizon,Max_Index);% Best egg size for
                                             host 2
    Choice_H1    = ones(Horizon,Max_Index);% 1 or 2 choices for host
                                             type 1
    Choice_H2    = ones(Horizon,Max_Index);% 1 or 2 choices for host
                                             type 2
% Start iterations
    Time      = Horizon;        % Initialize Time
    while ( Time > 1)
    Time     = Time - 1;     % Decrement Time by 1 unit
% Call OVER_STATES to get best values for this time step
```

```
Temp      = OVER_STATES (F_vectors, Xcritical, Xmax, Xinc, Npatch,
Psurvival, Max_Index, Wmax, A, Xegg, Xclutch, P1);
% Extract F_vectors
  TempF    = Temp(:,1:2);
% Update F1
  for J            = 2: Max_Index
  F_vectors(J,2) = TempF(J,1);
end % end j loop
% Store results
  FxtT(Time,:)                  = Temp(:,3);
  Best_Clutch1(Time,:)          = Temp(:,4);
  Best_Egg1(Time,:)             = Temp(:,5);
  Best_Clutch2(Time,:)          = Temp(:,6);
  Best_Egg2(Time,:)             = Temp(:,7);
  Choice_H1(Time,:)             = Temp(:,8);
  Choice_H2(Time,:)             = Temp(:,9);
end % End of Time loop
% Output information_ For display add states to last row of matrices
  Index                    = 1:Max_Index;
  FxtT(Horizon,:)          = (Index-1)*Xinc+Xcritical;
  Best_Clutch1(Horizon,:) = (Index-1)*Xinc+Xcritical;
  Best_Clutch2(Horizon,:) = (Index-1)*Xinc+Xcritical;
  Best_Egg1(Horizon,:)     = (Index-1)*Xinc+Xcritical;
  Best_Egg2(Horizon,:)     = (Index-1)*Xinc+Xcritical;
  Choice_H1(Horizon,:)     = (Index-1)*Xinc+Xcritical;
  Choice_H2(Horizon,:)     = (Index-1)*Xinc+Xcritical;
% Print Best clutch, best egg choice flag and decision matrix
  Best_Clutch1(:,1:Max_Index)      % Best clutch on host 1
  Best_Clutch2(:,1:Max_Index)      % Best clutch on host 2
  vpa(Best_Egg1(:,1:Max_Index),3)   % Best egg on host 1
  vpa(Best_Egg2(:,1:Max_Index),3)   % Best egg on host 2
  Choice_H1(:,1:Max_Index)    % 1=only 1 choice 2 =1+
  Choice_H2(:,1:Max_Index)    % 1=only 1 choice 2 =1+
  vpa(FxtT(:,1:Max_Index),3)% Print Fxt of Decision matrix: 3 sig
  places
```

Appendix 1

R functions used in this book with equivalent MATLAB codes where applicable.
Except for the first four rows, rows are arranged in alphabetical order of the R code
(na = not applicable for this book).

R	MATLAB	Operation
# Comment	% Comment	Comment
<-	=	Assigns variable
X%*%Y	X*Y	Matrix multiplication of X and Y
X*Y	X.*Y	Element by element multiplication
abs(X)	abs(X)	Absolute value of X
adapt	dblquad	Multidimensional integration
apply	use loop construct	Applies function to rows, cols or both
as.numeric(X)	na	Make X numeric
barplot(....)	bar(...)	Make a bar plot
Best <- X[Y[1]]	Best=X(I(1))	
cbind	horzcat	Bind columns
ceiling(X)	ceil(X)	Nearest larger integer
contour.(x, y, z. matrix)	contour(x, y, zmatrix)	Contour plot
contourLines	na	Set of x, y coordinates for user-specified contour lines
cor(X,Y)		Correlation between X and Y
c(x1, x2, x3...xn)	[x1, x2, x3.....xn]	Concatenate into a vector
data.frame	na	Matrix that can take variables of mixed type
dbinom(x=k, size=3, prob=Pi (PackSize))	binopdf(k, 3, Pi (PackSize))	Binomial distribution
deriv	diff	Derivative

(continued)

R	MATLAB	Operation
diag(X)	diag(X,0)	Diagonal elements of matrix X
dnorm(x=, mean=, sd=)	normpdf(x, mu, sd)	Density at x of the normal distribution
eigen(X)	eig	Eigen values and other stats of X
exp(x)	exp(x)	e^x
expand.grid(X,Y)	meshgrid	Matrix of all combinations of X and Y
floor(X)	floor(X)	Integer part of X
for (i in 1:n) { lines of coding}	for i = 1:n lines of coding end	Loop
FUNCTION NAME <- function(Input parameters) { Lines of code Return output parameters(s) }	function Output =FUNCTION NAME (Input parameters) Last line gives output parameters	Function definition
X <- FUNCTION NAME (input parameters)	X = FUNCTION NAME (Input parameters)	Function call
hist(X)	hist(X)	Histogram of X
if (X > Y) { Lines of coding }	if X>y Lines of coding end	If construct
if (X > Y) { Lines of coding} } else{ Lines of coding } Lines of coding}	if X > Y Lines of coding end else lines of coding end	If else construct
integrate	int, quad	Integration
length(X)	length(X)	Number of elelments in X
lines(x,y, optional parameters)	plot	Plot a line on an existing plot
lm(y~x)	na	Linear regression of y on x

log(X)	log(X)	Natural log of X
matrix(0,n)	zeros(n)	Column matrix of n zeros
matrix(0,n1,n2)	zeros(n1,n2)	n1 x n2 matrix of zeros
max(X)	max(X)	Maximum of values in X
mean(X)	mean(X)	Mean of values in X
min(X)	min(X)	Minimum of values in X
mvrnorm(n=, mu=, Sigma=)	mvnrnd(MU,SIGMA)	Random multivariate normal deviates
nlm, optimize	fminsearch, fminbnd	Non-linear optimization
ncol(X)	size(X,2)	Nos of columns in X
nrow(X)	size(X,1)	Nos of rows in X
order(X)	[C,I]=max(X)	Get indexes of X that indicate sort structure
outer(x, y, FUNC=)	na	All combinations of x and y applying FUNC=function
par(mfcol=c(1,2))	subplot(2,1,1)	Divide graphics page in two
par(mfrow=c(2,2))	subplot(2,2,2)	ivide graphics page into quadrats
persp(x, y, z. matrix)	surfc(x, y, zmatrix)	3D plot
plot(x,y, optional parameters)	plot, ezplot, fplot	2D plot
pnorm(x, mean=, sd=)	1-normcdf(X,mu, sigma)	Integral from x to infinity of normal distribution
points(x, y)	hold on plot(x,y,´:´)	Plot points on an existing plot
print(X)	X	Print X
print(c(x1, x2, x3))	[x1, x2, x3]	Print x1, x2, x3
qnorm(P, mean=, sd=)	na	normal distribution function
read.table (file="Filename. txt")	load Filename.txt	Read data from text file

(continued)

R	MATLAB	Operation
rep(x, times=)	na	Replicate x for times=
rbind	vertcat	Bind rows
rm(list=ls())	clear all	Clears workspace
rnorm(n, mean=, sd=)	na	Random normal deviates
rowSums(X)	na	Row sums of X
round(X)	round(X)	Round X to nearest integer
rpois(n=, lambda=)	na	Random deviate from a Poisson distribution
runif(n, min=X1, max=X2)	X1 + (X2−X1)*rand(n,1)	n uniform random numbers between X1 and X2
sample(x=, size=, replace=)	na	Random sample from X
sd(X)		Standard deviation of X
setwd("C:/……")	set directory in gui	Set path for output
set.seed(x)	rand('twister', x)	Set seed for random number
seq(from=x1, to=x2, length=n)	linspace(x1, x2, n)	Sequence generator
seq(from=x1, to=x2, 1)	x1:x2	Sequence generator
smooth.spline	na	Fits a cubic smoothing spline to the supplied data
solve(X)		Invert matrix X
sqrt(X)	sqrt(X)	Square-root of X
sum	symsum	Sum X
summary(X)	na	Summary statistics of X
table(X)	na	Tabulate X
t(X)	na	Transpose X
t.test(X, optional parameters)	na	t test
uniroot	fzero, solve	Find root
unlist(X)	na	reduce to a vector of atomic components of x

var(X)	na	Variance of X
while (Condition) { Lines of coding }	while (Condition) Lines of coding end	While loop
write(X, file="filename. txt")	save Filename.txt	Write to text file See setwd

Appendix 2

2.1 Brief review of differentiation

The calculus is particularly important for "Fisherian" optimality analysis, but it can also occur in other methods. While ways can be found to do most problems without the calculus, it is generally true that if the problem lends itself to the calculus it will be the most efficient approach. Both R and MATLAB have differentiation routines (see Chapter 2) but these can be frequently rather clumsy, particularly if one is searching for a symbolic solution. The following is an overview of the rules of differentiation that are likely to be used in the types of analyses presented in this book.

2.1.1 Differentiation of a sum of functions

$y = f(x) + g(x)$

$$\frac{dy}{dx} = \frac{df(x)}{dx} + \frac{dg(x)}{dx}$$

Examples:

1. $y = ax^2 + bx^3$

    $\dfrac{dy}{dx} = 2ax + 3bx^2$

2. $y = ax^n + be^{-cx}$

    $\dfrac{dy}{dx} = nax^{n-1} - bce^{-cx}$

2.1.2 The chain rule

An equation such as $y = (x^5 + 4)^3$ can be represented as two functions of x: $g(x) = x^5 + 4$ and $u = g(x)^3$. The derivative of y with respect to x can be obtained from the chain rule

$$\frac{dy}{dx} = \frac{dy}{du} \cdot \frac{du}{dx}$$

Examples:

1. $y = (x^5 + 4)^3$

    $u = (x^5 + 4)$

    $y = u^3$

    $\dfrac{dy}{du} = 3u^2 \quad \dfrac{du}{dx} = 5x^4$

    $\dfrac{dy}{dx} = (3u^2)(5x^4) = [3(x^5 + 4)^2](5x^4) = 15x^4(x^5 + 4^2)$

2. $y = (1 - e^{-kx})^2$

    $u = 1 - e^{-kx}$

    $y = u^2$

    $\dfrac{dy}{du} = 2u \quad \dfrac{du}{dx} = ke^{-kx}$

    $\dfrac{dy}{dx} = (2u)(ke^{-kx}) = 2(1 - e^{-kx})ke^{-kx}$

2.1.3   Differentiation of the product of functions

$$y = f(x)g(x)$$
$$\dfrac{dy}{dx} = f(x)\dfrac{dg(x)}{dx} + g(x)\dfrac{df(x)}{dx}$$

Examples:

1. $y = e^{bx}(1 - e^{-kx})$

    $f(x) = e^{bx} \text{ and } g(x) = (1 - e^{-kx})$

    $\dfrac{dy}{dx} = e^{bx}ke^{-kx} + (1 - e^{-kx})be^{bx}$

2. $y = ax^2\ln(x)$

    $f(x) = ax^2 \text{ and } g(x) = \ln(x)$

    $\dfrac{dy}{dx} = ax^2\dfrac{1}{x} + \ln(x)2x$

2.1.4   Differentiation of quotients

Done using the previous two rules. For example, suppose we have

$$y = \dfrac{f(x)}{g(x)}$$

then we write y as

$$y = f(x)g(x)^{-1} = f(x)u^{-1} \quad \text{where } u = g(x)$$

From the previous two rules we have

$$\frac{dy}{dx} = f(x)\left(-u^{-2}\frac{du}{dx}\right) + g(x)^{-1}\frac{df(x)}{dx}$$

Given that $\dfrac{du}{dx} = \dfrac{dg(x)}{dx}$ we can expand the above equation to

$$\frac{dy}{dx} = f(x)\left[-g(x)^{-2}\frac{dg(x)}{dx}\right] + g(x)^{-1}\frac{df(x)}{dx}$$

Examples:

1. $y = \dfrac{x^2}{1 + x^2}$

$$= x^2(1 + x^2)^{-1} \quad \text{where} \quad f(x) = x^2 \quad g(x) = 1 + x^2$$

$$\frac{dy}{dx} = x^2[-(1 + x^2)^{-2}2x] + (1 + x^2)^{-1}2x$$

$$= \frac{-2x^3 + (1 + x^2)2x}{(1 + x^2)^2} = \frac{1}{(1 + x^2)^2}$$

2. $y = \dfrac{ax^n}{1 - e^{-kx}}$

$$= ax^n(1 - e^{-kx})^{-1} \quad \text{where } f(x) = ax^n \text{ and } g(x) = 1 - e^{-kx}$$

$$\frac{dy}{dx} = ax^n[-(1 - e^{-kx})^{-2}ke^{-kx}] + (1 - e^{-kx})^{-1}nax^{n-1}$$

$$= \left[\frac{ax^n}{(1 - e^{-kx})^2}\right][-ke^{-kx} + (1 - e^{-kx})nx^{-1}]$$

2.1.5   Implicit differentiation

If the relationship between x and y is of the form $h(y) = f(x)$, where f and h denote functions and the equation cannot be converted into a form $y =$ some function of x, then implicit differentiation must be employed: For example, the equation $2y^3 + y^2 - 1 = x^5 + 3x$ cannot be so converted. Making use of the chain rule we can write

$$\frac{dy}{dx} \cdot \frac{dh(y)}{dy} = \frac{df(x)}{dx}$$

Hence

$$\frac{dy}{dx} = \left[\frac{dh(y)}{dy}\right]^{-1}\frac{df(x)}{dx}$$

Examples:

1. $2y^3 + y^2 - 1 = x^5 + 3x$

   $h(y) = 2y^3 + y^2 - 1 \quad f(x) = x^5 + 3x$

   $\dfrac{dh(y)}{dy} = 6y^2 + 2y \quad \dfrac{df(x)}{dx} = 5x^4 + 3$

   $\dfrac{dy}{dx} = \dfrac{5x^4 + 3}{6y^2 + y}$

2. $e^{ay} + y = \ln x + x^2$

   $h(y) = e^{ay} + y \quad f(x) = \ln x + x^2$

   $\dfrac{dh(y)}{dy} = ae^{ay} \quad \dfrac{df(x)}{dx} = \dfrac{1}{x} + 2x$

   $\dfrac{dy}{dx} = \dfrac{x^{-1} + 2x}{ae^{ay}}$

2.1.6 Putting it all together

The use of the above rules can be illustrated by the analysis of the optimal age of maturation in fish given in Roff (1984b; see also Roff [2002]). The assumptions of this model are

1. Growth can be described by the von Bertalanffy function:

$$L(x) = L_\infty(1 - e^{-kx})$$

where $L(x)$ is the length at age x and L_∞ and k are parameters.

2. Fecundity is proportional to the cube of length.

3. Assuming an equal sex ratio the number of female births at age x, $m(x)$, is

$$m(x) = c[L_\infty(1 - e^{-kx})]^3$$

where c is a species- or population-specific constant.

4. Mortality can be divided into two components: an "instantaneous" egg and larval mortality (i.e., this period is very short compared to the rest of the life and hence can be assumed to be a point event in time) and a subsequent constant instantaneous mortality rate. Thus the proportion surviving to adult age x is

$$l(x) = pe^{-Mx}$$

where p is the proportion surviving the egg–larval period and M is the mortality rate thereafter.

5. Fitness is measured by the Malthusian parameter r, which for a semelparous life history is given by (Roff 1992)

$$r = \frac{\ln l(\alpha)m(\alpha)}{\alpha}$$

where α is the age at reproduction. For the present model we thus have

$$r = \frac{\ln\{pe^{-M\alpha}c[L_\infty(1-e^{-k\alpha})]^3\}}{\alpha} = \frac{\ln pcL_\infty^3 - M\alpha + 3\ln(1-e^{-k\alpha})}{\alpha}$$

To differentiate the above, for convenience, we divide the equation into three components:

$$r = \frac{\ln pcL_\infty^3}{\alpha} - M + \frac{3\ln(1-e^{-k\alpha})}{\alpha} = f(\alpha) + g(\alpha) + h(\alpha)$$

$$\frac{df(\alpha)}{d\alpha} = -\alpha^2, \frac{dg(\alpha)}{d\alpha} = 0, \frac{dh(\alpha)}{d\alpha} = -\alpha^{-2}3\ln(1-e^{-k\alpha}) + 3ke^{-k\alpha}(1-e^{-k\alpha})^{-1}\alpha^{-1}$$

$$\frac{dr}{d\alpha} = -\frac{1}{\alpha^2} - \frac{3ke^{-k\alpha}}{\alpha(1-e^{-k\alpha})}$$

The value at which $\frac{dr}{d\alpha} = 0$ can be found numerically, using the methods described in Chapter 2.

To illustrate the use of implicit differentiation in addition to the other rules we make two changes in the model: (a) the life history is iteroparous, with α being the age at first reproduction and (b) growth ceases at α. The characteristic equation is

$$\sum_{x=\alpha}^{\infty} pe^{-Mx}cL_\infty^3(1-e^{-k\alpha})^3 = 1$$

The above construct is a geometric series (see Section 2.5.4), which can be solved to give

$$\frac{e^{-\alpha(r+M)}(1-e^{-k\alpha})^3 cL_\infty^3}{1-e^{-(r+M)}} = 1$$

For convenience we take logs to make an additive equation

$$\alpha r + \alpha M - 3\ln(1-e^{-k\alpha}) - \ln cL_\infty^3 + \ln[1-e^{-(r+M)}] = 0$$

Differentiating term by term
αr: This requires implicit differentiation

$$\frac{dr}{d\alpha} = r + \alpha\frac{dr}{d\alpha}$$

αM: This is simply

$$\frac{dr}{d\alpha} = M$$

$3\ln(1-e^{-k\alpha})$: Using the chain rule gives

$$\frac{dr}{d\alpha} = \frac{3ke^{-k\alpha}}{1-e^{-k\alpha}}$$

$\ln cL_\infty^3$:

$$\frac{dr}{d\alpha} = 0$$

$\ln[1-e^{-(r+M)}]$: Using implicit differentiation

$$\frac{dr}{d\alpha} = \frac{e^{-(r+M)}}{1 - e^{-(r+M)}}\frac{dr}{d\alpha}$$

Thus we have

$$r + \alpha\frac{dr}{d\alpha} + M - \frac{3ke^{-k\alpha}}{1 - e^{-k\alpha}} - 0 + \frac{e^{-(r+M)}}{1 - e^{-(r+M)}}\frac{dr}{d\alpha} = 0$$

Rearranging

$$\frac{dr}{d\alpha}\left[\alpha + \frac{e^{-(r+M)}}{1 - e^{-(r+M)}}\right] = \frac{3ke^{-k\alpha}}{1 - e^{-k\alpha}} - r - M$$

Provided the term in the parentheses on the left-hand side of the equation is not zero

$$\frac{dr}{d\alpha} = 0 \quad \text{when} \quad \frac{3ke^{-k\alpha}}{1 - e^{-k\alpha}} - r - M = 0$$

$$\text{i.e.,} \quad r = \frac{3ke^{-k\alpha}}{1 - e^{-k\alpha}} - M$$

We now have the optimum age at first reproduction, α, as a function of r. To find the optimum α we insert the function of r back into the original equation, or its log transform (which is more convenient):

$$\alpha G - 3\ln(1 - e^{-k\alpha}) - \ln L_\infty^3 + \ln(1 - e^{-G})$$

$$\text{where} \quad G = \frac{3ke^{-k\alpha}}{1 - e^{-k\alpha}}$$

The optimal value of α can now be found numerically.

References

Ayala, F. J., and C. A. Campbell. 1974. Frequency-dependent selection. *Annual Review of Ecology and Systematics* 5: 115–138.

Beauchamp, G. U. Y. 2000. Learning rules for social foragers: Implications for the producer-scrounger game and ideal free distribution theory. *Journal of Theoretical Biology* 207: 21–35.

Begon, M., and G. A. Parker. 1986. Should egg size and clutch size decrease with age? *Oikos* 47: 293–302.

Benton, R. A., and A. Grant. 1999. Optimal reproductive effort in stochastic, density-dependent environments. *Evolution* 53: 677–688.

Benton, T. G., and A. Grant. 2000. Evolutionary fitness in ecology: comparing measures of fitness in stochastic, density-dependent environments. *Evolutionary Ecology Research* 2: 769–789.

Bond, A. B. 2007. The evolution of color polymorphism: Crypticity searching images, and apostatic selection. *Annual Review of Ecology Evolution and Systematics* 38: 489–514.

Boulding, E. G., T. Hay, M. Holst, S. Kamel, D. Pakes, and A. D. Tie. 2007. Modelling the genetics and demography of step cline formation: Gastropod populations preyed on by experimentally introduced crabs. *Journal of Evolutionary Biology* 20: 1976–1987.

Brommer Jon, E. 2000. The evolution of fitness in life-history theory. *Biological Reviews (Cambridge)* 75: 377–404.

——, J. Merilä, and H. Kokko. 2002. Reproductive timing and individual fitness. *Ecology Letters* 5: 802–810.

Bshary, R., and R. Bergmueller. 2008. Distinguishing four fundamental approaches to the evolution of helping. *Journal of Evolutionary Biology* 21: 405–420.

Cade, W. 1975. Acoustically orienting parasitoids: Fly phonotaxis to cricket song. *Science* 190: 1312–1313.

—— 1984. Effects of fly parasitoids on nightly calling duration in field crickets. *Canadian Journal of Zoology* 62: 226–228.

Carranza, J., V. Polo, J. Valencia, C. Mateos, and C. de la Cruz. 2008. How should breeders react when aided by helpers? *Animal Behaviour* 75: 1535–1542.

Caswell, H. 1989. *Matrix Population Models*. Sinauer Associates, Inc., Sunderland, MA.

—— 2001. *Matrix Population Models*. Sinauer, Sunderland, MA.

—— 2002. *Matrix Population Models: Construction, Analysis and Interpretation*, 2nd edition. Sinauer, Sunderland, MA.

——, T. Takada, and C. M. Hunter. 2004. Sensitivity analysis of equilibrium in density-dependent matrix population models. *Ecology Letters* 7: 380–387.

Charlesworth, B. 1970. Selection in populations with overlapping generations. 1. The use of Malthusian parameters in population genetics. *Theoretical Population Biology* 1: 352–370.

—— 1972. Selection in populations with overlapping generations. III Conditions for genetic equilibrium. *Theoretical Population Biology* 3: 377–395.

—— 1993. Natural selection on multivariate traits in age-structured populations. *Proceedings of the Royal Society of London* 251: 47–52.

—— 1994. *Evolution in Age Structured Populations*. Cambridge University Press, Cambridge.

Charnov, E. L. 1993. *Life History Invariants*. Oxford University Press, Oxford.

——, and S. W. Skinner. 1984. Evolution of host selection and clutch size in parasitoid wasps. *Florida Entomologist* 67: 5–21.

Clarke, B. 1969. The evidence for apostatic selection. *Heredity* 24: 347–352.

—— 1979. The evolution of genetic diversity. *Proceedings of the Royal Society of London* 205: 453–474.

Clarke, C. W., and M. Mangel. 2001. *Dynamic State Variable Models in Ecology: Methods and Applications*. Oxford University Press, Oxford.

Clutton-Brock, T. H. (ed.) 1988. *Reproductive Success*. University of Chicago Press, Chicago, IL.

Cohen, D. 1966. Optimizing reproduction in a randomly varying environment. *Journal of Theoretical Biology* 12: 119–129.

Cole, L. C. 1954. The population consequences of life history phenomena. *Quarterly Review of Biology* 29: 103–137.

Crawley, M. J. 2002. *Statistical Computing: An Introduction to Data Analysis using S-Plus*. John Wiley & Sons Ltd., Chichester, UK.

—— 2007. *The R Book*. John Wiley & Sons Ltd., Chichester, UK.

Creel, S. 1990. How to measure inclusive fitness. *Proceedings of the Royal Society of London* 241: 229–231.

Crow, J. F., and M. Kimura. 1970. *An Introduction to Population Genetics Theory*. Harper and Row, New York.

Demetrius, L., and M. Ziehe. 2007. Darwinian fitness. *Theoretical Population Biology* 72: 323–345.

Den Boer, P. J. 1968. Spreading of risk and stabilization of animal numbers. *Acta Biotheoretica* 18: 165–194.

Dennis, B., R. A. Desharnais, J. M. Cushing, and R. F. Constantino. 1995. Nonlinear demographic dynamics – mathematical models, statistical methods, and biological experiments. *Ecological Monographs* 65: 261–281.

Dugatkin, L. A., and H. K. Reeve. 1994. Behavioral ecology and levels of selection – dissolving the group selection controversy. *Advances in the Study of Behavior*, Vol 23, pp. 101–133. Academic Press Inc, San Diego, CA.

——, and —— 1998. *Game Theory & Animal Behavior*. Oxford University Press, Oxford.

Eadie, J. M., and J. M. Fryxell. 1992. Density dependence, frequency-dependence, and alternative nesting strategies in goldeneyes. *American Naturalist* 140: 621–641.

Ebenman, B., A. Johansson, T. Jonsson, and U. Wennergren. 1996. Evolution of stable population dynamics through natural selection. *Proceedings of the Royal Society of London – Series B: Biological Sciences* 263: 1145–1151.

Endler, J. A. 1986. *Natural Selection in the Wild*. Princeton University Press, Princeton, NJ.

—— 1988. Frequency-dependent predation, crypsis and aposematic coloration. *Philosophical Transactions of the Royal Society of London B* 319: 505–523.

Ferriere, R., and G. A. Fox. 1995. Chaos and evolution. *Trends In Ecology & Evolution* 10: 480–485.

Ferriere, R., and M. Gatto. 1995. Lyapunov exponents and the mathematics of invasion in oscillatory or chaotic populations. *Theoretical Population Biology* 48: 126–171.

Fisher, R. A. 1930. *The Genetical Theory of Natural Selection*. Claredon Press, Oxford.

Fletcher, J. A., and M. Zwick. 2006. Unifying the theories of inclusive fitness and reciprocal altruism. *American Naturalist* 168: 252–262.

Fumagalli, M., R. Cagliani, U. Pozzoli, S. Riva, G. P. Comi, G. Menozzi, N. Bresolin, and M. Sironi. 2009. Widespread balancing selection and pathogen-driven selection at blood group antigen genes. *Genome Research* 19: 199–212.

Galvani, A., and R. Johnstone. 1998. Sperm allocation in an uncertain world. *Behavioral Ecology and Sociobiology* 44: 161–168.

Gardner, A., S. A. West, and N. H. Barton. 2007. The relation between multilocus population genetics and social evolution theory. *American Naturalist* 169: 207–226.

Gilchrist, G. W. 1995. Specialists and generalists in changing environments. I. Fitness landscapes of thermal sensitivity. *American Naturalist* 146: 252–270.

—— 2000. The evolution of thermal sensitivity in changing environments. In J. M. Storey, and K. B. Storey (eds.), *Cell and Molecular Responses to Stress*. Vol. 1, *Environmental Stressors and Gene Responses*, pp. 55–70. Elsevier Science, Amsterdam, the Netherlands.

Gillespie, J. 1974. The role of environmental grain in the maintenance of genetic variation. *American Naturalist* 108: 831–836.

—— 2006. Stochastic processes in evolution. In C. W. Fox, and J. B. Wolf (eds.), *Evolutionary Genetics*. Oxford University Press, Oxford.

Gillespie, J. H. 1977. Natural selection for variance in offspring numbers: A new evolutionary principle. *American Naturalist* 111: 1010–1014.

Grafen, A. 1982. How not to measure inclusive fitness. *Nature* 298: 425–426.

—— 1984. Natural selection, kin selection and group selection. In J. R. Krebs, and N. B. Davies (eds.), *Behavioural Ecology*, pp. 62–84. Sinauer Associates Inc, Sunderland, MA.

—— 1997. Selection pressures on vital rates in density dependent populations. *Proceedings of the Royal Society* 264: 303–306.

——, and T. G. Benton. 2000. Elasticity analysis for density-dependent populations in stochastic environments. *Ecology* 81: 680–693.

——, and —— 2003. Density-dependent populations require density-dependent elasticity analysis: An illustration using the LPA model of *Tribolium*. *Journal of Animal Ecology* 71: 94–105.

Greenman, J. V., T. G. Benton, M. Boots, and A. R. White. 2005. The evolution of oscillatory behavior in age-structured species. *American Naturalist* 166: 68–78.

Gross, M. R. 1982. Sneakers, satellites and parentals: Polymorphic mating strategies in North American sunfishes. *Zeitschrift fuer Tierpsychologie* 60: 1–26.

—— 1985. Disruptive selection for alternative life histories in salmon. *Nature* 313: 47–48.

——, and E. L. Charnov. 1980. Alternative male life histories in bluegill sunfish. *Proceedings of the National Academy of Sciencess, (USA)* 77: 6937–6940.

Guillaume, F., and M. C. Whitlock. 2007. Effects of migration on the genetic covariance matrix. *Evolution* 61: 2398–2409.

Haldane, J. B. S., and S. D. Jayakar. 1963. Polymorphism due to selection of varying direction. *Journal of Genetics* 58: 237–242.

Hamilton, W. D. 1964. The genetical evolution of social behavior. I. *Journal of Theoretical Biology* 7: 1–16.

Hammerstein, P. 1998. What is evolutionary game theory? In L. A. Dugatkin, and H. K. Reeve (eds.), *Game Theory and Animal Behavior*, pp. 3–15. Oxford University Press, New York.

Harley, C. B. 1981. Learning the evolutionary stable strategy. *Journal of Theoretical Biology* 89: 611–633.

Harris, W. E., and J. R. Lucas. 2002. A state-based model of sperm allocation in a group-breeding salamander. *Behavioral Ecology* 13: 705–712.

Hedrick, P. W. 2000. *Genetics of Populations*. Jones and Bartlett Publishers, Sudbury, MA.

Heino, M., A. J. Metz Johan, and V. Kaitala. 1998. The enigma of frequency-dependent selection. *Trends in Ecology & Evolution* 13: 367–370.

Houston, A. I., and J. M. McNamara. 1992. Phenotypic plasticity as a state-dependent life-history decision. *Evolutionary Ecology* 6: 243–253.

——, and —— 1999. *Models of Adaptive Behaviour*. Cambridge University Press, Cambridge.

Hutchings, J. A., and R. A. Myers. 1988. Mating success of alternative maturation phenotypes in male Atlantic salmon, *Salmo salar*. *Oecologia* 75: 169–174.

Johst, K., M. Doebeli, and R. Brandl. 1999. Evolution of complex dynamics in spatially structured populations. *Proceedings of the Royal Society of London – Series B: Biological Sciences* 266: 1147–1154.

Jones, A. G., S. J. Arnold, and R. Bürger. 2003. Stability of the G-matrix in a population experiencing pleiotropic mutation, stabilizing selection, and genetic drift. *Evolution* 57: 1747–1760.

——, ——, and ——. 2004. Evolution and stability of the G-matrix on a landscape with a moving optimum. *Evolution* 58: 1639–1654.

Katsukawa, Y., T. Katsukawa, and H. Matsuda. 2002. Indeterminate growth is selected by a trade-off between high fecundity and risk avoidance in stochastic environments. *Population Ecology* 44: 265–272.

Kawecki, T. J., and S. C. Stearns. 1993. The evolution of life histories in spatially heteroge-neous environments: Optimal reaction norms revisited. *Evolutionary Ecology* 7: 155–174.

Kerkoff, A. J. 2004. Expectation, explanation and masting. *Evolutionary Ecology Research* 6: 1003–1020.

King, O. D., and J. Masel. 2007. The evolution of bet-hedging adaptations to rare scenarios. *Theoretical Population Biology* 72: 560–575.

Kirkpatrick, M., and R. Lande. 1989. The evolution of maternal characters. *Evolution* 43: 485–503.

Koenig, W. D. 1988. Reciprocal altruism is birds – a critical review. *Ethol.ogy and Sociobiol.ogy* 9: 73–84.

——, S. S. Albano, and J. L. Dickinson. 1991. A comparison of methods to partition selection acting via components of fitness: Do larger male bullfrogs have greater hatching success? *Journal of Evolutionary Biology* 4: 309–320.

Kokko, H. 2007. *Modelling for Field Biologists*. Cambridge University Press, Cambridge.

Krause, A., and M. Olson. 2002. *The Basics of S-PLUS*, 3rd edition. Springer, New York.

Lack, D. 1947. The significance of clutch size 1. Intraspecific variation. *Ibis* 89: 302–352.

Lalonde, R. G., and B. D. Roitberg. 2006. Chaotic dynamics can select for long-term dorman-cy. *American Naturalist* 168:127–131.

Lande, R. 1980. Genetic-variation and phenotypic evolution during allopatric speciation. *American Naturalist* 116: 463–479.

Lande, R. 1982. A quantitative genetic theory of life history evolution. *Ecology* 63: 607–615.

—— 2007. Expected relative fitness and the adaptive topography of fluctuating selection. *Evolution* 61: 1835–1846.

Landes, D. S. 1983. *Revolution in Time*. Belknap Press, Cambridge, MA.

Leslie, P. H. 1945. On the use of matrices in certain population mathematics. *Biometrika* 33: 183–212.

Lessard, S. 2005. Long-term stability from fixation probabilities in finite populations: New perspectives for ESS theory. *Theoretical Population Biology* 68: 19–27.

Lessells, C. M. 2005. Why are males bad for females? Models for the evolution of damaging male mating behavior. *American Naturalist* 165: S46–S63.

Levene, H. 1953. Genetic equilibrium when more than one ecological niche is available. *American Naturalist* 87: 331–333.

Levins, R. 1969. The effect of random variations of different types on population growth. *Proceedings of the National Academy of Sciencess, (USA)* 62: 1061–1065.

Lewontin, R. C., and D. Cohen. 1969. On population growth in a randomly varying environ-ment. *Proceedings of the National Academy of Sciences* (USA) 62: 1056–1060.

Lotka, A. J. 1907. Studies on the mode of growth of material aggregates. *American Journal of Science* 24: 199–216.

Lynch, M. 1999. Estimating genetic correlations in natural populations. *Genetical Research* 74: 255–264.

Malthus, T. 1798. *An Essay on the Principle of Population*. J. Johnson, London.

Mangel, M., and C. W. Clark. 1988. *Dynamic Modeling in Behavioral Ecology*. Princeton Universi-ty Press, Princeton, NJ.

Mani, G. S., B. C. Clarke, and P. R. Sheltom. 1990. A model of quantitative traits under frequency-dependent balancing selection. *Proceedings of the Royal Society of London* 240: 15–28.

May, R. M. 1971. Stability in model ecosystems. *Proceedings of the Ecological Society of Australia* 6: 18–56.

—— 1973. Stability in randomly fluctuating versus deterministic environments. *American Naturalist* 107: 621–650.

Maynard Smith, J. 1982. *Evolution and the Theory of Games*. Cambridge University Press, Cambridge.

—— 1998. *Evolutionary Genetics*. Oxford University Press, Oxford.

Metz, J. A. J., M. Nisbet Roger, and S. A. H. Geritz. 1992. How should we define 'fitness' for general ecological scenarios? *Trends in Ecology & Evolution* 7: 198–202.

Mylius, S. D., and O. Diekmann. 1995. On evolutionarily stable life histories, optimization and the need to be specific about density dependence. *Oikos* 74: 218–224.

Nunez-Farfan, J., J. Fornoni, and P. L. Valverde. 2007. The evolution of resistance and tolerance to herbivores. *Annual Review of Ecology Evolution and Systematics* 38: 541–566.

O'Brien, E. E., and J. S. Brown. 2008. Games roots play: Effects of soil volume and nutrients. *Journal of Ecology* 96: 438–446.

Olausson, A., and K. Ronningen. 1975. Estimation of genetic parameters for threshold characters. *Acta Agriculturae Scandinavica* 25: 201–208.

Oli, M. K. 2002. Hamilton goes empirical: Estimation of inclusive fitness from life-history data. *Proceedings of the Royal Society of London – Series B: Biological Sciences* 270: 307–311.

Orzack, S. H., and W. G. S. Hines. 2005. The evolution of strategy variation: Will an ESS evolve? *Evolution* 59: 1183–1193.

—— and S. Tuljapurkar. 1989. Population dynamic in variable environments. VII. The demography and evolution of iteroparity. *American Naturalist* 133: 901–923.

—— —— 2001. Reproductive effort in variable environments, or environmental variation is for the birds. *Ecology* 82: 2659–2665.

Pepper, J. W. 2000. Relatedness in trait group models of social evolution. *Journal of Theoretical Biology* 206: 355–368.

Peterson, J. H., B. D. Roitberg, and R. C. Ydenberg. 2007. When nesting involves two sequential, mutually exclusive activities: What's a mother to do? *Evolutionary Ecology Research* 9: 1187–1197.

Queller, D. C. 1996. The measurement and meaning of inclusive fitness. *Animal Behaviour* 51: 229–232.

Rand, D. A., H. B. Wilson, and J. M. McGlade. 1994. Dynamics and evolution: Evolutionarily stable attractors, invasion exponents and phenotypic dynamics. *Philosophical Transactions of the Royal Society of London – Series B: Biological Sciences* 343: 261–283.

Ratnieks, F. L. W., and T. Wenseleers. 2008. Altruism in insect societies and beyond: Voluntary or enforced? *Trends in Ecology & Evolution* 23: 45–52.

Reeve, J. P. 2000. Predicting long-term response to selection. *Genetical Research* 75: 83–94.

——, and D. J. Fairbairn. 2001. Predicting the evolution of sexual size dimorphism. *Journal of Evolutionary Biology* 14: 244–254.

Roff, D. A. 1974. The analysis of a population model demonstrating the importance of dispersal in a heterogeneous environment. *Oecologia* 15: 259–275.

—— 1974. Spatial heterogeneity and the persistence of populations. *Oecologia* 15: 245–258.

—— 1980. Optimizing development time in a seasonal environment: The "ups and downs" of clinal variation. *Oecologia* 45: 202–208.

—— 1981. On being the right size. *American Naturalist* 118: 405–422.

—— 1984a. The cost of being able to fly: A study of wing polymorphism in two species of crickets. *Oecologia* 63: 30–37.

—— 1984b. The evolution of life history parameters in teleosts. *Canadian Journal of Fisheries and Aquatice Sciences* 41: 984–1000.

—— 1990. Selection for changes in the incidence of wing dimorphism in *Gryllus firmus*. Heredity 65: 163–168.

—— 1992. *The Evolution of Life Histories: Theory and Analysis*. Chapman and Hall, New York.

—— 1994a. Habitat persistence and the evolution of wing dimorphism in insects. *American Naturalist* 144: 772–798.

—— 1994b The evolution of dimorphic traits: Effect of directional selection on heritability. *Heredity* 72: 36–41.

—— 1996. The evolution of threshold traits in animals. *Quarterly Review of Biology* 71: 3–35.

—— 1997. *Evolutionary Quantitative Genetics*. Chapman and Hall, New York.

—— 1998a. Evolution of threshold traits: The balance between directional selection, drift and mutation. *Heredity* 80: 25–32.

—— 1998b. The maintenance of phenotypic and genetic variation in threshold traits by frequency-dependent selection. *Journal of Evolutionary Biology* 11: 513–529.

—— 2001. The threshold model as a general purpose normalizing transformation. *Heredity* 86: 404–411.

—— 2002. *Life History Evolution*. Sinauer Associates, Sunderland, MA.

—— 2006. *Introduction to Computer-Intensive Methods of Data Analysis in Biology*. Cambridge University Press, Cambridge.

——, and D. J. Fairbairn. 2007. Laboratory evolution of the migratory polymorphism in the sand cricket: Combining physiology with quantitative genetics. *Physiological & Biochemical Zoology* 80: 358–369.

Roff, D. A. and —— 2009. Modeling experimental evolution using individual-based variance-components models. In T. Garland, and M. Rose (eds.), *Experimental Evolution*. University of California Press, Berkeley, CA.

——, and D. Reale. 2004. The quantitative genetics of fluctuating asymmetry: A comparison of two models. *Evolution* 58: 47–58.

——, and R. Preziosi. 1994. The estimation of the genetic correlation: The use of the jackknife. *Heredity* 73: 544–548.

——, E. Heibo, and L. A. Vollestad. 2006. The importance of growth and mortality costs in the evolution of the optimal life history. *Journal of Evolutionary Biology* 19: 1920–1930.

Ronningen, K. 1974. Monte carlo simulation of statistical-biological models which are of interest in animal breeding. *Acta Agriculturae Scandinavica* 24: 135–142.

Rudolf, V. H. W., and M. O. Rodel. 2007. Phenotypic plasticity and optimal timing of metamorphosis under uncertain time constraints. *Evolutionary Ecology* 21: 121–142.

Ruxton, G. D., and M. Broom. 1999. Evolution of kleptoparasitism as a war of attrition. *Journal of Evolutionary Biology* 12: 755–759.

Sharpe, F. R., and A. J. Lotka. 1911. A problem in age-distribution. *Philosophical Magazine* 21: 435–438.

Sherratt, T. N., and I. F. Harvey. 1993. Frequency-dependent food selection by arthropods – a review. *Biological Journal of the Linnean Society* 48: 167–186.

Simons, A. M., and M. O. Johnston. 2003. Suboptimal timing of reproduction in *Lobelia inflata* may be a conservative bet-hedging strategy. *Journal of Evolutionary Biology* 16: 233–243.

Sinervo, B. 2001. Runaway social games, genetic cycles driven by alternative male and female strategies, and the origin of morphs. *Genetica (Dordrecht)* 112–113: 417–434.

——, and R. Calsbeek. 2006. The developmental, physiological, neural, and genetical causes and consequences of frequency-dependent selection in the wild. *Annual Review of Ecology Evolution and Systematics* 37: 581–610.

——, and C. M. Lively. 1996. The rock-paper-scissors games and the evolution of alternative male strategies. *Nature* 380: 240–243.

Slatkin, M. 1974. Hedging one's evolutionary bets. *Nature* 250: 704–705.

Smith, T. B., and S. Skulason. 1996. Evolutionary significance of resource polymorphisms in fishes, amphibians, and birds. *Annual Review of Ecology and Systematics* 27: 111–133.

Stearns, S. C. 1992. *The Evolution of Life Histories*. Oxford University Press, New York.

Tabachnick, B. G., and L. S. Fidell. 2001. *Using Multivariate Statistics*. Allyn and Bacon, Boston, MA.

Taylor, P. D., G. Wild, and A. Gardner. 2006. Direct fitness or inclusive fitness: How shall we model kin selection? *Jourunal of Evolutionary Biology* 20: 301–309.

Thorne, B. L. 1997. Evolution of eusociality in termites. *Annual Review of Ecology and Systematics* 28: 27–54.

Tuljapurkar, S. D. 1982. Population-dynamics in variable environments. III. Evolutionary dynamics of r-selection. *Theoretical Population Biology* 21: 141–165.

—— 1989. An uncertain life: Demography in random environments. *Theoretical Population Biology* 35: 227–294.

—— 1990. *Population Dynamics in Variable Environments*. Springer-Verlag, Berlin, Germany.

——, and S. H. Orzack. 1980. Population-dynamics in variable environments. 1. Long-run growth-rates and extinction. *Theoretical Population Biology* 18: 314–342.

Turelli, M. 1977. Random environments and stochastic calculus. *Theoretical Population Biology* 12: 140–178.

van Dooren, T. J. M., and J. A. J. Metz. 1998. Delayed maturation in temporally structured populations with non-equilibrium dynamics. *Journal of Evolutionary Biology* 11: 41–62.

van Tienderen, P. H. 2000. Elasticities and the link between demographic and evolutionary dynamics. *Ecology* 81: 666–679.

Venables, W. N., and B. D. Ripley. 2002. *Modern Applied Statistics*. Springer, New York.

Via, S., and R. Lande. 1985. Genotype-environment interaction and the evolution of phenotypic plasticity. *Evolution* 39: 505–522.

Wajnberg, E., P. Bernhard, F. Hamelin, and G. Boivin. 2006. Optimal patch time allocation for time-limited foragers. *Behavioral Ecology and Sociobiology* 60: 1–10.

Wakano, J. Y., and Y. Ihara. 2005. Evolution of male parental care and female multiple mating: Game-theoretical and two-locus diploid models. *American Naturalist* 166: E32–E44.

Weber, T. P., B. J. Ens, and A. I. Houston. 1998. Optimal avian migration: A dynamic model of fuel stores and site use. *Evolutionary Ecology* 12: 377–401.

West, A. S., I. Pen, and A. S. Griffin. 2002. Cooperation and competition between relatives. *Science* 296: 72–75.

White, A., J. V. Greenman, T. G. Benton, and M. Boots. 2006. Evolutionary behaviour in ecological systems with trade-offs and non-equilibrium population dynamics. *Evolutionary Ecology Research* 8: 387–398.

Wilbur, H. M., and V. H. W. Rudolf. 2006. Life-history evolution in uncertain environments: Bet hedging in time. *American Naturalist* 168: 398–411.

Wright, S. 1931. Evolution in Mendelian populations. *Genetics* 16: 97–159.

—— 1969. The theoretical course of directional selection. *American Naturalist* 103: 561–574.

Author Index

A

Albano, S. S. 14
Arnold, S. J. 231, 233, 268
Ayala, F.J. 15

B

Barton, N. H. 14
Beauchamp, G. U.Y. 339
Begon, M. 116, 120
Benton, R. A. 8, 12 13, 60, 172, 173, 180, 193, 203, 208, 222
Benton, T. G. 174, 195, 213, 222
Bergmueller, R. 14
Bernhard, P. 402
Boivin, G. 402
Bond, A. B. 271
Boots, M. 174, 195, 213, 222
Boulding, E.G. 269
Brandl, R. 222
Bresolin, N. 271
Brommer, Jon. E 3
Broom, M. 337
Brown, J. S. 337
Bshary, R. 14
Bürger, R. 231, 233, 268

C

Cade, W. 322
Cagliani, R. 271
Calsbeek, R. 271
Campbell, C. A. 15
Carranza, J. 14
Caswell, H. 8, 10, 165, 166
Charlesworth, B. 4, 5, 6, 59, 60, 86

Charnov, E. L. 4, 15, 376
Clarke, B. 271
Clarke, B. C. 233
Clarke, C. W. 341, 354, 367, 369, 376, 379, 389
Clutton-Brock, T. H. 4
Cohen, D. 10, 39, 40
Cole, L. C. 60
Comi, G. P. 271
Constantino, R. F. 173
Crawley, M. J. 1
Creel, S. 15
Crow, J. F. 5
Cushing, J. M. 173

D

De la Cruz, C. 14
Demetrius, L. 5, 11
den Boer, P. J. 11
Dennis, B. 173
Desharnais, R. A. 173
Dickinson, J. L. 14
Diekmann, O. 8
Doebeli, M. 222
Dugatkin, L. A. 14

E

Eadie, J. M. 338
Ebenman, B. 194, 221
Endler, J. A. 271
Ens, B. J. 401

F

Fairbairn, D. J. 50, 229, 233, 268
Ferriere, R. 7

Subject Index

A

Altruism 14

B

Bet-hedging 11
Beverton-Holt function 170, 173
binomial distribution 323, 368
Bourgeois strategy 276
Breeder's equation 224
Brute force approach 65, 71, 94
   And MATLAB 159–164
   and recursion 130
   example of 99–100, 129–139

C

Capital Breeders 375
Chain Rule 80
Chaotic behavior 170
Chaotic fluctuations 9
Characteristic equation 3, 4, 59, 87, 185
Clearing memory 18
Cole's paradox 60
Convergent stable ESS
   defined 174
Correlational selection 231
   defined 228
Critical age group 7

D

Darwinian fitness 3
Data frame
   defined 21
Decision Matrix
   defined 344
Demographic entropy 6
Demographic stochasticity 5–6
Demographic variance 6
Demographic weak ergodicity 10
Density-dependence
   and R0 8
Density-dependence and fitness 12
Directional selection 224
   IL model 251–255
   IVC model 248–251
Directional Truncation Selection 226
Dominant Eigenvalue 5, 8, 11
Dominant Lyapunov Exponent 7, 173, 174
Drosophila melanogaster 139
Dwarf mongoose 15

E

Effective equilibrium density 8
Eigenvalue
   and Leslie matrix 187
   and rate of increase 166
   and semidefinite positive matrix 228
   dominant 5
Elasticity
   defined 8
   example of 175
   of the invasion exponent 180
Elasticity analysis
   described 180–181
Epistasis 233
ESS 8, 16, 174, 177, 179, 180
Euler equation 3, 59
Evolutionary branching point 174–177
Evolutionary entropy 6
Evolutionary Stable Strategy 174
   defined 8, 16, 271

Coding Index

R Code (gives examples of the use of R and MATLAB code.
Some of the simpler codes have been omitted)

MATLAB code

contour 155, 161
dblquad 147
diff 63, 125, 140, 149, 151, 157
eig 166
ezplot 140
fminbnd 65, 141, 142, 418
fminsearch 128, 147, 150–153, 156, 159, 162, 164
fzero 103, 118, 145, 146, 149, 153
inline 65
int 106, 150

load 158, 416
meshgrid 161, 412, 415
pretty 143
quad 143, 144, 151
rand 26, 95, 146, 148, 404, 405, 416
save 158, 416
solve 64, 142, 144
sum 142, 413
surfc 46–50, 152, 155, 161, 412, 415
symsum 141